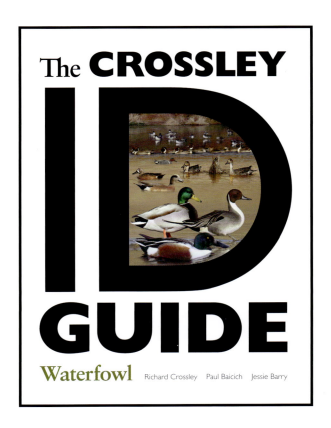

Waterfowl

Richard Crossley, Paul Baicich, Jessie Barry

Crossley Books

CONTENTS

Preface	5
Quick key to species	6 – 11
INTRODUCTION	12 – 31
PLATES	32 – 309
Wing cut outs	310 – 319
WRITTEN ACCOUNTS	320 – 482
Mystery Images: Answers	484 – 488
SAVING WATERFOWL & WETLANDS	489 – 502

Species Accounts	**Plates**	**Written Accounts**
Tundra Swan	34	320
Trumpeter Swan	36	324
Whooper/Bewick's Swan	38	329
Mute Swan	40	326
Snow Goose	46	330
Ross's Goose	48	333
Greater White-fronted Goose	52	336
Pink-footed Goose	58	342
Rare Gray Geese and Shelducks	59	339
Emperor Goose	60	345
Brant	62	347
Barnacle Goose	65	350
Canada Goose	68	351
Cackling Goose	72	357
Hybrid Geese	84	
Egyptian Goose	86	361
Black-bellied Whistling-Duck	90	362
Fulvous Whistling-Duck	92	365
Muscovy Duck	96	367
Wood Duck	98	369
Mallard	102	372
Mexican Duck	108	376
American Black Duck	110	378
Mottled Duck	114	381
Gadwall	118	384
American Wigeon	124	387
Eurasian Wigeon	128	390

Species Accounts	Images	Written Accounts
Northern Pintail	130	392
White-cheeked Pintail	134	395
Eastern Spot-billed Duck	135	396
Falcated Duck	135	397
Northern Shoveler	136	398
Blue-winged Teal	140	401
Cinnamon Teal	144	405
Green-winged Teal	148	408
Garganey	152	411
Baikal Teal	153	412
Hybrid Dabblers	156	
Canvasback	160	413
Redhead	164	416
Common Pochard	168	420
Tufted Duck	169	421
Ring-necked Duck	170	422
Lesser Scaup	174	425
Greater Scaup	178	428
Hybrid Divers	186	
Steller's Eider	188	431
Spectacled Eider	192	434
King Eider	196	437
Common Eider	202	440
Harlequin Duck	214	444
Black Scoter	218	447
Surf Scoter	222	451
White-winged Scoter	226	454
Common Scoter	231	450
Long-tailed Duck	236	457
Bufflehead	240	460
Common Goldeneye	244	463
Barrow's Goldeneye	250	466
Hooded Merganser	256	470
Red-breasted Merganser	260	473
Common Merganser	264	475
Smew	272	469
Masked Duck	273	478
Ruddy Duck	274	480
Exotics	304	

Mystery Images 42-45, 50 56, 66, 76, 80-83, 129, 154, 182-185, 212, 232-235, 254, 268-271, 278-281, 284-303.

'Looking Closer' Images 39, 78, 104-107, 200, 210, 230, 246, 282, 306, 308.

Wing Close-ups 310-319.

For those who love the outdoors

Copyright 2017© by Richard Crossley

All Rights Reserved. No part of this publication may be reproduced or used in any form. Requests for permission to reproduce material from this work should be sent to Crossley Books

Published by Crossley Books, 11 Pond Creek Lane, West Cape May, NJ 08204
www.crossleybooks.com

ISBN 978-0-692-90035-2

Printed in Hong Kong

Preface

I've been a hunter in some form or another since I was a kid. I was 7 years old when I started collecting eggs in Wykeham Forest, Yorkshire, England. It was a family tradition. My dad had done it as a kid, and so had his dad. Nowadays, admitting to being an egg collector is strictly taboo in Britain, as well as in the U.S.A. and Canada. However, I will always remember my dad repeatedly telling me, *"Only take one egg, lad, and be very quick doing it so you don't disturb the bird."* My father, who was a farmer, loves animals and the countryside; a conservationist! Wherever we went he would constantly be looking 360-degrees with his head on a swivel. He would repeatedly say *'just look at that.'* Whatever it was, was simply too beautiful for us to miss.

When I was 10 years old my school teacher, Mr. Sutton, changed my life forever when he took me birding for the first time. I was hooked. At first I 'hunted' for birds near where I lived, and by my late teens I went to other countries in Europe, and then around the world in my early 20s. I've lived permanently in the U.S. since 1991, and I've never stopped watching and studying birds. My 'hunting' has taken on many forms. Finding new birds has always been fun, particularly rare and vagrant ones. I have always embraced the challenge of identifying them at any distance and learning more about them. Most recently I have been obsessed with hunting birds with a camera and getting all the images for *The Crossley ID Guides* myself.

I have often looked back on those early days and asked why it was that birding took center stage rather than soccer, cricket, and other sports that had been my obsession into my early teens. Birds actually gave me license to travel anywhere and everywhere with a purpose – albeit an ever-changing one – to hunt birds to study, list, photograph, or some other reason, 24 hours a day. Actually, I have come to realize these are all just my own excuses. The reality is that I love being outdoors with nature. To be alone in a quiet place, the sun coming up, the noises, smells, and beautiful colors, nobody bothering me, with just a hope that something great and exciting could happen at any moment. If it doesn't, who really cares? It's just great to be back to my roots, with nature. After all, I am an animal!

Could my life story have been yours, if you had been me? Since you have this book in your hands, the answer may very well be yes. The reason I ask this is because I think that most people are basically the same at heart.

If we hunt waterfowl, carve decoys, go fishing, go birding, point a camera, simply love watching Mallards at your local park, or going for a walk outdoors, we are all the same. We have different vehicles to take us there, but there are at least three things that are critical to our common interest:

First, we must see ourselves as being on the same team.

Second, we must attempt to speak a common language – with a nature-based appreciative vocabulary.

Third, we must make a concerted effort to protect the things that we love – together.

This book has been something I have wanted to do for a long time. There has been no updated identification guide for North American Waterfowl in recent times and yet there is still much we don't know. My original interest in Old World birds formed the basis of my waterfowl curiosity. What's more, almost 70% of the commonly occurring waterfowl of Britain overlap with the common waterfowl of North America. In the 30 years I have spent in the U.S., this commonality has only been strengthened as I pursued appreciating all the waterfowl.

I had great help in this book from co-authors Paul Baicich and Jessie Barry. Paul has spent decades involved with a broad spectrum of people in the birding, hunting, and conservation communities. His passion and work for wetlands, waterfowl, and conservation is infectious. Jessie works for the superb Cornell Lab of Ornithology and is involved with several of the game-changing projects they are working on. Paul and Jessie wrote most of the species accounts in the text section. Paul also wrote *Saving Waterfowl and Wetlands*. I wrote most of the Introduction. I put together the plates and text – thankfully Paul was able help with all my mistakes.

My own passion has always been visual, and I enjoy expressing myself visually as well as writing the associated photo-accounts influenced by my Yorkshire tone. While many books strive for consistency, I am a fan of individuality and variety; it keeps things more interesting, in life and in books. Because I like to include something for everyone, the purists may find some topographical mistakes that we left for interest.

This book intends to move the needle. Most importantly, I hope it brings individuals and groups closer together by seeing themselves as the same, saving and enjoying waterfowl and waterfowl habitats. If we do this and form a more unified and coherent effort, there can be great benefits for conserving what we all love so much.

Richard Crossley

Tundra Swan p. 34
Trumpeter Swan p. 36
Mute Swan p. 40
Whooper/Bewick's Swan p. 38
Snow Goose p. 46
Ross's Goose p. 48
Greater White-fronted Goose p. 52
Rare Gray Geese p. 58/59
Shelducks p. 59
Emperor Goose p. 60

Long-tailed Duck p. 236

Bufflehead p. 240

Common Goldeneye p. 244

Barrow's Goldeneye p. 250

Hooded Merganser p. 256

Red-breasted Merganser p. 260

Common Merganser p. 264

Smew p. 272

Masked Duck p. 273

Ruddy Duck p. 274

INTRODUCTION

Everyone loves waterfowl. How could they not? Whether you call yourself a birder, hunter, wildlife photographer, naturalist, angler, environmental educator, artist, decoy carver, or just someone who loves to be out in nature, waterfowl have a particular attraction. Part of the appeal of waterfowl is their accessibility. They are everywhere from a creek in your backyard, to moist bottomlands in the South, to broad prairie potholes of the northern Great Plains, to open ocean, and to the vast Arctic tundra. A small lake in a city park is just not complete without several Mallards dabbling around its edges. These birds are often easy to observe too, because they are large, generally in the open, moving slowly, and even quite tame. Given that most waterfowl are simply beautiful, especially the showy males, it makes sense that they are universally admired. Their good looks and antics captivate anyone who stops to observe them. They have personality in spades!

According to the 2011 *National Survey of Fishing, Hunting, and Wildlife-associated Recreation*, by the U.S. Fish and Wildlife Service, approximately 18 million Americans, 16 years of age and older, will leave their homes for the specific purpose of watching birds. Of these, 13.5 million, or 75% will watch waterfowl (ducks and geese, primarily). This makes waterfowl the most-watched away-from-home birds in the U.S., followed by birds of prey (13 million), songbirds (12.2 million), and other waterbirds (10.8 million).

Waterfowl form an integral part of our common culture and history. Hunting waterfowl for food and sport is a long-standing tradition in North America, with its roots tracing back at least 2,000 years to Native Americans who used Canvasback decoys. Today, there are an estimated 1.2 million to 2.2 million waterfowl hunters in the U.S. and Canada.

Most significantly, waterfowl interest has probably done more for bird conservation and the conservation of wetland and grassland habitat in North American than any other interest in a group of animals in this hemisphere. Over the years, passionate waterfowlers have spent billions of dollars to ensure that waterfowl will continue to fill the skies for generations to come. And the efforts to save waterfowl have been examples for others – models for other conservationists and for other wildlife.

The focus of this book is waterfowl identification (ID) and appreciation. As with other *Crossley ID Guides*, its goal is to create a more comprehensive mental image of waterfowl and a celebration of the wetlands, grasslands, bottomlands, and tundra they inhabit. Birds, like people, have personality. This book shows their lifestyle, where and how do they live, how they move and why they do what they do. These are all important and interesting things to know for ID and, ultimately conservation. Hopefully this book will create a more inquiring and understanding waterfowl constituency, one able to ask better questions, interpret more of what we see, and defend the resource. In terms of understanding, by moving on from the days of the incredible Roger Tory Peterson, we can shift from the oversimplification of a white background and a few helpful arrows pointing at 'field marks' to a more realistic approach of a 'duck's world.' It is the discovery, working out the answer and not the answer itself, that is the real fun!

The next time you see a flock of ducks at your local park, take a closer look. Are they all Mallards? Are they all the same size and shape? While the identification of a stunning drake may be straightforward, what about the drab brown ones? Can you age and sex them all? Answering these questions keeps even the most dedicated observers curious for answers. The pages that follow will give you the tools to solve these puzzles.

The Crossley ID Guide: Waterfowl is organized in three main sections:

1) This Introduction gives you the foundation for how to get the most out of this book and better understand the world of waterfowl. The Introduction can best prepare you to approach the rest of the guide as a workbook. It is designed for you to get the most out of your outdoor experience through waterfowl, while thoroughly enjoying yourself!

2) The photographic plates of sitting or standing waterfowl are typically split into two seasons (winter/spring and summer/fall). Winter/spring is when most male ducks are in their distinctive bright (breeding) plumage and are at their easiest to identify (ID). These plates also have first-year (1st-yr) birds for easy comparison with the adults. Summer/fall plates show birds in eclipse plumage, in molt (partial eclipse), and with chicks in their breeding habitat. Eclipse is cryptic plumage most ducks have in summer. Each species is not only introduced using the common and scientific names, but is also presented with the 4-letter (alpha) banding code, as well as the average length and weight for the species.

A third plate (double page) is for birds in flight – the way we see them the most often. These flight plates are there to help us all. In particular, these will accelerate hunters' flight ID skills.

There are many quiz plates in the book (answers pp. 330-334). These are fun. They will prepare you for being in the field. Some of these quizzes are found just after the photo accounts of a similar looking group of species. Others at the end of the plates section have a larger number of species.

There are also a number of plates that should give you insight into a waterfowl's appearance and behavior, as well as celebrating their beauty. Examples include iridescence, females with male characteristics, hybrids, and mating.

Each image among the many plates has a specific purpose. Many illustrate the identification of a certain age or sex. Others provide close-up or distant views. A number of plates compare multiple species, while others were assembled to accentuate beauty. Until recently, identification in North America was largely based on color. This guide places an emphasis on size, shape, and behavior. By focusing on behavior and habitat, along with overall patterns of color, one is allowed a faster and more accurate identification. See pp. 15-16.

3) Species Accounts (pp. 320-482) have in-depth information for all North American waterfowl. If you want to take a step beyond the ID elements – among other things, understanding the yearly life of the species, diet and feeding behavior, nesting, and population and conservation – this book should provide essential details. We also include a section on areas of greatest continental significance for our waterfowl and a section on nestboxes for helping cavity-nesting waterfowl in North America.

The goal of *The Crossley ID Guide: Waterfowl* is to help all who open its pages to raise their knowledge of waterfowl to the next level. We also hope that the broad spectrum of varied waterfowl enthusiasts will recognize a shared common feeling, a love of waterfowl and a love of the outdoors, understanding the need to appreciate and preserve both.

Looking at Waterfowl

Ducks, along with geese and swans, are a family of waterbirds known as waterfowl. In Europe they are typically called wildfowl, and the word waterfowl is rarely used. In North America, the term waterfowl is sometimes used for other waterbirds such as loons, grebes, cormorants, and coots. While those waterbirds are often mistaken for ducks (see p. 40), under the scientific classification scheme they are not in the waterfowl family, Anatidae. Our guide to the waterfowl of North America includes all the species of ducks, geese, and swans that have occurred in North America.

Our modern-day ducks are abundant across the globe. But what makes them so successful? It's largely their ability to adapt to live in a variety of habitats with water. They are specially adapted with webbed feet for swimming, a thick layer of down to keep them warm, oil covering their feathers that keeps them dry, and unique bills for feeding on aquatic plants and animals. In many cases, they have also been able to adapt to the changes and challenges we humans have brought upon them.

Looking Versus Seeing

The biggest mistake most field observers make is rushing to get to a name for the bird rather than learning about the species, how it behaves and what it looks like. We often look rather than see!

When watching waterfowl, try to discover for yourself what it is rather than what someone else tells you it is supposed to be. We are all influenced or biased by the world around us and the things we have read or heard. Remember, the bird in front of you is your immediate reality. Watch it and you will learn. Believe your own eyes! You will understand the waterfowl in a way that books and photos cannot teach you. And remember, a bird's size, shape, and behavior usually do not vary too much from individual to individual, even though the plumage may. The same is true of humans. We change clothes seasonally, but underneath we remain the same.

Even if you are familiar with ducks, can you picture where the white patch is on an American Wigeon's wing compared to the white patch on a Gadwall? The wigeon's white patch is created by white upperwing coverts, but the Gadwall's is created by white in the inner secondaries. Knowing the exact terms for the feathers isn't as important as recognizing these differences, which will improve your ability to judge color patterns. A basic understanding of the parts of a bird will help you understand why a bird looks the way it does. Knowing a few key feather groups will significantly increase your ability to identify multiple species. This will all become clearer in the next few pages.

Field Identification

The tools and resources available for field identification have changed dramatically in the last century. Maybe you started studying waterfowl without binoculars or a handy field guide, but the times have changed. Now we have fantastic binoculars, high-powered spotting scopes, ever-changing new apps, and excellent field guides to make things easier.

For many decades, American bird identification books have focused on a very simplistic approach. Roger Tory Peterson (1908-1996) led the charge, with the historic 'field mark' method he introduced in *A Field Guide to the Birds* in 1934, a book which became the standard for guides in North America. Curiously, the "Peterson method" was influenced when Peterson was a mere youngster by the work of Ernest Thompson Seton, whose two black-and-white plates in *Two Little Savages* (1903) showed 24 species of river and sea ducks in a simplified and clear comparative fashion. After Peterson moved to New York City in 1927, he was inspired by the "dean of bird watchers," Ludlow Griscom (1890-1959), a master of sight-based field ornithology, who had, among many other things, written his master's thesis in 1915 on *The Identification of the Commoner Anatidae of the Eastern United States in the Field*. The initial presentation of Seton's ducks and Griscom's skills inspired Peterson and dominated his field-guide approach in his work for the rest of his life.

The Peterson method was enhanced – at least in the case of waterfowl – by Bob Hines (1912-1994) who, in 1963 came out with his breakthrough *Ducks at a Dis-*

tance, a booklet of fewer than 25 pages with 88 color drawings of waterfowl in flight. It was intended to instruct hunters in better identification of their quarry, but it reached many others. Several million copies were distributed and sold, and the work also appeared in Spanish and French.

By the start of the 1980s we saw the entry of photo-based field guides in North America. These were admirable, but had the disadvantage of capturing the bird in only one moment in time. Lighting and angles could limit the details previously shown in idealized artwork. Important identifying marks, visible in the field, might not appear at all.

But photography, however, has changed beyond all recognition since the start of the photo field guide. The digital age has now revolutionized and popularized bird photography, and, in fact, the day when a pair of binoculars was essential for any new field observer may be coming to an end. The camera could even bring millions of new participants into the field of bird appreciation. As digital cameras continue to improve at a dizzying pace, more people are becoming confident and proficient bird photographers, accelerating the trend of more photo-based guides. Still, even with a vast selection of individual images, these guides have essentially followed the same "static" formula which handicapped the artwork-illustrated books previously: concentrating on individual images isolated from the overall context of habitat, and from other birds. *The Crossley ID Guide* series changes this approach in a fundamental way.

Crossley-style plates

The color plates have been created to represent the way each waterfowl species appears in the field, or – put another way – as the layout might have appeared in an ideal piece of artwork! The images were chosen because they clearly portray each species' shape, plumage, and behavior. These images were "shaped," often after a considerable period of trial and error, to create an overall scene that is as lifelike as a printed image will allow. Over 5,000 images were used in the making of the approximately 300 pages of plates. Each plate contains a massive amount of identification information within a relatively small area.

Here is the rationale for this approach:

1) The mental picture. Today, photographic pixels create a lifelike, or 'apples to apples,' image. The brain is able to match this to reality. Painted artwork is idealistic and subjective; the brain sees it as 'apples to oranges'. Visually appealing, artwork helps emphasize shapes and color patterns but lacks the exact details of a photo that takes away any uncertainty in the identification.

It is much easier for the human brain to absorb information from a single photographic image, albeit a complex one, than from many separate and individual images. We are more likely to create and retain a mental picture from one image than from many. Moreover, the plates in this book are mostly in focus throughout their full depth, unlike all other photographic bird guides. This is how most of us perceive the world.

2) Reality Field Identification. One of the most important things to develop in becoming a good field observer is the ability to see the features that remain constant, regardless of distance. There is depth in the plates, and a bird's appearance changes with distance.

3) A picture is worth 1,000 words. And these plates contain many pictures, with a huge amount of information to process.

4) Practice makes perfect. The book is designed to be interactive. Use the captioned waterfowl in the foreground to try to work out the age and sex of birds in the background. This won't be possible for some birds, but for most it will. Besides, if you can't do it here, it will be very difficult with moving birds.

5) Inclusive plumages. All plumages are shown, included waterfowl in transition (molting). Many books will show birds in breeding and nonbreeding plumage. It may take weeks, sometimes months, and occasionally years, for a bird to molt the feathers that change its appearance. With a more thoroughgoing picture, it is easier to visualize and understand the workings of molt and how it affects appearance, and it gives you a better chance of finding a comparable image of that duck or goose you are trying to identify in the field.

6) Behavior. Many examples of waterfowl behavior are portrayed in the plates. Some, such as feeding behavior or unusual poses, are typical for that species. Flocking is usually depicted.

7) Habitat. Placing the bird in context plays a huge role in identification. The plates capture a habitat or environment typical for that waterfowl. This is sometimes difficult because waterfowl often live in a variety of habitats, and many ducks and geese breed in very different habitats from those they occupy during the nonbreeding season. In any case, you may recognize many of the famous locations across North America portrayed as ideal habitat.

8) Flying. Flight photos are provided; many species have multiple images. You may ask: "Why so many flight shots?" We see waterfowl in flight more than in any other pose. They can be relatively easy to identify, but it does require specific focus on size and shape, both on the ground and in the air.

Considering this reasoning, we can identify waterfowl in the same way we identify things we see every day. Take humans for example. If you spot your best friend walking under a street light at night, what will you notice first? Size. How tall is he or she? Shape is recognized almost immediately as well. Is it broad shoulders, long legs, or stocky stature that makes your friend distinctive? Size and shape are probably all it takes to recognize someone you know. If you still can't figure out who the person is, you'll look for other clues like a certain swagger or the unique color of that friend's favorite jacket. There you are, using behavioral clues and color pattern. In most situations, you would not use a single characteristic like eye color to name the person who is walking toward you, especially under a streetlight or jogging past. To the same effect, you wouldn't tell a Canada Goose from a Snow Goose using only bill color.

The probability of the sighting also comes into play. When it comes to picking out your best friend, you instantly consider the likelihood of that friend being in your neighborhood. Does your friend live in town? Or across the country? If he or she lives across the country and visits are few and far between, then the chances of that sighting in your neighborhood are rare. Spotting your neighbor, however, is expected. This relates to the probability of finding birds; it's unusual to find a bird out of its normal range or at an odd time of year.

In this analogy, identifying your friend by eye color or a logo on a jacket equates to using one plumage feature to identify a bird. It is far more difficult to spot those features, and you are more likely to be incorrect than if you use a combination of size, shape, behavior, and color pattern. This method does move away from the direction almost every other bird-identification book leads you, but it will prove a real benefit to your field skills. Size and shape, behavior, color, and habitat are the four most important clues for waterfowl identification.

Six Keys to Identification

We believe the ID of waterfowl can be broken down into the following six key areas, in order of importance: size, shape, behavior, probability, and color. Vocalizations are diagnostic if you know them. Some of you may be surprised by the low ranking of color. This is because much of the time, particularly when birds are distant, colors are often not visible. Color is also the most variable character. The best observers will always use a combination of all of the above.

1) Size. You may think it's hard to judge size in the field, but in this case we are talking relative size. Moreover, it turns out that we humans are remarkably good at judging other people's heights, in fact to within two percent accuracy on most occasions. The truth is that we spend most of our lives inadvertently practicing this skill. With a little adjustment, it can be applied to waterfowl.

Judging size is largely dependent on making comparisons with other birds and objects nearby. When you see a mixed-species flock of dabblers, you instantly make comparisons among individuals. In a mixed-species flock of Mallards and teal, the teal are tiny compared to the Mallards.

2) Shape. One of the most essential steps is to evaluate a bird's basic structure. This includes looking at head and bill shape, neck length and thickness, body and wing shape.

You'll notice shapes vary greatly within waterfowl, as they are specially adapted to fit various feeding strategies and migratory habits. This is particularly obvious with waterfowl bills. Each species has a distinctive bill shape, appropriate for survival in its environment. For example, dabbling ducks have bills designed to sift food from water off the surface, while most ocean-loving sea ducks have large, thick bills used to pry mussels off rocks. Given practice, you can identify nearly every species based on the head structure alone, though you have to be careful because head shape often changes, particularly after diving. The longer you observe, the more accurate your observation will be.

You can use these structural differences to your advantage by making comparisons between different parts of the birds. Are the wings longer than the length of the tail? Is the neck long, in relation to the rest of the body? Asking these sorts of questions also provides useful hints.

With practice, you can become accomplished at determining size and shape, which is critical since they are the least-variable characteristics in birds. Sometimes you will know you are very accurate with your assessment of size, but at other times it will be only a rough estimate. Naturally, we can also get this wrong, particularly when views are brief or distant. The secret is to know your limits and how accurate your assessment is.

A note on using measurements in this book: Measurements can be helpful, but relying heavily on exact length measurements often given in field guides – including this one – is not always the best approach. The weights can also give you an idea of stockiness and relative size of the waterfowl, when compared with other species. For example, Mallard and Northern Pintail have similar measurements, but Mallards are considerably heavier, appearing large and bulky relative to a sleek-looking pintail. If you use a combination of length and weight, they merge to create a more accurate picture of the bird's apparent size and shape.

3) Behavior is the way a bird acts. Learning the "personality" of a bird is hugely important. This takes longer to master than assessing a bird's size and shape. Knowing the behavior of birds with which we are familiar is essential in the field

This knowledge includes what habitat a bird chooses, how it feeds, the way it flies, what courtship ritual it performs and where it chooses to nest. Each species has a unique set of behaviors, most of which are genetically programmed. In other words, they are hard-wired into their system, so they are consistent for birds of the same species.

Have you ever seen a shoveler diving for fish? How about a flock of Snow Geese in the ocean feeding on mussels? These would be very strange behaviors for these species. But, you can count on the group of ducks at a sewage pond swimming in tight circles to be Northern Shoveler. Or if you watch Mallards displaying, you will notice each pair performs the same ritual every time. Remember, behaviors are consistent within a species, so it is worth taking the time to watch birds and think about how each species acts.

4) Color pattern is the overall impression of the basic colors. Looking at the patterns of blacks, whites, and browns helps sort through species quickly. It is much faster and simpler than trying to figure out specific groups of feathers, factoring in plumage details, molt strategies, and the effects of feather wear.

Judging color pattern is particularly helpful when identifying waterfowl in flight, or low light. When a bird is flying or a good distance away, we often can't see plumage details. Judging patterns of blacks, whites, and browns is far more practical and fast. When an American Wigeon passes overhead, you'll notice a white belly, with a dark band across the breast, dark rear, and gray head. If you catch a glimpse of the upperwing on an adult male, the white patch will stand out. You might even see the front of the head and notice the white blaze on the forehead. This is really more than you needed to identify it as a wigeon, so you're set to make the call.

Of course, we are naturally attracted by color. Despite this attraction, stick to identification basics: "Is the bird in front of me the correct size and shape for the species I believe it to be?" Color can be extremely variable, so it is important to focus less on the tone of the color itself and more on the overall pattern it creates, that is, the relative colors of different parts of the body. Seeing birds in 'shades of gray' will make you a much better observer!

Ultimately, color is undeniably important in bird identification, and for those new in the field, it will almost always be the first feature to attract the eye. But the secret is to learn how to use color in combination with all the other identification factors.

4) Habitat is the type of environment where a species is usually found. Brant prefer coastal areas – salt marshes, beaches, and estuaries. Fulvous Whistling-Ducks love flooded rice fields. These are species with distinct habitat and related food preferences, but if you take a close look, you'll notice each species has preferences.

Knowing what habitat a species normally occupies is very helpful for waterfowl identification. On the flip side, the ability to be at a location and predict what species you should encounter there is also valuable. When you're out scouting a new spot, you can often guess what you think should be there. Keying into habitat clues will help you find birds.

5) Probability is the likelihood of encountering a bird at a particular location given the time of year. It plays a big part in what you see in the field. With experience, this becomes intuitive. Part of probability has to do with habitat, covered above. You may already have an idea which species are likely to be at your favorite spot in the fall or winter, so when you see something new, you know it's unusual.

Knowledge of migration schedules and how common a species may be in the area are keys to waterfowl ID. Probability is helpful for identification because it narrows down the list of possible species from which to choose.

For example, if you are in eastern North America and see a very dark-colored duck it could be one of several species. If it is on an inland stream in Pennsylvania in winter picking at the surface you know it's an American Black Duck, so you eliminate sea ducks, like Black Scoter. Probability, in combination with the overall color pattern of the duck (dark), the habitat (inland stream), and behavior (feeding on surface) all helped you identify the bird. Using the four keys in combination with probability will help you identify more birds correctly.

6) Sounds that waterfowl make are often the first giveaway, even before seeing them. Some species make the most incredible sounds when you listen carefully. Sitting among a flock of Long-tailed Ducks chattering, almost laughing, with one another is an experience not easily forgotten. Gadwalls sound like they are up to something naughty. Their sounds often fit their large personalities. Sit in a marsh and make a conscious effort to locate every sound you hear; it will help you to learn and find more birds.

You can often detect and identify a flock of high-flying, honking geese before you even lift your head. Listen for dabbling ducks communicating as they come into land or take off.

Ducks are most vocal during courtship displays. Male ducks even have an enlarged trachea, known as the bulla, which acts as a sound chamber to help amplify their calls.

Also, listen for sounds that don't originate in the duck's syrinx, its voice-box. Included in these might be those of a goldeneye's whistling wings or as a Ruddy Duck beats its bill against air sac in its chest during a display.

Waterfowl Topography

Understanding is the key to success, so knowing what you are looking at is everything! Knowing the feather tracts of waterfowl is very important. Analyzing these, and the individual feathers within them, is arguably the key to becoming really good at knowing waterfowl. If you can do this, you will be able to age and sex most of the birds that you see.

On the facing page, we describe the essentials in the topography of ducks, which are, essentially, the same for geese and swans. In the two pages that follow the topography, we show images on how to use this book – the fundamentals behind the design of *The Crossley ID Guide* plates – and clues on how to age and sex birds. These pages have the same intent: to help you understand what you are viewing. Learning how to analyze something in context is far more important than learning individual answers.

Continued on p. 20

Waterfowl Topography

Primaries—waterfowl have 10 functional primaries. Numbered from outermost (p10) to innermost (p1).

Secondaries—usually 11 feathers, sometimes more, plus 3 or 4 tertials. Numbered from innerwing (p1) towards the body and the tertials. Number of feathers varies among species.

Speculum—iridescent patch on secondaries.

Tail—color is often important in ID. Waterfowl have 14-24 retrice or tail feathers (variable both among, and within, species). Often easily aged by heavily worn, faded, and narrow, juvenile feathers.

Greater covert bar
Primary coverts

Forehead
Throat
Neck
Collar
Breast
Flanks

Scapulars
Speculum—bright irredescent colors.
Tertials—innermost secondaries.
Tail—color important in ID. Feather shape used in aging. See p. 23.
Uppertail coverts
Undertail coverts
Mantle
Scapulars
Tertials—large and long, they protect the flight feathers. Sometimes the scapulars and tertials can be long and thin as in Northern Pintail.
Primaries—are there 8 showing?

Crown
Supercilium
Eyestripe
Cheek
Bill—made up of the upper and lower mandibles.
Nail

Breast

Flanks
Belly

Tail feathers (rectrices)
Vent
Primary coverts
Greater coverts—black, white and gray.
Wing (median and lesser) coverts
Rear flank
Alula

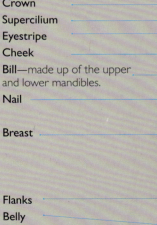

Nape

Nostril
Culmen—upper ridge of bill

Gape

Reality viewing – getting the most from this book.
Below are some other benefits of this type of life-like layout.

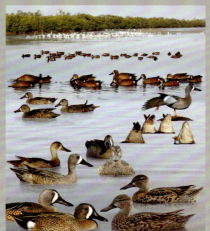

Unlike other books, Crossley ID Guides are designed to replicate reality in multiple ways. Understanding how to analyze something, rather than simply knowing the answer, is the key to being skilled. Here are some tips on how to gain more knowledge out of these information-packed plates.

Life is about patterns. Flock formations, habitat, feeding behavior, and color patterns are just a few shown here. Although we often get caught up in minutiae, it is understanding these simple patterns that is key.

Rectrice and undertail patterns are good for aging and sexing. Bold patterns with 'solid' colors are usually adult ♂ in bright plumage. 1st-yr ♂ and eclipse ♂ are intermediate. Females or juveniles are usually white with spots or streaks.

Looking at wing patterns is often the best way to sex and age many waterfowl. Bolder-patterned species tend to show the most variation. See pp. 310-19.

Both immature and eclipse males are dull or 'ghost' versions of adult males in bright plumage. Time of year is a good indicator of age. Adults are usually in bright plumage by late fall, 1st-yrs show signs of immaturity until the following summer.

Learn birds at all angles. The bill shape in species such as teal is very helpful. Face patterns, such as loral spots, can be striking head-on. Side on is not how we always see birds!

There is much variation in individual species, including adult ♂. Colors are variable, and just the tilt of a head can totally change head color. See p. 106.

Females and 1st-yrs are often very similar. Learning how to differentiate 1st-yrs from adults is tremendously helpful. See pp. 22-23.

Food is everything for waterfowl. Being able to feed allows them to successfully molt, breed, and migrate. Because of this, waterfowl move with the food, many traveling north in summer to different environments. Healthy birds grow new feathers that are better for insulation, camouflage, flying, and attracting mates, to name a few advantages. For these reasons, the plates in this book are mostly split into winter/spring and summer/fall. The priorities at these different times of year are different, and this is reflected in the lifestyle and appearance of the waterfowl.

Practice makes perfect! Repetition and learning variation while simplifying ID to a few basic patterns is the key to faster and more accurate identifications. When looking through an image, please try to create a clear picture in your mind of the lifestyle and appearance of all the birds as they grow from a few days old to males in eclipse plumage. Practise aging and sexing all the birds. The text below the plate will help with all of this.

Summer is when nearly all waterfowl breed. During this time, and in early fall, waterfowl are in eclipse or partial eclipse plumage. Many waterfowl molt their flight feathers on or near their breeding grounds. They finish their molt on, or on the way to, their wintering areas.

Notice how this open wing pattern is the same as the bird to the left in bright plumage. It is also an adult ♂ – but this one is in eclipse. Wing covert pattern is often the easiest way to sex birds in eclipse.

Juvenile plumage is the the first set of real feathers. These juvenile feathers are all the same age, texture, and appearance. As a result, you get a uniform-looking duck like this one. Look closely at all images in this book and try to find similar examples in the field.

This book shows most species of ducklings, goslings, and cygnets. Many species are shown at different ages so you can see their changing appearance as they grow-older. Visualizing and understanding the progression of changing appearances is a key to learning.

Adult ♂'s in full eclipse can be very similar to females. Multiple images will allow you to compare and create a better picture, a fuller understanding, of a bird's constantly changing appearance.

Plumages and Molts

Overview of Plumages

Have you ever wondered how old the duck you are looking at was? This is a common question, asked by the casual observer and waterfowl biologist alike. The answer is sometimes easily determined, but it can be challenging. Why is it important to age ducks? Well, these reasons range from answering conservation and management questions to satisfying your own curiosity.

If you are trying to figure out how old a person is you combine a set of clues. By incorporating a number of facts, such as a high-school graduation date, age of kids, and hair color (or how much of it is left!), we can make an educated guess as to a person's age. We basically do the same thing with ducks, putting together as many clues as we can.

You may be wondering: So, how does this relate to ducks as opposed to other birds? Well, ducks were caught in a plumage-terminology mess, because they have a somewhat different life-history schedule from those of most other birds.

The first aspect of this "mess" is that the pairing/mating schedule of waterfowl is shifted from that of other birds, as they select their mates months before breeding. A "breeding plumage" male Mallard will look spiffy and particularly handsome across most of the fall and winter, in order to make that essential connection with a female. In this case, the regular term "breeding plumage," is misleading. While most birds appear in "breeding plumage" in spring and early summer, if you want to see a male Mallard eager and ready for breeding, look in the winter!

The second cause of this mess is that ducks molt their wing feathers in an unusual way. In general, birds replace their wing feathers once a year, though they may replace their body and tail feathers more often. Most birds replace their primaries one or two feathers at a time, starting with the ones closest to the body, so that they can maintain flight during molt. Not so in waterfowl! Waterfowl (and some other waterbirds, including loons, coots, and grebes) have developed an alternate strategy to shed and grow all of their flight feathers at once, rendering them flightless for 4-7 weeks until their new feathers have grown. When flightless, the males will have a dull-looking – "eclipse" – plumage that helps them be more camouflaged when they can't fly to escape predators. They often venture to a safe area prior to dropping their flight feathers. So, many species have evolved an especially useful 'molt migration, in which species, like Northern Pintail, travel hundreds – even more than 1000 – miles, usually northward, to replace their feathers. These locations can be large lakes where the ducks can remain mid-lake where food is still potentially plentiful. Among ducks, the males are the first to depart on these molt migrations, joined by non-breeding females, and soon after by females whose early nesting attempts may have failed. Most females molt on their breeding grounds while incubating eggs and rearing the young. Among geese, which are species in which the sexes share parental care, the flightless period occurs while the parents are rearing their young. They all are basically flightless together. Besides geese, our swans and whistling-ducks may also look pretty much the same year round. Their flightless period also corresponds with their parental duties.

This molt migration is mostly a Northern Hemisphere phenomenon, particularly in the mid-latitudes. In the tropics and Southern Hemisphere, waterfowl typically only move away from their breeding areas when there is a shortage of food. Most ducks try to have 2 or 3 broods with males staying around to help the female with parenting. They tend to go into eclipse after the first brood is reared. By comparison, nearly all our waterfowl have only one brood and the males are quick to leave – and for reasons that are still not clearly understood.

And if this were not enough to make things a bit confusing, you should consider the reality that plumages and molts should be viewed as occurring in a continuum, an ongoing experience. It takes a lot of energy to molt and feathers grow only fairly slowly, so it makes sense that it is a long process. Plentiful food, good health, and periods when using less energy, will often result in increased molt.

To practice up on molt, we'll run through the molt timing for several groups of waterfowl. Let's start with the simplest molt strategy, and work through the more complicated ones.

Terminology

One area of confusion in bird books today is the different terminology used to describe waterfowl and other birds. This problem of terminology encompasses three features: age, plumage, and molt patterns. The reason for the confusion is due largely to lack of a clear and consistent terminology for describing each species' appearance.

Have you heard of these terms: eclipse, basic, non-breeding, prealternate, nuptial, formative, juvenile, first-winter, second calendar year and winter plumage … If you have, you've probably also been somewhat confused. Most people would find it difficult to put each of these terms in the correct category of age, plumage, or molt. Today we often see all these terms used simultaneously and, not surprisingly, incoherently. In an effort to help you sort things out, we're going to explain where some come from and what they mean.

The following systems are the ones most widely used in terminology:

1) The Life-Year System
Traditionally this has been the most popular system. We have used it in this book. The Life-Year system aims

to describe the way a bird looks based on the pattern and colors of the plumage taking into account the date of the observation. It originated in the early 1900s by Jonathan Dwight Jr., who made the first attempt to standardize plumage terminology. Dwight named plumages based on time of year, hence the name, the Life-Year System. This highly popular system describes birds as they appear, presumably figuring that molt patterns are linked to age and season and therefore a bird's appearance.

Fundamental to understanding how it works is that a bird starts its life in the summer (assuming it hatched in the Northern Hemisphere). To calculate a person's age we need to know his or her birthday. Knowing a person's age provides a better understanding of behavior and appearance; for birds it is the same. The following terminology relating to age is used in this book:

1st-yr: starts as a downy duckling, gosling, or cygnet in the nest, usually late spring or summer, hatched precocially and ready to leave the nest within 24-48 hours. Its contour or first set of 'real' feathers grow out within a month or two. This is juvenile plumage. Most birds molt a number of these juvenile feathers in fall, and they are replaced by adult-like or older immature feathers, creating the first-winter plumage (1st-w). In spring and summer, some birds can still be aged as first-year (1st-yr) due to retained juvenile feathers and, because of the time of year, can be labeled as first-summer (1st-s). The term "1st-yr," which we use in this book (though we occasionally use "immature"), encompasses all three plumages: juvenile, first-winter, and first-summer. In most cases, the terms immature and 1st-yr are interchangeable. Simply put, these are used for any bird that isn't an adult. On occasion, a bird such as Common Eider, will retain older immature feathers after the first year; in this situation, it can be aged as a second-year (2nd-yr) bird.

Though most bird species exhibit only one plumage a year, many wear different plumages in summer and winter. Typically, the bolder plumage is molted into in spring and retained through summer and is called breeding plumage. The complete molt occurs in late summer/autumn and results in a typically drabber appearance called nonbreeding plumage(nonbr.).

However, most ducks have a different strategy. Most male ducks have their 'breeding' plumage in winter, largely to attract a mate. For this reason, we normally use the term 'bright plumage' in this book, making no comment on whether this is in fact a breeding or nonbreeding plumage. Most male ducks have their 'nonbreeding' plumage in summer. This has traditionally been called 'eclipse' plumage, which is the term we use here.

While the Life-Year System describes an appearance or plumage, these appearances are variable. Do not necessarily think of these stages strictly as plumages, but rather as time periods in which the bird is of a certain age. Also, an awareness of the date afield – birding, photographing, or hunting – is critical when trying to age a bird.

2) The Calender-Year System

As the name implies, the calendar-year system uses language based on calendar dates, with January 1st being the first day of a new year. A Mallard that hatched this year, say, in June, would be in its second calendar-year on January 1st (but not in its second year of life). This is at odds with the way we age people, pets, and most things. This terminology has not been widely used in North America, but now occurs often enough to cause confusion with the life-year system. It is the commonest terminology used in Scandinavia and increasingly so in many other countries. One of the most commonly misunderstood terms in this system is "1st-s." (first-summer) which indicates a one year old bird in its second-calendar-year.

3) The Humphrey-Parkes System

The Humphrey-Parkes (H-P) system, formulated more than a half-century ago, is based solely on molt patterns. Because of the cyclical nature of annual molt and its relationship to physical appearance, use of this system has become more common. It is particularly valuable when molt patterns are used as the way to age birds, rather than physical appearance.

H-P system has nothing to do with color and is also independent of seasons, biology, and any other behavior that occurs within the annual cycle. Physiological processes within the body are independent of those that control when birds molt. Many ducks are at odds with color patterns of other birds. Most birds have a bright plumage in summer (summer or breeding plumage), and a duller appearance in winter (winter or nonbreeding plumage). Most duck species are at odds with this. Most ducks, such as Mallard or Wood Duck, have bright plumage in winter and spring to attract a mate. The shape and color of feathers is determined by the level of hormonal activity. As a result, there can be differences in color between similar feathers if they are being molted and grown in at different times, even though it is the same molt. Juveniles grow their feathers at the same time and so always have a uniform appearance. Ducks molt again in summer to a duller plumage that we call eclipse. This is more cryptic, though the difference are subtle in females and often hard to see; unlike males.

In the H-P system, there are only 5 major plumages: natal, juvenal, basic, alternate, and supplemental. There are also synonymously named molts. For example, the pre-alternate molt leads to the alternate plumage. Also, the first two early plumages – natal and juvenal – are worn just once in a lifetime. For the first year in swans, geese, and most species of ducks, the initial basic, and at times the initial alternate, plumages are different from the basic and alternate plumages of adults, and are, thus, also worn only once. These are sometimes called first basic (or Basic I) and first alternate (Alternate I).

After this, plumages do not change further with age, but virtually switch in sequence from one to the other.

While Humphrey and Parkes established long-lasting

consensus over molt, others, especially Steve Howell and Peter Pyle, have helped to popularize, improve our understanding, and modify the H-P system to add new knowledge. The sequences of molts – resulting in correspondingly defined plumages – are as follows:

First pre-basic molt/first basic plumage – This molt, occurring in the first few weeks after hatching, results in the first 'real' plumage and replaces the downy plumage. This plumage is dull and plain, and identified by the narrow and pointed feathers which are of loose texture, and prone to bleaching and wear.

Auxiliary pre-formative or supplemental molt/auxiliary formative plumage or supplementary plumage – This is a post-juvenile molt that is partial (conducted in July-Aug in some ducks, and involving some feathers on flanks, breast, back, neck, and head) and poorly understood. Many questions about it remain though it may be more common than we think.

Pre-formative molt/formative plumage – This partial and long-lasting molt may occur between Oct and Apr. It can involve nearly all the body plumage and results in an adult-looking appearance, though feathers are usually duller and some scattered juvenile feathers are usually retained. The period of this molt can be protracted further in some duck species, particularly long-distance migrants (Blue-winged Teal, Northern Shoveler) and some diving ducks (particularly mergansers).

Definitive pre-alternate molt/definitive alternate plumage – This partial molt generally involves flanks, scapulars, back, breast, neck, head, and sometimes other feathers. Extended in dabblers, especially females, but appears to be absent in scoters. This usually results in a useful cryptic plumage, helpful for nesting females.

Definitive prebasic molt/definitive basic plumage – This complete molt starts with the flight feathers. Once the replacement of these feathers is complete, or nearly so, the rest of the molt is conducted in the sequence head, neck back, and tail.

The above may seem very complicated. It is! As humans, we like to put everything in a box and tick it. After all, it is neat and tidy. However, nature is much more fluid. The large size and high energy demands of waterfowl, result in them molting through much, and perhaps all, the year. The amount of molt that takes place will fluctuate depending on other energy demands they have such as migration, breeding, keeping warm, as well as the supply of food. Look at almost any flock of waterfowl and you will see birds in different stages of molt. Thinking of the big picture, rather than plumage terminology, will probably give you a better overview and understanding of a birds appearance.

Again, in this book we use the Life-Year system. But a few further explanations are in order. You will see a number of images in the book, such as some of Canada Geese, in which the bird has mostly juvenile feathers but has molted a few feathers. (See if you can tell which they are.) These could have been labelled '1st-cycle' if we had chosen to write the book from the H-P perspective, or first-year. This is a judgment call. Where the bird has primarily juvenile feathers (>90%), we have usually called it a juvenile because it helps the viewer understand the appearance of the bird at this stage. Now you can look at all the bird's labelled juv and see if they have molted some of their juvenile feathers!

The major drawback of the Humphry-Parkes system is that it is at odds with other terminology, is an unfamiliar language for most people, and hard to grasp. However, understanding these molt cycles and the different appearance of different generations of feathers is often crucial in the correct aging of birds. At present, this terminology is poorly understood by most and often misused. It is best reserved for those with a solid understanding of molt, though if you have time, understanding molt will advance your skills immeasurably.

Birds spend varying amounts of time molting from one plumage to another and therefore will have feathers of both plumages at the same time. These transitional birds cause confusion; for this reason, we have treated transitional birds extensively in this book. Besides taking note of different colors and patterns, always remember: one feather may be new and another old, and different amounts of wear are often easy to see.

If you have had difficulty following these issues of aging, sexing, and molt in the last few pages, don't despair. The following pages, packed with photos, should help illustrate much of what has been covered. Use the photos to review the details and you will find out that you know more than you thought you did. These will put you in good stead for the remainder of the book.

Aging and Sexing Waterfowl

Young bird or adult? First-year male or female? It is often interesting and useful to know these things, and identifying some birds can be impossible without knowing them. Aging and sexing waterfowl usually requires piecing together several bits of information from the feathers and a few other characteristics. Each species is a little different, so there are different specifics to look for, but here are some things that are helpful for a number of species.

Juvenile plumage: This is the first set of "real" or "hard" feathers a bird has. The molt producing this plumage is the only one in which all of a bird's feathers are grown at the same time, resulting in a feather coat that is uniform in appearance and physical make-up. With practice, you can often recognize the differences between juvenile and adult feathers. Juvenile plumage tends to have low-quality feathers, ones that do not hold up as well as adult feathers. These feathers wear out and fade faster than the feathers of subsequent plumages, so they stand out next to new adult feathers.

Detecting a mix of juvenile and adult feathers is often a quick way to pick out a young bird. Remember, in all cases, the presence of one or more juvenile feathers means the bird is immature, and in the vast majority of cases, in it's first-year.

Eye color: Waterfowl are generally hatched with dark brown eyes. Eye color in young birds lightens with age in species that do not have brown eyes. Brightly colored eyes, whether they be yellow, red, or other shades, is an adult characteristic. Therefore, in the summer and fall, at least, birds with adult-colored eyes are adults. It is a great feature to look for in birds in eclipse plumage; males retain their often brighter iris color. By winter, sometimes as early as September, the eye color on first-year birds has often changed, and is no longer reliable for aging.

Body size: Young waterfowl are noticeably smaller than adults. Consider a familiar family flock of Canada Geese in which the fledgling youngsters are obviously slimmer, although plumage-wise they look much like the adults. While this is an extreme example, it does take geese and other young waterfowl several months to fill out to normal adult weights. Note also that females are generally smaller than males by species.

Tail: Look for juvenile feathers in the tail. They are narrower and have more pointed tips than do adult tail feathers. This difference in shape is typical of juvenile feathers compared to the following generations of feathers. If juvenile feathers are present, it is a first-year bird. Juvenile tail feathers, like juvenile body feathers, are weaker and wear out faster. They have soft fluffy tips (natal plumes) that break off at the tip resulting in a notch.

First-year dabblers sometimes replace their entire tail by the end of the fall. Diving ducks have more durable juvenile tail feathers and often retain some of them through the first year. Waterfowl replace the central tail feathers first. Looking for worn juvenile tail feathers that contrast with newer central tail feathers is a great comparative way to assess wear. However, some adult ducks can have different aged feathers in the tail so the presence of a molt limit (the contrast between feathers of different ages) does necessarily age it as a first-year. While tail feathers are most easily detected when the bird is in-hand, close and careful observation in the field, and from photos, should allow you to accurately age a large number of waterfowl.

Tertials: With some training, you can recognize the difference between juvenile and adult feathers in the wing. Juvenile tertials are narrow and frayed at the edge compared to broad, adult-like replacement feathers. These are often the most helpful feathers to detect juvenile vs. adult plumage in the wing.

Flight feathers: The outer primaries of juveniles are narrower, more-pointed, and often paler than those of subsequent plumages; they also wear more rapidly.

Juvenile secondaries are also narrower and more rounded at the tip than adult feathers: they are broader and more squared-off. This pattern is replicated in the coverts. However, these are averages, obvious in some birds but not others. Judging feather shapes and their age is easiest when there is a molt limit and feathers of different ages are adjacent for comparison.

Scapulars: These feathers average shorter and rounder in younger birds. While there may be variation in the shape among waterfowl, in many geese, at least, scapulars (and secondary coverts) can be very helpful in differentiating juveniles from adults. Juveniles have narrow and rounder-tipped feathers; adult's have almost square-shaped ends.

Flanks: The upper flank feathers are some of the last juvenile feathers to be replaced. As water has a stronger wearing effect than does air, so those feathers on the water line are usually replaced first. These upper flank feathers, particularly in dabblers, are narrow and pointed: adult-type feathers are broader and more rounded.

Bill: The bill shape of juvenile usually thickens more quickly at the base than it lengthens. A bill can appear thick and short in juveniles, with a culmen bulging in the center. This can be fairly well visible in some waterfowl, such as geese, well into the fall.

Bill color is typically uniform in juveniles ducks. Ducks frequently develop dark spots on the bill as they get older, some after only a couple of months.

In-hand Traits: The Bursa of Fabricius, or simply, "the bursa" is a sac-like lymphoid organ that is unique to birds. It serves to boosts a bird's immune system, but it recedes as the bird matures, so its presence serves as an indication of an immature bird. The size and condition of the bursa is useful to age waterfowl in-hand.

It takes a fair amount of experience to use bursa information effectively. The bursa is adjacent to the cloaca, with its opening just behind the cloaca. Generally, the bursa length reaches 8-10 mm to 30-50 mm in juveniles, depending on species size, and a mere 8-10 mm in adults.

Each species loses its bursa at a different time depending on the size of the bird and when it reaches maturity. In general, dabbling ducks lose the bursa in their first winter, because they breed in their first-year. Sea ducks and mergansers, which do not breed in their first year, will retain a bursa throughout their first winter and even into the following year. As a general rule, the presence of a bursa is indicative of a young bird, but the absence of a bursa in not necessarily indicative of an adult.

Females lose feathers just before incubation to optimise the transfer of heat from her body to the eggs. When present, this Brood Patch is diagnostic for females. Sometimes the belly is distended and the skin is noticeably wrinkled just after the eggs are laid.

Continued on p. 29

Aging and Sexing Waterfowl.
To ID waterfowl we often have to be able to age and sex them first. The following pages show you the best ways to do this. These patterns are consistent for most species, so learning them is very important. Once you know what to look for, it can seem surprising to observers how easy some of these features are to see.

Juvenile waterfowl have small rounded feathers, that are usually narrower than those of adults. They sometimes have prominent white tips that create wingbars. Juvenile feathers are soft and wear very quickly. The upper right Brant is darker and less worn because it is a young bird. The older juvenile (middle left) has worn feathers with frayed edges and faded colors. Notice the very small neat feathers on the belly of the top and bottom birds. These small juvenile feathers are some of the last feathers waterfowl molt and are a great way to age most waterfowl.

In waterfowl, males are usually larger than females. In direct comparison this can be useful in determining sex. In ducks, males also have larger heads. This can be particularly helpful sexing birds in immature and eclipse plumages.

1st-yrs

adult

Adult (middle right) has upperpart feathers that are pale-fringed, but much less so than juveniles. Adult feathers are larger, broader, and squarer-ended. The underparts lack the small and neat juvenile feathers, giving a strikingly different appearance. The larger flank feathers get more wear as they are at the waterline when the bird is swimming. They are replaced first, and the belly feathers replaced last.

1st-yr

Upperparts of 1st-yrs (bottom bird): All of the juvenile wing coverts are small and with broad, white tips and rounded ends. The scapulars are a combination of retained brown juvenile feathers, with white tips, and larger gray adult-type feathers. Notice how the upper left scapular is large and gray. The adjacent feather is a small, brown, white-tipped juvenile scapular.

Underparts of 1st-yrs (bottom bird): The feathers of the lower neck, breast, and belly are small and round-tipped. These juvenile feathers contrast with the much larger adult-type flank and vent feathers, which are soft and, often, transparent: one can see the dark wing coverts through them. The upper neck and head have new, black adult-type feathers that contrast with the brown juvenile plumage of the lower neck. It is easier to discern the individual juvenile feathers as they are pale-tipped; this pattern is replicated in all waterfowl.

Wing-covert patterns are a great way to age ducks. Adult ♂ have the boldest wing coverts, 1st-yr ♀ the dullest. Adult ♀ and 1st-yr ♂ are often very similar; or the young ♂ is the bolder, as is the case in the American Wigeon shown here. The iridescent colors at the base of the secondaries is the speculum. It is also brightest in adult ♂ and dullest, sometimes not visible, in 1st-yr ♀. Even when the speculum is bright in 1st-yr ♂, it is subtly duller and less iridescent than adult ♂. See pp. 310-319 for close-ups of spread duck wings.

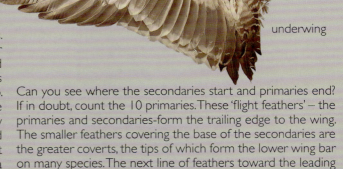

Most ducks have 10 primaries and 14-16 secondaries. The innermost 4-6 secondaries are modified to cover and provide protection to the folded flight feathers and are called tertials. Waterfowl usually molt their coverts from the innerwing outwards towards the wing tip. Adults have similar-sized and -shaped feathers after the fall molt. First-year waterfowl wing feathers usually show a contrast between worn, small, narrow, and rounded juvenile wing coverts and newer, adult-type feather, that will be larger and square-ended. This difference is called a molt limit. Retained juvenile tertials, when unmolted, are heavily worn and more pointed than adult feathers. They are brown in a lot of diving ducks.

Can you see where the secondaries start and primaries end? If in doubt, count the 10 primaries. These 'flight feathers' — the primaries and secondaries-form the trailing edge to the wing. The smaller feathers covering the base of the secondaries are the greater coverts, the tips of which form the lower wing bar on many species. The next line of feathers toward the leading edge of the wing are the median coverts, while the smaller darker feathers are the lesser coverts.

Ducks have 14-18 tail feathers (rectrices). Juvenile retrices (right image) are narrower, more pointed at the tip, and often have a 'V'-shaped notch cut out at the tip. These feathers are replaced quickly in a few species, not for a year in others; many have a combination of old and new. The soft make-up of juv feathers means they can be very easy to age, even in flight. Often skinny, faded, and a mess, compared to fresh-looking, broader, and larger adult feathers! Adult feathers (left image) are broader at the base and tip, more durable, are frequently colors other than brown, and often have well-defined pale fringes. You can also see the worn brown juv flank and uppertail feathers on the juv wigeon.

Adult ♂ Lesser Scaup (Feb). Most adult ducks are in 'bright' plumage by late fall. All the breast and tail feathers are black adult-type feathers. The flanks and back have no retained brown juvenile feathers. Most ducks are in their bold, bright plumage until early summer when they molt into their 'eclipse' plumage.

1st-yr ♂ Lesser Scaup (Feb). Superficially like the adult ♂. Look for old worn brown juvenile feathers. The tail, vent, flight feathers, and belly feathers are the last molted. The upper and rear flanks, breast, and back also are good places to look. The iris is already similar to adults. Feathers near or at the waterline are typically molted first.

1st-yr ♂ Lesser Scaup (Nov). Juvenile birds are initially all brown. Their soft feathers wear quickly, the edges soon becoming frayed. The upperparts on this bird have a few gray and white adult-type feathers; the iris is getting paler, and the bill is also fairly pale, all features suggestive of ♂.

1st-yr ♀ Lesser Scaup (Jan). Still in mostly juvenile plumage. The feathers are frayed, and the fringes are pale. It has grown a few darker adult-type feathers. See the dark brown flank feather in front of the fluffy and frayed juvenile vent and uppertail coverts.

1st-yr ♀ Lesser (left) with Greater Scaup (Feb). It would be very easy to call this Lesser an adult. Looking closely, we can see the tail looks quite pale, worn, and pointed – all juvenile features. It also has a few juvenile feathers in the flanks and a small paler brown patch at the base of the darker tail. Both are always great places to look for old feathers.

Adult ♀ Lesser Scaup (Nov). Adult *Aythya* have extensive gray and white flecking. Some feathers on the flanks are confusingly brown. Their color, shape, and texture show them to be adult. The dark tail matches the upperparts. In 1st-yrs the tail appears paler and ragged by this time of year. (Compare with image on the left.)

Eclipse ♂ Lesser Scaup (July). Eclipse birds are dull with lots of brown feathers. They look similar to 1st-yrs. Adults are in eclipse from Jun to about Oct. They molt their flight feathers in summer, the remaining feathers through fall.

Adult ♂ Lesser Scaup (Feb) The broad, dark, blunt-tipped tail feathers is an adult character; juveniles' tail feathers are narrower, pointed, more-worn, and brown and are typically notched at the tip.

Adult ♂ (Feb). Note the broad, blunt-tipped rectrices of an adult. The black on the bill tip restricted to the nail is a feature of most male Lesser Scaup and a few male Greater Scaup.

1st-yr. ♂ (Feb). A few birds keep juvenile feathers through much of the winter. Simply put, they look a mess! They tend to be pale or rufus. Note the still-dark iris color.

Adult ♂ (Feb.). This Lesser Scaup's completely dark wings and dark tail made up of broad rectrices are all adult features.

1st-yr. ♂ (Feb). The tail and wings are still all juvenile feathers. Some feathers on flanks and scapulars are adult-type.

Adult ♂ Surf Scoter (Feb). The broad tail feathers, bold colors, pale iris, bright bill are all adult ♂ features. Studying molt in scoters provides excellent aging (and sexing) clues, because of the clear differences among age and sex classes.

1st-yr. ♂ Surf Scoter (Feb). Bird sexed by bright bill and aged by small, pale belly feathers. Caution: Adults have white bases to these feathers, which are revealed by wear later in winter, often causing confusion.

1yr-old ♀ Surf Scoter (Aug). The bird sexed by dull bill and dark iris. Despite the late date, it is still largely in juvenile plumage, with just a few dark feathers on the breast; note also the emaciated tail. Juvenile feathers absorb stains more readily than do adult feathers.

1yr-old ♂ Surf Scoter (Aug). The bright bill, iris, and black feather are all adult ♂-like. The brown patches, particularly the belly and tail, are unmolted juvenile feathers, aging this bird as a 1st-summer. All, or almost all, of these juvenile feathers are typically replaced by about October.

1st-yr Blue-winged Teal (Oct). Blue-wings in fall are difficult to age and sex. This bird has already replaced much of its juvenile plumage with adult-type feathers, which are larger, have darker centers, and bolder edges. The large black central tail feather is new. The rest are juvenile feathers, which are narrower, lighter brown, with the tips frayed and even paler.

Adult ♀ Blue-winged Teal (Mar). The rectrices are all adult-like, being large, broad, and dark, with well-defined edges and little wear. Since all ♂'s show brighter colors and bolder patterns by March, this is a ♀. The tail feathers are all adult-like, large and broad, dark, well-defined edges, and with little wear.

Eclipse ♂ Green-winged Teal (Sep). Aging and sexing ducks is often difficult, sometimes impossible. The green coming in on the head, gray vermiculation on rear flank, and bold speculum bordered by copper are all male characters, while the large feathers with well-defined edges, including the tail, and the white underparts with dark blotches are adult features.

1st-yr. Green-winged Teal (Nov). Tougher still! Although the tail feathers look large, they are pointed with notched tips and do not have well-defined fringes, so are juvenile feathers. Evenly-patterned underparts are also a juvenile feature. Many juvenile feathers have a soft texture and can look fluffy: see the feathers behind the legs, and the tiny brown pale-tipped rump feathers. It's a youngster!

1st-yr ♂ Northern Shoveler (Dec). Wing patterns are a great way to age and sex birds; see pp. 310-319 for wing images. Adult ♂ Shoveler has a bold speculum with clean white greater coverts and blue forewing. This pattern is duller in 1st-yrs, like this one. The dull colors in Dec also suggest a youngster. The pointed and abraded tail feathers confirm it.

Eclipse ♂ Blue-winged Teal (Jun). By summer, feathers are old for both adults and 1st-yrs. They are also in heavy molt, often flightless. Such messy birds are hard to age. They often sit in the middle of large lakes or hide in the reeds. Birds out of their typical range in summer are often nonbreeding 1-yr-olds such as the scoters on previous page.

Age and sex these 3 birds – if it's possible. They were seen in Dec and Feb. Don't worry about identifying them! Answers p. 482.

The Life of Waterfowl

Just like us, swans, geese, and ducks have busy schedules. We pack a lot of activities into a year, which we all know takes up a lot of time and energy. Many of our human activities are physically demanding, and each has to be carefully timed to ensure success. The same applies to waterfowl.

The number one priority of waterfowl is to raise young. In order for this to happen, they, themselves, must survive. Survival depends upon a number of factors, from finding food and water to growing a new set of feathers to avoiding predators. Breeding – producing offspring that will carry genes onto the next generation – is simply essential. Success hinges on properly timing these events with the changing seasons.

Timing is everything for most species of waterfowl in North America. Think of it this way. If you are a Mallard that migrates north in the spring too early, before food is available, you may be hard pressed to survive. Or if you're a drake Mallard that grows in your sexy green head feathers a bit later because of poor nutrition, you may not be able to attract that desirable female. These life-history events are so closely tied to survival that there are strong selective pressures driving the evolution of these life history events. Each species (or population) has resolved a unique annual schedule that allows it to fit everything into the year.

Waterfowl have some basic needs: a need to breed, molt, and migrate. Let's take a look at each of these demands.

A Need to Breed: Living creatures have an innate drive to produce offspring, to pass their genes on to the next generation. For humans and waterfowl alike, finding a mate ranks high among the priorities of life. Humans put on their best clothes and are on their best behavior for a date. Ducks do the same thing. When the time comes, generally in winter, for ducks to form a 'pair bond' for the breeding season, the males compete for the females' attention by performing some crazy shows.

There are three characteristics of waterfowl breeding – from courtship through nesting – that are actually uncommon among other birds. The first is that pair formation largely occurs away from breeding areas, often during fall and winter. The second is that females are more philopatric – tending to return to a home nesting area – than the males. The third is that the hatched young are highly precocial, leaving the nest-site very soon after hatching.

As the days get shorter and winter's chill sets in, waterfowl are heating things up. The courtship displays of ducks, for example, are fascinating behaviors that we all can observe. You can watch pairs of Mallards in a city park pumping their heads or flocks of goldeneye stretching their necks and throwing their head back. These are just a couple of the displays, which range from subtle movements to dramatic actions that ducks perform to attract a mate and maintain a pair bond until the breeding season.

In the fall, the length of daylight (photoperiod) changes, which triggers shifts in hormone levels. With increased levels of hormones pumping through their blood and a new set of stunning feathers, males are ready to get the displays rolling. Competition is fierce. This is partly because there are significantly more drakes than hens in most populations. (When that number is known, we indicate the ratios in the book's individual species accounts.) Males often gather around the females to display and earn her approval. Females tend to pick older males in the first round. These guys tend to be large, physically stronger, and have the best plumage. It is thought that females select males that are better at performing the display (which may come from years of practice) and demonstrate strength, which is an indication of their ability to compete for food and other resources.

The age at which these females are ready to breed varies by group, and the general pattern – there are exceptions – is as follows: swans and geese (Anserinae) breed at 2 or 3 years after hatching, sometimes longer for swans; dabbling ducks (Anatini) breed the first spring after hatching; most pochards (Aythyini) breed at 1 or 2 years after hatching, and sea ducks (Mergini) breed at 2 or 3 years after hatching.

Each species has a unique set of behaviors, though many displays are shared among species. Generally, closely related species perform similar displays. When we break down the different displays performed within groups of ducks we notice there are certain displays that are commonly seen within a group. Dabbling ducks commonly perform the grunt-whistle, mock preening, drinking display, head-up/tail-up, nod-swimming, down-up, and inciting displays. Diving ducks commonly perform the neck-stretch, head throw, and inciting display. Geese and swans often perform a triumph ceremony.

Ducks have a radically different strategy than many other birds, finding their mate months before the breeding season. Which begs the question: Why so early? What's the advantage? There is not a clear answer to how this came about, but some observations shed light on this issue. For one, while on the wintering grounds, paired individuals are able to attain a higher social ranking, so they have better access to preferred foods. The male will defend his mate, so she is able to feed in peace. Therefore, when the time comes to breed, both members of the pair are in better condition for breeding, increasing their chances of fledging a brood.

Once the female has chosen a mate, the pair travels together, returning to the female's familiar territory. There she picks a spot to nest, and invests her energy into a single clutch (batch) of eggs. Ducks are smart though; they don't always put all their eggs in one basket. Females of many species are brood parasites, often laying eggs in the nests of other females. This increases the chance of her genes being passed on to the next generation. Waterfowl, like most birds, usually lay one egg a day. When the last egg is laid she begins to sit on them day and night, taking only short breaks to feed. After several weeks of incubating the eggs, ducklings begin to peep inside the egg, and all hatch nearly at the same time, even though the eggs are laid days apart! How this works is still a mystery to scientists, illustrating just one of the exciting discoveries yet to be made about this fantastic family of birds.

After the 'fuzzy' ducklings break out of the shell and dry off, the female leads them to water where they are able to find food for themselves. Young waterfowl do not demand much help from their parents; unlike songbirds they are able to feed themselves. Can you imagine a child that was ready to leave the house in just hours and left to fend for himself or herself in a matter of weeks? Female ducks typically leave their brood, about the time they are able to fly. Geese and swans are better parents, by our standards, staying with the young in their first year, leading the way on the migration to the wintering grounds.

The inclusion of breeding information for each of the species accounts in this book is no accident. Courtship displays, nesting sites, nest and egg descriptions, incubation period, and the role of parenting are crucial to the understanding of waterfowl life. It goes beyond species identification.

Hybrids are always a possibility. Have you ever seen a funky-looking duck? Sure, there are your various barnyard varieties and domestic types hanging around a city park or zoo, but what we are considering here are hybrid individuals among wild birds.

A hybrid is the offspring of parents of different species. Hybrid birds are rare among most waterfowl, but far more common than in most families of birds. Identifying hybrids can be challenging to impossible in the field, because there is variation within hybrids, even from the same parent species. Furthermore, at least a number of hybrid waterfowl are able to produce young, so there are second-generation hybrids or backcrosses. This adds even more potential variation!

There are several traits of waterfowl that lend themselves to hybridization. For one, there are more males than females in the duck population, so males have evolved strategies to compete to sire offspring. Forced copulation rates are very high in waterfowl, although these tend to be by males that already have mates. Females have developed exceptional defenses against forced copulations, including the shapes of their oviducts.

The strategy of forced copulation is certainly responsible for producing a number of hybrids, given that males will mate with females of different species. Mallard and Northern Pintail tend to be more promiscuous than other ducks, so it is no surprise they have hybridized with more species than other ducks. Some species, such as Northern Shoveler, are less likely to use forced copulation. A number of hybrid ducks and geese are illustrated in this book. However, hybrids take on many appearances, so learning how to analyze an unusual looking bird is the key to correct identification. In many cases, it should be realized that these birds are best parenthesized with probable (likely) or possible (could be).

Waterfowl are commonly kept in captivity in private and public collections where there is an increased chance of "unnatural" pairings that produce hybrids. Another factor that is speculated to contribute to hybridization is the practice of egg dumping. Young waterfowl imprint on the parent that raises them. Therefore, young that hatch from an egg laid in the nest of a different species can grow up thinking they are another species and be confused when it comes time to mate.

A Need to Molt: Why molt? Well, molt is one thing that keeps birds alive! It is the systematic replacement of feathers and a necessity, as feathers wear out. Without a good set of feathers, waterfowl (and other birds) are unable to regulate their body temperature, stay dry, find food, escape from predators or migrate. The process of molt also gets these waterfowl ready to breed, making them for attractive to the other sex.

Feathers provide birds with shelter, protection from the wind, rain, sun, sand, insects, etc. Humans buy clothes and build houses for refuge—ducks have their feathers. Feathers, like the shingles on the roof of your house, are only effective for a certain amount of time. Eventually, shingles and feathers wear out from physical abrasion and bleaching from the sun and need to be replaced. About once a year, all birds, from flamingos to penguins, molt to attain a set of fresh feathers, a new plumage.

The process was described in detail a few pages back, but the real need to molt is stressed here.

A Need to Eat: An understanding of what waterfowl need to eat to survive is also appropriate. An appreciation of what the birds eat blends well with the ability to identify the species itself. At the same time, some species will feed on a broad spectrum of foods; others are more exclusive.

For example, swans are year-round vegetarians, consuming large quantities of aquatic vegetation. Canada Geese will graze on leafy vegetation. Some Snow Geese populations have become almost dependent on waste grain during migration. Northern Shovelers strain small invertebrates. Blue-winged Teal often select seeds. Spectacled Eider in winter will gather by the thousands to feed in deep dives (up to 230 feet deep,) mostly on clams. Black Scoter in winter will feed mainly on animal life, including mollusks, crustaceans, and small fish, but with blue mussel often heavily favored.

As suggested, these diets can also change, sometimes

dramatically, between breeding and wintering. Meaningful shifts in diet can occur during egg-laying, particularly among female dabbling ducks with significant increases in consumption of animal matter. Ducklings, too, may rely heavily on invertebrates. And the energy (food) needs associated with the rigors of migration – between breeding and wintering – are just as important to appreciate. This is true, where considering agricultural foods (e.g., corn, wheat, soybeans, or rice), other plant (mostly native) foods, invertebrates (e.g., insects – including their larvae, snails, mussels – such as zebra mussels – or shrimp), or vertebrates (e.g., fish). And the study of winter feeding became increasingly important, starting in the late 1970s, as waterfowl researchers broadened their feeding interests beyond the investigation of breeding birds. Moreover, food-rich stopover locations are a real necessity.

As for the mix of agricultural waste grains, these are sometimes so readily accessible that waterfowl will spend less time on these grains in comparison to the time spent foraging on natural foods, be they animal or vegetable. Among the grains, however, soybeans are poorly suited to fulfil the nutritional needs of waterfowl, and soybeans also deteriorate rapidly when flooded.

Whether or not waterfowl consume agricultural foods, native plants, invertebrates, or vertebrates, the available data indicate that nonbreeding waterfowl spend most of their time feeding and resting. Moreover, feeding time increases in response to declining temperatures.

All of this helps make a case for presenting details on the diet and feeding behavior of the waterfowl in this book. Feeding demands are made clear in the species accounts and are even part of many photographic plates.

As we know, the right habitat is crucial for species, but habitat without food is meaningless. Being aware of the feeding ecology of waterfowl has been very important in conservation and management strategies. If anything, it will become more important in the future. It's always good to remember: no food, no birds.

A Need to Migrate: An understanding of the need to eat, leads directly to the seasonal movements in waterfowl, driven by that essential need to find food. Many of North America's waterfowl move throughout the continent to utilize food resources in northern regions as they become available in spring. Some move to a new location with ample food, and molt their wing feathers in a location where they do not need to fly to find enough food. In the fall, many species are pushed south as water freezes in the northern regions and food access becomes limited. Some species are fortunate enough to live in warm climates where they only move around locally during the year.

Waterfowl undergo some spectacular migrations day and night. Many individuals travel thousands of miles each year. In some spots, you can watch one flock after another pass, each flock hundreds or thousands strong. This not an unusual sight when geese, scoter or eider are on the move. Where are they coming from? Where are they going? You can't help but wonder how these birds can cover hundreds of miles in a nonstop flight, and take the same route each year. As amazing as that is, consider that others will go to a completely different area during the next winter.

Researchers are hard at work trying to answer these questions. Much of what is known about waterfowl migration has come from information from banded waterfowl.

Swans, True Geese, and Sheldgeese

Our first group of waterfowl in the book are the largest, and probably the most recognizable, waterfowl. They are grouped by ornithologists into three tribes, the swans, true geese, and sheldgeese. Their tribal characteristics are as follows:

Swans (Cygnini)
Unmistakable birds, the largest of the waterfowl, with long necks. Heavy, too. Our swans are white, but brownish immatures may be difficult to identify. Sexes similar in appearance. Long necks allow for deep vegetarian feeding. Their long and strong bills are well adapted for such feeding and grazing, with dabbling, head-submerging, and end-up feeding strategies. They do not breed until they are at least two years old, sometimes older (e.g. Trumpeter Swans in their 4th or 5th years), and they mate "for life." Both parents care for the young, with the offspring remaining with the parents as a family group into their first winter, sometimes to the start of the next spring. Only one body molt per year. They need a runway to take flight. The takeoff may look clumsy; the flight itself is elegant.

True Geese (Anserini)
Large, vocal, and sociable waterfowl, often found in large formations in the air and on the ground. They have proportionally shorter necks and longer legs than swans. Sexes also similar in appearance. They feed on vegetable matter on the water and land, their bills adapted to grazing, pulling, and picking. The sight and sounds of migrating geese in formation can be breathtaking. These waterfowl do not breed until they are at least two years old. They mate "for life," and both parents care for the young. The family group remains together through their first winter. Only one body molt per year. Short take-offs precede varying flight formations or lines once in flight. The ID of species and subspecies, especially among the 'white-cheeked' geese, can be a real challenge.

Sheldgeese, including Shelducks (Tadornini)
The Tadornini contains the sheldgeese and shelducks, moderately large waterfowl with short thick bills and usually bold coloration. The composition of this tribe has varied among authorities. They are intermediate between geese and ducks, these birds are represented by three birds in this book: one introduced species, Egyptian Goose, and two Eurasian rarities that might appear in North America, Common Shelduck and Ruddy Shelduck. Fairly long neck, legs, and wings. White upper wing patches. They are semiterrestrial, feeding in shallow water and are either vegetarian grazers and dabblers (with added minor animal matter) or they prefer animal matter. They are also up-enders. Bills are somewhere between those of true geese and dabblers. They reach maturity at two years and usually have long-term pair bonds. Unlike true geese and swans, they have two molts per year. They take off with short runways and fly with slow wingbeats.

Tundra (Whistling) Swan *Cygnus columbianus* TUSW L 52in W 15lbs **Winter | Spring**

A flock of Tundra Swans gracefully swimming on a shallow lake or grazing in farm fields is a beautiful sight. Serene and elegant, their mellow hooted *klooh* only adds to the atmosphere. They move south in family packs in long strung out 'V's, flocks varying from a few birds to dozens. Sometimes called Whistling Swan, this bird migrates late, usually November. A far-carrying call often announces the species' presence, a sure sign winter is on its way. Trumpeter Swans present a serious underappreciated identification challenge. Calls are distinctive. The Trumpeter's bugle, like a kid's tinny toy trumpet, is more strident than the softer Tundra. **ID:** Slightly smaller than Trumpeter, it looks less bulky and flatter backed. The neck is shorter and proportionally thicker. The head is sometimes peaked, sometimes flatter, but never seems oversized like in Trumpeter Swan. Adult: bill is black with most, but not all, having a diagnostic yellow spot at base – an easy way to be certain if there is doubt. Most Tundra Swans are identifiable by bill shape. The bill has a shallow 'U'

ad. with cygnets

Summer | Fall

shape between the eyes and is more curved at the gape. Judging these shapes can be tricky – beware! 1st-yr: bill shape similar to Trumpeter often with 'V' shaped forehead. 1st-yr birds are darker than adults, usually gray. Sitting or in flight they stand out, particularly the head and neck. Pink-billed babies quickly get dark tips, cutting edges and base. Very few get all dark bills before spring – most Trumpeters have all dark bills by the middle of winter. Tundra Swans molt earlier in the winter than Trumpeters and are often not easily aged from adults by late winter/spring. 1yr-old Trumpeters keep much of their juvenile plumage through the summer. Family groups return north together. One-year olds join other non-breeders at feeding and molting sites for the summer. Breeders nest on shallow tundra ponds and coastal deltas. They are large and tough, an advantage against predators such as foxes, Snowy Owl, Peregrine Falcon, and jaegers. After the young hatch, parents lead them to tundra pools and move along streams, toward the coast.

1st-yr. (late winter)
1st-yr. (early winter)
ad.

Trumpeter Swan *Cygnus buccinator* TRUS L 58in W 25lbs **Winter | Spring**

The world's largest waterfowl, this North American endemic is like a Tundra Swan on steroids – but with elegance. Successful reintroduction programs – especially in the Great Lakes region – have led to a large increase in numbers and range expansion – there were only 69 in the lower 48 states in 1932. The core of their wintering range remains with flocks of Tundra Swans in the Pacific NW. These Trumpeters breed mostly in AK. Mixed flocks forage in large flooded agricultural fields. They can also be found on water bodies of all sizes, rivers and estuaries. Two other populations in the Rocky Mountains and the interior – the only swans there. Named after distinctive deep trumpeted nasal *oh oh* – the quickest way to rule out Tundra. **ID:** The same size as Mute Swan. From Tundra by larger round-backed body. Longer thicker erect neck that somehow doesn't look right – it makes the head look over-sized. Long black straight culmen (top edge of bill) and sloping forehead create a pointed triangular look. Like Tundra, often shows salmon cutting edge

Summer | Fall

and has a noticeably shorter tail than Mute – a good hint when checking out sleeping birds. Adult: all white with all black bill. The 'V' shaped forehead and straighter edge to side of bill than Tundra. The black bill meets the eye broadly so the eye tends to 'disappear' into the bill unlike Tundra, where the eye is more prominent. Trumpeters don't have yellow at the base of the bill. 1st-yr: Cygnets are light gray and take 10 weeks to fully grow their juvenile plumage – larger birds take longer to grow feathers than smaller ones.

Gray or buff-gray juvs are much darker than adults. A few juvs are white in the Rocky Mountain population. Trumpeters have a more protracted molt than Tundra and one-year olds still have a combination of retained, worn and faded juvenile feathers, and new adult-type white feathers by summer. Pink bill has dark tip, cutting edge and base. It becomes darker more slowly than Tundra. Longer bill with straighter culmen noticeable as in adults, but the shape of feathering at bill base isn't useful until bill is fully grown.

Whooper Swan *Cygnus cygnus* L 60in WHOS **Tundra (Bewick's) Swan** *Cygnus columbianus* 52in TUSW

Whooper Swan is the Eurasian counterpart of Trumpeter Swan. Rare but annual visitor to the Aleutian Islands. Occasionally in Lower 48 with native swans. Extensive yellow on the bill should draw attention! Its call is most similar to Trumpeter, 3 notes in triplicate with a bit more farmyard goose quality. **ID:** Size and shape similar to Trumpeter – some still consider them the same species. The loral line is narrower where it meets the eye. The yellow on the bill extends past the nostril to a sharp point. Highly variable. 1st-yr birds have extensive pink base to bill somewhat mirroring pattern of the adult. Bewick's Swan (*C.c.bewickii*) is the Eurasian subspecies of Tundra Swan. Rare western visitor. Bewick's has extensive yellow on the bill unlike our Tundra, but slightly less than Whooper. The yellow stops short of nostril on Bewick's. Whooper also has a narrower loral line than our Tundra. 1st-yr has pinkish area at bill base that turns to yellow through winter. Escapes of both Bewick's and Whooper Swans occur.

MUTE SWAN

Distinctive patterns and colors. Smaller knob suggest adult ♀ or older immature.

Distictive orange bill. Very large black knob makes it a ♂.

Pale pinkish bill with bold triangular loral patch.

TRUMPETER SWAN

Large white forehead. Longer and less-curved cheekline creates narrower loral line. Eye appears farther back in face than Tundra.

'V'-shaped forehead often with indent at bottom.

Long pointed head with staright culmen (top edge of bill). Cygnets have pink bills, often with gray, quickly turning dark on tip, cutting edge, and base. Bill becomes all dark sooner than Tundra.

TUNDRA SWAN

Small white forehead and curved cheekline create a broad loral line. Most have a yellow spot.

Shallow 'U'-shaped forehead with no indent. Note the missing eye.

Steeper head than Trumpeter with cuved culmen. Bill color pattern similar or pinker. All young swans, except Mute, have pale 'V'-shaped foreheads. The bill grows and darkens through the first-year.

WHOOPER SWAN

Similar to Trumpeter but very narrow yellow loral line creating an isolated eye.

Yellow narrows to a point past the nostril. Often show narrow black base to bill.

Pale pinkish-white base to bill becomes yellow through winter as pink tip (not shown) becomes black. The pattern mirrors adult.

'BEWICK'S' SWAN

From our Tundra by more-extensive yellow and narrow loral line creating isolated eye.

Yellow on bill stops before nostril. Often shows narrow black base to bill.

Colors similar to Whooper – focus on size. Our Tundra Swan has dark base to bill. Bill becomes adult-like through winter.

Mute Swan *Cygnus olor* MUSW L 58in W 23lbs **Winter | Spring**

Familiar and unafraid introduced European species – often in urban areas. Mutes seem to change character from large graceful elegance to a brute ferocity when defending territory. Territorial ♂ (Cobs) frequently hold their wings high and arched moving with intent that is enough to scare any bird or human. The biggest and nastiest beast on the block comes with bad consequences for native nesting waterbirds. Besides the harassment, a pair eats enough aquatic vegetation to support a flock of teal. Nest is massive and usually conspicuous. In many states, culling programs, some covert, restore a natural balance of waterfowl. Stays near nesting site year-round if open water allows. Some shift to large bays and lakes in protected ice-free locales. Has a long, noisy running take off with wings thrashing water. Wings make a loud diagnostic whistled hum – other swans are very quiet. **ID:** Striking diagnostic orange bill and large black 'knob.' The largest swan with thick neck, bulky body, and square-headed look. The neck is often held curved, less 're-

on nest
territorial ♂
cygnets – 4-6 wks
ad. ♀
ad. ♂
cygnets – a few days old

Summer | Fall

gal' than the more erect postures of other swans. Mute's longer tail is a good way to ID it from 'wild' swans. Adult: always white, often with yellowish-colored neck. Knob is larger in ♂, usually apparent in direct comparison with the ♀. 1st-yr: Cygnets occur in two color morphs – dark and light ('Polish'). Dark morph birds vary in tone though they tend to be the same color within families. Some family groups have both light and dark morphs. Light 'Polish' birds have high mortality rates. Molts through fall/winter into white plumage with dark morph birds appearing piebald. The darker retained juv feathers contrast with the newly molted white feathers. Dark morph Mutes have gray bills, pale pink in white morphs. Bill becomes brighter, and small knob grows through winter. 1 yr-old birds (1st-s.) are similar to adults but with slightly smaller knob and duller orange bill. They form groups that loaf around while adults are in pairs, often with offspring. 2nd-yr's knob is slightly paler and smaller than adults'. Calls: variety of hisses, snorts, and gurgles.

Mystery Swans in February, Seattle, WA. The Pacific NW is the hotspot for Tundra and Trumpeter Swans. Large mixed flocks feed on estuaries, lakes, and particularly, large, wet fields. What a sight! While large and easy to study, they are one of the most underestimated ID challenges. If you don't think so, just give it a go. If this becomes difficult, you would be correct. So here are some pointers. One key is to keep be patient and keep studying. It's not worth doing if it comes too easy! Size and shape are always the best starter. Trumpeters are larger and heavier bodied, standing taller and more upright. Their longer necks are often kinked at the base, held straight up and tipped slightly backwards. Tundra's shorter neck is curved slightly forward as if sneaking a peek. Surprisingly difficult to judge is the thickness of the neck. Many will tell you Trumpeters are thicker-necked than Tundras, but judging this in the field is difficult. In fact many Trumpeter Swans look thin-necked, perhaps due in part to their extra length. A yellow spot on the bill is diagnostic for Tundras. Trumps have a hefty, long, all-black bill, triangular looking head and 'V' shaped forehead. The black skin swal-

lows the eye, so it blends into the bill. Tundra's bill is subtly slimmer, shorter, and can show a concave culmen. The black skin meets the bill at a narrower point, so the eye appears separate and smaller. There are a couple of standing gray birds and another in flight. Aging birds often helps to identify them. Trumpeters molt later, and the birds here appear to be in full juv plumage as all their feathers appear the same! But how about that bill color? Many of the birds here have muddy bills that make them look pale. Working out the real color is key. Then there are a couple of rust-stained birds. Or is it just dirt? It is easy to get sidetracked identifying birds, but always get back to the basics of size, shape, and, in this case, bills. Flight ID is tricky. Still focus on shape, also look for birds late-winter in juv plumage. These will be Trumpeters. Arguably, the true mark of really knowing your stuff is knowing when you know and knowing when you don't! Answers p. 484.

Mystery Swans in February, Great Lakes, NY. Consider the hints from the previous page. Probability, in this case location, has a massive impact on how confident we feel identifying all wildlife. We are always faster pulling the trigger when we know an area well and what species occur there. Trumpeter Swans are an increasing presence around the Great Lakes due to the highly successful reintroduction and conservation program. It has helped to save this species. Their range continues to increase, and they sometime wander out of range. Swans, like other birds, follow the food. Swans feed by

lead to dense concentrations of mixed groups – even Mutes are prepared to share! Mute Swan has a longer tail. Combine tail length with size, and it should be possible to identify all 3 to species. Aging birds in the middle of winter can be tough, though Trumps and Mutes are usually a mixture of retained juv and fresh adult-type feathers. Tundra Swans are usually further along in their molt cycle, but 1st-yr birds tend to have grayer necks. If you can't be bothered IDing or aging them, just enjoy the spectacle. Swans on and in the ice – now isn't that winter! Can you ID and age these 3 species of swan? Answers p. 484.

Snow Goose *Anser caerulescens* SNGO L 30in W 6lbs

Imagine yourself sitting in a field turned white by Snow Geese. An eagle appears in the distance. Heads go up, everything freezes, and there is silence. Blast off and mayhem, thrashing wings and honking – it's sort of frightening. You are beautifully stuck in one of nature's great spectacles. If you haven't experienced it, you simply haven't lived. Snow Geese breed on Arctic tundra in colonies, often with Ross's Geese. Snows arrive first, their nests are spaced further apart and on higher land. Large bills designed for digging plants leaves exposed peat in these areas, which is a big problem. Snow Geese's ability to adapt to agricultural practices have led to a population explosion. Locally common in winter, in agricultural areas, prairies or marshland, sometimes in flocks of 10,000s. Large skeins often fill the sky and lead you to where birds are feeding. Light (white) morphs are the most common except in Gulf states. Flocks are compact with 'lookouts' at the edges. **ID:** 2 populations recognized: Greaters breed in eastern Arctic Canada, win-

Winter | Spring

ter mid-Atlantic region. Lesser everywhere else. Medium-sized with heavy body and sloping head with large bill. Striking dark 'grin patch,' where mandibles meet, enhances 'mean' impression. Sexes similar, ♂ are larger. 2 morphs: light (white) and dark (blue) – 'Blue Geese'. Only Lesser has a dark morph. Light morphs are much more common everywhere except in the Gulf states. White morph: Juv: black bill, dingy gray with neat white-edged upperpart; Adult: white with black wingtips, pink bill. Often has orange ferrous (iron) staining on head (rarely in Ross's Goose). Blue morph: Juv: variably dingy dark brown-gray; Adult: gray-blue with white head, white extending on to neck. Intermediates are fairly common. Lesser averages slightly smaller in size but variation makes racial identity essentially impossible in the field – unless it's a dark morph. Occasionally hybridizes (1:500 in mixed colonies) with Ross's Goose, all features are intermediate. If they are not, forget it!

Ross's Goose *Anser rossii* ROGO L 24in W 4lbs

It's small and cute, the squidgy bill on a round head with black eye having lots to do with this. Like Snow Goose, the population is increasing rapidly, creating similar conservation problems in the Arctic. Distribution is local but often in large numbers, typically mixed in with Snow Geese. High Arctic breeder with a million birds alone nesting with Snow Geese at Karrak Lake on wet tundra. With such concentrations, the footprint is large and damaging. Winter birds are scarce but regular in the East, mostly in Snow Goose flocks (1:2000). **ID:** Much smaller with proportionally shorter legs and neck than Snow Goose. They have a small round head and stubby triangular bill that has a straighter border with the face than Snow Goose. This makes the small eye stand out. Gray area (wart) at base of pink bill is variable in size. It can get large and grotesque in older birds! In large flocks it is surprising how well they blend in with Snow Geese. Birds in flight are deceptively tricky to ID quickly. At other times they really stand out. Adult: white with black wingtips.

Winter | Spring

1st-yr: unlike Snows they are similar to adults and can be easy to overlook. Look for dark in the tertials, secondary coverts, duller bare parts, and gray wash to crown and rear neck. These dark areas can fade to white by late winter, making them difficult to age. Blue morph is rare; many are actually hybrids with Snow Goose, where the blue-morph gene is dominant. Blue-morph Ross's are much darker than blue-morph Snow Goose, with more dark on the crown. Check for typical Ross's features – size, shape, bill structure, and wart. In flight, the smaller size, short neck, and stubby bill combine with shorter wings and faster wingbeats as the best way to pick out in Ross's Goose in direct comparison. On the ground, it requires careful scanning to pick out individuals among the Snows. Hybridization is regular (1:500), reasonably straightforward in some individuals and virtually impossible in others. Look for a combination of intermediate characters in size and shape. The bill should have at least a reduced dark 'wart' and larger grinning patch than Ross's.

Looking for Rarities. What other species are mixed in this flock of Snow Geese in the mid-Atlantic in winter? Scanning for rarities takes patience and endurance, and it can seem overwhelming at times. Constantly on the move, these geese repeatedly come in and out of view from behind vegetation, or they are hidden behind other birds. Here they are in corn stubble. Snow and Ross's Geese have burgeoning populations, due to the availability of such surplus grains in winter and stopover areas. To ID these birds, you should create a search image for the 'odd one out' based on previous experience and knowledge. Ross's Geese can be found with Snow Geese anywhere. The smaller size and tiny bill are typically what most people look for, though the features are surprisingly easy to overlook. Stray geese are often on the periphery of

flocks. This may be because they are easier to see than in the center of the flock. Or it may be because they are harassed by the different 'carrier' species, forcing them to the edges. Take your pick! Ultimately, patience is the name of the game. Hunters are often better than birders at this. Test yourself: look carefully and find all the goodies in this flock. There are 6 Ross's, 2 White-fronts, 1 Canada, 1 Cackling, and 1 hybrid. Some birds will be controversial. The lower left goose is considered by some to be a Ross's, others to be a Snow/Ross's hybrid. It's bill is well within the variation of Ross's Goose, as are all other features. The atypical posture, shape, and possibly size, are suggestive of a hybrid. Birds such as this create endless discussion. Often the best answer is 'I don't know for sure'. All other answers p. 484

Greater White-fronted Goose *Anser albifrons gambelli/frontalis* GWFG L 28in W 5lb

Specklebellies are circumpolar. Fairly common Arctic tundra and taiga breeders in NA from w. AK to the Hudson Bay. Most people split into 2 groups based primarily on their wintering areas: *A.a.gambelli* in the mid-continent into Mexico and *A.a. frontalis/sponsa* the Pacific flyway. Tundra breeders average smaller and lighter; taiga breeders darker and larger; as you would expect! Clinally geese get smaller from the e. US to Siberia. They are best thought of as one subspecies that varies clinally and in response to their environment. The distinctive but scarce subspecies, Tule Goose (*elgasi*), breeds only in the Cook Inlet, Alaska, in taiga habitat. They winter in California's Central Valley. Greenland Whitefront (*flavirostris*) is a rare winter visitor to the East Coast. Large noisy flocks migrate through the Central and Pacific flyways in long lines and 'V's – the harbinger of changing seasons. Their high-pitched laugh or yodeled call – 2-3 syllables, *nil-LI-IK* – is quite different from other geese. Specklebellies winter in agricultural areas, prairies, and some coastal

Winter | Spring

regions, often in single-species flocks or with Snow Geese. They are scarce in other areas, usually mixed in with other geese. **ID:** The only common gray-brown goose. These are the palest and grayest subspecies, medium-sized geese with orange legs. They have mostly pink bills, though some have orange mixed in, usually at the base. The belly pattern varies from pale to almost solid black, but most birds have variably speckled black bars — hence the name, 'Specklebelly.' The white 'front,' accentuated by a dark border, is diagnostic. Extent of white is variable with some extending as far back as the eye. Young birds develop black belly and white face at varying rates through their first year. Even by spring, some birds have no dark on the belly and only limited white on the face, as well as some retained juv coverts. Black tail bordered by white and gray inner wings make the upperparts quite distinctive in flight. Orbital ring usually orange but variable. Beware of Graylag and other domestic gray geese combinations, particularly at the local pond!

'Tule' Greater White-fronted Goose *Anser albifrons elgasi* GWFG L 30in W 6lb

White-front subspecies are controversial, but not the distinctive Tule Geese. Their population is also the smallest of all geese subspecies, not more than 10,000 birds. **ID:** They are big, standing tall with tail down, chest pumped out, up, and proud. The thick neck is kinked back royally – a distinctive profile. The bill is long, and the head shallow, enhancing a snouty look. They are dark. Particularly striking is the dark upper neck and head. The white face really pops! They often have a capped look, though most White-fronts also do if you look closely. The central belly is really pale or white, contrasting with the dark neck and head, which is darker than any other subspecies. The belly is lightly barred, never solidly dark. A flock of similar-looking overhead White-fronts with solid-bellied birds automatically rules out Tule. Often touted field marks, bill and orbital ring color, are too variable to use! Found in family parties on ponds feeding on tubors: other white-fronts roost on ponds but don't feed there. Can you pick out the 6 White-fronts among the Tules?

'Greenland' Greater White-fronted Goose *Anser albifrons flavirostris* GWFG L 28in W 6lb

Greenland birds (*flavirostris*) are scarce winter visitors to the East Coast, typically in flocks of Canada Geese. **ID:** In some respects, they are closest in appearance to Tule Goose, being dark. Compared to Tundra White-fronts, the most likely stray specklebelly in the East, Greenlands are darker, particularly the head, neck, upperparts and flanks. They are the darkest white-fronts, browner in tone rather than gray and appear more uniformly colored, and they have the heaviest belly-barring. The bill is longer, and the bird as a whole can be more robust. The bill is usually pale orange but this feature can be difficult to judge, especially when there aren't other birds for comparison (see p. 62). Duller light tends to make judging colors easier. 1st-yr birds are paler than adults as in other White-front populations. Greenland White-front numbers have increased recently, and their occurrence here reflects this.

Mystery White-fronts in the West. Over the years, much has been made of subspecific ID based on bare part colors – orbital ring, legs, and bill. On closer inspection of these colors you will probably come to the conclusion that it is troublesome at best. What is orange and pink is subject to the individual's eye. Add to this that there is a great deal of individual variation and that most birds' bills are a combination of colors, and you will see this feature is of limited help. This is a West Coast scene where you get White-fronts (Pacific) and Tule Geese. Try to identify them using shape and color tones, with Tule having darker heads and necks that show a stronger contrast with the underparts. Solid belly patches are

only shown by Pacifics. Try to age birds 1, 3, and 4. 1st-year birds start with pale bellies, smaller white facial shields and less prominent orbital rings. Black belly feathers and the white facial shield are grown in through the winter and summer. By late winter some birds may not be easy to age using these features. With good views you can study the shape of the wing coverts and scapulars. Adults have larger, broader feathers that appear squared-off at the tips. Juvenile feathers are smaller and narrower. Looking for the two types of feathers is a lot easier than you might think. Give it a try. Get this sorted out, and you will quickly become a major-leaguer. Answers p. 485.

Pink-footed Goose Anser brachyrhnchus PFGO L 27in W 6-9lbs **Winter | Spring**

A rare, but now annual, visitor to the East in recent years. Usually found in flocks of Canada Geese from Newfoundland to Maryland. Many of these are returning adult birds. A fairly small compact goose with a dark head and neck that really stands out next to the paler breast. Frosty gray body, darker on the flanks. Short, thick neck and small rounded head. Legs and feet are always pink – as you would expect, given its name. Bill distinctly small, dark, and triangular with extensive pink toward the dark tip. All White-fronts always have orange legs and lack black in the bill. In flight, Pink-feet have a distinctive pale gray panel on the upperwing and a dark underwing. Broad white tail tip and uppertail coverts. 1st-yrs are aged by unmolted small juv coverts and belly feathers. The dark head, pink legs, and bicolored bill are usually obvious and distinguish them from any other possible rare or escaped gray geese. Call a distinctive *ang-ang-WINK-WINK*. Can you find all 6 standing Pink-footed Geese and a Snow x Canada hybrid?

Rare Gray Geese and Shelducks

Bean Goose was split into Tundra and Taiga Geese by the AOU in 2007. Both are very rare in w. AK, with a few records in the West, south to the Salton Sea. 'Middendorfs' Taiga Bean Goose is 10-15% larger than Tundra Bean with a more pointed flat head, long neck and bill. Tundras are Pinkfoot sized, shorter-billed, and rounder-headed. Both bean geese always have orange bare parts. Variation often makes ID contentious, perhaps impossible! Graylag has occurred in the NE and is rapidly increasing in Europe. Presence in captivity cloud sightings. Big and beefy. Thick neck, pale head, often with a noticeable orange orbital ring. Broad-based triangular bill, pink-orange with no black. A bruiser! Striking pale gray wing-coverts and forewing in flight. Lesser White-fronted Goose is small and cute-looking. Has occurred on the Aleutians. Bold orbital ring, white blaze extending high on forehead, stubby pink bill, and limited black on belly. It is common in captivity, as are Common Shelduck and Ruddy Shelduck, both of which may have occured as wild birds.

Emperor Goose *Anser canagica* EMGO L 27in W 6 lbs

A subtly beautiful coastal Alaskan species. 90% of the world's population breed on the Yukon-Kuskokwim Delta. This is a sea-goose found along intertidal zones and rarely straying far from coastal habitat. They are comparatively unique among geese because they eat large amounts of marine clams and mussels. They winter in single-species flocks along the Aleutian Islands and Alaska Peninsula. Rare farther south on the West Coast, often mixed in with other geese. Fairly common in captivity, sadly the best chance of seeing them for most observers. **ID:** A small charismatic goose. Compact, similar to Cackling Goose, with round head and stubby bill giving it a cute look. Lower mandible is black; bill in the male slightly larger. Iron staining results in a lot of orange-headed birds in summer. Can you find the one in this image? Adult: superbly intricate pattern, bold but subtle. Mostly silvery-gray plumage with barred upperparts, with those feathers having pale terminal and black subterminal band. The black and white head and neck is an

Winter | Spring

unusual and striking pattern. The legs are orange and the bill pink with a touch of purple at the base. A designer would be fired for such a design but it wins awards for the results. Juv: initially all gray. It quickly begins to molt adult-type feathers giving it a blotchy head and neck. The dark feathers around the distinctive loral patch are the last ones to go. Smaller juv feathers have a subtler pattern than adult feathers, more purplish-brown and less gray. Most 1st-yr birds retain extensive juv feathers on the underparts and wing coverts for much of the first year. A number of failed breeders and 1-yr-old birds have a molt-migration as far as Russia. In flight, Emperors look somewhat uniform except for the beautiful white head and upper neck contrasting with black throat; they are striking even at long range. It's easy to miss the white head and tail, particularly against the snowy and cloudy backdrops! Voice: fast and hoarse *chidee chideedee*. If you were an Arctic Fox, would these Emperors be camouflaged for the snow and gravel in their Alaskan world?

'Pale-bellied' Brant *Branta bernicla krota* BRAN L 24in W 3lbs

'Pale-bellied' or 'Atlantic' is the East Coast Brant. Rare in the West. A high-Arctic breeder, usually nests near the coast in colonies. Locally common in winter. Some remain until late May because their tundra breeding grounds are still frozen. They are found swimming in sheltered coastal bays, on barrier islands, or grazing in grassy areas – soccer fields are a favorite. They form large, dense, squabbling flocks that incessantly call a steady deep *cruuk cruuk*. The effect seems higher-pitched in mass chorus. It's a great sound on a quiet winter marsh. They often give each other a little nip as they waddle around on short legs – just to let each other know they are there! They fly in wavy, uneven lines – rarely in 'V's.
ID: Fairly small and compact with short, thick neck and pointed head. Overall, a dark goose with contrasting black neck and white underparts. Partial white necklace. 1st-yr aged by broad white fringes to coverts and scapulars, variable white necklace, and retained small juv belly feathers. Juvs are darker and browner than adults.

'Black' Brant *Branta bernicla nigricans* BRAN L 25in W 3lbs

Black, sometimes called Pacific, is the common West Coast Brant. A rare winter visitor in the East. It has the same habits, behaviors, and vocalizations as East Coast birds. Like them, it can be quite tame, often hanging out in marinas, estuaries, and on ball fields. **ID:** Black Brant are on average larger, longer-legged with a larger bill than other races. They are a strikingly dark bird. They are so dark that the contrast with the pale flanks and tail is what often stands out the most. If in doubt, notice how dark the belly is and how it extends past the legs. The back is equally dark; this difference compared to Pale-bellied is striking. Black Brant have a really broad, bold necklace with thick lines that meets at the front and wraps around most of the neck. The necklace does not meet at the front in other subspecies. 1st-yr birds are aged the same as other subspecies. 1st-yr birds in late winter can have pale underparts from old juv feathers that are faded and worn. These Black Brant are often misidentified as Pale-bellied.

Ad. and juv. Dark-bellied Brant

ad.

'Gray-bellied' Brant *Branta bernicla* BRAN L 25in W 3lbs

A recently discovered subspecies that winters only in the Puget Sound. A declining high Arctic breeder centered around Melville Island – there are about 8,700. **ID:** Taxonomically closest to Black Brant. Intermediate between its two NA counterparts in color, necklace shape, belly pattern, leg length, and bill size. It's a dead split! There is also considerable variation in all of these features adding to the difficulty in identifying them with certainty when out of their typical range. Presumed Gray-bellies have been seen on the East Coast and Ireland. Being certain is tough because it is particularly hard to rule out a dark Pale-bellied Brant or hybrids. Brant hybridize but we don't know how often. There are records of European 'Dark-bellied' Brent on the East Coast. They are slightly darker and grayer than Gray-bellied. The flanks show less white, sometimes almost none. The dark belly extends behind the legs. They tend to look thicker-necked. Individual variation among the subspecies, and the possibility of hybrids, makes ID of out-of-range birds a hornet's nest.

Barnacle Goose *Branta leucopsis* BARG L 27in W 4lbs

A beautiful medium-sized goose that breeds in NE Greenland and n. Europe. Numbers increasing in Europe, aided by self-sustaining feral flocks. They have become annual in small numbers in the East, usually showing up in winter with much larger Canada Geese. They are a commonly kept captive, but some birds are known to be from Europe, and many are probably legit. They are occurring with increasing regularity, and some return annually. Call a short high-pitched but shrill *kor*. **ID**: A striking black and white goose, compact with short thick neck, rounded head, and small black bill. The white or cream face stands out against black lores and neck. Strong contrast between breast and belly. Boldly intricate tricolored upperparts. The white U-shaped rump-band, is obvious when the goose is flying away.

1st-yr similar to adults with subtly less contrasting upperparts and barred flanks. Canada Goose can show similarly patterned faces – these are rarely hybrids! A hybrid should show some of the multiple differences between the two species.

Mystery Brant. The marshes of the mid-Atlantic coast are the winter home to large flocks of Pale-bellied Brant. They are one of the latest winter visitors to head north in spring, large numbers still being present in May. It's sometimes hard to believe that their high-Arctic breeding grounds are still frozen over at this time of year. For those of us who love looking for rarities, or something to do on a quiet day, finding 'odd' Brant can be a rewarding challenge. 'Black' Brant are rare but regular in the East, some returning annually. In fall and spring, the large turnover of migrants means that every day is different. Who knows what the real numbers of 'Black' Brant are actually in the East? When trying to ID Brant subspecies

you can look for the degree of contrast between the pale flanks and the rest of the body. The contrast in 'Black' Brant is accentuated because of the much darker colors. Always confirm your first impression with the size of the necklace and the extent of dark on the belly. If you keep watching, you should get a sense of a larger, more erect, and muscular bird with a longer bill. Beware of juv 'Pale-bellied' Brant, because they can be much darker than accompanying adults. If you suspect a 'Gray-bellied', look for intermediate characters including the color and extent of the gray belly, largish necklace,

Canada Goose – East *Branta canadensis* CANG L 36-45in W 6-10lbs

Abundant and familiar. Breeds throughout NA, except on tundra. Usually split into 2 groups. 1) Greater Canada Goose: Atlantic (*B.c.canadensis*), Interior or Todd's (*B.c.interior*), Giant (*B.c.maxima*), Moffit's (*B.c.moffitti*), Vancouver (*B.c.fulva*), and Dusky (*B.c.occidentalis*), and 2) Lesser Canada Goose: Lesser (*B.c.parvipes*). Only Giant, Atlantic, and Interior occur as 'wild' birds in the East. Reintroduction program on East Coast started in 1930's creating our feral populations. They are sedentary or short-distance migrants. Includes large western 'Moffit's' as well as eastern birds. These Canadas are familiar to everyone. Found in urban parks, lakes, golf courses, and everywhere you want to relax. Often tame, they readily hiss and honk, even attack you, if young'ns are about. They begrudgingly get out of your way. Wild populations are longer-distance migrants and less approachable. They prefer agricultural fields. Even slow drive-bys result in necks held erect 'to attention,' ready to be off, or at least to slink away between corn stalks. They head south in late fall

Interior, Atlantic, and intergrades

Winter | Spring

in large 'V'-shaped skeins and back north as the snow melts. They have a sixth sense for thawing fields to their north. They seem to know exactly when to migrate! Familiar honking call. Introduced populations molt in late-summer; wild populations later in fall. **ID:** Adult – Giant Canadas are very large, long-necked, have pale underparts, and are long-billed. The only subspecies sometimes safely identified. Interior is smaller, more compact, shorter-billed, and have darker neck and underparts. Atlantic Canadas average slightly smaller and paler than Interior but overlap, and are not safely separable. Introduced geese are a mix of all the above. The presence of a neck collar (white ring at the neck base) or a chin strap (dark line under the chin) is irrelevant in subspecific ID. Juv: small, soft-textured, brown feathers become frayed and are molted quickly. Climate change, different agricultural practices, and increasing adaptation to urban parks have all contributed to rapidly changing distribution, increasing populations, and behavior, no doubt including subspecific mixing.

Canada Goose – West *Branta canadensis* CANG L 36-45in W 6-10lbs

ID: Moffit's, also known as Western or Great Basin Canada Goose, is the *de facto* common and widespread Canada Goose in the West. It is large and medium-colored, often resident in both urban and rural areas. Some migrate. Like feral populations in the East, their numbers have increased and now account for two-thirds of all NA Canadas: it was less than 20% in 1970. Dusky Canada Goose is the darkest Canada. Medium-sized with a fairly small bill, they are variable in color and shape, making confusion with Vancouver and dark Lesser Canada an underrated problem. Dusky breeds only in Copper River Delta, winter in the Pacific NW. Vancouver Canada Goose is similar to Dusky, averaging slightly larger, paler, and longer-billed. Resident or local migrants from Glacier Bay, AK, south to n. Vancouver Island. Some will migrate as far south as OR. Lesser Canada Goose is a real head-scratcher with much unknown. Breeding range is only proven from AK: it was thought to breed widely in n. Canada. The dark Alaskan population, common

Anchorage Lesser Canada Goose

Winter | Spring

around Anchorage, overlaps in color with Dusky Canada. DNA and morphology appears to support them being their own subspecies. Intergrades occur where they meet with Dusky. The supposed light eastern population, found wintering east of the Rockies, of Lesser Canadas are probably all Richardson's Cackling × Interior Canada hybrids, and/or small Interior Canadas. All Canada populations are incredibly variable in size; birds only a little larger than Cacklers are regular. The darker Alaskan Lesser Canada is similar in size and shape to the noticeably paler Taverner's Cackling Goose. 'White-cheeked' Geese coloration is clinal; darker to the west, smaller to the north. Canadas hybridize with Cacklers where ranges overlap. Geographic ranges of Canadas is always a help in IDing subspecies. Geese travel in family groups; even these show much variation in color, posture, and size. However, there is much we don't know. Increased work will change the way we perceive the taxonomy, distribution, and clinal variation within white-cheeked geese.

Probable Interior Canada
ad. ♂ Mallard
juv.

Richardson's Cackling Goose *Branta hutchinsii* CACG L 25in W 3-5lbs

Cackling Goose was split from Canada Goose in 2004 by the AOU. Cackling breed farther north than Canadas on coastal Arctic tundra. They migrate long distances, hence longer wings that extend past the tail tip; Canadas' only reach the tail tip. Canadas are bigger-bodied, longer-necked, and nest farther inland and to the south. Cacklings are presently split in to 4 subspecies. Richardson's (*B.h.hutchinsii*) breed across much of the Canadian Arctic and winter mostly in the southern Great Plains, the western Gulf, and just into Mexico. 'Richies' are the Cackling Goose found in the Mississippi and Central Flyways with a few straying to the East Coast. The other 3 Cacklers are Alaskan breeders wintering in the Pacific NW: Taverners (*B.h.tavernii*), Aleutian (*B.h.leucopareia*), and Cackler (*B.h.minima*). Richardson's (the subspecies in the image) are known to hybridize with similarly-colored Interior Canada Geese where breeding areas overlap, presumably accounting for many of the birds we call Lesser Canadas. **ID:** Richies are smaller in size, bill

Winter | Spring

length, and skull size in the north of their range, and are darker to the west. All 'white-cheeked' geese (Canada and Cackling) get darker as you move west in response to their surroundings, like most other bird species. This clinal darkening creates questions about how many subspecies there really are. Richardson's are only a little smaller than the smallest Canadas. They typically look shorter- and thicker-necked, though the neck can look slender when stretched. The most important feature is the short bill; the length makes it look stubby. They tend to be fairly pale, often with a warm buff wash underneath. The upperpart feathers are gray at the base, shading to brown with a pale fringe. The gray base creates more of a 'silvery' appearance. White collars or black lines on the chin ('chin straps') are fairly common in all populations. The presence of collars isn't always obvious until the neck is stretched. Geese are usually in family parties through the winter; the 1st-yrs can be picked out by darker gray plumage and smaller rounded juv feathers.

Cackler, Aleutian, and Taverner's Cackling Goose Branta hutchinsii CACG L 24in W 3-5lbs

The Cackler (*B.h.minima*), Aleutian (*B.h.leucopareia*), and Taverner's (*B.h.taverni*) Geese all breed in AK and winter in the Pacific NW down to the Central Valley of California. Numbers have risen dramatically recently, a great conservation success. Strays occur away from these areas and are often head-scratchers. Cackling Geese winter in agricultural areas, sometimes with Canadas and other geese. They often stay with their own kind, particularly Aleutians, making ID easier. The tiny Cackler is the smallest; the Aleutian is mid-sized; the Taverner's is largest. **ID:** The small compact Cackler is distinctive, not only because of its size and shape, but also because of its boldly patterned feathers. Mallard-sized, it has a tiny bill, short legs, and long wings. The neck is short and proportionally thick. Cacklers are dark. On most, the upper breast is noticeably darker, often with a purplish tone. The under- and upperpart feathers have well-defined pale fringe, paler bases to the feathers, and dark subterminal bars. A distinctive pattern! Less than half have neck collars

Winter | Spring

of varying thickness; few are as broad as on Aleutians. Aleutians are slightly larger and lighter than Cacklers, appearing more uniform above and below, rarely showing contrast between the upper and lower breast. They are warm brown; some show orange tones on the breast. In flocks, over 90% of the Aleutians have striking broad white neck collars with a dark lower border; an easy and distinctive trait to see, even at a distance. The collars are usually broadest on the throat, and quite a few birds have white speckling extending onto the throat. Taverner's is the largest Cackling Goose, often Lesser Canada-sized and -shaped. Uniform brown pale-tipped feathers above similar to Aleutians. Uniform below except for darker flanks. Taverner's are large-chested, and can look long and thin-necked. They are more round- rather than square-headed. The bill is often quite long making it look narrow. W AK breeders perhaps slightly darker, winter in Pacific NW. E AK breeders presumably winter east of the Rockies. More study needed!

The Anchorage Conundrum. Going for a walk in a downtown park in Anchorage, AK at 11pm in summer is a great experience. The beautiful, saturated, evening light with its long shadows adds a different dimension to IDing birds. Understanding light and how it changes a bird's appearance is very important. Although colors appear a lot darker and richer, other features remain the same. Always go back to the basics of size, shape, and color patterns relative to other birds. The taxonomy of the Lesser Canada Goose is still uncertain. What are the 'dark' Lessers shown here that are common in Anchorage, AK? Many overlap in color with Dusky Canada Goose. Dusky Canadas breed just to the south, so one turning

up here is quite possible. Dusky averages slightly darker, larger, and stockier! Stragglers are often 1st-yr birds with retained old and faded juv feathers, most prominent as pale patches on the belly. Taverner's, Aleutian, and Cacklers are all possible here, as is the larger Moffit's Canada. Cacklers are tiny and dark with stubby bills; Aleutians slightly larger and paler with a good neck collar; Taverner's are the same size and shape as the local 'Lessers' but noticeably paler. IDing white-cheeked geese is fraught with difficulties. Knowing your limits, when to feel confident in your ID, and when to add words like 'possible' and 'probable,' is important. What other geese are mixed in with these 'Anchorage' Lessers? Answers p. 485.

4-6 weeks old: At this age, goslings are mostly down. The white specks on the wing are sheaths of feathers starting to grow in. These are the first 'real' feathers; they have hard shafts.

Giant Canadas: 1-week-old goslings are still covered in down.

A few days old: The eggs hatch within a few hours of each other. The goslings are brooded by the female for 1-2 days, then led by both parents to feeding areas.

Growing Up and Oddballs. Summer and early fall are fun times to watch the commoner birds that live near you. Watch how fluffy yellow goslings, a few days old, can grow so much and change their color to brown in the space of a 3-4 weeks. On closer inspection of these youngsters, the feathers look smaller and 'fluffy.' The soft down will be replaced by their first set of real feathers with hard shafts. These feathers will be the juvenile feathers. These juv feathers are all grown at the same time and, therefore, have the same appearance. At 4-6 weeks the short white wing-covert sheaths start to be visible. The flight feathers will grow in shortly afterwards. It takes about 8-10 weeks for a youngster to become fully grown. These juvs are the same size as adults, or very close to it. The upperpart looks very neat with small feathers, all uniformly sized with rounder tips. The soft, fluffier texture of juv feathers are noticeably different from the larger square-

ended adult feathers. Failed breeders and one-year olds often form large groups of loafing birds. In heavy molt, their old brown feathers often look remarkably worn and frayed. Newer feathers are cleaner and grayer. They will be different lengths while growing. Some birds will be rust-stained, so their colors will be all over the place. This often confuses those observers still obsessed with color! Checking through flocks, you will probably see some birds with white foreheads and atypical face patterns. This is particularly common in juveniles. Aberrant birds are not uncommon among geese. White-necked birds are often presumed to be hybrids with Snow Geese. Some of these birds are actually Canadas. The neck and head feathers are colored white instead of black. All the other Canada characters are typical. Taking a closer look at a familiar bird can teach you a lot. Discovery is what is fun, so always *look* and *question!*

Mystery Geese in Flight. Geese are often seen in flight and in large numbers as flocks fly majestically in lines or 'V's from one feeding area to another. They honk loudly as they go. What a sight and sound! These feeding areas can be 10 or more miles apart. If you are lucky enough to be on the flight line, thousands of birds may fly over in just a few minutes. Sifting through them to find the odd one out is great fun, but it takes focus, practice, and skill. In many ways it is easier than sifting through dense standing flocks, although you do have to be quick. Difference in size, shape, and color can be

more apparent in flight than when birds are standing. Size and color patterns are the most important features to key in on. There is some size and shape variation within each species, but it is usually slight. Ross's and Cackling Geese are noticeably smaller than their counterpart Snow and Canada Geese. Ross's and Cackling are more compact with shorter necks. The stubbier bills of the smaller species can be easier to judge than the comparative sizes of the bird. Try to look at both features. Answers p. 485.

North Slope Goslings. Deadhorse, Prudhoe Bay, AK. Identify the 4 species of goslings. They are all with their parents. Location is always a help! Deadhorse is the only town in NA where you can almost drive to the Arctic Ocean; the BP oil terminal is the only barrier. Contrary to what might be expected, the infrastructure of the oil refineries acts as a magnet for waterfowl as well as other types of birds and animals. Many seem oblivious to people and quite happily co-exist with humans. The tundra here on the North Slope is strictly off limits to people. Many of the waterfowl are flightless during their molt. They are often with offspring and are very adept at running to safety at the first sign of danger. They are really

fast when they want to be! There are large flocks of geese, often mixed. These nonbreeders comprise of adults and 1-year old birds. Breeding birds stay in family parties: 2 parents plus offspring. Birds preen every day (lower left). This White-front is an adult. See how all the feathers are large with squared-off ends. It has a few newly molted scapulars that are dark and pale-tipped compared to the worn and faded brown old feathers. The white-cheeked geese here are said to be Taverner's Cackling Geese. They are quite large, big-bodied, long-billed, and thin-necked; just like Lesser Canadas. Birds from Prudhoe usually winter east of the Rockies. Research in the next few years should be interesting.

Hybrid Geese. Geese form large mixed wintering flocks, sometimes carrying strays. Pair bonds are typically formed on the wintering grounds, sometimes with these strays. Also, geese breed colonially, often involving more than one species. Since the need to breed is strong, hybrids are regular. Snow and Ross's Geese frequently form mixed colonies where about 1:500 are hybrids. The two Snow/Ross's juvs shown here have several Ross's-like characters but are intermediate in size, bill length, and have more brown in the plumage than typical Ross's. Any bird that has a wart of any size, on its bill has Ross's Goose as one of its parents, even if the bill looks large. Some hybrids, however, don't show an expected

mix of characters from both parents. Clearly these often get overlooked. Cackling and Canada, Snow and Ross's are the species duos that have similar plumage patterns, so judging size and shape in IDing possible hybrids is critical. The flock in which the young hybrid is travelling will typically have at least one accompanying parent. This is a good hint! The color patterns produced are often surprisingly difficult to work out. If many of the birds above seem confusing, they are! Size and fellow-traveling geese are key to ID. In many cases the answer will not be certain and it is better to use words like 'possible' (a chance of) or 'probable' (a high likelihood).

Egyptian Goose *Alopochen aegyptiacus* EGGO L 27in W 5lbs

A well-established resident in select suburban areas in FL, but also in TX, AR, and s.CA. Recently (2015) added to the AOS list. Weirdly out-of-place African species first introduced in the 1980s. Feral population didn't become established in the 'wild' until the 1990s. Similarly established in w. Europe. Destined to become gangs of bullies that take over new hoods. They are nonmigratory, but like many adaptable introduced species are expanding their range. These birds are big and nasty, quite happy to chase anything as big as a human, with vicious intent when they have young ones nearby. They fly faster than you can run, and they have no problem trying to bite you! They will take over freshwater lakes, urban parks, golf courses, or just about anywhere with water and grass. They strut around in tight-knit pairs most of the year or in family packs after breeding. These are grazers, feeding both day and night, but mostly in early morning and at dusk. They are quite happy sitting in the tops of trees or on man-made structures, surveying the scene

All year

below. Equally at home swimming on ponds and lakes. They nest in holes in banks or trees, sometimes under bushes. They have peculiar wheezing call. **ID:** Unmistakable. Beautifully colored shades of gray and brown. An eye-patch gives it a professorial look, it goes with the bird being in charge! Some folks think it looks ferocious; others think it is goofy-looking. Decide for yourself. Large and robust with sturdy pink legs that look almost too long for such heavy body. Adults: sexes alike, with the ♂ only slightly larger. Chestnut 'shades' around eyes, chestnut nape and neck-ring, together with a large dark brown spot on breast, makes ID easy for this essentially gray and brown bird. Transformed in flight, with large, clean, white inner-wing patch both above and below, highlighted by dark trailing edge. The speculum is an iridescent green, beautiful in good light. Juv: Generally duller than adults, lacks dark breast patch and eye patch. The crown is dull brown, not pale gray-white.

Surface-feeding Ducks

These waterfowl consist of three tribes, all which are surface-feeding ducks. These ducks are dabblers and up-end feeders. In the past, the three groups have been divided by ornithologists into three tribes, the whistling-ducks, the perching ducks, and the classic puddle ducks. The perching ducks, of which we have two species, have been in flux, with ornithologists unclear how to categorize them. Nonetheless, their tribal characteristics are generally as follows:

Whistling-Ducks, formerly known as Tree Ducks (Dendrocygnini).

Long-legged and gangly waterfowl named for their whistling calls, whistling-ducks are primarily tropical, with the northern edge of their range in the U.S. Their long necks, long legs, and stance reveal affinity to geese. Other facets of their shape, behavior, and ecology liken them to geese, such as bone structure, one molt per year in adults, similar appearance of the sexes, and lifelong pair bonds.

Individuals typically first breed at the start of their second year, with, uniquely, the sexes sharing incubation. Young remain with their parents through fledging. With their slim bills, whistling-ducks feed by grazing and dabbling. Their loose wingbeats are faster than those of geese, slower than those of ducks. They have 10 primaries, with the outer five (p6-p10) being both notched and emarginated; 16 secondaries (including three tertials); and 14-18 retrices (usually 16).

Perching Ducks (questionable "Cairinini")

These waterfowl were previously treated as a group due to characteristic readiness to perch in trees. We have only two species, Wood Duck and Muscovy Duck, that have odd-enough features to prevent certain placement in either the shelducks or the true ducks. In either case, these are surface-feeding, omnivorous, woodland ducks with distinct nails on their bills and sharp claws on their toes (good for perching in trees), and their legs are placed farther forward on their bodies than are those of puddle ducks. They mature at one year, nest in cavities, and are seasonally monogamous. Perching ducks are broad-winged, agile flyers, with relatively long, squared tails. As with puddle ducks, they can take off nearly vertically from water or land.

Puddle Ducks, also known as Dabblers (Anatini).

The puddle ducks comprise the largest tribe of waterfowl, and have a classic "duck" shape. The legs are positioned near the center of the body, allowing for easy walking and, along with their large wings, nearly vertical take-off from water or land. The tipped-up feeding posture enables access to seeds, aquatic plants, and animal matter on the bottom of shallow water bodies. Although this feeding style is characteristic of Anatini, many species also graze extensively.

Puddle ducks conduct two molts per year, though only one replaces flight feathers. Nearly unique among ducks, dabbler wings are highlighted by the speculum, a patch of iridescent color on some to most secondaries, and usually bordered fore and aft by contrastingly paler color.

The sexes differ in voice (the females are usually the "quackers") and appearance, with males being more brightly plumaged. They reach maturity at the end of their first year and form seasonally monogamous pairs, usually broken during incubation when the male leaves to conduct his extensive molt. Females attend the brood until independence.

Puddle ducks flap more slowly than most other duck species, producing the illusion of slow flight in most species, the greatest exception being the whirring flight of the small teal.

Black-bellied Whistling-Duck *Dendrocygna autumnalis* BBWD L 19in W 1.8lbs

Rapidly increasing resident of Texas, common in Florida, spreading into other Gulf and southern Great Plains states. Prone to wander long distances as far north as Canada, particularly in late spring and summer. Found in wet areas such as agricultural ponds, rice fields, golf courses, and wetlands, particularly where birds can perch. Trees are their favorite, but also in unexpected places such as on farm buildings, railings, and places no other waterfowl would stand. Increasingly common in suburban areas in Florida. Paddles and searches for food with its head under water. Nests in tree holes or nestboxes. Often in noisy flocks, loud incessant 'whistling' calls carry long distances. You would probably get tired of hearing them if they lived next door. More often heard before seen. Most active at dawn and dusk (crepuscular) but also nocturnal. They fly around a couple of times in tight flocks, sometimes large, before dropping steeply with feet dangling down. **ID**: Exotic looking. Typical whistling-duck shape: fairly large and elongated with long

All year

legs, neck and bill, but fairly small head. Erect posture, as if it's listening and questioning you. Adult: sexes alike. A striking bird, two-toned with black belly contrasting with a mostly chestnut-brown breast, neck, and back. The face seems purposefully dull gray just to add contrast with its bold eyering and bright pink-red bill that stands out a mile away. Long pink legs are hard to miss. Unmistakable! Juv: mostly bright buff with pale fringes, gray bill and legs. Superficially similar to Fulvous Whistling-Duck, but Black-bellies are darker, and duller, with uniform brown back, and less contrasting underparts. The cheeks are grayer and lack prominent side streaks. Extended breeding season from Mar to Oct, peaking in mid-May to mid-Jul. Molts into adult-like plumage through winter. 1st-yrs average duller than ad. They are best aged by retained juv feathers; these create gray mottling on an otherwise black belly. Check out the bold tiger-striped ducklings! All whistling-duck chicks have a distinct T-stripe on the back of the head and neck.

ad. and juv. Black-bellied Whistling-Duck

ad.

Fulvous Whistling-Duck *Dendrcygma bicolor* FUWD L 18in W 1.6ibs

Mostly summer visitor in wetter areas, particularly in rice and flooded fields centered around LA and other Gulf States. Occasional ones stray to the North. Numbers have declined recently. They are scarce but sometimes occur in large flocks at favored traditional sites where the habitat is just right. They are usually in shallow water, where standing is as easy as sitting. Most arrive to wet fields in Feb-Mar when rice is planted. They usually nest in late summer when rice fields have lots of cover. Good luck finding the juvs; they are rarely seen. These are social ducks, occurring in fairly tight-knit flocks and rarely as individuals. Their habitat preferences overlap with Black-bellied Whistling-Duck, and they are often seen together. Like them, they are crepuscular and nocturnal, easiest to see and hear early and late in the day. Like other whistlers, they are also very noisy and are often heard before they are seen. Whistling call – a two-syllable *kit-Tee* or *pee-chee*. **ID:** Typical whistling-duck shape: fairly large and elongated with long legs and neck. They are

All year

fairly small-headed, recalling Pintail, though the skinny neck offsets this. The bill is large, and is variably colored between blue and black. They can stand tall and upright to attention like only whistling-ducks can. They are orange-brown with a darker back, though even these feathers are brightly tipped. Large white flank streaks are really striking and are often highlighted in black. The bold black-and-white rear end also stands out at a distance. Face patterns vary, with a lot being paler-faced and others less so. A dark line down the back of the neck extends round to form a large necklace on the neck sides. The only likely confusion is with juv Black-bellied Whistling-Duck, which are duller and more uniformly colored. Most importantly, Black-bellies are pale-backed, have bold eye-rings, and never have blue in the bill. Notice that all the whistlers have large eyes to take in more light to help them see at night.

Black-bellied and Fulvous Whistling-Duck

Black-bellied and Fulvous Whistling-Ducks are similar in size and structure. They are slim-bodied and round-winged, with very distinctive long slim necks and somewhat bulbous heads. The long legs protrude way past the tail, enhancing that long and skinny look. They usually hold their necks low making them look distinctly hunch-backed. Both species have striking dark underwings. Nothing else looks, or sounds, like them! Separating them apart in flight is straightforward, even from a distance. Black-bellies always have bold white wing bars and dark bellies that contrast with the paler chest, appearing distinctly two-toned even at distance. The bright bill is always hard to miss! Beware of Black-bellied in their briefly held juvenile plumage that lack the black belly and bright bill. Can you see the landing juvenile Black-bellied? Fulvous have fairly uniform upperwings, the flight feathers being darker and the only white being the uppertail coverts. The underparts are a uniform fulvous-brown, and they never have a black belly. They appear slightly more com-

Flight

pact than Black-bellies, with thicker necks and larger heads. Whistling-ducks can be seen at any time of day, but are most active at dusk (crepuscular) or night (nocturnal). Very vocal, their distinctive whistling calls are loud and a give-away, both night and day. Whistling-ducks are local, with large flocks spreading out in flight. Both species of whistling-ducks are often seen together, so look through flocks carefully. Looking at the image above, find the odd bird out on each page. If you can't find them, look again! Whistling-ducks spend a lot of time in trees and other closed-in areas where they need to parachute down steeply. Unlike most other ducks, they can drop from the sky vertically, with neck and legs down to make precise landings. In recent times Black-bellie's range and population have increased while those of Fulvous have declined. Out-of-range birds have mirrored this pattern. Black-bellied Whistlers frequently show up as far north as Canada, sometimes in flocks. Late spring and early summer are the best times to keep your eyes peeled.

Muscovy Duck *Cairina moschata* MUDU L 24–33in W 3.3–6.6lbs

Native Muscovies occur in Mexico, where it is considered endangered. It is rare and very local in the Lower Rio Grande Valley of Texas. A few pairs are most often seen flying over the Rio Grande, particularly at twilight. Wild birds are always black or very dark with green iridescence. They are slightly smaller, slimmer, and have more-angular heads than the feral Muscovy Ducks. Wild birds are very wary and are usually seen flying away, upriver or down. Large feral populations are established at a number of places; especially FL. Feral vs. wild birds can be separated by location, habitat, and habits. In FL, feral populations are common wherever there is water and people: parks, ponds, and where ducks are fed. They can also be found throughout the continent with other 'farmyard' ducks. They strut around the place as if they own it, and perhaps they do. Anything so big, bad, and ugly usually rules the roost! They waggle their tail from side to side as they walk. **ID:** Feral birds are very large and heavy with bulging sternum and sloping forehead. Wild birds are

ducklings; a few days old

All year

blackish with variable iridescent blue or green. ♀ are duller than ♂. Feral birds are highly variable. Colors range from all-black to all-white, many in between with brown. ♂ are 20% larger than ♀, are easy to sex by size alone. ♂ also have a larger head, thicker neck, and more-robust body. The bulbous wart protrudes from the top of the bill, gets larger with age. It's grotesque. The warts can extend around the eye and bill. The warty face is usually red but sometimes black. The bill is typically bicolored pink or gray with black. Wild birds have a small warty area just around their bill and eye that is largely dark. ♀ are much smaller and slimmer with fewer warts. Without the protruding wart, the bill can appear longer. It isn't. Juvs tend to look ♀-like but are more uniformly colored, have smaller feathers, and are duller with less iridescence. Juv have a dark iris, reddish-brown in ♀, yellow-orange in ♂. Striking white patches on underwing and forewing (lacking in very young birds) are obvious in flight.

ad. ♂ ad. ♀

Wood Duck *Aix sponsa* WODU L 19in W 1.3lbs   **Winter | Spring**

Woodies are fairly common freshwater ducks but often hard to see. They live in swampy woodlands or any combination of water and trees. They can find the smallest hidden wooded pond where no other duck goes. These ducks tend to sit high in the water and swim with head jerking backward and forward. They flush easily; they see you before you see them. A few get 'urbanized' and wimp out to the soft life in city parks, usually because they get fed. Most often seen in flight, typically in compact groups, particularly dawn and dusk. Nests in cavities or nest boxes. The spread of nest boxes helped save this species in the 20th century. Heard giving squealy calls: ♂ with a wheezy *szeeeEEP*, ♀ in a rising *ooo-EEK*. Woodies are beauties; its scientific name translates to 'bridal dress.' **ID:** Fairly small duck. Adult ♂: bushy crest creating bulbous back to head. Iridescent array of greens peppered with purple, accentuated by lines of white. The iris and orbital ring are a brilliant red. It's hard not to focus on the head pattern of ♂, but notice how subtly

Summer | Fall

stunning the rest of the plumage is with some more white lines thrown in for good measure. How many are there? Adult ♀: neatly patterned in an artist's palette of browns. Such subtleties makes the large white 'tear' around and behind the eye really stand out, even at the longest distances. The unique head shape, with a small crest and white chin, gives ♀ Woodies a somewhat comical look. Both sexes are long-tailed, a particularly useful feature in flight and for silhouetted birds. Woodies happily perch on branches, sometimes very high up in trees. The ducklings, like other tree-nesting ducks, famously parachute in a leap of faith to the ground when only a day or two old. Where do they get the nerve to do that? Woodies frequently sit on logs and branches on pond edges – a great ID clue. Whistling-ducks are the only other ducks that make this a standard practice. Woodies usually associate in small groups out of breeding season, but rarely with other species.

Wood Duck

You are having a nice walk on a trail in a swamp, shady forest, or around the town pond when all of a sudden a loud horror-movie shriek startles you. Several ducks take off steeply, finding a way through the trees, seemingly just as rattled as you. Their habitat, squeal, and behavior instantly give their identity away. Wood Ducks fly in tight family packs, with even spacing. They have a very distinctive shape; most striking is the long squared-off tail. Flock shape and long tails are immediately distinctive. Also notice how uniform the upperparts appear. The blue secondaries can look brown at a distance, and the white trailing edge can disappear into the sky. Woodies are ducks lacking strong contrast on the underparts except for the ♂ tail, but they always have a pale belly. Despite an elaborate plumage, the dark coloration in Wood Duck allows them to blend in surprisingly well to almost any darkened pond or wooded swamp they may inhabit. Late summer and fall can provide a wide array of plumages that can make aging and sexing seem confusing.

ad. ♂ (left) and ♀ (right) Mandarin Ducks

eclipse ♂

eclipse ♂ with ducklings

ad. ♀

Summer/Fall

Some ♂ are still in full eclipse when the first ♂ have molted out into their stunning colors. Eclipse ♂ retain their red iris and red on the bill even when everything else is drab. The gaudy plumage is usually attained by about Oct. Ad ♀: brown, a striking white eye patch, dark bill, and diffuse white streaks on the breast. They don't show 2 pale lines from the throat extending round the neck and onto the cheek like other plumages. Juvs: brown, like adult ♀. Differs in having a complex head pattern, more finely streaked breast, and less bulbous head. 1st-yr ♂: develop a dull orange iris and orbital ring, pale orange bill, but retain juv brown-and-white breast-streaking. Most 1st-yr ♂ look adult-like by mid-winter and become difficult to age. Mandarin Duck is the gorgeous Asian counterpart of Wood Duck. Common in captivity, occasional escapes occur. ♂ is unmistakable. ♀ have more boldly spotted underparts and a grayer head with a narrower but better defined spectacles around and behind the eye than ♀ Woodie.

ad. ♂ Domestic Mallard

ad. ♀

ad. ♂

Mallard *Anas platyrhynchos* MALL L 23in W 2.6lbs   **Winter | Spring**

The familiar and common duck, found in city parks, farm fields, water bodies of whatever size, to the wildest Arctic places. Mallards are the best known and commonest waterfowl, a favorite with moms and their kids, farmers, lunch-break shoobies, and just about anyone who likes to get close and observe personality. These are the classic dabblers, up-ending to feed, picking on the surface, putting their heads and necks under water, just fun to watch. Yes, character they have in spades, and a sex drive that makes you wonder if they take Viagra. 'Greenheads' can take the heat and the cold, often bunching up in winter in approachable flocks, wherever there are handouts to be had. The 'Mallard complex' also includes American Black, Mottled, and 'Mexican' Duck. They are all of similar size and shape, have similar DNA markers, hybridize wherever they come in to contact, and sound similar. Mallard is actually the odd one out, the ♂ having a distinctly different bright plumage. It's the boss! Mallard is also the ancestral stock of many domestic ducks. Do-

Summer | Fall

mestic Mallards are larger and chunkier with an abdomen like it's wearing a diaper. Some are colored like Mallards, but they come in all sorts of colors, and they are always tame! Pinpointing truly wild birds is often tough. Call: the stereotypical quack-quack duck call is given by ♀ only. ♂'s call note is quieter. **ID:** Fairly large, well-proportioned, and muscular. Blue speculum (can appear purple) bordered by black and white. Adult ♂: striking green head with white collar; funky upturned black central uppertail coverts. Bill is bright yellow to yellow-olive with black nail. Eclipse ♂ (Jun–Sep): retains yellower bill. 1st-yr ♂: identical to adult ♂. ♀: dullish gray-brown, paler on head and neck with dark crown and eye-stripe. White outer tail feathers. Variably yellow-orange bill with mottled dark center. Juv: briefly held plumage similar to adult ♀ but warmer brown with darker neatly aligned centers to feathers. These juvs molt into bright plumage over the next 2-3 months. By mid-fall they are identical to adults except for retained juvenile flight feathers and coverts.

Attracting Mates! Mallard seemingly copulate more than other ducks. Perhaps this is one of the factors why it is the commonest duck in the Northern Hemisphere. They copulate most often in winter and spring, but also summer, and occasionally fall. The ♀ may do an incite display, getting her mate or pretenders to display by quacking, stretching out her neck, or moving her bill to the side and down. He starts to swim a little faster with neck held more erect. The ♀ knows: they swim around a little, as if she is playing hard to get. They stop, face each other, and start energetically synchronized bobbing. This may go on for about 20 seconds. The ♀ cooperates partially submerges allowing the ♂ to mount her. The ♂ grabs the back of her neck, pushes her head under water impregnating

her in a matter of seconds. It's quick and ruthless. The ♂ dismounts, swims off with neck outstretched and held close to the water. Both then give a little shake, and then raise up and flap their wings. This may be in part to show off the speculum; the bright feathers in the secondaries. They are done. Life gets back to normal. Flight is another constant of a duck's life. They all land in similar ways but with some variations. Most come in at roughly a 30- to 60-degree angle, use their wings to slow them down, and their legs act as shock absorbers as the birds hit the water. Heavier birds, such as sea ducks, have a longer 'landing zone' to stop, need to use their wings and feet more, and create a longer splash zone. The smaller ducks, such as teal, and whistling-ducks come in the steepest

What Creates Color in Feathers? Color in feathers is created in a few ways. Browns, blacks, grays, and 'earth tones' are created by melanin. Oranges, reds, yellows, and purples by carotenoids. Porphyrins are responsible for some greens, reds, and a range of browns. Combining these results in a wide spectrum of colors. A feather's surface, is made of a tough protein called keratin. It is also found in legs, feet, and bills. When the translucent keratin is layered, it reflects short wavelength light creating stunning metallic greens, blues, and purples we view as 'iridescence'. We can see this in speculums and head colors. The remaining light rays are absorbed by the melanin layer beneath. In many feathers color is a result of light reflected by the keratin and pigments in the feather

Here, with the sun to your right, notice how the 'green' head of a Mallard looks purple or black! It appears black when the feathers are in the shadow, as there is no sunlight to reflect the beautiful metallic colors. The head is usually purple or blue when you are looking toward the sun, and green when the head is backlit. With a quick tilt of the head, the colors change. This is even more apparent on a duck's speculum. Subtle wing repositioning can result in a mosaic of blues and purples in seconds. Check this Mallard out! Go to your own local duck pond, and watch a few 'Greenheads' for a while. One interesting thing to remember is that across all species of birds, the color blue is never created by pigment, but always by the crystal feather structures that create iridescence

'Mexican' Duck *Anas (platyrhynchos)- diazi* MEDU L 21.5in W 2.2lbs

Considered a subspecies of Mallard by the AOU, though they are more closely related to Mottled Duck and probably best thought of as a full species. It is treated equivalent to a full species here. Found most commonly close to the Mexican border from AZ to w. TX. Birds are occasionally found farther north. Mexican Ducks have adapted to man, occurring at water treatment facilities, stock ponds, town parks, and other wetlands. Mallards are also found in these areas, and the degree of hybridization is not certain. **ID:** Mexican Duck is best thought of as being intermediate between a pale Black Duck and a ♀ Mallard. Similar to Black and Mottled Ducks. Both sexes look alike. Adult ♂: averages darker than ♀, slightly more rufous on the chest, green tinge to crown, and most importantly, have dark yellow to olive-green bills. Adult ♀: have orange bills, sometimes with extensive gray on the upper mandible, particularly in summer. The tail is dark, fading to rufous, with narrow white edges. Mallard always has an extensive white outer tail. Mexican Duck's speculum usu-

All year

ally appears blue with 2 fairly broad white wing bars, nearly as broad as Mallard. Some variation is clinal, birds becoming darker and with less white to the south: in central Mexico they usually show no white in the greater coverts. The influence of Mallard genes, is uncertain. Compared to ♀ Mallard, Mexican Duck has darker and simpler-patterned body feathers with narrower and darker feather fringes. Tertials are more uniformly brown. Mexican Ducks have dark-spotted upper- and undertail coverts; smaller spots and paler borders in ♀ Mallard. They rarely show a purple sheen to the speculum, and often have an all-orange bill. The underwing is all white, lacking the dark spotted lesser coverts of Mallard. Mottled Duck is slightly darker, has a dark spot at the base of the bill, and narrower white border to the speculum. Mexican x Mallard hybrids have curly uppertail coverts, extensive green on the head, extensive white in the tail, and average paler. ID is often tough and knowing if there is Mallard influence can be difficult.

American Black Duck Anas rubripes ABDU L 22in W 2.6lbs

Winter | Spring

A darker cousin of Mallard, these birds are the same size and shape. Found in the East, in the South only in winter. Scarce in most areas, though locally common in saltwater marshes where they form sizeable single-species flocks in winter. Most breed farther north in a variety of forested wetlands as well as coastal marshes. Beaver-altered wetlands are particularly popular. They tend to be very wary and easily flushed, usually the first to take flight when in mixed flocks, an adaptation to us pursuing them over the years. Open coastal marshes make it a real challenge trying to get close. Declining, largely due to encroachment from Mallard with which it frequently hybridizes. Working out which are 'pure' birds is difficult and is always a headache. **ID:** Size and shape just as Mallard. At all times of year always look for the really dark unicolored body. It should really be called 'Dark Brown Duck.' The head and neck are conspicuously paler than the body, and they stand out at distance. The dark eyeline and cap are distinct. The cap appears almost black, but with very

ad. ♀ with juvs; about 6 weeks old

ad. ♂

ad. ♀

Summer | Fall

close views usually shows slight green iridescence – this is normal. Extensive green in the cap is a sign of hybridization, and these birds often show other features – see next page. Sexes similar in color, though ♂ is sometimes subtly darker. Most reliably sexed by bill color: yellow in ♂ with black nail, ♀ paler with duller olive-green bill. They are frequently in pairs making comparison easy. In summer bill color typically darkens, some being completely dark. Black Ducks never show white outer tail feathers – Mallards always do. If in doubt, always check this out! In flight the bold, often gleaming, white underwing contrasts strongly with the body, the key to ID at any distance. Paler head also a good confirming character. Purple/blue speculum bordered by black with narrow or no trailing white edge to secondaries (compare Mallard). Any white on the leading edge to the speculum marks it a hybrid with Mallard. Seen far off, the wing often looks uniformly dark. Smaller juv feathers are quickly replaced making ageing difficult.

Mallard x American Black Duck Hybrid

Sadly, wherever you see American Black Ducks (Black Ducks), there is a real possibility that they will have some Mallard genes. Genetic differentiation between the two species has dramatically changed, presenting major problems for the Black Duck's species integrity. This happens when unpaired ♂ Mallards join Black Duck courtship groups. Mallards are competitively superior, with ♀ attracted to the brighter colors. The dominant ♂ Mallard is adept at keeping the ♀ Black Duck's attention from subordinate ♂. Offspring are fertile, being able to breed with either species. Long term, this is a real conservation problem, as Black Ducks continue to decline significantly. Too many hybrids and Mallards filling the void! **ID:** the upperwing in these hybrids has white borders to the speculum. Black Ducks can have a narrow white trailing edge to the speculum, but never a white leading edge, although it can have a duller gray or beige border. Black Ducks usually have 10 or more dark underwing coverts, creating a band on the leading edge of the wing. This Black Duck

All year

feature is strongly suggestive, but not diagnostic, of hybridization. A slight green iridescence on the crown is quite common in pure Black Ducks. Many ♂ hybrids have intermediate characters. If these show strong Mallard features they are either Mallard × Black Duck or Mallard × hybrid. Most striking is a half-green head. Compared to purebred Black Duck, other features include brighter chest and more intricately marked body feathers. Always look for the Mallard's white outer tail feathers and kinked black uppertail coverts, unique among ducks to Mallards. Hybrid × Black Duck backcrosses have some green on the crown, but this is often tough to evaluate at distance. Orange fringes to the body feathers are a good indicator of hybridization. Most of these birds show the kinked black uppertail coverts. Identifiable ♀ hybrids are dark, similar to Black Duck but show a Mallard-type bill and reduced white in the tail. ♂ hybrids outnumber ♀ by 6:1. The true status of hybrids is not known. How many hybrids don't show any intermediate features is anyone's guess.

ad. ♀ with ducklings

ad. ♀

ad. ♂

Mottled Duck *Anas fulvigula* MODU L 22in W 2.4lbs

Replaces American Black Duck (Black Duck) in the extreme SE and the Gulf Coast, occurring from SC to TX. Occasionally wanders as far north as Canada. Fairly common in the range. Thankfully, its range rarely overlaps with Black or Mexican Ducks. It has a similar fondness for coastal marshes, but it is also common in freshwater wetlands, rice fields, canals, and ditches. Mottled Ducks are typically seen in pairs. After breeding, the pair bond breaks, though couples often renew. Because they are paired most of the year, larger flocks are rare. **ID:** Intermediate in color between Black Duck and Mallard with warmer tones due to broad warm brown feather fringes and internal markings. The head usually has warmer buff tones, with unstreaked buff throat and often less streaking on the cheeks than other Mallard-complex species. The crown has less dark streaking and less of a capped look. These features create a pale-headed look that contrasts strongly with the body. Other species can have unstreaked buff throats, so this character

Summer | Fall

is not diagnostic on its own. A black spot at base of bill (gape) is the boldest of the Mallard complex. It can actually be easy to see at distance. ♂: slightly darker version of ♀ with brighter yellow bill. ♀: bill yellowish to orange, a few greenish, with or without a saddle. In summer the bill often turns dark, particularly in ♀. Shows complex feather-center pattern as ♀ Mallard (typically solid in Black Duck). Speculum blue, but can appear purple with narrow white trailing edge. Slightly shorter wing-point than Mallard and Black Duck. (Longer-distance migrants usually have longer wings.) There are 2 subspecies: *A.f. fulvigula* is the paler and most warmly colored, occurring mostly in Florida. These are the 'blonds' of the dabbling ducks. *A.f. maculosa* occurs from Alabama down in to Mexico, averages narrower buff fringes and looks darker and more Black-Duck-like. In flight looks most like Black Duck with striking white underwing, similar speculum colors, and an all-dark tail. The white on the trailing edge of the speculum varies from absent to quite broad.

ad. ♀s

Mottled Duck x Mallard Hybrid

Wherever Mallards come in to contact with Black, Mexican, or Mottled Ducks, hybrids will occur frequently. In FL, for example, Mottled Duck x Mallard hybrids are increasingly common, and species integrity has become a real conservation issue. Hybridization rates in different parts of Florida have been as high as 24%. The ♂ Mallard's competitive superiority, because of their bright colors, is already becoming a problem for the Mottled Ducks, as the Mallards continue to increase in the Mottled Duck's range. Mallards are dominant close to humans in ponds surrounded by apartment complexes, local parks, golf courses, and anywhere where people are too familiar. The Mottled Duck population is at particular risk since over half the Florida population of that species may occur in urban and suburban areas. Mottled x Mallard hybrids can be found anywhere, particularly in these areas. The hybridization issue is not serious in the Gulf Coast population of Mottled Ducks, since pairing of Mottled Ducks in Louisiana and Texas, for example, occurs before wintering

ad. ♂'s

All year

Mallard arrive. By Nov-Dec, when Mallards arrive in large numbers, 93-96% of Mottled Ducks are already paired on the Gulf Coast. **ID:** The Florida hybrids are highly variable in appearance and show the same traits as Mallard × Black Duck hybrids (see p. xx). ♂ typically show distinct features of both species, notably partial green heads, rufous breasts, gray in the flanks, kinked black uppertail coverts and a variable amount of black on the undertail and rump. The white outer tail, a great Mallard feature, is always prominent. ♀ are often trickier to ID. The first clue is the bill, usually being partially dark rather than uniform green. The head usually has more streaking and is less buffy than in Mottled Duck. The body color is usually darker than Mallard but not as warmly colored as most Mottled Ducks. There is little or no white in the outer tail feathers. The speculum typically has broader white borders than Mottled Duck. It is quite noticeable how Mallards, or Mallard hybrids, are more approachable than Mottled, American Black, or Mexican Ducks.

What are these?

Gadwall *Mareca strepera* GADW L 20in W2lbs

A common duck of shallow wetlands, found just about everywhere. Superficially nondescript, Gadwalls are often approachable, though unobtrusive, and can easily be overlooked, particularly when mixed in with other more-obvious dabblers. The neck is usually held tucked in, making the species look bulkier and more compact than other dabblers. The ♀'s mischievous Donald-Duck-like gurgly *quack* is very distinctive, and they call a lot! ♂ give a deep *aark*. **ID:** Adult ♂: a beautifully subtle array of shades and patterns of gray, with rich brown scapulars for emphasis. It's no accident it's sometimes called the 'Gray Duck'. With a square, over-sized Frankenstein head, complete with a bulge at the rear, the ♂ sits high and proud in the water with lots of flank showing. The overall gray appearance makes the black rear end extra striking. Notice that most ducks with black butts have the black fronted by white (see the American Wigeon on the left). A brown cap sometimes extends to eyeline and has a purple iridescence on the sides. Adult ♀: noticeably smaller

Ring-necks, American Wigeon, and Canadas

1st-yr ♂'s

ad. ♀

Winter | Spring

and more petite than ♂, and often sit lower in the water. The hen is often confused with Mallard and other ♀ ducks, but look for the smaller size, slim neck, and small square head. ♀ and 1st-yr Gadwall usually have distinctive orange-sided bills, emphasizing the dark ridge. It's noticeable, even at a long distance, though it is a highly variable pattern. Pale head, particularly the throat, contrasts with darker upperparts. Solid dark feather centers have diffuse pale fringes. Tail is all brown, in contrast with the Mallard's distinct white outer tail feathers. Upperwing shows unique white square bordered by black, boldest in ♂. This can often be seen on some sitting birds. How many birds show this in the plate? Equally striking is its white central belly. Gadwall molt out of eclipse plumage early, and most are in bright plumage by Oct. 1st-yr ♂ grow adult-type feathers through first year. They have a highly variable combination of retained juv feathers and newly molted adult-type feathers through winter, and most are easy to separate from spiffy, clean adults.

Gadwall

Gadwall breed in a variety of freshwater habitats from seasonal wet areas to large lakes. They nest in fields, ditches, islands, and wetlands with plenty of cover. Principal breeding range is in the Prairie Pothole Region; they have a high success rate which probably helps to explain their expanding breeding range. They eat large amounts of submerged aquatic vegetation and spend a lot of time feeding.

Adults usually arrive on the breeding grounds in Mar or Apr in bright plumage. The ♂ typically start to molt into eclipse in Jun and are at their dullest in late-Jul and Aug. This molt pattern is typical of many dabbling ducks. Many birds, mostly ♂, take a molt migration to the north. Flightless Gadwall sit out on larger lakes while they molt. This is the safest, and the best strategy, for waterfowl to molt. It is also why we don't often see eclipse ♂. They keep the old upperwing coverts with lots of chestnut and the bill typically gets orange sides like the ♀. Most eclipse ♂ shows few remnants of bright plumage. These are often bars on the breast and flanks, and

ad. ♀ with juvs.

a few days old

juv. – about 6 weeks old

late-summer ad. ♀ with new eclipse feathers

worn mid-summer ad. ♀

juv. – about 3 weeks old

Summer | Fall

black on the uppertail coverts; the belly is white and contrasts more strongly with the flanks. Some ♂ may retain extensive brown eclipse feathers into Oct and are confused with advanced 1st-yr ♂. Adults will have newly molted broad gray tail feathers and larger flank feathers than the brown and narrow juv feathers on the 1st-yr birds. ♀ are remarkably variable, with no two alike. Some are pale brown and washed-out, others dark brown. Some have complicated internal feather markings, though most are dark centered with pale fringes. ♀ and juvs are often warmer brown than Mallards. The smaller size, different shape, orange bill sides, pale head, and all-brown tail always stay the same. These are all great features for separating from Mallard! Juvs are not easy to age, but it's always good to see if they are in family parties when the odd one will be the adult. Look for the uniform plumage with same-age feathers smaller and rounder than in adults; dark centers; and broad, pale fringes. Breast spotting is also smaller and more uniform than in adults.

Gadwall

A medium-sized dabbler that looks a bit smaller and slighter than Mallard with a slimmer neck and smaller head.
The wings are quite broad-based, pointed, and angled back at the carpal: everything is intermediate! They are usually in small flocks; groups of over 50 are scarce. When the bird is overhead, always look for the white central belly patch. It is neatly bordered by brown in ♀ and shades of gray in ♂. The bright white underwing contrasts with the flanks, creating a very distinctive look. Add to this the ♂'s black vent area and lack of bright colors, and the combination gives the Gadwall a pattern that simply pops at a distance. The square white secondary patch on the trailing edge of an otherwise fairly uniform dark upperwing is also obvious at any distance. Nothing else looks like it! This mark can be subdued on some breeding and juv. ♀ but is always present. Ad ♂ are most striking because of the bold contrast with the black border. Maroon medium and lesser coverts also add color to this duck. Young ♀ have the narrowest white

Flight

patch, smaller subdued dark border, and no chestnut. 1st-yr ♂ and ad ♀ have similar wing patterns with some chestnut on the median coverts, but they can be sexed by using other characters. Pair bonds are usually formed during the fall. Often groups of 5-6 ♂ will woo a ♀. Things are at their most active in the morning when one of the ♂ constantly harasses her, including trying to mate. The other ♂ all form a surrounding pack, but they never intrude. The ♀ constantly tries to swim away, only to be blocked off until she eventually flies. The whole group follows, going around in circles, often turning sharply with belly sideways and wings as broad as possible to negotiate the turns. She can't win, and so eventually she puts back down. But nothing changes. This ritual can go on for hours. When the pond seems noisy, check to see if this is what is actually going on!

American Wigeon *Mareca americana* AMWI L 20in W 1.8lbs   **Winter | Spring**

This is the duck that 'whistles.' Widespread and fairly common. Breeds in shallow marshy lakes and ponds with submergent vegetation and reedy edges, some in the far north. They form large noisy flocks in winter in wet areas or grazing in agricultural crop and grass fields. 'Pepper-heads' or 'Stealer-ducks' can be surprisingly tame, loitering around local ponds and city parks with Coots and gulls. Not quite as big as Mallard, this slight duck sits low in the water. **ID:** Flat-backed and small-headed with a short broad neck. They have a steep forehead, peaked forecrown, and a tendency to lean forward as they peer into the water. It's a distinct profile that can look dainty and elegant, particularly if the neck is held stretched! At a distance, flocks appear as a variety of pinks and burnt oranges with contrasting speckled gray heads. A small, pale blue bill, framed by black tip and base, is shaped for grazing. Adult ♂: bright plumage is pink with a distinctive black butt fronted by a white patch. It is striking at any distance and emphasizes its long, pointed tail.

Summer | Fall

Creamy yellow forehead and crown (it usually looks white) give the duck its old colloquial name, 'Baldpate.' Some also show creamy throats. The beautiful iridescent green stripe behind the eye appears black at distance. Eclipse ♂: ♀-like; most easily sexed by prominent white wing patch, brighter bill, and larger head. Adult ♀: orange-brown with gray flecked head. The hen usually has a smudgy patch around the eye. In summer, ♀ are faded and worn with tones tending to brown rather than orange. the bill darkens. Ad's molt into bright plumage through Oct-Nov. Juv/1st-yr. is similar to ♀ and can be aged by retained juv feathers. The blue bill often shows smudginess and a less-defined black border. From fall through winter adult-type feathers are molted in, and ♂ are sexed by pink flank and scapular feathers. The scapulars often cover the wing coverts and speculum. When visible, most birds are quite easily aged and sexed by their upperwing covert pattern.

American Wigeon

The beautiful whistled calls, sometimes described as squeaky-toys, are often the first thing that draw your attention to overhead Baldpates. Medium-sized, they are a well-proportioned duck, though a bit pot-bellied. Wings are fairly narrow, angled back at the wrist, and pointed. They fly with their heads held high, as if always ready to chatter to one another. The head looks large, emphasized by the small bill. Their striking white bellies stand out at any distance as they fly in compact tight-knit flocks. They are agile with fast deep wing beats. The white wing linings add to the white appearance, but are always divided from the white belly by darker flanks. It's a distinctive pattern you should always look for. Wigeon are often in large flocks, occasionally in the 1000s. An overhead raptor will create an incredible spectacle. The compact flock will explode and cover the sky: a mosaic of fall colors with white bellies and black butts. The ♂ have a striking black vent and long central tail feathers, like Pintail but shorter. American Wigeon's neck and up-

Flight

perparts look uniform at distance, except for the inner wing patterns. The dark ear patch is noticeable when closer. Most birds can be aged and sexed quite easily by the upperwing covert pattern. Adult ♂ have bold bright white wing coverts. 1st-yr ♂ also have white in the coverts, though not as clean white as Adult ♂, and they also have a dark trailing edge to the greater coverts. The speculum is green at the base in ♂, brightest in adults. The speculum lacks green in ♀. Beware: the green shows only in ♂ in certain light, and the speculum looks black for all birds most of the time. Adult ♀ have white on the greater coverts, but the median and lesser coverts are usually brown: a few show a pattern similar to 1st-yr ♂. A few 1st-yr ♀ have only white tips to the greater coverts, so they look quite dark-winged in the field. ♂ show the distinctively-shaped black in the tail from fall onwards in adults and later in fall, winter, or summer, in 1st-yr birds. ♀ are always brown-tailed.

Eurasian Wigeon *Mareca penelope* EUWI L 19in W 1.5lbs   **Winter | Spring**

Small numbers winter in the Pacific NW. Regular migrant in w. AK. Mostly singles elsewhere, usually with American Wigeon. A big flock often has one! **ID:** ♂ has vermiculated gray flanks and back. The burnt red head often shows green iridescence behind the eye – it's not necessarily a sign of hybridization with American Wigeon. Look for patterns of both on the flank and back for suspected hybrids. ♀, juvs, and eclipse ♂ are similar to American Wigeon. Eurasians have a browner head; its the same color as the body. Head shape is subtly different: flatter- and deeper-headed, otherwise structure and behavior similar. Additional ♀ Eurasian features are the lack of black around the base of the bill and more uniformly dark centers to the upperpart feathers. 1st-yr ♂ similar to ad ♂ by winter. They are most easily aged by gray-centered wing coverts – white in ad ♂. In flight, or ith wing raised, the clincher is the gray axillaries (armpit), which are strikingly white in American (though beware misleadingly quick views).

Mystery Wigeon

Wigeon regularly form large flocks. Their autumn colors and far-carrying whistled calls are one of winter's most beautiful experiences. Listen carefully for Eurasian Wigeon, it's a higher pitched and less two-noted; it stands out. These wigeon seem to call a lot! Eurasians are often mixed in with the Americans, particularly in larger flocks. The ♂ head colors always stand out. Hybrids do occur but are over-reported. The presence of green behind the eye is common in Eurasian Wigeon. Hybrid males typically show extensive green behind the eye, paler lower face and throat, pink extending on to the vermiculated black-and-white flanks. The hybrid underwing pattern is whiter than in pure Eurasians. The ♀ Eurasian's head has warmer red-brown tones that are similar in color to her body. She will have a larger and more bulbous head with a thicker neck. ♀ American Wigeons have a much grayer head that contrasts with the warmer body colors. Americans show some black at the base of the bill; Eurasians don't. Identify all the wigeon. Answers p. 485.

Northern Pintail *Anas acuta* NOPI L 23in(♂+4in tail) W 2.1lbs **Winter | Spring**

Breeds in US heartland, throughout most of Canada and AK, north to tundra. Winters mostly in the US or farther south, largest numbers in the West. Fairly common in shallow freshwater and brackish coastal marshes, usually swimming in flocks numbering from a few to 1000s. Graze in agricultural fields and even parks. Sometimes form very large tight single-species flocks. Droughts and loss of grassland habitat in the Prairie Pothole Region has led to substantial declines in population. **ID:** Usually best to ID by unique structure: slim, long-necked, long-tailed, with erect posture creating very distinctive elegant appearance: a really beautiful duck! Silhouette is distinctive even as specks in the distance. Long gray bill and legs. Eyes look small. Adult ♂: striking with brown head and white neck stripe; a very 'thoughtful' and somewhat dapper look. In nice light, shows a beautiful iridescent purple patch behind the ear coverts. Otherwise, many intricate patterns and shades of black, white, and gray, with yellow on the vent. Long tail with black

Summer | Fall

butt distinctive at long range. Boldly patterned gray bill. Ad ♀: Plain-looking, even for a ♀. Underparts vary in color from pale brown to white. Uniform face and neck; simple but elegant. Bill blue-gray, darkest in center, lacking the ♂ strong contrast. Eclipse ♂ (Jul–Oct): similar to ♀ but retains bolder covert pattern, gray-and-black-striped bill and has longer gray scapulars until it starts molting new adult-type feathers about Sep – the vermiculated gray-and-white flank feathers are typically the first to appear. Most adults are in bright plumage by Nov. Juv: similar to a warm-toned ad ♀. Aged most easily by looking for neatly patterned short streaks on the underparts – usually present on the belly through the winter, smaller feathers with less-complicated internal markings. In fall they can be aged by newly-molted, adult-type flank feathers. 1st-yr ♂ are best separated from eclipse ♂ by retained juv feathers on the underparts. Any ♂ not in full bright plumage by Dec is most likely a 1st-yr. By Feb, only a few 1st-yrs show signs of immaturity.

Northern Pintail

Long, slim, and very elegant, Pintails stand out in a group by their shape alone. Nothing else is like them. Their wings are narrow, long, and pointed, and angled back falcon-like from the carpal more than in other duck species. Not surprisingly with such a build, their flight is fast and direct but effortless – true athletes. With closer inspection, you will notice quite an unusual shape, with hunched back and a belly with the bulk of its weight at the rear, close to the vent. Sprigs or Pinnies often hold their body tipped up like the Concorde as if to counter-balance the extra weight near its derriere. Although slimmer than other ducks, Pintails are large, being longer than species such as Mallard and Shoveler. Pintail often form straight lines or 'V's like geese, particularly on longer flights. They frequently fly in single-species flocks and tend to fly higher than other species. Pintail are always pale. The upperparts look uniform except for the contrast with the dark speculum and broad white trailing edge; a distinctive pattern. The Pintail underwing is intricately patterned

Flight

gray, lacking bold contrast; the white trailing edge to the wing on the secondaries is the most prominent feature. Adult ♂: bold white underparts and neck. The white goes to a narrow point behind the brown head. The black rear end with long pointed central tail feathers. The long feathers disappear at distance. The bird's dark green speculum can look purple or brown. It is bordered by a broad white trailing edge and rufous-tipped greater coverts. 1st-yr ♂: similar speculum pattern but slightly duller. ♂ are bigger than ♀, the neck and head obviously thicker and larger with careful observation. ♀ are not much darker than buff — the palest duck! Hens have more brown in the speculum, narrower white trailing edge, and copper-tipped greater coverts. Even far off, the bold white trailing edge is distinct on what is often known as the greyhound of ducks. What other 3 duck species are mixed in with the Pinnies? Answers p. 485.

White-cheeked Pintail *Anas bahamensis* WCHP L 18in W 1.2lbs

A West Indian and South American species. Caribbean birds occasionally show up s. FL, most likely in drought years where they live. White-cheeks are a common captive bird so their true status here is controversial. Most are presumed escapes, perhaps too hastily. It's a beautiful and exotic-looking duck, a pintail but lacking the grace of Northern Pintail. White-cheeked Pintails have a supersized head that could be called square in ♂ but round in ♀. It's two-toned brown-and-white, making the bird really stand out. The bill is large, but it is the red base that is unique. Also notice that red eye. In direct comparison, ♂ are noticeably larger than ♀, particularly the head, and have more-boldly-marked flanks which are brighter orange. ♂ average more-extensive and brighter red on the bill and are slightly longer-tailed. All these differences are subtle. Juvs are similar to adults but duller with smaller spotting on the underparts. The dark bill soon turns red. They molt into larger and bolder adult-type feathers quickly.

Eastern Spot-billed Duck *Anas zonorhyncha* **ESBD** L 23in W 2.4lbs

Asian species that has shown up about a half dozen times in w. AK. Mallard size and shape. Yellow-tipped black bill is visible at distance and makes ID straightforward. Bold face pattern stands out on the pale head and neck. Otherwise, it's a dingy brown duck with narrow pale fringes to upperpart feathers. Broad white tertial fringes conspicuous on an otherwise Mallard-like wing pattern. Bold white underwing coverts like Black Duck.

Falcated Duck *Mareca falcata* **FADU** L 20in W 1.4lbs

Rare but almost regular to w. AK. A few wintering ♂, some returning annually, in Pacific states. ♂ are stunningly patterned and unmistakable with unusually shaped head. Look at the crazy tertials! 1st-yrs molt into adult-like plumage in fall. ♀ are very easy to overlook as Gadwall: they often mingle. Noticeably warmer-toned, particularly on underparts, but it's the large head, tapered at the back that is most distinctive. The bill is gray or black, lacking orange of Gadwall. ♀ have gray tertials with white outer fringes. Upperwing pattern similar to Green-winged Teal.

Northern Shoveler *Spatula clypeata* NSHO L 19in W 1.5lbs **Winter | Spring**

Common in a variety of shallow wetlands, with a real penchant for water treatment plants. Usually found in small loose groups, it can also occur in larger numbers in suitable habitat. Shovelers are large, heavy ducks that sit distinctively low to the water. Its massive, spatulate bill can be swished from side to side as it 'shovels' and sieves out food. The bill, combined with short neck and broad head, adds to its distinctive bulkiness and should be enough to ID most birds. They often feed in tight packs that move in circles like killer whales shoaling prey. Extensive white in the outer tail. Orange legs. **ID:** Adult ♂: unmistakable. Bright white accentuates iridescent green head and chestnut flanks. Nothing else is this color combination. Depending on light, the head can look purple or black. Bill is all black except in eclipse. Eclipse ♂ (Jul–Oct) similar to a warmly colored juv./1st-yr ♂. Ad ♂ always has a bright yellow-orange iris. Birds in partial eclipse in early summer and early fall are intermediate with darkish heads often showing a pale crescent in front of the eye

Summer | Fall

recalling Blue-winged Teal. The bolder bright plumage grows in gradually, and many ♂ don't reach full bright plumage until Jan (later in the East than other areas). 1st-yr ♂ (Jul–Jun): Similar to eclipse ♂, their appearance is also very variable. Ad ♂ are in bright plumage by mid-winter; birds not in bright plumage after Christmas are likely imm. 1st-yr ♂ irises become light around Oct, and although subtly duller than adults, they are difficult to judge in the field. 1st-yrs retain more-pointed, brown upperparts feathers and pale-tipped, brown flank feathers until spring. ♀: a pale-looking duck, due to broad buff fringes to feathers. Spoonies appear brown; typically warmly colored with strong orange-buff tones, particularly on the flanks. Bill orange, brightest at the edges, and duller on top. 1st-yr and eclipse ♂ also have orange bills. The iris appears dark in ♀: brown, often with a yellow hue. Although the plumage variation in Shoveler is great, and not fully understood, thankfully its shape and behavior is very distinctive for this bruiser of a duck.

Northern Shoveler

Aptly named and thick-set, muscular ducks, Shovelers' wings are broad-based, pointed, and angled back, almost falcon-like, tending to make them look slim. The head and neck suggest a dabbler on steroids, able to carry a massive bill: it's obviously large, apparent even at a distance. The massive bill helps to make it appear long-necked. The bill is held tilted slightly downward. Wing beats are fast, the flight powerful and direct. Shovelers are often in single-species flocks that are compact but in no particular shape. They often create short lines or 'V's. They do fly in mixed flocks with other dabblers and are commonly seen among Blue-winged Teal. Blue-wings are noticeably smaller but have very similar wing patterns and, sometimes, face patterns, making ID a problem for the unwary. The differences in size and shape should always be obvious if you focus on this. The underwing in Shoveler has obvious white median and lesser coverts contrasting strongly with the darker trailing edge and body. ♂ Shoveler's upperwing has an emerald green speculum that

Flight

can appear black at distance. The bold white greater coverts patch tapers significantly toward the body. The forewing is powder blue in ♂. The colors are subtly brighter and more iridescent on adult ♂ compared to 1st-yr ♂. But field confidence takes some practice! Adult ♀ upperwing is relatively dull with gray-blue wing coverts and a speculum that has some green but usually appears black. 1st-yr ♀ are similar but duller, with browner coverts. When ♂ are in bright plumage, the dark head and chestnut belly contrasting with white neck and underwing is a unique pattern that stands out at any distance. Other plumages are quite similar to ♀ Mallards in color with warm brown underparts, orange bill, and white outer tail feathers and underwing. But the structure is always strikingly different. Are there 3 Blue-winged Teal and 3 Mallards mixed in with these Shovelers?

Blue-winged Teal *Spatula discors* BWTE L 15in W 0.9lbs

Winter | Spring

A welcome common summer visitor, hence often called Summer Teal. Some winter in the South. Usually in pairs or small parties, often announcing itself with a high-pitched 'kip'. Found on variety of shallow marshy wetlands, big or small. Usually near vegetation, where they dabble, upend, or pick food off the surface. They are often quite tame and are found in fairly tight-knit groups as they fidget around, though they all look like they are pals. They readily mix with other species, particularly other teal and Shoveler.

ID: Small dabbler; slightly larger than Green-winged and smaller than Cinnamon Teal. They sit low and long in the water, with a wide, slightly rounded head. Neck is often held upright, and slightly tilted forward, seemingly extra-observant as they look nervously from side to side. The bill is fairly large, broad, and all dark, though shorter than on the flatter-headed Cinnamon Teal. Adult ♂: Unmistakable, beautiful half-moon face is striking at long range. Some birds even show the white extending along the crown sides and

Summer | Fall

down the nape. The flanks and breast are buff spotted black, but every bird has a different color and pattern. The black undertail, fronted by white flank patcvh, is striking at any distance. Adult ♀: All plumages of Blue-winged Teal, other than older ♂ in bright plumage, are similar to ad ♀, making aging and sexing tough. All are dark brown, sometimes appearing grayish, with well-defined white or buff feather fringes. Always look for the distinctive pale area at the base of the bill. In summer, adult ♀ tend to get darker and have bolder markings on the underparts. Eclipse ♂ are similar to ♀ but usually show a 'ghost' of the 'half-moon' face pattern. Ad ♂ don't attain bright plumage until around Dec, later than most dabblers. 1st-yr ♂ are a dull version of adults through most of the winter: date is a great clue to help in aging. Juv plumage is monotone but neat. They quickly start molting head and flank feathers. Birds on migration have similar looking, but different-aged feathers. Ageing is tricky; look for unmolted juv tail and belly feathers.

Blue-winged Teal

Our longest-distance waterfowl migrant, with many wintering as far south as n. South America, though good numbers winter in the s. US to FL, most along the Gulf of Mexico. They move south early, with flocks arriving as far south as the Gulf Coast by Aug. Most arrive back on their favored prairie breeding grounds in Apr, some earlier. Blue-wings are small and slim, but their lean athletic shape can make them look deceptively large. The undercarriage is nicely rounded, the wings slim and angled back. Very similar to Cinnamon Teal in size, shape, and upperwing pattern. Noticeably slimmer and slightly larger than the very dark and compact Green-winged Teal. As you would expect, they are fast and agile flyers with rapid wingbeats, seemingly in a hurry. They take off steeply and quickly. They fly in small groups, but on migration, can form large flocks that are closely knit but spread out. Distant ♀-type Blue-wings look quite dark. The dull bill stands out because of the contrast with the pale subloral spot. On ♂, the white upperwing coverts are really

Flight

obvious at any distance. The powder-blue forewing can be striking, but the iridescent green speculum usually appears black. 1st-yr ♂ are similar, but the blue is slightly duller, and they often have a few dark spots on the white wing coverts. ♀ are noticeably duller, and the wing coverts are black and white. They don't stand out at distance as on ♂. Looking for retained juv belly and tail feathers is often the easiest way to age them. All Blue-wings have a dark leading edge to the underwing. It contrasts strongly with the white underwing coverts and axillaries. Look at how striking the underwing looks! Summer Teal often fly with Shovelers which have a similar upperwing pattern. To differentiate, concentrate on the size, underwing pattern, and the shoveler's massive bill. Green-winged Teal are slightly smaller, noticeably more compact, and darker, without the blue 'wing.' Cinnamon Teal have the same wing pattern as Blue-wings, so they can be safely identified in flight only by other plumage patterns.

Cinnamon Teal *Spatula cyanoptera* CITE L 16in W 0.9lbs **Winter | Spring**

Breeds throughout w. US, extending north to s. Canada and south through Mexico, mostly in shallow alkaline wetlands. The Great Basin and mountainous region is their stronghold. Most winter in Mexico south. Rare in the East. They arrive and leave early. A few winter in s. US in a variety of shallow wet habitats. Nowhere are they common, usually in pairs or small groups, but often tricky to find at all. Sometimes found in single-species groups, but often with Blue-winged Teal and Shoveler. Quite similar to Blue-winged in many ways with a friendly demeanor, quietly moving around in groups picking food off the surface and occasionally tipping. **ID:** Cinnamons are very similar to Blue-winged Teal in size and shape. They average slightly larger, their head tends to be flatter, the bill longer, and the neck thicker. This is sometimes distinctive but these are all average differences so be careful! Adult ♂: uniquely chestnut, even the black upperparts have striking orange fringes. Bold red eyes in all ♂ (usually by Oct in 1st-yr ♂). Eclipse ♂ are similar to ♀

Summer | Fall

but look for the red iris. The brown feathers are replaced by chestnut feathers through early fall and most adults are in full bright plumage by Nov. 1st-yr ♂ get some chestnut feathers and red iris from around Oct but are easily aged by signs of immaturity through the winter. Adult ♀: similar to Blue-winged Teal. Cinnamons are noticeably blander-faced which enhances the longer-billed look. The pale loral spot and dark eye-stripe, obvious in Blue-wings, are almost lacking in Cinnamons which have a more-complete eye ring. It is the warmer, brown-toned plumage with broad buff fringes that initially stands out on most. Ad ♀ in summer are more similar to Blue-wing with darker brown-centered feathers, narrower and whiter fringes. Juvs are very similar to ad ♀. Like adults, juv Cinnamons are variable in color, but only a few overlap with the colder tones or face pattern of Blue-wings. Most birds are identifiable, but a few are best left unidentified. A number of reports of out-of-range Cinnamons are misidentified rust-stained Blue-wings.

Cinnamon Teal

Cinnamon Teal are very similar to Blue-winged Teal in just about every way, the most notable exception being the stunning ♂ in bright plumage. Although there is overlap, some Cinnamons are longer-billed, thicker-necked, and flatter headed, giving them an even-more-slender appearance than Blue-wing, for those with an acute eye. The warmer tones, more uniform appearance, and, particularly, the plainer face pattern, are other good features to look for. However, all these differences are subtle, and some birds are best left unidentified. The upperwing patterns mirror Blue-winged Teal. Cinnamons are frequently found together in flocks with Blue-wings, so seeing a couple of easy-to-identify gaudy males does not mean the accompanying birds are the same species. Aging sitting Cinnamons, like Blue-wings, is very difficult and being able to see juv belly feathers is a good way. Here you can see all the finely speckled underparts of the bird labelled '1st-yr'. This appearance is typical of most 1st-yr ducks and with ever-improving cameras and

Flight

powerful scopes, it is something we can see in the field as well as on specimens. Adults usually have unmarked underparts or larger blotches that are irregularly spread. The large bill and bold wing pattern have similarities with Shoveler – and they are often seen together. Shovelers are noticeably larger, and the bill is really massive. If you are not sure, you can look for the dull upperwing coverts on ♀ Shoveler; it's powder-blue on all Cinnamons. Shovelers also have a pale leading edge to the underwing. Most Cinnamons can be aged and sexed using wing covert patterns. 1st-yr ♂ are like adult ♂ but have pale tips to the dark, greater coverts, and narrower tertials. ♀ have extensive dark (brownish-blue) bases to the greater coverts, with broader white edges on the outer ones. It's sometimes quite surprising how often we can see features like a red iris, belly, and tail feathers to help age and sex birds when we focus on specific characters. Are there any Shovelers or Blue-winged mixed in with the Cinnamon Teal?

Green-winged Teal *Anas crecca* GWTE L 14in W 0.7lbs **Winter | Spring**

The commonest small duck in many areas. Breeds in permanent ponds with lots of emergent vegetation near boreal forests and in prairie potholes. Found in most wetlands, agricultural fields, and tidal mudflats in winter. They favor shallow pools, near muddy edges and dense cover a lot more than many dabblers; they can be a devil to find. They happily waddle over muddy shores and estuaries to feed. Green-wings are often in compact groups and can form large flocks away from the breeding grounds. The ♂ can often be heard giving short, football-whistle calls: *krik*. It's one of the marshes most distinctive noises. **ID:** The smallest dark brown duck in the marsh. Compact and deep-bodied, it sits high in the water. Look for a large square head on a short neck with small bill – the rubber duck of ponds. A distinctive shape! Adult ♂: Rich chestnut head with green mask, finely patterned body. Green-wings (*A.c.carolensis*) have a white vertical flank line and black-bordered yellow butt that stand out. Eurasian Teal (*A.c.crecca*) is considered

Summer | Fall

a separate species in Europe. It is scarce, but regular, in the East with its cousin, (perhaps 1:1000). Bright-plumaged ♂ lacks the white vertical stripe between the breast and sides. Instead, look for a bright horizontal line that runs along the bottom edge of the scapulars. Also look for bolder lines that help frame the face. It's a more striking bird. Asian subspecies (*A.c.nimea*) almost identical to *crecca*. Intergrades with both the vertical and horizontal white lines occur regularly. ♀: Focus on dark color and distinct shape, particularly the large head. Bold eyeline, usually with a cheek stripe (normally lacking in *crecca* and *nimea*). The easiest Green-wing ID feature : a horizontal pale yellow (often appears white) line at the base of the tail. It is obvious, even far off. Juv: most easily aged by finely patterned underparts. 1st-yr ♂: best sexed by new vermiculated flank feathers and yellowish vent. Most attain full bright plumage about Nov/Dec, 1-2 months later than adults. The brown flank feathers are molted in last. Aging and sexing Green-wings in fall is difficult on many birds.

Green-winged Teal

A small, dark duck with a square head! They often stay quite well hidden close to dense cover and are easily flushed with fast, vertical take-off. Surprisingly, they have a long landing zone: a flock landing has water splashing everywhere. Their small size enables them to be very agile, allowing for the steep ascent, though it is a bit of a struggle to get going. The compact body with short tail, short neck, and bulky head all add to the impression of it being small. The bill shape adds to the smooth concave forehead – other teal look flatter-headed. They appear dark at a distance, lacking bright colors with a relatively indistinct wing pattern. The green-and-black speculum, bordered by copper and white is the same for all Green-wings. The rest of the upperparts are unicolored. When mixed in with other teal, they are the small, dull ones! They are often in larger flocks of a 100 or so, although it doesn't look like that many. They will flush vertically if a passing eagle gets too close. The water explodes everywhere, and the teal wheel off in a compact ball.

Eurasian Teal

juv.

Flight

Their wingbeats are fast and agile, and they move tightly in unison, staying close together. Their wings are narrow and angled back. Greenies often roll from side to side recalling a swift. Although a freshwater species, many will migrate over the ocean, usually in single-species flocks, but small numbers happily mix in with scoter, Bufflehead, other teal, and additional species. They sometimes hold their heads up as if peering around for a better view. ♂ in bright plumage are easy to sex, but all others are tough. The underparts show incredible variation in patterns, and the upperparts show none. All ages and sexes of Green-winged Teal have the same upperwing pattern. The speculum is emerald green and black, with a white or buff trailing edge. The green iridescence can look blue, purple, or black. The greater coverts form an orange or copper bar of similar width to the white trailing edge. In 'Eurasian' or Common Teal, the covert bar is white and much broader than the trailing edge; no other teal has a pattern like this.

Garganey *Spatula querquedula* GARG L 15in W 0.8lbs

Eurasian species, rare in w. AK, accidental everywhere else. Often found with the similar Blue-winged Teal — they are the same size and shape, and are found in similar habitat, though they tend to be a lot easier spooked. Not surprisingly, most records are of ♂, mostly in spring. **ID:** ♂ have a unique head pattern and have beautifully patterned gray and white flanks and scapulars. Unmistakable! Eclipse ♂, ♀, and juvs are similar to Blue-winged Teal. Look for Garganey's darker and colder colors; bolder face pattern, particularly the horizontal cheek stripe emphasized by a pale loral area; and pale throat. The white supercilium is boldest behind the eye. Beware of Green-winged Teal, which can show a similar face pattern though not as strong as Garganey. Green-wings are smaller and more compact with a smaller bill and have the pale bar edging the tail. Garganey have paler and grayer upperwing coverts, and the green speculum is bordered fore and aft by striking, broad, white lines; very different from Blue-winged Teal.

Baikal Teal *Sibirionetta formosa* BATE L 16in W 1lb

This Siberian species has been increasing in numbers recently, so it may become more regular. Most records from w. AK, but does show up on the West Coast with other wintering ducks. It is kept in captivity, so beware! Slightly larger than other teal, with a large, distinctively shaped head, peaked at the rear. Bright ♂ are stunning and unmistakable – though a couple of hybrids have caused confusion, so double-check carefully. Other plumages are more subtle, but still distinctive. They have a strong face pattern. A white loral spot with a unique dark border. Reddish eyeline is broadest behind the eye. White throat extends as a pale area up to the eye. They are warmer reddish brown on the breast, and the warm tones are replicated in the upperparts feather fringes; feather centers uniformly brown. The upperwing pattern is similar to Green-winged Teal. Baikals have uniform upperwings except for a narrow green speculum because the white trailing edge is very broad. Striking wing pattern in flight is reminiscent of Pintail.

Mystery Teal – ID, age, and sex these fall birds. The key is to take your time and proceed systematically. Teal typically form fairly tight flocks and quite readily coalesce with similar species. Mixed flocks are great for direct comparison. Green-winged Teal, in particular, can be quite easily spooked, so be careful trying to sneak up close. In late fall, you can get a full array of plumages: young, eclipse, and bright ♂, as well as ♀. Identifying them to species is mostly straightforward, but aging and sexing can be really tough. Identify the boldest-marked birds first; you can use these for comparison. Green-wings are the smallest and most compact, hint of horizontal cheek stripe, with square head and thick

neck. Pale vent line is usually obvious; a great feature. Blue-wings are sleeker with pale loral spot, much larger bill, and conspicuous eye-lids. Flank feathers have broader fringes that appear more rounded than those of Green-wings. Cinnamon Teal look slightly larger, flatter-headed, and a little larger-billed than Blue-wings. A red iris is diagnostic. Cinnamon typically has warmer tones and a blander face pattern. Watch out for rust-stained birds or strays, such as Garganey – they are colder brown with a horizontal cheek line. As mentioned, take your time. It's often surprising how you can keep seeing new features despite looking at a flock of birds several times. Answers p. 486.

Hybrid Dabblers. Hybridization is quite common in waterfowl. Just about any combination of parents you can think of has occurred. This is not uncommon in captivity, where there is a higher chance of unnatural pairings. Hybridization also occurs from forced copulation. Only 3% of birds have penises; ducks do. They are long and corkscrew like. The hen's oviduct is also corkscrew-shaped, but in the opposite direction, to counter ♂ aggressive behavior. In waterfowl, many species inhabit the same places and form pairs when flocks are mixed in winter, so opportunities to crossbreed occur. Brood parasitism sometimes occurs in groups like goldeneyes and Redhead. Shortage of mates, such as in out-of-range waterfowl, also encourages hybridization. Between laying eggs hens promiscuously mate with any drake they can find for the egg to be fertilized. Some of these offspring can breed creat-

♂ Pintail x Mallard

ad. ♂ Blue-winged x Cinnamon Teal

♂ and ♀ American Widgeon x Mallard

ad. ♂ American Widgeon x Redhead

♂ Pintail x Mallard

ing backcrosses that are even harder to ID, but many are infertile. Most hybrid waterfowl show characters that are intermediate between the parent species. Size and shape are very important characters and are hard to assess in photos. Color patterns are also critical. Beware of senescent ♀ showing ♂ characters, eclipse and molting birds, rust-staining, as well as birds that are aberrant. Male dabbler hybrids often have anomalous pale areas on the head not matching either parent's pattern. It is impossible to work out the parents of some 'couples', but many can be sorted out by adding all the pieces of the puzzle together. It is a challenge and fun. Mallards are notorious for pairing and hybridizing with, particularly, Black, Mottled, and Mexican Ducks (see p. 108/112/116). See if you think all the birds above are correctly captioned. What is the name of this famous marsh in Manitoba? Answer p. 486.

Diving Ducks, also known as Bay Ducks or Pochards (Aythyini)

Medium-sized, accomplished diving waterfowl with mostly short bodies and large heads. Their legs are set far back on the body and far apart, which helps them dive underwater, sometimes to 20 ft. Their leg-positioning, however, makes them awkward walkers. They usually feed on vegetable matter but can be omnivorous. Bills are somewhat heavy, usually about as long as the head, and sometimes with a distinctive tip. The males are more brightly colored than the females, but not as much as the contrast in most puddle ducks. No speculums, but with a more-or-less contrasting wing stripe formed by paler bases of the flight feathers. They mature at one year. They form seasonally monogamous pair-bonds, usually broken sometime during incubation when the males depart. The females take care of the ducklings until they fly, at which time the young are on their own. They have two molts per year, with one wing molt. They are heavy in relation to the surface area of their wings, which reduces lift. With relatively heavy bodies, they usually run along the water for some distance to gain enough lift for takeoff.

Sea Ducks (Mergini)

This is a varied tribe, called "sea ducks" as most species are associated with salt water, at least in winter. Males and females look different, with some really stunning males (e.g., Harlequin Duck and Spectacled Eider) They are all expert divers, primarily feeding on animal matter. Most can dive to feed at depths much deeper than those reached by Aythyini, the standard divers. Bill shapes are highly variable, depending on the subgroup adaptability (see below). Unlike the Aythyini, they do not breed until the end of their second or third year. Their seasonally monogamous pair bonds end with the breeding season, but some are known to re-form during the following winter. Females rear their broods until the young birds can fly. Almost all the diving ducks have two molts per year with one wing molt. They need a runway to take off, not unlike the diving ducks. Sea ducks can be considered in a few subgroups:

Eiders — bulky, hardy, heads large, wings relatively short, and flight heavy, usually low over water. All four species winter and molt in marine waters.

Scoters — stocky, dark, short-necked, migrate and winter in large flocks, flying in lines, low over the water. Mostly coastal and northern.

Goldeneyes (including Bufflehead) — chunky or large, big-headed, cavity nesters.

Mergansers — slender and relatively long-bodied. Appear particularly slim in flight. Classic fish-eaters with long, thin, serrated bills; cavity nesters or ground nesters.

Others — Harlequin Duck (unique little divers are northern river-breeding specialists and rocky-coast winterers), Long-tailed Duck (hardy divers, occurring in large flocks in migration and winter; unique molt sequence with three body molts).

Stiff-tailed Ducks (Oxyurini)

We have only two species in this unique tribe, Ruddy Duck and the rare Masked Duck; both are shallow divers. They are chunky ducks with short, rigid tail feathers that serve as a rudder for these diving ducks; the tail is often held cocked, particularly when sleeping. Their bodies are broad and short, necks are short, feet are adapted for diving, and legs are placed farther back on their bodies than in other waterfowl; they are poor walkers. Stifftails are omnivorous, with bills about as long as the head, broad, widened, and flattened at the tip. Ruddy Ducks have unique courtship display, but courting behavior is virtually unknown in Masked Duck. They mature at one year and pair bonds are seasonal, with some males being polygynous. Young stay with the female, but males may linger. Two molts per year, with one wing molt. Shape apparent in flight: thick neck; pot belly; long tail; and short, broad wings. Wingbeats are swift and direct. Ruddy Duck needs very long runway, but Masked Duck lifts off almost vertically, without a running start.

Canvasback *Aythya valisineria* CANV L 20in W 2.7lbs

Winter | Spring

The 'king of ducks' is a NA endemic. Locally fairly common. Breeds on deep freshwater marshes surrounded by emergent vegetation. Winters in flocks, usually in deeper rivers and lakes inland, and brackish water in coastal areas, on both coasts. Frequently with other bay ducks, particularly Redhead and scaup. Wide-ranging, with favored wintering areas, where flocks in 1000s from the Great Lakes to Mexico; also large stretches of range with very few individuals.
ID: The largest bay duck, with a diagnostic, long, evenly-thick neck, its head just an extension of this. The angular head has a wedge-shaped profile lacking a forehead. It is accentuated by its long, all black bill, which gives this duck its distinctive shape. Adult ♂: at a distance, ♂ Cans look two-toned — pale gray with a black head and rear. Up close the pale gray is actually white with very fine darker vermiculation. The head and neck are chestnut, the face and forehead are darker, and the eye is vivid red. 1st-yr ♂: quickly molt out of all-brown juv plumage into adult ♂-like appearance.

Summer | Fall

With close views, some can be aged by any retained brown juv tail feathers and tertials; these are ragged and pointed. A few have noticeably duller heads and brown mixed in the upperwing and body. Eclipse ♂: brown-headed, and the light gray body and upperpart feathers become a mixture of brown and gray. Like in other ducks, it keeps its bright iris — a great clue for sexing birds. ♀: have brown heads and necks; often darker on the crown. They are pale-throated, with a distinctive pale smudgy teardrop behind the eye. In winter, the upperparts and flanks are somewhat ♂-like, but with coarser vermiculation. The brown feather bases often show, as the gray tips wear off through the winter, and by spring they look much browner. Young ducklings are similar to Redhead chicks but quickly become darker brown and look like a fresh ♀ with a bold eyering. Even the young ones have the distinctive head profile when they are a few weeks old!

Canvasback flight

The fastest flying duck ... once it gets going. It takes quite a bit of running and flapping to get airborne. Its large size, big body, angular aerodynamic head and long wings are built for speed. They fly with fast powerful wingbeats in a straight line always giving the impression they are in a hurry to get there. Their long neck is held straight, seemingly stretched out as much as possible, but occasionally held down as if checking you out, not unlike a Red-throated Loon. The wings are held straight out rather than angled back as in most other species. ID is relatively straightforward if you focus on the above characters, but particularly the long, stretched neck and large bill extending onto the sloping forehead. It's a unique profile! They typically fly in straight lines or 'V's, in groups of a few to 25. Large flocks tend to be made up of small packs. They are more widely spaced than other ducks; perhaps they need a bit more braking room! Cans are frequently found with Redheads, and they do sometimes fly together. Given their somewhat similar

Flight

plumage patterns, it's very easy to overlook the 'wrong' species mixed in. Redheads are slightly smaller with a shorter and thinner neck and more bulging head that lacks the wedge shape of Canvasback. ♂ Cans are very pale above lacking strong contrast. ♂ Redheads show a strong contrast on the upperwing, a less extensive red head, but a more-extensive black neck. ♀ Cans share the same distinctive shape as ♂. Although not as boldly colored as ♂, they are equally distinctive. They have a brown neck and slightly paler head that contrasts nicely with the white underparts. The little pale smudgy tear drop behind the eye is really helpful. The upperparts are darker than ♂ but still paler than Redhead. Canvasbacks can sometimes be aged in flight by retained brown retrices and vent feathers. Also look for a molt limit; darker, retained juv wing coverts contrasting with newer, and paler adult-type feathers. The contrast between the dark wing coverts, and the paler mantle and scapulars, is the strongest. Adults look uniformly pale.

Redhead *Aythya americana* REDH L 19in W 2.3lbs

Winter | Spring

Locally fairly common diving duck, sometimes in big winter flocks on rivers, deeper water inland, and coastal lagoons. Close to 90% of Redheads winter at Laguna Madre in Texas and Mexico. Large flocks are also in the Great Lakes area, but there are large areas of US with only a few. Often with other diving ducks, particularly Canvasback and scaup. They breed in open-country freshwater marshes with dense emergent vegetation. **ID:** A fairly large diving duck with a supersized head that looks puffy and rounded and with a steep forehead. They sit high in the water and are round-backed. Focus on shape if you are confused by color patterns, though also look for the distinctive tricolored bill, with its large, black tip. The ridge of the bill and forehead create a concave shape from the bill tip to the crown. It's nearly straight in Canvasback. Adult ♂: boldly patterned with a chestnut head and black lower neck and rear. The back and flanks appear medium gray; up close you can see they are coarsely vermiculated black-and-white. Orange iris. 1st-yr

Summer | Fall

♂: similar to ad ♂ by late fall. Most easily aged by retained juv feathers, particularly the tail and belly, but these brown feathers can occur anywhere on birds through the winter. Black breast feathers usually show narrow, pale tips. Eclipse ♂: brown-bodied with a dull red head. Adult ♀: quite variable in color patterns. They are brown with pale-tipped feathers. When with scaup and Canvasback, focus on the bill and head pattern. Redhead has a pale throat often extending round the base of the bill like scaup. They have a distinctive pale ring around the eye with a diffuse pale line arching down behind that often sets off a slightly darker crown. Redhead commonly show white patches on the head, particularly the nape; these can be quite extensive. In summer, ♀ are more uniform brown, the pale eye-ring often lacking the pale area behind. 1st-yr ♀: hard to differentiate from ad ♀, but average paler. Look for retained juv feathers, particularly in the tail and belly.

Redhead

A fairly large and powerful duck, big-bodied, with a deep, rounded undercarriage. Redhead has a nipped-in neck that accentuates its large head, a feature to note in the field. The convex forehead matches all its other smooth curves. The wings are quite broad and blunt-tipped; they are held fairly straight even though there is quite a strong carpal angle. Because the majority of Redheads winter in very large localized flocks, they are often seen flying in good-sized groups. Raptors, such as Peregrine Falcon, quickly learn where breakfast is and have no problem taking ducks as big as, or even larger than, themselves. An overhead Peregrine will put a flock into a frenzy. Being a heavy bird, a Redhead needs to create speed by running over water before taking off. There's a lot of frenzy and splashing water when a flock explodes into the air. Once aloft, Redheads have a powerful and direct flight. Redheads size and shape, with wingbeats slower than most divers, can recall Gadwall; the relatively dull wings of GADW assist in that similarity. At close range, air

1st-yr. ♂'s
ad. ♂
ad. ♀

Flight

can be heard whooshing through their feathers. They often fly in 'V's or lines. Even-larger groups tend to be stretched out, two- or three-birds wide. They often drop out of the sky rolling steeply from side to side, legs splayed apart before putting their feet down and pulling back, as if they are frightened of overshooting the landing site. ♂ Redhead's bold color pattern is striking and distinctive in flight. ♀ are trickier. All Redheads have a broad gray or brown wing-stripe. The stripe broadens and darkens toward the wing-tip, as does the dark trailing edge, though the secondaries have barely-visible white tips. Only Ring-necked Duck has a similar wing pattern. ♀ Ring-necks are smaller, paler above, and have different face and color patterns. Canvasbacks are longer and leaner, the long, all-black bill striking. Both sexes are quite obviously paler. Both ♀ scaup have whiter wing stripes, the easiest feature to see. Scaup are also smaller, slimmer-winged, with faster wingbeats, and have a different face pattern. They typically fly in more-compact flocks.

Common Pochard *Aythya ferina* COMP L 18in W 2lbs

Eurasian stray to w. AK, particularly in spring. Sometimes in flocks, showing up with Tufted Ducks. A few records elsewhere. Escapes have occurred. **ID:** Common Pochard is intermediate between Redhead and Canvasback in just about all respects, notably head shape and bill pattern. Always focus first on shape, the key feature, though body color of ♂ also useful. Redhead × Canvasback and other hybrids occur that look very similar. Look at exact details of the bill shape, iris color, and all color patterns, including the forehead (Canvasbacks have black). ♀ Common Pochards are most similar to Redhead, the bill pattern being the first feature to draw attention. In winter, they are more two-tone, the head and neck contrasting with the grayer body. Summer and 1st-yr birds are more-uniform brown like Redhead – both species can have all-dark bills in summer. Similarly patterned to Redhead in flight, the paler color reduces the wing contrast in Common Pochard and is somewhat more Canvasback-like. Check that bill pattern!

with Greater Scaup and Redhead

1st-yr. ♂

1st-yr. ♀

eclipse ♂

ad. ♂

ad. ♀

Tufted Duck *Aythya fuligula* TUDU L 16in W 1.7lbs

Scarce, but regular, w. AK, sometimes in small flocks; rare elsewhere. Annual on West Coast (especially Pacific NW) and East Coast (especially in Atlantic Canada and NE states), often in flocks of scaup or Ring-necks; returning individuals occur. **ID:** A chunky duck with a short neck and big head, about the size of Lesser Scaup or Ring-necked Duck. ♂'s diagnostic black back, white flanks, and striking head tufts are easily seen. Eclipse ♂ have brown flanks but still show an obvious crest and a yellow iris. ♀ are tougher to ID and, not surprisingly, are reported less frequently. ♀ are similar to scaup, often with extensive white around the base of the bill. They have a short, but obvious, tuft, flatter head, and uniform dark-brown plumage. 1st-w are paler, initially have a dark iris, and no white at the "... base of the bill, and at least a slight tuft. Like all Tufted Ducks, the bill is tricolored, with the dark tip bordered by a pale band. In flight, the wing pattern is similar to Greater Scaup. Can you ID the pair of Tufties sitting with the Greater Scaup and Redheads?

Ring-necked Duck *Aythya collaris* RNDU L 17in W 1.6lbs **Winter | Spring**

This is a fairly common, medium-sized duck, about the same size as Lesser Scaup. They breed in freshwater ponds and marshes surrounded by trees, often at higher altitudes. In winter, usually found in small groups, sometimes with other diving ducks. Seen in a variety of freshwater wetland areas, often in ponds surrounded by trees where it is the only species. Occasionally found in large numbers, particularly when staging on migration. They dive in relatively shallow water and are often found with dabblers as a result. The maroon 'ring-neck' on ♂ is hard to see, and is not a good field mark. **ID:** A variable-looking duck that often gets people scratching their heads. Always focus on the distinctive sloping forehead and peaked rear crown, but beware of 'flattened-out' wet diving birds. They sit high in the water, with short neck and that large, peaked head. Perhaps 'ring-billed duck' would be a better name as all Ring-neck bills have a white ring emphasized by black bill tip. Adult ♂: appear black with gray flanks. Look for the diagnostic white

Summer | Fall

'spur' at the front of the vermiculated gray flanks; it jumps out at a distance. The iridescent blue-purple head usually appears black. The bill is boldly marked, and the white line around the base adds emphasis. Orange iris. Eclipse ♂: brown flanks and look dingy. Adult ♀: have dark brown backs, contrastingly paler-brown underparts, and gray head. Distinctive narrow spectacles and pale around base of bill. Yellow-brown iris. ♀ often show a pale patch at the front of the flanks. ♀ Ring-necks are boldly-marked dull ducks!

Juv: all brown; initiate molt into adult-like plumage by late fall. By mid-winter, 1st-yr ♂ a duller version of ad ♂, with retained brown juv tail and flank feathers and subdued bill pattern with less white at base. Most 1st-yrs are hard to age by Feb/Mar. 1st-yr ♀: browner than ad ♀ with a duller bill pattern. 1st-yr birds can often look smaller- and rounder-headed than ad. Look at images of the distant Ring-necks to see what features really stand out.

Ring-necked Duck

Ring-necks are often seen in compact flocks of 6 to 15 in winter. They frequent seemingly sterile forested ponds where little else lives, where no other ducks are present for comparison. At other times, odd ones are mixed in with both dabblers and divers, making ID more interesting. They tend to stay away from the ocean. On migration, they have favorite staging sites where 100s, sometimes 1000s can occur. These places can vary from large marshes, such as Montezuma NWR in n. New York, to a seemingly innocuous gravel pit in the middle of nowhere. They are smallish, about Lesser Scaup-size, so when flushed, they need only a short running take-off. They fly in short lines or compact flocks, rarely in 'V's. They are fast, agile flyers, with quite deep, but rapid wingbeats. The wings are bunt-tipped, held straight out, and not as swept back as many similar species. They are compact, pot-bellied, with short thick necks, and large heads. Given their haunts, they can drop down steeply into confined spaces. From below, they are striking, with

Flight

white underwing and belly. This is obvious in ♂, the white belly and underwing contrasting strongly with the dark tail and neck. The upperparts are uniform for both sexes with a large, but low-contrast, wing bar, just like Redhead. The flight feathers are gray, becoming browner on the primaries, with a broad dark trailing edge. The secondaries have a very thin, white trailing edge that isn't usually noticed. Even far away, the overall impression of both sexes is just a darker-looking species than scaup. In fact, ♂ Ring-necks are often misID'd as scaup. The Scaup's pale mantle and whiter, high-contrast wing bar in flight should be evident. Ring-neck's bold bill pattern is always a good feature. ♂ Tufted Duck is dark-mantled and quite similar, but focus on the Tuftie's white wing bar and flanks. ♀ Ring-necks are also best separated from scaup by the same darker wing bar. Their bolder eyering and grayer head are also good features. The color patterns of ♀ Redhead are similar to Ring-neck, but look for the Redhead's larger size and longer 'nipped-in' neck.

Lesser Scaup *Aythya affinis* LESC L 17 in W 1.7lbs **Winter | Spring**

The little bluebill is a widespread diving duck, and the only scaup that breeds outside of AK and n. Canada. Widespread in winter, with a preference for fresh water, but also on coastal estuaries and bays. Usually occurs in small flocks, although some are larger. Rarely found in massive concentrations like Greater Scaup. Frequently mixes with Greater Scaup and other bay ducks. **ID:** Compared to Greater Scaup, Lesser is roughly 10% smaller and looks slighter-bodied, lacking the muscularity and bulk of Greater. The different head shape is critical: peaked at rear crown due to long crown feathers, giving Lesser a more-balanced and square-headed look than Greater. This is difficult to judge on 'slicked-back' diving birds. By comparison, Greater is larger-headed, with steep forehead peaking above the eye, then gradually tapering back. The neck is thicker and, from in front, the cheeks more 'jowly.' Lesser's bill is more parallel-sided with black usually confined to nail. Greater's is broader, flared toward the tip with black bleeding off the nail. Adult ♂: Lessers can ap-

Lesser Scaup *Aythya affinis* LESC L 17 in W 1.7lbs **Summer | Fall**

pear purple-headed (mostly in summer) or green-headed like Greater; often appearing just black. Iris yellow. Lesser ♂ have more coarsely vermiculated upperparts. Greaters appear uniform gray because of the narrowness of the markings. ♂ Lesser's light gray flanks have brown juv. or eclipse feathers mixed in through fall and much of the winter. Adult ♂ Greaters are in full bright plumage by fall; a strongly suggestive ID point. Eclipse ♂: brown flanks and necks; the head, though often purple, can be green, brown, or just grungy-looking. Adult ♀: brown with gray flecking on the flanks and back. Bold, clean-cut white around base of bill. ♀ in summer are lighter brown with a pale neck, cheek, and face – very confusing for those familiar with winter birds. Juvs are all brown with a darker iris. 1st-yr ♂: molt in adult-like feathers through winter. Most show worn pale brown juv feathers in the tail, flanks, or belly until spring and have darker eyes (paler in adults). 1st-yr ♀: browner, less white at base of the bill, darker bill, and retained worn juv feathers.

Lesser Scaup

Lesser Scaup have a large breeding distribution and can feed in a variety of habitats, from shallow to deep. They migrate long distances and can show up anywhere. Lesser Scaup often fly in tight, compact flocks, but will create loose long lines or 'V's on longer journeys. They are medium-sized, compact ducks with a rounded undercarriage and pointed wings that are angled back. They have fast wing-beats – to be expected, as they are not as large and powerful as most other bay ducks. Most winter in the south, particularly FL, with some going as far as South America, so making long jaunts is not a problem. Many migrate over the ocean as well as inland, often mixed in with other *Aythya* or other waterfowl. They can look very small at a distance; the fast wing beats and compact shape can recall Green-winged Teal. Far off, ♂ in particular look very two-toned black-and-white, the white in the secondaries standing out. Although very similar to Greater Scaup, there are several other species that also need to be eliminated. Ring-necked

Flight

Duck are of similar size and shape, but appear darker and the wingstripe is duller on the secondaries. Lesser Scaup's gray back in ♂, and different face pattern in ♀ are good additional characters. Redheads have darker wing stripes, like Ring-necks, and are also larger. IDing Lesser from Greater is very difficult, sometimes impossible. In mixed flocks the difference in size and shape are noticeable; Lessers are about 10% smaller. They are slighter, with a thinner, nipped-in neck and smaller head. The two-toned wing bar with the brown-washed primaries contrasting with the white secondaries is the best feature to look for. This can be quite easy to judge. The white extends onto the primaries in Greater Scaup, but only barely in some. They lack the clear two-toned impression of Lessers. Poor or limited views can be misleading – and so can photos. Don't put a name to every bird. Try to sex all the birds above. Ad ♂ have an orange iris. 1st-yr ♂ also get paler through the winter and they grow ♂-like darker head and gray back feathers.

Greater Scaup *Aythya marila* GRSC L 18in W 2.2lbs **Winter | Spring**

Fairly common breeder from the Hudson Bay north, 75% breed in AK. Found on the tundra and in boreal forests, often nesting on islands in large lakes. More southerly summer scaup are almost certainly Lesser Scaup. Greaters form large, dense flocks in winter in deepwater coastal bays, estuaries, and sometimes on the ocean. 80% winter in the urbanized north-east. Often mixes with the very similar Lesser Scaup, and other bay ducks. **ID:** Greater is large diving duck, with a broad head, thick neck, and bulging cheeks. The forehead is often steep, with crowns peak above the eye. From there, it gradually tapers to a thick, muscular neck. The bill is broad, flaring at the tip, black typically extending off the nail onto the leading edge (black usually restricted to the nail in Lesser). Nearly all Greater Scaup can be identified from Lesser Scaup with practice, the different size and shape being key. Greaters, with a stretched neck, tend to be the most confusing. Sleeked-back 'hairdos' of diving birds also make ID tricky. Yellow iris. Adult ♂: iridescent green head, often

Summer | Fall

appearing black, but never purple. Upperparts vermiculation usually noticeably finer than on Lesser, looking uniform gray at any sort of distance. Fall Greaters are usually in clean bright plumage, whereas most Lesser show brown on the flanks until at least Christmas. Eclipse ♂: like other eclipse *Aythya*, ♂ are dull with brown in the head and flanks, and look grungy. Adult ♀: brownish, typically a shade darker than Lesser. Vermiculated gray body feathers increase with age, as in other *Aythya*. The well-defined white patch around the base of the bill in Greater averages broader than Lesser at the sides, so they look whiter-faced at a distance. In late-winter and summer with a distinct white ear-covert patch. They are paler and warmer brown, lacking gray vermiculations: Lessers usually look quite different. Juv: uniform brown, with a dark brown iris and darker bill. 1st-yrs molt adult-type feathers from fall onwards. ♀ white face is molted in through the fall, some confusingly dark until Nov. 1st-yr ♂ highly variable, becoming harder to age by late-winter.

Greater Scaup

Big bluebills occasionally form huge, closely knit rafts that can number as many as 10,000. Most of these are in the Northeast, close to urban areas, such as Long Island Sound. Concentrations like this always provide potential for problems. However, getting to see such mass spectacles, by sight and sound, always leaves a lasting impression. Greaters are hardy, as their northerly distribution would suggest. Like a gull, a Greater Scaup's larger and heavier bill may allow it to handle and extract more food in frozen conditions. Greaters fly in angled lines or 'V's that are evenly spaced. Sometimes they are in more-compact flocks. Greater Scaup are thick-set ducks with bulky heads, large bills, and broad necks. The Greater is a bit of a brute compared to the smaller and thinner-necked Lesser. Big bluebills are powerful flyers, and, like other large *Aythya*, they land with a splash, their big bodies taking some slowing down (as you can see from the landing birds on the right). They look two-toned, the dark neck contrasting sharply with the white belly, and the white

Flight

wing stripe standing out against the dark upperparts. The ♂ gray mantle is obvious – if you look for it. But it is easy to think they are all dark if you don't look carefully when they are distant. The pale bill is set off by the dark head. The white face in ♀ is clean cut and striking even far away. Greaters are slightly larger than Lesser, although this is a tough thing to judge. The wing stripe is the most important character to focus on. The secondaries are white and this extends onto the inner web at the base of the primaries. It fades out toward the wing tip. The overall impression is of a white wing stripe extending out onto the primaries. For Lesser, the impression is a white secondary stripe contrasting with a brown primary stripe – clearly two-toned. It's usually easier to judge this when birds are not too close. It's a better character to study in the field than in photos. The stripe on Greater Scaup is also broader; this is most noticeable on the outer wing. What are the other species of ducks at Irondequoit Bay, Rochester, NY? Answers p. 486.

Mystery Aythya Sitting. Food and the need to breed are the two primary driving forces in life. Large flocks of *Aythya* ducks will often gather where food is plentiful. These flocks are often dense, although they do sometimes break up into groups. These flocks usually involve multiple species of diving ducks and are sometimes joined by smaller numbers of dabblers. At first glance, the mosaic of different colors can be confusing, particularly to those new to the scene. However, the ability to see lots of seemingly different species and plumages together is a great way to learn birds and be more certain

of your identifications, if only because you can carefully compare their sizes and shapes. Patterns of color are also important. Greater Scaup are larger, bulkier, and have a different head shape. Although Redhead and Canvasback both have red heads, they are very different in shape and color patterns. ♀ Redhead can be trickier, largely because the pale face often gets people thinking scaup. Slowly and carefully try to ID, sex, and age every bird in this image. There are four flocks of bird

Mystery Aythya Flight. Bay ducks often form large flocks in winter, sometimes on ponds, but often in coastal bays and harbors. In many ways, the Great Lakes could be considered freshwater oceans, and large flocks often concentrate in sheltered sites where the water is not frozen. These birds are often disturbed, or they move to different feeding grounds, so there is plenty of opportunity to practice flight ID. Most of the species fly in single species flocks, but they do mix frequently enough that you need to be looking at every bird. Most species fly in loose lines or 'V's. Because ♂ are boldly marked in winter it is often quite easy to age 1st-yr ♂ by their bright colors molting in on an otherwise ♀-like brown

Although it's easy to get carried away and focus on colors, the size, shape, and flight styles are always the first keys to look for. Sometimes, if the weather is dull, or you are looking into the sun, ducks are simply dark. The great thing with looking at waterfowl without optics is that it helps to focus on what is truly important. You are mastering the basics! While it's fun and challenging to ID birds zipping by overhead, there's nothing like having a load of bay ducks dropping out of the sky in front of you and crash landing into a small area of open water. If you look carefully, you can see the narrow bedraggled tail feathers of the 1st-yr birds compared to the broad, neat and dark adults. Can you ID them all? Answers p. 486.

ad. ♂ Common Goldeneye x Hooded Merganser (3)

juv. King Eider x Common Merganser

♀ Barrow's x Common Goldeneye.

Barrow's x Common Goldeneye (3)

Hybrid Diving Ducks. Hybrid diving ducks are rare but regular. They are difficult to ID because of the large amount of variation in plumages. Most have characters of both parents. What intermediate characters do you see in the hybrids shown here? The 3 goldeneye are all hybrids. The intermediate shapes of the white on the face and back are the obvious clues. Head and bill shapes are more subtle. This captive ♀ hybrid would be extremely tough at best to ID in the wild. The (captive) brown juv behind the goldeneye with its neat broad feather fringes recalls King Eider in face pattern, shape, and coloration, but the long hook-tipped bill and long tail are Common Merganser features. Hooded Merganser and Common Goldeneye hybrids are striking, with a fair number of records. Is it because they are visually bold or because

♂ Ring-necked x Redhead

♂ Ring-necked x Tufted Duck

♂ Ring-necked x Lesser Scaup (3)

ad. ♂ Tufted Duck x unknown

ad. ♂ Ring-necked Duck x Lesser Scaup

the parents' lifestyles are very similar? *Aythya* with vermiculated flanks and backs are variable and deceiving. Bill pattern, head shape, and flank coloration/pattern are key. Notice the variation in the 2 different Ring-neck x Lesser Scaup hybrids and how head shape changes on the same bird. The head shape is also important in the ID of the other hybrids shown. The brown-flanked hybrid has a Tufted Duck head shape, the brown flanks making the other parent a Redhead, Common Pochard, or similar. Wing bars are often intermediate, so keep watching as they fly off! The Ring-necked Duck characters are not very strong on the Redhead and Tufted Duck hybrids, though the bill pattern remains strong and both show the white at the front and edges of the pale flanks.

Steller's Eider *Polysticta stelleri* STEI L 18in W 1.9lbs

Winter | Spring

A unique and incredible-looking duck, Steller's breed on coastal ponds in n. and w. AK. In winter Steller's cling to sheltered harbors and inlets with rocky foreshores in s. AK. Rare and declining. A reintroduction program on the Yukon Delta will hopefully help. They form tight packs in winter, huddled up and turning in synch like a flock of starlings. Suddenly, they will hurriedly swim in a close-knit line to another spot. They are quite small for an eider and look nervous, the group regularly changing direction for seemingly no reason. They dive together, water splashes everywhere, before they bounce back to the surface like rubber ducks. They are so serene and gentle. How could you not love them? Watching ♂ with their eyes circled in black on a white face, you get the feel they are looking back at you. A clown with a lime-green bobble on the back of his head, wanting to entertain! With dots, lines, and colors unlike any other bird, it makes one ponder what the logic is behind it. All ♀ are mundane by comparison, but still fascinating. Their bills have

Summer | Fall

a unique 'catamaran' shape, with turned-down edges when viewed head on, presumably to help feed, as they dive for mollusks. Surprisingly for a sea duck, they commonly dabble and up-end, picking food off the surface. They often waddle on rocky seaweed-laden shores to feed, preen, and rest. **ID:** smaller than other eider and a totally different shape. They are one-of-a-kind, flat-headed, and with a short, muscular neck. They look compact, but with quite a long, spiky tail. The bill, quite large, is blue or gray, with that odd shape.

Adult ♂: Nothing looks like them. 1st-yr ♂: molt into unmistakable bright plumage after a year. Adult ♀/1st-yr: similarly brown with a distinct eyering and two bold white wingbars. 1st-yr can be aged with difficulty by smaller and duller tertials; white-edged blue in adults. Some 1st-yr ♂ show paler, spotted underparts and a darker chin. There is lots of subtle variation, if you are looking closely. Eclipse ♂: Jul-Sep, highly variable amounts of brown and gray, often with remnants of bright plumage and retained white wing coverts.

Steller's Eider

There are days in Alaska when the cloud formations over the mountains are indescribable, the mist is rolling in over the water, and you can only ask yourself, 'Does it get any better than this?' The answer is 'Yes,' if a flock of cheerful Steller's Eider comes flying past. Their wings produce a loud whistling sound – louder than that of goldeneye. From a distance, you will notice they are packed tightly, but often organized into lines. They are steady flyers, purposeful without being in a hurry, flying in a straight line. Steller's often feed in harbors and where space is tight. They will circle around until the time is right to land and are quite agile. They land feet first, and use them, rather than their bellies, to do most of the braking. Water flies in all directions. Steller's are an unusual shape, not quite an eider, any other diver, or a dabbler: perhaps a combo shape of all three. The thick neck in Stellers is evident, accentuated by quite a small head with large bill. The tail is quite long and noticeably pointed from some angles. Stellers don't have much of a belly, so the

Flight

undercarriage looks smooth. The neck is held slightly down, giving them a bit of a hunch-backed look. The wings are held noticeably straight out and are blunt-tipped; not surprising for a bird that doesn't fly far. At a distance, the flocks are distinctively two-toned: the brown ones and those other ones that are almost indescribable. Steller's rarely mix with other ducks! The brown ones all have dark blue speculum, (usually looking black), clearly bordered in white, equally on either side. The white underwing, contrasting with the brown body is obvious, like in other eiders. The bold eyering is the only other thing that might catch your eye. Ad ♂ are strikingly patterned and also have white underwings. Even more noticeable are the all-white forewing and white trailing edge. These strange beauties, officially designated as Threatened under the Endangered Species Act, deserve all the help we can provide.

eclipse ♂'s

ad. ♂

Spectacled Eider *Somateria fischeri* SPEI L 21 in W 3.3lbs

Another officially Threatened eider that nests on coastal tundra ponds in n. AK. Only in 1995 were their unique wintering grounds discovered: Large groups of Specs, jammed into open pack-ice leads in the Bering Sea, their heat helping to keep the water open. They dive down 100-200 ft for clams. This is in sharp contrast to summer, when they lazily mill around shallow ponds with head submerged to feed. They often sit on the edges, imperiously looking around, seemingly without a care in the world. With a head like that you have to be the king! **ID**: A medium-sized eider. They have a triangular head (except bright males) and smaller bills than Common. They seem to sit high in the water, accentuating a round-backed appearance. Adult ♂: words can hardly do justice to their beauty. His head is dominated by an array of lime and seafoam greens, seemingly put there to accentuate a flowing mane and fluffed-up face. Sandwiched in between are his large 'spectacles' bordered in black, just in case you were missing something. The subtle

nuances of it all are remarkable. You have to wonder if this is not the 8th wonder of the world. Like some other eiders, the body is basically black-and-white, with small sails (raised scapulars), long tertials, and an obligatory spot — a white one on the vent. Eclipse ♂: Jul to Oct, the head and body are medium brown. Much of the white upperparts and eye stay largely white or pale brown. 2-yr-old Specs have dark tertials, but otherwise look the same as adults. Adult ♀: Like Common and King ♀, brown with wavy black bars. They are warm-colored in fresh plumage, much like ♀ King. They wear paler through the winter and summer with narrower feather fringes. Always look for the pale spectacles which are similar to those on ♂, but buff and open on the bottom and with the buff color extending to chin and neck. The dark forehead mask looks like a band-aid over the bill. Juv: dark-centered feathers with narrower buff fringes than ad ♀. The ♂ bill turns pink to orange quickly; ♀ are blue. Adult feathers are molted in slowly through the winter.

ad. ♂

ad. ♀ (notice the newly molted flank feathers)

Spectacled Eider

Given their far northern haunts, Specs are rarely seen in flight by most people, even by most Alaskans! Arguably the best places to see them are nesting in the remote Yukon/Kuskokwin (Y-K) Delta or off places like Gambell, on St Lawrence Island, where 100s, occasionally 1000s, fly past in late-Sep/Oct on route to their wintering grounds in the Bering Sea. Ad ♂ pass first, ♀ and juv later. Interestingly, there are none present some years; presumably, they take another route. Returning birds are seen as late as mid-Jun on the way back to their possibly frozen breeding grounds. Like other eider, their size and power allow them to handle their often harsh environments. They are a fairly large and heavy sea duck, about the size of King Eider, a little smaller than Common Eider. Large sloping head with a relatively small bill for an eider: a distinctive shape. Thick neck, rounded undercarriage, and medium length tail. The wings are broad-based and quite blunt-tipped. These are held straight out, rather than swept back. This is somewhat similar to other northern species, like

♀ King Eider

ad. ♀ with ducklings a few days old

Flight

Steller's Eider, that don't move far. These are characteristics that favor maneuverability and allow Specs to fly in windy weather. Long, pointed, and angled-back wings are better for flying far and fast. Spectacled Eider fly in lines or 'V's, usually in groups of a few to 30, rarely in larger groups. Ad ♂ Spectacled Eider are best identified by their bold black and white patterns. These are most like Common Eider with dark tail and extensive white upperparts. There are two features to key in on. First, the more-extensive black underparts extend past the leading edge of the wing and nearly to the neck. This black breast is striking. Second, the distinctive green head with bold 'spectacles.' Adult ♀ and 1st-yr are brown like other eider. The pale spectacles are the easiest feature to separate them from King and Common Eider. They are often seen with King Eider. Specs are similarly-sized and colored, but a little slimmer, longer-necked, with a more pointed head. Like other similarly-plumaged eider, they have white underwings with a darker trailing edge.

King Eider *Somateria spectabilis* KIEI L 22in W 3.6lbs **Winter | Spring**

Uncommon high-Arctic breeder, nesting on small shallow tundra ponds, often quietly sitting around surveying the scene with their mates. They will feed for a while, diving or tipping for food. Life seems unhurried and good. In winter, a few move south, but are scarce everywhere, just in ones and twos, and nearly always 1st-yrs. Kings are always a good find, usually hiding, or diving, among Common Eider on the ocean, near jetties or in harbors. There are always in a few in the Great Lakes! The majority stay in the far north wherever there is food and open ocean. They form large, compact rafts, some many 1000s large, often miles offshore. They can be a devil to find, even when you know they are there. **ID:** Noticeably shorter and more compact than Common Eider. They are a chunky bird that sits high in the water; this is noticeable at any distance. The neck is short and thick, the head blocky and square. Add to this a bill that is small for an eider, and you have a shape that is very different from its longer and snouty-headed cousins. The forehead and culmen

Summer | Fall

are concave, straighter on other eider. Adult ♂: the head is a surreal mosaic of pastel blues, greens, and orange. The orange knob gets larger with age, full size at about 3 years old. A large, pale upper-eyelid mark that arches down the side of the neck, present in all plumages, gives a distinctive and somewhat regal look. They have the most prominent 'sails' (scapulars that protrude from back) of all the eiders. 2nd-yr ♂: aged by smaller shield and subdued head colors. Eclipse ♂: mostly dark brown but bill still boldly colored bill. Adult ♀: appear brown, some grayer, with intricate internal markings. Bill always black. From Common Eider by warmer brown colors. The prominent pale area around and behind eye is the best feature at distance. Much discussed chevrons on flanks have limited ID value. Paler in summer. Juv: from ad ♀ by duller colors, narrower fringes to upperparts, and retained small juv underpart feathers. 1st-yr ♂: Darker with pale breast, brown body, and orange bill. The shape is always key for IDing Kings if you are in doubt. Gyrs' love to eat them.

King Eider

A few King Eider show up in the northeast, usually occurring in 1's and 2's. Most stay to the far north where they form large, dense flocks, some of over 10,000. If you're close, you can hear their wings whistle as they fly by. At Point Barrow, AK, during one 10-hour period, 360,000 passed by on migration, with 113,000 passing by in half an hour. Kings are found far out to sea, or wherever there are open leads in the pack ice. They dive down to a remarkable 150 ft, eating mostly animal matter (they eat mostly vegetable matter in summer). If the Kings all take off, they provide a stunning spectacle that only the bitter cold can temper. The heat shimmer coming off the ocean will destroy any shots you take. These ice-free zones make great feeding habitat for Snowy Owls. Kings will co-habit with these owls; they seem to keep away gulls which might threaten the Kings' brood in summer. **ID:** The ♀, like the ♂, look stocky with a thick neck, blocky head, and small bill, at least for an eider. They are deep-bellied and short-winged, the tips quite blunt. The ♀'s

Flight

head contrasts with the darker body and particularly with the black bill. In direct comparison with Common Eider, the smaller size, warmer tones, and different structure are quite noticeable. The underwing coverts are white, contrasting with the rest of the underwing, like other eider. The ♂ are exquisite. The rear half of the bird is black with a bold white patch extending from the rear flanks onto the rump sides. It's difficult to miss. Black upperwings have bold white wing-covert patches: beacons at the longest of ranges. The multitude of soft pastels on the breast, neck, and head can look just light orange at a distance. In the image above, there is a ♂ and a ♀ (left lower center, ♀ above) Common Eider mixed in with these Kings. They are very difficult to pick out, but patiently look for the larger size, slimmer build, bold pattern in the ♂ and paler ♀. Notice how the bill looks black and small in ♀ Kings. In ♀ Commons, the bill is a lot longer and is a bit paler so it doesn't contrast with the head.

What is He Doing? King Eider is a gorgeous duck, ♂'s with their boldly patterned plumage and beautifully subtle head colors. The yellow-orange knob grows larger with age. The ♂ courtship display is similar to that of a number of other duck species. They lean forward with rear-end thrust in the air and bill in the water. With chest proudly pumped out and head still pointing down, they throw their head back while making a soft wooing 'coo' sound. After repeating the process a number of times, they will often 'stand up' on the water and flap their wings – hopefully mission accomplished with a suit

ably impressed hen. Preening birds will use their bill and feet to help get the job done. Contorting their head backwards, they move feathers into place and will run them through the bill to put the barbules in place. When finished, they will often repeatedly dunk under the water with beads of water droplets running off their water-resistant feathers. All eider species can handle extreme cold temperatures. Hence, the high cost of 'eiderdown.' Try to work out what each bird is doing, and study the incredible face and chin patterns.

'Dresser's' or 'Atlantic' Common Eider *Somateria mollissima* COEI L 24in W 4.5lbs **Winter | Spring**

Common Eider is a hardy, circumpolar sea duck. Nests are partially harvested for famous eider-down, less so now than previously. In NA, there are 4 subspecies: Dresser's *(S.m.dresseri)*, Hudson Bay, *(S.m.sedentaria)*, Northern *(S.m.borealis)*, and Pacific *(S.m.v-nigrum)*. Variously called Dresser's, American, and Atlantic Common Eider (we call it Dresser's because it removes ambiguity), this is the common East Coast eider from Labrador south to Maine, nesting colonially on the ground on rocky islands. Commoner to the north, familiar to anyone who lives in range on the coast. Large creches – cooperative nurseries – often found close to the beach. These are sea ducks found primarily on rocky coastlines. Any duck sitting on a rocky outcrop is likely to be this species. Dresser's love rock jetties and harbors, sharing them with the shoobies, fishermen, Oldsquaw, and scoter. They habitually dive, seemingly in a hurry to get back down there for more. They eat animal foods; mostly blueshell bivalves. A few Dresser's wander south in winter

partial eclipse ♂ – June
partial eclipse ♂ – fall
eclipse ♂ – July
ad. ♀

'Dresser's' Common Eider — Summer | Fall

in small parties of mostly immatures to favored jetties. **ID**: Largest NA duck. Unique profile; sturdy, long, hefty body; long thick neck, sloping forehead, and peaked forecrown! They sit proudly upright, chest pumped forward. Adulthood acquired after 3 years and 8 molts. Adult ♂: boldly marked black and white duck with a lime-green hair-do. Dresser's have largest raised scapulars, known as 'sails'. Even ♀ have them, though smaller. ♂ lobes, a facial extension of the bill, are usually yellow or yellow-green, averaging larger, broader, and greener with age. To describe lobe shape and color as 'variable' in eider is an understatement! 2nd-yr ♂: dark-edged tertials, otherwise like ad ♂. Eclipse ♂: all brown except for white wing coverts. 1st-yr ♂: brown, becoming pied, as adult-type black and white feathers molt in. Pale bill. Adult ♀: highly variable, most rufous brown in winter; more cryptic in summer. 1st-yr ♀: similar to adults; narrower wing bars and trailing edge to secondaries, smaller and narrower-fringed wing coverts, and average darker and grayer.

'Pacific' Common Eider *Somateria mollissima* COEI L 25in W 5.4 lbs   **Winter | Spring**

Pacific Eider breeds from AK to Nunavut on barrier Islands and coastal tundra. A northern bird, most winter in the closest unfrozen waters, particularly in w. AK. **ID:** The largest and most distinct Common Eider; perhaps it's a separate species. The head is even longer and more pointed than other subspecies. Adult ♂: almost unique to Pacifics is a black 'V' under the chin. Pacifics also have the most squared-off black crown at the back of the head, and narrowest white crown stripe; the most extensive green on the face, and the least on the nape. The frontal lobes are relatively short, narrow, and pointed. The black down the side of the bill is broader and more prominent than on other subspecies. The bill is bright, lollipop orange. The tertials are very long and downcurved. Pacific ♂ are very distinctive! Adult ♀: shares the ♂, long sloping head, accentuated by the short bill. The long feathered 'forecheek', often has a distinctive pale patch where it meets the bill; is more rounded, and less pointed, than other subsp. Colors variable; grayer in summer, browner in winter.

'Hudson Bay' Common Eider *Somateria mollissima* COEI L 23in W 4.2lbs **Summer | Fall**

Sedentaria, as the name suggests, are Hudson Bay residents. Large die-offs can occur when region is frozen, so it makes sense some would move south. Because of similarity to Dresser's, IDing them on current knowledge is impossible; some consider Hudson Bay and Dresser's to be the same subspecies. Adult ♂: lobe shape similar to Dresser's, averaging more orange and less yellow-green; slightly narrower, shorter and more parallel-sided. 1st-yr ♂: both subsp have paler bills that are narrower and more parallel-sided than adults. ♀ Hudson Bay birds are considered more distinctive than ♂; in summer most are gray-toned, though their cryptic nature makes ♀ highly variable in color; some are browner. The underparts have narrower dark bars than Dresser's, and they molt later. Very little is known about their appearance in winter. ♀ of other subspecies are browner and less cryptic in winter; *sedentaria* may be the same. Lobe shape is shorter and narrower than Dresser's, though this character is hard to judge in the field.

ad. ♀

'Northern' Common Eider *Somateria mollissima* COEI L 23in W 3.9lbs

'Northern' or 'Boreal' Eider, breeding in arctic Canada and Greenland, is the smallest COEI. Most winter off NL and Greenland. They are commonly hunted and are much more wary than other races. Where the breeding grounds overlap with Hudson Bay and Dresser's, intergrades are regular. **ID:** Northern Eider have the shortest and narrowest lobes; they are relatively pointed. Adult ♂: bill has a strong orange tone and looks quite different from other subspecies. They have a narrow crown stripe like Pacifics. The green on the head is usually distinct and is restricted to the hindneck and nape; it doesn't extend onto the cheek. Adult ♀: in summer have creamy underparts and broad, brown fringes to upperparts. In winter they are darker, usually brown. Looking at this wintering flock of Northerns off Newfoundland, you can see how most ♀-types are brown. However, a few birds are strikingly grayer and there is lots of variation. The ad ♂ are more consistently patterned, but if you look closely you will see variation in lobe shapes, particularly in the width.

There is also a ♂ Dresser's 3 birds left of the 1st-yr ♂ (top, centre, left page). When thinking of Common Eider as a whole, their lobes get smaller, more pointed, and more orange as they move north. This variation is typical in all populations. Even within Dresser's, more-northerly populations are smaller-billed. You can also see the variation in color in ♀. Some birds are significantly grayer. Just as in grouse, owls, and other cryptic birds, the relationship between gray and brown may not be as different as humans perceive it. Other species, such as Long-tailed Duck, also appear to show differences in color of feathers, such as scapulars, from brown to gray. While the term 'morph' is often used to classify these differences in color, they are typically clinal, with many intermediate in color, or showing a combination of colors. Shorebirds, such as Sanderling and Red Knot, with similar breeding habits, also show similar variation in these cryptic color patterns. The word 'morph' may be an inappropriate term in many cases.

Common Eider

Their large size and weight means these eiders need a heck of a long runway to get airborne, water splashing everywhere. Once up and going, they fly fast and with great power. They look like tough sprinters, solidly built but lean and muscular. It's as if their long, sloping foreheads were designed to cut through the air, and their deep, but long, bodies, ready for carrying fuel. The wings are long, quite pointed, and broad; they are only angled-back only slightly. As you would expect from their build, they are powerful flyers, able to handle tougher climates in the north and fly through even the strongest winds. Quite comical in flight, it's as if they are peering at you with their beady eyes. The eye is located at the top of the bulging forehead, on a wedge-shaped head; it is accentuated by a pale spot arching over it, in all but Ad ♂. As they fly past, you will notice their huge size and distinctive shape, with long head held at 45 degrees to the water. They fly in lines or 'V's, also in sorted packs of 10 or 20. Where they are in numbers, larger flocks of over

Flight

a 100 are not uncommon. They fly low to the water; typical of birds used to flying in windy weather. It's best to stay low! **ID:** Adult ♂: arresting black-and-white plumage. The black belly and white flank patch is only matched only by King Eider. Commons have more-extensive white on the upperparts, neck, and head; a much whiter bird. Eiders are commonly seen with scoter. The ♂ pied plumage is a giveaway at any distance. Ad ♀/ Juv are similar in flight. All brown, the only other color you will notice is the white in the underwing. The narrow white wing bars and trailing edge to the secondaries are easy to miss. The pale area above the eye is always conspicuous: it really affects its appearance. ♀ Common Eiders are best separated from other eider by their larger size, different head shape, and the face pattern. King Eider, the species that Commons are most often seen with, are not only smaller, but obviously shorter and thicker-necked, have a blocky face with a small bill that is boldly black. Head features are key to the ID!

Eider Beauty. Is there anything weirder, wilder, and yet as wonderful as the adult ♂ eiders? Their flamboyant palette of colors is unique. Look at the colors closely – they will make any interior designer drool. Notice the hard orange 'knob' of the King Eider – it gets larger with age. Seafoam green cheeks, coastal-blue crown and nape but, as if this is not enough, the colors are divided by white and black lines. Who the heck designed that? The Spectacled Eider can't match the hard orange knob of the King Eider – but how about that foam green pom pom on its face? Drakes have a long hairdo on the nape to match. Between is the large round bulging white 'spectacle' on the face, bordered by black, presumably to add

emphasis to the spectacles! Steller's Eider has an emerald 'bobble' hat. Head on, it has a staple-shaped bill and unique colors. They all have black around the eyes. Why is that? Perhaps for attracting hens. Is it to help with visibility in a snowy environment? What do you think? Yet, despite all their beauty, eiders are some of the toughest birds known, able to endure extreme cold temperatures with its once heavily collected 'eiderdown'. Can you identify and count them all? There are lots of birds huddled-up, so look closely. If not, just think about their incredible beauty and ask yourself how and why. Please remember several of these species are our most imperiled species of waterfowl in N.A. Are they worth saving?

Mystery Eider. There's nothing quite like eiderdown to keep you warm. It is light to boot. Simply put, it is the best. This is why eiders can be the true arctic ducks, able to withstand the coldest and harshest of conditions that dark northern winters offer. Eider form large flocks in winter, concentrated where the sea remains unfrozen. Heat and movement of these mass flocks can help to keep the ocean open. Rafts 10,000s large can form, often far offshore. Huddled up, flocks can be hard to spot among the waves. The use of transmitters, and a plane, led to the discovery of the Spectacled Eider wintering grounds in 1995. Eider are circumpolar and they do show up outside their regular range. The lower right ♂

with its bright bill and pointed lobes is a Pacific Eider. The other adult ♂ to the left is Dresser's or Hudson Bay-based on lobe shape. White tertials indicate that both are adults. The ♀ Common Eider behind the Pacific is an adult, based on the white wing bars. The short bill and lobe shape suggest *borealis* or an intergrade. The rest of the eider on the right page are Kings, except for a ♀ Common in flight. I see three 1st-yr ♂; notice how black the bills are on ♀. Left page has two ♀ Common Eider close, an adult and a 1st-yr (both Dressers). Which is which? A Spectacled Eider is flapping behind, just in front of a pack of Stellers. There are few more distant Common Eider and Long-tailed Ducks. Can you ID all the eider?

Harlequin Duck *Histrionicus histrionicus* HARD L 17in W 1.3lbs

Winter | Spring

An appealing duck with a gentle personality, Harleys are often tame and approachable. They breed on fast-flowing mountain streams, swimming against the current with head submerged as they snorkel for food. In winter they head to rocky coasts and jetties. They are hardy, happily embracing the roughest weather. Harlequins are usually found in small flocks feeding close to shore, either diving for food or picking at mollusks on rocks. They spend lots of time standing or sitting on rocks, surveying the terrain and are adept at jumping in and out of the water. They have a little squeaky call, chattering a lot for a duck, but you need to be close to hear them. **ID:** Habitat and behavior alone are often distinctive. Structurally, they don't look like anything else. Fairly small, with a short, really thick neck. The small bill curves up onto the steep forehead. The back of the neck forms a smooth arch from the crown to the mantle; the ♂ head stripes only emphasize this. The angled, bulky neck makes Harlequins look like they are always leaning forward. When

Summer | Fall

swimming, they look cute and never in a hurry; perhaps it's because they look pudgy and non-athletic. They swim in lines when heading somewhere. Only when catching a wave or riding torrents do they move quickly. They have a long tail that is often held raised at 45 degrees. Adult ♂: Metallic blue with a mosaic of white lines and spots. Rusty flanks and border to crown. They are simply stunning; their tameness and character are other reasons for making them one of the most charismatic and popular ducks. At distance, or in bad light, the dark colors can look black. Eclipse ♂: duller, browner, and with less white. 1st-yr ♂: brown juv quickly molt and are similar to adult ♂ by fall but are duller and lack the crisp whites of adults. The belly retains pale juv feathers until summer. Adult ♀: smaller-headed than ♂. Uniform brown, slightly darker on the back. The head is clearly marked with white patches in front, above, and behind the eye. 1st-yr ♀ have the same color patterns as adults and can be aged by smaller juv feathers.

Harlequin Duck

Harlequins are so tame, they rarely fly to get away from you. They clearly prefer swimming to flying and tend to fly for longer journeys only. Flock size is usually in small; large flocks are very rare. They are sometimes seen with other species, particularly scoter. Harleys are noticeably smaller than scoter; about the size of Lesser Scaup or Long-tailed Duck and are noticeably larger than teal. Their unique shape is also evident in flight. The thick neck and steep forehead make them look almost headless, the small bill adding to this unique look. They usually fly with their head slightly raised, the steep forehead emphasizing this, often bobbing their head as if inquisitive. Although stocky with a nicely rounded undercarriage, they are long-tailed, giving them an attenuated appearance. The neck extension in front of the wings is barely longer than the tail extension behind. The wings are quite broad, short, and pointed; wings are held straighter than most species. They tend to fly with purpose when they do fly, though their short wings are not made

with Surf Scoters

Flight

for speed and long-distance flights. They are agile, quite able to maneuver rocky outcrops to land in confined spaces. The runway for landing and takeoff is shorter than that for the larger sea ducks – as you would expect. ♂ Harlequins can look dark from afar, but the white lines and spots stand out. The two dark-bordered white breast lines are the easiest to see, the white face at times disappearing into pale skies and seas. 1st-yr ♂ are easily aged in flight by their pale juv belly feathers. All ♀ have pale bellies, though they are not always easy to see. Otherwise, a uniform brown duck with a boldly spotted face. The distribution and boldness of these white face patches are not in any other species. ♂ distinctive marking makes them hard to miss for careful observers. With scoter, Harlequin's smaller size should be obvious. Always confirm with the longer tail and color patterns. Long-tailed Duck's size and proportions are quite similar but they are lighter with different color patterns.

Black Scoter *Melanitta americana* BLSC L 19in W 2.1lbs

A common sea duck that breeds in grasses near tundra ponds. In winter, found off both ocean coasts, rare inland. They can be well offshore (several miles), but also in sheltered bays and estuaries where mollusks and other animal matter is plentiful; jetties and rocky shorelines are a favorite. On migration, particularly in the East, American Scoters form spectacular wavy lines, often with Surf Scoters and other ducks. Through winter and spring, ♂ give an incessant wailing call, hence its name the 'Whistling Scoter'. It's a sound that can be non-stop and carry a long way; really distinctive once you have learned it. Flocks are ♂ dominated. Often divided into small groups of half-a-dozen birds, five ♂ all wooing a single ♀. It is harassment from her perspective, and it can go on for hours. **ID:** The smallest and chunkiest of the scoters with diagnostic, over-sized, round head. The neck is quite thick, but short, giving Black Scoter a distinctive profile. Fairly long, spiky tail sometimes held up at 45 degrees. A scoter with smooth, round body edges, arched

Winter | Spring

back, rounded head, and pot belly. Adult ♂: All black with a shiny luster in good light: every tiny head feather stands out. Bulbous orange bill knob is a beacon, even at long range. Narrow orbital ring is orange. Scoter don't have eclipse plumage; replacement feathers are the same colors. Adult ♀: all brown, with a pale face contrasting with dark crown giving it a capped appearance. The ♀ bill has a smaller version of the ♂ bulbous knob. They always show some yellow after the first year, mostly on the knob, but also the edge of the lower mandible. The knob size and amount of yellow increases with age. Juv: all brown with a paler belly. The bill is all black. 1st-yr ♂: start to develop adult-like bill and molt new black feathers mid-winter. 1st-yr ♀ have all-black bills, except for nostril, through most of the first year. All 1st-yr scoter are usually very easy to age; old pale juv feathers contrast with new dark adult-type feathers until they molt in to adult plumage in late-summer. .

Black Scoter

Black Scoter is the least common of the 3 scoter, but you would never know that watching along the mid-Atlantic coast in late Oct or Nov. They pile past in their 1000s, sometimes 10,000s. They form long, wavy lines and loose 'V's that snake up and down, the flock always morphing into another shape, often with a cluster up front. Large and powerful, they seem to like a slight headwind to help with uplift. Early-morning flights to feeding grounds are less organized. Black Scoter will fly anywhere from just above the waves to 30 ft up, occasionally higher. It's not unusual for them all to drop suddenly to change altitude. Which bird decides that? They prefer to fly over water, but will cut over land. Some migrate inland from their tundra breeding grounds and are seen on larger bodies of inland water, particularly after storms. They are regular on the Great Lakes. Black Scoter are fast, direct flyers; maintaining speeds of 30- 40 mph is no problem. They are much more compact than other scoter. They have a rounded undercarriage, deepest toward the back of

Flight

the body; it comes up steeply, adding to a short-tailed look. The wings are broad-based, shorter, and not as swept back as other scoter. The neck is short and thick, with that 'big' head. The head is held straight, but the steep forehead and bill shape create the illusion the bird is looking down. Black's shape is very distinctive. Surfs look much slimmer with attenuated head and tail, wings angled back; distinctive at long range. The ♂ Black's orange bill stands out, though it does disappear with distance. The primaries, particularly on the underwing, are pale. They reflect light and can stand out, though there are more-distinctive field marks to use than this one. The ♀ pale face is the easiest color pattern to see – at almost any distance! 1st-yr scoter are very easy to age by their pale bellies, and can be sexed by bill pattern. See if you can find a Surf Scoter; and age and sex all the Blacks going past Cape May Point, NJ.

Surf Scoter *Melanitta perspicillata* SUSC L 20in W 2.3 lbs

A common sea duck, breeding in boreal forests in dense cover near shallow-water lakes. Common in winter on both ocean coasts; the default scoter in the West. They are rare but regular inland; often 'downed' after big storms. Often with other scoter. They feed primarily on mollusks, and other animal matter; they like rocky coasts and jetties, also bays, harbors, inlets, and can be farther offshore. Usually in flocks, from a few to 100s. Like White-winged Scoter, they dive a lot, using wings and feet to swim under water; Blacks use only their feet. **ID:** Larger, longer, and sleeker than Black Scoter; smaller with a subtly different head shape than White-winged Scoter. A large duck, Surfs swim tall and proud, neck upright. The bill is large, the profile wedge-shaped — a distinctive feature at a distance. They look square-headed at times, rounded at others. Adult ♂: their incredible head pattern has to make it the clown of ducks: the white eye, forehead, and nape all add to this caricature. Its bold colors can be seen at distance; the white nape is the best feature

Flight

for clinching the ID. The crimson legs help with IDing diving birds. **Adult ♀:** All brown; averages darker than 1st-yrs. Most have a white nape, varying from subtle to obvious, though not as eye-catching as ad ♂. They look capped, and have white patches in front and behind eye. The bill is typically dark, but older birds can show a ghost pattern of ♂. Iris brown. **Juv:** all brown, slightly paler than ad ♀, increasingly so through the winter, particularly the belly. By late winter, retained juv feathers can fade to white. **1st-yr ♀:** aged by lack of pale nape and juv feathers; they contrast with the darker newly molted ones. **1st-yr ♂:** most become sexable around New Year when the iris becomes paler brown, black feathers start to molt in, and the bill turns paler and patterned. After the summer molt, a few can be separated from ad ♂ and labeled 2nd-yr; they have a little less white on the forehead, nape, and bill, the last sometimes dark-flecked at tip. A beautiful duck! Like Blacks, small packs of ♂ Surfs are often chase single ♀s in late-winter.

Surf Scoter

It's the last week of October. You are at Avalon seawatch, NJ, but it could be anywhere along the mid-Atlantic coast. A cold front is a day away. Ahead of it are typical light southeast winds. The head-on southerlies help provide uplift, and they are light enough not to sap the scoters' energy. The easterly component drifts the birds close to shore. Undulating lines, lots of them, are snaking across the sea. Behind them are even more lines. In fact, they are as far as the eye can see. They constantly change shape and altitude. They veer out past the jetty, and suddenly you get a sense of how fast these birds are really moving. The scale of it is just breathtaking! Drinking in the spectacle, you didn't focus on IDing them. Most were Surfs, also a few Blacks. What else is mixed in? It's easy to separate the close birds: ♂ Surf's obvious bill and white nape; ♀ darkish head with pale patches. These are hard to miss. The pale bellied 1st-yrs are easy to pick out, some ♂ already showing distinctive patterns. The ♂ Black's orange bill, the ♀ pale throat, also easy to see.

Flight

Looking at distant birds gets more difficult. Distant scoter can look all dark, the ♀/juv Black's pale face the easiest feature to see. Surfs are slightly longer, but noticeably slimmer. They have a longer neck, small head, and long bill. The pale nape and forehead in ♂ disappears into the background adding to the streamlined appearance. Black's large head, steep forehead, and small bill is in marked contrast to Surf's wedge-shaped profile. Always focus on this. The undercarriage is centered farther forward than Black's, and they are not as deep-bellied. The rear end is longer and more pointed, the wings slimmer, longer, and more angled back. This very different shape can also be visible when other features are not. Head on, key on the color patterns. White-wings are larger and similarly shaped to Surfs, but it is their bold white wing patches that you should always look for — and see quite easily! Surfs often fly with other species. Picking out odd ones in hundreds of birds can be challenging, IDing them is usually the easy part. How many Blacks can you ID?

White-Winged Scoter *Melanitta fusca* WWSC L 21in W 3.1lbs

White-wings nest in dense cover, often on bushy islands, on large boreal lakes, as far south as Redberry Lake, Saskatoon, SK. Fairly common on both ocean coasts in winter; also the commonest scoter on the Great Lakes, eating introduced zebra mussels. They dive to depths of 100 ft, explaining why they are often farther offshore and in deeper water than other scoter. Also in bays and harbors in small groups. When close to shore, they are usually outnumbered by other scoter. **ID:** The white secondaries are hard to miss in flight, and usually visible on sitting birds, with patient observation. Big birds, can be picked out by their larger size from other scoter. White-wings have a neck on steroids, particularly broad at base, and an overall 'mean' demeanor. They are anything from round- to square-headed, the neck tilted forward, the nape-line at 45 degrees. Long, pointed face is slightly concave from forehead to bill. Frequently tip their head back and point their bill skyward. Adult ♂: surprisingly small-billed on close inspection. White eye patch is usually visible at long

1st-yr. ♂

1st-yrs

ad. ♀s

Year round

range. Brown flanks, tough to see at distance, otherwise all black. Distinctive bill. Pale iris. 2nd-yr ♂: some can be aged by less white next to eye and smaller protrusion above nostril. A few records of Siberian form, Stejneger's Scoter (*M.f.stejnegeri*), in w. AK. Ad ♂ has black flanks, yellow-orange edge to red bill, and larger 'kinked' protrusion above nostril. Head shape is quite different: wedge-shaped like Common Eider. Adult ♀: uniform dark brown in winter. Most developing pale loral and cheek patches in summer, occasionally in winter. Juv: Brown wearing paler through winter. Round pale loral and cheek patches; average bolder in ♀. 1st-yr ♂: most easily aged by brighter bill, paler eye (Feb/Mar), and pale juv belly. 1st-yr ♀: Black bill, pale belly, and the largest white face patches. ♀/juv is easy to overlook in Surf flocks. Look carefully for small bill with a large feathered area between the bill and eye. Surf Scoter has a capped appearance, much stouter squared-off bill, with vertical loral patch oval, rather than rounded.

White-winged Scoter

About 10 % larger than Black and Surf Scoter. The size difference is noticeable when in mixed flocks, but it is the White-wings that always catch your eye. Even at long distances they typically stand out, in part because of the strong contrast with the dark body and rest of the wing. Occasionally, it's easy to overlook a bird or two in large scoter flocks, but if you keep watching, it is surprising how they will appear out of nowhere. In areas where they are fairly common, White-wings tend to be in small groups of 3-15, and don't mix so much. Flocks fly in evenly-spaced lines. White-wings are big, strong, and powerful, though wing-beats slow, deep, and purposeful – typical of larger sea ducks. The wedge-shaped face with peaked crown is very much like Common Eider. Other similarities are the balanced proportions with rounded undercarriage centered slightly to the rear. The neck, broadest at the base, is stouter than in other scoter. The head blends into the neck, accentuating the long sloping forehead, bump above the eye, and

Year round

bill. White-wings are quite long-tailed. Their wings are broad, strongly angled back at the carpal, and quite pointed. As expected for such a large and heavy duck, they need a long runway to get airborne with lots of splashing. Landing, they hold their wings distinctively open at 45 degrees; Surfs hold theirs almost vertical. All White-wings have the same basic wing pattern with white secondaries. They can be aged and sexed by the amount of white on the greater coverts: all white in adult ♂, 1st-yr ♀ have the least white. Color patterns are also useful for aging and sexing. Aging birds using pale belly is tricky. Ad White-wings have pale bases to their belly feathers, the amount of white visible is variable. Later in winter, as the belly feathers become worn, some birds are strongly white-bellied and very difficult to differentiate from 1st-yrs using this feature. Slightly larger size, different structure, particularly the head shape, and those white wing patches, separate from other scoter. Shape and power most similar to Common Eider; color patterns are different.

Scoter Landing Styles. Imagine a ski jumper launching down a giant hill in the Olympics and you will wonder if they copied the Black Scoter. As they sail downward, they keep their body at 40 degrees. Just before landing, they put their feet out and stand tall and proud with neck stretched upright and chest pumped out, the wings held back! On touchdown, their wings, feet, and chest are thrust forward, all acting as brakes. They do a kamikaze-like bellyflop, with water flying everywhere. This 'crash landing' is distinctive among the sea-ducks even at the longest distances. Surf Scoter has a more-sedate and economical landing than the Black Scoter. It stands tall with feet pushed forward, wings held almost upright for several seconds until it slows down enough to slip into a sitting position. White-winged Scoter's landing style is similar to Surf Scoter, but its wings are held at about 45 degrees.

Common Scoter Melanitta nigra COSC L 23 in W 2.3lbs

Common Scoter recently made its long-overdue first appearance in NA in California. This Eurasian species was recently split from Black Scoter. Compared to Black Scoter, Common has a longer and more pointed tail. The neck is also longer and slimmer, the head smaller. These features are noticeable, even at a distance. ♀ have a longer and narrower-based bill with a straight culmen. It's all-black, other than a yellow nostril, and it stands out against the steeper forehead. All but juv Black Scoter show orange on the bill. Ad ♂ Common Scoter are the easiest to identify. The bill shape and the pattern of orange on the bill are obviously different. The yellow orbital ring is more prominent. Jet black feathers surround the base of the bill. The bird in CA was less approachable than the other scoter present and rarely mixed with them. That's centuries of persecution for you!

Mystery Scoter on the Coast or Great Lakes. All 3 species of scoter often form mixed flocks. These can number in the 1000s and, on rare occasions, 100,000s if there is an abundance of mussels or other food. The ocean moves constantly, and areas of plentiful food also change. Jetties are often good places to look, but flocks can often be miles offshore. Identification is straightforward in adult ♂, even at a very long range. The white nape and bill pattern on Surf, orange bill in Black, and white eye-patch on White-wings are all easily spotted. ♀ are a little trickier. The two-toned face pattern of Black Scoter juvs and ♀ make them a straightforward ID. Juv and ♀ White-wings and Surfs, however, are the easiest to

overlook. White-wings are noticeably larger than the other scoter but can be surprisingly tough to pick out. The White-wings are striking, but are not always visible. Missing these two characteristics, look for the capped appearance, larger bill, and square-looking head, sometimes with pale nape of Surf Scoter. White-winged are uniformly brown-headed, some with two bold pale face patches, others with none. Check through this flock to see if there really are five White-winged Scoter. Also try to identify, age, and sex most of these birds. The key is being patient, taking your time and doing your due diligence. Practice makes perfect!

Mystery Scoter. Lines of scoter twist up and down, in and out, as they pass offshore. It is spectacular. In Oct and Nov, they move south. They are quite happy to fly into the wind, their heavy bodies seemingly enjoying the uplift. They occur in winter in large numbers, occasionally in massive concentrations of 100,000s if there is an abundance of food. They regularly shuttle between feeding grounds, often miles apart. Lines of scoter frequently include all three species. White-winged Scoter are easy. They are noticeably larger and most importantly, the white wing patches are usually evident at any distance. Blacks are slightly smaller than Surfs and appear more compact. The head is larger, the neck shorter and thicker

the bill shorter, with a pot belly. The orange knob in ♂ can be obvious at a distance. Surfs look slimmer with a longer neck, smaller head, and pointed bill. The lowest point of the underparts is closer to the rear, and the wings are angled back more. The slimmer appearance is exaggerated in ♂ by the 'disappearing' white nape. The different head patterns in ♀ is striking. However, distance and bad light changes things and there always becomes a point where these are best left as 'scoter sp.' (scoter species unknown). See if you can work out most of the birds in the photo. Answers p. 486.

Long-tailed Duck *Clangula hyemalis* LTDU L 16in(♂+5in tail) W 1.6lbs **Winter | Spring**

This is a common, northern diving duck that often nests by tundra ponds. Long-tails winter on oceans, bays, and in river mouths on both ocean coasts and the Great Lakes. They are often the closest ducks on the ocean, diving in or just beyond the surf line. You will often hear them first; a beautiful yodeling call that carries a long way. Long-tails live in loose groups, one minute diving for food, the next chasing each other, or flying 1000 yards to a better site. Packs are a constant buzz of energy one minute, but then will settle down into loosely spaced pairs. When not feeding, they form compact flocks, sometimes large, recalling Ruddy Duck. At a distance, they appear as a mosaic of browns and whites that don't seem to fit any particular pattern. A closer look and you will see that the shape, behavior, and color all contribute to a very dainty, but elegant, appearance. Sometimes they sit tall and proud, particularly the ♂ with his head and long tail, held erect. **ID**: Long-tails are smallish (Lesser Scaup-sized). Thick neck and round

ad. ♂ bright
ad. ♀
1-2 weeks old

Summer | Fall

head (female's squarer and smaller) and small, broad-based bill. They sit high in the water. Color patterns variable and poorly understood. Some are gray, others rufous or brown; cryptic variability perhaps in response to environment, like some arctic-nesting shorebirds. Superficially different head patterns also add to confusion. Adult ♂ winter: boldly patterned browns and whites, with long tail. Pink in bill a ♂-only character. Adult ♂ summer: molts spring into much darker upperparts with white mask and crown. Adult ♀ summer: pale mask like ♂ otherwise paler, and duller (but with dark breast), and short-tailed. Bill lacks pink in ♀. Adult ♀ winter: very similar to juv/1st-yrs. Almost all have cheek spot and dark crown stripe, upperparts, and breast. Head and breast patterns and colors, gray to rufous-brown, highly variable. 1st-yr ♂ can be sexed when they get pink in bill and longer scapulars. Differentiate adults from 1st-yrs by differently shaped juv feathers, as coloration of scapulars and other feathers, is not indicative of sex.

Long-tailed Duck

Oldsquaw often forms large flocks, sitting quietly, neck down. They spend a large amount of time preening; seemingly more than other sea ducks. At other times, they will be spread out in small groups or pairs, necks and tails up, full of action and raring to go. They often chase one another low across the water before plunging in, an avalanche of water briefly surrounding them. Agile, they roll side to side, with neck held straight and deep wing beats as if to compensate for the big belly. They dive steeply, wings held partly out; wings and feet are used to propel themselves underwater after mollusks and other animal matter. All this action is often accompanied by noise; a yodeling up and down, *ow-owdelee*, repeated. It's a classic sound, relaxing and a call to action, all in one. Long-tails are an unusual and unique shape. Compact, with a very deep pot-bellied undercarriage that rises abruptly near the tail. They are thick-necked, with a high, rounded head in ♂; smaller and squarer in ♀. The bill is small for a duck, compared to the size of the

Flight

head. The wings are quite slim, angled at the carpal and pointed. Only ad ♂ are long-tailed; in flight, the tail streamers are held straight or slightly tilted up, as when sitting. Long-tail flight is fast, often rocking from side to side. Wing beats barely get above horizontal; it's all in the down-stroke, recalling bats, swifts, or swallows. They fly in evenly-spaced lines, usually close to the water, birds sometimes changing altitude, making waves in the line. Flocks are always a mish-mash of browns and white. This alone is distinctive. All Long-tails have uniform dark underwing coverts that contrast strongly with mostly white underparts. Both ♂ and ♀ are mostly white in winter; distant flocks appear as distinctive tiny white dots. The fast flight, deep belly, two-toned colors, and all-dark underwings can get you thinking of alcids at a distance. Aging and sexing is the same as in sitting birds. The long tail, cheek patch, and dark chest are clear adult ♂ features. The pink and black bill is indicative of all ♂. Others are often safest left as juv or ♀.

Bufflehead *Bucephala albeola* BUFF L 14in W 0.9lbs **Winter | Spring**

Buffleheads are our smallest ducks, but with boatloads of character. They breed in cavities near wooded deepwater lakes, ponds, and rivers, mostly from MB west, north to AK. They can be found in lowlands or mountains. In winter, look through estuaries, marinas, and bays, even out on the ocean. They are gregarious, associating in 2s or 3s, up to groups as many as 100, often loosely spread out and rarely in tight flocks. They bob up and down, the rubber duckies of waterfowl. Although short, they are chunky, sitting high on the water with a deep body, making them easy to spot. They dive smoothly, jumping up and entering the water cleanly with barely a splash. They often resurface quickly, bobbing up with a bounce. **ID**: A small, compact duck with an oversized head. They frequently look square-headed with a steep forehead. This is accentuated by a small blue-gray bill. The culmen is curved. The tail is fairly long, very broad, and sturdy. When diving at certain angles, this is quite easy to see. Adult ♂: White patch from the eye back set off by

Summer | Fall

an otherwise dark head of beautiful iridescent blues, greens, and purples. Backlit birds typically appear purple, but often black at a distance. The large head bulges at the back. Much of the back is black, the rest white. At a distance, white is the dominant color, the white on the face tending to stand out most. Eclipse ♂: some of the white areas become duller, but ID is still straightforward. Adult ♀/1st-yr: Head brown with a white cheek patch. Upperparts brown, flanks and tail paler brownish gray. The bill averages darker than ♂. Although superficially the same, some birds are slightly larger, with a bigger head; larger white cheek patch that starts closer to the eye. Some of these larger birds have bluer bills and paler breasts. These are 1st-yr ♂. With practice, some can be quite easy to pick out. Bufflehead is a good example of ♂ having larger heads than ♀. Distant ♀-types can initially appear all dark, but sudden shifts in angle reveal their pale cheek or underparts. Notice how similar the chicks are to those of Common Goldeneye.

Bufflehead

Butterballs prefer to swim away, but when they do fly, they are all action. Their running take off is long for such a small waterfowl, an indication of their high wing-load (ratio of weight to wing area). This shows in their landing, too. They come in at 45 degrees, bubble-gum pink legs splayed wide, chest pumped out, and leaning far forward as they can. On landing with feet down, they pull back hard, leaving a long wake behind. Even so, the landing zone is long for such a short bird. In flight they appear fat-bodied, with a rounded undercarriage and quite a long and noticeably broad tail. The tail shape is distinctive, head-on or from behind. The neck is short but thick: what you would expect in such a large-headed bird. The wings are somewhat average, reasonably broad, quite pointed, and slightly swept back at the carpal. The overriding impression is its chunkiness, with rounded head and body. The name "Butterball" is fitting. Buffleheads have a distinctive flight style. Their wings are fast; often a blur. They rock from side to side like a Spotted Sandpiper. With

Flight

stiff wings, they flap from the shoulder; wingbeats almost all in the downstroke, and little in the upstroke. Head-on, or from behind, the wings are noticeably curved down. Buffleheads always seem to fly as fast as they can, but don't get very far fast. They fly just above the water, rarely getting much above the water surface, but agile enough to maneuver between any waves. They are often in pairs, sitting and flying. They are also commonly in small compact flocks, only occasionally in lines. Adult ♂: Focus on the bold gleaming white ear patch on a dark head. Upperparts are mostly dark with a broad white band from front to back on the innerwing, and an inconspicuous scapular stripe. The underparts are the opposite of the upperparts: nearly all white. Adult ♀/1st-yr: Appear dark at distance; in contrast to adult ♂. Brown above with a dark head with white ear patch. Small white wing patches on the upperwing (usually 4 secondaries and greater coverts). 1st-yr ♀ can be aged by dark greater coverts. The underwing and head contrast with the paler breast and belly.

Common Goldeneye *Bucephala clangula* COGO L 18in W 2lbs   Winter | Spring

Common and widespread. Breeds on deep lakes and rivers in forested areas, nesting in nearby tree holes or nest boxes, many to the north in Canada and AK. In winter, they are found on both coasts on estuaries and bays, and in cold landscapes where open water remains. Smaller numbers found as far south as FL. Often alone, though sometimes large congregations occur where there is plentiful food. Roosts communally in winter. Named after the color of their eyes; ♀ often greener-toned; they look white at a distance. Goldeneyes dive a lot and deeply, feeding in deep waters that stay open longer in cold weather. Depth of 15-20ft is typical. Always alert, ready to dive or fly, they are easily spooked. By mid-winter, they start to display, with head tossed back and body contorted, a great winter scene. **ID**: Medium-sized duck with an oversized head that juts out from the back of the neck, but not so extreme as in the scarcer Barrow's Goldeneye. The head shape is variable depending on posture and how the feathers are

Summer | Fall

held: sometimes rounded with sloping forehead and crown flatter (especially after diving); other times conical with steep forehead and raised crown. Large bill is longer than it is deep; Barrow's is triangular and stubbier-looking with shorter nostril. Adult ♂: round white face spot, dark green head. The head often looks black, occasionally purple when backlit. Black and white appears more white than black, the white scapulars blending into the underparts except for thin black lines. Common lacks the flank spur shown by Barrow's, often showing a dark spot here. Eclipse ♂: like ♀, best sexed by retained extensive white wing-covert pattern and darker brown head. Adult ♀/juv: Dark brown head and mostly gray body. Bill black in juv and most breeding ♀. Ad ♀ usually have variably-shaped yellow tip to bill in winter. Rarely extensive yellow (past nostril) like Barrow's. 1st-yr often darker- and duller-headed; darker iris lightens from outer edge through winter. 1st-yr ♂ grow adult-type feathers through winter and are a dingy version of adults.

Displays. Waterfowl often have incredible displays. They are varied and short, typically lasting from a few to about 30 seconds. They involve different contortions such as in the Common Goldeneye and Red-breasted Merganser. Some, such as Mallard, head-bob up and down in an exaggerated fashion; others head-shake, moving their head from side to side. Some birds tail-shake, sometimes simultaneously while moving their head. These actions are sometimes followed by short flights; often triggering a chain reaction from nearby males. They sometimes end in copulation. This usually happens in late winter and spring, although it does sometimes happen in fall. ♀ also copulate between laying eggs, the eggs being fertil-

ized between laying (the ♀ is often not monogamous). ♂ Common Goldeneye swim quickly with their neck repeatedly pumped out at 45 degrees, occasionally they just sit still. Suddenly they recoil, head thrown onto its back and bill pointed skyward. (This takes between one and two seconds); often they give a shrill squawk. Sometimes the throw back or head throw is exaggerated with rump in the air and chest submerged. Waterfowl displays are usually distinctive, probably reducing hybridization. Barrow's Goldeneye has a similar but different display with more head-bobbing and doesn't throw its head back so far. Hybridization is rare. Mallards and Black Duck have similar displays → with lots of hybrids!

Common Goldeneye

Common Goldeneye's scientific name – clangula – comes from the whistling the drake's wings make in flight. 'Whistlers' are often seen flying overhead alone or in pairs as they shuttle between feeding areas. In flocks, rarely large, they tend to be evenly spaced, somewhat far apart and sometimes in irregular lines. They are wary and will fly or dive quickly. They are medium-sized, muscular-looking ducks. The very large heads; big, broad-based bill; and the particularly thick neck create a profile distinct from all but Barrow's Goldeneye. Commons are heavy-bodied with a deep undercarriage centered toward the rear. The dark tail is broad and usually appears rounded and stands out in strong contrast with white underparts. The wings are quite short and held straight, with noticeably blunt tips. Wing beats are stiff, flapping from the shoulder, adding to the muscular appearance. They tend to look quite hunch-backed and slightly tipped-up with the head held higher than the tail. Commons appear two-toned with dark head and upperparts with

Flight

white wing patches and mostly white underparts. Among the striking features are the dark underwing coverts. Shape and color patterns make this a distinctive species. Told from ♂ Barrow's Goldeneye most easily by round eye-spot and green head. Eye-spot shape also good ID for 1st-yr ♂. In ♀-type Commons, focus on darker bill and shape. Barrow's brown head extends farther down the neck and appears more squared-off, particularly on the throat. Underwing coverts average darker. Barrow's Goldeneyes also average less white on the median and lesser coverts, some showing no white; Commons always do. Commons can usually be aged and sexed by a combination of head, iris, and wing-covert patterns. Ad ♀ have two distinct wing bars and the most white on the lesser coverts; 1st-yr ♀ narrow wing bars and the least white on the coverts; 1st-yr ♂ are intermediate.

Barrow's Goldeneye *Bucephala islandica* BAGO L 18in W 1.7lbs **Winter | Spring**

Scarcer cousin of Common Goldeneye, found mostly in the Rockies and to the west. Both are similar in many ways. Usually breeds by relatively fishless lakes and ponds, often at high altitudes in boreal forests. Most winter in flocks on tidal coastal bays with mollusks. Some winter on inland lakes and rivers. They sometimes are found with Common Goldeneye, flocks tending to segregate. Often more approachable than Common. **ID**: Size and structure very similar to Common Goldeneye, except for bill and head shapes. Always focus on these in ♀-types. Bill in Barrow's is shorter and therefore more triangular. Head-on it is broad-based, tapers narrower in center and comes to more of a point at the tip. Common bill is longer, broader, and more spatulate. Head shape often obvious with steeper forehead and much more puffed-out nape area when neck is held erect. The dark head extends farther down the neck in Barrow's; noticeable when the neck is stretched. This makes the neck collar in ♀-types narrower than in Common. Judging this on all birds

Summer | Fall

may be difficult. Adult ♂: ID is straightforward. Head shape, typically purple iridescence to head (not green), black vertical flank spur, smaller white scapular spots, and white face crescent, are all easy to see. Overall impression of ♂ Barrow's is of a dark duck with some white, the opposite of ♂ Common. Eclipse ♂: like ♀ with ♂ wing pattern. Black bill, averages paler-breasted. Adult ♀: Bill color variable; typically yellow to yellow-orange in winter, most with some black in basal half; mostly black in summer, palest toward tip. Icelandic birds have darker bills; use multiple ID characters. Brown head is often darker and duller than Common Goldeneye. Body gray with paler fringes, often paler on breast; like Common, they are variable. 1st-yr ♀: most easily aged by duller yellow bill and darker iris. 1st-yr ♂: adult-type white facial and breast feathers start to be molted in from early winter. Darker iris. Beware of hybrids, occurring regularly enough and showing intermediate features. Goldeneye ducklings are best separated by bill shape.

ad. ♂

Barrow's Goldeneye

Barrow's are similar to Common Goldeneye in flight, with the same muscular build, undercarriage deepest at the rear and strikingly dark underwing coverts. The rounded, dark tail contrasts strongly with the pale underparts. Barrow's are subtly more compact than Commons with broader wings. Barrow's have a larger head with steeper forehead, and much thicker neck, quite noticeable in flight. This super-sized head accentuates the smaller stubby bill. Barrows, in general average slightly darker than Commons. The head tends to be held higher than the tail. Goldeneyes regularly form mixed flocks. Always ID the ♂ first; they are the easiest. The 'half-moon' face pattern is noticeable at long distances. Most goldeneye can be ID'd by the pattern of white on the upperwing, particularly if they can be aged and sexed. The innerwing appears completely white, or almost so, on ♂ Common Goldeneye. On Barrows the white is less extensive and is broken by a broad black bar, creating 2 white patches. On many ♂ Barrows the white on the co-

Flight

verts has lots of black spotting mixed in, a darker and less-clean look than in Commons. The black tips to the greater coverts are hard to see on ♂ of both species. The dark head of both ♂ and ♀ Barrow's extends farther down the neck, especially on the throat, emphasizing the square-headed look. The longer, bushy-brown or purple feathering on the nape often sticks out above the neck, or farther down the nape. The yellow bill is quite obvious in ♀-types; an easy feature to look for. ♀-type Barrows have less white on the upperwing than Commons. Adult ♀ have only one black bar (2 in Commons) and bases to median and lesser coverts are dark with white mixed in; similar aged Commons have more-extensive white. Most 1st-yr Barrows lack any obvious wing bars and have one square white patch; Commons have one or two wing bars and lots of white. 1st-yr ♂ can be also aged by face pattern, duller iris, and black bill; ♀ by dull iris and yellow bill. Like other divers, Barrows have a fairly long take-off and splash-landing.

Mystery Goldeneyes. Common and Barrow's Goldeneyes often mix together in winter. Ad ♂ are relatively easy to identify. Many people search for the different face patterns, though the more-extensively dark upperparts in Barrow's is usually what stands out the most. The black breast spur, along with head and bill shapes, are great backup features. Hybrids do occur, and it is always worth checking for birds that don't quite 'add up,' with intermediate features. These are most easily judged using the shape of the facial and scapular spots. 1st-yr ♂ usually show 'ghost' features of adult ♂ by early winter and have black bills. ♀ and juveniles are much tougher with some best left unidentified. The longer bill of Com

mon, more rounded and less pointed at the tip, is sometimes obvious, other times it is confusingly difficult to judge. The yellow bill tip in Common is usually well demarcated and rarely extends beyond the nostril. The subspecies of Barrow's from Iceland often has less yellow than NA birds, though it usually extends beyond the nostril. Supporting features for Common are longer nostril and warmer-colored and paler brown head that doesn't extend as far down the throat, larger white collar, and darker bill. In flight, Common also shows more-extensive white on the median and lesser coverts and a more-pronounced dark median-covert bar. Can you ID all these goldeneyes? Answers p. 486.

Hooded Merganser *Lophodytes cucullatus* HOME L 18in W 1.6lbs   **Winter | Spring**

Hooded Mergs breed in the far west, across much of southern Canada, and eastern US. They live in forested swamps, staying well hidden on small lakes, ponds, and streams, usually in areas with lots of cover, and are often hard to see. They nest in tree cavities and nest boxes. They winter on both coasts on estuaries and creeks; some inland, and are common on the Mississippi Flyway. The smallest NA merganser. Secretive, even in winter. They are in tidal creeks and channels, often between houses and trees, and can be tough to see. Icy weather can lead to dense concentrations in open water. Flushed easily, they have a very distinctive flight style, shallow wingbeats so fast they are a blur. They dive for fish and other animal matter. 100s sometimes gather at favored roost sites, often tucked up to pond or river edges with trees. **ID**: A small merganser that sits long and low in the water with a long bushy crest. They are beautiful and distinctive. Rounded back tapers to the rear, accentuated by long tail usually in water. When cocked, the tail is quite

Summer | Fall

long and pointed. Oblong-headed. It is the bushy crest that grabs attention. ♂ opens like a Victorian fan, simply stunning. When sleeping, the steep forehead and long flat head is still uniquely-shaped. Adult ♂: distinctively patterned black and white head and breast; the white behind the eye is striking at any distance. Rich chestnut flanks. Eclipse ♂: ♀-like. Always look for the yellow-orange iris and wing covert pattern. Adult ♀: Dark brown, grayer on the neck and head, darkest on the forehead and with a much brighter orange-brown bushy crest, paler at the back. Extensive yellow on bill; ♂ is usually black. Red iris (usually appears dark) is much darker than ♂. Tertials are striped black and white. In summer, Hoodies ♀ often show more spiky crest recalling Red-breasted Merg and are more uniform brown. 1st-yr: Like ad ♀ with smaller and browner juv feathers, tertials lacking bold white stripes, and shorter crest. ♂ molt adult ♂-type feathers from fall onwards. Iris becomes lighter, bill darkens and crest is longer; most can be sexed by early-winter.

Hooded Merganser

Fairly small, particularly for a merganser. Slim but compact with a long tail. They fly past like a bat out of hell with really fast shallow wing beats a blur. There is nothing else like them! Their back is often hunched up and neck tilted down as though ready to attack. At other times their head is held higher – it looks a lot more relaxed! Thin bill is accentuated by the steep forehead. The body is sleek, with a fairly long tail. Wings are forward on the body, slim, pointed and held straight out from the body. The speed of the wing beats alone makes them distinctive, and their shape just adds to this making them easy to ID. When coming in to land they often tilt at 45 degrees, like a cyclist coming round a bend, with wings half tucked in before dropping to land with feet first. Fast and agile, they get in and out of tight spots with ease. They fly in tight single-species groups, usually in small numbers though groups of 20 and 30 are not uncommon,

Flight

particularly when areas of open water become restricted due to icy weather. They roost communally and are often seen flying to and from these sites at twilight. Their shape and flight style still gives them away! Flocks are compact, often as deep as they are long. From below, Hoodies are dark with white belly patches and underwing coverts (they are divided by a narrow dark flank line); this is a distinctive pattern when flying overhead. The upperparts appear uniform with black borders to white in the speculum and greater secondary coverts. 1st-yrs have slightly smaller white spots than ad ♀ but aging using this feature is very difficult in the field. Ad ♂ have gray median coverts, though this is only really a key ID feature in eclipse plumage. Size, long tail and flock formations are similar to Wood Duck, but Hoodies are much slimmer and have faster wingbeats. Occasionally occur with other mergansers, but are noticeably smaller.

Red-breasted Merganser *Mergus serrator* RBME L 23in W 2.3lbs   **Winter | Spring**

Common northerly breeder on boreal streams, rivers, islands, and lakes. Ground nester, in shallow cavities, under cover, in protected spots. In coastal areas they breed in burrows on dune systems. One of the commonest ducks in winter on both coasts and the Great Lakes, both in sheltered and exposed areas. Usually in small groups of 2 to 40, sometimes strung out in lines. Other times they are widely spread, often in pairs. They dive with a jump, often clearing the water; sometimes snorkeling, with head underwater. **ID**: Noticeably smaller and slighter than Common Merganser. The spiky crest, longest in ♂, is often the first thing to stand out. The bill is long and thin along the whole length: deep red, it averages paler in 1st-yrs. Common Mergansers are much broader, particularly at the base. Beautiful red iris. Mergs usually sit long and low in the water; rounded back tapers gradually to the tail. Red-breasted Mergs can usually be ID'd by structure alone. Adult ♂: Green head with long spiky crest, making them look large-headed: smaller

Summer | Fall

when the crest is down. White collar contrasts strongly with brown-streaked breast and black back. It stands out at any distance. Body different patterns of black and white. Eclipse ♂: ♀-like with white median coverts. Molt into bright plumage on wintering grounds, as late as Dec. Adult ♀: Extremely variable. Body mostly gray, some browner; paler on the chest. Reddish brown head; spiky crest varies from short to nearly as long as ad ♂. Red iris. Some show dark loral spot bordered by white; older birds show more-extensive black around the eye like older 1st-yr ♂. Tertials usually gray, some whiter. 1st-yr: Like ad ♀ but averages browner. Look for orange-brown eye, retained smaller juv feathers, particularly pointed brown tertials. 1st-yr ♂ grow in dark feathers around eye through winter, hard to separate from older ad ♀. Common Mergs are larger and bulkier. Commons have a much broader base to the bill. Larger and brighter head contrasts strongly with the white chin and underparts. Differences are mirrored in ad ♂.

Red-breasted Maerganser

Red-breasted Mergs are just one of several species of mergansers or 'sawbills'; named after the serrated or saw-like edges to the bill. These are shaped to better help grip fish. Can you see the 'saws' on the two close birds? And notice the stunning red eyes! They display in late-winter and early spring. With their heads at an angle and slightly tilted back, crests along the back, they suddenly thrust their heads forward and upwards, as far as they will go. They hold it in place for a second or two with crests spiked. They tip forward, neck submerged, head up, rear-end even higher before sitting back down. This is enough to get all the ♂ worked up. Often the ♂ will all run 3 or 4ft across the water; if one goes, the others follow suit. Red-breasted Mergs are fairly large sleek birds, with long slim necks and small heads. The head is shallowly-rounded and the throat sticks out below the long skinny bill. The wings are quite far back in the body; the neck is longer than the tail; you get the feel they are stretching their necks as far forward as they can. Wings are

Flight

slim, pointed and slightly angled back at the carpal. Mergs are fast and direct flyers with rapid, fairly shallow wingbeats, emphasis on the downstroke. The head is held straight, occasionally higher, or tipped down. They fly in straight or angled lines, even if only 2 or 3 birds. Larger flocks may form 'V's or more haphazard groups before becoming more organized. Adult ♂: besides shape, the broad white collar sandwiched between the dark head and brown-speckled collar is key. The extensive white upperwing has 2 black bars; all other plumages have a wing bar and less white. Adult ♀/1st-yrs: from below they have a large white belly patch extending to the tail and the underwing is extensively white. Orange-brown head becomes grayer on the rest of the body. 1st-yr birds average narrower or no greater covert bars, and browner plumage, but this is very hard to judge. Traditionally birds with black around the eye were called 1sy-yr ♂, many are actually older ♀. Did you find the 2 American Wigeon with the eclipse ♂ merg sandwiched between them?

Common Merganser *Mergus merganser* COME L 25in W 3.2lbs Winter | Spring

Widespread and fairly common breeder on larger lakes and fast-flowing rivers in northern forests and mountains. They nest in cavities in trees, cliffs, nest boxes, or under some cover on the ground. Very hardy. They winter most commonly in the north where fresh water remains open, gathering in large concentrations where the food is plentiful. They swim in tight packs, snorkeling and diving for food. They often sit in groups on floating ice, banks, and are particularly fond of power plants. Rare near salt water. Like other mergansers (also known as sawbills), has serrated bill for holding fish. **ID**: Comfortably, the largest merganser. Typically sits low in the water, looking slimmer than it really is. The tail is usually in the water making it a very long-looking bird. The head is long and large; flat-crowned with deep crest typically held flattened-down on the hindneck. The crest is less ragged than Red-breasted, the head larger, and the neck thicker. The bill is large, broadening onto head, and bright red. This combination makes the bill far more conspicuous than in the thin-

Summer | Fall

billed Red-breasted, a great ID feature. Adult ♂: Clean cut white with black back and green head (often appears black). The underparts often have a pink or peach wash. Eclipse ♂: from ♀ by retained white coverts, browner upperparts and darker head. Many ♂ have noticeably larger and broader-based bills than ♀. Adult ♀: rich chestnut heads and well-defined white chin. The strong contrast is very different from all other mergs. Also differs by uniform light gray back and flanks. All Common Mergs are 'clean-cut'. 1st-years: Very similar to adult ♀; best separated by loral pattern; pale line bordered by dark. 1st-yrs also have a paler iris, average duller. Some ♂ start to become more adult-like in spring, separating them from eclipse birds is very difficult. In bright plumage by about Nov. Eurasian 'Goosander' is a vagrant to AK. It has a noticeably squarer head, much narrower bill, with feathering at the bill-base more pointed and less 'squared-off' at the face. The tip is strongly hooked, the nail a different shape. Ad ♂: greater coverts are all white.

Common Merganser

Common Mergs are large, long, and sleek. Their boldly marked color patterns and pale colors adding emphasis to their large size. Although slim, they are solidly built. As you would expect, they are powerful and fast flyers. The neck is long and very thick, the head barely any thicker. The crown usually slopes into the broad-based bill. Red-breasted Mergs have very thin necks and obvious foreheads. The bill is so slim, that it is often hard to see. Common Merg undercarriage is gently rounded and the tail medium-lengthed, though it looks short relative to the length of the neck and head. The tail usually looks rounded or even pointed at times. Wings appear quite far back on the body, broad-based, angled at the carpal, and pointed. Typical of mergansers, stiff wingbeats are fast, and relatively shallow, with emphasis in the downstroke. Common Mergansers, like Red-breasted, prefer to fly quite high above the water, and low only on shorter flights. They are usually alone or in small groups. Flocks usually travel in evenly spaced angular lines.

Flight

Adult ♂: easily separated from Red-breasted Merganser by clean-cut white underparts; the green (often appears black) head stands out and the bill often stands out at distance due to its bright color and large size. The white innerwing extends to the median and lesser coverts, the simplest way to age eclipse ♂. Adult ♀ and 1st-yrs Common Merganser have dark chestnut heads contrasting strongly with the pale neck and throat; Red-breasted Mergansers show weak contrast, are noticeably slighter with a thin bill, a dingier-looking bird. The head contrast is always the key feature to look for on Common Mergs on an otherwise clean-cut gray and white bird lacking brown tones. Wing patches are restricted to the secondaries and greater coverts. The dark tips to the greater coverts on 1st-yrs are narrower and paler than adults. Some 1st-yrs can be safely sexed: ♂ by larger bill and paler gray median and lesser coverts; ♀ smaller, narrow-based bill and darker coverts. Bald Eagles are often found sitting on ice when there are bountiful food sources nearby.

Mystery Mergansers. Hoodies, Red-breasts, and Common Mergs are sometimes seen together, particularly when areas of water are frozen over and they are concentrated in remaining open patches. When the fishing is good there will always be a crowd! ID is quite straightforward when birds are not sleeping. When the head is tucked in, the ID gets tougher. It's always best to start with the easiest birds to identify, usually boldly patterned ♂ and birds showing their faces and bills. If you are certain of a bird's identity, these are great reference points for size, shape, and subtle plumage patterns you might not have otherwise noticed. Hooded Mergs are small and are the only merganser with a dark bill. Of course

never rely on just one feature, always check that size, shape, and color patterns are all okay. Red-breasts are about 20% larger than Hoodies, and are also dingier browns. The spiky-headed Red-breasts are chestnut-headed in ♀-like plumages. By comparison, Common Mergs are bigger and cleaner gray-and-white. Describing differences in size is hard to quantify and subjective. Commons are about 10% longer and 25% heavier than Red-breasts; but we often perceive the same things differently! To my eyes Commons look about 20% larger than Red-breasts. What do you think? Identify all the mergansers. Answers p. 487. Did you notice the 'sawbill' on the bird to the left?

Mergansers in the Bay. The biggest driving force in nature is food. A hungry, or unhealthy, bird does not have the energy to carry out the functions such as migration, molting, and breeding, that are vital to the individual and species. As a result, you will rarely find wildlife where there is very little food, even if the habitat looks great. Sometimes there a lot of food available, and, therefore, more birds, in the most unlikely places. Deep snow, or icing of both water and land, will sometimes make feeding impossible, and groups of waterfowl will move to new areas. Salt water remains open longer than fresh water. Where water remains open, mixed waterfowl will gather, including freshwater species like Common Merganser and there are feeding frenzies where food is concentrated. Watch how the birds move with the food. It can be interest-

ing watching schools of bait fish move, is it in response to the waterfowl, or visa-versa? Also watch varying behavior within, and between, species. For example, Red-breasted Mergs will often jump almost completely out of the water when diving. Other times they will slip straight under without a splash, like Common Merganser. Most people assume that we know much more about wildlife than we do. There is still so much we can learn from careful study of behavior that will help us manage better for conservation. As food is the driving force, understanding water temperatures, sun aspect, salinity, and water depths are just a few examples of things we need to know better to manage effectively. Try to paint a more complete picture for yourself the next time you're out. It's interesting! How many of each species are there? Answers p. 487.

Smew *Mergellus albellus* SMEW L 16in W 1.4lbs   Winter | Spring

A rare Eurasian visitor throughout NA, mostly to w. AK and the West. Most occur late-fall, sometimes in small groups, or with other wintering waterfowl. Found in deeper freshwater lakes, but also on rivers and coastal bays. Common in captivity, clouding some records. Unusual monotypic diving duck, somewhere between a small merganser and goldeneye. A small compact duck with short thick neck, short crest. Unique small pointed bill with tiny hooked-tip. Adult ♂: unmistakable black and white duck sometimes called 'white nun'. Adult ♀/1st-yr: color patterns superficially like Common Merg, but much smaller and a different shape. Chestnut head and white throat contrasts with mostly gray body. By late-winter 1st-yr ♂ start to show adult-like characters such as black eye patch, white breast and scapulars. 2nd-yr ♂: some can be aged from ad by gray-tipped scapulaurs and subdued color pattern. In flight all have white wing patches (smaller in 1st-yr ♀) and 2 narrow wing bars, the white trailing edge often difficult to see against pale skies.

Masked Duck *Nomonyx dominicus* MADU L 14in W 0.8lbs

Rare stiff-tail, mostly found in TX and FL, sometimes in groups (invasions). Nomadic, breeds any time of year. A skulker in weedy overgrown ponds, lakes and ditches. They dive a lot. Slightly smaller than Ruddy Duck, Masked are similarly shaped. Has large pale broad-based bill and big 'neck-less' heads without a forehead. Adult ♂: can be in bright plumage any time of year. Obvious bright chestnut-brown with black face and random black spotting/flecking. Nonbr ♂, ♀, and juvs are all similarly intricately marked brown and buff. Dark cap, eyeline, and cheek pattern form three stripes (two on Ruddy), a unique face pattern. ♂ has stronger orange tones, particularly on nape and chest, but sexing birds is difficult. Masked and Ruddies are not as similar as many think. Ruddies need a long runway for takeoff. (The bird has high wing load.) Masked Duck will lift off the water almost vertically, without a running start. This practice lets Masked feed secretively in small ponds and wetlands. They are crepuscular, fly mostly at night, and prefer to swim out of trouble.

Ruddy Duck *Oxyura jamaicensis* RUDU L 15in W 1.3lbs **Winter | Spring**

The common stiff-tail, breeding in ponds, marshes, and lakes, usually where there is plenty of vegetation for cover. They disappear for periods in even the smallest of ponds, suddenly reappearing; and often there are several pairs! Ruddies are divers feeding on a wide variety of plant and animal life. In winter, they form flocks on rivers, coastal bays, and lakes, where they sit in compact flocks, often with heads tucked-in. They will sometimes mix with Lesser Scaup, Canvasbacks, Redhead, and other diving ducks; then their small size becomes obvious. Although only teal-size, they are compact and sit high in the water; they can look deceptively large. They often swim with their tail held cocked at 45 degrees, hence the name 'stifftail.' Ruddies prefer to swim away from trouble: they rarely fly. They have to run across the water a long way before they can get airborne, with big feet dragging behind. **ID**: Small, chunky ducks with a distinctive shape. Big broad head and very large bill with concave culmen creates a distinctive headshape. They sit high in the

ad. ♀ with ducklings about 2 weeks old

ad. ♂ breeding

ad. ♀ with ducklings a few days old

Summer | Fall

water, and the rounded back tapers to the rear, its long tail often barely visible when in the water. The tail is dark, and when held 'stiff,' contrasts strongly with the white undertail. Adult ♂ br: powder blue bill, with varying amounts of dark at tip, rich chestnut body (the pale belly, often mixed with black, is rarely seen), and bold white face bordered by black. Unmistakable! Adult ♂ nonbr: molt into ♀-like plumage in fall but look for the white face with dark border. The bill is dark, though often with some blue visible. Body feathers have narrow vermiculations and pale spots. Transitional birds show more chestnut and bluer bills. Adult ♀ br: brown, usually with strong chestnut tones to the body and head. The cheek stripe is always conspicuous. Bill varies from dark to paler gray and black. Adult ♀ nonbr: darker brown above, paler below, some with chestnut fringes, bold cheek stripe, and dark bill. 1st-yrs: ♀-like, ♂. Ageing 1st-yrs from ad ♀ nonbr is difficult. Look for fewer spots and vermiculations than adults, and particularly retained juv tail feathers birds.

♀s fighting

Ruddy Duck

A small quiet pond, no doubt with sleeping Ruddy Ducks in the reeds, suddenly becomes alive as ducks swim out to the middle. Everything they do seems hurried, perhaps emphasized by their small size. They preen fast and excitedly, jabbing themselves as though it's a matter of life and death. Then with heads held high, they peer around proudly, as though they are the sole owners of their domain, even though they are not. Head-on or from behind, his head has a deep furrow. It gives him a thoughtful, or is it devil-like, look. Several pairs may be in one small area, increasing territoriality. All of sudden, he is off, banging the water repeatedly, faster and faster, with bubbles frothing. He makes a *blub blub blub bla* sound – like flicking fingers up and down over your lips, to entertain babies. His tail is stuck high, appearing to add to his authority. As the battle intensifies he shudders, presumably to demonstrate his intent. It goes on for a short while, and then he runs across the water toward his foe with his back up and with bad intent, only to back off.

Display and Flight

He has made his point. They dive under the water, sometimes with a splash, sometimes slipping quietly without a trace. The ritual happens again, but you think you have them worked out. He slaps the water, and off he runs. This time though, he has had enough. No bluff this time and he engages. They duke it out, standing tall and pounding each other with their feet. They are nasty, and they mean business. They break up and swim away. Were the ladies impressed? The two ♀ are eyeing the drakes but also each other. They want their mate. They put their heads down low to the water and swim toward each other. Suddenly and ferociously they rear up and the tussle really starts. Their bills lock as they grapple for supremacy, as if one is trying to pull the other's head off. Judging the winner is not easy, but you can only be struck by how ferocious this looks. The pond returns back to normal. The battles have settled down. Everyone is sitting quietly. All of a sudden a head goes up, and, surprise, surprise, it doesn't look happy. Oh those nice little Ruddies!

Distant Ducks on a Mountain Pond. Aeautiful mountain pond, the smell of fresh air, and sounds that travel for miles. The solitude where you can hear yourself breath and think, a lifetime from most of our reality. Escape at its finest, a place where we can leave behind the rat race. It's not somewhere chock-a-block with birds. Habitat, it can be called probability, is a key factor in bird ID. Mountain ponds or lakes are the regular home for only a few species. See if you can work them out. We are often intimidated by distance, thinking that not being able to see the close up minutiae is a hin-

drance to being able to identifying birds. Often 'less is more,' and this is often the case with bird ID. We often get caught up in all the details and lose sight of the big picture. Focus on the shape and the simple color patterns. The features you notice when a bird is still speck in the distance can be the most important things to consider. These are frequently different from what the field guides may tell you. Knowing what you can't see at a distance is just as important as knowing what you can see!

Prairie Potholes. You don't need a guide to tell you where to go in the Prairie Pothole Region of the US and Canada. Any road that goes through the rolling countryside will lead you past a mosaic of grasslands and accompanying wetland potholes. Formed after glaciers retreated 10,000 years ago, almost half of NA waterfowl breed here. It is not just the wetlands that are critical, also the surrounding grasslands that where most of the waterfowl nest. The loss of these wetlands and grasslands continues to be a major conservation problem for waterfowl and all wildlife. Some ponds will be tiny; some will be bigger. Typically they all have their fair share of birds on them. By Jul, it's not just the adults but the young ones as

well. Overhead Black Terns, Bank (brown-backed, shallow forked tail and breast band) and Barn Swallows (blue-backed, dark throat and steeply-forked tail) hawk insects. Pied-billed and Red-necked Grebes are often mixed in with the waterfowl, and Great Blue Herons fish the edges. Jul is prime time for an abundance of food in these areas and the reason why so many birds move north in summer to breed. It is also no coincidence that this is when most birds hatch their young. Try and identify all the ducks. How many Bank and Barn Swallows, Great Blue Herons and Black Terns are there?

Senescent Hen Waterfowl – Old, or senescent, ♀ waterfowl that show ♂ characteristics are scarce. They usually pass as eclipse or first-year ♂, even hybrids. These ♀ are commonly mislabeled as 'intersex.' This term is used for animals that have both ♂ and ♀ organs. These birds do not. As birds age, their estrogen level declines, just like in women. Estrogen keeps the ♀ appearance in place, but without it, color patterns revert back toward the 'default' ♂ in sexually dimorphic ducks. This happens in all birds, not only waterfowl. It is common in captive birds and at those local ponds where they live long lives. It is easiest to look for senescent ♀ in Mallards. Since ducks are often in pairs, look for the 'bright' ♀. They have intermediate characters like an immature or eclipse ♂. ♀-like bill pattern is often the biggest clue – see the two Mallards above. Time of

year is also a big clue. The Long-tailed Duck images were all taken Dec 24, but the brown ones appear to be most similar to a ♂ in summer with a ♀-like bill. Presumably this is a ♀. The Wood Duck is also a senescent ♀; look at the bill and iris color. Other birds are easy to call ♂, but as our knowledge evolves, this may change. Labeling everything is not always possible! Red-breasted Mergansers with black around the eye have always been thought to be 1st-yr ♂. Most of these birds are actually older ♀. Of course, a number of birds may show subtle ♂ characteristics of older birds such as a dark breast in Gadwall, more color in Ruddy Duck, or perhaps this is just variation. In this world of humans wanting to give everything a label and a nice square box to put every item in, much of what we do is not possible. There is so much we don't know. Now isn't that fun?

Rust-stained Birds. Some birds, notably the Sandhill Crane, apply mud, rich in iron-oxides, to their feathers that gives them a rusty appearance. Rust-stained waterfowl are quite common. Unlike the cranes that apply the staining on purpose, it happens by accident in waterfowl. Waddling around in mud or water, the iron oxides that are present stain the feathers. It seems to be particularly prevalent in juv and white feathers on the belly. It's also more prevalent in summer. These softer and presumably more absorbent feathers are the ones with most contact with the iron oxides. These feathers are older than the newer second generation feathers and have had longer to absorb the stain. Notice on many of the ducks here

how the small rusty juv feathers contrast strongly with the cleaner large flank feathers that have recently been molted in. This atypical appearance can confuse even the best. Many Cinnamon Teal that have been identified out of range are often simply rust-stained birds, particularly the structurally similar Blue-winged Teal. Rusty staining is also quite common in adult waterfowl in summer in the iron-rich far north. Emperor Geese are frequently rusty-faced and other birds with lots of white feathers are particularly prone to it. What are all these species, and which ones are not 1st-yr birds?

Mystery Freshwater 'Bellies.' A marsh full of waterfowl feeding quietly can quickly change to a kaleidoscope of mayhem when a Bald Eagle comes by. Most, if not all, the birds will quickly take to the air in a tangible state of panic. Many of the birds will stay as single-species flocks; others will be in mixed groups. With hundreds, sometimes thousands, of birds circling the air, knowing where to look first in the mayhem can be confusing. Look at the closest birds with the sun behind you. Weather and lighting conditions are always an important factor in the birds' appearance. Beware of birds in the shadow of trees, buildings and other birds. Size is always crucial. Having several species nearby is great for comparison

With the exception of the Mallard complex, every other duck has a unique size and shape. Learning them is vital, with bill, head, neck, undercarriage, and tail shapes being particularly important. Many are quite striking in the field such as the large spatulate bill of Shoveler, the long tail of Wood Ducks, or the sleek appearance of mergansers. Color can be a big help in bird ID, but in poor light conditions it is of little use. Knowing the color patterns is critical for fast ID. It is better to think of birds in terms of tones or shades of gray rather than color. Then the lighting conditions don't matter! Can you ID all these overhead waterfowl? Answers p. 487.

Overhead 'Bellies.' A Prairie Falcon with its dark armpits flies over somewhere just west of the Rockies. A storm looks like it's brewing, and all the ducks from the nearby shallow marsh start circling overhead, seemingly happy to stretch their wings up in the clouds. As always, most of the ducks separate into single-species flocks or with similar species. The standard basics of size and shape always apply. Directly above, the upperwing patterns are not visible, but it is not a problem. Their head patterns, particularly in drakes, are where you should focus. Tail color can be very useful, though, remember, they are usually different depending on what age and sex the duck is. Underwing patterns can be useful. Most teal have dark

leading edges to the wing creating a contrasting white inner wing stripe. Green-winged Teal are not as boldly patterned as Blue-winged and Cinnamon Teal, and are similar to species like American Wigeon. These American Wigeon also have white armpits or axillaries. Its similar Eurasian counterpart, Eurasian Wigeon, has gray axillaries creating a more uniformly gray underwing – a great feature to look for if you aren't sure! And then there are the different specks where it's tempting to tell yourself that they are too far away and you won't be able to work it out. Of course, that is just an excuse. Slow down, systematically look at every little detail you can see, and put the clues together. Can you work them all out. Answers p. 487.

Mystery Teal in Flight. A gunshot goes off and all hell breaks loose. The birds are in the distance with not enough time for your mind to focus. They are close, you hadn't seen them and now you have about 15 seconds to ID as many as you can. But just how good are you? Let's find out. Get a stopwatch, close the page and then just see how many birds you can ID in those 15 seconds. Do you think you can run through them all in 15 seconds. Yes or No? For those of you who had the courage to take the challenge, well done. So how did you do? For those who really have their 'eye in', is 15

seconds long enough to identify all the birds, or at least narrow it down to a couple of species for the tougher ones? If you are way off this time, try it a few more times. Your time should keep coming down. As in any outdoor sport, practice makes perfect. As you familiarize yourself with patterns and they become more solidly imprinted on to your brain, the recognition becomes almost instantaneous. Answers p. 487.

Mystery Flight in Fall. The beautiful colors of the trees and marsh make fall a favorite time for most people. It's also a time when there are many immature birds, and many drakes are in partial eclipse. If the marsh is big enough, and it's a year when there is plenty of food, numbers of waterfowl can be fantastic, with many species that change on a daily basis. It can be a devil to see everything hidden in the vegetation but a passing Bald Eagle changes all that. It's a juvenile, so it's all brown with some white on the underwing — nothing like the white-headed and tailed birds we are always shown on

TV. With everything in the air, it is time to really focus, because you have limited time to look at and identify everything. Often birds will separate out into single-species flocks. Once you have ID'd a couple of birds, ♂ are usually easiest, quickly look to see if any of the flock look 'wrong' for that species. Sometimes it's just mayhem, and there is a mosaic of species, and there is no other way to do it other than one by one. There is great variety in this flock. See if you can ID them all. Answers p. 487.

Flying Away in Buffalo, NY. The Great Lakes Region can be superb for waterfowl in winter. The more frozen the lakes are, the more the more tightly packed the concentrations will be in any remaining open water. The ice on the lakes, rivers, and bays is constantly on the move, and so are the birds. Wind direction, tides, and temperatures all in effect where leads open up, a very dynamic environment. Birds pour in. In mild winters, many birds stay offshore, many out of sight in the middle of the lakes. In harsh winters, any remaining open areas can be chocked full of birds. Every day is a different day.

and you just never know when it's going to be simply great. With such concentrations of birds, mix is often impressive, and it's possible to see lots of different species in the air at once. Watch for decoys, some are incredibly life-like. When everything else is flying, those Canvasbacks still sitting might need double-checking. Even when a mass of ducks all take off at once, they tend to split up into same-species groups. See if you can ID all the ducks here on the Niagara River in Buffalo, NY. Answers p. 487.

Flying Away Bay Ducks. It's likely that we see all birds from the rear-end more than at any other angle. They usually see us before we see them, and it is their instinct to fly away from us. Under those conditions, we get to see fewer features than from other angles, and things don't get easier as they disappear frustratingly into the distance. Size and shape are tougher to judge, but they are still possible. It simply takes a bit more focus. Judging size and shape is still key. Relative comparison to other birds is vital, as are other clues, such as wing-beat speed — slower wingbeats on larger birds, faster on smaller Birds such as mergansers still look slim-bodied relative to scaup or scoters. Depending on the angle, we can

still see the upperparts or the underparts. Trying to see the head and upperwing patterns is always important, and staying focused on these features may be all that time allows. Occasionally, the 'from-behind' angle is a big help, for example, judging the pattern of the wing stripe in scaup. Flank and underwing patterns can also be useful. Factor in the habitat and where you are – this is AK. Yes, rear ends can be brief and hard, but stay focused, think quickly remembering and analyzing every feature you can see. Just like when you ID people from behind, you can do it with birds when you know them well. Good practice is always the key! Can you ID all of these? Answers p. 488.

Squadrons. You notice lines of ducks in the distance. It's cold, and you've not seen anything for hours. You pray for them to come your way. Lo and behold, they do. Within seconds they are right in front of you. There is a *whrrr* of wings as squadrons of ducks, at different altitudes, fly toward and over you. You know you have seconds to ID them – simply not the time for so many birds. You have to play the percentages. Each squadron, chances are, will be one species or perhaps two. Focus on the easiest, usually boldly patterned adult ♂. Once you have identified one, see if there is anything in the

flock that stands out as being out of place, and then quickly move on to the next group. Of course we will often have things we are specifically looking for. For example, we know that Barrow's and Common Goldeneyes sometimes form mixed flocks in winter. Also look for the massive differences in underwing patterns. Often when we are asked for specific patterns, we don't know them. However, when we are familiar with a specific type of waterfowl, we know it looks right,

Landing. A Peregrine comes by, and all the birds take to the sky. Everything disappears – it seems like an eternity. 5 minutes go by, and your decision to wait doesn't look like it will pay off. Suddenly, they appear, and all come crashing in, seemingly at once. Safety in numbers! As they drop out of the sky, it's clear the dabblers are dropping down steeply, wings accelerating as they get closer to water to slow themselves down. They hit the water feet-first and are quickly able to settle down. There are a couple of divers mixed in. They come in at a shallower angle and need a longer runway for their splash landing. The birds lean forward, their undercarriage helping them to stop, as do their feet. IDing birds in flight

is often less difficult than many think. The same basics apply: look first at size, shape, flock formations, followed by color patterns. Waterfowl usually stick to their own kind. It's always good to look for the loner. Look carefully through all the landing birds and identify the odd ones. If you want an extra challenge, try to age and sex as many of these birds as possible. Many are showing spread tails. Adult feathers are broader, less pointed, often darker with well-defined pale fringes, and show fewer signs of wear. They molt the central tail feathers first. Also check the speculum, wing covert pattern, and overall plumage aspect. Answers p. 488.

Dabblers Taking Off. You come round the corner. You haven't seen them, and they haven't seen you. And then 'there they are', but it's too late. For their part, these ducks are expending lots of energy! Indeed, take-off is one of the most energetically demanding aspects of flight. Water is exploding. You grope for your camera, binoculars, or shotgun knowing all too well that it's going to be too late. The ducks are dabblers; they were able to rise steeply after a few panicked flaps to get away. There are several reasons why they can do this and diving ducks can't. Divers are bulky and heavy relative to the surface area of their wings. This high wing load ratio reduces their lift so they need to run atop the water to help gain

enough lift before takeoff. With their small wings and large body weight the Ruddy Duck has the highest wing load ratio of our waterfowl, and, therefore, needs a long runway. The similar Masked Duck, has a low wing-load ratio, allowing it to fly in and out of ditches and other tight locations it inhabits. Dabblers also have a low wing load, and with their proportionally large wings, they are able to lift almost vertically from the water. Using a larger wing-structure, these puddle-ducks also usually employ fewer wing beats per second than divers (with teal the exception) ID all the ducks Answers p. 488.

Exotics. Thousands of miles of train track criss-cross the continent. Always higher than the surrounding land, they form embankments that wet pools and marshes often form against. These wetlands are often great for waterfowl. Locally bred domestic varieties are often found at local parks, sometimes in wilder places, and are a constant source of confusion. Domestic varieties of waterfowl, such as Mallards, are usually larger and bulkier than wild birds with a deep body, particularly by the vent. Pekin Duck, is a white form of Mallard originating in China. Many intermediates are a vast array of colors, usually darkest on the head and browner on the body. Domesticated Geese mostly originate from Swan Goose (an Asian

species) and Greylag Goose. Often called 'farmyard' geese, they tend to boss groups of birds and are noisy. White forms are quite common. Intermediates are a variety of colors, and hybrids between the two species are quite common. Shape and location are always good starting points when suspecting domesticated ducks and geese. There are several other species that can occur as escapes – some regulars are shown here. The duck standing on a rock just behind the Swan Geese is a ♂ Labrador Duck (♀ were fairly uniform brown). Their habits were quite similar to Harlequin Duck with a bill shaped like Stellar's Eider. They were found in the north-east and became extinct in the late 1800s.

Duck Look-alikes. There are a number of wetland species that swim and fly that are not classified as waterfowl. Most dive for food, too. They will share habitat — and often food requirements — with waterfowl. Quite obviously, however, none will have duck-like bills! Nor do they have webbed feet. Still, some of these waterbirds, such as loons, grebes, gallinules, and cormorants, can be mistaken for waterfowl, particularly at a distance. These are all swimming birds; some sit low in the water (e.g., cormorants and loons); others sit higher (e.g., gallinule), and many dive. Also like ducks, most of these waterbirds have two distinct plumages: a bright pattern for summer and a duller non-breeding plumage that is also similar to

juvenile plumage. Try to recognize these birds on your local patch. Perhaps you already know them! Look at each bird and work out which is in breeding plumage. Where there is only one plumage shown it means that the species has the same appearance throughout the year. Most of the species are fairly common over much of North America. Another species which shares habitat, but doesn't look much like waterfowl is the Osprey. Wherever there is food, such as fish, Ospreys are usually lurking around. Ospreys dive 'talons-first' and rotate the catch for improved aerodynamics. They will fly with their prey head first! If you're fishing, hunting, boating, or looking at waterfowl, there is always lots to enjoy!

Widespread and Common. It's a glorious day in the prairie pothole region, though it could be just about anywhere in NA. Snowy Egret, with it's yellow feet and dark bill, is much smaller than the yellow-billed and snake-necked Great Egret. Great-Blue Heron is even larger and mostly gray. Similar-sized Sandhill Cranes tend to be in the fields, rust-staining causing some to be brown rather than gray. Black-crowned Night-Heron are chunky and boldly black, white, and gray, except in juvenile plumage. Youngsters are always a similar size and shape to adults when 2 months old. Night-Herons are brown and white but a subtly different shape and less boldly patterned than the skulking American Bittern. ♂ Ring-necked Pheasants

water to drink and bath. Red-winged and Yellow-headed Blackbirds names are self-explanatory. Bill shapes in shorebirds can be helpful: Snipe are long and straight, Avocets upturned, Black necked Stilts straight with long pink legs, and Wilson's Phalaropes needle-like as they spin on the water. Orange-rumped Killdeer feign injury to protect their young. Tiny Marsh Wrens straddle reeds. Distant raptors include Red-tailed (rounded wing tips) and Swainson's Hawks (pointed wing tips). Kestrels hover and Turkey Vultures have dihedral wings. Coopers Hawk dash through looking for unsuspecting prey such as Yellow Warblers. Massive White Pelican swim as White-faced Ibis fly by. Herring is the largest gull, Ring-billed is smaller. Forster's Tern are smallish with narrow pointed wings. Mourning, White winged, and Eurasian Collared-Doves fly by.

Age, sex, and identification of ducks using in-hand upperwing patterns.

Most waterfowl can be aged and sexed with careful study of upperwing patterns in hand, the field, or from photos.

In summer/early fall, most ducks are in eclipse plumage. During this period, they retain their wing coverts. In many species of duck, each age and sex has a unique wing pattern, making many quite easy to age and sex when the upperwing is seen. The duck bill and iris patterns are other particularly good features for helping with aging and sexing at this time of year. It should also be remembered, that by summer, many of the feathers are nearly a year old, and they are typically heavily worn and abraded.

In fall/winter, learning to differentiate juvenile from adult-type feathers is often critical for aging. Juvenile feathers have a softer texture, are duller, and wear more quickly. Flight feathers and tertials are narrower and more pointed; wing coverts are smaller, with more rounded tips, than adult feathers. Tertials are shorter and narrower; even more so in females. These characteristics are the key tools for aging, not only waterfowl, but all birds. With practice, all of these features can be quite easy to see, not only in the hand, but also in the field. Please read the introduction (pp. 22-28) for a more complete discussion on aging and sexing waterfowl.

Waterfowl molt from the inner wing first, replacing the tertials and innerwing coverts before replacing feathers toward the outerwing. First-years usually retain some juvenile feathers through winter. The contrast with newer adult-type feathers is a *molt limit*. Understanding these basic principles of molt are always key to aging birds in the field, and in the hand. Always look for these characters, as well as the features shown in the upperwing patterns shown in the following pages. It is also important to remember that males average larger than females – some measurably so.

The wings shown here are examples, and it should be remembered that variation within many species is large. It would take many examples of each age and sex if we wanted to get a thorough representative sample of the variation within each species. Some of the birds have molted many of their feathers, and even though a few retained feathers can age them as first-years, in many respects, they are adult-like. In an ideal world, a series of images would show the molt progression in stages from juvenile plumage, through to bright-plumage, and would include eclipse-plumage. To do this topic justice would take another book. The following wing cut-outs are courtesy of the Slater Museum of Natural History (University of Puget Sound) and the University of Washington Burke Museum (UWBM). They are included to provide a very basic overview of in-hand wing patterns. It is also useful to cross-reference them with the many images of waterfowl in flight that are used in this book. The page number of the flight plates for each species are included for quick reference.

Wood Duck p. 100 (flight plate)   Mallard p. 104

311

Narrow even trailing edge to secondaries.

ad. m.

White greater covert bar rarely extends past speculum. Outer greater coverts lack white on outer edge; 1st-yr. ♂ typically show a white edge.

Broader white trailing edge to secondaries; mostly on outer web.

ad. f.

White greater covert bar extends onto tertial coverts.

Aged from ad. ♂ by retained juv feathers. Most retain some juv. coverts for a year until they molt into bright plumage.

imm. m.

Similar to ad. ♂, though some have white on tertial coverts and look similar to imm. ♀. Narrow juv. ♂ tertials replaced by mid-fall.

Narrowish trailing edge to secondaries; mostly on outer web.

imm. f.

Similar to ad. f., but white is less extensive. Imm. m. and ♀ have pale edges to inner webs of 4 distal primary coverts.

American Black Duck p. 110   Mottled Duck p. 114

Tertials longer, broader, and less frayed than juv. feathers. All juv. tertials can be replaced as early as September.

ad. m.

Tertials longer, broader, and less frayed than juv. feathers.

ad. f.

Coverts narrow, rounded, and worn in juv. Middle greater coverts have broadest black tip in ad. m.; intermediate in ad. ♀ and 1st-yr. ♂, narrowest in 1st-yr. ♀.

imm. m.

Coverts narrow, rounded, and worn in juv. Middle greater coverts have broadest black tip in ad ♂, intermediate in ad. ♀ and 1st-yr. ♂, narrowest in 1st-yr. ♀. Pale at base of black on the greater coverts is more extensive in Mottled Duck than in American Black Duck.

imm. f.

Gadwall p. 122

Extensive chestnut and black on wing coverts.

Variable amounts of black and chestnut on wing coverts; less than ad. m. and often similar to 1st-yr. ♂.

Similar to ad. ♀; look for noticably slimmer and rounder-tipped juv. feathers.

Very little (sometimes none) black and chestnut on the wing coverts.

American Wigeon p. 126

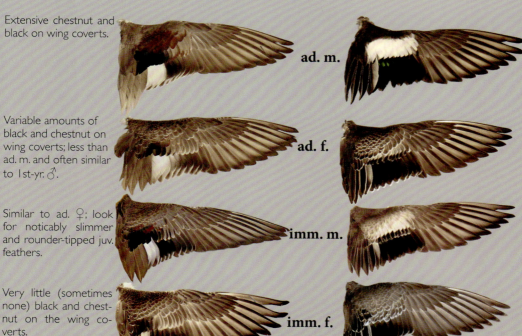

ad. m.

ad. f.

imm. m.

imm. f.

Extensive white wing coverts contrast strongly with black-tipped greater coverts and secondaries.

Wing coverts checkered; pale edged, gray subterminal tip, and paler toward base. Some are less checkered like 1st-yr. ♂.

Wing coverts typically somewhat uniform with pale gray panel at base to greater coverts.

Wing coverts somewhat uniform with pale tips.
Note: the auxillaries and underwing coverts are white; duller gray in Eurasian Wigeon.

Eurasian Wigeon p. 128

Extensive white wing coverts contrast strongly with black-tipped greater coverts and secondaries.

Wing coverts checkered; pale edged, gray subterminal tip, and paler toward base. Some less checkered like 1st-yr. ♂.

Wing coverts typically somewhat uniform with pale gray panel at base to the greater coverts.

Wing coverts somewhat uniform with pale tips.
Note: upperwing pattern similar to American Wigeon; they average slightly less white.

Northern Pintail p. 132

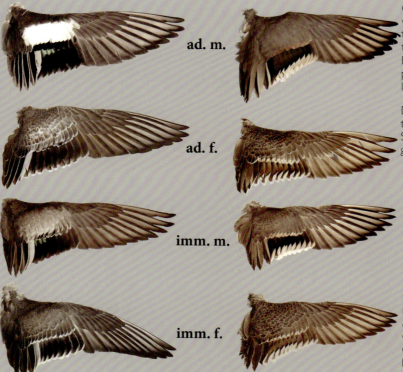

ad. m.

ad. f.

imm. m.

imm. f.

Gray wing coverts with very narrow or no pale tips. Broad chestnut tips to greater coverts. Bright bronzy or purplish sheen to speculum.

Distinct white or buff tips to wing coverts. Speculum has some gloss.

Similar to ad. ♂ but often with broader pale tips to coverts. Greater covert tips usually buff, not chestnut. Duller speculum.

Similar to ad. ♀ but have indistinct white or buff wing tips to wing coverts (buff in Greater's). Speculum lacks gloss.

Northern Shoveler p 138   Cinnamon Teal p. 146

Aging and sexing similar to other 'blue-winged' teal; note the longer wing bar by age and sex. Bright blue coverts. Bold white greater covert bar. Bold green sheen to speculum.

Tertial coverts tipped white. Blue wing coverts more glossy than 1st-yr. ♀. Some gloss on speculum.

Tertial coverts usually all dark. Blue wing coverts lack gloss of ad. m. Outer greater sec. covs. same or more white than ad. ♀. Some gloss on speculum.

Tertial coverts tipped white or buff. Median and lesser coverts dull blue-gray, usually pale-fringed. Long distinct greater covert bar. Dull speculum.

Upperwing pattern similar to Blue-winged Teal by age and sex. Bright blue coverts. Bold white greater covert bar. Bold green sheen to speculum.

Tertial coverts tipped white. Greater coverts edged white. Median and lesser coverts less dingy than 1st-yr. ♀. Some gloss on speculum.

Tertial coverts usually all dark. Blue wing coverts lack gloss of ad. m. Outer greater sec. covs. same or whiter than ad. ♀. Some gloss on speculum.

Tertial coverts tipped white. Median and lesser coverts dull blue. Outer greater secondary coverts have little white. Dull speculum.

Blue-winged Teal p. 142   Green-winged Teal p. 150

Bright blue coverts. Bold white greater covert bar. Bold green sheen to speculum.

Tertial coverts tipped white. Median and lesser coverts less dingy than 1st-yr. ♀. Some gloss on speculum.

Tertial coverts usually all dark. Blue wing coverts lack gloss of ad. m. Outer greater sec. covs. same or whiter than ad. ♀. Some gloss on speculum.

Tertial coverts tipped white. Median and lesser coverts dull blue. Outer greater secondary coverts have little white. Dull speculum.

Scapulars vermiculated and/or barred. Outer edge to outer tertial black with well-defined edge.

Outer edge to outer tertial black or brown with diffuse edge. Ad. have broader and more extensive pale tips to outer greater coverts than imm.

Scapulars barred. Some ad. ♀ and all imm. have narrow pale edges to coverts and tertials.

Birds with fewer than 4 secondaries with completely green iridescent outer webs are ♀; those with five or more are ♂. Intermediate birds are best left unsexed.

'Eurasian' Common Teal p. 151   Canvasback p. 162

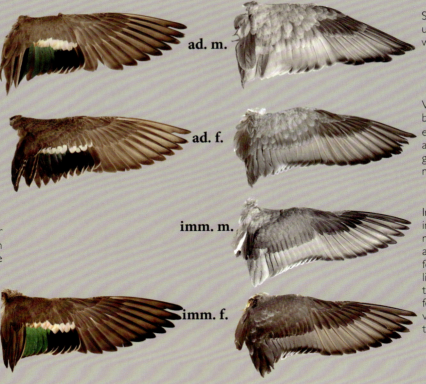

Age and sex as Green-winged Teal. Separated from Green-wing by dusky shaft streaks to tertials; little or none in Green-wings. Pale tips to greater coverts are also noticeably broader by age and sex. Outer greater coverts whiter, particularly in ♀. These features can be seen under careful field observation.

Imm. ♂ most similar to ad. ♀, typically with more bronze in the greater covert bar.

Striking fine vermiculations make the wing look gray.

Vermiculations broader and browner than ad. ♂. Older adult birds are often grayer and more male-like.

Initially brown, many imm. quickly molt many feathers that are adult-like. Look for contrast (molt limit) between retained, brown juv. feathers and grayer, vermiculated adult-type feathers.

Redhead p. 166   Ring-necked Duck p. 172

Black-and-white vermiculations make the wing look gray. In *Aythya* ducks, white in the vermiculations on the greater coverts are most extensive on ad. m. and least extensive on imm ♀.

Vermiculations are browner on ad. f. than ad. ♂. Older adult birds are often grayer and more male-like.

Initially brown, many imm. quickly grow new feathers that are adult-like. Always look for contrast (molt limit) between the retained, brown juv. feathers and very different, adult-type feathers; they are vermiculated, grayer, and, of course, differently shaped.

Ad. ♂ has the blackest wings with iridescent tertials.

Ad. ♀: Brown-black wings; tertials lacking or with little iridescence.

Imm: Brown-black wings. Look for a molt limit between brown and narrow juv. feathers and blackish adult-types. Tertials have little or no iridescence.

315

Lesser Scaup p. 176

Broad black-and-white vermiculations on coverts; imm. ♀ brownest wings with no vermiculations; ad. ♀ and imm ♂. intermediate (♂ averaging darker and with more white flecks.)

Imm: Look for molt limits between narrow, brown juv. feathers and broader, darker adult-type feathers with more fine vermiculations.

Greater Scaup p. 180

Aging and sexing the same as Lesser Scaup.

ID from Lesser Scaup by white extending from the secondaries onto the bases of the inner primaries. Lesser Scaup does occasionally show this pattern.

Steller's Eider p. 190

Ad. ♂: Boldly marked.
2yr. old ♂: Similar to ad. ♂ with more diffusely marked tertials that are narrower and with less white. Some have brown on the greater coverts.
Ad. ♀: Compared to imm. ♀, has narrower, rufous-fringed coverts, broader white wingbars, and some iridescence on the speculum.
Imm. ♂: Similar pattern to ad. ♂ with brown on some coverts and tertials; less iridescent speculum.
Imm. ♀: Compared to ad. ♀, more boldly rufous-fringed coverts, narrower white wingbars, and dull speculum.

Spectacled eider p. 194

Ad. ♂: Boldly marked.
2yr. old ♂: Similar to ad. ♂. with tertials brown and white; all-white in ad. Some 2nd-yrs. have brown on the greater coverts.
Ad. ♀: Rufous-fringed coverts with dark subterminal bars.

Imm. ♂: Similar pattern to ad. ♂ with brown on some coverts and tertials.

Imm. ♀: Narrow white-fringes to brown coverts. Look for molt limits later in the year.

King Eider p. 198

Ad. ♂: Coverts mostly white; an odd median, and many lesser coverts darker. Median coverts more extensive brown in 2-yr-old birds.

Ad. ♀: Rufous-fringed coverts. White wing bars to secondaries and greater coverts.

Imm. ♂: Dark-brown coverts, narrow pale tips (wingbars) to greater coverts and secondaries.

Imm. ♀: Compared to ad. ♀, more uniformly brown coverts. Also, much narrower wingbars, broadest in the middle secondaries and corresponding coverts; still often hard to see.

Common eider p. 208

Ad. ♂: Boldly marked. 2 yr. old ♂: tertials mostly brown; white in adults (beware of birds in eclipse). Some birds may have brown on the greater coverts.

Ad. ♀: Pale-fringed coverts with dark subterminal bars. White wing bars to secondaries and greater coverts.

Imm. ♂: Similar pattern to ad. ♂ with brown on some coverts and tertials; less iridescent speculum.

Imm. ♀: Compared to ad. ♀, more uniformly brown coverts. Also, much narrower wingbars, broadest in the middle secondaries and corresponding coverts. Still often hard to see.

Harlequin Duck p. 216

Ad. ♂: the only plumage with white in the wing. Some imm. ♂. Harlies grow tertials with white later in the winter.

Ad. f.: All-brown like imm.

Imm. ♂: Dull medial stripe to longest tertial (ghost pattern of ad. m.) – not present in f.

Imm. ♀: As with all waterfowl, the best way to age Harlies is to be able to identify juv. feathers. They are short, narrow, with a soft texture that is prone to wear. Also, usually paler, browner, and more pointed than adult-type feathers.

Surf Scoter p. 224

Ad. ♂: All black wings.

Ad. f.: Dark brown wings.

Imm: Dark brown wings. As adult-type feathers are molted in through winter, molt limits become quite obvious. Juv. feathers fade and wear quickly, contrasting with new adult-type feathers; brown in f. and black in ♂.

White-winged Scoter p. 228   Black Scoter p. 220

Ad. ♂: Blackish wings with white secondaries. Greater coverts have black bases and white tips, create a saw-tooth pattern.

Ad. ♀: Dark-brown wings. White tips to greater coverts are rounded at the base; not serrated.

Imm. ♂: Smaller spots to tips of the greater coverts than ad. Usually grow some black feathers later in the year. Molt limits are often striking.

Imm. ♀: Smallest white spots to tips of the greater coverts.

Ad. ♂: Strikingly-thin outermost primary. Black coverts, black-brown flight feathers.

Ad. ♀: Dark brown; imms usually slightly paler.

Imm.: Brown, fading paler through winter. Molt limits often striking, particularly in m.

Long-tailed Duck p. 238   Bufflehead p. 242

Imm. ♂: Black-brown. Innermost tertials black. Outer tertials and speculum rufous tinge.

Ad. ♀: Dark-brown, with broad fringes to coverts, usually rich brown, but highly variable. Rufous tinge to tertials and secondaries.

Imm: Similar to ad. ♀. Highly variable, particularly in spring/summer when covert fringes become broader, brighter, and presumably more cryptic.

Ad. ♂: White creates a solid stripe across the wing.

Ad. ♀: Like imm and only sepsrable by feather shape and texture.

Imm.: Like ad. f. through winter. Imm. f. often lacks white spots on the greater coverts. Imm. ♂ rarely shows any adult m-type feathers until summer.

Common Goldeneye p. 248   Barrow's Goldeneye p. 252

Ad. ♂: All-white wing patch bordered by black coverts.

Ad. ♀: 2 distinct wingbars formed by dark-brown tips to coverts. White lesser coverts usually more extensive than imm.

Imm. ♂: Usually 2 wingbars formed by medium-brown tips to coverts.

Imm. ♀: Similar to imm. ♂ but typically with browner lesser coverts.

Ad. ♂: White wing patch divided by black bases to greater coverts, unlike Common Goldeneye. Other coverts black.

Ad. ♀: wings dark brown, not black. Limited white on lesser coverts.

Imm. ♂: Like other Barrow's, less extensive white than Common Goldeneye.

Imm. ♀: The least amount of white on the upperwing.

Hooded Merganser p. 258   Red-breasted Merganser p. 262

Ad. ♂: Pale-gray median and lesser coverts. All tertials black-and-white striped. Extensive white on the greater coverts.

Ad. ♀: 3 tertials black-and-white striped. Typically more white in the greater coverts than imm.

Imm.: Similar to ad. ♀ but tertials more brown than black, and white greater covert spots average smaller particularly in ♀.

Ad. ♂: Extensive white on the median and lesser coverts, divided by 2 dark wingbars. The leading edge to the wing is always black.

Ad. ♀: Similar to imm; averages slightly darker greater coverts. Note how the greater covert bar extends farther across the wing than Common Merganser.

Imm: Similar to ad. ♀ but average narrower dark greater covert bar — sometimes almost absent.

Common Merganser p. 270   Ruddy Duck p. 276

Ad. ♂: Extensive white on the lesser coverts to the leading edge of the wing. Dark bases to greater coverts form a wing bar.

Ad. ♀: Very similar to imm. with wing bar created by dark bases to greater coverts. These feathers are also dark-tipped, creating another wingbar that is usually broader than in imm. birds, particularly ♂.

ad. m.

ad. f.

imm. m.

imm. f.

Ad. ♂: Look for signs of bright chestnut breeding plumage to sex as ♂.

Aging and sexing Ruddies on wing criteria can be very difficult.

319

SPECIES ACCOUNTS

Reading the Accounts:

The species accounts that follow are almost self-explanatory. Almost, but not quite... Some explanation is necessary. These species accounts are supplemental to the photo-based pates in the front of this book, add more details, and fill in pieces of information that need to be further explained — or simply can't be shown visually. They will often take the reader far beyond ID, into an area of appreciation and even conservation. The species accounts include the following headings:

The species common name, four-letter code, scientific name, and common or regional names, including those used in Quebec, Mexico, and Arctic native communities. Those arctic native regions are indicated as follows:
YK – Yukon-Kuskokwim Delta of Alaska.
NS – Norton Sound of Alaska.
NWS – Northwest Arctic and North Slope from the Kotzebue region, eastward across the Arctic National Wildlife Refuge.
N – Nunavut, Canada, comprising a major portion of Northern Canada, and most of the Canadian Arctic Archipelago.

Measurements, for lengths, wing, and weight (each for male and female)

First impressions or First impressions and similar species (for Eurasian and other rarities)

ID: in depth and similar species

A year in the life of the species
Geographic variation
Sounds (mainly vocalizations)
Diet and feeding behavior
Nesting, including site, nest description, clutch size, egg description, incubation, and brood parasitism
Hunting
Population and Conservation

These headings are often truncated for real rarities, especially because they do not nest in North America and are – by definition – less likely to be found here!

The North American map color codes are as follows:
pink — summer/breeding range
blue — wintering range
purple — permanent range

Many species have two maps: one for breeding, the other for wintering. In these cases, the paler tones (pale pink or pale blue) indicate areas of lesser breeding concentration or lesser wintering concentration. Also, waterfowl do not always have firm range-boundaries, depending as they do on food availability and weather. Therefore, the value of these maps can be limited. Finally, there are some map sets for distinctive or important subspecies.

TUNDRA SWAN (WHISTLING SWAN) — Plates Page 34
Cygnus columbianus TUSW

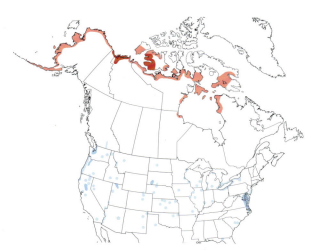

OTHER COMMON OR REGIONAL NAMES
Whistling swan, whistler, tundra, wild swan
(Arctic: qugyuk [YK, N], qugruk [NS, NWS], qubruk [NWS], qugjuq [N])
(Québec: cygne siffleur)
(Mexico: cisne de tundra)

MEASUREMENTS
Length: Male – 48-57 in, av 52.0 in (132.1 cm); Female – 47-58 in, av 51.5 in (130.8 cm)
Wing: Male – average 21.2 in (53.8 cm); Female – av 20.9 in (53.1 cm)
Weight: Male – av 16.0 lbs (7257 g); Female – av 13.9 lbs (6305 g)
Bill: Male – av 103.7 mm; Female – av 101.1 mm

FIRST IMPRESSIONS
An elegant species of Arctic wetlands in the summer, Tundra Swans winter on estuaries and agricultural fields along parts of both coasts and interior U.S. They travel in pairs, family groups, and sometimes in flocks of hundreds and announce their presence with rolling bugles. Adults are pure white, sometimes with some rusty stains on the face. The bill is black, often with a small yellow patch at the

base just below the eye. First-years transition from gray to mostly white. Size and shape: Tundras have a long, slender neck and large body. The head is rounded and tapers into a wedge-shaped bill. When swimming, the neck is often held straight or with a gentle curve. They are smaller than Mute and Trumpeter Swans. Flight: Notice Tundra Swans sleek white body and long neck. Tundras lack the potbellied look of Mute Swans and the heft of Trumpeters. However, it is difficult to separate Tundras from Trumpeters in flight without direct comparison or unless they are calling. Tundras need a considerable runway to take off, creating a stir as their wings and feet slap the water; however, they are graceful on liftoff. When moving around their wintering areas, Tundra Swans often fly fairly low, in pairs or family groups, falling into an oblique line, V-formation or U-shape. During migration, they may be in larger flocks, sometimes numbering in the hundreds. They sometimes mix with Trumpeter Swans, particularly on wintering grounds in the Pacific Northwest. Wingbeats are slow and powerful, yet a bit faster-paced than Trumpeter or Mute.

ID: IN DEPTH AND SIMILAR SPECIES

Tundra Swans are easy to age as first-years, but they are not reliably sexed in the field. Males (cobs) are slightly larger than females (pens) and are more aggressive when defending their family and feeding areas. Cygnets are light gray, quickly fading paler, usually with pinkish bills. Juvenile plumage is gray overall, slightly darker on the head and fully-grown at about 9-10 weeks.

First-years replace their light gray juvenile plumage throughout the winter, starting with the sides and back, followed by the head and neck. The result is a transition from a pale gray to mostly white plumage. Early in the fall they are mostly pale gray; by mid-December they have a considerable amount of white feathers on their body. Most individuals have replaced more than 80% of their body feathers by late December. Only a few wing coverts are replaced, therefore washed out pale gray wing coverts remain until they are about a year old. Their bill pattern and color shifts from pink to black as winter progresses. Some two-year-olds can be distinguished by gray flecking on head and neck.

Adults are white overall with small yellow patch on their otherwise black bill. The amount of yellow varies from a small dash right below the eye to covering about a tenth of the bill. A few birds show no yellow at all and occasionally it is quite extensive. Birds in the west average more yellow than eastern birds.

On Bewick's Swan, the Eurasian subspecies of Tundra Swan, the yellow is more extensive, covering up to nearly a quarter of the bill and 42% of its length. The bill is slightly shorter and thinner, and the culmen often noticeably more concave. All Bewick's Swans at Slimbridge Wildfowl Trust, England, are identified individually by their unique bill pattern. Bewicks are slightly smaller than American birds and tend to be more petite. There seems to be very little, if any, overlap in the amount of yellow on the bill between the two subspecies, though more research iis needed.

Adult Tundras start their wing molt in late July and are flightless for 33-34 days. Pairs stagger their wing molt with males starting first. This allows for at least one adult to be functional, facilitating in territorial and brood defense. Non-breeding or failed-breeders start their wing molt earlier than breeders. After wing molt, body molt continues for several months. Iris is dark brown. Legs black, or can be pale yellow or orange on leucistic individuals as in other swans. Rust or iron staining tends to be quite common, particularly in summer on their northerly breeding grounds.

Similar species: Mute and Trumpeter Swans are fairly widespread species that are candidates for confusion. Mute Swans have a heftier shape build. Since bill structure is a key ID character in swan identification, look for Mute's striking orange bill and accompanying black knob on the head. Be aware of a thicker neck, pot-bellied body, and longer pointed tail. Mute Swans almost always hold their pointy tail out of the water, while Tundras more often slopes into the water.

Separation from Trumpeter is far more troublesome because its general body and head shape is very similar. Remember, if you see that yellow spot by the bill, it's a Tundra. Trumpeter has a larger bill (it's huge) and will have a more peaked or triangular head shape. Their head slopes evenly into a straight-looking bill, whereas Tundra isn't as smooth a transition. Tundra has a rounder head and just a bit of a concave slope to the bill. Trumpeter Swans often have a different posture, holding the neck with a kink backwards over the back. Trumpeters also have a larger, round-backed body. Tundras have a bit shorter neck, which is often held straight or with a smooth curve. Although difficult to discern, Trumpeters tend to rest lower in the water and appear to move more deliberately. On land, Tundras appear shorter-legged with proportionally larger feet.

On adult Tundra Swans you can clearly see their eye, whereas on Trumpeters the eye is more connected with the black facial skin and bill, and it essentially blends together, with the black almost swallowing the eye. Also, when looking at an adult head-on, look to see if there is a V-shape on the forehead where the bill meets the white feathers or a broad U-shape. Trumpeters show a V-shape and Tundra U-shaped but is not always obvious because some Trumpeters look U-shaped.

Juvenile Tundra and Trumpeter Swans can appear very similar, but the overall body coloration is a light silvery-gray in Tundras and a darker gray or gray-brown, in Trumpeters, especially about the head and neck.

First-years are even more difficult to identify. There is a tendency for first-year Tundra Swans to molt into a whiter plumage earlier in the winter than Trumpeters. Many Tundra Swans have largely white bodies and grayer head/neck by January, whereas Trumpeter Swans lag behind and will be largely gray well into February and beyond. This molt-timing difference is best used in association with other characteristics.

Voice is also helpful. Tundras sound scared, and Trumpeters announce their presence with confidence. (See Sounds below.)

Hybrid Tundra x Trumpeter Swans are extremely rare. Captivity may be the primary source of the hybrids, which are intermediate in bill size and shape and other structural characteristics. A tiny amount of yellow in front of the eye may be present.

Sex ratio: Limited information is available, but males probably outnumber females, if only slightly.

YEAR IN THE LIFE

Tundra Swan is an Arctic breeder that winters across the U.S. and Eurasia. Some Tundras move through each flyway, but they are in greatest numbers in the Pacific and Atlantic Flyways. To see the largest concentrations head to Mattamuskeet NWR in North Carolina, Bear River NWR in Utah, Upper Mississippi NWR in Wisconsin, Lower Klamath NWR in California, Long Point in Ontario or Middle Creek WMA in Lancaster County, Pennsylvania.

In winter, Tundras head to areas with shallow water, including ponds, lakes, rivers, and estuaries to feed. They also forage in agricultural fields

Tundra Swans are long-lived species that normally mate for life, but there are rare cases of divorce. If one member of the pair dies, the other will find a new mate. Courtship rituals begin to be observed in late winter when young, unpaired swans begin to form pair bonds. Pair bond displays, used year round, include a forward call with extended head and neck, quivering wings, head-bobbing, and ritualized bathing. This forward thrusting of head and neck is in contrast with the Trumpeter Swan's up-and-down vertical display. Once the two- and three-year-old swans pick a mate, it will be another 1-2 years before they actually breed for the first time.

Spring migration gets off to an early start with pairs taking off from their wintering grounds in mid-March. Pairs push north as the snow melts and ice thaws in the wetlands where they breed. Their arrival on the breeding grounds varies by location, spanning from late March to mid-May. Pairs breeding in the Yukon-Kuskokwim deltas begin arriving in late April and most are present by mid-May. They prefer tundra lakes, pools and ponds in coastal deltas. Tundra Swans are uncommonly found breeding farther inland or south to the tree line.

Each year pairs return to the same breeding territory and defend their site even in years when they are not breeding. In some cases, they may not breed if their nest fails or if they are a young couple. Tundra Swans lay only one clutch a season and do not lay replacement clutches like many ducks will do when eggs are lost to predators. Females perform about 70% of the incubation duties and males fill in the remainder of the time. Shortly after the cygnets hatch, the adults begin molting, pairs stagger the timing to minimize the number of days when they are both flightless. Young fledge in 40-45 days.

Fall migration for Alaskan breeders begins with staging on ice-free brackish waters on the coast, leaving the breeding grounds in late September. Family groups stick together during fall migration and throughout the winter. Tundras begin arriving on their wintering grounds in mid-October with numbers building through November and early December.

GEOGRAPHIC VARIATION

Tundra Swan has two subspecies that were formerly considered distinct species and may be split again someday. Whistling (Tundra) Swan, *C. c. columbianus* is widespread in the U.S. and Canada. Bewick's (Tundra) Swan, *C. c. bewickii* breeds in Eurasia from the Kola Peninsula to arctic northern Siberia and winters in western Europe and southern Asia. The subspecies are known to interbreed in eastern Siberia, however, the extent of overlap is not well-known.

Bewick's Swan has more extensive yellow on the bill and is slightly smaller overall. Slimbride W. T. showed that the amount and shape of the yellow varies enough that with very careful study, you can actually recognize individuals by their bill patterns. The yellow patch is even classified into three different patterns—black neb, yellow neb, and pennyface. When viewing them head-on, yellow nebs have yellow across the front of the bill, black nebs have a dark patch, and pennyface have a circle right in the center. First-year Bewick's have an extensive pale area on the bill that changes from a pinkish pale color to yellow during the winter.

Bewick's Swan is very rare in the winter in Washington, Oregon, Montana, and northern central California where large concentrations of Whistling Swans are found. There are also a handful of records from Utah, Idaho, Yukon, Saskatchewan, and British Columbia. There are over 165 records of Bewick's Swan in western North America, excluding Alaska records. Bewick's is also rare in the Pribilof Islands of Alaska in the spring and is likely to turn up elsewhere in Alaska. In general, records in North America have increased since 1980, reflecting a population increase and range expansion of Bewick's Swan in Eurasia. There are also a handful of reports of apparent intergrades.

SOUNDS

Tundra Swan is a highly vocal swan that frequently calls in flight. Wintering flocks have a constant chorus, as family groups vocalize on feeding territories and new pair bonds form. Vocalizations of both sexes are similar. They give a loud, rising *oU* or *oH* or mellow *klooh* that is higher-pitched and not as rough as that of Trumpeter Swan. This call is most frequently given in flight or before take off. Sometimes they give a three-syllable *ou-OU-oo*. (First-year birds are more highly pitched.) Tundra Swans also deliver a number of soft conversational calls, clucks and rolling, bugling *oo-oo-oo* in flocks during spring migration. They give a loud, piercing *whiiiinnk hiiink hiink* in succession with their neck stretched in an aggressive posture. A hiss is given as a threat, often when defending a brood. Parents give a *kuk kuk* contact call to their cygnets.

Trumpeter Swans really sound like a bugle giving a couple of distinct notes, whereas Tundra Swans are more like wailing notes slurred together. From a distance, a flock of calling Tundra Swans can sound like a pack of baying hounds or distant "whoops and hollers." And when non-calling Tundra Swans pass close overhead, the whistle of their wingbeats can be heard.

DIET AND FEEDING BEHAVIOR

Tundra Swans feed as family groups or in a flock by dabbling, submerging head and neck, up-ending, and grazing. They are vegetarians, consuming seeds, leaves, shoots, roots, and tubers by plunging their head into water and up-ending to reach submerged vegetation. During migration and in winter, they are often found in large flocks feeding in open water and grazing in fields among agricultural crops, waste grains, and winter cereal grain crops. Corn and rice fields are particularly attractive at this time.

Traditionally, the Tundra Swan diet consisted primarily of submerged aquatic vegetation and benthic organisms, but declines in such vegetation at some migratory stopover sites and at wintering areas fostered a shift where this species would feed extensively in grain fields, sometimes leading to conflicts with farmers alleging crop damage

NESTING

Site: Arctic tundra near water (e.g.,, lakes, ponds, and pools), primarily in coastal delta areas, less frequent inland to the tree line, and sometimes while the snow is still present. Nest usually built on an islet or at the water's edge, or as a floating mass in the water, but land sites may be used before melting snow has surrounded them with water. Pairs nest singly.

Nest description: On the ground, a conspicuous mound of moss, grass, dead leaves, and other plant material, all acquired within about 9 feet of the nest. Very little down. Old nest mounds, used in previous years, are frequently used. The nest, usually about 12-18 inches high, may be as high as 24 inches. Other dimensions can be quite variable, from 10-20 inches to 48-72 inches in outside diameter at the base and 8-15 inches or 36-64 inches at the top. The depth may be 4-8 inches.

Clutch size: Usually 3-4, sometimes 5-7.

Egg description: Subelliptical. Smooth and slightly glossy with some fine granular texture. Creamy white. 107 X 68 mm.

Incubation duration: 29-32 days, ostensibly by both birds, although the male has no incubation patch.

Brood parasitism: Not known.

HUNTING

Tundra Swans were particularly popular game birds during the market hunting days in the Chesapeake Bay region. The MBTA of 1918 closed the hunting season on Tundra Swans, but in 1962, Utah became the first state where western birds could be legally harvested. In the 1980s, other states (e.g.,, Montana, North and South Dakota, and North Carolina) opened highly limited seasons and bag limits. Today they are hunted by permit in a few other states, including Alaska, Nevada, and Virginia. Permit holders are allowed to harvest one swan per season. Harvests of both populations are small. In the eastern population, almost 70% of the birds are shot in North Carolina, which remains a center of hunting activity. In the West, 67% of the hunting occurs in Utah.

Substance harvest is larger, with the western population estimated at 6,000-10,000 swans harvested by native people and the eastern population probably under 1,000 harvested.

POPULATION AND CONSERVATION

Tundra Swans populations are monitored during the annual Midwinter Survey, which divides them into eastern and western populations. The latter breeds solely in Alaska. Both populations increased in the twentieth century. The average population for 2002-2011 was 99,680 for the eastern population and 87,370 for the western population. These numbers are well above the NAWMP management goals of 80,000 for the eastern population and 60,000 for the western population. Count numbers fluctuate significantly annually, which can be attributed in part to the fact that in some years the swans are not present in the survey area (they are wintering farther south or north) and the numbers may not be not entirely due to dramatic annual population changes.

The population wintering in the Chesapeake Bay has decreased since the late 1960s when there was a significant decline in submerged aquatic vegetation. These birds apparently shifted to North Carolina where the number wintering has gone up and more are feeding in agricultural fields. Canvasback and Brant followed a similar movement away from the Chesapeake as a main wintering site.

Hunting has an impact on adult survival. Regulated hunting accounts for the annual mortality of about 4,000 Tundra Swans. That number doubles for unregulated hunting, including the subsistence harvest in Arctic and unsanctioned take by hunters elsewhere. Continued lead poisoning, from spent shot and fishing sinkers, is a problem. Mortality rates from lead poisoning were higher for Tundra Swans than for many other waterfowl. An estimated 7,200 swans succumbed over a five-year period in the late 1980s and 1990s on wintering areas in North Carolina alone.

Oil and gas drilling on Arctic breeding grounds and loss of critical migratory stopover sites are also threats to the Tundra Swan population.

TRUMPETER SWAN
Cygnus buccinator TRUS

Plates Page 36

OTHER COMMON OR REGIONAL NAMES
Trumpeter, wild swan

MEASUREMENTS
Length: Male – 56-62 in, av 59.0 in (149.9 cm); Female – 55-58 in, av 57.0 in (144.8 cm)
Wing: Male – av 24.3 in (61.7 cm); Female – av 24.5 in (62.2 cm)
Weight: Male – av 27.9 lbs (12655 g); Female – av 22.6 lbs (10251 g)
Bill: Male – av 112.5 mm; Female – av 107.0 mm

FIRST IMPRESSIONS
Thanks to successful recovery and reintroduction programs, family groups of Trumpeter Swans grace North America's landscape once again after their close call to the edge of extinction in the 1930s. Families feed in freshwater wetlands and graze among other waterfowl in agricultural lands in winter. Pure white adults with their black bills will sometimes have rusty stains on their faces, particularly in summer, but they will not have yellow patches of at the base of their bills like most Tundra Swans. First-years transition from an all-gray to gray-and-white plumage through the winter. During that time, first-years bills also darken from mostly pinkish to mostly black. Size and shape: The Trumpeter Swan is a huge bird, the largest of North American waterfowl. It has a honking-big bill and long neck on a hefty body, with thick legs and big feet. Pay special attention to the bird's large bill, which is particularly important for separating Trumpeter from Tundra Swans. Flight: A Trumpeter's heft and long-necked appearance is particularly apparent in flight. As opposed to the all-white adults, first-years have a gray head/neck and variable amounts of white and gray on the body. Trumpeters need a long runway to take off and make an incredible racket as their feet and wings pound the surface of the water before liftoff. In flight they are especially difficult to separate from the more slender and smaller Tundra Swans without direct comparison. Their wingbeats are steady and powerful.

ID: IN DEPTH AND SIMILAR SPECIES
Trumpeter Swans look like adults when they are just over a year old; however, they typically do not breed until they are 4-7 years old, rarely when they are two or three. On average males (cobs) are slightly larger than females (pens), which is sometimes noticeable in the field within pairs. Adults are heavier than first-years. Cygnets are pale gray with pinkish bills. Juvenile plumage is a plain mouse-gray and grows in when the cygnets are 6-10 weeks old. About one in ten juveniles of the Rocky Mountain population will be white or leucistic. The cygnet bill is pink with a dark tip and dark at the base. Sometimes they have olive on the legs and feet. First-years slowly replace their dusky-gray juvenile body feathers throughout their first winter, starting sometime between August and October. Some individuals have a few white feathers on the back in December. In February, they are oftentimes still primarily dusky-gray on the head and neck with white bellies and mottled white backs. By spring, their retained gray juvenile wing coverts, tertials, and tail feathers have faded significantly. Their bills transition from mostly pink to black by the time they are a year old. Second-years are distinguishable if scattered gray feathers or gray shaft streaks are present on the scapulars or other feathers. Two-year olds and other nonbreeders replace wing feathers on the molting grounds, as early as May. They complete their molt on the wintering grounds wrapping up from November-January. Adults are entirely white with black bills. Their bills have a line at the corner of the bill, visible at close range. Rarely, they have a dash of pallid yellow at the base of the bill. Curiously, their legs and feet can be almost any likely color, from black, to gray, to gray-pink, for example. As their youngsters are growing, adults begin a wing molt and they become flightless for about 30 days when they replace all of their primaries and secondaries. Females molt earlier than the males in most regions. Thus, both parents are not flightless at the same time. They continue to molt body feathers into February.

Similar species: Tundra Swans can be easily confused with Trumpeter Swans. Separation from Tundra is difficult because their general body and head shape is similar. Trumpeter, however, will have a larger, round-backed body. The best approach is to focus on call, size, the head-shape, bill, and face pattern. To see specifics, see the treatment for Tundra Swan on p. 320. Hints can also be found in the section on Sounds below.

The structurally similar Whooper Swan is a very rare visitor to North America. The major difference between the two species is that half of the bill of Whooper Swan is yellow. A bright yellow patch covers the base of the bill, ending at a point below the nostril. Even on first-years this is apparent as a large pale area contrasting with a darker bill tip. Beware of Trumpeter Swans with mud caked onto the base of their bills, giving the impression of a Whooper Swan.

There are a few records of hybrid Tundra × Trumpeter Swans though they are possibly under-recorded because of the difficulty in identifying them in the field. Captivity may be the primary source of the hybrids, which are intermediate in bill size and shape and other structural characteristics. A tiny amount of yellow in front of the eye may be present.

Sex ratio: Limited data exists, but males generally outnumber females.

YEAR IN THE LIFE

Trumpeter Swans are increasing in their localized ranges in North America, thanks to substantial conservation efforts in the 1900s. Restoration programs and increasing populations have caused a huge expansion in their wintering range. These birds can turn up almost anywhere in the Lower 48. Trumpeter Swans rarely wander beyond North America, however. There is one documented record from Japan (winter 1991-1992), a report from Russia (June 1991), and four reportedly shot in England in 1886. They are most common on the Pacific Flyway, where the bulk of their population winters at relatively few sites. Winter high counts of over 500 are mainly from Skagit, Samish, and Butler Flats in western Washington, near Monticello in Minnesota, and Fraser Valley in British Columbia. The highest counts, exceeding 2,000 at times, are from Marsh Lake and Tagish in the southern Yukon in April.

Trumpeter Swans prefer to winter on muddy fields where they graze on waste grain. They also use areas with small bodies of freshwater, where they feed by up-ending and reaching for submerged aquatic vegetation. They are often in small flocks, but gather by the hundreds in the core of their wintering range in the Pacific Northwest. There they mix with Tundra Swans, large flocks of pintail, wigeon, and Mallards.

Trumpeters are long-lived and go through an involved process to establish their pair bonds. Most pairs initiate their bond in late March to mid-May. These may begin when the birds are two years old, but firm pair bonds are not established until their third or fourth winter. In display, the pair swims together, dipping bills in water, and may blow bubbles as bill is withdrawn. They may also face each other bobbing their heads and shake their wings while calling. This up-and-down vertical display is in contrast with the Tundra Swan's forward thrusting of head and neck. Once firmly established, pairs remain together year-round. It is generally assumed that they mate for life and are likely to form another monogamous bond when a mate is lost.

Spring migration begins very early, with many birds departing from their wintering sites in late February or March. Pairs often arrive on their breeding grounds with freshwater marshes, ponds, and lakes before the ice thaws from mid-March to mid-April and begin to defend their territory. Young pairs, those 2-4 years old, will sometimes hang out at a wetland and not initiate nesting there until years later.

The cygnets take a long time to mature; it is at least 100 days before they are able to fly. Broods occasionally will join to form crèches. Breeding adults molt near the nesting site, while they are with their brood. Some failed breeders and nonbreeders undergo a short molt-migration. Red Rock Lakes NWR in Montana and Grays Lake NWR in Idaho are two well-known molting sites.

Family groups stick together during fall migration and throughout the winter. When the water freezes, families begin to head toward their wintering grounds, leaving between mid-October and late November. Some flocks do not travel very far or are sedentary as long as they are able to find open water in the coldest parts of winter. The "Interior Population," the introduced/reestablished population, usually has undeveloped and unpredictable migration patterns, perhaps because traditions have yet to be well-developed. Out-of-range birds are becoming increasingly regular.

GEOGRAPHIC VARIATION

No subspecies are recognized. Some authors consider Trumpeter Swan to be conspecific with its Eurasian counterpart, Whooper Swan.

SOUNDS

Their confident bellowing call is often heard in flight and from wintering flocks on the ground. The most commonly heard call is a bugling *oh-OH*. It is deep and nasal. The calls of the female are higher-pitched than those of the male. This difference is heard in comparison during their triumph display or in courtship behavior when the pairs face each other, quiver their wings, bob their heads, and trumpet.

A Trumpeter really sounds like a bugle or trumpet, hence its name (even the specific name: *buccinator*, from the Latin for trumpeter). This swan will give a couple of distinct notes: resonant, deep, sonorous, and trumpet-like. Tundra is more of a combination of wailing notes slurred together. Trumpeters announce their presence with confidence, whereas Tundra almost sounds scared or hesitant.

A Trumpeter's wings and feet may also slap the water's surface noisily during takeoff. And when close, such as when passing overhead, the whoosh of the wings can sometimes be heard.

DIET AND FEEDING BEHAVIOR

Trumpeter Swans feed by up-ending or by dipping; they will also dabble along the water's edge and graze on land. They are often observed feeding in family groups or, especially in winter, in large flocks. Adults eat a highly varied diet of submerged, floating, and emergent vegetation (e.g.,, leaves, stems, roots, seeds, and tubers), occasionally fish (e.g. salmon) and fish eggs. Grazing on pasture grasses, small grain fields, and tuberous crops is common in some locations.

NESTING
Site: Breed on large inland waters with a nest on water's edge or on a muskrat den and over water at least 2 feet deep. They will nest in scattered pairs.

Nest description: A very large mound of emergent or submerged aquatic vegetation with some white down and feathers. Height of 18 inches. Other dimensions are variable, but may be about 10-16 inches in inside diameter, 60-132 inches in outside diameter (at the base), and 4-8 inches in depth.

Clutch size: Usually 5, sometimes 2-9.

Egg description: Subelliptical to long subelliptical. Smooth, slightly glossy, with slight granular surface. Creamy white to pale yellowish. 111 X 72 mm.

Incubation duration: 32-37 days, perhaps by both, but the male may occasionally just sit at the nest for protection without actually incubating.

Brood parasitism: Probably not extensive, although Canada Geese have been known to lay eggs in Trumpeter Swan nests.

HUNTING
Trumpeter Swan is a protected species whose population has been off-limits to hunting since the Migratory Bird Treaty Act of 1918. Where Trumpeters overlap in areas where Tundra Swans can be hunted, accidental take is a possible issue.

POPULATION AND CONSERVATION
The recovery of Trumpeter Swans is a conservation success story. The population continues to increase after crashing to a very small number of individuals in the early 1900s. They were formally widespread and abundant, but their numbers dwindled during the fur trade and European settlement in the 1600s-1800s. By 1932, only 69 individuals were known to be alive in the Lower-48. Fortunately, there were others unrecorded in remote areas of Alaska and Canada. (There were, perhaps 1,000-2,000 in Alaska and 200 in Canada and the Yellowstone area.) After help from protection from hunting, as well as, habitat preservation and restoration programs, their numbers have increased substantially. The population was estimated at almost 35,000 by 2005: the Pacific Coast Population was 24,928, Rocky Mountain Population was 5,228 and the Interior Population was 4,647. And they continued to grow.

The extent of their former range is not precisely known, because in many cases they were extirpated by hunting (commercial and subsistence) and habitat loss before early ornithologists were keeping records of Trumpeter Swans. The species was not described until 1831, and they were frequently mentioned simply as "swans" in the earliest records.

Restoration programs are underway in parts of their presumed former range, including Iowa, Arkansas, Wisconsin, Minnesota, Michigan, Ohio, and Ontario. Thanks to these programs and their increasing population size, in winter they can occur just about anywhere in the Lower 48. The current winter distribution is thought to reflect their historic wintering range.

A serious mortality issue is lead poisoning (from old lead shot on the bottom of ponds, pools, and shallow lakes, or from lead fishing sinkers lost in wetlands and lakes), especially on the Washington and British Columbia coasts. Other current threats include wanton shooting (not hunting) or species misidentification resulting in accidental mortality by hunters, powerline barriers near wetlands or riverways, predation of cygnets (by everything from snapping turtles to red foxes), and continued habitat degradation and loss.

In 2015, a record 63,016 of these swans were tallied in North America. For comparison, in 1991 there had been only 15,600 in the wild.

MUTE SWAN
Cygnus olor MUSW

Plates Page 40

OTHER COMMON OR REGIONAL NAMES
Mute, park swan
(Québec: cygne tuberculé)

MEASUREMENTS
Length: Male – av 59 in (147 cm); Female – av 57 in (143 cm)
Wing: Male – av 23.3 in (59.2 cm); Female – av 21.7 in (55.1 cm)
Weight: Male – av 25 lbs (11340 g); Female – av 21 lbs (9525 g)
Bill: Male – av 103.5 mm; Female – av 97.7 mm

FIRST IMPRESSIONS

It might be hard to imagine that such a peaceful-looking and lovely bird wreaks havoc in marshes and ponds wherever it is established. Yet, these aggressive swans out-compete native waterfowl, by eating their food and pushing them away from nesting sites. Pairs of these non-native swans stake out their territories and defend them relentlessly for most of the year, until water freezes over and they move into larger wintering groups. Adults of both sexes are entirely white with an orange and black bill. First-years vary from gray-brown to white. Size and shape: A huge bird! Mute Swans are heavy-bodied with long, thick necks that are often held in a graceful arched curve. Their small head is often held tilted downwards. Adult Mutes have a dark knob on top of their obvious orange bills. Wings are sometimes held high and arched over the back, particularly when a bird is in an aggressive posture. Their tails are relatively long and taper to a point. They hold their tails out of the water more often than other swan species. Flight: Mutes, like other swans, have a very long neck, big body, and broad wings. They look particularly robust in flight, because they have a more rounded undercarriage and overall chunky body. In flight, their feet fall short of their tail tip. When taking off they make a thunderous clattering noise as they run along the water and their wings beat the water's surface. Once airborne, their wings will produce a whistling hum, much louder than any other waterfowl. Small flocks, with fewer than 10 individuals, are seen traveling between feeding sites. They stick fairly close to the surface of the water and string out in a line or V-formation. Wingbeats are methodical, shallow, and lumbering.

ID: IN DEPTH AND SIMILAR SPECIES

Mute Swans are capable of breeding in their third year. They are relatively easy to age, and it is possible to sex most birds. If you see a mated pair, look for a slightly bigger knob on the male (cob), along with aggressive behavior and threat posture with his neck tucked back, wings raised. Not a bird to be messed with! The female (pen) will also sometimes use this posture when warranted. Cygnets come in different color forms, dark (gray or brown) and light (white). The dark cygnets have light gray-brown down with dark gray bills and legs; they are grayer and browner than Tundra and Trumpeter cygnets. The light morph, common among North American swans, has white down with light brown to pinkish bills and feet. These cygnets are brighter white than other North American swans. This light color morph, also called the 'Polish' morph is the result of a single sex-linked gene and is more prevalent in some populations than others. Originating in the nineteenth century from coastal Polish birds with an inherited leucitic mutation; their white color was more attractive for captive birds so these were deliberately bred, particularly in England. A single family group can often have goslings of both morphs. Juvenile plumage starts to grow-in gradually at about six weeks, and is either gray-brown or white. First-years are in juvenile plumage until they are about four months old, at which point they start growing white adult-like feathers. By late December, they usually have white sides, scapulars, head, and neck, and they attain pinkish bills. They may continue to molt body feathers into the early spring. At about one year old, they start to shed any remaining dark juvenile feathers (and newer white feathers) to grow an entirely new set of feathers. This complete molt spans May to October, with some body molt continuing into December. Their bills have a small swollen knob and is duller colored. Second-years begin body molt in June and are flightless during their wing molt, starting as early as June. They form large groups to do this and can be seen loafing around ponds and lakes. Nearby nesting adult birds stay as tight-knit pairs and don't mix with these birds. Most are flying again by August or September. They tend to have smaller knobs and pallid red bills, but by this age they are not always reliably distinguished from adults. Adults are clean white with large black knobs on the top of their bright orange to reddish bills. Breeding adults undergo wing molt and replace their body feathers while their young are growing. Nonbreeders (along with second-years) are pushed away from a breeding pair's territory and congregate to molt starting in late May, most are actively replacing flight feathers from June to August when they are flightless for 6-8 weeks. Body molt continues until December or January. 'Polish' adults have paler legs, pinkish-gray to pale gray, opposed to black.

Similar species: Mute Swans can be confused with other species of swans and possibly Snow Geese or white domestic geese. Their extremely long neck and long body rules out any confusing white geese. Tundra and Trumpeter Swan have a fairly similar shape, but Mute Swan tends to hold its neck in an arched curve and angles its head and bill down giving them a more submissive look. The native swans tend to hold their bill horizontal to the water. Mute Swans have a more pronounced forehead than Tundra and Trumpeter, which have smooth head profiles with wedge-shaped bills, sloping foreheads, and gently peaked heads. In flight, Mute Swan looks like a heftier bird with its rounded undercarriage. Tundra and Trumpeter have a sleeker look in flight with thinner necks and flatter bodies.

Sex ratio: It is male-biased, usually 54-58%, but sometimes as high as 65%.

GEOGRAPHIC VARIATION

No subspecies are recognized.

SOUNDS

Contrary to its name, Mute Swan is a fairly vocal species although their calls are not as loud and do not carry as far as other swans. Adults have 8-10 different calls, various grunts, snorts, hisses and whistles. The main call given on the water and in flight is a weak, trumpeted, descending *Heeorrf*. The diagnostic whistling hum of their wings is very loud as they pump through the air. Other swans are much quieter in flight. They also make quite a racket slapping their wings and feet on the water as they take off.

YEAR IN THE LIFE

Mute Swans were introduced to North America from Europe in the late 1800s as decorative waterfowl for parks, zoos, and country estates. Their native breeding range is across north and central Eurasia, from the British Isles to Russia and China and south to Africa, but they are a common ornamental species worldwide. Since their introduction, they have established large populations in the Great Lakes region, Long Island Sound, and Chesapeake Bay. They are now established on the southeast portion of Vancouver Island, in British Columbia. The largest winter concentrations are on the Detroit River where counts of over 500 are regular. Also, Jamaica Bay on Long Island has held several hundred in winter. The Chesapeake Bay formerly held the highest counts, but numbers have been seriously reduced after the success of population control measures in the region. Sightings extend south to Florida. There are increasing numbers in Washington and California, and there is a peppering of records elsewhere, demonstrating that these swans can get around and are not all coming from recent captive origins.

Mute Swan is an invasive species that has devastating impacts on the marshes and lakes where they feed and breed. Aggressive by nature, their hostile territoriality, especially intolerance of other waterfowl during nesting and brood-rearing times, allows them to out-compete native nesting birds for food and nesting sites.

They forage primarily on submerged aquatic vegetation (SAV) that would otherwise be available for native waterfowl. If not for their aesthetic appeal, it's no doubt that Mute Swans would not be tolerated due to the significant detrimental effects on the biodiversity of the areas they inhabit. Culling takes place 'quietly' at some locations.

They are considered year-round residents on their breeding grounds in North America, although there is considerable local movement as water freezes and non-breeders undergo a molt-migration. Some populations in Eurasia are migratory, wintering from northern Africa to India and southeast China.

In the winter, if their breeding grounds freeze-over, they move around and tend to congregate in areas where there is open water and food. There is also an annual dispersal of young birds, which do not breed until they are 2-3 years old.

Pair bonds initially form sometime from January through March. In courtship display, the two birds will face each other, upper neck-feathers raised, bills pointing down, sometimes with raised secondaries, and with mutual head-turning (accompanied by dipping motion of neck toward the water).

They will setup a territory not far from where the female was born. Unlike ducks, the male selects a nest site, sometimes several, before the female picks just the right spot. They do not undergo a molt migration, but will often congregate at traditional molting sites.

Pairs remain together year-after-year. Depending on ice conditions, they return to their breeding territory as early as possible from late January to early April. Females endure a long incubation before the cygnets hatch. Young are able to fly when they are four-five months old (about 17-21 weeks). Family groups often remain together until the following spring, when adults push them away from their nesting territory. From late May to late August, non-breeders and failed breeders congregate and molt in large shallow bodies of water.

In the fall, if necessary they move to ice-free ponds, bays and lakes for the winter. This shift often takes places from October to mid-December.

DIET AND FEEDING BEHAVIOR

Mute Swans mainly feed in water up to 3 feet deep by up-ending or by dipping, immersing their heads and necks. They will also dabble along the water's edge, and they will graze on land, but not as often as other swan species. A wide selection of submerged aquatic vegetation (SAV) – with little preference – is the main diet. These swans can reach bottom in far deeper water than other up-ending waterfowl. As such, the species' effects on native ecosystems are of major concern, especially since they feed in place all year, reducing the food supply for other waterfowl, either migrating or wintering. While feeding, the swans uproot and dislodge three times the amount of SAV they ingest. They will each eat an estimated 6.6 – 9..0 pounds of vegetable matter per day. Animal matter (e.g.,, frogs, toads, tadpoles, mollusks, worms, and insects) is sometimes taken, especially during annual molt and in cool springs.

NESTING

Site: Mute Swans will use many wet areas to nest, large or small, fresh or brackish, and in swamps or even drainage ditches. They prefer to breed in coastal ponds, estuaries, inland ponds, creeks, and slow-moving rivers that flow into large bodies of water. They will nest on water's edge on land or on small islands, or built in shallow water in reedbeds.

Nest description: A large mound of woven vegetation (e.g.,, tree twigs and branches, reeds, cattails, cord-grasses, bulrushes, and various other grasses and sedges) with a raised hollow in the center. Height of 18-26 inches. Other dimensions are about 15-18 inches in inside diameter, 48-66 inches in outside diameter (at the base), and 3-4 inches in depth.

Clutch size: Average 5

Egg description: Subelliptical to long elliptical. Smooth, slightly glossy, with slight granular surface. Some almost white, but more often with a pale blue-gray of blue-green tint. 112 X 74 mm.

Incubation duration: 34-38 days, basically by female. The male may sit on the nest when the female is at recess, but without a brood patch probably does no real

incubation.
	Brood parasitism: Not known.

HUNTING

Mute Swans are not hunted throughout most of North America simply because they are not listed as a species that is huntable. Hunters granted a swan permit in Virginia may harvest one Mute or Tundra Swan per year. Their status actually varies by states, in some states they are specified as protected. In others they are by law considered a nuisance, invasive feral species and not protected, yet not actively harvested. These include New Hampshire, Delaware, Minnesota, North Carolina, Oregon, and Washington. Curiously, in Canada, Mute Swans are a protected species.

POPULATION AND CONSERVATION

These swans were first brought to the U.S. in the late 1800s. Introduced as decorative waterfowl in the northeastern U.S., Mute Swans were first recorded breeding in the wild along the lower Hudson River in 1910 and on Long Island, New York, shortly thereafter. More than 500 Mute Swans were imported to the U.S. between 1910 and 1912, leading to multiple introductions and escapes, especially along the Atlantic coast.

The Mute Swan population grew from fewer than 1,000 birds in the mid-1950s to more than 14,000 in 2002. Today the numbers are probably closer to 22,000-25,000.

Michigan swans, brought to the state in 1919 have proliferated. The state may now have the largest number of Mute Swans in the country; over 15,400 were counted in 2011.

In 1962, five mute swans escaped from a private collection in Talbot County, Maryland, on the Chesapeake Bay's eastern shore. Their numbers remained low into the 1970s. By 1986, 264 were recorded in the state, concentrating on the Chesapeake Bay. But by 1999, the number had jumped to almost 4,000. Culling programs, although contentious, have been encouraging, with only about 50 mute swans in Maryland waters today. But on the Virginia side of the Chesapeake Bay, up to 500 of the swans continue to reside.

Reduction programs vary by region and state. Concentrations of these geese can be detrimental to the welfare of other species. By controlling the swan population, it decreases competition for nesting areas, food and other resources for native nesting birds, and it increases biodiversity in wetlands as a whole. Swans eat or destroy significant amounts of submerged aquatic vegetation each day, limiting food availability native migratory birds.

Coordinated flyway-wide approaches are probably a real necessity for effective Mute Swan management. Individual state programs are insufficient. Protection in Canada, however, makes control and management difficult.

WHOOPER SWAN
Cygnus cygnus WHOS

Plates Page 38

OTHER COMMON OR REGIONAL NAMES:
Whooper

MEASUREMENTS Length: Male – av 60 in. (150cm) Female – av 57 in (144 cm)
Wing: Male – av 24.1 in (61.1 cm); Female – av 23.2 in (58.9 cm)
Weight: Male – av 19.5 lbs (8850 g); Female – av 12.3 lbs (5600 g)
Bill: Male – av 106.0 mm; Female – av 99.0 mm

FIRST IMPRESSIONS AND SIMILAR SPECIES-

This very rare Eurasian visitor can stand out in large swan flocks in western North America because over half of a Whooper Swan's bill is yellow. Look for the extensive bright yellow patch that extends from the base of the bill and comes to a point just below the nostrils. Whooper Swans, like their North American counterparts, Trumpeters, often hold their neck in an erect posture or kinked backwards. Adults have entirely white bodies. Juveniles are cinnamon-gray overall with a pinkish base to the bill. First-year birds have bills and lores that are pale yellow to pinkish at the base, pinkish in the middle, and dark at the tip. Trumpeter Swan has dark lores and base to the bill. Size and shape: The entire head and bill on these huge, long-necked birds will appear wedge-shaped and elongated. They have a flat forehead that smoothly tapers to a long bill. Whooper Swans are similar in size and shape to Trumpeter Swans and noticeably larger than Tundra Swans, but with a longer neck. Flight: Whooper Swan resembles Trumpeter Swan, given they are both very large white birds with exceptionally long necks, and both need a long runway on the water to take off. A Whooper Swan's wingbeats are even, powerful, and slow.

Similar species: Adult Whooper Swans share a large yellow patch on the bill with Bewick's (Tundra) Swans which is also very rare in North America. Whooper Swan is larger and longer-necked than Bewick's and has more yellow at the base of the bill. The yellow on the bill of Whooper covers roughly half of the bill, extending below the nostrils toward the tip, whereas the yellow on Bewick's bill does not extend below the nostrils.

Sex ratio: assumed to be equal.

BACKGROUND AND TIPS
Whooper Swan is a Eurasian counterpart of our Trumpeter Swan. They are very rare in western North America. Whoopers are almost annual winter and early spring visitors to the outer Aleutian Islands of Alaska (including Attu, Adak, Amchitka, and Shemya). Max. 31 on Amchitka 10 April 1970. There are some other records for Alaska and more than two dozen reports from elsewhere in the West (including locations in British Columbia, Alberta, California, Oregon, Idaho, Montana, and Wyoming). Records for eastern North America have all been treated as escapes. Whooper Swans in captivity have hybridized with Trumpeter Swan; something to be aware of when looking at a suspected vagrant.

Most vagrant swans detected in the Lower-48 are lone adults in large swan flocks.

The global population, estimated at 180,000 individuals, is thought to be decreasing dramatically, although breeding numbers in some regions are increasing. Whooper Swans are threatened by habitat loss and degradation, including the reclamation of coastal and inland wetlands, draining of wetlands for irrigation, and oil pollution.

SOUNDS
Whooper Swan is a highly vocal species with a loud, three-syllable or four-syllable bugling call. The calls lack the somewhat nasal or muffled quality of those by Trumpeter Swan. They have a bit of a farmyard-goose quality. Males sound slightly lower-pitched than females.

DIET AND FEEDING BEHAVIOR
Feeding behavior, in fresh and saline waters, is similar to other swans, including up-ending, dipping, and head and neck immersion They may forage on land, eating grain. Predominantly vegetarian, their diet consists of leaves, stems, and roots of aquatic plants, grasses, sedges, and horsetails. Adults may take marine and freshwater mussels.

NESTING
Notes included here only because of two recorded nesting on Attu, Alaska (1996 and 1997). Site, nest description, clutch, and eggs very similar to that of Trumpeter Swan. Incubation slightly longer (35-42 days).

SNOW GOOSE
Anser caerulescens SNGO

Plates Page 46

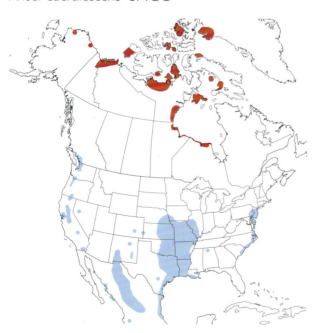

OTHER COMMON OR REGIONAL NAMES
Wavie (alternately, wavy), white goose, white brant, blue goose or eagle-head (for the dark morph)
(Arctic: kangniq [YK], kafuq [NS, NWS], kanguq [YK, NS, N])
(Québec: oie des neiges)
(Mexico: ganso nevado, ganso blanco)

MEASUREMENTS
Length: Male – 28-33 in, av 30.0 in (76.2 cm); Female – 27-32 in, av 29.0 in (73.7 cm)
Wing: Male – av 18.0 in (43.7 cm); Female – av 17.3 in (43.9 cm)
Weight: Male – average 6.60 lbs (2994 g); Female – av 5.80 lbs (2631 g)
Bill: Male – Greater – 59-73 mm; Lesser – 51-63 mm; Female –Greater – 57-68 mm; Lesser – 50 – 61 mm

FIRST IMPRESSIONS
Snow Geese are increasingly numerous, traveling in huge wavy flocks between their crowded Arctic breeding colonies and their temperate wintering grounds. Their spectacular skeins can sometimes fill the sky. Snow Geese are pure white on their bodies with black wingtips and pink bills. Their faces are often stained with a rusty to orange wash, the result of the birds foraging in mud containing iron oxides. Look for first-year birds that have dusky smudging on the head and body. In some populations "Blue Geese" – actually blue-morph Snows – are prevalent, mostly down central North America; these adults have dark bodies and white heads. Size and shape: A medium-large goose, about the same size as White-fronts. Pink bill size varies with population, but generally robust with striking "grin patch," where the mandibles meet. Head is wedge-shaped and neck is thick. Flight: Short-necked and long-winged goose. Snows are white with black wing tips. Some flocks are mixed with blue-morph

geese, which have dark bodies, white head (and half of the neck), upperwings are silver-gray on the coverts and dark on the flight feathers. Snows are able to spring into the air more easily than other geese, those that make use of a runway. When landing, Snow Geese will drop their necks and dangle pink feet as they approach, taking their time when they get close to the ground. Snow Geese can often be seen flying in long waving and irregular lines, with individuals numbering into the thousands. They travel high during migration, but lower when moving between feeding sites on the wintering grounds. They will fly in an undulating fashion, and seldom in well-formed Vs. They are not as steady on the wing as Canada Geese, tipping side to side a bit more. They certainly cover some serious ground with strong and consistent wingbeats.

ID: IN DEPTH AND SIMILAR SPECIES

Males are slightly larger than females, which can be noticeable in direct comparison. Distinguishing adults from first-years is not very difficult. Snow Geese breed for the first time at two years old. Goslings are warm yellow with a dusky wash on the body. Juvenile plumage begins to appear at 2-3 weeks and is fully grown by 6 weeks. In white Snow Geese, juvenile plumage is gray overall, palest on the breast and belly. Blue Geese are dark, dusky-brown overall with limited white speckles on the face. First-years transition from gray to mottled white as they replace juvenile plumage through the winter. Blue Geese are mostly dark gray. They will attain additional white speckles behind the bill and around the eye. Their wing coverts are dark-centered with white edging (much like adult Blue Geese), paler gray than the sides and back. First-years and second-years (non-breeders) migrate north and molt their primaries and body feathers in the Arctic from June through September. They undergo wing molt earlier than successful breeders. Adults have clean white body plumage but with black wingtips, often with rusty stains on the face. Successful breeders start their wing molt when their goslings are about three weeks old. Females start 3-4 days before the males. Adults are flightless for about three weeks, and regain flight about the time their goslings begin to fly. Their body molt continues through November.

Similar species: Ross's Goose looks like a miniature, small-billed version of Snow Goose. Ross's Goose is best separated by its smaller overall size, petite rounded head, and stout triangular bill that lacks a "grinning patch." As part of Ross's Goose petite appearance, they will also have a dainty ambience. Ross's Geese usually lack rusty staining on the face (which is common in Snow Goose) because they pluck at grasses, grazing carefully, opposed to digging into mud to feed on roots and tubers like Snow Goose. Beware of hybrids, however, which are intermediate in size and bill shape.

Snow Goose can also be confused with white domestic geese and ducks, including the white Peking ducks and white Graylag-type geese, which have orange bills and feet. Domestics also lack the black primaries of Snow Goose. Also, look for shape differences, including the heavy bottoms and unattractive waddle of domestics.

Sex ratio: Basically equal during all stages of the life cycle.

YEAR IN THE LIFE

Snow Geese vacate their Arctic breeding areas, traveling across much of North America to reach their wintering grounds, which span southward even to Veracruz, Mexico. Winter counts flourish in several parts of the country, including Arkansas, Sacramento NWR in California's Central Valley, Prime Hook NWR in Delaware. Breeders from Wrangel Island, Russia winter in two distinct areas in the Fraser and Skagit River Deltas of British Columbia and Washington and in a portion of southern Oregon and Central Valley of California. The population breeding in northwest Greenland, winters along Atlantic Coast. Snow Goose occasionally winters in Hawaiian Islands, also Greenland, Iceland, Norway, Finland, British Isles, continental Europe, Azores, and Korea.

In winter, before the mid-1970s, Snow Geese fed on marsh vegetation. However, they adapted quickly to feed in agricultural lands when large-scale farming led to a large and increasing supply of surplus corn and cereal grains.

During migration, Snows often move during the day and at night, often taking off at dusk. Listen for their calls at night during migration.

Spring migration kicks off to an early start and is in full swing in late February and early March in the East. In the west, they are also moving in March and early April. Pairing usually takes place in spring, sometimes in winter. Courtship displays are not complicated, with males enlarging their body contours, adopting an exaggerated erect posture and closely follow females.

Once family groups arrive on their Arctic breeding grounds, the first-year birds head off on a molt-migration. Interestingly, if the parents do not breed or if they lose their clutch early on, some first-year birds will reunite with their parents and remain with them until the following winter. Adults do not attempt to nest again.

Females select a nest site by the coast. Large Snow Goose colonies are bustling with activity as parents defend their nests against predators and other Snow Geese. Sometimes pairs will approach the nest of another pair with intent of laying a parasitic egg in the nest. The males often fight as they intruding female tries to dislodge the incubating female. The curiosity is that if the egg is laid close to the nest, the incubating female will roll the egg into her nest, adopting the egg. Typically, in brood parasite systems, the host is developing strategies to get rid of the parasitic eggs!

Young fledge about 43 days after hatching. Adults molt their wing feathers while tending to the brood in brood-rearing areas that may be more than 45 miles from nest locations. Nonbreeding geese, including one year-old birds, travel a molt-migration heading north as far as 150 miles where they molt their primaries.

During fall migration, Snows often travel in large skeins numbering in the thousands. Snow Geese congregate in incredible numbers, for example, as they pass through Cap Tourmente, Québec, and Saskatoon, Saskatchewan in October. They begin arriving on their wintering grounds in large flocks starting in October with numbers building through November.

GEOGRAPHIC VARIATION

Two subspecies are recognized: Greater Snow Goose, *A. c. atlantica* and Lesser Snow Goose, *A. c. caerulescens*.

A. c. atlantica: Greater has the more limited breeding and wintering range, breeding in the Canadian High Arctic from northernmost Baffin Island and Ellesmere Island, to western Greenland. Greaters winter along the U.S. Atlantic coast from New Jersey to South Carolina, concentrating in the Delaware and Chesapeake Bays. On average, they are larger, particularly with a larger, more robust bill.

A. c. caerulescens: Lesser constitutes the remainder of the population, mid-continent and western breeders. Some authorities point out, sufficient overlap in size may warrant dropping subspecific designation. In the parts of the east where both subspecies occur, most individuals are not reliably separable in the field.

There are two color morphs that were formerly treated as distinct species: Snow Goose, *Chen hyperborea* and Blue Goose, *C. caerulescens*. Genetic studies in the 1960s determined that the color dimorphism is controlled only by a single locus. Distribution of color morphs varies regionally; Blue Goose, a dark morph of the Lesser, is abundant in central North America, including dominating on the central Gulf Coast, comprises only a few percent of geese along the Atlantic Coast, and is rare west of the central Great Plains. These distributions reflect the ratios on the breeding grounds.

SOUNDS

Listen for their noisy, high-pitched flocks passing overhead, day and night. These are probably the most vociferous of all waterfowl. Males and females give similar calls in a chorus of raspy honks, *whonk* or *whouk* that are given almost incessantly when they are in migrating and in winter flocks. First-years are distinctly higher-pitched, giving more of a whistle. Snow Geese also give guttural feeding calls, a series of *gah* notes. Adults call to their goslings with a quiet *uh-uh-uh* notes. Alarm calls on are a deep *kaah-aaah*.

DIET AND FEEDING BEHAVIOR

Snow Geese are intensive foragers, preferring to feed in water-logged soil or in shallow water (usually under 6 inches). In winter, they often forage in large flocks for long periods of times. The diet of Snow Geese consists entirely of plant material, with a foraging strategy that involves probing for underground rootstalks, tubers, and roots. The "grinning patch" on the goose produces a strong grip for extracting underground tubers and rootstalks of marsh plants. Snow Geese also graze on new shoots of aquatic and agricultural plants. In breeding season, they often favor leafy parts of grasses, sedges, rushes, willows, other aquatic plants, and tundra shrubs. During migration and on the wintering grounds, they actively scavenge agricultural areas for excess grain (e.g., corn, barley, wheat, and rice), an activity that has contributed to the phenomenal spread and increase of this species. One shift became evident in the 1960s and 1970s in rice -country in Arkansas and Louisiana. Today, snows will migrate in more of a stepping-stone manner, corresponding with key areas with excess grain.

NESTING

Site: Snow Geese breed on tundra, near the coast on relatively grassy or featureless terrain, near ponds, shallow freshwater lakes, streams, or islands in braided deltas. They breed in colonies, sometimes with Ross's Geese. Areas with a slight rise and that are clear of snow early and not flooded in a spring thaw are preferred. Ross's Geese nest in the lower areas and arrive a week or two later.

Nest description: A hollow on the dry ground, often in taller vegetation, lined with plants and dried grasses and built up at the rim, with an inner lining of small white feathers and pale gray down. Nest size averages 9 inches in inside diameter, 18 inches in outside diameter, and 4 inches in depth.

Clutch size: Usually 2-6 eggs.

Egg description: Elliptical to subelliptical. Smooth with a fine granular texture. White to creamy-white. 79 X 52 mm.

Incubation duration: Averages 22-25 days.

Brood parasitism: Frequently lays in the nest of other Snow Geese; rarely Canada Goose or Common Eider eggs are found in their nest.

HUNTING

Wavies are notoriously difficult to bring into decoys; it may take hundreds of decoys or white flags to pull them in. They are accustomed to moving with and settling into large flocks of geese. If they lock into a field, they form an impressive tornado of birds spiraling down from great heights to land an incredible experience with thousands of birds spiraling in and landing!

Bag limits have been liberalized dramatically in recent years, through the Light Goose Conservation Order, to compensate for the remarkable Snow Goose population explosion. Here is a prime example of hunting as a serious waterfowl management tool. There are even spring hunts underway across the country where electronic callers are legal. The discontinuence of employing a plug (reducing the capacity to three shots or less) is also allowed in some areas. Despite these actions, the harvest of Snows has not kept pace with the dramatically increasing population. Other techniques need to be considered, since increasing harvest opportunities is probably the only viable option to control the Snow Goose population. At the same time, younger birds are almost twice as likely to be taken as adults, which does not directly help cut down the breeding adult population.

POPULATION AND CONSERVATION
The Snow Goose population has exploded in recent years, perhaps the most abundant waterfowl in the world. Their numbers have increased in response to a warmer climate, better average weather in the spring, increased nesting success, and, especially, their ability to adapt to agriculture—utilizing agricultural lands and excess grain during migration and winter. Current population estimates range from 4.5 million to 6.7 million, where there were only about 1.3 million in the early 1970s. Some stunning population estimates have gone as high as 18.7 million birds. NAWMP population objectives are just under 2.5 million, continent-wide.

In the mid-1990s, biologists discovered that vast areas of the arctic were being destroyed because there were simply too many Snow Geese crowding the habitat. When traditional and fragile tundra breeding habitat was degraded, the Snows would shift to new area where conditions were better. The process would begin anew, and it continues today. The remarkable increase in Snow Goose numbers also causes significant management concerns and a shift to a population-regulation attitude. Even liberalized hunting regulations have failed to check either the growth of Snow Geese or the adverse impact on their breeding habitat.

New or increased harvest techniques have been recommended to control overpopulation. These include revisiting limits, hours, calls, bait, and decoys, issuing cross-state-province-country Snow Goose hunting permits, and permitting more egg-collecting by native peoples on the tundra breeding grounds.

ROSS'S GOOSE
Anser rossii ROGO

Plates Page 48

OTHER COMMON OR REGIONAL NAMES
Little wavie, horned wavie, warty-nosed wavie (in each case alternately spelled "wavy"), rosser
(Arctic: kangunnaaq [N])
(Québec: oie de Ross)
(Mexico: ganso de Ross)

MEASUREMENTS
Length: Male – 24-26 in, av 25.0 in (63.5 cm); Female – 22-24 in, av 23.0 in (58.4 cm)
Wing: Male – av 15.5 in (39.4 cm); Female – av 14.8 in (37.6 cm)
Weight: Male – av 4.00 lbs (1814 g); Female – av 3.56 lbs (2522 g)
Bill: Male – av 43.4 mm; Female – av 40.1 mm

FIRST IMPRESSIONS
A small, white goose with black wingtips and a pink triangular bill; often mixed in with flocks of Snow or White-fronted Geese. On the ground, they have a clean and cute impression from their rounded-head that lacks the rusty staining often seen on the face of Snow Geese. Blue-morph Ross's Geese with almost black backs and dark necks are extremely rare. Size and shape: Smaller than Snow Goose, similar in size to Cackling Goose. Their bills are petite and triangular on a small rounded head. Short, thick neck, compared to Snow Goose. Flight: Ross's small size stands out when singles or small groups are mixed in with Snow or White-fronted Geese. The size, short neck, and stubby bill are great indicators. This goose can be difficult to separate from Snow Geese, however, if there aren't Snows to use for comparison. Flocks are typically strung out in single wavy lines, in loose V, or even W-shaped formation. Their wingbeats, with shorter wings, are faster than those of Snow Geese.

ID: IN DEPTH AND SIMILAR SPECIES
Males are slightly larger than females and first-years look much like adults at first glance, but with closer examination they are not hard to age. Ross's Geese typically breed in second or third year.

Goslings are remarkably variable, from pale white to warm yellow to gray with a dark hood. Juvenile plumage is grown by 5-6 weeks. Juvenile plumage is similar to adult, but has dusky smudges on the head, in front and above the eye, and on the nape and back. Also look for gray-brown tertials and secondary coverts on the juvenile. First-years are separated from adults by the dusky markings on their wing coverts. Ross's Geese replace juvenile plumage during a protracted molt that can span from September to April, mostly taking place on the wintering grounds. They return to the Arctic for the summer and replace all their wing and body feathers June-October at an Arctic molting site. Adults are clean white with black primaries. Their stubby bill is pink, with a bit of bluish-gray at the base. Adults replace body feathers from July through November, sometimes wrapping up body molt on the wintering grounds. Nonbreeders and yearlings begin wing molt earlier than breeding adults. Most adults drop wing feathers shortly after body molt starts, when their brood is able to move with them downstream, toward the coast to a suitable molting site. Adults are flightless for 4 weeks and able to fly again by mid-to-late August.

Very rarely there are blue morph Ross's Geese that are like miniature blue Snow Geese with the dark coloration coming farther up on the neck and blacker backs. Their tertials and upperwing coverts are white with dark edges. Juvenile blue-morph Ross's are also dark overall, most of their head, neck, back and sides is smoky-brown. They will have variable amounts of white flecks on the head, particularly around the eye. The origin has been thought to be the result of interbreeding with "normal" Ross's and blue-morph Snow Geese, where the blue-morph gene is dominant. However, a high percentage of "blue-morph" birds show no features of Snow Goose and more research is needed before we should assume that most birds are hybrids.

Similar species: Ross's Geese are only likely to be confused with Snow Geese. When it comes to picking out a Ross's Goose, it's helpful to make comparisons with other geese in the flock. Ross's is significantly smaller with a petite bill. They usually do not show any dark staining on the face like Snow and lack a dark "grin patch" where the upper and lower mandibles meet. The birds that cause the most confusion are hybrid Snow x Ross's Geese. Identifiable hybrids are intermediate in body size, but also bill length and grin patch. Apparent blue Ross's Geese, particularly away from west are reasonably likely to be hybrids, so double check the bill structure and that the white on the head is really only on the back. Also, ensure the back is really dark – approaching black – before identifying the bird as a blue-morph Ross's.

YEAR IN THE LIFE

Ross's Goose has been a little-known, often overlooked North American species. The species' range has been shifting eastward in recent years, resulting in increased numbers of sightings beyond their historical breeding and wintering ranges. A goose of the Central Flyway, the traditional core of its wintering range has been the Texas coast, New Mexico, and Chihuahua, Mexico, with other concentrations in California's Central Valley. Highest wintering counts are from California in the Salton Sea NWR, Merced NWR, and Klamath Basin (also on the Oregon side). Also, Bosque del Apache NWR in New Mexico and along the Texas panhandle and coast. Large numbers can be seen migrating through south central Saskatchewan in late September. Recently, and with an increasing population, these traditional wintering areas have spread, covering some areas in-between and, especially, spreading eastward.

In winter, they forage in agricultural fields and shallow wetlands. They roost on reservoirs, lakes, and other wetlands.

Spring migration progresses in stages. They begin moving north in early March, passing through eastern Oregon in early April and concentrating in Alberta in mid-May. There is very little information on courtship and pairing displays, but males may assume a dainty walk, short prancing rushes, fluffed neck feathers, and head-dipping.

Breeds on remote arctic tundra. They are inclined to nest colonially and prefer to nest on inland islands. By avoiding river edges, lake shores and the coast, it relieves some predation pressures. Jaegers and gulls are more numerous on the coast, and foxes rarely swim to islands. Unlike Snow Geese, however, they are too small to fend off foxes. Their inland nest sites were off the path of early Arctic explorers as well. In fact, Ross's Goose breeding grounds were not discovered until 1938, because explores traveled along coasts and rivers.

Much of the population has nested in the Queen Maud Gulf Migratory Bird Sanctuary of the central Canadian Arctic in Nunavut. Two large colonies (Karrak Lake and Colony 10) alone account for an estimated 1.3 million birds. The Ross's Goose population has been growing and shifting in recent years. For example, an increasing number of Ross's Geese now nest eastward on Southampton and Baffin Islands, westward on Banks Island, and southward along the western coast of Hudson Bay. Nesting usually begins around the second week of June, depending on weather. After hatching, family groups gather in large marsh-edged lakes or move downstream toward the coast where the adults molt. Young and adults are flying by late August.

Fall migration begins earlier than other arctic species. Ross's begin their journey in September about the same time as White-fronted Geese. For example, most have arrived on Tule Lake, California by mid-October. Large numbers arrive in Texas by mid-November.

GEOGRAPHIC VARIATION

No subspecies are recognized.

SOUNDS

Quieter than other geese, Ross's Goose is generally less vocal, but higher-pitched, than Snow Goose. Its flight call is softer with less inflection, a simple *keek keek keek*. Gives a one-syllable and almost duck-like *kowk* when disturbed. On breeding grounds, adults give a threat call that is a high-pitched squawk or grumbling *nnaagg* along with other weak grunts. Females call to goslings with a soft *kuk* calls. Also hiss when approached by potential predator.

DIET AND FEEDING BEHAVIOR

Ross's Geese, strictly vegetarian, graze on grasses, sedges, legumes, shoots, and domestic grain adjacent to roosting wetlands. During breeding season, they forage close to or within their nesting colonies. Their small bills are ideal for grazing on short blades or shoots of plants while Snow Geese have larger bills perfect for digging roots and tubers. Ross's Geese forage while standing or walking on land or in shallow water. In migration and in winter Ross's Geese will take advantage of varied surplus grain (e.g., wheat, barley, millet, corn, and rice). Quite simply, they have benefitted from the spread of grain-agriculture on their wintering and stopover areas, particularly feeding on waste wheat, barley, and corn. This grain abundance has been facilitating their spread eastward and their winter holdover in areas often north of their traditional wintering grounds.

See "Population and Conservation" for feeding behavior implications involving Ross's Geese.

NESTING

Site: Ross's Geese nest on the ground usually on sparsely vegetated islands and surrounding mainland areas of shallow arctic lakes, but less frequently on islands in rivers or offshore. Their nests are in the open, next to rocks, or among dwarf shrub (e.g., willow and birch). Ross's Geese nest in colonies, often interspersed with nesting "Lesser" Snow Geese. The Snow Geese typically arrive 2-3 days earlier and take nest sites on higher terrain that thaws first.

Nest description: A hollow lined, thick at times, with vegetation from nearby (birch and willow). The nest is often built up with a thick rim several inches high. It is lined with white down. Nest size averages, 6 inches in inside diameter, 19 inches in outside diameter, and 3 inches in depth.

Clutch size: Usually 3-4 eggs.

Egg description: Elliptical to subelliptical. Smooth with a fine granular texture. White to light cream-colored. 70 X 47 mm.

Incubation duration: 21-23 days.

Brood parasitism: Mixed clutches with the eggs of Ross's Goose and "Lesser" Snow Goose are not uncommon.

HUNTING

Little wavies have been protected from hunting at various times and have not been as commonly hunted as Snows. With the boom in Ross's Geese and the eastern expansion of the species, however, harvest rates and adult mortality have increased significantly. In 1999, the USFWS introduced a Light Goose Conservation Order for "white geese," with the intention of staving off the populations by means of increasing harvest mortality. A spring hunt, starting with the Mississippi and Central Flyways, allowed for hunters to use unplugged shotguns and electronic calls under extended hours and a very liberal bag limits. Combined, these efforts add up to the use of hunting as a core conservation and wildlife management mechanism.

The behavior of Ross's Geese is much like that of Snows. It is difficult to get Ross's Geese to commit to coming into the decoys. They will often drift by, just out of range. It might take 300-1000 decoys to bring them in. Traditional hunting locations include National Wildlife Refuges and surrounding areas in California's Central Valley, Texas, and New Mexico.

POPULATION AND CONSERVATION

Surprisingly, Ross's Geese were thought to be close to extinction in the early 1900s; in the 1930s there were only thought to be 5,000-6,000. But by 1965, the total population estimate was closer to 30,000 birds.

Clearly, the population has been steadily increasing, at least since the mid-1950s. Spring counts in the central Arctic increased from 34,000 in 1966 to 567,000 in 1998. The total spring population in central and Eastern Arctic estimated as 805,000 in 1998. The large colony at Karrak Lake was estimated at 12,000 birds in 1965; it included 709,000 adults by 2010. Winter counts in California's Central Valley rose from fewer than 30,000 in 1962-1963 to an average of 200,000 between 1988 and 1992. By 2008, the number was over 282,000; by 2014 it was over 365,000. With the population growth, expansion of the Arctic breeding grounds both westward and eastward beyond the Queen Maud Gulf Migratory Sanctuary, and increased numbers wintering outside central California, there have been an eastern migration through the center of Canada and the Great Plains and an increased number of sightings in the East. Before 1970, almost all Ross's Geese wintered in California's Central Valley. According to the NAWMP, the total numbers exceed a million birds, well over the target population objective of 100,000. Continental numbers may actually be over 1.5 million birds.

The availability of waste grain on migration and at wintering areas has supported a tremendous increase in Ross's Geese. In turn, this has allowed more youngsters to reach adulthood and more adults to return to arctic breeding grounds. Breeding grounds have expanded, almost to the point of exceeding the landscape's carrying capacity. The breeding expansion of Ross's Geese has impacted tundra habitat, not unlike the imp[act of Snows. But it is difficult to separate the damage done by both species; the two nest together. Moreover, the small bill of the Ross's Goose (compared to Snow Goose) allows it to graze very close to the ground, which can slow or prevent tundra-plant recovery. This habitat degradation has also negatively impacted additional species — songbird, shorebirds, and other waterfowl. Thus far, harvest management (i.e., expanded hunting) has failed to keep up with the boom in Ross's Geese.

GREATER WHITE-FRONTED GOOSE
Anser albifrons GWFG

Plates Page 52

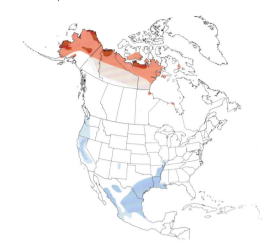

OTHER COMMON OR REGIONAL NAMES
Specklebelly, white-front, speck, laughing goose, white-fronted goose, bar-belly, tar-belly
(Arctic: neqlepik [YK], liqlivik, neqlek [NS], niklivik, niblivik [NWS], nirlivik, niglik, niglervi, akto [N])
(Québec: oie rieuse)
(Mexico: ganso frente blanca, ganso careto mayor)

MEASUREMENTS
Length: Male – 27-31 in, av 29.1 in (73.9 cm); Female – 26-29 in, av 27.3 in (69.3 cm)
Wing: Male – av 17.3 in (43.9 cm); Female – av 16.5 in (41.9 cm)
Weight: Male – av 6.29 lbs (2853 g); Female – av 5.53 lbs (2508 g)
Bill: Male – av 51.4 mm; Female – av 48.4 mm

FIRST IMPRESSIONS
Noisy flocks of brown geese in the Central and Pacific Flyways are bound to be White-fronts. At first glance, flocks appear uniform in size and coloration. In the early fall, however, adults are a bit larger with more splotches on their bellies. These birds are gregarious, occurring in large flocks and often found with white geese and Canadas, as well as with puddle ducks. This is plain grayish-brown goose with a paler brown breast, darker brown head, neck, and back, and with those distinctive speckles – or barring – on the underparts. The legs are orange. The bill appears pink to wholly or partly orangish with a white-feathered border. That border is highlighted in the bird's binomial. *Albifrons* comes from Latin: *albus*, meaning white and *frons*, meaning forehead. Size and shape: A medium-sized and stocky goose, roughly the same size as Snow Goose, but White-fronts have a bit longer and thinner neck than Snow Goose and a slender-looking bill. Flight: Greater White-fronted Geese have more rounded bodies than other geese, giving them a bit of a pot-bellied look. Their loose wingbeats and relatively long thin wings often make them appear unstable, tipping from side to side in flight. Members of a flock are often not on the same beat, a flight behavior which gives them a distinctively disorganized appearance, even at long distances. Canada Geese, by comparison, have stable and steady wingbeats. In flight, Greater White-fronted Geese are brown-bodied with a two-toned upperwing. They have white on the undertail, a white extending to the uppertail, and a thin white band at the tip of the tail. Flocks travel in lines and in V-formations. Their loud, piercing flight calls are also a giveaway to their identity. They carry well, so you often hear a flock before you see it.

ID: IN DEPTH AND SIMILAR SPECIES
The challenges of White-fronted Goose ID lie in separating subspecies and distinguishing juveniles from the closely related Pink-footed and bean geese, both very rare visitors to North America, so these are not everyday problems. However, watch out for separating White-fronts from the slew of domestic Graylag-type geese, which are all over city parks and barnyards!

Goslings are variable, but generally green-yellow in coloration with grayish eyestripes that can look like a mask on darker individuals. Juvenile plumage begins to emerge at three weeks old, and young they are fully feathered and flying by about 6 weeks. Juveniles are an even, plain gray-brown, lacking black splotches on the belly and white border at the base the bill in the early fall. The birds develop their splotches and the white around the bill base at variable rates, from September through the winter. The bill also starts a dull yellow, later becoming pink. First-years replace juvenile body feathers throughout their first winter and spring, acquiring some white behind the bill and limited black belly-speckling. In the winter, look for mottled appearance on the breast and belly, a mix of juvenile feathers that are becoming worn and faded, contrasting with fresh, rounded adult-like plumage. Their bills are orangish at least through October, becoming more pink by the winter. Adults of each sex are similar, although males are larger with darker bellies than females on average. Breeding adults undergo a complete wing molt from July to mid-August on the breeding grounds. They often shed their flight feathers 2-4 weeks after their goslings hatch and are flightless for 20-30 days. Pairs stagger their wing molt, males usually starting first, but it varies among pairs.

Adults complete their body molt in the fall. Tail molt is variable and in the fall, some replace their tail, others have 2-5 worn tail feathers. This plumage is held until the next July or August. Nonbreeders and unsuccessful adults typically molt at molting areas from June to September, and may still be completing body molt in October.

Similar Species: White-fronts are not likely to be confused with other regularly occurring species. Domestic varieties of Graylags and other barnyard geese are frequently misidentified as White-fronted Geese. Beware! Separating Greater White-fronts from very rare visitors to North America can be more challenging. For our coverage on the separation from these rare geese, see the next few species accounts as ll as the treatment of geese on pp. 58-59 for Pink-footed, Graylag, and Lesser White-fronted Geese, as well as the Taiga and Tundra Bean Geese.

Also consider that mottled-looking hybrids of White-front/Canadas, as well as White-front/Snows, have been occasionally reported.

Sex ratio: With males at 51-52%, they slightly outnumber females.

GEOGRAPHIC VARIATION

The names and number of subspecies is in contention. Four to six subspecies have been recognized, of which three to four breed in North America. There is significant geographic variation and clusters have formed. Overlaps and clinal changes are found between some populations. While subspecific identification is sometimes straightforward, many individuals present a more significant challenge than is commonly appreciated or suggested by other references. Lone birds, in particular, are often very difficult to identify to subspecies with accuracy and confidence.

Subspecific naming and field identification is unclear with the populations breeding in Alaska (not including those in the Cook Inlet) and the Canadian Arctic—these are *gambelli* and *frontalis*. Some authorities have renamed the western Alaskan population of *A. a. frontalis* to *A. a. sponsa*. *Gambelli* and *frontalis/sponsa* separate out in the breeding and wintering grounds, but they look very similar and are not readily distinguishable in the field. In the future, *frontalis/sponsa* and *gambelli* may be lumped as one subspecies. Their large variation in appearance, irrespective of subspecies, is in part clinal and mostly in response to the environment they live in. Some nest in taiga, most on the tundra, ranging from western Alaska to eastern Canada, so variation is to be expected. Just like in white-cheeked geese, much work needs to be done before we have a much better understanding of North American Greater White-fronted Geese.

A. a. gambelli, Tundra White-fronted Goose, is the most widespread subspecies in North America that breeds from west and northwest Alaska across northwestern Canada. They migrate via the Central Flyway to wintering grounds primarily in Texas and northern Mexico. They average larger than *frontalis*, but there is significant overlap. Interestingly, birds breeding in places such as Barrow, Alaska, winter in the Gulf Coast region. They cross paths on migration with more easterly breeding birds that winter west of the Rockies.

A. a. frontalis, sometimes labelled *A. a. sponsa*, Pacific White-fronted Goose, winters in western North America and averages the smallest and palest of the subspecies. It overlaps with *gambelli* in appearance, and separating them in the field by appearance is typically not possible. *A. a. frontalis* is a mostly tundra breeder, stretching between northwest Alaska and Arctic Canada. They travel via the Pacific or Central Flyway, staging in southern Saskatchewan, continuing on to winter in California and western Mexico.

A. a. elgasi, Tule Goose, is a distinct subspecies that breeds just south of the Alaska Range and north of Cook Inlet in Alaska, surprisingly among trees, a site only discovered in the late 1970s. They will stage the Columbia Basin of Oregon and Washington and the Summer Lake Basin of Oregon and winter in the marshes of the San Joaquin-Sacramento River Delta and Sacramento Valley. Look for them in pairs or family groups on ponds with lot of tules (rushes) and willows. Tule Goose is larger and big-headed, with a longer bill, longer and darker neck, thicker legs, and broader-wings than White-fronts from other parts of Alaska and the Canadian Arctic. They stand tall with a protruding sternum. The dark head can really accentuate the white face. The dark head extends down the neck and creates a very strong contrast with the pale underparts. They also average less extensive black on the bellies than other White-fronts; the underlying belly color is pale, contrasting with browner sides. Tule Goose also has darker feathers around the white patch behind the bill and occasionally shows a yellow-orange eyering. These unique characteristics have lead some authorities to consider full-species status for taxa. The Tule Goose population numbers an estimated 7,500.

A. a. flavirostris, Greenland White-fronted Goose, breeds in western Greenland on glacial plains and alpine bogs on plateaus, and this subspecies normally winters in Ireland and northwest Britain. It is occasionally found in the Atlantic Flyway. Greenland birds have a distinctly longer, orange-colored bill. Their heads and necks are larger and bulky with a darker and more uniform brown. They appear to be a more robust bird. In the East, where both birds from the Canadian Arctic and Greenland can occur, one must use caution when identifying to subspecies This is particularly true for first-years, because *gambelli* often appear to have orange-colored bills. Greenland birds also have narrower white border on the side feathers, less conspicuous pale tips on the greater and median coverts, and narrower edging on the tertials. Juveniles are remarkably gray with dark feathering at the base of the bill and broad white tips to the greater coverts. Genetic studies suggest that *flavirsotris* may be genetically distinct enough to warrant separate species status from American and Canadian birds. Their population estimate is 33,000.

A. a. albifrons, European White-fronted Goose, is the Eurasian subspecies, breeding on the tundra in Russia from the Kanin Peninsula to the Taimyr Peninsula. Winters in northeast Europe. It has not been recorded in North America, although it is likely to have occurred undetected. It is smaller and paler-headed then *A. a. flavirostris* and *fron-*

talis with a pinkish bill. The base color to the breast and belly is grayer than North American birds. The population estimate is 1.3 million.

A. a. albicans, Asian White-fronted Goose, is found in the Eastern Palearctic. It breeds on the tundra in Siberia between the Khatanga River and Bering Strait and winters in southwest Asia. It is often considered to be part of *frontalis*. This questionable subspecies, too, has not been recorded in North America. The population estimate is 80,000.

SOUNDS

The high-pitched, laugh-like flight call is distinctive and familiar to those who often encounter these geese. (Calls of Tule White-fronted Geese are said to be coarser and harsher.) The call is 2-3 syllables, *nil-LI-IK*. The notes are rising with an accent on the last syllable. In a flock, the voice of an individual can ring out, loud and clear. During aggressive encounters these gees give low, murmuring, *gang-gang*, used as a threat and in triumph ceremony. The alarm call is a loud mew. Occasionally given in duet is a *gig-gog*. A series of vocalizations are given during the triumph ceremony when greeting family members. Also, they will emit a typical goose-like honk.

YEAR IN THE LIFE

Greater White-fronted Goose breeds almost across the entire Arctic region. In North America, across the year they will span from the northern tip of Alaska to central Mexico. With considerable geographic variation in the populations they have segregated migration, breeding, and wintering areas, which makes for some interesting life history strategies.

They concentrate in winter along the Central and Pacific Flyways. Large numbers are found in Texas and the central plateau of Mexico, and California's Central Valley, where they often gather in agricultural areas. There are an increasing number of individuals found in eastern North America. Prior to 1980 there were no reports from Atlantic Canada; they were mostly from the Hudson-Delaware region (DE, PA, NJ, NY). They are now annual in the Atlantic Providences and Eastern Seaboard. A number of these sighting are of birds from the Greenland population. As one would predict, the vast majority of these sightings are from winter and spring.

Once spring hits, White-fronts take off to their breeding grounds. White-fronts nest in a range of habitats from tundra to forested regions in taiga, hummock marshes, and spruce bogs. Unlike other arctic-nesting geese, Specs pairs are solitary or dispersed breeders. The female selects a nest site on the ground, normally in areas with little surrounding vegetation.

Pairs stick together year after year to defend their nest sites and broods from intruders. They breed when they are two years old, so congregations of one year-old nonbreeders and failed breeders gather to molt their wing feathers. Breeding adults molt while they are still attending their brood. Usually the pair staggers their wing molt so both members of the pair are not flightless at the exactly same time. About the time adults are able to fly again, the young are ready to fledge by about 6 weeks. Then the family departs together on fall migration.

White-fronts are the first of Arctic breeders to head south in the fall. Thousands can be seen at staging areas in Alberta and Saskatchewan in late September. The family group remains together until the following breeding season. Some offspring will stay with parents for multiple years, longer than any other geese.

DIET AND FEEDING BEHAVIOR

Greater White-fronted Geese Greater are basically vegetarians, grazers of wetland and agricultural grasses. Most of the year (summer, spring, and fall), they will feed on grasses, berries, and sedges, selecting a "fresher" or more tender menu during the breeding season. Specs depend heavily during parts of migration and in winter on agricultural foods. Rice, in particular, and waste grains are favorites. The Tule subspecies, true to its name, often prefers to feed on underwater tubers of tule (*Scirpus robustus*) in winter, while the other White-fronts forage in open grassy fields or in rice. Greater White-fronted Geese are often observed walking head-down, picking at the ground. When feeding in the water, they will up-end or simply submerge their heads.

NESTING

Site: On the ground near water. On the tundra, may be in short vegetation, sometimes on islands in rivers, in spruce bogs, taiga transition zones. In interior forested areas, often near willow or spruce. Typically nest singly or in loose aggregations, but not colonially.

Nest description: A shallow scrape with a lining of local vegetation, down, and, occasionally, feathers. About 7 inches in inside diameter, 15 inches in outside diameter, and 3 inches in depth.

Clutch size: Usually 5-6, sometimes 4-7

Egg description: Elliptical to subelliptical. Creamy-white and smooth. 79 × 52mm

Incubation duration: 22-27 days.

Brood parasitism: Uncommon, sometimes by Emperor Geese.

HUNTING

Specklebllies decoy like a charm, particularly the clear-bellies (immatures). This makes them popular geese to hunt, particularly given the challenges of hunting white geese. Fewer decoys are needed, perhaps just a dozen. In fact, many hunters in the South use only four or fewer. A high-pitched call often helps. Their meat is considered by many to be superior in taste to that of Canada and Snow Geese.

The harvest has paralleled their population growth. In the U.S., the annual average in the 1960s was 134,000; in the 1990s it was 225,000. In the U.S. over two years

(2013 and 2014), the average is almost 300,000 birds. In Canada, while the harvest numbers in early 2000s was 73,000 birds, the 20013 and 2014 average is at 81,300.

Texas and Louisiana top the charts as popular hunting locations, with the greatest harvest of Specklebellies in the U.S. There is also quality Speck hunting in Arkansas and California's Central Valley. Others are harvested migrating through Alberta and Saskatchewan in late September and early October.

POPULATION AND CONSERVATION
The average North American population of Greater White-fronted Goose has been growing and is estimated at slightly over 1,180,000 birds, based on 2002-2011 numbers. Still, populations have fluctuated since the early 1950s; some subspecies are declining. Specks may have developed a dependence on agricultural grains. At the same time, changes in agricultural practices (e.g., more soy which is of poor nutritional value) and more efficient harvest (reducing the waste remaining) could present problems.

In poor breeding years, when fewer juveniles are present more adults are taken by hunters on the wintering grounds. If this persists for consecutive years, it can take a toll on the population of these long-lived adults.

The Tule Goose population is about 7,500. The Pacific breeding population, those nesting on the Yukon-Kuskokwim Delta in Alaska and wintering in the Central Valley, declined in the 1970s and 1980s. They are recovering now, estimated at about 515,000. This population increased an average of 6% per year from 1999-2008. The mid-continent population, nesting from central and northwestern Alaska to the central Arctic and Foxe Basin, is counted on a fall survey in Alberta and Saskatchewan. It totaled 764,000 birds in 2007. Numbers reported from this survey from 1998-2007 has declined an average of 5% per year. The current estimate is about 660,000.

LESSER WHITE-FRONTED GOOSE
Anser erythropus LWFG

Plates Page 59

OTHER COMMON OR REGIONAL NAMES:
None used in North America

MEASUREMENTS
Length: Male – 23.7-25in, av 24.2 inches (61.5 cm); Female – 22.7-24in, av 23.8 in (60.5 cm)
Wing: Male – av 14.9 in (37.9 cm); Female – av 14.7 in (37.4 cm)
Weight: Male – av 4.68 lbs (2125 g); Female – av 3.91 lbs (1775 g)
Bill: Male – av 31.5 mm; Female – av 30.0 mm

FIRST IMPRESSIONS AND SIMILAR SPECIES
A petite version of a Greater White-fronted Goose with a swollen yellow eyering and more extensive white on the face, this goose is extremely rare in North America. Lesser White-fronts are dark grayish-brown with a large white slash on the forehead, pink bill and orange legs. A yellow eyering is distinct if you are close enough to see it. A Lesser White-front will tend to have fewer irregular dark blotches on belly than a Greater White-front. Slightly darker on back and wings, lacking the silvery wing coverts of Greater White-front. Size and shape: A dainty, round goose that is long-winged, with wing tips often extending past the tail, small head, and a short neck. Similar in size to Brant or Ross's Goose. The pink triangular bill is clearly small and short. Flight: Small rounded body, with short neck, compact overall. Wingbeats are faster and even a bit more maneuverable than Greater White-fronts.

Similar Species: Greater White-fronted Goose is the most similar species. Lesser White-fronts are smaller, shorter-necked, stepper forehead, with a smaller head and bill than Greater White-fronted Goose. The white on the forehead extends higher than it does on a Greater.

Sex ratio: Presumed to be equal.

BACKGROUND AND TIPS
There is one accepted spring record from Alaska, on Attu (1994). A reoccurrence may be unlikely, but it seems possible on the edges of Alaska (e.g., Attu, Adak, and St. Lawrence Island). One might appear again in early summer as geese are moving back toward their breeding grounds. There are more birds in the Asian population, so one is more likely to appear in the West than in the East. These high-latitude breeders are long distance migrants, often traveling with Greater White-fronts and Barnacle Geese. Reports from the East may involve escapes. They are fairly common in captivity.

Lesser White-front is a globally threatened species whose numbers decreased dramatically since the 1950s and have not recovered well, a problem exacerbated by the fragmentation of its breeding range.

SOUNDS
Yelping flight call, an *ay-ay-ay*, is higher-pitched and squeakier than the vocalization of Greater White-fronts.

DIET AND FEEDING BEHAVIOR
During winter and on migration – seasons when it might appear in North America – this goose feeds on open short grasslands, particularly by seashore pastures and farmland. They will graze by rapid movements (faster than

Greater White-fronts) and will forage in shallow water. They are herbivorous, feeding on shoots, leaves, and stems of grasses of aquatic and terrestrial plants, as well as roots. In winter they will also feed on available agricultural grains.

GRAYLAG GOOSE
Anser anser GRGO

Plates Page 59

OTHER COMMON OR REGIONAL NAMES
Graylag
(Québec: oie cendrée)

MEASUREMENTS
Length: Male – 35 in (88 cm); Female – 29 in (74 cm)
Wing: Male – 18.4 in (46.8 cm); Female – av 17.7 in (44.9 cm)
Weight: Male – av 7.83 lbs (3550 g); Female – av 6.61 lbs (2950 g)
Bill: Male – av 63.5 mm; Female – av 62.0 mm

FIRST IMPRESSIONS
The domestic variety of Graylags are scattered throughout parks, farm ponds and zoos in the Americas, but the wild Graylag from Eurasia is extremely rare in North America.

Graylag is a very hefty, thick-necked, grayish-brown goose with darker head and paler breast with slight black speckling on the belly. The dark grooves along the neck are often obvious. Within a pair, males are larger than females. The huge, triangular, pink-to-orangey bill, without any markings, is distinctive. Size and shape: Rotund, bulky geese that are the largest of the Anser geese. They have a deep bill, big head, long thick neck, chunky body—heaviest in the rear. Rear end rides high in the water. Flight: Graylag is a big-bodied bird, even wild ones have robust undercarriage, with broad, blunt wings. Flight can appear slow and ponderous. The head is large and rounded with a hefty bill. The neck appears almost pinched-in behind the large head and bill. Look for silvery wings with light blue-gray upperwing coverts. Graylag also is distinctively two-toned in the underwing, with pale gray underwing coverts, contrasting with dark flight feathers. Wingbeats are slow and heavy.

Similar species: In North America, wild Graylags are most likely confused with the domestic variety and with Greater White-fronted Geese. Domestic Graylags frequently hybridizes with Canada Goose, producing strange plumages that are often confused with White-fronted Goose. But it is separating domesticated Graylags with a wild bird that will be the most obvious problem. If a wild Graylag is very large, then a domesticated Graylag is simply huge, big-bellied and large-breasted.

Sex ratio: assumed to be equal.

BACKGROUND AND TIPS
There are only a handful of convincing reports from easternmost Canada and New England.

Graylags are breeders in northern and eastern Europe. They have recently started to show up in Greenland and are a summer resident in Iceland, with populations at of about 40,000 pairs. Birds from Iceland are relatively short-distance migrants (mostly wintering in Scotland). Graylags are among the latest fall migrants, named because they "lag" behind other species. Many populations are migratory, although some Scottish breeders and those in northwestern Europe are mainly resident.

Hopes for finding a Graylag in North America may depend on location, timing, and association. As for location, the eastern seaboard from Newfoundland to the Chesapeake Bay may be likely. Timing suggests late fall or wintering birds, perhaps early spring but not summer. Association may be highly convincing, such as in flocks of geese coming from Greenland. For example, check groups of Greenland Greater White-fronts (*Anser albifrons flavirostris*) in the winter months. Candidate Graylags could also accompany neck-banded geese that can be tracked back to their points of origin.

There are healthy populations of Graylags in many parts of their range; their overall numbers are increasing. The population estimate is 1.0-1.1 million.

SOUNDS
Graylag Goose gives a low, nasal, and rough cackle, a varied repertoire. Some calls shrill, others deep, but not unlike that of domestic geese.

DIET AND FEEDING BEHAVIOR
Graylag Geese feed on plant items such as grass and leaves, roots, stems, and shoots, whether in water or ashore. During winter, they will also graze to take grain. They will up-end in water, to pull up submerged aquatic vegetation and will probe in soft mud, to reach plant roots.

TAIGA BEAN GOOSE
Anser fabalis TABG

Plates Page 59

OTHER COMMON OR REGIONAL NAMES
None used in North America

MEASUREMENTS
Length: Male – 34 in (87 cm); Female – 29 in (73 cm)
Wing: Male – 19 in (48.6 cm); Female – 18.1 in (46.1 cm)
Weight: Male – av 7.1 lbs (3198 g); Female – av 6.3 lbs (2843 g)
Bill: Male – av 63 mm, Female – av 60 mm

Please see the Tundra Bean Goose account for more details.

TUNDRA BEAN GOOSE
Anser serrirostris TUBG

Plates Page 59

OTHER COMMON OR REGIONAL NAMES
None used in North America

MEASUREMENTS
Length: Male – 32 in (82 cm); Female – 29 in (73 cm)
Wing: Male – 18.5 in (46.9 cm); Female – 17.6 in (44.7 cm)
Weight: Male – 5.9 lbs (2690 g); Female – 4.8 lbs (2220 g)
Bill: Male – av 66 mm; Female – av 63 mm

FIRST IMPRESSIONS AND SIMILAR SPECIES
These two Eurasian species are very rare visitors to North America. They are closely related, poorly understood, very similar but variable, and based on the lack of current knowledge, are best treated together.

They are generally beefy dark brown geese with pale breasts, orange legs, and dark gray bills with small orange-yellow bands before the tips. These are the basics, and it can be extremely challenging to separate the two bean geese. Many of the differences are clinal, and these two taxa may be relumped in the future.

Adults of both species have dark grayish-brown heads with contrasting grayer bodies. They have well-defined ribbing on the neck, not unlike some other gray geese, and an even gray body. Their back feathers are broad, square-tipped with pale tips. They have a bold white line bordering the feathers on the side that rest over the wing coverts, giving the look of a white line down the side of the body. Size and shape: Bean geese are long-billed and long-necked relative to other geese. They also have a broad-based and heavy bill with an unusually thick lower mandible. There is significant variation in the bill (size, shape and pattern) and overall body size within bean geese. When it comes to separating Taiga and Tundra Bean Goose, consider these points: Taiga is the Bean Goose with the heavy wedge-shaped bill. It is 10-15% larger, longer-billed, with a more pointed flat head and longer neck than Tundra. It has an upright stance and longer legs than Tundra. Some *middendorffi*, the E Asian race of Taiga Bean Goose, are strikingly long-billed and flat-headed. A bean goose with features that include a rounded head, short and thick neck and not particularly long-looking bill all point toward Tundra Bean Goose. Some are intermediate and may be best left unidentified. Flight: Large, heavy-bodied geese with broad wings. The upperwing is uniform in coloration; it does not contrast with the forewing. The underwing is all dark, which contrasts with unspotted pale gray-brown belly. Wingbeats are slow and loose.

Similar species: In North America, the bean geese are most similar to Greater White-fronted Goose. Bean geese lack the dark splotches on the belly of an adult White-fronted Goose. White-fronted Goose has a more slender bill that is uniform in color, whereas bean geese have an orangey band across their otherwise dark bills. Both Taiga and Tundra Bean Geese can have a hint of white showing at the base of the bill, suggesting Greater White-front (but first-year White-fronts average smaller and have mostly pink or orange bills).

Pink-footed Goose is also extremely rare in North America. It can be separated from bean geese by the Pink-footed Goose's pink legs and pink band across the top of the bill as well as grayer underparts. Bean geese have orange legs and orange in the bill.

Taiga and Tundra Bean Geese can be almost impossible to separate. A larger, longer neck, flatter head and longer-billed look to bean goose all point to Taiga Bean Goose. Related to the long, sloped bill, Taiga has little or no "grinning patch" where the mandibles meet. Tundra is generally smaller with a shorter neck, rounded head, and is not especially long-billed. Tundra has more restrictive orange on the bill (the outer third in Tundra, but extending back well past the midpoint in Taiga). It also has a "grinning patch" on the bill.

Sex ratio: assumed to be equal.

BACKGROUND AND TIPS
Split by the AOU (now AOS) in 2007 from Bean Goose into Taiga Bean-Goose and Tundra Bean-Goose. Some prefer to treat Bean Goose as a single species. (We use the names Taiga Bean Goose and Tundra Bean Goose.)

Very rare visitors to North America, these Eurasian geese are most likely to be found associating in large flocks of White-fronts, Cacklings, or Canadas. With luck, either goose might be found in spring, or perhaps fall, in the outer Aleutians (Shemya, Attu, or Adak might do the trick), the Pribilof Islands, or St. Lawrence Island. Exceptional elsewhere.

Taiga Bean Goose breeds in swamps and lakes of northern forested regions in dense coniferous forests or birch scrub across Norway, Sweden, Finland and Russia east to eastern Siberia. They winter in Great Britain, Europe, the Middle East, and southern Asia to eastern China and Japan. Taiga Bean Geese are very rare away from their main wintering sites.

Tundra Bean Goose breeds in the tundra zone of Siberia. They winter in open country, marshes, coastal wetlands, and agricultural fields of northern Europe and Russia, Turkestan, China and Japan.

Taiga Bean Goose includes the formerly recognized subspecies *A. f. fabalis, johanseni,* and *middendorffii*. There is clinal increase in size from east to west. *A. f. fabalis* has a mostly orange bill, *middendorffi* is larger and darker billed. *A.f. johanseni* is intermediate in size between the other two and darker-billed.

Some authorities regard Tundra as monotypic. Others consider two subspecies: *A.s. serrirostris* and *A.s. rossicus*. Size increase in clinal from east to west, from the smaller *rossicus* to larger *serrirostris*.

The bean geese have distinct wintering groups and they overlap on the breeding grounds, but without a large zone of overlap due to their different habitat preferences between the forest and the tundra. Both species show clinal variation in size, bill color, and body tone. (This is a similar to what we see in Greater White-fronted Goose.)

The entire bean goose population is estimate at 830,000-850,000. While their population overall is declining, some populations appear to be stable.

SOUNDS
For both species, listen for their nasal cackle, a two-note *gang gang* with emphasis on the second syllable. They are not as vocal as other *Anser*. Taiga is lower-pitched than Tundra.

DIET AND FEEDING BEHAVIOR
Bean geese are known vegetarians, mainly grazing on moist grasslands, agricultural field, and livestock pastures and feeding while wading in shallow waters in winter. On their breeding ground they will feed on fresh green parts of plants, flowers, and fruits, seeds, and rootstocks. In is unclear, but Taiga Bean Geese may prefer shallow lakes and freshwater marshes and mudflats for winter feeding, with Tundra Bean Geese having a preference for grasses, cereal grains, and other crops for winter feeding.

POPULATION AND CONSERVATION
In the past, bean geese have declined due to many threts: hunting, habitat loss, degradation of habitat from oil pollution, peat-extraction, decreased grazing and mowing of meadow (causes too much scrubby overgrowth for their liking), and pesticide poisoning on agricultural land.

PINK-FOOTED GOOSE
Anser brachyrhynchus PFGP

Plates Page 58

OTHER COMMON OR REGIONAL NAMES
(Québec: oie à bec court)

MEASUREMENTS
Length: Male – 27.5 in (70 cm); Female – 25.5 in (65 cm)
Wing: Male – av 17.5 in (44.5 cm); Female – av 16.5 in (42.0 cm)
Weight: Male – av 5.73 lbs (2600 g); Female – av 5.40 lbs (2450 g)
Bill: Male – av 47 mm; Female – av 43 mm

FIRST IMPRESSIONS AND SIMILAR SPECIES-
Pink-footed Geese will very rarely, wander from Greenland or Iceland and end up grazing with flocks of Canada Geese on the East Coast.

Look for darker geese with dark brown heads, dark brown necks with grooved markings, frosty blue-gray backs, and distinctly paler buffy breasts, contrasting with the head color. The smallish bill is dark at the base with a pinkish band near the tip. Legs are always pink. Size and shape: A medium-sized goose, similar in size to White-fronted, though slightly smaller. Thick bill, relatively short neck, and body also differentiate it from a White-front. Flight: Small, rounded head and compact body. Upperwings are silvery, appearing gray overall, even though they look much browner on land. Underwings are dark. There is a white band almost all the way around the rump and a broad white tip to the tail.

Similar species: Most easily confused with bean geese (even rarer) or Greater White-fronted Goose in North America. The pink legs are distinct, a helpful mark when geese are grazing or at close distance, although judging color can be difficult with far-off birds. Adult Greater White-fronted Goose has a larger pinkish-orange bill, white on the forehead and black markings on the belly and orange legs, all features not exhibited in Pink-footed. In comparison with bean geese, Pink-footed has a slightly shorter neck and smaller head; it is more compact overall. The overall color is a bit lighter with paler back and forewings. Pink-footed has more white on tail than bean geese.

Sex ratio: assumed to be equal

BACKGROUND AND TIPS
Sightings of this rare visitor are increasing in the northeast, reflecting a dramatic population increase in Greenland, Iceland, and Svalbard (Norway). Birds reaching Atlantic Canada or the Northeast U.S. in winter are probably coming from the first two locations, where breeding populations increased from about 10,000 pairs at the end of the 1980s, to about 135,000 pairs by 2005. Currently, hunting in season is popular in Iceland and has not done any damage to the growing population.

SOUNDS
Particularly vocal in flight, giving high-pitched honks as they travel. The typical *ung-ungk* of this species, or its distinctive *ang-ang-WINK-WINK*, are not as high-pitched or like the friendly rolling laugh of White-fronted.

DIET AND FEEDING BEHAVIOR
Pink-footed Geese are herbivorous but opportunistic when foraging. They feed mainly by grazing on land (often farmlands and grasslands in winter), but will feed while floating on water and, occasionally, by up-ending for SAV. On land, they will probe soft mud for stems and roots. In their wintering areas in Europe, Pink-footed Geese spend most of their time foraging on grasses as well as grain and other leftover crops on agricultural farmlands.

COMMON SHELDUCK
Tadorna tadorna COMS

Plates Page 59

OTHER COMMON OR REGIONAL NAMES
Shelduck

MEASUREMENTS
Length: Male – 28 in (71 cm); Female – 25 in (63 cm)
Wing: Male – av 13 in (33cm); Female – av 11.8 in (30 cm)
Weight: Male – av 2.70 lbs (1225 g)
         Female – av 2.20 lbs (1000 g)
Bill: Male – av 56.0 mm; Female – av 49.0 mm

FIRST IMPRESSIONS AND SIMILAR SPECIES-
This very rare visitor – or escapee from aviculturists – is a handsome and striking waterfowl, looking like a slim goose or a longish duck! Its status in North America is confounded by also being a popular bird in captivity.

Adults are boldly-patterned with an almost gaudy appearance, complete with a bright pinkish-red bill, dark green head, and largely white body with a broad chestnut band across the breast and a thick black line down the belly. Males have reddish-pink knobs on top their bills, which is lacking or is smaller in females. Females also have duller colored bills, not as crisp of plumage and are smaller than males. First-years lack dark markings on the breast and belly and have white around the base of the bill. Size and shape: This is a large-bodied, goose-like duck, bigger than Mallard about the same size as a Brant. Bill curves up at tip, big head on a long neck. Flight: Looks basically black and white, with lots of white on the body (breast, belly, neck and underwing) and a dark head. Upperwing coverts are white and flight feathers black. Chestnut band across the breast and dark stripe down the middle of the belly is present on adults. Steady, relaxed wingbeats, almost goose-like. Often holds head high, but sometimes holds it down, like a Red-throated Loon, giving a hunchback look. Wings are relatively long and narrow. Square tail. Shape is almost reminiscent of Northern Pintail with its long neck and sweptback wings.

Similar species: Common Shelduck, long-necked with bold color patterns, is very distinct. A male Northern Shoveler has a vaguely similar color pattern, but, among other things, a Northern Shoveler lacks the white belly and sides of shelduck. And Northern Shoveler has a very different shaped and colored bill: large spatulate and never deep reddish-pink!

Sex ratio: assumed to be equal.

BACKGROUND AND TIPS
Common Shelduck breeds in northwestern Europe; there also are local populations around the Mediterranean and Black Sea, stretching east to China. Numbers have increased substantially in Iceland since the first breeding in 1990, from a few pairs to a few hundred. This mirrors an increase in reports on our East Coast. Most Icelandic Common Shelducks are thought to be migrants, but their wintering areas are unknown.

Many Common Shelducks found in North America for years have been presumed to be escapees from aviculturists, but surely some wild birds may have made it here on their own. This may be true, particularly for locations that are coastal estuaries with tidal mudflats, the habitat they frequent in Europe. Common Shelducks could show up anywhere on the eastern seaboard from Newfoundland to Maryland. There are almost 50 records for this region. Of these, about a third have been from Quebec. A pattern of occurrence is emerging, with early August to December birds being the most likely candidates for valid individuals.

The global population estimate is 580,000-710,000.

SOUNDS
Males give a variety of breathy whistles. Females give a series of short raspy quacks. Sometimes they start slowly and speed up into a chatter. These can sound like a series of belly-laughs with a sarcastic ring.

DIET AND FEEDING BEHAVIOR
Common Shelduck feed in shallow water (usually salt or brackish), wet mud, grassy shores, and less often on dryer inland areas (including agricultural fields). They wade in shallow water or dabble at surface mud, while moving their heads from side to side. They also up-end to feed on salt-water mollusks, other aquatic invertebrates (e.g., crustaceans, insects, and worms), small fish, and plant matter (e.g. algae, seeds, and agricultural grain).

RUDDY SHELDUCK
Tadorna ferruginea RUSH

Plates Page 59

OTHER COMMON OR REGIONAL NAMES
Brahminy duck (a common name from India, also used in the trade)
(Québec: tadorne casarca)

MEASUREMENTS
Length: Male – 25.5 in (65 cm); Female – 24 in, (61 cm)
Wing: Male – av 14.5 in (36.9 cm); Female – av 13.6 in (34.5 cm)
Weight: Male – av 3.15 lbs (1430 g); Female – av 2.67 lbs (1213 g)
Bill: Male – av 46mm; Female – av 40mm

FIRST IMPRESSIONS AND SIMILAR SPECIES-
Ruddy Shelducks are popular in captivity, and those seen in North America are presumed to be escapees from collections. But natural vagrancy from the Old World is not inconceivable, and has been presumed to have already happened!

The color of this large waterfowl is mostly an orange-brown, with a buffier head. The relatively small bill is black. In the breeding season, the male has a blackish ring around his neck, a ring that is lost or indistinct in winter. The female, without the ring, has a slightly more distinctive white face-pattern from the chin to above and behind the eye. Size and shape: This is a large-bodied, almost goose-like, duck with fairly long neck and legs. Flight: Long and somewhat narrow wings. The rump, tail, and flight feathers are black, and the inner-forewings (both above and below) are white with black flight feathers. The two-toned wings are obvious in flight. The black, examined closely, has a greenish gloss.

Similar species: Ruddy Shelduck is distinctive. It might be confused at long-range with Egyptian Goose, especially in flight. (Both species are a pale brown with large white forewing-patches.) Both species are popular in captivity, and the Egyptian Goose has an established wild population in Florida and can be found elsewhere. Cape Shelduck, another regular escapee, is gray-headed but otherwise very similar.

Sex ratio: assumed to be equal.

BACKGROUND AND TIPS
Ruddy Shelduck has a main breeding area from southeast Europe and southern Russia, across central Asia to Mongolia and western China.

Observers in Atlantic Canada and in the northeastern U.S., will want to be on the alert for this species. While Ruddy Shelduck is regularly found in captivity, interesting individuals and small groups have been observed in a number of states and provinces. Among these, six birds at remote Southampton Island, Nunavut, in late July 2000, during a big westerly displacement in Europe, proved highly convincing. Presumably, the same flock was seen passing through Cape May that same August. (In western Europe, the occurrence of Ruddy Shelducks has also been contentious, with escapees from aviculturists complicating matters.) Future patterns would need to be tracked, especially observations in late summer, corresponding to molt-migration and post-breeding dispersal, particularly in drought conditions.

Numbers have been uneven throughout the Ruddy Shelduck range. Western populations are in general decline. The global population is estimated at c. 170-000 – 220,000.

SOUNDS
A series of loud, nasal honking notes, given on the ground or in the air. Listen for a rolling *aakh*, given repeatedly. The call can be often repeated before taking wing. Male said to favor an *O* sound, while the female gives a louder, slightly deeper, and harsher *A* sound.

DIET AND FEEDING BEHAVIOR
Ruddy Shelducks feed, often at night or during twilight hours, by grazing like geese, wading in shallow water (usually fresh, but also brackish), dabbling at the muddy surface, and up-ending in shallow water. They feed on a diet of green shoots and the seeds of terrestrial vegetation, agricultural grains, and a variety of aquatic invertebrates (e.g., crustaceans, insects, and worms), and small fish.

EMPEROR GOOSE
Anser canagicus EMGO

Plates Page 60

OTHER COMMON OR REGIONAL NAMES
Emperor, beach goose, emp
(Arctic: nacaullek [YK], nazaujik [NS], mitilugruaq [NS, NWS])

MEASUREMENTS
Length: Male – 26-28 in, av 27 in (68.8 cm) Female – 26-28 in, av 26.8 in (68.1 cm)
Wing: Male – av 15.3 in (39.0 cm); Female – av 14.5 in (36.8 cm)
Weight: Male – av 6.12 lbs (2776 g); Female – av 6.25 lbs (2835 g)
Bill: Male – av 44.5 mm; Female – av 37.5 mm

FIRST IMPRESSIONS
Emperor Geese are exceedingly handsome geese with stately white heads, black throats, and frosted gray bodies. The body appears silvery-gray with upperpart barred. These hardy sea geese have a very limited range in tidal areas around the Bering Sea. Flocks are often peppered with dark sooty juveniles until late in the winter, birds which look very adult-like by March with dusky smudging on the face. Outside of their normal range, one or two will mix in with flocks of white-cheeked and white geese. Size and shape: A small and stocky goose with a petite bill. Its fairly short wings do not reach the tip of the tail. Flight: This is a small goose with a short neck, rotund body and relatively broad wings. Aloft, it gives a gray overall impression with white head and white tail, with gray in between, accentuated by black lines along the trailing edge of the wings (formed by mostly black primaries and secondaries). This goose is paler overall than you may otherwise expect at a distance. They often fly in pairs or small groups, except during fall migration when flocks can number in the thousands. They often cruise just above the water, with wingbeats that are quick, shallow, and consistent.

ID: IN DEPTH AND SIMILAR SPECIES
Emperor Geese only have a few different looks: adult, juvenile, or somewhere in between. So, they are fairly easy to age. Males have slightly larger bills, which is a good indication of sex when comparing a mated pair.

Goslings are pearly gray and white, but darkest about the eye. Look for their short wide black bill and black legs. Juvenile plumage is usually fully grown at about 7 weeks old. It is gray overall, especially dark about the head, with a generally scaly appearance. Juveniles have dusky bills and grayish-yellow legs. First-years replace juvenile plumage gradually, beginning on head and neck in early September, largely finishing October through mid-December at which point they look mostly like adults. Look for dusky smudging on the white head, particularly in front of the eye, which indicates a first-year bird. They often have a dark loral smudge through most of the winter. First-years also often have traces of juvenile plumage retained on the belly or elsewhere. They replace tail feathers in early October, finishing in winter. They retain smaller and duller juvenile wing feathers until summer wing molt.

Adults have prominent white heads in the winter, but on the breeding grounds their heads often turn a rusty orange from iron staining. Non-breeders and failed breeders initiate body and flight feather molt in mid-to-late June or early July, completing flight feather molt by late June or early August, body molt continues into late August or September. Successful breeders molt on breeding grounds, drop wing feathers 2-3 weeks after young hatch. They are flightless for 32-35 days, flying again in mid-August. Body molt initiated in mid to late July, finished by early October; it may continue into December. Some males start to wing molt just after the young hatch, completing the molt before their mates.

Similar species: Emperor Goose could be mistaken for dark morph Snow Goose. Emperor Goose, however, has a much smaller bill and black throat not seen in Blue Goose. Juvenile Emperor can be separated by juvenile Blue Goose by its smaller bill, more scaly appearance on the body.

Sex ratio: assumed to be equal.

YEAR IN THE LIFE
This elegant goose could have been named the "Bering Sea Goose" because its range is within coastal waters bordering the Bering Sea. They are locally common within their small range of southwest Alaska and coastal Russia. They are found in Russia from Anadyr to Bering Strait and along Chukotsk Peninsula to Kolyuchin Bay. Some winter on the Commander Islands, along southeast coast of Kamchatka. Their main wintering concentrations in the US are on the central and outer Aleutians. They are uncommon east to the Alaska Peninsula. Kodiak Island is one of the more accessible spots to view them in winter. From late October through April they are rare visitors to the Pacific Northwest and northern California. There are also records from Hawaii, Japan, and Wrangel Island, Russia.

Emperor Geese winter around rocky areas of coastal salt marshes and brackish lagoons.

In the spring, birds wintering in western Aleutians move east in March and early April to stage. Birds from throughout the Aleutians arrive in lagoons on the north side of Alaska Peninsula by mid-April. Mutual courtship displays – including triumph ceremonies – include lateral head movements and threat displays to rivals, and known to occur over the winter. Pairs return together each year on their largely uninhabited breeding grounds in Yukon-Kuskokwim Delta by mid-May, the Seward Peninsula and St. Lawrence Islands by late May-early June, and Russian breeding grounds by mid-June.

During the breeding season, grazes in marshy areas above tidal flats and even in drier tundra.

Adults undergo wing molt as the young are growing. The timing is such that both adults regain flight about the time the juveniles can fly. This is usually in early August, 50-60 days after the young hatch. Immatures, nonbreeders and failed breeders, molt earlier than adults, and they are already at sites en route to wintering grounds in mid- to-late August. Individuals undergo a northward molt-migration; there is a concentration on the n. Chukotsk Peninsula, Russia, with a few molting on St. Lawrence Island.

Beginning in late August or early September, family groups embark on the first leg of fall migration to staging areas on the Alaska Peninsula (e.g., Izembek Lagoon). They feed there through the fall, and by late November most have departed to winter in the western Aleutians. A few thousand head to Kodiak Island.

GEOGRAPHIC VARIATION
No subspecies are recognized.

SOUND
When in flocks, they frequently give high-pitched calls that are reminiscent of other small geese. Emperor Geese have two main vocalizations that are frequently given. In flight, they give a fast and hoarse *chidee chideedee*. If alarmed, they utter a deep, ringing *u-lugh, u-lugh*.

DIET AND FEEDING BEHAVIOR
With early arrival on the nesting grounds, Emperor Geese will feed on such vegetation as overwintering bulbs and plant roots and shoots. During the breeding season the geese may graze to consume arrowgrass, alkali grass, sedge, and even crowberries in drier areas. Winter diet is poorly known, but may consist of eelgrass, sea lettuce, grasses, and sedges, with a heavy reliance on intertidal invertebrates, mostlyu mussels and clams. Feeding is in shallow waters connected to the sea. They feed by dipping their head in water about one-foot deep or by walking through shallow water, mudflats, and sandy beaches (hence its nickname, "beach goose"), and feeding with only their bill in the water.

NESTING
Site: On the ground on coastal tundra, by ponds or lagoons, on coastal shores, or estuarine islands. They prefer sites farther inland than those chosen by Brant and Cackling Goose, near lines of driftwood debris that provide cover for incubating females, or even in low rolling hills.

Nest description: A hollow thickly lined with grass and plants with an inner lining of small feathers and down. About 8 inches in inside diameter, 15 inches in outside diameter, and 3 inches in depth.

Clutch size: Usually 5-6 eggs, sometimes 3-8.

Egg description: Elliptical to subelliptical. White to creamy white and smooth. 78 × 52mm.

Incubation duration: 24-25 days.

Brood parasitism: Common, typically parasitized by conspecifics, but occasionally by Cackling Goose, Greater White-fronted Goose, Brant, and Spectacled Eider.

HUNTING
In response a declining population of Emperor Geese, authorities in Alaska reduced, and then closed, Emperor Geese hunting in the mid-1980s. First, the bag limit was reduced from 6 to 2 in 1985; then, managers closed the regular hunting season in 1986; finally, subsistence hunting was closed in 1987. The importance of migratory birds to native peoples has been long recognized by authorities, and a reopening of subsistence hunting began in 2017, witha bag limit of one, since the population topped 80,000 birds. In the meantime, unauthorized subsistence take continues, with annual harvest estimates ranging from 1,200 to 4,500 geese and most taken in the spring.

POPULATION AND CONSERVATION
An estimated 90% of the world's population nests on the Yukon-Kuskokwim (Y-K) Delta in Alaska. The state's population declined by nearly two-thirds from 139,000 in 1964 to 42,000 in 1986. Subsequently, the population has increased slightly, to about 70,000, a 2002-2011 average, and has recently approached 86,000. The factors that caused the sharp decline and marginal recovery in remote Alaska are not well understood, but they include subsistence hunting and coastal oil pollution in wintering intertidal areas. While Emperor Geese numbers are increasing slowly, the population remains below the target number of 150,000. The International Union for the Conservation of Nature (IUCN) has classified Emperor Goose as Near Threatened and lists climate change as an additional threat to their population and states that it is expected to undergo a moderate population reduction in the future due to climate change.

BRANT
Branta bernicla BRAN

Plates Page 62

OTHER COMMON OR REGIONAL NAMES
Sea goose, brant goose, white-bellied brant, pale-bellied brant, Pacific brant, brent, wavie
(Arctic: neqlernaq [YK], niqliqnaq [NS], niblinbaq [NWS], nirliq, nigliknak , nechlernak [N])
(Québec: bernache cravant)
(Mexico: ganso de collar)

MEASUREMENTS
Length: Male – 22-26 in, av 24 in (61.0 cm); Female – 22-25 in, av 23 in (58.4 cm)
Wing: Male – av 12.0 in (30.5 cm); Female – av 11.4 in (29.0 cm)
Weight: Male – av 3.30 lbs (1497 g); Female – av 3.00 lbs (1361 g)
Bill: Male – av 33.6 mm; Female – av 31.9 mm

FIRST IMPRESSIONS
This compact sea goose travels in flocks, moving between Arctic breeding grounds and foraging sites on coastal wintering grounds. In winter, they are often not far from the water's edge, foraging by casually by walking along beaches, salt marshes, tidal areas, and occasionally grazing in grassy areas. Flocks have a uniform look, but juveniles can be picked out by their frosty wing coverts and mottled belly. Brant have black heads, necks and breasts; they are dark brown above and conspicuous white on their rear ends. The coloration of the sides and belly is variable between the subspecies ranging from pale gray to very dark gray bases with contrasting white feather-tips. Size and Shape: A small goose, Brant are larger than a Mallard, but smaller than Canada Goose and only slightly smaller than Cackling Goose. They are actually similar in size to Common Eider. Brant have rectangular shaped heads, petite bills, and short thick necks for a goose. Flight: Small, dark geese with long wings. Compact body, thick neck, small head, and even tinier bill are apparent. Flocks often call in flight. They tend to fly in looser formations than Canada Geese. They will often cruise low over the water, and they typically migrate in flocks of 30-200 individuals. Brant fly with floppier, less consistent wingbeats than Canada Geese.

ID: IN DEPTH AND SIMILAR SPECIES
Identifying Brant is not difficult, because they are petite and so much darker than Canada and other geese. Identifying them to subspecies, however, can be perplexing. There are four distinct subspecies of Brant, which are genetically different and reproductively isolated. These populations are described in the Geographic Variation section below. It is important when identifying a tough Brant that the bird's age is considered. Fortunately, aging Brant is straightforward.

Goslings are pale gray with black caps. Juvenile plumage is usually fully grown by 42 days. These birds are most readily distinguished from adults by the whitish tips on their upperwing coverts. Juveniles initially also lack a white necklace, and this is grown in through the winter. First-years replace juvenile plumage throughout the winter. They can be picked out by the presence of worn juvenile plumage, which contrasts with fresh adult-like feathers. By spring, most of the juvenile plumage has been replaced, often with the exception of some upperwing coverts, belly, and tail feathers. At about a year old, they are not of breeding age, so they head to molting sites to undergo a complete wing and body molt from roughly June-October.

Adults have a clean, sleek plumage with more extensive white necklaces than first-years. Adults drop their wing feathers about 14 days after their brood hatches. They are able to fly again about three weeks later, when the young take wing. A complete body molt begins after the wing feathers are fully grown, which can last until November.

Similar species: Brant are most like Barnacle and Cackling Geese in size and shape, but their overall color pattern is quite different, so they generally do not present identification challenges.

Sex ratio: The limited information sometimes indicates male bias (e.g., 57%) but sometimes female bias (e.g., 55%).

YEAR IN THE LIFE
Brant, or Brent Goose, as they are known in Europe, travel long distances each year to and from their Arctic breeding grounds. They are typically found only in the Atlantic and Pacific Flyways. Major wintering areas on the Pacific Coast include Morro Bay, California and the Puget Sound of Washington.

In spring, Brant have the latest departure of all Arctic nesting waterfowl from the Lower 48, with large flocks still seen moving north in mid-May. Their spring migration route shifted in the 1930s in response to eelgrass die-off. By the mid-1930s two-thirds shifted from a coastal route, to an overland route, because the geese were no longer dependent on coastal eelgrass beds. An inland route is still in use for flocks heading directly to James, Hudson, and Ungava Bays, then fanning out to nesting grounds. Brant are among the last waterfowl breeders to arrive on their Arctic nesting grounds, typically in late May to early June when their nesting habitat finally clears of snow.

Arctic summers are short, so Brant have only a small window of time to raise their brood.s Brant are very sensitive to the timing of their arrival on the breeding grounds, after snowmelt. Females are ready to lay their clutch within days of arrival. But if the ground is still covered in snow they must delay nesting and the females reabsorb their maturing eggs. In such cases, once the snow clears, they are not able to lay a full clutch. and broods tend to be smaller. Alternately, the Brant will skip nesting entirely and go to molt a month early. Fortunately, adults that molt early will end up being stronger during the winter and are more likely to survive into the following nesting season.

The majority of population breeds in the second-year, nearly all by the third-year. Once a pair bond forms, it lasts until one member of the pair is no longer living. Pair bonds are thought to be formed in the second year. Displays are presumed to be subtle.

Unlike Snow Geese and other larger waterfowl, Brant are too small to fend off Arctic foxes, so foxes are a real threat to colonies, especially in years when lemming numbers are down. Once the goslings hatch, the parents defend them until they are capable of flight in 45-50 days. Adults finish their wing molt at about the same time as when their goslings can fly. Shortly thereafter, the family group begins to head south.

In fall, Atlantic Brant begin to congregate in coastal areas near breeding and molting grounds by early September, timed with first heavy snow and freeze-up. In the East, they head south over Hudson and James Bays to the Atlantic coast, to vicinity of New Jersey. Western populations move along Arctic coast to Bering Sea, with many Black Brant flying directly from the eastern Aleutians to northern California. There is also a very concentrated movement through the Great Lakes, passing Lake Ontario in a three-week period, starting about 15 October, with peak days typically one day after the passage of a cold front. Fully 70% of the season's individuals pass through in an average of 8 days.

GEOGRAPHIC VARIATION

Three subspecies are recognized, although a fourth discrete population awaits a subspecific designation. In short, Black Brant is found on the West Coast. Pale-bellied Brant (or Atlantic Brant) is on the East Coast. Gray-bellied Brant (or Western High Arctic Brant) winters a few locations in the Pacific Northwest, however, it has not been officially described as a subspecies. Dark-bellied Brant winters in Europe. Research suggests these populations are genetically distinct and reproductively isolated populations, which do not exhibit widespread intergradation and potentially could be separate species.

B. b. hrota, Pale-bellied or Atlantic Brant, winters along the Atlantic Coast of North America from the tip of Nova Scotia and southern Maine to North Carolina. The group breeding in the Canadian Low Arctic, near Foxe Basin, heads to the Eastern US to winter. Breeders in the Canadian High Arctic, from Melville Island eastward, winter mostly in Iceland. There is also a population in northern Greenland, Spitsbergen, and Franz Josef Land that go to Denmark, northeast England, and Ireland for the winter.

As the name implies, it has the lightest belly color of all the subspecies. They are gray-brown above with gray and white sides. Their belly is white between and behind the legs. Adults have a white necklaces. It is typically broken in front of, and always behind, the neck. Any sightings on the West Coast should be carefully examined for the possibility of Gray-bellied Brant, which can overlap in coloration.

B. b. bernicla, Dark-bellied Brant, or as its known in its native lands of Europe, Dark-bellied Brent Goose, breeds in northwest Siberia (primarily on Yamal, Gydan and Taaymyr peninsulas, islands in the Kara Sea). It winters in Europe on both sides of the North Sea and English Channel, from Denmark to France and in southeast England, with some on Atlantic coast of France. There are a few unconfirmed reports of Dark-bellied Brant in North America. Dark-bellied has cold gray upperparts, typically lacking brown tones, lighter in overall color than other subspecies. They lack much contrast between the upperparts and underparts. Their sides have faint pale bars. The dark belly color extends behind the legs.

B. b. nigricans, Black Brant or Pacific Brant, winters on both sides of the Pacific coast, in North America and parts of Russia, Korea, China, and Japan. In North America, they winter from Alaska to California with some individuals wintering as far south as Baja California Sur and Sonora. It breeds in northwest Canadian Arctic to Alaska and northeast Siberia west to the Taymyr peninsula. Siberian birds are smaller than other Black Brant.

Black Brant is relatively large and robust, larger than other subspecies, with a black belly; sides are boldly marked with wedges of black and white. This subspecies has a thick white necklace which typically meets on the foreneck. Bills of Black Brant are slightly longer, and the overall appearance is more "muscular," with an erect posture. It is also longer-legged than other subspecies. Upperparts are very dark. There is little contrast between the breast and the dark belly color that extends past the legs.

"Gray-bellied" Brant *B.b barryi* breed in the Parry Islands in the Canadian Arctic, primarily on Melville Island, which puts them north of breeding Black Brant and west of the High Arctic population of Pale-bellied Brant. They stage in the Izembek Lagoon of Cold Bay with Black Brant, and then migrate to the Puget Sound of Washington, specifically Padilla Bay, for the winter. They have a small and declining population of only about 8,700 individuals.

Gray-bellied is best thought of as intermediate between Pale-bellied and Black Brant. Gray-bellied Brant have upperparts just slightly darker in color than Pale-bellied and often show strong brown tones. There is strong contrast between the black breast and gray-brown belly. Gray-bellied Brant are intermediate in belly color between Black and Pale-bellied, and are quite variable, showing more variation than Black or Pale-bellied. They have fairly extensive white on the flanks. Importantly, the dark belly coloration extends beyond the legs; noticeably farther than Pale-bellied. The white necklace is intermediate in size between Pale-bellied and Black Brant; it doesn't quite make it all the way around the front of the neck.

Their identification outside the Puget Sound of Washington must be done with great care. Structurally Gray-bellied Brant are smaller bodied than Black Brant. They can appear particularly small-billed with a sleeker look to the head. Their distinction from Black Brant is typically not a problem when other birds are nearby for comparison. The two subspecies don't typically mix. Little is known about this mysterious taxa. Genetic studies (Shields and Cotter, 1998) indicate this population is not of hybrid origin and are temporally and reproductively isolated. Recent DNA work on Gray-bellied has shown it to be closer to Black than to Pale-bellied Brant.

SOUNDS

Brant are very vocal in flocks. The gutteral chuckling of a flock can be heard from great distances. Both sexes give a rolling *cronk* or *cruuk-cruuk* in flight or on the ground. It may seem higher-pitch in a mass chorus. Males: Lower-pitched than females. Sometimes they give a rolling *cut cut cut cronk* in flight. Drawn out *crrronk* and instense *cruk* are given as an alarm call. Also hiss and growl in defense of a nest or brood.

DIET AND FEEDING BEHAVIOR

Brant have more specialized diet needs than other geese, feeding almost exclusively on marine plants and short native grasses, sedges, mosses, and forbs. During breeding and molting, Brant will eat short arctic grasses, forbs, and mosses. Eelgrass is its main winter food, but when that is unavailable, the birds will shift to sea lettuce, wigeon grass, and rockgrass. Brant have adapted to occasionally forage on lawns, pastures, and golf courses in winter at locations on both coasts. They have well-developed salt glands for coastal life during the winter; then they switch to freshwater habitats for breeding where they graze on shrubs and grasses.

NESTING

Site: On coastal tundra on the ground near water (on small islands, raised beaches, sometimes on rocks and points of inland lakes). Some populations nest in the low Arctic in dense colonies; other nest in the high Arctic where they tend to spread their nests out a bit more.

Nest Description: A hollow on the ground, often lined and built up with moss and lichens, with a thick inner lining of down. The thick pillow of down insulates the eggs from the permafrost that lies just below the nest. About 12 inches in inside diameter, 18 inches in outside diameter, and 2 inches in depth.

Clutch size: 3-5 eggs, sometimes 2-8.

Egg description: Elliptical to subelliptical, often long, Smooth and slightly glossy. Creamy-white to yellowish. 71 X 47 mm.

Incubation duration: 23-24 days, sometimes 22-26 days.

Brood parasitism: Infrequent.

HUNTING

Historically, Brant was a prestigious game bird on the East Coast, but they lost their status when the eelgrass die-off in the 1930s forced a shift in diet and their meat became less palatable. There was also a West Coast die-off of eelgrass in the early 1940s. Brant decoy well, and calling works. These geese often come in large flocks.

The harvest of Brant in the U.S. over two years (2013 and 2014) averaged at about 13,700 birds. Subsistence harvest in Canada in the recent past, however, has been estimated at 7,400 birds.

Hunting of "Gray-bellied" Brant wintering in the Puget Sound, Washington is very restricted. The season is open for seven days in January only if surveys earlier in the month indicate the wintering population is over 6,000 (2007-08).

POPULATION AND CONSERVATION

Populations are in a slow, long-term decline, although they are not at a particularly high risk. The estimated continental population may total about 315,000 birds. Black Brant populations may have declined by 60% in the 1980s; their numbers today are at about 150,000, a 2014-2016 average. The Atlantic Brant population declined drastically in 1931 following sudden die off of eelgrass from a disease, though they adapted to other food sources and population recovered. Since 1970, the population has ranged from a low of 40,800 in 1973 to a high of 184,200 in 1992. They are now estimated at 150,000. The Gray-bellied Brant has ranged from a low of 2,100 in 1983 to a high of 16,900 in 1995. The 2002-2011 population average has been put at 8,700.

These are long-lived geese, so even though they do suffer years with very poor reproductive success due to weather and depredation by Arctic foxes they have adapted to sustain through tough years.

Counts at breeding colonies have decreased steadily since 1960s for reasons that are not well-understood. Competition from Snow Geese on some nesting grounds may be one factor. Brant are particularly susceptible to breeding failures and starvation. Therefore, populations are closely monitored and hunting is strictly regulated, which significantly affects population size.

BARNACLE GOOSE
Branta leucopis BARG

Plates Page 65

OTHER COMMON OR REGIONAL NAMES
(Québec: bernache nonnette)

MEASUREMENTS
Length: Male – 26 in (66 cm); Female – 24.5 in (62 cm)
Wing: Male – av 16.1 in (40.9 cm); Female – av 15.5 in (39.3 cm)
Weight: Male – av 4.08 lbs (1850 g), Female – av 3.53 lbs (1600 s)
Bill: Male – av (30 mm); Female – av (29 mm)

FIRST IMPRESSIONS AND SIMILAR SPECIES-
This little silvery goose occasionally wanders to North America where one will often join a flock of Canada Geese. Barnacle Geese can blend in surprisingly well in large flocks of Canada Geese on the ground, but in flight their small size and overall color stands out.

Barnacle Goose looks basically like a silvery-bodied, white-faced Brant. Adults are light, silvery gray, with primarily black head, neck, and breast. The white patch on the head is reminiscent of Canada Goose, but larger, encompassing the eye and extending onto the forehead. That patch is part of this goose's scientific name: *leucopis* is from the Greek, with *leucos* being white and *copsis* referring to the face. Plus, Barnacle has an additional white band on the forehead. Size and shape: Similar to Brant. This petite goose is small-billed with a small head and shorter neck than Canada Goose, closer to the size of Cackling Goose. Its body is also small compared to Canada Goose, but their wings are proportionally long. Flight: Body shape is more like Brant or Cackling Goose, given the long wings and shorter neck, compared to Canada Goose. Pale gray back stands out in a flock of Canadas. Note the white U-shaped rump-band in flight. Note, also, the sharp contrast between the black breast and the white belly. Frequently calls in flight.

Similar species: These little geese are generally distinctive, between their small size, white face, and silvery-gray coloration. Look out for Canada or Cackling Geese suggesting a similar face pattern (almost regular in juveniles). Hybrids, though uncommon, are probably most likely to generate an ID puzzle.

Barnacle x Canada Goose or Barnacle x Cackling can have a head pattern similar to Barnacle with the white band across the forehead, white cheek, black neck. They also have a dark brown breast, with a barred back, and gray sides. You will need to look closely at the patterns and colors on the plumage, because the hybrids lack the crisp-looking silvery-gray backs. They also have darker sides than Barnacle, with brown tones, and they tend to have larger bills. Backcrosses of this paring (offspring of Barnacle x Canada paired with Barnacle) look much like that of a Barnacle Goose, but still have more brown tones in the body and larger bill. They may also have reduced white in the head and slightly paler breast.

Sex ratio: Assumed to be equal.

BACKGROUND AND TIPS
Barnacle Goose is abundant in parts of its range in Europe. These attractive geese are often kept in captivity, which puts many sightings into the "origin uncertain" category. While some seen in North America have surely originated in captivity, many have found their way to North America by pumping their wings thousands of times.

Barnacle Geese hail from four breeding populations, three of which are in the Arctic. Each of these populations has a different migration timing and route. One population of roughly 56,000 of these geese nests in eastern Greenland and winters in western Scotland and Iceland. This increasing Greenland population may be the source of many of our winter sightings in the Northeast.

Barnacle Geese banded in Scotland have been encountered in the Northeast, while others have arrived accompanying Greater White-fronted Geese from Greenland.

Barnacle Geese now show up at least once a year in most Atlantic Provinces, New England, and the mid-Atlantic states. There is a regularly occurring pattern of sightings from this region from late September through April, and, especially between November and March. This strongly suggest that many of these geese are natural vagrants, opposed to escapees from captivity. A number of records from states such as Oklahoma, Indiana, California, and Wisconsin are suspect (and some are known escapees). But, increasingly, more inland records are falling into a convincing pattern.

Barnacle Geese are gregarious by nature, they often found in flocks in their homelands. In North America, thus far, they are basically loners; they will often join flocks of Canada Geese. Most reports are of a single Barnacle Goose (opposed to a pair or a family group) and they are almost all adults.

Populations are increasing in Europe, in large part due to conservation efforts. The estimated world population is at about 500,000, with over 10% of these in Greenland.

SOUNDS
Like other geese, Barnacle Goose is a vocal species; flocks are often not silent for long. They frequently give a one note, dry, barking *gunk* given on land and in flight. They will also give a high-pitched *kor*. A flock resembles a group of small, yapping dogs. Their note is drier note than a Brant call. Also, utter muffled, lower pitch feeding call *hoog* or *hogoog*.

DIET AND FEEDING BEHAVIOR
Despite its name, this species does not feed on barnacles.

Instead, the Barnacle Goose diet is mainly vegetarian, with leaves and stems of grass dominating. In winter, it will also resort to eating seaweed, mollusks, and shellfish. It will also forage in pastures and stubble, often in search of leftover grain and seeds. This goose, an efficient grazer, will also pull and tear at SAV. With plants covered by water (e.g., at high tide), the Barnacle Goose will up-end or seek food with its head and neck below the surface.

CANADA GOOSE
Branta canadensis CANG

Plates Page 68

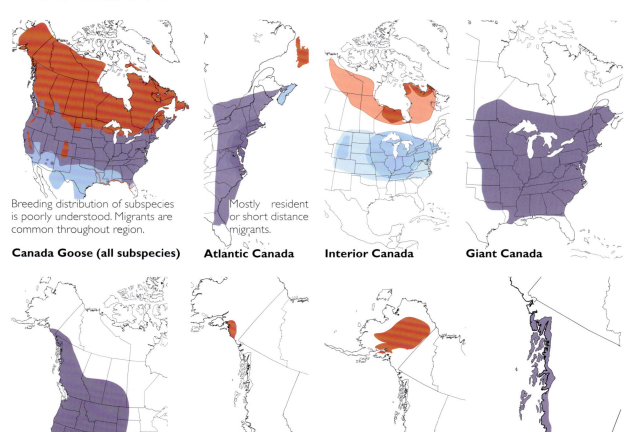

OTHER COMMON OR REGIONAL NAMES
Canada, honker, Canadian, white-cheek giants, greaters (Arctic: tuutangayagpak [YK], tuutalhusig [NS], nibliq [NS], niglivik [NWS], uluaralik, uluagullik [N])
(Québec: bernache du Canada)
(Mexico: ganso Canadiense)

MEASUREMENTS (highly variable in populations)
Length: Male – c.36-37 in, av 36.7 in (93.2 cm); Female – c.33-35 in, av 34in (86.4 cm)
Wing: Male – av 19.3 in (49.1 cm); Female – av 18.3 in (46.5 cm)
Weight: Male – av 9.40 lbs (4264 g); Female – av 8.10 lbs (3674 g)
Bill: Male – 42.4-60.7mm; Female – 40.6-57.3 mm

FIRST IMPRESSIONS

Canada Goose is one of the most widely recognized birds in North America, with its classic honk, black head and neck, and distinctive white-cheek patch that wraps under the chin. These familiar geese live in wetlands across the continent, traveling in large flocks or family groups that are uniform in color pattern, but vary slightly in size.

Many of the newer feral populations are permanent residents, while the northern migrant populations exhibit impressive movements. The whole white-cheeked goose complex – the baffling mix of Canada and Cackling Geese – has significant geographic variation; some subspecies are readily separable while others are impossible to distinguish in the field. For our purposes, we have seven geographic forms treated in some detail in "Geographic Variation," including the smallest, but most controversial, subspecies, *B. c. parvipes,* or Lesser Canada Goose. Size varies greatly with subspecies, but also within populations. Flight: Large-bodied and long-necked with wings set back on the body. They appear dark at a distance. The black tail with white U-shape on rump is apparent in flight. The larger the subspecies, the more measured and slower the wing-beat will appear. Flocks frequently travel in V-formation or long skeins of 20-200 birds, sometimes with other waterfowl mixed in.

ID: IN DEPTH AND SIMILAR SPECIES

Males are noticeably larger than females (12-19% heavier) with longer bills (5-11%), depending on subspecies, a fact which is noticeable when pairs are together. In the fall, immature birds can be distinguished, but it becomes very difficult after they molt out of juvenile plumage.

Goslings have warm yellow faces and olive-brown bodies. Juvenile plumage begins to appear at 3-4 weeks old, by 8 weeks it is fully grown. Juvenile plumage is evenly marked on the body with rounded edges on the body feathers, which gives the breast and sides a scalloped appearance. Wing coverts are narrow and have a round tip, unlike the square-tipped adult feathers. The black on the neck is also duller and there is not as crisp of a line between the black breast and belly. Overall, they are duller with less contrast in their markings. Juveniles are also noticeably smaller and more slender until the winter, by which point they put on significantly more mass. First-years replace juvenile plumage in the fall, most of which has been replaced by November. Sometimes, worn juvenile belly feathers can be seen until the early winter or even into spring. In general, larger subspecies Canada Geese tend to replace their juvenile plumage faster than smaller ones. (Cackling Goose retains significantly more juvenile plumage into the winter than Canada.) Northern migratory populations also molt later than more southerly resident birds. Yearlings do not breed, so come summer, they go on a molt-migration to a region where they undergo a complete molt of body and flight feathers, resulting in an adult plumage. One study showed 45% of two-year olds, and 75% of three-year olds had brood patches so, presumably, some join first-year birds and nonbreeding adults in a northward molt-migration in the summer.

Adults never have perfectly even wing coverts because they do not grow in at precisely the same time, unlike juveniles when all the wing feathers grow at once for the first time. Adults undergo a complete molt of body and flight feathers, starting in later stages of raising the brood. They are flightless for 5-6 weeks and regain the ability to fly at about same time as their brood's first flight. While their plumage does not change appreciably throughout the year, it is likely that they are replacing head/neck and some body feathers multiple times a year, such as in the spring.

Similar Species: In light of the general similarities to Cackling Goose, refer to the "Similar Species" section for that species on p. 358. The real problem, as previously mentioned, plagues observers when dealing with smaller Canada Geese, an issue explained further in the "Geographic Variation" section which starts on the next page. At the same time, remember that juvenile Canada Geese can also be a pitfall for the unwary who are trying to find Cackling Geese. Juvenile Canadas are smaller than their adults (so there is contrast in size within the flock), and they don't fill out to a full-size goose until the winter.

Sex ratio: Basically equal

YEAR IN THE LIFE

Canada Goose is an extremely successful species that has adapted to live in farm fields, town parks, golf courses, airports, corporate office complexes, and varied wetlands across the continent. Their highly migratory habits have shifted, many becoming largely resident in some areas. They are one of the few species that is able to cope with the conversion of wetlands to golf course ponds and city parks. The green slick from goose-droppings left on a golfer's shoes or a kid's soccer cleats, and the crying kids petrified when a gander bites them on the butt when they came too close to his nest have invariably led to this goose's status as a pest in some areas.

In many ways it's remarkable that Canada Geese are so common these days. At the end of the nineteenth century, their population was in serious trouble and facing extirpation in some areas. Hunting regulations, federal laws, and habitat protections (e.g., the rise of a meaningful refuge system) had real results. Once live decoys were outlawed in hunting in 1935, many captive Canada Geese were released. Also, reintroduction programs, starting in 1930s and seriously in motion by the mid-1960s, led to remarkable rebounds in populations. Stocking programs began as efforts to reestablish seriously depleted or extirpated populations. What threw a wrench in the whole process was that the birds that were introduced by one or another means were not necessarily from the same population as the native birds, reslting in a jumble of unintended consequences.

Not surprisingly, Canada Geese were also introduced and established in Great Britain, Iceland, southern Scandinavia, and New Zealand. The genie, in many places, is now out of the proverbial bottle.

Habitat preferences and behaviors are variable among the subspecies, but some are consistent throughout the populations. In the winter and during migration, populations will spend their days feeding in agricultural fields, grassy areas, or in marshes. There are increasing numbers of resident Canadas found at this season, as well as through much of the year, in suburban areas with large grassy areas, particularly golf courses.

Some populations no longer follow their historic migratory patterns. Other populations winter within their breeding area. Reverse migrations occur in spring or fall, if geese come across adverse weather conditions. Migratory Canada Geese exhibit strong philopatry to specific migration-stopover sites and wintering areas, a strong evolutionary force usually keeping management units and subspecies distinct. Spring migration begins as early as late January, with departures from the most southerly wintering grounds; migration timing follows receding snow in the spring. For example, the Hudson Bay/Interior Canada Geese *B. c. interior* begin heading north from southern Illinois in late January to mid-February, peak arrival in northern Illinois in late February to mid-March, arriving in Wisconsin mid-March, first arrivals in northern Ontario late March, peak in mid-April, average time for radio-tagged geese from southern Illinois to arrival in northern Ontario is 54 days. Giant Canadas, *B. c. maxima*, wintering in Rochester, Minnesota, depart mid-March to mid-April and arrive on their breeding grounds a Marshy Point, Manitoba, from late-March to mid-April, with an average traveling duration of 10 days, ranging from 6-14 days.

Canada Goose breeds near water in a range of habitats from temperate regions to arctic tundra, and semi-desert. They nest individually or semi-colonially. Life-long pair bonds typically form during the second or third year. Courtship displays are subtle, but "triumph ceremonies," used by pairs in recognition and in fending off rivals, cement pair and family bonds. The female selects and prepares nest site, which can be reused multiple years. The nest is built out of vegetation gathered near the nest site and is added throughout laying. Down is added when the second or third egg are laid. Males and females tend the brood, even after they are able to fly at 8-10 weeks. Families stick together for a year, migrating and wintering together.

Nonbreeding, first-years, second-years, and some adults undergo a molt-migration. The distance ranges from several miles to more than 1,000 miles. These geese generally move north for molt-migration to forage on plants in earlier stages of growth. Many re-established populations of the Giant *B. c. maxima* have become non-migratory, but they still participate in a several-hundred-mile molt-migration. At least a few molt-migration routes are apparent for these birds in southern Ontario and the northeastern U.S. These include routes to Hudson Bay, Ontario, and James Bay, a western route to Hudson Bay, Manitoba, and a northeastern route to northeastern Québec. Distances can range from 350 miles to 1,200 miles. Some geese even stage for this migration.

Fall migration begins in the most northerly nesting grounds beginning in late August-September, with most birds reaching the northern U.S. by late September-early October. Individuals wintering farthest south typically arrive on their wintering grounds by early to mid-November through mid-December. Majority of the arctic and boreal Interior Canada Geese (*B. c. interior*) from the northern Ungava Peninsula of Québec, will depart for their main winter range along the Atlantic Coast from New Jersey to North Carolina in under seven days, with some traveling over 700 miles in a single day. The Interior Canadas from the west coast of James Bay and the southwest coast of Hudson Bay will depart northern Ontario in late September to mid-October, arriving at Horicon Marsh, Wisconsin from late September to early November. Their departure timing is variable, starting late September, peaking in early November.

GEOGRAPHIC VARIATION

The white-cheeked goose complex has a complicated and controversial taxonomic history. Authors differ greatly in their interpretations, ranging from the description of seven to over 80 morphometric groups. Formerly there were 19 management units of white-cheeked geese that overlapped little during breeding, migration, and wintering. Today, as numbers increase, and ranges expand, many of their wintering management areas are being amalgamated. These days population descriptions are more often based on their breeding distributions rather than their wintering ones.

There are seven subspecies of Canada Geese that are fairly broadly accepted today: *B. c. maxima* (Giant), *moffitti* (Moffit's/Western/Great Basin), *canadensis* (Atlantic), *interior* (Interior/Hudson Bay), *fulva* (Vancouver), *occidentalis* (Dusky), and *parvipes* (Lesser). Be aware that only Giant, Atlantic, and Interior occur as "wild" birds in the East.

A short study and cross-reference with the seven subspecies range maps on p. 351 should help to clarify our presumed geographic ranges as we describe these seven subspecies.

When considering identification, *B. c. maxima, moffitti, canadensis*, and *interior* are sometimes separable in the field by range or a particularly distinctive group. However, if you spend any length of time watching flocks of Canadas, you will notice an incredible range of variation in size, shape, color, neck collar, bill shape and just about any feature you study. In short, the more you look, the more you will realize the futility of attempting subspecific identification much of the time.

We don't go into detail over chin strap and neck collar when describing Canadas because these are not reliable indicators for subspecies. While there are extremes within subspecies when considering these two features, they are never useful.

B. c. fulva and *occidentalis* are distinctive in their extremely dark coloration; however, they are not reliably separated, except by range. And, lastly, *B. c. parvipes*, the smallest of our Canadas, is troublesome enough to be regularly misidentified as a Cackling Goose, *B. h. taverneri* or *B. h. hutchinsii*. In fact, we question the existence of Lesser Canada Goose, as it is now known, believing that many small Canadas are either just small Canadas or possibly hybrid Cackling-Canadas. See *B.c parvipes* for a clearer explanation. Often times, these white-cheeked geese are simply impossible to distinguish in the field. And over the years, there has been significant mixing, with clines of integration between some of these populations. Future research and DNA analysis will probably reveal that distinct populations no longer exist in most areas. The following Canada Goose subspecies descriptions, along with *average* measurements, in conjunction with the accompanying range maps, may help bring some clarity to the situation.

B. c. maxima, Giant Canada Goose, the world's largest goose subspecies, is long-necked, long-billed, particularly pale-breasted (gray or whitish), with a large white cheek patch extending farther up the head than Atlantic Canada Goose, *B. c. canadensis*, and it can have a white band or mark on forehead. The large size and pale appearance make the extremes of this subspecies one of the few populations that can often be identified with some certainty. Giant Canada Goose was nearly extirpated in the early 1900s, but since the 1960s have been reestablished across their former range (across the Mississippi and Central Flyways) and now breeds in all states east of the Mississippi. They are especially amenable to these efforts, since they are easily propagated in confinement, readily use artificial/floating nest structures, and have high rates of nest success. Giant is similar to Western Canada Goose, *B. c. moffitti*, and intergrades with *moffitti* and other subspecies, so it is difficult to discern a clear status and distribution for this subspecies.

Wing: Male – c. 22 in (55 cm); Female – av 19.5 in (49.6 cm)

Weight: Male – av 10.71 lbs (4858 g); Female – av 10.6 lbs (4825 g)

Bill: Male – 60.7 mm; Female – 57 mm

B. c. moffitti, Moffit's, Western, or Great Basin Canada Goose, is slightly smaller and lighter in general coloration than *maxima*. This is the widespread goose in the West, a common resident in urban and rural areas. These account for two-thirds of the Canadas in the West. Moffit's Canada Goose intergrades extensively with Giant Canada Goose, to the east, and other Canadas northward. This creates many mixed offspring ranging across much of the central part of the continent, with many geese best left unidentified to subspecies or simply grouped as *moffitti/maxima*. Its breeding range has even spread beyond, with individual introduced populations in Oklahoma, northeast Texas, and elsewhere, and with some wintering populations moving to southern-most California and south Texas.

Wing: Male – av 20.5 in (52.1 cm); Female – av 18.8 in (47.8 cm)

Weight: Male – av 8.6 lbs (4017 g); Female – av 7.6 lbs (3450 g)

Bill: Male – 50 mm; Female – 46 mm

B. c. canadensis, Atlantic Canada Goose, is large-sized and long-necked. The Atlantic Canada Goose is similar to Interior or Hudson Bay Canada Goose, *B. c. interior*, but averages slightly larger and paler. In fact, there is gradual intergradation with *interior* westward into the Ungava Peninsula of eastern Quebec. This is the commonest subspecies wintering in the northeast.

Wing: Male – av 18.8 in (47.7 cm); Female – av 18.1 in (45.9 cm)

Weight: Male – av 10.9 lbs (4931 g); Female – av 9.4 lbs (4280 g)

Bill: Male – 57 mm; Female – 54 mm

B. c. interior, Interior or Hudson Bay Canada Goose, has a wide distribution and is highly variable. They average slightly smaller and darker than the previous subspecies, Atlantic Canada Goose, *B. c. canadensis*. Widespread wintering grounds no longer extend as far southeast as in the past.

Wing: Male – av 19.6 in (49.7 cm); Female – av 17.6 in (46.6 cm)

Weight: Male – av 9.9 lbs (4472 g); Female – av 8.10 lbs (3759 g)

Bill: Male – 56 mm; Female – 54 mm

B. c. fulva, Vancouver Canada Goose, like the next subspecies, Dusky Canada Goose, *B. c. occidentalis*, is decidedly dark. Vancouver Canada Goose is chocolaty brown bodied, averaging slightly larger and paler than Dusky Canada but otherwise very similar in appearance, to the point where they are not reliably separated except by range: they are good canditates to be lumped. Vancouver Canada Geese are essentially non-migratory, wintering in southeast Alaska southward throughout coastal British Columbia, occasionally wintering into south-central Washingtona and even Oregon, at which point their identification from *occidentalis* becomes muddled.

Wing: Male – c. 20.3 in (51.6 cm); Female – c. 20.3 in (51.7 cm)

Weight: Male – av 8.1 lbs (3690 g); Female – av 6.7 lbs (3043 g)

Bill: Male – 51 mm; Female – 48 mm

B. c. occidentalis, Dusky Canada Goose, like the previous subspecies, Vancouver Canada Goose, is dark, but Dusky is the darkest subspecies. The Dusky is a medium–large goose that is brownish overall on the body. Underparts on Duskys vary a lot from tawny chestnut to dark chocolate brown. *B. c. occidentalis* breeds on the Copper River Delta, southeast Alaska, and on several islands in the Gulf of Alaska and Prince William Sound, wintering in Willamette River valley of western Oregon and lower Columbia River valley of north-central Oregon and south-central Washington.

Wing: Male – av 19.3 in (49.1 cm); Female – av 18.5

in (46.9 cm)

Weight: Male – av 7.1 lbs (3233 g); Female – av 5.8 lbs (2640 g)

Bill: Male – 46 mm; Female – 44 mm

B. c. parvipes, Lesser Canada Goose, is a medium-sized goose that overlap extensively in size with cackling goose. The type specimen, collected in 1852, is the size of a Cackling Goose! From this inauspicious start, Lesser Canada Goose has been a constant source of confusion. As a general rule, what have been called Lesser Canadas are expected to be small Canadas with graceful necks. Also, Lessers are depicted with a longer bill and more sloping head than Cackling. This is different from "short-billed" or "square-headed," descriptors used for Cackling Goose. In fact, *parvipes* is only considered a Canada goose because it has (maternally inherited) mtDNA that is characteristic of Canada geese, but that is not found in cackling geese. This combination of characteristics (small body size and Canada goose mtDNA) could be expected to occur in hybrids between the two species.

The existence of 'textbook' small, pale, and slim birds, that theoretically winter commonly in the western Great Plains, is questionable. Many appear similar to smaller Interior Canadas. Similar looking Canadas are quite common elsewhere.

With its true status unknown, a number of questions exist over what Lesser Canada Goose actually is. DNA work from Alaska is distinctive for a smaller Canada Goose; it is distinctive from Cackling. We now know that Alaska is the only place these Canadas are known to breed. (Previous literature had shown them breeding as far east as Hudson Bay and as far south as northern Alberta and Manitoba; this supposed distribution probably helped with the confident identification of many geese as Lessers.) Unfortunately, measurements, weights, photos or descriptions were not systematically taken to match to the DNA samples leaving field-ID questions unanswered. Even the measurements in the present literature, including those below, should be considered tentative:

Wing: Male – av 18.1 in (46.0 cm); Female – av 16.6 in (42.2 cm)

Weight: Male – av 7.2 lbs (3266 g); Female – av 5.4 lbs (2450 g)

Bill: Male – 42 mm; Female – 41 mm

These perplexing geese may all be darker Alaskan birds, geese that are best known from the Anchorage area, where they are common. (We call them Alaska 'Lesser' Canadas here.) Over the years there has been much discussion about these geese and where they fit in the big picture. At this time, it makes sense to assume that these are the Lesser Canadas with the different DNA that are restricted to breeding in Alaska. These Alaska 'Lesser' Canadas are variable in color; they tend to be quite uniform underneath, some being as dark as paler Duskys. Very few birds in the western Great Plains have similar structure to these darker Alaska 'Lesser' Canadas that winter in the Pacific NW; yet, they are typical of the shape of birds depicted in much of the literature. Personal observation of dark Anchorage Canadas with supposed Taverner's Cacklers on the North Slope at Deadhorse, Alaska, showed no noticeable difference in size or shape, though their coloration was strikingly different. Perhaps the pale Lesser Canadas seen in some areas are Taverner's Cackling Goose; a bird that over the years has been considered almost identical to Lesser Canada goose and at one time deemed conspecific.

Furthermore, to add to the confusion, the dark Alaksa 'Lesser' Canada subspecies intergrades with Taverner's Cackling Goose in western interior of Alaska. This helps to explain the wide variation in color, with some birds being quite pale.

Analyses of band recoveries indicate that medium-sized white-cheeked geese originating from interior Alaska (presumed *parvipes*) and the North Slope of Alaska (*taverneri* complex) will winter primarily in eastern Washington and Oregon, while small white-cheeked geese originating in far western Alaska (*taverneri*) winter primarily in western Washington and Oregon, and northern California.

All along, it should be remembered that the other geese we consider generally grow smaller as the population extends northward, and darker as they go westward. This variation can be considered clinal. This is why when looking at groups of subspecies such as Vancouver, Dusky, and the Alaska 'Lesser' Canada, we should have an open mind. It is also clear that birds from different populations interbreed, and hybridization with Cackling Goose occurs. Clearly, there is a lot to unravel among these taxa. One would think that continued studies of small Canada Geese and Taverner's Cackling Goose throughout the year, allied to DNA work, would help clarify a number of remaining questions. For now, looking at small Canadas with a fresh perspective seems to make sense.

SOUNDS

The Canada Goose gives its raucous honks both in flight and from the ground. They are noticeably lower-pitched and louder than the high-pitched Cackling Goose, a very useful identification tool. Canadas give over a dozen different calls. Generally, larger males will give a lower-pitched honk. Also, the smaller the subspecies, the shorter the call, the higher the pitch. For example, the calls of *B. c. parvipes* are higher-pitched than *B. c. moffitti*, useful to know when they are together. Males: Known for classic honk contact call given alternatively with female's call. Females: Gives *hrink* contact call in duet with male. Differences in pitch between sexes is apparent when in pairs.

DIET AND FEEDING BEHAVIOR

Perhaps more than any other waterfowl on the continent, Canada Geese have benefitted from the agricultural activity of humans, as the birds feed on waste grain (e.g., corn, oats, buckwheat, sorghum, and soybeans). Agricultural crops and grasses comprise the main portion of their diet in migration and wintering. This feeding activity was recorded as early as the 1880s. Midwestern geese that historically migrated to the Gulf Coast will use freshwater marshes in refuges and agricultural lands for feeding, sometimes cutting short their migration. Aquatic plants – e.g., in the mid-Atlantic region – have been largely spurned by Canadas in favor of nearby upland crops. Still, *B. c. fulva* will supplement its vegetable diet with a menu of clams, salmon eggs, and even dead salmon. On northern breeding grounds, Canada Geese feed on native grasses, sedges, and berries.

NESTING

Site: Highly variable locations and usually by water, including in marsh grasses, on the tops of muskrat houses or beaver lodges, or on wetland dikes. The vegetation surrounding tundra nests is generally short and includes sedges, dwarf shrubs, and lichens. Nests in interior forested regions are frequently near taller willow, and other trees. Islands generally seem to be favored, on lakes, reservoirs, rivers, or streams. Some subspecies (e.g., *B. c. moffitti* or *B. c. maxima*) will take readily to raised man-made structures such as baskets or galvanized washtubs on posts or trees, or to floating wooden platforms. Natural above-ground sites include cliffs, tree stumps, and even abandoned nests of large birds, including Osprey and various herons. *B. c. moffitti* often use these abandoned nests.

Nest description: A hollow, lined with a variable amount of plant material, including twigs and plant stems, and at times built up to a substantial structure well above the water-line. There will be an inner lining of down and some feathers. About 9-13 inches in inside diameter, 17-48 inches in outside diameter, and 3.5-6 inches in depth.

Clutch size: Usually 5-6 eggs, ranges from 4-10

Egg description: Elliptical to subelliptical. Dull creamy-white and smooth. Variable by subspecies, but averages 86 x 58mm

Incubation duration: Typically 25-30 days.

Brood parasitism: Lays in nests of other Canadas and other waterfowl.

HUNTING

Canadas often come into goose decoys and calling, whether over field or open water. Calling Canadas into a decoy spread generally takes some skill, and they are more responsive to good calling than other species. (There is an incentive to be a particularly good goose caller!) In the East in the fall, the first major Canada migration day often falls in the first week of December on the day of a massive cold front.

Bag limits are generous in many regions, with special hunting seasons in some areas to decrease resident populations. These seasons (usually in September) may precede the arrival of migrating Canadas, helping to automatically differentiate the populations. Some recent harvest numbers (e.g., 2013 and 2014) for these seasons average 170,000 resident geese for the Atlantic Flyway, 240,000 resident geese for the Mississippi Flyway, and 42,000 resident geese elsewhere. (It is unclear, however, how many resident geese may be harvested during regular geese seasons.) Hunting, however, is not allowed in areas – suburban and residential – where these birds may be expanding the most. In these localities, the geese are virtually invulnerable to harvest. Moreover, there simply may not be enough waterfowl hunters to make this a real solution to the problem of expanding resident Canadas.

At the same time, hunters in the Pacific Flyway, especially, need to be able to identify subspecies of non-resident Canadas and Cacklers. Hunting of Dusky Canada Geese is very restricted in Pacific NW. Hunters should beware, as Duskies tend to fly low and drop quickly into decoys. They are particularly unwary and easy to lure. With such a small population and vulnerability to over harvesting, their harvest is closely monitored.

Body size and voice can be very helpful identifying geese as they are coming into the decoys. High-pitched yelps of Cackling Geese are readily distinguishable from larger Canada honks. Cackling Geese, like Dusky Canadas, are also tightly regulated in the regions they occur. See the treatment for Cackling Goose, on p. 360.

POPULATION AND CONSERVATION

Canada Goose populations are increasing overall. There may be more Canada Geese in North America today than any time in history. Management programs focus on specific geographic units or subspecies. The population of Giant Canada Goose in the Mississippi Flyway was recently estimated at 1.7 million, an over-abundant population that has grown at an average rate of 3% annually (2001-2011).

Lesser Canada Goose populations are increasing in the last decade, and considered stable. On the other hand, Dusky Canada Goose population has been about 10,000 to 18,000 since the 1980s, but it was estimated in 2005 at 21,800. It was estimated at about 11,000, considering a 2002-2011 average.

Some populations of Canada Geese were formerly migratory and are now resident and considered a nuisance in some areas. Geese grazing at or near airports can create serious flight-safety issues. Depending on location, some molt-migrants may mix in with resident Canadas, further confusing the origins issue. In any case, resident Canada Geese can be a wildlife management problem wherever they occur. The birds can bedevil communities in the East – New York, for example, has an estimated population of 260,000 geese – or more rural areas – South Dakota has an estimated 270,000 Canadas. The New York population goal of 85,000 is optimistic and may never be reached. Pest control programs, including treating eggs with oil to kill the embryos but keep adults attempting to incubate, have been implemented to decrease local populations in many areas. Higher bag limits, extended hunting hours, unplugged guns, and electronic callers have also been part of the effort to reach regional management objectives.

CACKLING GOOSE
Branta hutchinsii CACG

Plates Page 72

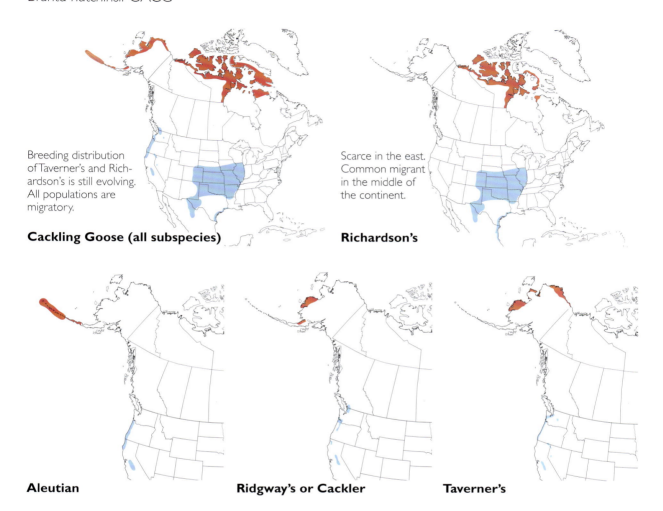

OTHER COMMON OR REGIONAL NAMES
Cackler, Ridgway's, Ridgway's Cackler, honker, Aleutian goose, Richardson's goose, Richies, Taverner's goose, Tavs, Canadian
(Arctic: lagilugpiaq [YK], iqsragutilik [NS], iqsrabutilik [NWS], neglerk, necklerk [N])
(Québec: bernache de Hutchins)
(Mexico: ganso cascareador)

MEASUREMENTS
Length: *B.h.minima* c. 23 in (58.4 cm); *B.h. leucopareia* c. 25 in (63.5 cm); *B.h. hutchinsii* c. 31 in (78.2 cm); *B.h. taverneri* c. 33 in (83.8 cm)
Wing: Male – av 14.8 in (37.5 cm); Female – av 12.7 in (32.3 cm)
Weight: Male – av 4.70 lbs (2132 g); Female – av 3.80 lbs (1724 g)
Bill: Male – 29.7 – 39.0 mm; Female – 28.1-37.7 mm

FIRST IMPRESSIONS
These geese, looking like miniature Canadas, are adorable with their small size and little bills. Wintering flocks and family groups are often grazing in fields with other geese or traveling in flocks of twenty or more in between feeding and resting areas. In 2004, they were elevated to the status of a full species, split from Canada Goose. The whole white-cheeked goose complex – including both Cacklers and Canadas – can be difficult to unravel, but most Cackling Geese at least can be approached with some degree of certainty. Cackling Goose has impressive geographic variation, encompassing four subspecies. All will show a black head and neck with a white cheek patch and their overall body color ranges from pale brown and even silvery, to darker brown and purplish. A Cackling Goose will have a stubby bill, short neck, squarish head, and a long primary projection, compared to a Canada Goose. The subspecies, of course, are described in the "Geographic Variation" section below. Note that some

individuals can be impossible to identify to subspecies or species in the field, particularly single birds that are out of range.

Size and shape: A petite goose with a short thick neck and small bill. Individuals in some populations are larger with more slender necks and slightly longer bills. Cackling Geese can range in weight from just over 2 pounds to 5 pounds, and length can vary from 21 to 29 inches. Many of them are not really much larger than a Mallard. Flight: Short neck, long wings and rounded body characterize Cacklers. They look compact, but with proportionally long wings. Again, coloration varies by population from silvery wings to darker brown or pale brown upperparts. Flocks string out in a V-formation, like Canadas. Cackling Geese often traveling in flocks of 5-75 when moving around wintering grounds. They migrate in flocks of hundreds, high in the sky, day and night, often mixed in with flocks of Canadas. Their wingbeats are looser than Canada Goose, and their long wings have tendency to flop from side to side make them look like they are a bit out of control.

ID: IN DEPTH AND SIMILAR SPECIES

Aging Cackling Geese isn't too hard with practice by looking for juvenile plumage, which is often retained well into the winter. Cacklers usually don't breed in their first-year. Males are larger than females (about 20% heavier), which is noticeable when pairs are together.

Goslings vary with subspecies. They are generally pale yellow with dusky markings on the back and head. On average, they have more dusky wash on the body than most populations of Canada Goose. Ridgway's Cackling Geese, *B. h. minima*, are darkest with a dusky wash on most of the body and around the eye. Goslings also have a very stubby bill. Juvenile plumage has a scalloped look on the belly and breast, where each feather is rounded and narrower. Wing coverts are also more rounded at the tip, whereas adults' feathers are square-tipped. The black on head and neck is a bit duller black than on the adults. Juveniles lack white neck collars. First-years replace juvenile plumage from September-April; therefore, they have a mix of juvenile and adult-like feathers often well into December or even later in the winter. These long-distance migrants hold more juvenile plumage into the winter than do Canada Geese. First-year Cacklers will often replace all of their tail feathers. Many first-years obtain at least a partial white neck color in the winter. One-year olds (nonbreeders) molt their wing and body feathers from June-November.

Adults have a smooth look on the breast and belly, except when they are molting in late summer and early fall. Adult *minima* have a nice purplish sheen, unlike most first-years. A significantly greater percentage of adults have white neck collars, compared to first-years. Breeding adults shed wing feathers after their brood hatches. They usually stagger their molt, with the males replacing primaries first. After their wings have regrown, they replace all of their body feathers by December. Nonbreeding and unsuccessful adults presumably undergo a molt-migration for their molt.

Similar Species: Generally, the Cackling Geese can be separated from Canadas by their smaller size, thick neck, head shape, and stubbier bill. Still, it can be difficult to separate smaller Canada Geese (*Branta canadensis*) from some Cackling Geese, particularly from Richardson's Cackling Goose (*B.h. hutchinsii*) or, especially, Taverner's Cackling Geese (*B. h. taverneri*). At one time, *parvipes* and *taverneri* were treated as a combined subspecies of Canada Goose. Today, the true status of pale Lesser Canada Geese is uncertain. For the Cackler/Lesser-Canada problems, see the treatment of *parvipes* under the Canada Goose "Geographical Variation" section starting on p. 353. The staggering variation in size and color often adds to the oversimplification of identifying many birds. In the East, for example, the smallest Canadas are very similar in color to Cacklers, and are only slightly larger in body and bill size. As with gulls and other bird species, smaller Canadas are usually more compact with rounder heads, more compact, and have smaller bills; like Cacklers. If you occasionally have to scratch your head in confusion, it probably means you are looking carefully!

Many observers are interested in figuring out the subspecies of white-cheeked geese, in part because they are distinct. For hunters, it may also be out of necessity, because some subspecies have restricted bag limits.

In flight, Cackling Goose is shorter-necked and longer-winged than Canada Goose. Juvenile Canada Geese can be a pitfall for the unwary who are looking for Cacklers, because juveniles are smaller than adults (so there is contrast in size within the flock), and they don't fill out to full-size until the winter.

Sex ratio: Assumed to be equal.

YEAR IN THE LIFE

Cackling Geese breed in the Arctic and winter mainly in western and midcontinent North America. They are most abundant in the Pacific Flyway, with one subspecies (Richardson's, *B. h. hutchinsii*) regularly found in the Central and Mississippi Flyways, rarer but regular in the Atlantic Flyway. Richardson's high counts are in Lake Sule in Illinois, Hughes county in South Dakota. Some of the largest wintering concentrations of Aleutian Geese are in Humboldt Bay NWR and San Joaquin River NWR, both in California. Ridgway's Cackler numbers in the thousands at William L. Finley NWR in Oregon, Ridgefield NWR, and Nisqually NWR in Washington. Taverner's concentrate in northwest Oregon, the Puget Sound and just east of Cascades in Washington. They are known to wander as far south as Florida, Baja California Sur, and Hawaii. There are records from Europe. However, Cacklers are quite common in captivity, escapes are quite likely, and be carefully considered anywhere out of range.

Winters in open areas with large grass fields and water. Some have adapted to winter in suburban parks where they graze on grass and loaf in man-made ponds.

Hundreds, or even thousands, will congregate in areas with good habitat where they graze on grasses and feed on agricultural waste grain. Even in large flocks of "white-cheeked" geese, family groups of Cackling Geese tend to segregate and cluster with other families of their own kind.

Spring migration kicks off for these long-distance migrants in February as family groups begin to retreat from the southern limits of their wintering range. Ridgway's Cacklers, are on their wintering grounds longer, departing their wintering areas in mid-to-late April, heading to coastal regions of south-central Alaska, reaching the Cook Inlet in late April to early May. They arrive on their breeding grounds on the outer Yukon-Kuskokwim Delta from late April to mid-May. Band recoveries indicate that minima follow two routes, one passing over the Alaska Range from the Cook Inlet and down the Yukon River drainage and the other a coastal route over the Alaska Peninsula.

Little is known about their initial pair formation, but once pairs are formed they last "for life" or until one member of the pair dies. One particular display used by the pair, the "triumph ceremony," acknowledges mutual recognition and is also used upon fending off rivals; it secures pair bonds. Pairs arrive on their breeding grounds as snow and ice melts. Arrival on the breeding grounds varies with subspecies, latitude and ice conditions each year. Ridgway's juveniles are able to fly at a very young age, 6-7 weeks. Richardson's youngsters will fly at 7-8.5 weeks. Parents remain with young throughout their first year, migrating and wintering in family groups. Molt-migration not well-documented but surely occurs, presumably in non-breeders and failed breeders.

Once young fledge in mid-August, *B. h. minima* stay on the Yukon-Kuskokwim Delta until early September. When they start heading south, they stop briefly in southern portions of the delta, then continue on to staging grounds on the Alaska Peninsula, where they pause from late September to mid-to-late October. Next, they continue directly to Oregon and California arriving only 2-4 days later.

GEOGRAPHIC VARIATION

Currently, there are four subspecies recognized as Cackling Geese. The smallest and darkest, Ridgway's Cackler, breeds in western Alaska. The Aleutian, breeding on those islands, is slightly larger and paler, with a large neck collar. Taverner's, from northern and western Alaska, is the largest. Finally, Richardson's, breeding right across Northern Canada, is similar to Taverners but averages slightly paler and smaller. See the range maps for additional details. and the fuller explanations below.

B. h. hutchinsii, Richardson's Cackling Goose, is found primarily in the Central and Mississippi Flyways and was the first subspecies to be described, therefore bears the subspecific name of the species, *hutchinsii*. Richardson's is on average the palest-breasted subspecies. The upperparts are also paler on average than the other Cacklers and often have gray bases to the upperpart feathers that can make them appear silvery compared the other subspecies, and even most Canadas. Larger Richardson's are similar to Taverner's Cackling Goose in size and the two are difficult to separate. Richardson's is intermediate in size for a Cackler and has a proportionally longer bill. Richardson's is also the only subspecies that is expected to occur in the East. (Bill length average: M – 33.7mm, F – 31.6mm; Bill width average: M – 21.6mm, F – 20.6mm.) Richies average darker in the west and smaller to the north of their breeding range. Although wintering birds may concentrate mid-contiinent and along the Texas coast, as per the map on p. 357, individuals and small groups may range widely, especially eastward, even to the Atlantic coast.

B. h leucopareia, Aleutian Cackling Goose, is mid-sized with a distinct migration route from its breeding grounds on Aleutian Islands mostly to wintering areas in the Central Valley of California, particularly the Sacramento-San Joaquin river deltas. Within its normal range, it is relatively easy to identify. Most have a distinctive, broad, white collar. The collar has dark feathering at its base. Such a collar – though usually a lot more indistinct – is occasionally present in other subspecies. The breast is pale, usually brown-gray. Distinct island populations of *leucopareia* Cacklers have been described, including extirpated breeding populations from the Kuril and Commander Islands, which were once considered their own subspecies, *B. h. asiatica*. There is also a disjunct Simidi-Island population – slightly larger and darker-necked – of a few hundred birds that winters on the Oregon coast (Nestucca Bay NWR). (Bill length average: M – 34.7mm, F – 32.5mm; Bill width average: M – 15.2mm, F – 14.6mm.)

B. h. minima, Ridgway's Cackling Goose, is the original "Cackler." Its common name was usurped and used to name the entire species. It is the smallest and darkest Cackling Goose; the adult will have a dark breast that is purplish to bronzy. It sometimes has a partial, thin, or pale collar (in about 10% of the individuals). Rarely is it thick.

Nests on the Yukon-Kuskokwin Delta of western Alaska and winters primarily in the Willamette Valley of Oregon. (Bill length average: M – 27.3mm, F – 28.2mm; Bill width average: M – 17.1mm, F – 16.6mm.)

B. h. taverneri, Taverner's Cackling Goose, is a large Cackling Geese subspecies, breeding in northern and western Akaska, wintering mostly in Oregon and Washington. and is quite variable in size and plumage coloration, leading to real identification problems. It, too, can have a complete white collar, though not as distinctive as that of the Aleutian Cackling Goose. Taverner's Cackling Goose may intergrade with Richardson's Cackling Goose. (Bill length average: M – 37.9mm, F – 36.9mm; Bill width average: M – 19.0mm, F – 17.8mm.)

SOUNDS

This is a very vocal species, with large flocks sounding like a group of yappy dogs. Always higher-pitched than Canada Goose, but also characterized by alternating high and low honks. The high-pitched yelping of the Cackling

Goose is distinctive, particularly of Ridgway's Cackler that gives a yelp that varies little. Richardson's is very similar to Ridway's Cackler, in that it is high-pitched, but it has more of a real honk. Aleutian's call is deeper than Ridgway's Cackler and is often double-noted. Taverner's most frequently gives a Ridgway's-type yelp, but lower-pitched, and gives a deep *whoop* most often given during take-off or landing, reminiscent of some Canada Goose calls. Identifying an individual or flock to subspecies solely by voice is not reliable, but it can lend another clue in the identification.

DIET AND FEEDING BEHAVIOR

Cackling Geese forage in winter primarily by grazing on grasses and agricultural waste grain. For example, in Aleutian Cackling Geese, wintering in California frequent harvested cornfields, winter wheat, alfalfa, and irrigated pasture grasses. Cackling Geese in spring and early summer will select leaves high in crude protein and low in fiber. The diet shifts in the late summer to sedges seeds and berries to increase fat reserves for fall migration, rather than on green leaves, which is the preferred food at other times in the year, helping to increase fat reserves for migration.

NESTING

Site: Prefers small island locations on tundra, surrounded by water, close or nearby. Small peninsulas extending into tundra ponds may also be used. Hummocks are often preferred. Some subspecies (e.g. Aleutian) will nest on hillsides or steep slopes and in colonies. Richardson's will also nest in colonies with Ross's and Lesser Snow Geese.

Nest description: A hollow, lined with a variable amount of mosses, grass, and leaves. There will be an inner lining of down and a few feathers. About 6-10 inches in inside diameter, 11-14 inches in outside diameter and 2-4 inches in depth.

Clutch size: Usually 5-6 eggs, ranges from 4-8 with subspecies

Egg description: Elliptical to subelliptical. Creamy-white and smooth. Varies by subspecies, but averages 76 × 51mm

Incubation duration: Averaging 26 days, but sometimes 24-30 days.

Brood parasitism: Very low rates..

HUNTING

Harvesting is restricted in states. Ability to distinguish between subspecies is necessary in order to adhere to regulations. Subspecies managers would like hunters to target Taverner's, as opposed to Aleutian and Ridgway's Cackler, though hunting emphasis has shifted to Ridgway's Cackler because they are most readily identified. They are very wary and tend to fly higher than other subspecies. Cackling geese are among the most difficult geese to lure into decoys.

Harvest trends for Cackling Goose are not described here as they are for many other species in this book. That is because the data for Cackling Goose and Canada Goose are still combined by the USFWS.

POPULATION AND CONSERVATION

Richardson's Cackling Goose, populations nearly doubled from 1971 to 1993 and were estimated at 225,000 in 2012. By 2016, the number was nearly 3 million.

Aleutian Cackling Goose, was listed as Endangered under the ESA from 1967 to 2001, after the population reached 34,200. Numbers in 1967 may have been as low as 1,000 birds. A control program on arctic fox – not native to the Aleutians – on selected breeding islands and hunting closures in important wintering areas resulted in a remarkable rebounding of the populations. This has been a real conservation success story. Aleutian population reached 79,500 in 2009 and was close to 103,000 by 2011, and estimated at over 156,000 in 2016.

Population of Ridgway's Cackling Goose, was 400,000 in the late 1960s, but fell below 25,000 by the mid-1980s, decline attributed to subsistence harvest in Alaska and sport harvesting on wintering grounds. B. h. minima formerly wintered primarily in the Central Valley of California, now 95% in Willamette Valley and lower Columbia River, and expanding north each year into the Puget Sound region. The population estimate was 156,900 in fall 2005 and 327,500 by 2016.

Taverner's Cackling Goose, has not been accurately distinguished from Lesser Canadas, B. c. parvipe, during surveys, but there was a combined 2005 population estimate of 63,800. Taverner's population is considered stable, although accurate winter counts are not available.

EGYPTIAN GOOSE
Alopochen aegyptiacus EGGO

Plates Page 86

OTHER COMMON OR REGIONAL NAMES
African sheldgoose

MEASUREMENTS
Length: Male – c. 27.9 in (70.9 cm); Female – c. 25.9 in (65.7cm)
Wing: Male – av 15.5 in (39.2 cm); Female – av 14.5 in (37.1 cm)
Weight: Male – av 4.57 lbs (2075 g); Female – av 3.63 lbs (1650 g)
Bill: Male – av 48.6 mm; Female – av 47.9 mm

FIRST IMPRESSIONS
Egyptian Geese appear ferocious, or almost goofy, depending on your point of view. This feral resident of southeast Florida looks gray-brown overall, with an orange-buff tone to the breast and orange eyes surrounded with obvious chocolate-brown "shades." Also note the "dirty" brown collar around the base of the neck and a dark center-patch on the lower breast. The particularly long legs and bill are pinkish. Size and shape: This is a stocky long-legged waterfowl that appears to be almost part-goose and part-whistling-duck. The odd shape is distinctive. Flight: The flight appears heavy, strong, and goose-like, with relatively slow wing-beats. Egyptian Geese may fly together in an irregular V-shape formation or in a long line. The large, clean, white, inner wing-patches (both above and below) are easily observed in flight. The primaries are dark, and the speculum an iridescent green.

ID: IN DEPTH AND SIMILAR SPECIES
Adult Egyptian Geese are similar, with the male slightly larger than the female. The female often has darker markings on the pink bill and a lighter-colored head. A degree of individual variation among these birds exists, however, with some birds being grayer and some browner.

Goslings are dull brown above, grayish-white below with a broad pale eyestripe. They have white patches on the wings. Bill, legs, and feet are dark gray. Juvenile plumage is duller than the adults, lacking the dark brown around the eyes and the dark brown patch on the lower breast. The white upperwing surface is tinged with a sooty coloration. The crown is dull brown, not pale gray-white. These birds become sexually mature at two years.

Adults also will have dark mottling on the back of the neck and crown, sometimes appearing reddish-brown. The bill has black on the tip; the back, rump, and tail are black. The undertail coverts are cinnamon. In breeding season, the pink legs and feet become brighter.

Similar species: It's hard to mistake an Egyptian Goose, but be aware of the brown and gray variations and the juvenile plumage among adults. Hybridization with resident Canada Geese has been recorded in the U.K., so be aware of such possibilities in North America.

Sex ratio: Assumed to be equal.

YEAR IN THE LIFE
Since the species is popular as an ornamental species, escapes are relatively common and feral populations have become established, especially in southeastern Florida. The species is dependent on human-altered habitats that present a mix of shallow wetlands and extensive lawns for foraging. They are present in urban parks, golf courses, freshwater ponds, and associated large grassy lawns. This bird could rival resident populations of Canada Geese as the "suburban goose" in some areas. These non-migratory Egyptian Geese are usually gregarious, except when nesting. They will remain in small flocks of family units throughout much of the year. The geese will often be seen roosting in trees or on buildings.

Courtship is noisy, with a mix of elaborate displays, honking, and neck-stretching on the part of the male. Pair formation involves much male-to-male and female-to-female confrontation. Pair bonds are presumed to be permanent.

The breeding season varies with location, but extends from February to December in Florida where pairs may raise more than one brood per year. Breeding pairs of Egyptian Geese are usually well dispersed, each maintaining relatively large, discrete, and well-defended nesting territory.

Adults undergo molt after breeding, during which time they can form large flocks, becoming more sociable.

GEOGRAPHIC VARIATION
No subspecies are recognized.

SOUNDS
Males produce a husky, wheezy breathing sound, or a hoarse, subdued quack which is seldom heard unless the male is agitated. Females will produce a noisier harsh quacking or trumpeting, which can be loud, quick, and strident.

DIET AND FEEDING BEHAVIOR
Mostly, Egyptian Geese feed by grazing on short grass, typically eating grasses, seed-heads, leaves, berries, and plant stems. In shallow water, they will consume tubers and aquatic shoots. Occasionally, they will eat locusts, worms, or other small animals. They feed both day and night, but mostly in the early morning and at dusk, at times far from water.

NESTING
Site: Highly variable: on the ground in concealed sites (e.g., under bushes), in high vegetation, or in tree cavities, crotches, or on buildings.

Nest description: A scrape with a lining of nearby vegetation, lined with gray down. About 10 inches inside diameter, 16-20 inches outside diameter.

Clutch size: Usually 5-8 eggs, sometimes 4-14.

Egg description: Subelliptical to oval. Creamy white and smooth with slight gloss. 70 × 50mm.

Incubation duration: 28-30 days.

Brood parasitism: Unrecorded in North America.

HUNTING
Egyptian Goose is not a regulated species in the U.S. Occasionally, feral or escaped birds have been shot by hunters.

POPULATION AND CONSERVATION
The Egyptian Goose is a widespread waterfowl in Africa, south of the Sahara, particularly in eastern and southern Africa, and it also occurs in the Nile Valley into Egypt. These birds were domesticated by the ancient Egyptians, who included the birds in their artwork and came to consider them sacred. Introduced populations occur in locations in Western Europe, including Britain (East Anglia and spreading), Belgium, Denmark, and the Netherlands. British populations date back to the 18th century. In 2009, Egyptian Goose was officially included in the "general license" of birds in the U.K. that can be culled without individual permission. It is also an offense there to release or allow the escape of this species into the wild.

In the U.S., Egyptian Geese began to be seriously recorded in the early 1990s. They are currently established in southeastern Florida, but there are feral birds in other parts of the state and in Arkansas, California, Texas, and elsewhere where birds may spread and incidental releases may continue.

Because of their adaptability and aggressive territorial behavior, Egyptian Geese could possibly prove to be troublesome in locations (upscale residential developments, county or city parks, and around gold courses) where they breed in the U.S. Any competition with native species here has yet to be recorded, however.

BLACK-BELLIED WHISTLING-DUCK
Dendrocygna autumnalis BBWD

Plates Page 90

OTHER COMMON OR REGIONAL NAMES
Black-bellied tree-duck, gray-breasted tree-duck, red-billed tree-duck, whistling-duck, tree-duck, cornfield duck (Mexico: Pichichi, pato maizal, pato pijije ala blanca, pichi-huila)

MEASUREMENTS
Length: Male – 18.7-19.8 in, av 19.4 in (49.3 cm); Female – 18.5-20.0 in, av 19.1 in (48.5 cm)

Wing: Male – av 9.4 in (23.9 cm); Female – av 9.3 in (23.6 cm)

Weight: Male – av 1.80 lbs (816 g); Female – av 1.85 lbs (839 g)

Bill: Male – av 51.5 mm; Female – av 50.8 mm

FIRST IMPRESSIONS
These noisy and garish tropical waterfowl are often seen in flocks at dawn and dusk as they travel between foraging and roosting sites, from tree-lined ponds, to marshes, even to golf courses. Adults have plain, pale gray faces, with dark brown bodies and black bellies. Look for their obvious, stunning, electric salmon-colored bills. Flocks often appear uniform because males and females look alike, although juveniles are less boldly-marked. Size and Shape: A long-necked and long-legged duck with a short tail and upright posture, this species is the most erect of our waterfowl. It appears dark with a prominent white upperwing stripe on the wing. Black-bellied Whistling-Ducks have broad wings and long necks, with tails practically nonexistent, so their long legs and feet stick out. Sometimes, their posture, tree-perching, and legs can even leave the impression of a heron. Flight: The long legs can be easily seen in flight in this long-necked bird. The white upperwing is obvious, as is the striking black underwing. At a distance they appear broad-winged and hunch-backed, with their heads slung low in flight. Flocks also travel in loose lines, never really holding a single file line or V. Wingbeats are slow and steady, but somewhat jerky and loose.

ID: IN DEPTH AND SIMILAR SPECIES
Black-bellied Whistling-Ducks are bold-looking waterfowl, with distinctive plumage. Males and females look alike throughout the year, and juveniles are usually readily distinguished. Whistling-ducks have some novel traits among waterfowl that allow for flexibility in their molt timing.

They molt only once a year, have long-term pair bonds, and do not undergo long migrations, and, thus, have fewer constraints normally associated with molt. The exact timing of molt in adult Black-bellied Whistling-Ducks is poorly understood and probably variable. Except for northern breeders, they appear to undergo most of their molt away from the breeding grounds, unlike other waterfowl. Ducklings are black and fairly bright yellowish-white, with a dark cap, and dark stripe through their white cheek. As in all *Dendrocygna*, they have a distinct dark T-stripe on the back of the head and neck. These ducklings are yellower than those of Fulvous Whistling-Duck. They have a white breast and a few white spots on their dark body. Don't be fooled into thinking that you are viewing a female or first-year male Masked Duck simply because of a similar face pattern. Look for the pale yellow spots on the body of juvenile Black-bellied ducklings, not present on Masked Ducks. Juvenile plumage, fully acquired when the ducklings are 10-13 weeks old, lacks a black belly. The juvenile has a dull gray belly and all-gray bill. At 13-14 weeks, just after being fully grown, they also begin replacing juvenile plumage with an adult-like plumage that is retained for about a year. At 13-14 weeks old, they begin replacing juvenile tail feathers, then head, neck, breast, back, and rump. In the middle of this molt, they appear mottled, as they are growing black belly feathers. The amount of juvenile plumage replaced is variable. Some late-hatching individuals replace a few body feathers, while other replace all their body feathers. This molt also includes all tail feathers and some wing coverts and usually spans from August-March, depending on how early in the season they hatched. Most birds are inseparable from adults at one-year old.

Adult males and adult females cannot be reliably separated in the field. If you are comparing a mated pair, you may notice females tend to be a little duller on the belly with a browner face and have pinker legs, opposed to a male's whitish or yellowish-pink legs. Both sexes will have a bold pink, almost red, bill with grayish tip. Adults have one plumage that is worn all year, so they have one complete molt, including a 20-day flightless period. For some individuals this takes place in August and September, prior to fall migration, but others apparently molt away from the breeding grounds. Their molt tends to be protracted and the timing is more flexible than in other waterfowl.

Similar Species: Juveniles are most likely to be confused with Fulvous Whistling-Duck. The Fulvous Whistling-Duck, however, will have a warm brown face and underparts. Downy young have a similar head pattern to female and first-year male Masked Ducks. Look for the pale yellow spots on the body of juvenile Black-bellied ducklings, not present on Masked Ducks. When in the Rio Grande Valley of Texas, don't be misled by the bold white stripe on a Black-bellied Whistling-Duck's wing, thinking you have seen a wild Muscovy Duck. At first glance, the white wing patches make both species appear similar, but Muscovy is a much heavier bird, with a long thick tail, and, perhaps most importantly, the white on the wing is on the forewing.

Sex ratio: It is more balanced that in other ducks, virtually even.

YEAR IN THE LIFE

From parts of the southern United States to northern Argentina, Black-bellied Whistling-Duck is fairly common. This species is expanding in the United States, where individuals or small flocks are prone to wander – especially in late spring and summer – to unexpected states such as California, Wisconsin, North Dakota, Pennsylvania, Maryland, Massachusetts, New Jersey, and even Nova Scotia. The species is frequently kept in captivity, so escapes make the true origin of some of these birds very tough to assess.

Black-bellied Whistling-Ducks are migratory only in the extreme northern part of their range. Birds inhabiting the limits of their range outside of Texas will retreat between August and October to spend the winter in northern Sinaloa and farther south. Some flocks remain on the coast of southern Texas for the winter. Winter congregations form in the lowlands of Mexico in shallow, freshwater lakes and ponds with dense emergent vegetation. Sometimes they use open areas and other habitats including mangrove swamps, rivers and lagoons. They even hang out in grassy residential areas with ponds including suburban parks and golf courses.

Black-bellied usually form pair bonds in the winter and remain with the same mate for subsequent years. Young birds are able to attract mates and breed when they are about one year old. Their courtship displays are simpler than those of dabbling ducks, more like those of geese and swans, with neck-stretching and head-dipping. In one display, they fling their heads up and splash water over their backs.

In the spring, they arrive in Texas from early March to April, and in Arizona in mid-April. Like many tropical species, their breeding is more closely tied to the availability of water and other resources, rather than a particular season.

Nesting in Texas is initiated from early April to mid-October, peaking in mid-May to mid-July in years with normal rainfall. In Texas, broods hatch from mid-May to late September. If there are drought conditions, nest initiation is pushed off later in the season. The pair cares for their brood until long after the young are capable of flight at 8-9 weeks old. In Forida, however, those whistling-ducks are late-summer breeders, with most broods found in August and September.

GEOGRAPHIC VARIATION

Two subspecies are recognized, one of which occurs in North America, *D. a. fulgens*, which breeds from the southern United States to western Panama. The northern birds of this subspecies average larger than those farther south. Nominate *D. a. autumnalis* breeds from eastern Panama to central Argentina, which is also known as *D.*

a. discolor in some literature. They are smaller with a gray brand across the breast, wrapping around the base of the neck, so they have more limited brown on the neck and breast than *D. a. fulgens*.

SOUNDS
This very vocal species, as the name implies, has a whistling vocalization that can carry long distances. The soft and wheezy whistle, *pee-che-che-ne*, is frequently given in flight and while perched. They are also often heard at night as flocks travel to feed in flooded fields. Black-bellied Whistling-Ducks also utter *chit-chit-chit* in flight. When taking flight these birds occasionally give a single *yip* or a series of notes. Their distraction call *oo-eek* is similar to that of a female Wood Duck.

DIET AND FEEDING BEHAVIOR
Black-bellied Whistling-Duck forages both day and night, with much crepuscular feeding in shallow water and fields. These waterfowl are primarily terrestrial grazers, as opposed to aquatic sievers. The birds will eat grains and plant materials, especially Bermuda grass and sorghum seeds, as well as, smartweeds, and millet. They also forage in corn and rice fields where they can become a problem. Black-bellied Whistling-Ducks will also forage for small treetop fruit. Animal matter (snails and insects) makes up less than a tenth of the diet. The birds will feed in shallow water, along shorelines or mud bars, but seldom beyond leg depth.

NESTING
Site: In wooded areas with lakes and ponds and by subtropical lagoons and marshes with surrounding mesquite, also agricultural areas and tree-lined suburbs. Nest in cavities (often in live oaks, ebony, and willows) between 8-30 feet, and readily use nestboxes, occasionally nest on ground. Pairs may nest far away from water (even up to 1,000 yards away). Nestboxes that are predator-proof have double the nesting success. See the appendix at the end of this book for Black-bellied Whistling Duck nestbox details and dimensions.

Nest description: Cavity nests unlined, with no down present (a unique practice among waterfowl by whistling-ducks). Ground nests composed of bent-down stems and grasses.

Clutch size: average 13, as few as 8, sometimes up to 18.

Egg description: Short elliptical. White to creamy white. 52 x 39 mm.

Incubation duration: 27-28 days, by both sexes (along with Fulvous Whistling-Duck, virtually unique among our waterfowl).

Brood parasitism: Commonly lay in nests of other Black-bellied Whistling-Ducks, sometimes with dozens of eggs present. In some studies in Texas, about 70% of the nests have been parasitized by other Black-bellied Whistling-Ducks. Closely-placed nest-boxes can exacerbate the brood parasitism. In Mexico, mixed clutches in nestboxes have been reported with Muscovy Duck.

HUNTING
"Pichichies" are under little hunting pressure in the Unites States, partly because many individuals depart the U.S. prior to the opening of hunting season, and partly because the species is also moving into hunt-free suburbs. They also were legally protected from hunting until 1984. Not surprisingly, today about two-thirds of the U.S. harvest occurs in Texas.

Hunting pressure is greater in Mexico for the "pato maizal." On a broad-scale, hunting does not appear to be significantly impacting populations. They are not a particularly wary species by nature, but they do become distrustful in areas where hunting is prevalent. For northern hunters who are encountering tree-ducks for the first time, it's a completely new experience to see gangly "shorebirds" with oddly loose wingbeats drop into a spread.

POPULATION AND CONSERVATION
Populations have been significantly increasing in the United States. In the early 1900s the core of their U.S. breeding range was in the Lower Rio Grande Valley. Starting in the 1960s, they spread to areas north of Corpus Christi. Now, they are breeding across Texas into southeast Oklahoma, Louisiana, and southwest Arkansas.

The increase in range may be at least partially explained by the spread of irrigation impoundments and stock ponds for cattle. Small post-breeding flocks and individuals have wandered north to the Great Lakes and east to the Mississippi River Valley and along the Gulf Coast where they have been recorded from many eastern states and provinces. They have also pushed into Arizona since the 1960s. In Florida, they are uncommon to locally abundant and increasing resident. This population is believed to have spread initially from a single flock arriving from the Yucatán, or perhaps from Texas, in the early 1980s. Escapes from zoos may also have enhanced the Florida population. Whatever the case, since then, they have moved through Florida to coastal Georgia and have bred in southeast South Carolina. According to Breeding Bird Surveys their populations increased an average of 8.8% annually from 1966-1998. The Christmas Bird Count data for 2009-10 totaled 20,396 birds in the U.S, with 73% in Texas, 20% in Florida, 6% in Louisiana.

The addition of next boxes in areas where there are few natural cavities has greatly contributed to the success of local populations. Their status in the U.S. certainly seems secure, and their spread has been a real success story. In Mexico, nesting habitat is being lost through deforestation and the alteration of habitat for cultivation.

FULVOUS WHISTLING-DUCK
Dendrocygna bicolor FUWD

Plates Page 92

OTHER COMMON OR REGIONAL NAMES-
Fulvous tree-duck, long-legged duck, Mexican squealer, squealer
(Mexico: pijía, serrano, pato silvón, pato pijije ala negra, pijije canelo)

MEASUREMENTS
Length: Male -17.7-18.5 in, av 18.1 in (46.0 cm); Female – 16.0-18.3 in, av 17.3 in (43.9 cm)
Wing: Male – av 8.6 in (21.9 cm); Female – av 8.1 in (20.7 cm)
Weight: Male – av 1.72 lbs (780 g); Female – av 1.49 lbs (676 g)
Bill: Male – av 46.6 mm; Female – av 45.5 mm

FIRST IMPRESSIONS
Noisy flocks of these orange-buff birds dropping into flooded rice fields to feed is a regular site in southwestern Louisiana and other spots along the Gulf Coast. Look for warm colors overall, with a tawny head and neck, dark brown back scalloped with rufous covert edges, and rusty below. Size and shape: The words long and lanky characterize these ducks. They have a long goose-like neck, small-looking heads, and long legs. Tail is very short. The stance is less erect than that of Black-bellied Whistling Duck. Flight: Hunch-backed, broad wings, long thin neck, and trailing legs are noticeable. Legs disappear at a distance. The head and neck are warm pale brown. Distinctive black underwings really stand out. Upperwing coverts are rusty. A white U can be seen at the base of the tail, and white in the vent area. Comes into land with neck drooped, legs dangling, and feet outstretched- a whistling-duck distinctive posture. Flocks move in loose V-formation between feeding sites. Often migrates at night, but flocks are seen off Texas coast during the day, fairly low over the water, often calling in flight. Fulvous Whistling-Ducks look like they are moving slowly on floppy wingbeats with an emphasis on the down stroke.

ID: IN DEPTH AND SIMILAR SPECIES
Ducklings are gray-bodied with a black caps and napes, white cheeks and white bands that wrap around the back of the head. Like the Black-bellied Whistling-Duck, this duckling has a dark T-stripe on the back of the head and neck. But these ducklings are overall paler. Juvenile plumage begins to appear at three weeks and is fully grown at 9-10 weeks. The plumage is only slightly paler and duller than that of the adults, with narrower feathers and a looser texture. First-years that hatched in the U.S. replace their juvenile body plumage in from mid-October to November. This is retained until the following summer, about July. Adults are very similar to first-years; males are slightly larger than females. The black stripe on the hindneck is continuous in female, usually broken in male. Not much is known about molt among the U.S. breeders. Both sexes have a similar molt schedule and undergo just one molt a year. They are flightless during their wing molt, which is likely to take place in November or December, well after the breeding season. They undergo a protracted body molt, which is most intense during the wing molt. Adults have more broadly rounded upperwing coverts than immatures.

Similar species: Their gangly appearance is only similar to our other species of whistling-duck, the Black-bellied. Fulvous are unlikely to be confused with other ducks given a good view. One potential pitfall is confusion with a juvenile Black-bellied Whistling-Duck, which is somewhat similar but very dull and plain-colored. Black-bellied, however, quickly obtains significant amounts of black on the sides and belly and will have a darker breast.

Sex ratio: It is slightly male-biased (c. 53%).

YEAR IN THE LIFE
Fulvous Whistling-Ducks are becoming increasingly scarce in many parts of their range in the U.S. However, it is still one of the most widely distributed species of waterfowl in the world. They are found from the Gulf Coast and Florida, throughout the Caribbean, south to central Argentina and in the Old World in East Africa, Madagascar, India, Sri Lanka, and southwest Burma. They are resident breeders in the Hawaiian Islands.

Fulvous Whistling-Ducks expanded north to the southern United States from Mexico beginning in the late 1800s. They became established in California and U.S. Gulf Coastal Plain and Florida in early-to-mid-twentieth century. Their expansion into the U.S. coincided with the expansion of rice in Texas, Louisiana, and Florida. The biggest concentrations have been of over 2,000 birds found in southwestern Louisiana (at Lacassine NWR) and in Vermilion Parish in March and April. Also, winter counts at Stormwater Treatment Areas in Hendry County Florida and in the Rio Grande Valley (Hidalgo County, Texas) in

July are exceptional.

Fulvous Whistling-Ducks are migratory only in the northern parts of their range, mainly the central US (Texas and Louisiana). These whistling-ducks arriving in Louisiana are either migrating along the rim of the Gulf or fly across the west end of the Gulf. Many Florida birds are resident, however, and a portion of the birds banded in Florida have been recovered in Cuba. After the nesting season, they often engage in irregular northward post-breeding movements, which result in sightings in the Florida Panhandle and very rarely along the Mississippi River basin and the East Coast.

In spring, the birds arrive on Gulf Coast nesting areas in February and March, coinciding with planting in rice-growing areas. Formerly arrived in early to late March in California; since the mid-1980s the earliest arrivals have been in April. Pairs bonds are at least for multiple years, if not for life. Courtship displays are subtle, with regular bill-dipping. Whistling-ducks don't put on much of a courtship show like the dabblers do. At least a post-copulatory display by both is more elaborate, a "step-dance" where they face the same direction, rise up, tread water and hold their necks almost S-shaped.

The main courtship action occurs when the birds arrive on their breeding grounds until mid-April.

Once the brood hatches, the male remains to care for the young as they grow, not unlike geese and swans. Adults molt away from breeding grounds.

Fall depart U.S. breeding grounds in September and October. Staging birds at Lacassine NWR, Louisiana, peak from late August to late September.

GEOGRAPHIC VARIATION
No subspecies are recognized.

SOUNDS
This is a vocal species, heard day and night. Their typical call is a high-pitched, two-syllable whistle, *kit-Tee* or *pee-chee*. It is often given in flight and from ground while feeding and before roosting. They also give a variable, soft, four-syllable chatter, *cup-cup-cup-cup*. During hostile behaviors, a single, harsh *kee* note is rapidly repeated. The female calls are softer and lower and slightly rougher than the males..

DIET AND FEEDING BEHAVIOR
Fulvous Whistling-Duck will dabble at or below the water surface, up-tipping or snatching items on the surface or on low vegetation (e.g., aquatic insects in the breeding season), and will even engage in shallow diving. These birds feed almost exclusively on different moist-soil and aquatic plant seeds, with a special fondness for rice, but also on some aquatic invertebrates. Feeding water-depths when diving are mostly between 18–45 inches, but in ricefields under 18 inches.

NESTING
Site: Nests constructed in dense floating or flooded emergent vegetation (often in rice) or on the ground on low levees or in weedy fields.

Nest description: The foundation usually consists of a weak platform of bent-down stems and other plant material found nearby. There is no down lining (a unique practice by whistling-ducks). Nest sizes average about 10 inches in inside diameter, 14 inches in outside diameter, and 4 inches in depth.

Clutch size: Range 8-14.

Egg description: Short elliptical to short subelliptical. White to creamy-white. Smooth and non-glossy, with a finely pitted surface. 53 x 41 mm.

Incubation duration: 24-25 days, by both sexes (along with Black-bellied Whistling-Duck, virtually unique among our waterfowl).

Brood parasitism: Several females may lay in the same nest with up to 16 eggs found in a nest.

HUNTING
Fulvous Tree Ducks are not widely hunted in the U.S., largely due to their limited distribution, relatively small population and early departure from the country, often before the season kicks off. On a global scale, they are popular game birds and hunting is a major factor in population management. For example, the harvest is considered sustainable in Venezuela, but in other areas, the population is threatened by commercial and subsistence harvests.

POPULATION AND CONSERVATION
Fulvous Whistling-Duck numbers in U.S. have fluctuated dramatically since the early twentieth century. Populations may actually ebb and flow over the long term. These shifts are attributed to the species' irregular movements, changes in rice agriculture, pesticide contamination, habitat loss and degradation, disturbances associated with agricultural practices, and hunting. The 1974 EPA banning of aldrin, extensively used in rice agriculture, resulted in a rebound of Fulvous Whistling-Duck numbers.

The California population has been in steep decline. In the early to mid-1900s they were regular breeders in coastal areas from the San Joaquin Valley to the south side of the San Francisco Bay and in southeastern deserts. By the late 1970s nesting was limited to the Imperial Valley. Twenty years later, there were fewer than five pairs nesting in the region. They are now rare in southern California (Imperial and Los Angeles Counties).

The southern Florida population has also crashed since the 1970s and is now only found in a few favored locations. Fulvous Whistling-Ducks, however, are expanding in the central portion of their U.S. range, even nesting in southeastern Arkansas.

MUSCOVY DUCK
Cairina moschata MUDU

Plates Page 96

OTHER COMMON OR REGIONAL NAMES-
Muscovy, musk duck
(Mexico: pato real, booxpato, pato criollo)

MEASUREMENTS
Length: Male – c. 31.7 in (80.5 cm); Female – c. 26.5 in (67.3cm) Note: Feral birds are significantly larger, especially males.
Wing: Male – av 14.8 in (37.5 cm); Female – av 12.1 in (30.8 cm)
Weight: Male – av 6.50 lbs (2950 g, but domestic birds may be over 4000 g); Female – av 2.75 lbs (1250 g)
Bill: Male – av 67.9 mm; Female – av 51.4 mm

FIRST IMPRESSIONS
Muscovy Ducks are black with prominent white patches on the forewing on adults. The bill of a Muscovy Duck is pinkish with a dark band. Wild birds have a small warty area just around their bill and eye that is largely dark. Domestic birds have more extensive red warts around the eye and bill, and their overall body color comes is a variety of shades. These hefty, goose-like ducks are difficult to find in their wild form in the US, where they occur only in the Lower Rio Grande Valley of Texas, particularly in Starr County along the Rio Grande. However, if you head to a city park in Florida, or elsewhere in some of the warmer parts of the U.S., you're likely to find the domestic variety, covered in warts and waddling about. The closest relative in North America is the Wood Duck which shares the behavior of perching and roosting in trees. Muscovy Ducks are most active in the early morning and evening, so that is the best time to look for the wild birds flying up and down the Rio Grande. Size and shape: A bulky-bodied duck, with a long broad tail, long, thin neck and somewhat crested head. The domestic variety are larger and heavier-looking; males are much larger than females.

These ducks can erect a crest on their head and produce a very steep forehead. Flight: Appears massive with very broad wings and large white patches on the upperwing and underwing on adults. Wild birds are agile in flight, despite their relatively heavy bodies, with slow, steady, but snappy wingbeats. First years have very small white patch on wing. They have a long, thick tail and small head on a thin neck. They typically occur in pairs or small groups traveling shyly and silently for short distances between feeding sites. They sometimes roost communally at tops of large trees.

ID: IN DEPTH AND SIMILAR SPECIES
Ducklings are dark brown with a bright yellow face and breast. They have a dark brown stripe behind the eye and yellow forehead. Juvenile plumage is dark overall, duller than adult females. First years replace juvenile plumage in their first-year. They are dark brown with some iridescence in the wing. Their breast is pale brown and bill is paler than adults. They lack extensive warts around the eye and do not acquire a white wing patch until their first winter

Adult males are dark iridescent green on the back, which appears black in many conditions. They have a light pink tip to the bill and dark facial skin in between the eye and bill. The reddish warts are limited to a line where the facial skin meets the feathers. Adult females are smaller and duller than males. They lack a knob on the top of their bill.

The timing and extent of molts are not well-known in wild Muscovy Ducks. Concentrations of molting birds have not been reported. Given they do not have strong seasonal pressures, molts are likely protracted and timing is somewhat flexible. Adults likely undergo a complete molt after the breeding season. They may replace some body feathers at other times of the year, but their appearance does not change.

Similar species: Their structural oddities and atypical behaviors, make them unlikely to be confused with most other ducks. The domestic vs. wild birds can usually be separated quickly by location, habitat, and habits. Domestics are often in city parks or around other domestic mutts. In Florida and Brownsville, Texas, there are large populations of feral birds. Domestic-type males also have extensive red, warty skin around the bill and are even larger than wild Muscovies. Some varieties of domestic Muscovies have white blotches on the head and body or are mostly white.

Black-bellied Whistling-Duck is the most likely species for confusion when they are cruising down the Rio Grande flashing their big white wing patches. Black-bellieds have white all the way down the center of the wing, opposed to just the forewing. With a quick glance, they seem similar, but another look to see the pale face and dangling pink feet of Black-bellied is usually enough to resolve confusion.

Cormorants are also cruising down the Rio Grande, which are basically dark overall like immature Muscovies, but they hold their neck kinked in flight.

Sex Ratio: Unknown.

YEAR IN THE LIFE

A wild Muscovy Duck is wary and hard to find north of Mexico. They are scarce and difficult to see in Lower Rio Grande Valley along the river from San Ygnacio to Roma. They are even less frequently seen farther downriver at Bentsen-Rio Grande State Park and Santa Ana NWR. Muscovy Duck ranges from extreme south Texas, through eastern Mexico south to northern Argentina.

Like other tropical waterfowl, Muscovy is not migratory and has a more flexible annual schedule because of fewer seasonal changes to deal with during the course of a year. This is especially true farther south in the core of their range.

Timing of the breeding season varies throughout their range, but is basically during the wet season. In northern Mexico, breeding lasts from late April to September with the peak laying in May and June.

Muscovy does not form strong pair bonds even in the way that dabblers do, certainly not like the long-term pair bonds seen in geese. Still, Muscovy Ducks reportedly have courtship rituals including head-bobbing, crest-raising, tail-wagging, and bill-clapping. Males do not play a role in parental care or nest defense.

GEOGRAPHIC VARIATION

No subspecies are recognized.

SOUNDS

Muscovy Ducks are usually quiet. They are not often heard unless they are disturbed when they give a short, flat *huh*, which is often repeated. While courting, they repeat a low *ha-ha-ha* gasping chuckle. Males give a hiss. Ducklings give high-pitched peeps in rapid succession.

DIET AND FEEDING BEHAVIOR

Muscovy Ducks are omnivorous, eating plant matter and animals on the surface or dipping their heads underwater to access shallow-lying food. They eat roots, seeds, and stems of a variety of terrestrial and aquatic plants and will also eat agricultural crops. Among animal matter that Muscovy Ducks eat are small fish, frogs, snails, and insects, with termites being a favorite. They feed by dabbling and up-ending, mainly in shallow water. They will also graze on land.

NESTING

Site: Cavities, holes in trees or banks, or nestboxes. Traditional sites in northern Mexico are often near small farm ponds, streams, areas with flooded timber, forested swamps, and other wooded areas around water. See the appendix at the end of this book for Muscovy Duck nestbox details and dimensions.

Nest description: A hollow, lined with little plant material (grass and dry leaves) and with down and feathers. Down tufts are light brown with pale centers. The size is variable, depending on the natural cavity, but the outside diameter may be c. 11 inches.

Clutch size: 9-15 eggs normally

Egg description: Subelliptical to elliptical. Pale creamy to pale buff. 61 × 45mm

Incubation duration: 30-31 days in wild, 35 days for domestic birds.

Brood parasitism: Common, dump nests frequently occur, sometimes have Black-bellied Whistling-Duck eggs in the nest.

HUNTING

Muscovy Ducks are frequently hunted and poached throughout much of their range in Central and South America. Year-round hunting is known to occur in Mexico. The birds are typically secretive and especially wary in areas wherever they are hunted.

POPULATION AND CONSERVATION

Little is known about the about the population of wild Muscovy Ducks. Numbers declined significantly or disappeared altogether over much of its range in Mexico, presumably because of year-round hunting and clearing of riparian habitat for agriculture. In response, biologists set up the first experimental nestboxes in 1981. Their success prompted a widespread nestbox effort, primarily led by Ducks Unlimited de Mexico, A.C. (DUMAC), an effort which was very successful in restoring the Muscovy Duck population in northern and eastern Mexico. Through 1994, 7,400 boxes were set.

The birds are considered endangered in Mexico, and they are officially protected. (Year-round hunting and the continued clearing of riparian habitat are considered two main threats to the species in Mexico.) Expanded nestbox programs on both sides of the U.S.-Mexican border, in appropriate habitats, would probably contribute to the conservation of this species.

The highest number of wild birds along the Rio Grande – about two dozen individuals – have been found in Starr County, between Falcon Dam and Roma.

The birds are also protected under the Migratory Bird Treaty Act since they occur in Hidalgo, Starr, and Zapata counties in South Texas. Introduced populations in Florida and elsewhere in the U.S. are considered invasive species that compete with native waterfowl for food and nesting areas. In Florida and anywhere outside their natural range, they are not protected and may be removed without a federal migratory bird permit.

WOOD DUCK
Aix sponsa WODU

Plates Page 98

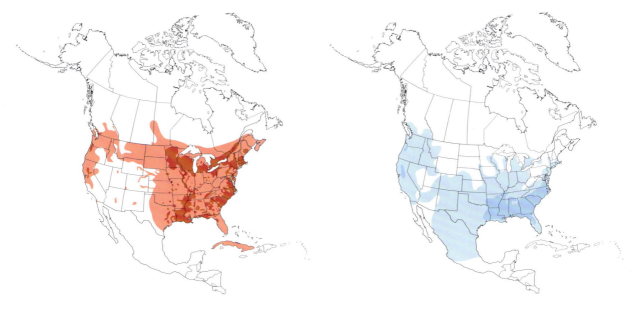

OTHER COMMON OR REGIONAL NAMES
Woodie, summer duck, Carolina duck, acorn duck, swamp duck, squealer, spring duck, water pheasant
(Québec: canard branchu)
(Mexico: pato de charreteras, pato arcoiris, huyuyo)

MEASUREMENTS
Length: Male – 18.8-21.2 in, av 20.0 in (50.8 cm); Female – 18.5-20.1 in, av 19.5 in (49.5 cm)
Wing: Male – av 8.9 in (22.6 cm); Female – av 8.6 in (21.8 cm)
Weight: Male – av 1.53 lbs (694 g); Female – av 1.43 lbs (647 g)
Bill: Male – av 33.0 mm; Female – av 34.5 mm

FIRST IMPRESSIONS
Males have a rainbow of iridescence about the head and back that is simply stunning up close. Despite their elaborate plumage, Wood Ducks' dark coloration allows them to blend in surprisingly well with the wooded swamps they inhabit. They are dark ducks, males with paler sides and white belly. Females are gray-brown overall, short-crested, with a white chin and white tear-drop-shape eye patch. Pairs and small flocks, consisting of fewer than 20 birds, feed in bottomland forest by picking and dabbling from the surface, moving quickly while jerking their heads. Frequently bob head backward and forward when swimming. Unlike most other ducks, they frequently perch on logs and branches. Size and shape: Wood Ducks have small bills, crested heads and skinny necks, slender bodies and long, broad tails. They ride high on the water, with the rear of their body tipped up. Flight: They are long-bodied and short-winged. Their long and squared-off tails, in particular, and their skinny necks are distinctive in silhouette. They easily gain height upon take-off. At a distance they appear uniformly dark, with white bellies. They distinctively bob their heads up and down in flight. Flocks cluster in ovals and generally do not shift positions. They maneuver well through dense woodlands, aided by their long tails.

ID: IN DEPTH AND SIMILAR SPECIES
Wood Ducks typically breed when they are a year old. They usually replace all of their juvenile plumage through fall, after which they are difficult to age. Ducklings are similar to Mallard, but they are darker brown on the body with paler cheeks and smaller bills. Their face is not a warm yellow like Mallard. Juvenile plumage is fully grown at about 9-10 weeks. It is basically the same color pattern as adult females, but the crest is not as full and coloration is muted and patterns are more diffuse, particularly about the face. Their bellies are streaked and mottled, rather than white. First-years replace juvenile plumage from about 14-21 weeks. This molt includes all body feathers and most (to all) wing coverts, so first-years are essentially identical to adults by the end of the summer. Timing of this molt varies depending on when the brood hatched, but it often takes place in July-August.

First-year females are very difficult to impossible to distinguish from adult females once they replace juvenile plumage. If any juvenile wing coverts or other juvenile feathers are present, it's safe to call it a first-year. Adult females are gray-brown overall with prominent white patches around the eyes – and appearing almost like tear-drops – and white throats. Adult females molt some body feathers late-winter to early spring.

First-year males are almost indistinguishable from adults after they molt out of juvenile plumage. But they will have a duller orange iris and orbital ring, pale orange bill, and retained juvenile brown-and-white breast streaking. Some birds can also be aged in-hand if some juvenile wing coverts are retained. Rarely, some males will retain some juvenile plumage on the flanks or a tertial or two. Adult males are stunning, with their brightly marked and distinctive bushy crests and the bulbous backs of their heads. Their white neck-rings, and chin straps, along with their red eyes and red-and-silver bills are unique. The males are in eclipse plumage from June-September. Eclipse males have brown sides and breasts; they loose the crest on their heads, leaving a shadow of the breeding head pattern, particularly the white neck-rings and chin-straps. Their eyes are still red and the bills are colorful, but duller than in the breeding season. During wing molt males are flightless for about 3 weeks.

Similar Species: Their shape and distinctive plumage readily separates them from most other ducks, except Mandarin Duck, a native of Asia, which is often kept in captivity. The colorful male Mandarin Ducks is unmistakable, with its wide white band from the eye to the rear of its fluffy-looking crest, its bright chestnut-orange cheeks and distinctive fan-shaped chestnut-orange tertials. Female Mandarin Duck is similar to a female Wood Duck, but it has a lengthy thin eye-stripe extending behind the eye and a thin white eyering that is far narrower than the tear-drop of the Wood Duck. The female Mandarin's nail is pale, while the female Wood Duck's is dark. Released Mandarin's have breed in the wild, for example in Sonoma County, California.

Sex ratio: Males dominate at 56% across wintering banding sites.

YEAR IN THE LIFE

Wood Ducks are common in wooded swamps and freshwater marshes of much of North America. You are unlikely to find them in the arid regions areas of the southwest, but they do occasionally show up in the winter or during migration. It's a rare bird in southeast Alaska. Wood Ducks are most abundant in the Atlantic and Mississippi Flyways. Wintering concentrations in the southeast in parts of Arkansas, Louisiana, and Mississippi can reach impressive numbers with over a thousand in a single location. Wood Ducks are denizens of bottomland forests, swamps, riparian habitats, and freshwater marshes.

Wood Ducks are both migratory and resident in North America. It is the only North American waterfowl with both a large migratory population and a nonmigratory one. Approximately one-third of the eastern population and three-quarters of the western population are permanent residents. Migratory birds will begin moving north in February, with the majority of spring migration taking place in March and April. Wood Ducks get an early start on the courting season, forming pair bonds earlier than other ducks, beginning in late summer, continuing through to the early spring. Courtship displays will include a wide variety of elaborate actions, including the male's "turn-the-back-of-the-head" where the nape is oriented to the female, the associated "incite" action by the female, as well as ritualized drinking, crest raising, wing preening, vocal burps, head-shakes, and essential display shakes with head-and breast movements and whistling.

Upon selecting a mate for the season, females lead their mates to their breeding grounds. Females search wet woods for nest cavities in hollow trees, Pileated Woodpecker holes, and man-made nestboxes. Finding the right cavity is key to nesting success. Experienced females nest 11-19 days earlier than rookies, first-year breeders. Wood Duck is the only duck in North America that can pull off two broods in a season, especially at southern latitudes where there is a long window in the year open for nesting. Given their southern distribution, females can raise the first brood from January to April and start a second clutch shortly after. As you may expect, it is normally the older, more experienced females that attempt two broods a year. Males abandon their mate shortly after the females begin incubating the clutch. Most males undergo a northerly molt migration. The average time females remain with brood varies from 4.5-8 weeks, depending on the region and at what point within the nesting season the clutch hatched.

As northern nesters begin heading south in the fall, numbers build up from mid-August until in late September in regions where counts can exceed one thousand birds in wetland. Wood Ducks are not hardy, cold weather ducks, so they head out relatively early compared with the majority moving through the Midwest in early October. Some migrate offshore and join flocks of scoters on the Atlantic coast. Numbers on the wintering grounds in southern states increase steadily through December.

GEOGRAPHIC VARIATION
No subspecies are recognized.

SOUNDS
Males: They will infrequently give a high, thin, and wheezy *szeeeEEP*. Females: Squealing flight call given by females is distinctive and readily recognizable. The most frequently heard call is a rising squeal, *ooo-EEK*, often given as flushed. A variation of the female call is *ter-WEEeeoh*. Gives a quivering *who-who-who who-oh-oh* to call ducklings. Ducklings: Alarm call is a high-pitched *Peep* often repeated. They begin vocalizing 2-3 days before hatching, which may allow the clutch to hatch synchronously.

DIET AND FEEDING BEHAVIOR
Wood Ducks are omnivores with a varied diet. They dabble, dip, and up-end in habitat that is often flooded timber (which may often be beaver-associated) and relatively shallow wetlands with emergent vegetation. They occasionally dive, but they more often feed in waters that

are 7-16 inches deep, consuming seeds, fruits, and aquatic and terrestrial invertebrates, a diet not dissimilar to that of many dabbling ducks. Depending on season and locality, they may favor nuts, especially acorns, and waste from harvested fields.

NESTING

Site: Wood Ducks nest near mature forest streams and pools. Nests are found in natural cavities in tree trunks and in nestboxes, 6-30 feet up (average: 24 feet). More rarely, they will nest at a similar site but in a building, such as a barn. See the appendix at the end of this book for Wood Duck nest-box details and dimensions.

Nest description: Cavity nests are lined with white down.

Clutch size: Average 13 eggs for first brood, 10 eggs for second brood. Usually 8-10, sometimes 6-15.

Egg description: Subelliptical to oval. Smooth and fairly glossy. White or creamy-white to tan. (See Hooded Merganser.) 51 x 38 mm.

Incubation duration: 28-32 days.

Brood parasitism: Commonly lay in nests of other Wood Ducks (nests with 16 or more Wood Duck eggs is assumed to be parasitized) and is regularly parasitized by Hooded Merganser.

HUNTING

After a remarkable 20th-century population recovery, one made possible in part by 23 years of federally-mandated closed hunting followed by two decades of periodic state closed hunting, Wood Ducks thrive again. Starting around 1960, the Wood Duck harvest increased steadily.

This species today is greatly sought after by hunters, especially in the Atlantic and Mississippi Flyways, where it comprises more than 10% of annual waterfowl harvest in United States. Their feathers are also highly sought-after by fly fisherman for their flies. Hunters in pursuit of Wood Ducks often have success by jump-shooting or pass-shooting. They react unpredictably to decoys and are generally wary and shy to begin with. However, they don't necessarily flush right away when they are startled. Squealer duck calls are available, and are most appropriate in settings in which the species dominates.

The harvest of Woodies in the U.S. over two years (2013 and 2014) averaged at about 1,120,000 birds; and for Canada the corresponding number was 76,800.

Prime Wood Duck hunting can be found in the southeast.

POPULATION AND CONSERVATION

The recovery of Wood Duck populations from near extinction in the early 1900s is a spectacular success story. George Bird Grinnell, grand ornithologist of the time, remarked in 1901 that the species was being shot at all seasons, becoming very scarce, and "likely to be exterminated before long." Populations had been devastation by the destruction of bottomland hardwood forests, overharvest from market hunting, and loss of wetlands. In fact, prior to signing of the Migratory Bird Treaty Act in 1918, Wood Ducks were hunted from September to April. In 1918, their harvest was halted nationwide. As populations rebounded, their season was reopened in 1941.

The implementation of strict hunting regulations and an ambitious nestbox program – starting seriously in the late 1930s, presumably at the Chatauqua National Wildlife Refuge in central Illinois – were the key to recovery. The practice grew significantly in the years following WWII. Across North America, it was estimated in 1988 by Frank Bellrose, the foremost expert on the subject, that 100,000 Wood Duck nestboxes might produce 300,000 ducklings annually. By 1994, he estimated that 150,000 of these ducklings per year would reach flight age.

The population is strong and has been expanding across the northern Great Plains over the last 50 years. Their spread – particularly northward and westward since the 1970s – has, at least in part, been due to the expansion of beaver populations, and their corresponding flooded wetlands.

Loss and degradation of forested habitats and limited cavity availability are still major threats to Wood Duck populations. Wood Ducks are impossible to survey using traditional aircraft methods because they cannot be seen through the forest. Therefore, precise population-wide data is limited. Their populations are monitored primarily through the Breeding Bird Survey, nestbox monitoring, the annual Wing Bees, hunter harvest reports, and band recoveries. The current population is probably between 3.0 and 4.6 million, with at least 2.8 million bird in eastern North America and Cuba, 665,000 in interior North America, and 66,000 in the West.

MALLARD
Anas platyrhynchos MALL

Plates Page 102

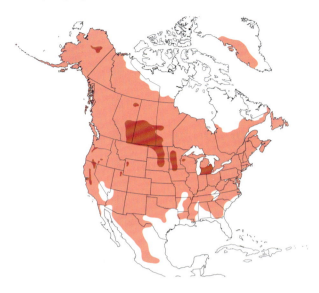

OTHER COMMON OR REGIONAL NAMES
Greenhead (drake), gray duck (hen), susie (hen), green-headed mallard, northern mallard, redlegs
(Arctic: uqsuqerpak [YK], ivugasrugruk [NS, NWS])
(Québec: canard colvert)
(Mexico: pato de collar, pato galán)

MEASUREMENTS
Length: Male – 20.4-27.5 in, av 24.7 in (62.7 cm); Female – 21.7-24.7 in, av 23.1 in (58.7 cm)
Wing: Male – av 11.4 in (29.0 cm); Female – av 10.6 in (26.9 cm)
Weight: Male – av 2.75 lbs (1247 g); Female – av 2.44 lbs (1107 g)
Bill: Male – av 41.7 mm; Female – av 38.7 mm

FIRST IMPRESSIONS
Mallards might be the most adaptable of all ducks. They are certainly the most abundant, studied, and recognized wild ducks in the world. They thrive around the globe, surviving a wide variety of habitats, including city parks and areas with lots of people. They also occur in some of the wildest places, from open prairie wetlands north into the Arctic. This makes them the most recognized and readily identified duck in North America. As such, they are the standard for learning all dabbling ducks. Pairs of green-headed males and patterned brown females in small neighborhood ponds are a familiar sight across the continent. In the Mississippi Flyway, massive flocks can cloud the skies. Wherever you see Mallards, spend some time studying them. Familiarize yourself with their size and shape, flight style, feeding behaviors and courtship rituals, because it will allow you a reference point of comparison for other species. Males have a green head with a thin white collar, chestnut breast, primarily gray body, and black butt with a white tail. Also note the curious upturned black central uppertail coverts. His bill is bright yellow to yellow-olive with a black nail. Females are a medium brown, with patterned body feathers and a paler head and neck. Note the whitish outer tail feathers and a yellow-orange bill with a dusky saddle. Size and shape: A big puddle duck a long bill and broad wings set back on the long body and a tail. Mallard is the "typical" duck shape. Flight: Hefty and powerful in flight. Large-bodied with a longish neck and well-proportioned head. Wings are set back on the body, which tapers at the end, but the tail is not long. Male's head is dark, body pale, and butt dark. Females are an even brown, a bit lighter on the head and neck, with a darkish crown and eyestripe on the face. Both sexes have white tips to the greater coverts and secondaries, framing their blue speculums with two white lines. Glaring white underwings on both sexes. When taking off, they spring straight up out of the water. Wings are distinctly cupped when they come in for a landing—feet outstretched and head down. Flocks range from two to hundreds and fly high, sometimes taking on lines and V-formations for longer flights or looser clusters for short trips. Wingbeats are strong and steady, but a bit slower than most other dabblers.

ID: IN DEPTH AND SIMILAR SPECIES
Mallards attain a mature adult plumage and often breed as yearlings, so they are very difficult to age after they molt out of juvenile plumage. Mallard follows a typical dabbling duck strategy for feather replacement, which makes them an excellent species to learn molt cycle and apply the pattern to other dabblers. Ducklings are dark brown above with warm yellow faces, a dark crown, brown stripes

through the eyes and small dark ear spots. Juvenile plumage starts growing from 18-21 days after hatch and is usually fully grown by 8-10 weeks when they are able to fly. Juvenile plumage is warm brown (particularly on the breast) with even streaks on the breast. Patterns are crisp and uniform, because all the body feathers grow at the same time. Their bills can be noticeably smaller and are a strange olive color, unlike any adult color. They begin to molt out of juvenile plumage in August or September, continuing into November. By December they have replaced most of their head and body feathers and look like adults.

First-year females are difficult to separate from adult females, once they replace all their juvenile plumage, usually by late November or early December. They can be aged prior to that time by the presence of any juvenile plumage, which looks worn and paler. Typically, juvenile wing coverts are all replaced, but when in the hand, look for narrow and more tapered tertial coverts that are sometimes are retained. Adult females (and first-years) molt some body feathers from February to April to be more camouflaged while incubating. Look for new tertials in the spring that are brown (opposed to grayish) with buffy internal markings. After the brood fledges, females initiate a complete molt of wing feathers, typically on or near the breeding grounds, followed by a body molt that finishes up in the fall.

First-year males are difficult to separate from adult males; once they replace all their juvenile plumage, usually by late November or early December, they blend right in with the rest of the flock. They can be aged prior to that time by the presence of any juvenile plumage, which looks abraded and faded. Typically, the juvenile wing coverts are all replaced, but when in hand, look for narrow and more tapered tertial coverts that sometimes are retained. Adult males (and first-years) start molting body feathers to acquire an eclipse plumage in mid-May to June, or after they leave their incubating mates. They migrate to a suitable location to shed their wing feathers and are flightless in July and August for 4-5 weeks. Wing molt is followed by a complete body molt into their bright breeding plumage, which is usually wrapping up in late October. This plumage is held until the following June when they start to molt into eclipse plumage and have brown mottling on their gray sides and green heads. Eclipse males look generally like females in the summer (lacking green heads, gray sides and black butts), but they have much grayer faces and darker bodies. Their bill is usually duller than in the winter, dull yellow or olive rather than bright yellow, but still an even color. Males are larger than females, which is more apparent when they are in eclipse plumage. At almost any time from June-October, adult males have a mottled appearance on their breast and body. Juveniles are around at the same time of the year, but their plumage is very even with uniform patterns. When the juveniles start to molt into an adult-like plumage, they can be separated from eclipse males by looking for juvenile feathers on the sides, which by late summer/early fall are worn, faded and pointy. Adults coming out of eclipse, have body feathers that are not particularly worn and are more rounded pattern with a different internal pattern. Timing is also helpful for separating youngsters from adults; adults attain a clean breeding plumage much earlier, almost a month earlier on average.

Similar species: Female paler than Mottled Ducks (especially the western subspecies) and American Black Duck, bill brighter orange, tail and rump clearly paler, with distinct white borders to the blue speculum. From the smaller female Gadwall by rounded head shape, lacking a distinct forehead, larger, deeper based bill, iridescent speculum with white borders. Much larger than female teal with a larger, extensively orange bill.

Feral and semi-domestic birds are local residents, often found in those popular city and suburban parks. These birds, often behaving quite tame, can also appear discolored, blotched, or even misshapen, Since the Mallard is the ancestral stock for many domestic ducks, all observers should be aware of the potential variability in the look of Mallards.

Other odd-looking Mallards may be hybrids. Mallards commonly hybridize with American Black Duck, and have been known to hybridize with Mottled Duck, Northern Pintail American Wigeon, Northern Shoveler, and other species..

If it is not a hybrid, it may be senescent. These older females with male characteristics are scarce but regular. They are easy to overlook and often suggest hybrids (see pp. 282-283). These female Mallards might have curved, but not curled, black uppertail coverts, heads that are green and brown, and bills that may be yellow, but with the female-looking dark saddle.

Sex ratio: Males dominate, but numbers vary with season and location. Males are usually at 53-56%, but sometimes as high as 58%.

GEOGRAPHIC VARIATION

Mallards have colonized and been introduced in many parts of the world. Moreover, the relationships between the widespread Mallard and their wide-ranging sister subspecies and taxa are often controversial and change as genetic research unveils new information.

There is some geographic variation within the "normal" green-headed Mallards that span the northern continents. North American Mallards are slightly larger than those in Eurasia. Mallards in Greenland are significantly larger and classified as a weakly differentiated subspecies, *A. p. conboschas*.

Another subspecies that has been considered a separate species in the past (and may be again the future) is the Mexican Duck, *A. p. diazi*. Mexican Ducks are found mostly in southern Arizona, New Mexico and Texas, often along the Rio Grande Valley. Both males and females closely resemble a female northern Mallards. This taxa is treated as a full species in the next account on p. 376.

There is a significant amount of interbreeding between Mallards and Mexican Ducks at the northern edge of Mexican Ducks range. Therefore, there are a number of hybrids in the population, and there is concern that Mallards will continue to infiltrate Mexican-Duck territory and over time could out-compete their southern counterpart.

SOUNDS

The descending quacks of Mallards are often heard in parks, ponds, and pastures where they congregate. Contrary to popular belief, it is the loud female call that is most often heard. Active feeding flocks often give a soft chuckle, *duga-duga duga-da-da-dug*. Males: Less vocal than females and utter shorter, raspy *gaack*, which is often drowned out by the calls of the females. Given singly or in series, in several contacts including if alarmed, during courtship, and as a contact call with mate. Also, give rapid double-note sets of *Rabrab* when alarmed, during courtship, or in aggressive situations. During the courtship, the grunt-whistle display give a piercing high-pitched whistle followed by a soft grunt. The whistle and accompanying motions of the display are will catch your attention. Females: Classic quack call, given in a series of loud, descending *QUACK, QUack, Quack, quack, quack*. Wide array of calls given around brood, including an alarm call, a single *quaaack*. Also, gives persistent quacks in the spring, before laying when settling in at her breeding site. Persistent quacks are evenly spaced, repeated monotone notes. Ducklings: Give distress calls, a series of loud, evenly repeated *peep peep peep* and soft *pi-pip* notes when content.

In flight, it has a slight whistle to the wings.

YEAR IN THE LIFE

Mallards are abundant and widespread in the Northern Hemisphere and in each flyway. Their adaptability has led to successful introductions, for example, to Australia, New Zealand, and the Hawaiian Islands. In the North America, Mallards range south to northern Mexico. There are large concentrations often in November and December at such places as Squaw Creek NWR and Clarence Cannon NWR, Missouri, Bear River refuge, Utah, Sandusky Bay, Ohio, Shiawassee NWR, Michigan, Bonney Reservoir, Colorado and Samish Island, Washington.

In winter, Mallards forage and rest on nearly any body of water, dabbling and up-ending to feed. Their courtship rituals begin in the late fall, as soon as the drakes come out of eclipse plumage they have a surge of testosterone and displays begin. Courtship activities are elaborate, involving ritualized shaking movements (including the swimming-shake), bursts of activities (e.g., grunt-whistle, head-up-tail-up, or down-up), and catch-up jump-flights. The female will often respond with incitement moves beside the male and by nod-swimming with an erect neck. Most pair bonds form early in the fall and winter, often between September and November.

Mallards and Northern Pintail are the first spring migrants, pushing north as water thaws. They are frequently forced to retreat under freezing conditions. Mallards are a highly migratory species, even though in some areas urban populations are sedentary. Some linger in Mexico until March and until late April in California.

Mallards join Northern Pintails as the earliest nesters, reaching the breeding grounds in late February or early March in the southern portion of their range or in late April in northern areas. A very large portion of the Mallard population heads to the duck factory of the prairie-potholes and parklands to the north. Others move farther north into the boreal forest. They able to breed in a range of habitats with nearby wetlands, which is one reason why they are so widespread in the world.

Mallards, and other ground nesting ducks, frequently loose a clutch to a predator. Mallards, however, are masters at renesting; they will renest up to 5 or 6 times if needed. In about 10 days, a female can be ready to lay another clutch. This is another reason why they are so cosmopolitan. Still, populations in the prairies are getting hammered by predators (e.g., raccoons, foxes, and skunks) whose numbers are unnaturally high due to a lack of larger predators in the ecosystem.

Hens stay with their brood until they fledge, which can fly at 8-10 weeks. Females start their wing molt right after the ducklings fledge or the brood is lost, often molting on or close to (within ~30 miles) their nesting site.

Fall migration is the most protracted of any duck. They typically head south as water freezes and food is covered in snow. They will move south when conditions are harsh, then come north again and push south if needed in the course of a winter.

DIET AND FEEDING BEHAVIOR

Mallards are omnivorous and opportunistic feeders across their range. They dabble on the surface of the water, dip their heads and necks, or up-end to reach seeds and grains, mostly of agricultural sources, in the fall and winter. These seasons they will eat moist-soil plants, acorns, aquatic vegetation, and cereal crops (e.g., corn, barley, sorghum, soybeans, wheat, and rice). Agricultural foods will sometimes dominate the diet, especially in winter, depending on the availability of alternatives. (With the decline of southern bottomland hardwood forests, Mallards moved from an acorn-dominant diet in the past to a waste-crop diet today.) Mallards use agricultural food sources more than any other ducks. In the spring and summer, they shift their diet, feeding heavily on invertebrates (e.g., insects, aquatic invertebrates such as snails and freshwater shrimp, and earthworms).

NESTING

Site: Mallards breed near almost any type of freshwater area, in a wide variety of habitats: marshes, farmland, forests, and urban parks. They will even use brackish habitats along the coast. Nest usually in cover among tall vegetation, grasses, shrubs, etc., and on small islands; or in raised sites in tree crotches or holes, in old nests of large birds, on buildings and ruins. The nest may even be far from water.

Nest description: A shallow depression on the ground lined with plant debris, leaves, grass, etc, the lining mixed with down and feathers. Down tufts are brown, with pale centers and tips. (Compared with American Black Duck, the pale centers are more conspicuous.) Nest size averages, 6-8 inches in inside diameter; 10-12 inches in outside diameter; and 2-6 inches in depth.

Clutch size: Average 9. occasionally 1-13.

Egg description: Elliptical to subelliptical, fairly short. Smooth and waxy rather than glossy. Usually pale green to blue-green, sometimes creamy with green tinge, buffish-green, or almost blue. (Eggs of Mallard, American Black Duck, Mottled Duck, Northern Pintail, Northern Shoveler, and even Redhead can appear very similar.) 58 X 41 mm.

Incubation duration: Average 28 days, ranges from 23-30 days.

Brood parasitism: Occasionally parasitized by other species including: Redhead, Ruddy Duck, Gadwall, Northern Shoveler, Northern Pintail, Common Goldeneye. Also, in areas with many Mallards, occasionally parasitized by other Mallards.

HUNTING

"Greenheads" are a favorite duck among waterfowlers across the continent. These Mallards are key target in all the flyways. More hunters set up to hunt for Mallards than any other species of waterfowl and are at the top of the list for harvest totals. Mallards are wary by nature. Everything needs to be just right to get them to decoy. They are particularly enticed by flapping motorized decoys, although these are illegal in a number of states. Calling as Mallards approach decoys is often effective tactic. Responsive to good calling of the "high ball quack." The heart of Greenhead hunting is Arkansas, but Mallard hunting is prime throughout the Mississippi Flyway.

The harvest of Mallards in the U.S. over two years (2013 and 2014) averaged at about 3,777,000 birds; and for Canada the corresponding number was 523,450.

The release of game-farm Mallards, an activity encouraged by some hunters, has had a negative impact on some other species. Releasing captive-reared Mallards is an oversimplified and short-term approach to increasing hunter opportunities; it fails to address problems concerning duck populations and habitat loss. See Population and Conservation.

POPULATION AND CONSERVATION

This is the most abundant duck in North America. Mallard populations, nontheless, fluctuate greatly based on water conditions on the prairies. Prior to twentieth century Mallards were only found in the west and central region of North America. Populations in various regions have fluctuated, particularly in first half of the 1900s. In more recent years, their population is generally stable, changing in response to dry and wet periods. Still, Atlantic Flyway numbers have slipped, perhaps by 19% since 2000. North American population estimate was 10.6 million in 2012, 40% above the long-term average. By 2015, the number was over 11.6 million. The region of greatest abundance extends between the Appalachian and Rocky Mountains.

Mallard populations are carefully monitored and managed. Their adaptability to human-influenced habitat has certainly contributed to their success. They benefited greatly from the Conservation Reserve Program of the Farm Bill, converting millions of acres of cropland to perennial cover. The continuation of the CRP and similar programs is important to maintain their population. Mallards are continually in need of better nesting cover, predator management, controlled water levels in wetlands, nesting islands, and even hen houses.

There is concern for exposure to pesticides and other contaminants. Mallards feeding habits lend them to be particularly vulnerable to ingesting lead shot. This risk has been greatly reduced since lead shot was initially banned in the Mississippi Flyway in 1977 and nationally in 1991. However, lead is still present at high levels in some areas.

Continuing the efforts to preserve habitat is imperative for continuing to have a healthy Mallard population. The conversion of wetlands to agriculture, urban encroachment, the draining of wetlands, and turning grasslands into croplands are all serious, large-scale threats for Mallards. Among these, the conversion of upland nesting habitat to agricultural cropland (particularly into corn fields for ethanol production) is among the very top problems. Often, this transformation also accelerates the spread of predators (e.g., red foxes).

Finally, the release of game-reared Mallards has complicated conservation efforts in some areas. While it is difficult to estimate the total number of captive-reared Mallards that are released annually, it could be many tens of thousands. Most of these are small-scale releases where the Mallards are thought to augment hunting opportunities and/or to increase viewing opportunities. Problems abound, with increased risks of genetic introgression and hybridization, disease transmission, and confounding established waterfowl management programs. Pairing and interbreeding of captive-reared Mallards with wild Mallards, Mexican Ducks, Mottled Ducks and, especially, with American Black Ducks, have been documented. This is likely contributing to putting those species at some risk.

MEXICAN DUCK
Anas (platyrhynchos) diazi MEDU

Plates Page 108

OTHER COMMON OR REGIONAL NAMES
Mexican mallard, New Mexican duck
(Mexico: pato triguero, pato Mexicano, pato nixtamalero)

MEASUREMENTS
Length: Male – c. 22.4 in (56.9 cm); Female – c. 19.3 in (49.0 cm)
Wing: Male – average 10.7 in (27.2 cm); Female – av 10.0 in (25.4 cm)
Weight: Male – av 2.27 lbs (1,028 g); Female – av 2.00 lbs (908 g)
Bill: Male – av 42.0 mm; Female – av 38.8 mm

FIRST IMPRESSIONS
Mexican Duck is the southwestern stand-in within the complex including Mallard, American Black Duck, and Mottled Duck. This taxa is officially treated by the American Ornithological Society as a subspecies of Mallard, but here is treated as a species. Although Mexican Ducks have their core range in the interior plateau of central Mexico, they are found in the U.S. mostly in southern Arizona, New Mexico, and along the Rio Grande Valley in Texas. Both males and females closely resemble female Mallards. Mexican Ducks are a rich brown in body color with buffy internal markings on the feathers. The face of a Mexican Duck will be lighter gray-brown with a darker eyestripe. These ducks usually have thin white lines bordering their blue speculums, bordering that is much reduced in comparison with Mallard. But be aware that the width can sometimes be broad on the leading edge. Males and females are generally alike, except males are slightly darker overall with yellow to yellow-orange bills. Females have duller olive-yellow or dusky orange bills. The tail color is gray-brown with rufous fringes, not whitish. Location and range has become the default way to separate Mexican Ducks from female Mallards, but this is insufficient and unreliable. For one, depending too much on location muddies up the consideration of out-of-range birds. For another, there are many hybrids involving Mexican Ducks in the U.S. Size and shape: A large dabbling duck, shaped like Mallard without the male's curly uppertail feathers. Males are larger than females. Flight: A big puddle duck, with broad wings set back on the body. The body is an even brown with a paler face. Take a close look at the upperwing. Mexican Ducks will have gray leading edges to their wings and will have white tips to the greater coverts and secondaries, like Mallards. Look for well-defined, but thin, white borders to the blue speculum. The presence of this white is one characteristic of Mexican Ducks that is not nearly as strong in Mottled Ducks. When taking off, these wary Mexican Ducks spring straight up out of the water. Mexican Ducks are usually in pair or small groups of fewer than 20 moving between feeding locations. Wingbeats are strong and steady.

ID: IN DEPTH AND SIMILAR SPECIES
Mexican Ducks attain a mature adult plumage and often breed as yearlings. They are very difficult to age after they molt out of juvenile plumage. Like other more tropical ducks, they do not have intense seasonal pressure dictating when they molt, migrate, and breed. They breed and move locally according to the cycle of wet and dry seasons. Mexican Duck molt has not been well-studied; however, they presumably follow a similar strategy as other *Anas*, such as American Black Duck where their appearance changes little throughout the year.

Ducklings are dark brown above with warm yellow faces with dark crowns, brown stripes through the eyes and small dark ear spots. Juvenile plumage is streakier and poorer quality than subsequent sets of feathers, so it fades and wears out quickly (the bulk of it is also replaced quickly). First-years can be distinguished if there are any remnants of juvenile plumage. Presumably they begin replacing juvenile plumage about two months after hatching.

Adult male Mexican Ducks are slightly larger than females and have even-colored yellow to yellow-orange bills, opposed to the olive-yellow or dusky-orange bills of females. Females sometimes have a dark saddle or mottling on the bill, like female Mallards. Their plumages change little throughout the year, but it is likely that females replace their tertials before breeding, attaining tertials with internal markings that are more camouflaged. Presumably, after breeding, they undergo wing molt and are flightless for 3-4 weeks and then replace their body feathers. The distance traveled from their breeding areas is not well known.

Similar species: Mexican Duck has several identification challenges – separation from female Mallard, Mottled Duck, and a slew of hybrids. Female Mallards can be distinguished by their lighter overall body color; Mallards have paler and more extensive internal markings on the body feathers. Compared to female Mallards, Mexican Ducks have darker and simpler-patterned body feathers, with narrower and darker feather fringes. Female Mexican Ducks tend to have more evenly colored olive-yellow bills, whereas female Mallards have dark brown spots in the center of their orangey bills. Female Mallards also have mostly white with buffy markings on the tails, whereas Mexican Ducks have dark gray-brown tails. The undertail coverts in Mexican Duck are dark, while they are pale in Mallard. The presence of second- and third-generation hybrids can complicate things further.

Distinguishing pure Mexican Duck from a Mexican × Mallard hybrid can be very difficult and sometimes impossible. The presence of domestic-type or released Mallards doesn't help matters. Many Mexican × Mallard hybrids have half green heads with buffy cheeks. These males are relatively easy to pick out as hybrids, and they are frequently seen at some locations, such as the Sweetwater Wetlands in Tucson, Arizona. Hybrids usually have darker brown tones on their breasts, contrasting with paler brown sides. Some male hybrids look just like Mexican Ducks, but will have slightly curled uppertail coverts.

Mexican Ducks are a touch paler than a pure Mottled Duck (especially the western subspecies of Mottled Duck found in Texas and Louisiana). Mexican Ducks will show a darker and more extensive brown crown with a dark eyeline. Remember, Mottled Duck would lack white tips on the greater coverts and secondaries entirely and have that small black gape-spot.

In the Lower Rio Grande Valley there are Mottled × Mexican Duck hybrids. These hybrids tend to have reduced white tips on the greater coverts and secondaries compared to pure Mexican ducks.

Sex ratio: It appears to be even, although the information is sparse.

YEAR IN THE LIFE

In the U.S., Mexican Ducks are the southwestern counterpart to Mottled and American Black Duck. Their status as full species or as a subspecies of Mallard has changed over the years, with the AOU (now AOS), since 1983, considering them conspecific. There is very little overlap between wintering Mallards and Mexican Ducks in the U.S., and Mexican Ducks likely pair early, often as early as September, well before wintering Mallards arrive. Moreover, Mexican Ducks may have lengthy pair bonds, conceivably into multiple years.

Courtship displays include lively rushes across the water, splashing, ducking, and wing-flapping.

The core of their range is in the plateaus of central Mexico, where over 90% of the population occurs. They span south roughly to Mexico City, with some sightings in Oaxaca. Several records reach north all the way to the front range of Colorado. Mexican Duck is often in pairs or small flocks; it's unusual to see more than forty or fifty in one location. Some of the largest concentrations numbering only around a few hundred are in Chihuahua, Durango, and in Presidio County in west Texas.

They move short distances seasonally, dispersing during the rainy season in the summer to breed at small wetlands. In the drier, nonbreeding, seasons, they gather at larger bodies of water, and they may be somewhat nomadic during nonbreeding seasons.

GEOGRAPHIC VARIATION

Currently, Mexican Duck is considered by the AOS as a subspecies of Mallard, although it was considered a separate species in the past. It may again be considered a separate species, especially since genetic studies have indicated that Mexican Duck is actually more closely related to Mottled Duck and American Black Duck than it is to Mallard. Another possibility, of course, might be the removal of Mexican Duck from Mallard and have it combined with Mottled Duck. In any case, the situation is far from resolved.

SOUNDS

The descending quacks of a Mexican Duck are heard in ponds and slow-moving rivers where they congregate. Active feeding flocks often give a soft chuckle, *duga-duga duga-da-da-dug*. Males: Less vocal than females and utter shorter, raspy *gaack*, which is often drowned out by the calls of the females. Females: Classic quack call, given in a series of loud, descending *QUACK, QUack, Quack, quack, quack*.

DIET AND FEEDING BEHAVIOR

Mexican Ducks forage by filtering the surfaces of wetlands for seeds and vegetable matter. Like other puddle ducks, they will dabble on the surface of the water, dip their heads and necks, or up-end to reach seeds and grains. Crops consumed in the past included alfalfa shoots, corn, wheat, barley, and oats. In Mexico they even ate garbanzo beans.

NESTING

Site: Found in freshwater wetlands, often small and seasonal — including meadows of salt grass, sedge, and rushes. These sites may also be some distance from a ditch, stream, or other water (averaging 215 yards from the water).

Nest description: A depression filled with compact grass fragments and concealed with an arch of vegetation. It will be lined with down. Nest size is about 5-8 inches in inside diameter, 10-13 inches in outside diameter, and 2-6 inches in depth.

Clutch size: Normally 4-9 eggs.

Egg description: Elliptical to subelliptical. Smooth. Greenish-white or pale green. (See Mallard and Mottled Duck egg descriptions.) 55 × 41 mm.

Incubation duration: Presumably very similar to Mottled Duck, averaging 25-26 days.

Brood parasitism: Not reported

HUNTING

Given that Mexican Duck has a restricted range, there is not much hunting in the United States. Moreover, the decision to lump what had been two species (Mallard and Mexican Duck) into a single species negated any special harvest management actions by authorities. Mexican Duck is more of a popular gamebird in the core of its range in Mexico, although the size of the harvest there is unknown. Old studies from the 1920s suggested that Mexican Ducks were decoy-shy, preferring to feed some distance away, in contrast to the actions of Mallards.

POPULATION AND CONSERVATION

Since Mexican Duck was relegated to the status of subspecies of Mallard, it has not received sufficient management attention. Mexican Duck had been considered endangered in 1967 and was removed from the ESA list in 1978. There is significant interbreeding between Mallards and Mexican Ducks at the northern edge of the Mexican Duck's range. As such, Mexican Ducks share the same challenges as American Black Ducks and Mottled Ducks where Mallards (both released and wild) continue to infiltrate and out-compete their monochromatic cousins. Mexican Duck population trends in Mexico are still positive.

These ducks readily adapt to man-made water sites (e.g., storage reservoirs, stock ponds, and farm ponds) that are created in arid areas. At the same time, natural wetlands have been eliminated or reduced in size in these areas, presenting a need to consider serious habitat restoration.

The overall population estimate in 1980 was 55,000, although winter counts in Mexico typically record 15,000-20,000 (with a high of 49,000). It is assumed that the population has never been much higher than this. About 98% of the population is estimated to occur in Mexico, and the U.S. population is said to be under 1,000. Clearly, further study is justified.

AMERICAN BLACK DUCK

Anas rubripes ABDU

Plates Page 110

OTHER COMMON OR REGIONAL NAMES
Black duck, black mallard, red leg, red-legged black duck, dusky duck
(Québec: canard noir)
(Mexico: pato sombrío)

MEASUREMENTS
Length: Male – 21.6-24.2 in, av 22.5 in (57.2 cm); Female – 20.0-23.7 in, av 20.8 in (52.8 cm)
Wing: Male – av 11.4 in (29.0 cm); Female – av 10.7 in (27.2 cm)
Weight: Male – av 2.76 lbs (1252 g); Female – av 2.45 lbs (1111 g)
Bill: Male – av 54.2 mm; Female – av 51.1 mm

FIRST IMPRESSIONS

Small flocks and pairs of Black Ducks can pepper salt-marshes on the northeast Atlantic Coast. Inland in the East, they are often with Mallards and will stand out because they are so much darker than female Mallards. They look like Mallard darker cousins. They are a dark-chocolate brown overall, which appears black at a distance. Look for their contrastingly paler face and neck, a cold gray-buff. Size and shape: Same as Mallard, but lacking the curly uppertail feathers found on male Mallard. Flight: Body is dark overall, but with a paler face and striking white underwings in a contrast sharper than that of female Mallard. Speculum is dark purple to blue, lacking Mallard's prominent white borders. (There will sometimes be a narrow white trailing edge to the speculum on American Black Ducks, but never a white leading edge.) American Black Duck often migrates in high-flying flocks with Mallards. They have strong and steady wingbeats, just like Mallards.

ID: IN DEPTH AND SIMILAR SPECIES

American Black Ducks are difficult to age and sex. Typically, females have dusky yellow to dusky yellow-green bills, which are duller than the males' yellow bills. Both have black nails. American Black Ducks breed in their first-year; in the field, first-years look just like adults after molting out of juvenile plumage in the fall.

Ducklings have dull yellow faces and breasts with dark brown crowns. They have bold stripes through the eyes and often lack dark ear spots. They have pale patches on their brown bodies which are often buffy, opposed to the yellower patches on Mallards.

Juvenile plumage begins to grow when the birds are about three weeks old. Once their body feathers are fully grown at 6-8 weeks, juveniles can be separated from adults by paler streaks, particularly on the side feathers, which are more prominent than those of adults. Juvenile plumage is not held for a more than a couple months and wears out and fades quickly. First-years molt almost completely out of juvenile plumage from July to November. Some birds retain juvenile tertial coverts until the end of April. On average, first-year males molt earlier and replace more tertial coverts than females.

First-year females are separated from adult females by the presence of any juvenile plumage. By spring they have similar molt timing as adults. Adult females undergo a partial body molt from February-May. They raise broods and initiate complete molts of wing and body feathers after their brood fledges. This molt typically takes place on or near the breeding grounds between June and October.

Males are distinguished from females by the males' yellow green bill color. Their larger size is noticeable within pairs. First-year males are separated by the presence of any retained juvenile plumage. Adult males undergo partial molt of body feathers from May-July. Then they head out on a molt-migration to a safe site where they replace wing feathers simultaneously and they are flightless for 4-4.5 weeks. They also replace body feathers in the summer; most of their molt takes place between June and September. In the summer, the bill color darkens and they have even less pale edging on their body feathers.

Similar species: Within their range, American Black Ducks are most often confused with female Mallards, however, American Black Ducks are always significantly darker overall on the body – including the tail and belly – with less pale patterning on the body feathers. Mottled Ducks approach the darker body color of American Black Ducks, but Mottleds have considerably warmer-colored buffy faces and bordered blue speculums. American Black Duck × Mallard hybrids are becoming increasingly common. Many individuals show intermediate features. Typical looking hybrids are Black Duck-like with a large green patch behind the eye and uneven body color—more rusty on the breast and lighter on the sides and belly and silvery tertials. They may show white-bordered speculums. There is a lot of variation in hybrids, some will look almost just like a Black Duck, but with a slightly curled uppertail feather. Finding "pure bred" American Black Duck can sometimes be a challenge.

Sex ratio: Males dominate at 55-62%.

YEAR IN THE LIFE

A bird of the Atlantic Flyway, American Black Ducks winter primarily in mid-Atlantic salt marshes and in wetlands throughout the northeast south to South Carolina. They occasionally wander to western gulf states and western North America. American Black Ducks are very rare visitors to the British Isles and Iceland. Winter high counts are from Forsythe NWR in New Jersey in January, Long Point in Ontario, Sandusky Bay in Ohio, and coastal Massachusetts at Parker River NWR and Plymouth.

Black Ducks in winter can be found in large groups, often only sharing habitat with Brant.

Courtship rituals start in the fall and many pair bonds have solidified by December. Males will give three main kinds of courtship displays: the grunt-whistle, the head-up-tail-up with its head-stretching and tail-cocking, and the down-up display. Like other puddle ducks, additional displays are also involved, including the female incite response. Some pairs will reunite on the wintering grounds and stay together for more than one breeding season.

Spring migration is underway in early February, proceeding gradually as ice thaws. For example, they concentrate at Abbagadasset River, in Maine, in early April. American Black Ducks arrive on the freshwater wetlands where they breed in Maine in early April, late May in northern Quebec. They often choose remote areas including quiet beaver ponds, lakes and bogs throughout mixed hardwood and boreal forests, and salt marshes.

On the breeding grounds, American Black Ducks are wary of human disturbance. Females will often abandon their nests if they are flushed before the clutches are complete. Once females settle in with their clutches, males defend feeding territories and remain with the females until midway through incubation. Females usually stay with their broods full-time for 2-3 weeks, decreasing the amount of time spent with them in the following weeks. Eventually females leave when their broods are 6-7 weeks old. At that time, the females find safe spots near the breeding grounds with dense emergent vegetation, often black needlerush, and molt their flight feathers.

Breeding and nonbreeding males congregate in late May and early June for a molt-migration. Many head north of their breeding site, for example, to coastal Labrador, Ungava Bay, James Bay, southern Hudson Bay, and northern Manitoba; others may undergo more local movements to Lake Erie marshes in Ohio. There are particularly high counts from Cap Tourmente in Quebec during August and September.

Fall migration begins in mid-September to early October, depending on latitude. Peak migration in the mid-Atlantic region is in early November, peak in the western Great Lakes is in mid-November. Many reach wintering sites in coastal marshes in from mid-October through November.

GEOGRAPHIC VARIATION
No subspecies are recognized.

SOUNDS
Their calls are probably not reliably distinguishable in the field from those of Mallards. Some quacks are slightly lower and raspier. Males: Most common call is a low *raeb*, given to as a warning signal, sometimes as a two-note call *raeb-raeb*. During the grunt-whistle display, they give a high-pitched whistle, followed by low grunting. Females: Most frequent call is loud *quack*. Their decrescendo call is typically about 6 notes long, *quaegeageageageag* with accent on second syllable, decreasing in volume. During inciting, *ggeggeggeggegge* is given in variable lengths. They utter quick, low chucklings, similar to Mallard feeding calls. Females also give a series of rough *gaeck* calls when incubating or with brood and being harassed by males. Single, long, *quack* alarm calls are uttered if they are disturbed. A low-pitched, soft *quai quai guai* is given on nest as hatching nears.

DIET AND FEEDING BEHAVIOR
American Black Ducks typically forage by dabbling, pecking at surface of water or ground, and up-ending to reach submerged vegetation. Sometimes they even dive 6-12 feet to reach tubers in winter. They eat a wide array of foods including seeds, roots, tubers, stems, and leaves, corn and other grain if available. Animal foods (e.g., larvae, flies, dragonflies, isopods, snails, and clams) are essential prior and during egg-laying. In marine habitats in particular, they eat aquatic insects, crustaceans, mollusks, and fish.

NESTING
Site: On the ground near woodland lakes and streams, tidal or freshwater marshes. Sites are highly variable. While river or lake islands are also often used, sites may not always be close to water in uplands.

Nest description: A hollow of grasses, leaves, and other debris, lined with down. (Down not unlike Mallard down, but pale centers less conspicuous.) Nest size averages, 7 inches in inside diameter, 12 inches in outside diameter, and 2-3 inches in depth.

Clutch size: 8-10, sometimes 6-15.

Egg description: Elliptical to subelliptical. Variable color, from green, greenish-buff, yellowish-buff, to creamy with a green tinge. (See Mallard egg description for comparison.) 59mm X 42mm.

Incubation duration: 23-33 days (usually 26-28) varies with ambient temperatures.

Brood parasitism: Infrequently parasitized by other species.

HUNTING
American Black Ducks are associated with a rich hunting tradition, but also a history of exploitation, which has led to very strict bag limits since 1983. Fortunately, these bag limits have helped lead to a tentative stabilization in the population. They are popularly hunted in the mid-Atlantic states, and the harvest of American Black Ducks in the U.S. over two years (2013 and 2014) averaged about 86,300 birds; and for Canada the corresponding number was a similar 86,200.

American Black Ducks are wise and wary. They prefer marshes with tidal influence, and they will move around creeks and shorelines with the tides. A few decoys (fewer than a dozen) in a calm spot will usually be sufficient. The ducks will come into Mallard decoys and in response to good calling. Big flocks are rare. Birds will often make their way to the fields and seldom decoy. Watch for small groups approaching from windward. They round out downwind and slowly come in as they scout the area. The last hour of the day can be the best time for American Black Ducks.

POPULATION AND CONSERVATION
The American Black Duck population declined by more than 50% between the 1950s and 1980s. Since the mid-1990s the numbers continued to drop, although not as steeply. In the Atlantic Flyway the decline was 55%, between 1955 and 2005, and in the Mississippi Flyway the drop was a shocking 86% for the same period. The species' long-term decline has been ascribed to number of reasons.

There are no conclusive studies pointing to overharvesting. Contaminants and lead shot have been considered. On-the-ground habitat changes — including urbanization, wetland alteration, deforestation, agricultural expansion, and wetland destruction — are certainly contributing factors, whether considering breeding or wintering alterations.

Large-scale habitat alterations in North America have also facilitated Mallard range expansion from the central plains into American Black Duck territory in the Northeast. This opened the door for interbreeding and competition with the more aggressive Mallard and insertion of dominant Mallard genes. Such hybridization threatens the long-term future for American Black Duck, especially since there seem to be no behavioral or habitat-related isolating mechanisms between Black Duck and Mallard.

The situation becomes complicated with the release of game-farm Mallards at major wintering areas of American Black Ducks.

Even with some recent stabilization, the American Black Duck population is still only estimated at half of its historical size. Their wintering habitats in the Chesapeake Bay and mid-Atlantic region, for example, have seriously degraded. A long-term decline in counts of wintering populations corresponds to habitat changes. The wintering population in the 1950s was estimated at 800,000, but only 300,000 in the 1990s. By 2008, the population estimate was 271,200. The NAWMP target population is 385,000 ducks for the midwinter surveys.

The estimates were higher during for the breeding ground estimation, which was 550,000, 13% below the long-term average in 2011. The total continental population, according to the NAWMP is close to 1.2 million, based on a 2002-2011 average.

Mottled Duck
MODU *Anas fulvigula*

Plates Page 114

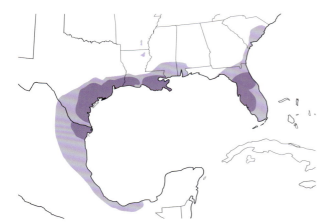

OTHER COMMON OR REGIONAL NAMES
Florida mallard, Florida duck, black mallard, mottled mallard, summer mallard, canard d'ete (Louisiana) (Mexico: pato monteado, pato tejano)

MEASUREMENTS
Length: Male – 19.8-24.0 in, av 22.4 in (56.9 cm); Female – 17.5-23.4 in, av 20.9 in (53.1 cm)
Wing: Male – av 10.3 in (26.1 cm); Female – av 9.7 in (24.6 cm)
Weight: Male – av 2.50 lbs (1134 g); Female – av 2.30 lbs (1043 g)
Bill: Male – av 65.0 mm; Female – av 60.0 mm

FIRST IMPRESSIONS
Pairs and small groups of Mottled Ducks can be found tucking away to rest and up-end to feed in calm marshes along the Gulf Coast and Florida. They have dark brown bodies, approaching the shade of American Black Duck, with a buffy face. The Florida birds appear almost as the blonds of the dabbling ducks. The Mottled Duck speculum is blue-green with a hint of white tips on the secondaries. Look for two ducks or a group of fewer than 10 dark ducks that all appear similar. This is the usual profile for Mottled Duck. You may notice a difference in bill color within the pair; males have dull yellow bills and females have olive to drab orangish bills with black splotches. Both will have a black nail and also a small oblong black spot at the lower base of the bill (gape). This spot and often be seen at a distance. Size and shape: Mottled Ducks are large-bodied with a large round heads. They are about the same size and the same shape as Mallard and American Black Duck. Flight: Shape in flight is much like Mallard and American Black Duck with a large body and broad wings but with a shorter wing-point than either. Mottled Ducks appear dark-bodied with a pale face; the upperwing is dark with a very thin white trailing edge (or none at all) on a blue-green speculum. Their white underwing coverts contrast strongly with the dark body. Mottled Ducks are often in small groups, flying low moving in between feeding and roosting sites. Their wingbeats are slow and steady compared to smaller dabbling ducks.

ID: IN DEPTH AND SIMILAR SPECIES
Mottled Ducks are likely to breed in their first-year. They mature into an adult plumage very quickly and are often tricky to age and sex. In general, males have broader, grayer tertials and yellower bills than females. Ducklings are just like downy Mallards with yellowish faces and dark brown bodies with a couple of yellow spots on the back.

Juvenile plumage presumably starts appearing 18-21 days after hatching and is usually fully grown by 9-10 weeks when the young are able to fly. Juvenile plumage is streakier on the breast than adult plumage. In general, juvenile feathers are narrower, and buffy edging is not as prominent. First-years replace juvenile plumage starting in August, spanning through November for some individuals.

First-year females can be distinguished from adult females by the presence of any lingering juvenile plumage. On adult females, besides the helpful bill-color – olive to drab orangish with splotches – look at the breast tone. Adult females look somewhat paler brown on the breast than the males, due to the presence of more buffy brown on the breast feathers. Females undergo a partial body molt from February-April. Their bills are darker when they are incubating and with their broods. After their broods fledge, they are flightless for about 27 days as they replace their wing feathers. They continue molting body feathers for several months after the wing molt.

First-year males can be picked out from adult males if they have any remaining juvenile plumage, which is mostly gone a couple months after they fledge. Adult males have solid, dulll yellow bills. When pairs are together, the male's larger size is noticeable. Males will also appear subtly darker on the breast. Males undergo their partial molt in mid-May to June. Eclipse males look like adult males in July and August.

Similar species: Mottled Duck identification can be tricky when it comes to separating female Mallards and figuring out if an individual is a pure bird or a hybrid. Female Mallards aren't too tough if you look at the overall color, which is darker for Mottled Ducks, and especially for the Gulf Coast birds. Also look for white on the tail of female Mallards along with their blackish saddles on their bills. For more complications, see Geographic Variation.

Sex ratio: Close to even, with slight male bias.

YEAR IN THE LIFE OF A MOTTLED DUCK

Mottled Ducks occur in coastal habitats along the Gulf of Mexico from Alabama to Tamaulipas and throughout Florida (except the panhandle), north to South Carolina. Mottled Ducks are essentially non-migratory, although they undergo local and seasonal movements as habitat conditions change. This is unlike most North America puddle ducks that are highly migratory. Mottled Ducks do occasionally wander outside their normal range and may even breed in northeast Texas, southern Arkansas, and Oklahoma. There have even been a handful of sighting in Kansas, Colorado, Kentucky, Tennessee, Iowa, Ontario, and Wisconsin. There is also an introduced population near Delta Santee Wildlife Management Area and ACE Basin of South Carolina. About 1,200 were introduced (1975-1982) for hunting opportunities. These were from the western Gulf Coast population. They are now established and moving south into Georgia.

Courting rituals start earlier than most other ducks. They involve the head-shake, the head-up-tail-up, the grunt-whistle, the down-up display, and the turning-the-back-of-the-head. The female may respond by inciting displays. Nearly 80% of the Mottled Ducks will have a mate by November, so pairs are together for most of the year, and they appear to be less "social," non-flicking, than other dabblers. They are seasonally monogamous, and it is suspected, but not confirmed, that they may renew their pair bonds with the same mate regularly.

In winter, Texas and Louisiana populations move south from rice prairie to adjacent coastal marshes. They forage in freshwater marshes, lakes, and less frequently in brackish bays and estuaries. The largest winter concentrations are in the prairies of southern Florida, particularly near Lake Okeechobee and in agricultural areas south of Okeechobee, Everglades Agricultural Area, and upper St. Johns River marshes. Finding just a couple of hundred in one spot constitutes a large number of Mottled Ducks, unlike most other puddle ducks that can regularly gather in groups of hundreds.

Nesting begins in the early spring, peaking March through May. Some pairs start as early as January and others as late nest as July. In the breeding season, the female selects a nest site, builds the nest and incubates. Males remain with females well into incubation. These ducks do not undergo a molt-migration, but they will move a short distance where the male undergoes molt and is flightless for about 27 days. On the western Gulf Coast, they head to harvested rice fields to molt. Florida bird molt in flooded agricultural field and also wastewater treatment impoundments. Meanwhile, after the ducklings hatch, the female leads them to shallow wetlands nearby where they can feed on invertebrates. The young are able to fly at 65-70 days.

There is not a significant fall migration, but birds are moving before and after their wing molt.

GEOGRAPHIC VARIATION

Mottled Duck has two distinct populations that look slightly different. *A. f. fulvigula* is endemic to peninsular Florida and used to be called Florida Duck. *A. f. maculosa* is on the western Gulf Coast from Alabama to southern Tamaulipas.

The western Gulf birds are darker overall with thinner buffy edging on the sides. The Florida birds have thicker buffy edging, so their entire body appears lighter colored. There is overlap, but western Gulf coast birds generally look more like American Black Ducks, while Florida birds are less likely to be mistaken for Black Duck.

Mottled Duck has a confusing taxonomic history. It was first described as a subspecies of American Black Duck, later elevated to two full species, followed by designation as a subspecies of Mallard, currently (since 1983) considered one species with no subspecies by AOS. Some authorities consider Mottled Duck to be a subspecies of Mallard; others view the two separate Mottled Duck populations as potentially species-distinctive.

Recent genetic studies concluded the two populations are isolated, without gene flow between the populations. Moreover, the closest relative of Mottled Duck is actually Mexican Duck, which is a closer relative to American Black Duck than Mallard is. There is one additional complication; those previously mentioned Mottled Ducks introduced in southern South Carolina, using stock from the western Gulf, are spreading south and creating a gene flow issue which previously had not existed.

SOUNDS
Listen for their quacks, which are much like Mallard calls. Male: Gives low, raspy *Raeb*. One note is as an alarm call, but two notes given during courtship or conversation. During courtship, utters single sharp whistle during the Head-up-tail-up Display and Grunt-whistle. Female: Produces loud, raspy, Quacking Decrescendo Call, often six notes, second loudest and highest pitched. Also, gives a muffled *Tickety-tickety-tickety* while feeding and sometimes in flight. Utters 3-4 harsh *quacks* if alarmed. During Inciting Display, gives irregular *Gagg* note. *Gaeck-gaeck-gaeck-gaeck* call sometimes heard during Gesture-of-repulsion Display.

DIET AND FEEDING BEHAVIOR
Mottled Ducks will filter the surfaces of wetlands for seeds (e.g., wild millet, rice, delta duck potato, and spike rush), other vegetable matter, and animal matter (e.g., insects, snails, small fish, and crayfish) while sitting on the water. They usually feed in waters 10 inches deep or less, but occasionally, they will tip up to a foot deep or feed while in very shallow water. Breeding females eat primarily aquatic invertebrates. Mottled Ducks will leave coastal marshes for interior fields in the fall to feed on the seed heads of grasses and rice. They will usually be found feeding in pairs or very small flocks, characteristically in winter and spring.

NESTING
Site: Found in freshwater and brackish wetlands – including natural and human-made ponds, ditches, and impoundments – in both rural and, increasingly, suburban areas in the eastern part of its range, sometimes in agricultural fields. Also coastal marshes and inland freshwater wetlands (including ricelands) in the western Gulf Coast part of its range. Nest usually on or near the ground, though may be in cordgrass or under a bush.

Nest description: A depression filled with grasses, reeds, and leaves. The rim of the cup lined with down, which is brown. Nest size averages, 6 inches in inside diameter, 11 inches in outside diameter, and 1.5-3.5 inches in depth.

Clutch size: Normally 8-10 eggs, sometimes 5-12.

Egg description: Elliptical to subelliptical. Smooth. Creamy-white to greenish-white. (See Mallard egg description.) 55 X 41 mm.

Incubation duration: Averages 25-26 days.

Brood parasitism: Not reported

HUNTING
The "Florida Ducks" or "Black Mallards" have a limited range, so they are not hunted widely. Hunting, however, is a main source of mortality. Still, little is known about the overall impact of hunting on the populations. Over two years (2013 and 2014) the annual harvest averaged about 45,800 birds. Popular areas of high concentration include the Gulf coast of Louisiana, Texas, and Florida.

POPULATION AND CONSERVATION
Mottled Duck was not monitored very closely until recently when more concern and studies have arisen. It is a species of special conservation concern throughout its range. Their populations fluctuate in response to water conditions, declining during droughts. The total continental population, according to the NAWMP, is estimated at 260,000.

They are vulnerable to loss of habitat through the drainage of coastal marshes for development, as well as, saltwater intrusion on coastal marshes and erosion in Louisiana and Texas. Saving coastal marshes and sustaining agricultural rice lands is very important to maintaining healthy populations of Mottled Ducks. Most Mottled Duck habitats occur on private lands. The influx of Mallards (both wild and through introductions) into the South is also a threat, because there is increased hybridization. Many biologists would argue that additional action needs to be taken to stop the flow of Mallard genes into the Mottled Duck populations. Educating the general public about the negative effects of releasing domestic Mallards would be one step. Preserving the identity of Mottled Duck is an urgent conservation concern.

Lead ingestion has been declining since the ban, but the species' non-migratory status keeps Mottled Ducks exposed to lead longer than migratory waterfowl.

Understanding local and seasonal movements will also play a key role in managing habitat for Mottled Ducks. The western Gulf-Coast population is estimated to be at least 200,000 (perhaps much higher), while the Florida population is estimated at 56,000-60,000.

Gadwall
GADW *Mareca strepera*

Plates Page 118

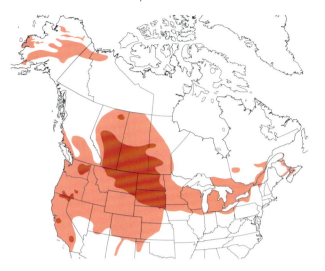

OTHER COMMON OR REGIONAL NAMES
Gray duck, gray mallard, gaddy
(Québec: canard chipeau)
(Mexico: pato pinto, pato friso)

MEASUREMENTS
Length: Male – 19.5-22.5 in, av 20.9 in (53.1 cm); Female – 18.2-20.2 in, av 19.2 in (48.8 cm)
Wing: Male – av 10.7 in (27.2 cm); Female – av 10.1 in (25.7 cm)
Weight: Male – av 2.10 lbs (953 g); Female – av 1.80 lbs (816 g)
Bill: Male – av 41.5 mm; Female – av 39.0 mm

FIRST IMPRESSIONS
When you see a pair of ducks, and you think one looks like a female Mallard, but the accompanying drake is gray with a black butt, you need not go further than Gadwall. Among the first ducks to pair up in the fall, Gadwalls are often seen in pairs. The male is gray with a black butt and dull-silvery tertials. The female looks superficially like a Mallard but a little grayer, with a thinner bill that has an orange stripe running along the bottom edge. Also, look for the Gadwall's white belly, seen when standing and in flight. Size and shape: Similar to Mallard, appearing somewhat smaller and slimmer, yet comparatively muscular. Gadwall has a squarer head, characterized by a steeper forehead, and with a bit thinner or nipped-in neck. It sits high on the water. Flight: They are similar to Mallards in shape, but with slightly thinner wings. The white in the inner third of their secondaries stands out from other dabblers. In males, the white is bordered by black and then a rufous or dull chestnut on the forewing; in females, the white bordered by a hint of black and a trace of the dull chestnut on the forewing. At a distance, Gadwall appear similar to Mallards, but the distinctive bold white patch in the wing usually stands out, as does the white belly of the hens and drakes. In flight, the white underwing coverts contrast brightly with grayish primaries and secondaries. Gadwall usually migrates in flocks of fewer than 100, often under 50. They are often mixed with American Wigeon or other puddle ducks. They have even wingbeats, again like Mallard. All of these characteristics are somewhat similar to Mallard, which is why Gadwall appears nondescript and is often overlooked and underappreciated.

ID: IN DEPTH AND SIMILAR SPECIES
The males and females look different and the males have an eclipse plumage, so telling each of these plumages apart can be difficult at certain times of the year. Most Gadwall breed in their first year, although some first-year males are not able to succeed in attracting a mate given there is so much competition because the sex ratio is skewed.

Ducklings are like pale Mallard ducklings. They have a less-pronounced eyelines and lighter brown backs, and little yellow tones in their buffy patches.

Juvenile plumage is similar to adult female, although a bit buffier. The breast spotting is smaller and more uniform than in adults. The patterns are even and fresh in August and early September, a time when adult females are looking worn and mottled. First-years molt out of juvenile plumage starting in July-September, continuing until December. During this molt, they attain an adult-like plumage by replacing all of their body feathers, some of their secondary coverts and none to all of their tertials and tail. Most first-year males acquire a clean adult plumage by November and they are ready to attract a mate. Like Mallards, Gadwall form pair bonds early on in the courting season, often in the late fall.

First-year females can be separated from adult females by the amount of rufous on the wing coverts. Young females also have the narrowest white patch and a smaller subdued dark border. Adult females have more rufous-tipped feathers than first-years. They are remarkably variable, some pale brown and others dark. Females replace some body feathers in January-April to become slightly more camouflaged before incubation. They grow a set of narrower brown tertials with buffy internal markings, which are strikingly different than the broad gray tertials they have in the fall and winter. After raising their broods, females will move to nearby lakes, not far from where they raised their broods, and there they grow new wing and body feathers.

First-year males have a body plumage just like adult males by about December after they have molted out of juvenile plumage. In their first year they can be separated by their upperwing pattern. First-years have less rufous on the median and lesser upperwing coverts and short, brown tertials. Adult males have extensive rufous tips on many of the median and lesser coverts and more extensive pure black greater and median coverts. Their tertials are also longer, coming to a sharp point and are silvery gray. Shortly after leaving an incubating mate, males replace at least half of their body feathers, and attain a camouflaged eclipse plumage sometime in May-July. Eclipse males look much like females, acquiring brown side and back feathers with buffy edges. Their heads lose some puffiness and are lightly speckled about the face. Their bold chestnut and black wing coverts are retained. If visible, this is a surefire way to pick out an adult male. Upon arrival to the molting grounds, they shed their wing feathers and are flightless for about 25 days while they grow a completely new set of primaries and secondaries. They undergo a complete replacement of body feathers mainly from July-September. Some males continue to grow new body feathers through November. However, the majority of adult males come out of eclipse by late September and are ready to find a mate in the fall, months before most ducks.

Similar species: Females Gadwall are often misidentified and overlooked for female Mallards. Many observers need either a good look at the bill or a nearby drake to tell them apart. Female Gadwall have squarer heads, thinner necks, and a thinner bill than Mallard. IN swimming birds, look for an even orange stripe that runs along the bottom of the bill, unlike Mallard's orange-brown mottled bill. The smaller size, different shape, orange bill sides, pale head, and all brown tail are all great feature when considering female Mallard. Also, look for a white belly, often visible unless the bird is swimming. Look for the white inner secondaries on Gadwall, which are sometimes visible on swimming birds.

Sex ratio: Males dominate at 52-58%

YEAR IN THE LIFE

Gadwall are practically everywhere, but they are often passed over. They are widespread and common across much of the Northern Hemisphere where small bodies of water are found, stretching in the Americas from the Arctic to Guatemala. They are a common winter visitor to reservoirs, beaver ponds, farm ponds, and coastal marshes where waters remain open. They flock through the Mississippi and Central Flyways, where the largest wintering concentrations are found on the Gulf Coast in Louisiana and Texas.

Courtship begins very early in the season, contrary to their spring migration, which begins relatively late in the season. Most pairs are together by November, a whole 4-5 months before they reach the breeding grounds in southern prairies. Counts on the wintering grounds start to drop in March. The courtship displays include introductory shakes (preludes to major displays), head-up-tail-up with head-stretches and tail-lifting, bill-tipping, grunt-whistles, burp displays, chin lifts, and turning-the-back-of-the-head. These varied male moves are often followed by a favorable female "incite" response, replete with neck and head actions toward the water and tossing the head back and forth.

Most pairs head north in April to the ponds, lakes, and marshes they call home during the breeding season. Gadwall are actually late nesters, even though they arrive on the breeding grounds relatively early in late April and early May. They will remain in place for a month or so until they start nesting. Even if their first clutch fails, they are persistent renesters and will continue renesting through July. This is a great adaptation when coping with high predation rates.

On the breeding grounds, the male defends a moving territory around a female. He has to keep a close eye on his mate, because other males will attempt to copulate with her. While a male Gadwall is a good mate-guarders for much of the year, he will leave the female after she selects a nest site and begins incubating the clutch. Once the eggs hatch, the female leads the brood to an area where they can find food. She remains with the ducklings until they are about 10 weeks old, at which point she will find a body of water near where she raised the brood to replace her wing feathers.

Males, nonbreeding females, and females that are failed breeders undergo a molt-migration to remote, shallow bodies of water. The timing depends on when the pairs split and the distance traveled depends on the availability of suitable wetlands. Particularly large numbers gather in mid-June, for example, in Delta, Manitoba, and early July in North Dakota.

Upon regaining flight, fall migration begins in September. Gadwall migrate again, along corridors through the plains and Mississippi River alluvial valley to the Gulf Coast of Texas and Louisiana. Concentration can be found at refuges including Tule Lake NWR (California), Great Salt Lake (Utah), Lacreek NWR (South Dakota), Valentine NWR (Nebraska), and Squaw Creek (Missouri).

GEOGRAPHIC VARIATION
No subspecies are recognized.

SOUNDS
Gadwall are fairly vocal dabblers, similar to Mallard but harder-toned. You'll often hear the female's flat, muffled *quack*. Males: They call mostly during displays, as they give a very low, nasal, burping *araeaeb*, uttered in series of 2-3 that increasing in length to 4-5 in pursuit flights. During grunt-whistle display they utter a nasal, piercing whistle *geee* given as well. Females: A *quack, aack*, is more nasal and higher-pitched than that of Mallard; it is sometimes given in descending series of 4-7 notes. Both sexes give chatter in flight or while feeding.

DIET AND FEEDING BEHAVIOR
A true dabbler, Gadwalls feed at the surface and tip up to gather aquatic vegetation, seeds, and invertebrates. Like American Wigeon, they have a weakness for succulent stems and leaves. Gadwalls will eat leafy parts of pondweeds, water milfoil, wigeon grass, parts of smartweeds, and some invertebrates. But unlike American Wigeon, they rarely graze on grass pastures or upland grain fields. Still, they are often found in areas where other dabbler species are nearby. Also like American Wigeon, they will snatch food from coots and diving ducks as they surface. They are almost entirely herbivorous in winter.

NESTING
Site: Gadwalls, breed mainly in mixed prairie, but also shortgrass prairie, tallgrass prairie, and, less frequently, in sub-Arctic habitats. They nest on the ground, in dense areas of vetetation, often under tall vegetation, preferring islands by freshwater lakes, pools, or slow streams with waterside vegetation. They tend to have higher nest success rates than other prairie-nesting ducks.

Nest description: A scrape lined with plant material, down, and some feathers. (The down is dark with small pale centers and distinct pale tips. It is darker than down of American Wigeon.) Nest sizes are about 7-8 inches in inside diameter, 8-12 inches in outside diameter, and 3 inches in depth.

Clutch size: Usually 8-12 eggs, rarely 7-16.

Egg description: Elliptical, subelliptical, or sometimes oval. Cream colored, sometimes with a green tint. (Very similar to that of American Wigeon.) 54 X 39 mm.

Incubation duration: 24-27 days.

Brood parasitism: Fairly common (e.g., by Lesser Scaup, Redhead, and Mallard).

HUNTING
"Gray Ducks" are generally not at the top of a hunter's list of species to attract to decoys, but they are near the top of the list for most harvested species (third, behind Mallard and Green-winged Teal in the 2014-2015 season). The harvest of Gadwalls in the U.S. over two years (2013 and 2014) averaged at about 1,629,000 birds; and for Canada the corresponding number was 52,800.

With their numbers on the rise, they are an increasingly popular target among hunters in the Southeast. Techniques for hunting Gadwalls are close to those for Mallard or Black Ducks. Mallard decoys (especially hen decoys) work just fine; some hunters say Gadwall decoys are also worth a try.

Using a Gadwall caller will also increase the odds of attracting Gadwall. Gadwall callers give a note that is softer than Mallard. Popular hunting areas include coastal Louisiana and Texas, Arkansas.

POPULATION AND CONSERVATION
Gadwall populations remained stable when other waterfowl species declined in the 1970s and early 1980s. Over the last century, their range has expanded in the East and west of the Cascade Mountains. The population has grown since the late 1980s to today's record levels. Much of this has been attributed to Conservation Reserve Program (CRP) grasslands in the Dakotas. Increases in populations of small predators (e.g., raccoons, foxes, skunks, feral cats) may have less of an impact on Gadwall nesting success because these ducks are persistent renesters and favor nesting on islands. The North American population estimate was 3.6 million in 2012, 96% above the long-term average. By 2016, the estimate had increased to 3.7 million.

American Wigeon
AMWI *Mareca Americana*

Plates Page 124

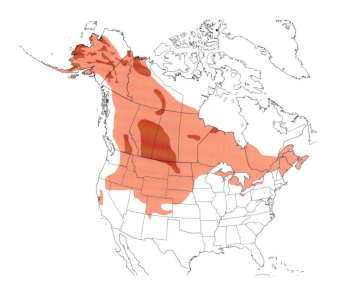

OTHER COMMON OR REGIONAL NAMES
Baldpate, gray duck, wige, stealer duck, pepper-head (Arctic: qatkegglig [YK], uuwiuhiq [NS, NWS], ugiihiq [NWS])
(Québec: canard d'Amérique)
(Mexico: pato calvo, pato chalcuán, pato panadero, pato poolnuxi)

MEASUREMENTS
Length: Male – 18.4-23.0 in, av 20.3 in (51.6 cm); Female – 17.7-20.3 in, av 19.0 in (48.3 cm)
Wing: Male – av 10.4 in (26.4 cm); Female – av 9.7 in (24.6 cm)
Weight: Male – av 1.80 lbs (816 g); Female – av 1.70 lbs (771 g)
Bill: Male – av 40.5 mm; Female – av 35.1 mm

FIRST IMPRESSIONS
American Wigeon are colorful and somewhat chunky-looking dabblers that have a particular propensity to graze on land (particularly grassy fields) like geese. Their stubby bills and legs in the center of their body are ideal for scarfing grass. They are equally as comfortable on land as in the water. They often travel in large flocks that can be detected by a chorus of high-pitched whistles. Males have a distinctive head pattern, including a peaked forecrown and white forehead, which gives them their old colloquial name, Baldpate. Also in males, look for the striking black vent and long central tail feathers – a rear-end pattern like a Northern Pintail, but shorter – bordered in front by white. Breast and flanks are almost pinkish. Females have gray-brown heads with smudgy patches around the eyes, sometimes giving the impression of a bruised, or "black" eye. The head also contrasts with a warmer-colored body.

Both sexes have bluish-gray bills with small dark tips. Size and Shape: They are slightly smaller than Mallards, which makes them a mid-sized dabbler with a fairly long, pointed tail. Their head is rounded with a distinctly small bill. Flight: At a good distance, wigeon can be hard to distinguish from other species. Males have more white on the upperwing that any other duck. Still, they share a white wing patch like large mergansers, pointed tail and narrow, sweptback wings like pintail, and are similar overall to the indistinct Gadwall. Listen for their high-whistled call that often given in flight. On the East Coast, if ducks are seen flying with Canada Geese they are most likely wigeon. American Wigeon fly swiftly with deep wing beats and narrow sweptback wings, but they are more erratic in flight than other larger dabbling ducks.

ID: IN DEPTH AND SIMILAR SPECIES
American Wigeon have more variable plumages than most other ducks. You can even find males with all white cheeks and black or pale creamy throats and variations up to their typical face patterns. They are one of the few dabbling ducks that you can age and sex in the field well into the winter. They can be readily aged by the pattern and color of the upperwing coverts. After they flap their wing, before the wing is nestled in back into their side feathers, take a peek at the median and greater coverts.

Ducklings are similar to those of Mallard, but they lack a dark brown eyeline, so their faces appear plain with warm-yellow coloration. Juvenile plumage begins to grow at two weeks, so by the end of six weeks it is fully grown, and the birds are flying by eight weeks old. At that age, they look much like adult females. By late August, they are replacing juvenile plumage; the majority of it is shed by December. They replace most of the juvenile body feathers, some upperwing coverts and a variable number of tail feathers.

First-year females are distinguished from adult females by the dull pattern of their median and lesser coverts. Their median and lesser coverts are dusky brown and lack a distinct white edge. Their greater coverts lack a white base. Also, look for any retained juvenile plumage, which starts to look worn by the fall. Adult females have crisp white edges to their lesser and median coverts, which contrast with dark brown centers. Their greater coverts are white at the base with a black tip. They replace some body feathers in February-May and become slightly more camouflaged before incubation. After raising the brood, she will migrate from where she raised her brood to a larger lake to grow a new set of wing feathers, followed by new body feathers from July-December.

First-year males have dusky upperwing coverts, not as clean white as adults, with a dark trailing edge to the greater coverts. They often retain bits of orangey juvenile plumage on the sides through the winter. Adult males are readily distinguished, by clean white upperwing coverts year-round. Shortly after leaving their incubating mate, males typically replace over half to all of their body feathers to attain a camouflaged eclipse plumage in mid-June. Upon arrival to the molting grounds, they grow their new wing feathers in July and August and are flightless for 35 days. They molt into their bright plumage through September and October. This plumage is kept until the following summer. In eclipse plumage they look very much like females with white wing coverts. They are slighter darker on the upperparts than females and have a rich orange breast and sides.

Similar Species: Eurasian Wigeon is uncommon to rare in North America (depending on locale). The occasional hybrids can cause confusion, though they are much rarer than reported. Female Eurasian Wigeon are often seen next to a male Eurasian Wigeon. This is often a good clue! They are noticeably richer brown on the head with less flecking than American Wigeon. Head shape is subtly different appearing flatter-headed. They lack black around the base of the bill. The clincher, if you can see it, is the median coverts and axillaries (wingpits) – white in American Wigeon but gray in Eurasian Wigeon. See the Eurasian Wigeon accounts (pp. 128 and 390) for a more in-depth treatment of separating females.

Hybrid American × Eurasian Wigeon tend to be misidentified as Eurasian Wigeon. Hybrids vary in their appearance. Males often have a rusty head, but paler cheek than pure Eurasians. Extensive green iridescence on the head is indicative of hybridization, though beware, many, if not most, Eurasian Wigeon show some green behind the eye. The body color should also be examined. Hybrids often have purplish breasts that bleed into gray sides (that means more purple than on pure Eurasians, but more gray then on pure Americans).

In flight, American Wigeon can look really similar to Gadwall. They share a white belly and fairly similar shape and white patch in the wing. American Wigeon have white on the upperwing coverts, whereas Gadwall have several white secondaries close to where the wing meets the body.

Sex ratio: Males dominate at 52-60%.

GEOGRAPHIC VARIATION
No subspecies are recognized.

SOUNDS
American Wigeon is a highly vocal duck. Large flocks of wigeon are quite noisy, sometimes sounding like a mass of rubber squeaky-toys. The male frequently gives a whistle that likely serves as a signal to his mate to keep them together in hectic flocks. Males: Give a high, two- or three-part whistle *chu-CHU* or *chu-CHU-chuu*. Given in many contexts to communicate with mate. Intensity of call varies as threat level increases. Whistle calls are often given in flight. Females: Infrequently give a nasal croak on land and in flight. Soft, low *errr* calls are given in many contexts, as alarm call when disturbed with brood, leading mate in flight, and during the distraction display. A *squak* call is given when disturbed with brood. Rarely gives a decrescendo call, similar to Mallard and Northern Pintail, which is uttered less frequently than other dabbling ducks.

YEAR IN THE LIFE
American Wigeon are common and widespread in winter, but they have a definite bias for the West. They are at home in habitats ranging from large coastal marshes to city parks. Watch for wigeon in celery beds with Canvasback, American Coot, and other adept diving species from which aggressive wigeon often steal a meal. Wigeon are often frequently seen grazing in fields and suburban parks where their grazing may call to mind a flock of petite geese.

Nearly half the population winters along the Pacific Flyway in California's Central Valley. Large numbers are also found in the Mississippi Flyway where they concentrate in coastal marshes. Smaller numbers are found south to Panama and the Caribbean. Some regularly winter in Hawaii. Wandering birds have been found as far as Europe, the Azores, and Japan.

Courting rituals begin upon arrival at the wintering grounds, where they establish pair bonds before the onset of spring migration. Intricate courtship displays include a swimming-shake, bathing and wing-flapping, wing-raising, and the burping, turning the back of the head, and jump-flight (to get ahead of other displaying males) that is seen in other puddle ducks.

Aside from Northern Pintail, American Wigeon has the northernmost breeding distribution of any puddle duck. They are also one of the latest puddle ducks to move north. By early May, most wigeon have arrived at southerly breeding grounds in North Dakota, but birds in Nunavut may not arrive until late May or early June.

Once pairs reach the tundra pools, river deltas, boreal lakes, and prairie potholes where they breed, the female selects a nest site. Males take off, leaving their incubating mate often in their second or third week of incubation, to undergo a molt-migration, some males only move several miles, while others travel up to several hundred miles to reach suitable lakes and marshes for their wing molt.

Females remain with their ducklings until they are 6-7 weeks old and then migrate to a larger lake to molt.

In the fall, American Wigeon are one of the first species of ducks to start heading south. Migration kicks off in Alaska in mid-August, peaking in early September. Numbers in western Washington are on the rise in October and November, where many birds stay for the winters. Others continue onto California and Mexico where numbers grow through December.

DIET AND FEEDING BEHAVIOR

American Wigeon feed in shallow wetlands and are distinguished from other dabbler species by bill dimensions that will facilitate grazing, both for aquatic and terrestrial plants (e.g., stems and leaves of aquatic plants, upland grasses and clovers, and leafy parts and seeds of agricultural crops. Their diet consists largely of these plant materials (with females relying on large proportions of animal matter during breeding). In winter and migration, they will engage significantly in grazing in upland agricultural areas. Their goose-like bill is indicative of their feeding strategy, primarily as grazing herbivores, especially in winter.

They will feed on vegetation from the surface to only about 8 inches deep. American Wigeon are also fairly aggressive and opportunistic foragers. In winter they may closely associate in the water with American Coots and species of diving ducks (e.g. Redhead), taking plant material brought to the surface by these species since the American Wigeon themselves are not effective divers.

NESTING

Site: Breeds by shallow, freshwater wetlands (ponds, sloughs, small lakes, marshes, and rivers). Prefers areas where there is upland cover. This is typically in a dry meadow with some cover, well concealed, and within 50 yards of water. In forested areas, may be in leaf litter by a tree or bush.

Nest description: A slight depression lined with dry grasses or other plant material. The nest is well lined with light gray down and feathers. (The down is smaller and lighter than that of Gadwall.) The inside diameter is about 8 inches.

Clutch size: Average 8 eggs, range 6-11

Egg description: Elliptical to subelliptical. Smooth. Cream colored. (Very similar to that of Gadwall.) 54 X 38 mm.

Incubation duration: 23-25 days.

Brood parasitism: Rare host.

HUNTING

Baldpate are wily ducks that are often wary and quick to flush. They tend to drop in toward decoys from high altitudes approaching from downwind, but they often approach very far out. They usually flare into the wind and drift back. They can change their course faster than most ducks. They come into dabbling, diving duck, and goose decoys. Wigeon whistle calls or pintail whistle calls are available and helpful for some hunters.

The harvest of American Wigeon in the U.S. over two years (2013 and 2014) averaged at about 624,600 birds; and for Canada the corresponding number was 32,700.

Favored hunting localities include: Arkansas, Missouri, and California's Central Valley.

POPULATION AND CONSERVATION

American Wigeon populations have increased since a decline in early 1980s when the population dropped from 3.5 million to 1.8 million due to a widespread drought. The more recent increase is attributed to improved habitat conditions in the western breeding grounds and an eastward expansion of the breeding range, but their numbers are still below the NAWMP target population. The population estimate was 3.4 million in 2016, which is 31% above the long-term average (1955-2015). Still, the population estimate in 1959 was 3.8 million.

American Wigeon certainly benefit from our modern habitat protection plans, as they suffer from loss of wetlands to agriculture and development. Carefully monitored bag limits are important to sustaining their population. They are also at risk of ingesting lethal amounts of organophosphate herbicides while they graze on lawns, particularly turf on golf courses.

Eurasian Wigeon
EUWI *Mareca penelope*

Plates Page 128

OTHER COMMON OR REGIONAL NAMES
European wigeon, redhead wigeon, wigeon, wige (Québec: canard siffleur)
(Mexico: pato silbón)

MEASUREMENTS
Length: Male – 18.2-20.5 in, av 19.3 in (49.0 cm); Female – 16.5-19.5 in, av 17.9 in (45.5 cm)
Wing: Male – av 7.6 in (19.3 cm); Female – av 7.2 in (18.3 cm)
Weight: Male – av 1.60 lbs (726 g); Female – av 1.41 lbs (640 g)
Bill: Male – av 34.5 mm; Female – av 32.5 mm

FIRST IMPRESSIONS AND SIMILAR SPECIES
Eurasian Wigeon are rare, but regular visitors in North America.

The bright burnt red head and gray body of a male Eurasian Wigeon really stands out in a flock of hundreds of American Wigeons. The breast is pinky-brown, the belly white, and the flanks are finely barred gray and white (Americans never show this flank pattern.) In dense flocks, it can actually be easier to find via flank color rather than head color. Females are trickier. Look for a browner head contrasting little with the body.

Both sexes have bluish-gray bills with small dark tips. Size and shape: Large rounded head of males, along with round body and long pointed tail characterize all wigeon. But the Eurasian is shorter-tailed than American, and the head shape is subtly different – flatter and deeper-headed. Flight: Slender, swept back wings, long neck with rounded head, and long pointed tail are traits shared with American Wigeon, along with the white forewing patch. The Eurasian male's rusty head color and gray body can be readily apparent in flight, even at considerable distances. Picking out females in flight is difficult, but you can look for the gray wingpits (axillaries) and underwing coverts in all plumages in Eurasian, something that is striking white in American Wigeon. Also, the upperwing – the greater coverts – will be darker on Eurasian than on American.

Similar species: Bright-plumaged male Eurasian Wigeon are easy to identify. Eclipse and female Eurasian Wigeon are more difficult to distinguish from American, but with a little practice it can be done reliably and with confidence.

The overall body and head color of female Eurasian is warm brown. There is little or no contrast between the color of the head, breast, and sides; look for uniformity. In American, though, the head is grayish with more pronounced streaking. It contrasts strongly with the breast and flank color; they look noticeably two-toned. Both wigeon have warm breast and flank colors that vary from pinkish-brown to chestnut. It is the head color and the contrast that is the key.

A squarer head, flatter and deeper, is good supporting evidence for Eurasian. It often appears short-necked, holding its head not very high off its body much of the time. Also on the head, look for a lack of black around the base of the bill on Eurasian.

Eurasians have more uniformly dark centers to the upperpart feathers. Americans have complex internal feather markings. Eurasian Wigeon have dark brown greater coverts with thin white edges. American has a black base and white tip to the greater coverts. They can also be aged based on wing covert differences. Remember to look for the gray axillaries on flying, flapping, or preening birds. They are gleaming white in Americans.

Male hybrid wigeon will also throw people off as well, because they can have the rusty head and mostly gray body. Some hybrids will have on the flanks a mixture of gray and pink, an excellent indicator of a hybrid individual. Other hybrids look more like Americans with a lot of green on the head and purplish bodies. The presence of a bit of green iridescence behind the eye is not necessarily a sign of hybridization, however.

Sex ratio: Males dominate in Northern Europe at 52-60%.

BACKGROUND AND TIPS
Hundreds of Eurasian Wigeon spend the winter in North America and probably return to Eurasia to breed. They are regular migrants through western Alaska (not indicated on map). It's possible that some of them actually breed somewhere in North America, but a nest has yet to be documented. Still, they have been recorded in nearly every state and province, with a majority of records from October to May.

They are most common in the Pacific Flyway where

they are in the greatest numbers in the Puget Sound region and British Columbia; they are uncommon along the Pacific coast south to southern California. They are scarcer in the interior and eastern half of North America.

Band recoveries suggest that Atlantic coastal birds originate in Iceland, while Pacific coastal birds may be from the Kamchatka-Andyr area in Russia.

In winter, Eurasian Wigeon are found mainly along these coasts in shallow, sheltered waters with tidal mud, sand or saltmarsh, also in freshwater and brackish lagoons and flooded grasslands. Some will linger in the Lower-48 until the spring, with most headed north by May. In fall, Eurasian Wigeon begin to show up again in the Lower-48 starting in September, with numbers picking up in October. Individuals often return to the same areas to winter for multiple years. They are almost always found in American Wigeon flocks.

Eurasian Wigeon are occasionally taken by hunters, particularly in the Pacific Northwest where they are often present in large flocks of wigeon. They are common enough now in North America to occur in harvest surveys, and the average annual harvest in the U.S. for 2006-14 was about 1,800 birds. For Canada, it has been closer to 200 birds in the recent past. When traveling with American Wigeon, these birds will come into decoys but will typically land far out. They are often wary and quick to flush.

Eurasian Wigeon reports in North America have been on the rise certainly in part due to observer awareness. They are abundant and populations are stable or increasing throughout most of the breeding range in the Old World. Winter counts in northwest Europe have increased significantly in the last 20 years. The global population estimate is 2,800,000-3,300,000.

SOUNDS

Wigeons are generally vocal species. A male's Eurasian's higher-pitched whistle is can be readily heard over a flock of noisy American Wigeon. Male: Gives piercing whistle, *WheEEOO*. The Eurasian whistle is three syllables, unlike the American, with two. Also, unlike American's more constant whistles, Eurasian is usually heard only once at a time and sticks out from a flock of calling Americans. Female: Gives a harsh call, grating call, often given repeatedly during aggressive encounters.

DIET AND FEEDING BEHAVIOR

Eurasian Wigeons will feed by grazing on land (e.g., fields) and dabbling on the surface of shallow water. Less often, they will feed to a depth of about 8 inches. They eat a mainly a vegetarian diet of leaves, stems, rhizomes, seeds, stems and root bulbs of pond weeds, fine grasses, horsetails, eelgrass, and algae. Animal materials are rarely taken (although recorded in breeding season) and usually incidental to plant matter or seeds.

Like the American Wigeon, the Eurasian Wigeon will supplement its diet with food snatched from diving ducks.

NESTING

While there has been no verified nesting of Eurasian Wigeon yet in North American, its increasing annual occurrence and numbers — especially wintering in the West — leads to the conclusion that nesting will be found somewhere — perhaps in the Canadian northwest or in Alaska — soon. Hybridization with American Wigeon is probably just as likely. Eurasian Wigeon nest in a variety of habitats but more often by freshwater lakes and streams, or on lake islands, occasionally away from water. The nest description, clutch size, and egg description is very similar to that of American Wigeon (p. 389).

Northern Pintail
NOPI *Anas acuta*

Plates Page 130

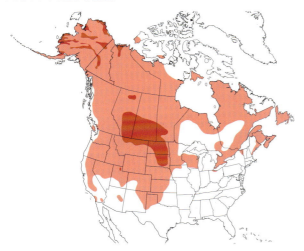
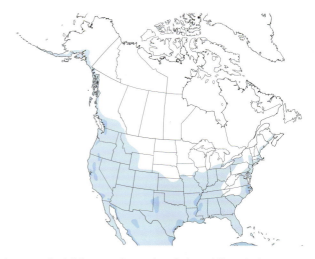

OTHER COMMON OR REGIONAL NAMES
Pintail, American pintail, sprig, bull sprig, pinny, spike, spike-tail, picket-tail
(Arctic: uqulegaq [YK], uqsuqaq [NS], kurugaq [NWS], qummnajunq, kchomukchayuk [N])
(Québec: canard pilet)
(Mexico: pato golondrino, zakaal, pato rabudo)

MEASUREMENTS
Length: Male – 23.6-30.1 in, av 25.2 in (64.0 cm)*; Female – 20.6-24.8 in, av 21.4 in (54.4 cm)
Wing: Male – av 10.7 in (27.2 cm); Female – av 10.1 in (25.7 cm)
Weight: Male – av 2.26 lbs (1025 g); Female – av 1.91 lbs (866 g)
Bill: Male – av 51.2 mm; Female – av 46.8 mm
*Includes up to 4 in (10 cm) of tail extension in males.

FIRST IMPRESSIONS
This is an elegant duck, long and lean. It can be identified by structure alone. The male's brown head, white neckstripe, extremely long central trail-feathers, and gray body, patterned with contrasting blacks and whites, gives it a stately and sleek appearance. The long tail and black undertail of the male is distinctive, even at a long range. The female's soft and seemingly warm brown tones along with her trim figure combine to project a graceful look. The bill, also slim, is blue-gray and distinctive, darkest in the center. Size and Shape: Pintails have a distinctive slender and, when in the water or on the land, erect appearance characterized by a long neck and long tail. Not coincidentally, the bird's specific name, "acuta," is a reference from the Latin to the sharp tail of the male. Flight: Northern Pintails in flight also appear slender, long-bodied, long-winged, and long-tailed. This combination of features gives Northern Pintails a distinctive silhouette—the reason that they have been called "the greyhounds of the air" and, thus, can often be identified at greater distances than other dabblers. The head is often held high, tipped slightly upward. The swept-back wings might suggest a wigeon, but note that Northern Pintails have much longer necks and tails. The male is white-bellied with gray upper flanks. In mixed flocks of flying dabblers, Northern Pintails also appear paler than other ducks. Flocks are often strung out in a line or in a V. They tend to travel in fairly large flocks; it is not unusual to see flocks of several hundred birds. The birds are fairly common in freshwater and coastal marshes, even agricultural fields, but they avoid wet wooded areas. Pintails often fly higher in sky than other ducks and will often form lines or Vs. Northern Pintail moves swiftly with medium-deep wing beats and swept-back wings.

ID: IN DEPTH AND SIMILAR SPECIES
Northern Pintail breed in their first year. Some males, however, do not find mates in their first year because of intense competition and a skewed sex ratio.

Ducklings are grayer overall compared to other dabblers. They have a dark gray crown and back and a lighter gray to slightly whitish face and breast. Legs are brownish-gray or greenish-gray, sometimes bluish-gray. Bill gray to bluish-gray by the second week. Juvenile plumage begins to appear at about 3 weeks and is fully grown by 7-8 weeks, sometimes later. It looks much like adult female plumage. However, look for perfectly even patterning on the sides, flanks diffusely spotted and barred. This particular patterning doesn't last long, but is useful for a time frame around July, before the birds begin replacing juvenile plumage, a time when adult females look very worn and motley. Look for neatly patterned short streaks on the underparts — usually present on the belly, smaller feathers with less complicated internal markings. The trailing edge to the speculum may look like that in the adult female but narrower. First-years begin replacing juvenile plumage in August-September. It is not long before they have molted most of their body feathers and are transitioning into an adult-like plumage. First-year males are best separated from eclipse adults by retained juvenile feathers on the underparts. Any male not in full bright plumage by December is most likely first-year. By February, only a few first-year birds show signs of immaturity.

First-year females can often be distinguished from adult females by their duller tertials and any retained juvenile plumage. Adult females have a warm brown, face with even patterns on the body. The simple but elegant look is enhanced by a speculum that is a dark gray-brown with a white trailing edge. Females replace some body feathers in February-April and become slightly more camouflaged before incubation. This often includes replacement of the tertials, which change from an even dark brown-gray feather with a thin white edge to a dark brown feather with either strong buffy internal markings or buffy barring that extends from the edge to the shaft. After their broods fledge, females usually move to a nearby body of water to molt not far from where they raised their brood. For about 4 weeks they are flightless, as their primaries and secondaries grow. Body molt continues until the fall.

First-year males look like adult males by winter, but they molt into that plumage a month or so after the adults. Males with mottled brown feathers on the side in the end of October or later are likely young birds. Some first-year males do not attain a clean, adult-like plumage until December, although most have an adult-like appearance by November. After this point, they are unlikely to have any juvenile plumage, and they become difficult to separate from adult males.

Adult males are as previously described and are best identified by structure, including an erect posture. Also note the speculum, which is brown, bordered by chestnut in front and a white trailing edge.

Shortly after leaving their incubating mates, males will replace at least half of their body feathers to attain a camouflaged eclipse plumage. The molt into eclipse plumage usually takes place sometime from May-August. Eclipse males have plain gray-brown heads and a dull-colored body with dark barring on the sides. Overall, their grayer appearance and barring on the sides will separate them from females and juveniles. Upon arrival to the molting grounds, males shed their wing feathers and grow a completely new set of primaries and secondaries in July and August. Some males are still growing the last of their new body feathers in November. Many, however, have finished their body molt by October. This plumage is kept until the following late spring/early summer.

Found an odd Northern Pintail? It may be a hybrid. Northern Pintails have been recorded or presumed hybridizing in North America with American Black Duck, Mallard, Gadwall, Northern Shoveler, American Wigeon, and other species.

If it is not a hybrid, maybe it is a senescent female. These females often have barred sides and dull gray-brown heads. At first glance, they appear similar to eclipse males, but if it's not the time of year when drakes are normally in eclipse plumage, take a closer look, particularly for the pattern on the sides, for head color, and bill pattern.

Similar Species: Learn the size and shape of Northern Pintails, because they have a unique, slender appearance that will help separate them from other ducks. The only other North American duck with such a proportionally long tail is the male Long-tailed Duck. Northern Pintails may appear smaller than Mallards or American Black Ducks, or longer, even though their measurements are actually similar.

Look for the rounded head in a Northern Pintail that curves into a long, graceful neck and long, attenuated body. Females are most similar to wigeon, Gadwall, and Mallard, but female Northern Pintails are a paler, warm brown overall. Their pale bellies are a blended cream color, not a sharply delineated white belly like a Gadwall or wigeon or darker-bellied Mallard.

In flight, at a distance, their shape most closely resembles wigeons, but the overall color pattern of wigeons is quite different, with the drake's white patches on the wing and white bellies contrasting with darker sides.

Sex ratio: Males dominate at 53-59%, but may vary due to season and location.

YEAR IN THE LIFE

Northern Pintails are common and widespread in the Northern Hemisphere. The species' range covers more of the earth's surface than any other duck. During the fall and winter, Northern Pintails are most often found in shallow wetlands with little cover or in harvested grain fields. They also commonly frequent flooded agricultural fields, inland reservoirs, bays, and tidal wetlands. They are almost always one step ahead of other ducks. They are one of the earliest ducks to begin fall migration and to arrive on their wintering grounds.

Nearly half the population winters in central California. They are found in particularly large numbers in the marshes of the Sacramento and San Joaquin valleys in California. The Sacramento NWR is a great place to enjoy lots of pintails. Large numbers are also found around the Chesapeake Bay, western Washington, Gulf Coast, rice regions of Arkansas, west coast of Sinaloa, and the Mexican Plateau. Smaller numbers winter regularly south to Costa Rica, Cuba, and the Bahamas.

Pair formation will have begun in early fall or early winter. Male courtship display behaviors include burp (most common display involving vertical neck-stretching), grunt-whistle (often performed after burp), chin-lift, head-up-tail-up, turning-the-back-of-the-head, and ritualized preening revealing the speculum. They also have a characteristic aerial courtship which involves a female and several males. Females prefer males with the whitest breast color and the longest scapular feathers.

Northern Pintails are also among the first ducks to head north in spring. They certainly have a long way to go to reach their breeding grounds. They have the northernmost breeding distribution of any puddle duck. The largest concentrations of breeders are usually in the Prairie Potholes, prairie parkland, and in Alaska. If it is a drought year on the prairies, however, they will move farther northward; up to 60% may breed in Alaska or even continue onto Siberia (typically some 25% of pintails breed in Alaska). Therefore, they are perhaps the most nomadic of any of our ducks.

Once a pair finds suitable nesting habitat, which is usually in an open area near shallow water on the prairie or tundra, the female selects a nest site. Northern Pintails are the only dabbling duck that actually prefers tilled cropland for their ground-nesting. Nesting in marginal habitats may sound like a good thing, but, unfortunately, many of their nests are discovered by predators or destroyed by agricultural activity. One study in North Dakota found that nearly half of all nests were destroyed by farming operations. Almost all Northern Pintails will renest at least once and many twice, but not more, because they tend not to breed late in the season.

For successful broods, the females remain with their ducklings until they are 6-7 weeks old, at which time the females migrate to a larger lake to molt. Males often travel an even greater distance to find a suitable place to molt. Part way through the incubation, the male abandons his incubating mate and takes off, often heading south but sometimes north, to a larger body of water. On average, drake Northern Pintails will undergo the longest molt-migration of any puddle duck, sometimes traveling hundreds of miles.

GEOGRAPHIC VARIATION
No subspecies are recognized. There is an isolated population, "Eaton's Pintail," on the Kerguelen Islands of the Indian Ocean, which is considered a separate species by some.

SOUNDS
Northern Pintails are fairly vocal, at least for dabblers. Males: Short, mellow *proop-proop* is most frequently heard, along with a high, whining *mee-meee* or *wheezy whee* note, heard throughout the year These can be most often heard when groups of Northern Pintails are courting. The whistled *proop-proop* is similar to that of Green-winged Teal, but lower-pitched and more musical. During the burp display males utters high-pitched, burping *ee hee*, followed by a trilled whistle. Females: Give a hoarse, weak *kuk* throughout the year, singly or in series. They give a *kuk-kuk-kuk-kuk* during the inciting display. Also, utter a loud, *gaak* given as an alarm call. She will give a hoarse descending *queeack* if the pair is separated or in response to other Northern Pintails.

DIET AND FEEDING BEHAVIOR
Northern Pintails will make wide use of cereal grains (e.g., after wing molt is completed on the Northern Great Plains before a southward migration and when wintering in California). Foods taken include waste grain barley, rice, wheat, sorghum, and corn, and Northern Pintails are often seen grazing in these agricultural fields. (Reductions in rice growing in Texas may adversely affect these birds.)

The species also has an appetite for natural food: aquatic plant seed, pondweed, three-square bulrush, burr reed seed, etc. Northern Pintail is a habitual up-ender when feeding, with long neck facilitating a reach to the bottom in slightly deepr water.

Nesting hens find animal foods particularly important — aquatic insects, crustaceans, worms, snails — though less so in the Arctic. Individuals may forage alone or with their mates in the nesting season, but in flocks — sometimes very large flocks — in nonbreeding seasons. Feeds while walking in fields or in very shallow water. Dabbles for food at water surface, but may even dive to reach bottom seeds. Flocks of Northern Pintails will often make regular feeding circuits in fall and winter — dry fields in the morning and early evening, flooded fields and wetlands at night.

NESTING
Site: More than any other duck, Northern Pintails will select open areas and sparse vegetation for their nests. The nest will be on the ground, sometimes under some cover and sometimes near water. Northern Pintails will also tend to locate their nests farther away from water than other ground-nesting ducks. Vegetation at the site will vary with the locality.

Nest description: A hollow, lined with plant material, down, and some feathers. (Down tufts can be longish, light brown with pale centers, not unlike Northern Shoveler's). Nest sizes are variable, 5-7 inches in inside diameter, 7-10 inches in outside diameter, and 2-4 inches in depth. May be flush with, or even below, ground level, but high nests have been found — 7 inches above the ground — in Alaska in tidal areas.

Clutch size: Average 7, range 3-12.

Egg description: Subelliptical to oval, occasionally long. Variable color: yellowish-cream to greenish- or grayish-buff or even bluish. (See Mallard egg description.) 54mm X 37mm.

Incubation duration: 22-24 days.

Brood parasitism: Occasional host, sometimes by Redhead or Ruddy Duck, most commonly parasitized when nesting on small islands.

HUNTING
"Sprigs," also nicknamed "Pinnies" or "Spikes," are a favorite duck of many hunters. Northern Pintails tend to be warier than other waterfowl, so they will often be the first dabblers in a mixed species flock to flush. In the Atlantic Flyway, they are more difficult to attract to decoys than other dabblers, although hens and immature males will decoy more readily than adult males. They often fly high, but will drop down into the decoys by cupping their wings

from 200-300 yards up. They often make an initial high pass over the decoys, but only one pass by the decoys once they are within range. Using pintail decoys is not a necessity, but adding a few to any spread adds to variety and realism.

They are often hunted in larger ponds and bays, but also in fields or marshes, like Mallards. Northern Pintails do respond to commercially manufactured "pintail whistles" but some hunters have better luck with these calls than others. To call Northern Pintails into decoys with a caller, hunters will give two quick shots followed by a tongue-trill over and over.

The harvest of Northern Pintail in the U.S. over two years (2013 and 2014) averaged at about 505,000 birds; and for Canada the corresponding number was 61,000. The population decline for this species has lead to restrictive hunting seasons, at least since 1987.

Favorite hunting locations include: California's Central Valley, Gulf Coast of Texas and northern Mexico, and coastal Sinaloa, Mexico.

POPULATION AND CONSERVATION

North American populations fluctuate in response to conditions on the breeding grounds more than other species of waterfowl. This species, once one of our most abundant ducks, is particularly susceptible to drought and loss of grassland habitat in the Prairie Pothole Region. Population was lowest during a prairie drought from 1988-1991 and highest in the 1950s and 1970s. North American population estimate was 2.6 million in 2016, 34% below the long-term average (1955-2015). In fact, this species has declined more dramatically than any other of our North American Ducks over the past 40 years. This long-term decline, generates deep concern for the Northern Pintail population and further demonstrates a need to protect and restore grasslands.

There are two groups in the North American Northern Pintail population. One population, which is stable, nests in the high Arctic, concentrating at the Mackenzie River Delta. The other population nesting in the Prairie Pothole Region is declining and probably accounts for the population-level declines. (In contrast, however, other dabbling ducks in the region have been rebounding.) One explanation is that Northern Pintails often choose nest sites with little cover, e.g., in crop stubble. They will arrive on the breeding grounds and initiate nesting early in the season, before the farmers beginning tilling in the spring. Once the tilling is underway, many clutches are destroyed and hens are run over by farming equipment. If the nests are in winter wheat, however, the nesting is usually successful, since winter wheat is planted in the fall and not harvested until mid-summer, after nesting is over. CRP lands can be beneficial, but as that habitat becomes taller and thicker it becomes far less appealing to Northern Pintail.

At the same time, nest losses due to predators are correlated with the degree of nest concealment.

Northern Pintails also seem to be more susceptible to disease outbreaks than many other waterfowl. While avian botulism and cholera can impact all waterfowl, 13% to 40% of waterfowl with these diseases have been Northern Pintails. In some years, die-offs have been as high as 350,000 Northern Pintails, a significant percentage of the continental population.

White-cheeked Pintail
WCHP *Anas bahamensis*

Plates Page 134

OTHER COMMON OR REGIONAL NAMES
Bahama pintail, Bahama duck, Bahama teal

MEASUREMENTS
Length: Male – 16.9-20.4 in, av 18.7 in (47.5 cm)
Female – 16.1-19.3 in, av 17.7 in (45.0 cm)
Wing: Male – av 8.4 in (21.4 cm); Female – av 8.0 in (20.4 cm)
Weight: Male – av 1.2 lbs (524 g); Female – av 1.1 lbs (503 g)
Bill: Male – av 43.0 mm; Female – av 41.5 mm

FIRST IMPRESSIONS AND SIMILAR SPECIES
This tropical rarity has a striking white cheek, chin, and throat, contrasting with a darker forehead and cap. Otherwise, the White-cheeked Pintail has a warm brown pattern. The tail is mainly cream-colored; the warm brown body is speckled with black markings. The grayish bill, with a red base, has a strongly curved culmen. Although quite distinctive as a species, separating males and females is not easy. Females are smaller, slightly paler, and with shorter tails. Larger males have more extensive red at the base of the bill, puffier heads, more pronounced crown, have more boldly marked flanks (brighter orange), are slightly longer-tailed. Juveniles are similar to adults but duller with smaller spotting on the underparts, with a dark bill. Size and Shape: This species is somewhat similar in size and shape to Northern Pintail, but with a thicker neck and shorter tail. The large head suggests a square shape in the male, but a rounder shape in female. Flight: In flight, it is similar to Northern Pintail, but with a longer neck and shorter body. The cream-colored tail and uppertail coverts are distinctive in flight, especially when landing or banking. The broad, buffy color on the trailing edge of the

secondaries is prominent. This species is graceful and swift in flight with sweptback wings.

Similar Species: White-cheeked Pintail always has a large white cheek patch, so it is generally distinctive. Winter male Ruddy Ducks also have white cheek patches, but their entire bodies are much more compact than the graceful lines of White-cheeked Pintails.

Sex ratio: Unknown.

BACKGROUND AND TIPS

The "Bahama" White-cheeked Pintail was formerly abundant throughout the West Indies, but it is now threatened. It is declining in the West Indies, with the exception of the population in Cuba, which has benefited from rice farming since the 1960s. The nominate "Bahama Pintail," *A. b. bahamensis*, is the subspecies that has reached the United States. It spans the West Indies and northeast South America, and is the brightest subspecies.

White-cheeked Pintail is not considered a migratory species, but it will travel in flocks, making short movement between islands throughout the year. Moreover, about half the pairs stay together for multiple years.

Be on the alert for this rarity in south Florida. Most of the records are from late November through early May, with multiple records from Everglades National Park. This is a popular duck kept in captivity, so the origin of individuals, even in Florida, is often in doubt. There is a good chance that most birds seen beyond south Florida originated in captivity despite intriguing reports from far-flung locations including Alabama, California, Delaware, Illinois, Louisiana, Nevada, New Jersey, North Dakota, Ontario, Québec, Texas, Virginia, West Virginia, and Wisconsin.

White-cheeked Pintail is nominally protected from hunting in some areas, including the Bahamas and Puerto Rico. This pintail can be locally common in some areas that have extensive areas of ideal habitat (e.g. in the Bahamas on Abaco, Andros, and Great Inagua) and bird refuges (e. g. Paradise Island, Bahamas).

SOUNDS

The male produces a low, soft, wheezy whistle *mhee-mhee*. Also, gives several wheezy whistles as a warm-up for *peep-peep-pu-pu* similar to the vocalizations given during displays of other puddle ducks. The female gives weak descending *quacks*.

DIET AND FEEDING BEHAVIOR

White-cheeked Pintails favor brackish or saltwater ponds and mangrove marshes where they forage by dabbling. They will feed on aquatic plants and small animals, mostly invertebrates. Some of these include shorefly larvae, brine shrimp, water boatmen, aquatic nematodes, and midge larvae. White-cheeked Pintails also eat seeds of foxtail grass, panic grass, wigeon grass, and wild millet

Eastern Spot-billed Duck
ESBD *Anas zonorhyncha*

Plates Page 135

OTHER COMMON OR REGIONAL NAMES
Spot-billed Duck

MEASUREMENTS
Length: Male – c. 26.0 in (66.0 cm); Female – c. 24.0 in (60.9cm)
Wing: Male – av 10.8 in (27.4 cm); Female – av 10.0 in (25.3 cm)
Weight: Male – av 2.65 lbs (1202 g); Female – av 1.95 lbs (865 g)
Bill: Male – av 55.8 mm; Female – av 49.8 mm

FIRST IMPRESSIONS AND SIMILAR SPECIES

Eastern Spot-billed Duck, an Asian species, is dark brown on the body with a contrasting, paler buffy breast, neck, cheek, and eyebrow. The black bill is yellow-tipped. Its body is lightest on the head and breast, progressing to a very dark brown butt. Look for white tertial edges. This feature helps set Eastern Spot-billed Duck apart from female Mallard and other dabblers. Females are slightly paler. Size and shape: Similar in size to Mallard with a touch longer, more pointed tail. Flight: Large and dark with a heavy body and broad wings, striking white underwing coverts, not unlike American Black Duck, and dark upper wing with narrow white borders to the purplish-blue speculum. It has white borders on its dark brown tertials. Steady wingbeats. The yellow tip on the black bill can be visible at a considerable distance.

Similar species: Where these birds are most likely to turn up, a female Mallard would be the most similar-looking duck. Mallards are paler overall on the body, with more subtle facial patterns. They lack the striking, clean pale cheek and lines on the face of Eastern Spot-billed. Occasionally, Mallards are sighted with a hint of a Spot-billed face-pattern, with a short dark line extending from the base of the bill up into the cheek. Look for other Spot-billed characteristics such as the white border on the tertials and the dark butt. Also, notice Eastern Spot-billed does not have any internal markings on the body feathers; they have thin buffy edges to the back and side feathers, but lack prominent internal chevrons seen on many other dabblers. Indian Spot-billed Duck, formerly conspecific and quite a common captive, has an orange-red lobal area (absent in juv), lacks a cheek stripe, more extensive yellow bill, and averages paler with more boldly-fringed feathers.

Sex ratio: Unknown.

BACKGROUND AND TIPS
Eastern Spot-billed Duck is a very rare visitor to the Aleutian Islands of Alaska. It is a relatively short-range migrant, making is resident in much of Japan, Korea, and eastern China. Most records are from spring for the central and western Aleutians, but there are also records there for fall and winter. (There is also a specimen record from Kodiak Island.) Moreover, some records might represent the same individuals for long intervals. There is always a chance that one could show up elsewhere in Alaska or farther south.

Spot-billed Duck populations are not carefully monitored. They appear to be declining slightly, with habitat loss a main threat to population (estimated at 910,000-1,800,000).

DIET AND FEEDING BEHAVIOR
The Eastern Spot-billed Duck feeds like other dabblers. It is mainly vegetarian, eating plants at the surface and leaves and seeds on the ground. On occasion, it feeds on aquatic organisms. It is commonly a crepuscular or a nighttime feeder.

SOUNDS
Listen for their Mallard-like quacks. Males: Give flat, raspy *kreep*. Females: Give a loud *quack*, much like Mallard.

Falcated Duck
FADU *Mareca falcata*

Plates Page 135

OTHER COMMON OR REGIONAL NAMES
Falcated teal, bronze-capped teal

MEASUREMENTS
Length: Male – c. 20.0 in (50.8 cm); Female – c. 25.9 in (65.7cm)
Wing: Male – av 10.2 in (25.9 cm); Female – av 18.9 in (48.0 cm)
Weight: Male – av 1.57 lbs (713 g); Female – av 1.29 lbs (585 g)
Bill: Male – av 41.0 mm; Female – av 39.0 mm

FIRST IMPRESSIONS AND SIMILAR SPECIES-
This exquisite Asian rarity is everything a Gadwall might have wished it was – with graceful tertials so long they droop in the water, a crested head, delicate black bill and each feather with ornate patterns. The male has a gray body, a dark chestnut forehead and crown, glossy green cheeks, a small white dot just above the base of the bill, and a white chin and throat crossed by a black collar. The female is brown-bodied with warm brown breast and grayer head with just the hint of a crest. Hens have plain gray tertials that are also unusually long. Eclipse males are gray-brown overall, not unlike females, but with darker crowns and napes. They have shorter tertials than winter males, but the tertials are still longer than those of other puddle ducks. Size and shape: Similar to Gadwall with a smaller thinner bill, large shaggy head, and short thick neck. Males have distinct sickle-shaped tuft draping down back of head and those elongated tertial. Females are brown overall with a tan face and pale belly. Flight: Males are dark headed, with a gray body, darkest on the chest. White throat with black collar may also be apparent in flight. The upperwing is light gray above with dark secondaries. The underwings are striking white. Females are brown-bodied and with plain gray upperwings. Both sexes will show a green speculum flanked by white lines.

Similar species: Adult males are unlikely to be confused with other ducks. The green on the head is only superficially like a Mallard's, and body plumage much like a Gadwall. However, Falcated Ducks have so many unique features- crested head, long terials, stripes on the throat— that their ornate plumage is distinctive. Females on the other hand, are more challenging to separate from female Gadwalls. Take a close look at the shape, particularly Falcated's longer, thinner, and dark bill, the hint of a crested nape, uniform head color, and subtle dark fringes on the body feathers. Falcated's dark thin bill combined with a large puffy head eliminate other female dabblers. Also, notice the warmer-tones, particularly on the underparts.

There are Gadwall × Falcated hybrids out there (mostly in Asia). Male hybrids have a gray body, big black butt and light gray elongated tertials. Larger bill than a pure Falcated and a squatty-looking mostly brown head.

Sex ratio: Unknown.

ID: IN DEPTH
Falcated Ducks reach their mature plumage early in the winter, much like Gadwall and are difficult to age in the winter.

Juvenile plumage is buffier and browner than adult females. Tertials are plain brown with a narrow, buffy edge. Males tend to have broader, grayer edge than females. Scapulars are dark brown with a paler edge. Males are, on average, a bit darker and richly colored. Juveniles are readily sexed by their upperwings. Males have gray upperwing coverts, greater coverts are gray with a white tip. Females have dusky upperwing coverts with pale edging with dull greater coverts.

Adult females are similar to first-year females. They can be aged by any retained juvenile feathers.

First-year males appear much like adult males by mid-winter, but their tertials are shorter until the following summer. Also aged by any retained juvenile feathers.

Adult males have a stunning plumage with obvious, sickle-shaped crest and tertials long enough to reach the water when swimming. The head also has a dark chestnut forehead and crown, glossy green cheeks, a small white dot just above the base of the bill, and a white chin and throat crossed by a black collar.

BACKGROUND AND TIPS
Falcated Duck is an uncommon duck of Eastern Asia. Nearly 90% of their population winters in China (c. 78,000), with the remainder in Japan (c. 9,000) and Korea (c. 2,000). They are rare migrants to the western Aleutian Islands (mid-May to mid-June, sometimes late September into November)), even rarer on the Pribilofs, and there are a handful of records from the West Coast (e.g., Puget Sound, Oregon, and Central Valley of California). Fortunately, some of these sightings represent repeat winter appearances over multiple years.

While some records are known or likely escapes, building evidence suggests that West Coast records are of wild origin. Although, records outside of Alaska are likely to be treated with some justified caution.

Falcated Duck numbers in Asia are declining. The rate of decline in China is fairly rapid according to surveys, with a high percentage of their population harvested in China each winter. Hunting for food, for subsistence and local markets, poses the greatest threat to the Falcated Duck population (estimate at 89,000 by BirdLife). The species was listed as Near Threatened by the IUCN in 2006.

SOUNDS
Generally quiet, unless on breeding grounds. Males give a brief, low whistle, followed by *uit-trr*. Females utter a hoarse *quack*.

DIET AND FEEDING BEHAVIOR
Falcated Duck feeds mainly by dabbling and, less often, by up-ending in open and relatively shallow water. It often associates closely – including feeding – with wigeon, Gadwall, and Northern Pintail. It normally stays close to emergent vegetation, but sometimes grazes in fields near the shore. The species is mainly vegetarian, feeding on grasses, aquatic plants (e.g., tubers and leaves), seeds and fruit and sometimes on insects and other aquatic organisms.

Northern Shoveler,
NSHO *Spatula clypeata*

Plates Page 136

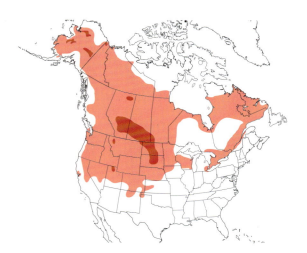

OTHER COMMON OR REGIONAL NAMES
Shoveler, spoonbill, spoonbilled duck, spoony, Hollywood mallard, smiling mallard, neighbor's mallard
(Arctic: curcurpak [YK], curcurpet [NS], alluutaq [NWS])

(Québec: canard souchet)
(Mexico: pato cucharón, pato cucharón norteño, cucharón, pato bocón, pato cuaresmeño)

MEASUREMENTS

Length: Male — 19.0-20.2 in, av 19.4 in (49.3 cm); Female — 18.0-20.0 in, av 18.7 in (47.5 cm)

Wing: Male — av 9.6 in (24.4 cm); Female — av 9.0 in (22.9 cm)

Weight: Male — av 1.50 lbs (680 g); Female — av 1.40 lbs (635 g)

Bill: Male — av 63.0 mm; Female — av 61.0 mm

FIRST IMPRESSIONS

Bunching tightly on the water, groups and pairs circle around each other as they sift invertebrates from the surface. No other duck in North America has a bill the size of a shoveler, nor one so specially adapted to filter. Shovelers seem to love sewage ponds and water treatment facilities, but you can also see them in a wide variety of inland and brackish wetlands. Males are one of the very few white-breasted, chestnut-bellied ducks. Their heads are dark green sometimes appearing blackish and blending into the unremarkably dark-colored back. Females are a light brown, almost frosted overall, with a plain head; each body feather has a buffy edge, producing a crisp pale look. Size and shape: This is a heavily-built duck with a massive spatulate bill, short neck, and long body. It sits low in the water, and when foraging, the breast usually sinks low, and the bill is held at or just below water level. Flight: Northern Shoveler suggests a large Blue-winged Teal with sweptback wings. Wingbeats are a bit slower due to the shoveler's larger size, but the flight is still powerful and direct. The head is held slightly downward in flight. The chalky blue upperwing coverts and quick maneuvers lend to the Blue-winged Teal impression. With such a large bill, longish neck, and pointed sweptback wings, they have a distinctive shape. If you don't see the massive bill, look for the male's chestnut belly (dark at a distance) and white breast, which are diagnostic. Males and females have big pale blue forewings, like Blue-winged and Cinnamon Teal; but the rest of the body coloration is very different on males and the bill is much larger. The male has an obvious blue, white, and green innerwing. Extensive white in the outertail. At a distance, the color pattern of a male may be most noticeable. Often migrates in smallish flocks of 10-25, often in small and well-defined V-formations. Sometimes singles mix with other puddle ducks.

ID: IN DEPTH AND SIMILAR SPECIES

Shovelers breed in their first-year, but they form their pair bonds form later than other dabblers. A late courting season correlates with a late molt into a crisp, bright plumage. Most individuals can be aged and sexed by differences in their upperwing coverts.

Ducklings have large bills and a color pattern similar to Mallard, some are darker with bold ear spots. Juvenile plumage begins to appear at 3 weeks and they are fully feathered by 6 weeks, obtaining full flight a week after. When juvenile plumage is fresh (in the summer) it is darker than adult females (a time when they are very pale and worn). Fresh juveniles have dark brown crowns with brown wash on the face and brown eyes. The breast is evenly patterned with a delicate pattern, again darker brown than an adult female. Their eyes are brown and bills are olive on top with an orangey brim and are not quite full length. By September, some individuals are starting to look paler and worn as males are starting to become distinguishable. First years undergo a slow molt to an adult-like plumage. They often retain some juvenile plumage, on the sides in particular, well into the winter.

First-year females can be separated from adult females by their browner upperwing coverts in some cases. The presence of any juvenile plumage is always indicative of a first-year bird. Females undergo a partial body molt February-April. After raising a brood, they undergo wing molt and are flightless for 3-4 weeks. As the regain flight, they go through a complete replacement of body feathers.

First-year males start to acquire some male characteristics in September, usually revealed by incoming white breast feathers, chestnut side feathers, pale yellow eyes and dark bill. Often it is well into the winter, or even spring, before they shape up to look like adult males. It seems as though they replace a lot of juvenile body feathers fairly quickly, but grow another set of reddish-brown side feathers with some internal markings. These feathers are not the same color or pattern as seen on adult males. Adult males have bright white greater coverts and bright yellow eyes year-round. Breeding males undergoes a partial molt into eclipse plumage in early to mid-June. Most males are flightless by early July and spend 3-4 weeks growing new primaries and secondaries. Males are exceptionally secretive during their wing molt, hiding in vegetation almost all the time and feeding little. Eclipse males look a lot like females. One of their obvious features separating them from juveniles and females is a yellow eye and overall grayer head, sometimes showing a hint of a pale crescent behind the bill (Blue-winged Teal style). Their breast and sides are warm brown — specifically dark brown centers with broad pale edges (lacking internal markings). They obtain spotted feathers on the undertail. Their bill can lighten to olive and have orange tones on the edges. After regaining flight in early to mid-August, males flock up again and feed before migrating. They initiate a body molt into bright plumage before end of the flightless period, which is worn throughout the winter until after the next breeding season. These adult males molt out of eclipse plumage well before (perhaps 2-3 months before) most first-year males acquire a white breast, solid green head and even chestnut sides.

Similar species: The male's green head may suggest Mallard, but other characteristics easily correct that impression. The honking bill on shoveler makes it hard to confuse this bird with other ducks, given a good view. Even in flight, the bill is prominent, making the entire head look large. Shoveler shares the chalky blue upperwing coverts with Blue-winged and Cinnamon Teal, however, even when comparing females, the whopping bill of a shoveler stands out. (Even the species name draws attention to this character: *clypeata* from the Latin for shield-like, *clypeum*.)

Sex ratios: Clearly male-dominated at 60-65%, sometimes as high as 70%.

YEAR IN THE LIFE

Northern Shovelers are common throughout the Northern Hemisphere. They commonly winter south through Central America, the Caribbean, northern Colombia and Venezuela, and rarely in Trinidad. They are most abundant in the Pacific Flyway. The largest wintering concentrations are in California, coastal Louisiana, Texas, and coastal and interior mashes of Mexico. A few hundred winter on the main Hawaiian Islands.

During the winter, shovelers prefer shallow wetlands and open lakes with dense aquatic vegetation, from freshwater ponds to brackish coastal marshes, as well as industrial cooling facilities and agricultural wastewater ponds. They forage by swimming and swishing their big spoon-like bills from side-to-side.

Pair bonds form on wintering grounds, later than other dabblers. Courtship activity primarily takes place in December. Male behaviors include repeated calls, turning-the-back-of-the-head, lateral dabbling, head dipping, up-ending, and jump flight. Most of the females select a mate by January and pair bonds cement by February.

Shovelers are late migrants in the spring. Migration begins in late March or early April, with the masses moving through Arkansas in March, Missouri early April and the Great Lakes in early April.

They arrive on their prairie breeding grounds in mid-April to early May, many head to eastern North Dakota. Shovelers seek shallow wetlands with muddy bottoms and abundant invertebrates, including saline ponds and sewage treatment plants. They nest later than other puddle ducks. The female selects a nest site and scrapes away an area to lay the eggs. Male shovelers are extremely territorial, guarding their territories and mates fiercely. The males also stick around longer than other ducks. Sometimes they even begin to molt into eclipse plumage when they are still on territory. Unlike most other ducks, males usually do not undergo a molt-migration. Instead, they molt on the breeding grounds or at nearby lakes. Females tend to their brood, leading them to suitable water bodies to feed. Young are able to fly at seven weeks.

Fall migration begins earlier than other dabblers, in late August or early September for adult males, followed by females and first year birds. They migrate from the prairie potholes via the Pacific and Central Flyways, with prime stopover areas in the Great Salt Lake, Malheur Basin, and Carson Sink.

GEOGRAPHIC VARIATION

No subspecies are recognized.

SOUNDS

Fairly quiet, but hollow, hoarse *took-took* calls are distinctive. Males: Give a repeated low *took-took* and *wheezy*, ascending *wheehe* during courtship and loud, nasal *paaay* post copulation. *Took* calls given with head pumping and aggressive displays. Gutteral *took-took* often heard as bird takes flight. Decrescendo call given in fall and early winter, *paaay…took-took…took-took*. Females: Give various flat quacks, often evenly spaced, given in singles or doubles, *chuck* or *chuk-ha*. When mated females are chased by other males give a repulsion call, a single loud quack, followed by series of quieter *gaek* notes. Decrescendo call variable, 1-4 long notes, each lower pitched, followed by a series of 3-9 shorter notes of even pitch.

Although not a vocalization, the low whistling sound of the bird's powerful wings is distinctive, and it can take off with drumming or clattering wingbeats.

DIET AND FEEDING BEHAVIOR

Unlike other puddle ducks, Northern Shovelers feed solely in the water. Also, unlike most dabbling ducks, these birds have bills ideally suited for straining small swimming crustaceans from the water while holding their bills in the water and continually dabbling. They will partially or fully immerse their heads when feeding, and they will sweep their bills from side to side while moving. The water is taken in at the bill tip and pushed out at the base through long, comb-like lamellae that trap food. Groups may even feed together in tight packs and swim in circles to help stir up nutrients from below the surface.

In summer, Northern Shovelers will eat small crustaceans, easy obtained by straining the water. They will also consume seeds, larvae, and aquatic insects. During breeding season, they will especially favor water fleas (Cladocera). In winter, the diet is principally made up of floating organisms and aquatic seeds. Proportions of animal to vegetable matter in the diets are poorly known, but those Northern Shovelers foraging in freshwater habitats generally have better-quality diets than those foraging in saline habitats.

NESTING

Site: Breeds in a variety of wetlands by still of sluggish fresh water with vegetation at the edges, by shallow or overgrown ponds, marshes, bogs, sloughs, or slow creeks. Nest on ground, in grassy areas, usually in short vegetative cover and often not close to water.

Nest description: A simple scrape on the ground lined with plant material, down (particularly around the rim), and some feathers. (The down, added during incubation has tufts that are brown with whitish centers, not unlike those of Northern Pintail.) The scrape is about 8 inches in inside diameter, and 1 inch deep.

Clutch size: average 9-10 eggs, sometimes 7-14.

Egg description: Elliptical. Smooth. Creamy buff to olive tinted. (See Mallard egg description.) 52 X 37 mm.

Incubation duration: Average 25 days.

Brood parasitism: Little known.

HUNTING

Spoonies are among the ducks that are easiest to decoy, and they often are harvested incidentally by hunters in pursuit of Mallards and Gadwalls. They are not considered to be very palatable. Flocks lock onto decoys, cup wings, and come right in as if they aren't ever suspecting any trouble. They typically do not balk but head straight in. Readily identifiable on their way into the decoys, with their large bill, and cupped, swept back wings set back on the body. Wings rattle during takeoff. Calling is not particularly helpful or necessary.

The harvest of Northern Shoveler in the U.S. over two years (2013 and 2014) averaged at about 763,300 birds; and for Canada the corresponding number was 26,800.

POPULATION AND CONSERVATION

The North American population has remained fairly steady since the mid-1950s, while recent numbers, since 2007, have mostly been high. Their breeding range has expanded eastwards in recent years, perhaps in part due to their ability to adapt to wastewater treatment plants. Shovelers depend on wetlands for breeding and wintering; habitat loss is one of the biggest threats. They are also at risk of agricultural pollution; Northern Shovelers in California have been subject to reproductive impairment as a result of selenium accumulation in liver tissue. Populations are now rising consistently. The 2016 North American population estimate was almost 4 million, 56% above the long-term average (1955-2016).

Blue-winged Teal
BWTE *Spatula discors*

Plates Page 140

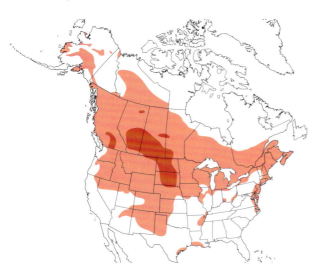

OTHER COMMON OR REGIONAL NAMES

Bluewing, summer teal, white-faced teal, teal
(Québec: sarcelle à ailes bleues)
(Mexico: cerceta de alas azules, chichito)

MEASUREMENTS

Length: Male – 15.0-16.2 in, av 15.6 in (39.6 cm); Female – 14.7-15.5 in, av 14.3 in (36.3 cm)

Wing: Male – av 7.3 in (18.7 cm); Female – av 7.1 in (18.0 cm)

Weight: Male – av 1.02 lbs (463 g); Female – av 0.83 lbs (376 g)

Bill: Male – av 41.0 mm; Female – average 39.0 mm

FIRST IMPRESSIONS

These petite dabblers are often seen in pairs or small courting groups. They have squeaky-toy voices, a friendly expression, and are often more approachable than other ducks. The male's striking white crescent behind the bill stands out from other dabblers. The male has a slaty-blue head, bold white crescent behind the eye, spotted breast and sides (appears brown from a distance), and an obvious small white patch in front of the black butt. Females-types are trickier to identify, but they are a cool brown color overall, with a plain face. Size and shape: A small dabbler with a wide, flattish head, slim neck, and long and modestly-shaped spatulate bill. They sit low and long in the water. Their heads look wide and slightly rounded, but they appear long-necked when their heads are held high. Blue-winged Teal are a lot smaller than Northern Shovelers, slightly smaller than Cinnamon Teal, but larger and longer-bodied than Green-winged Teal. In flight they fall somewhere between Northern Shoveler and Green-winged Teal. They have long, pointed wings that are swept back, a thin neck and rounded head. Their body is not as compact as Green-winged Teal, and they appear more front-heavy. As their name suggests, in all plumages they have a large chalky blue patch on the wing, a feature shared with Northern Shoveler and Cinnamon Teal. Male Blue-winged Teal have even brown body coloration, while Cinnamon is darker. Shovelers have contrasting bodies, white breasts, dark bellies, and dark heads. Blue-winged Teal fly in fairly tight groups that do not shift as frequently as do Green-winged Teas. Blue-winged Teal are a bit erratic in flight, but steadier on the wing than Green-winged Teal. They are very fast!

ID: IN DEPTH AND SIMILAR SPECIES

Blue-winged Teal present some identification challenges – they are difficult to age and sex in the field and even in-hand. Female-plumaged birds are easily confused with Cinnamon Teal, and to a lesser extent, Green-winged Teal. Blue-winged Teal molts follow a similar pattern to other dabblers. However, the timing is shifted slightly from that of other dabbling ducks, presumably because Blue-winged Teal are long-distance migrants. They breed in their first year as one-year olds.

Ducklings are very similar to those of Mallard, but they are smaller and have a narrow yellow band right above the bill. Mallards have a dark stripe from their crown to the bill. Juvenile plumage begins to appear at about 2 weeks and is fully grown by about 6 weeks. Initially, juvenile plumage is crisp with even patterns. First-years molt out of juvenile plumage starting in July. They often replace their head feathers first and continue with body feathers, molting out of juvenile plumage throughout the winter. The males molt into a bright, adult plumage later than other dabblers. These birds appear dull, or like eclipse males in late winter or spring. The "ghost" of a crescent on the face usually starts to become apparent by the end of December. Some first-year males are still molting into an adult-like plumage into March.

First-year females can be separated from adult females by the presence of any juvenile plumage. In hand the pattern on the greater coverts can be helpful, which is pictured on p. 313. Adult females replace some body feathers in February-April to become slightly more camouflaged before incubation. After raising her brood, she will move to a nearby water body to grow a new set of wing feathers. She will continue growing body feathers into the winter, most of which are replaced on the wintering grounds. She will look neatly patterned, brown-gray with well-defined fringes to her feathers, with a crucial distinctive pale area at the base of her blackish bill. Her broken white eye-arcs and dark eyeline through the face should be visible.

First-year males look like females for the fall and part of the winter. They have more white on their greater coverts than females. Once they molt into a male-like body plumage they are difficult to separate from adult males. But these bird may be easier to age in winter by default – when the adults are in clean bright plumage. Males, with their crescent-moons appear on their gray heads and their black-and-white butts, are identifiable at a great distance. Their flanks and breast are buff spotted black, but variable by individuals. They are in their bright plumage for a short period of time compared to other ducks. From about January through mid-July they are readily distinguished from females and juveniles by their slaty-blue heads and white crescents behind their bills. At other times of the year, when they are in eclipse plumage, look for their completely (or nearly) white greater coverts on the males. About 12 days after leaving an incubating mate, breeding males will take off for the molting grounds where they begin to replace at least half of their body feathers and where they attain a camouflaged eclipse plumage in mid-May to June. After arriving at the molting grounds, they shed their wing feathers and are flightless for about 3 weeks until they grow a new set of primaries and secondaries in mid-July to mid-August. The extent to which males grow a new dull-colored body plumage in the fall is unclear. They typically don't acquire a slaty-blue head and breeding plumage until January-March. It's unlikely they are entirely in their eclipse plumage during this time frame.

Similar species: It can be difficult to separate female-type Blue-winged and Cinnamon Teals, especially at certain times of the year. In the fall, until October, young Blue-winged Teal have a warm coloration more like Cinnamon. Some individuals can be exceptionally bright due to rust staining on their body plumage and identical in coloration to Cinnamon teal. These birds can be extremely difficult to separate and are very easily misidentified.

As with most difficult identifications, it is useful to start with size and shape when it comes to Blue-winged vs. Cinnamon. Notice that Cinnamon Teal has almost no forehead, the head slopes directly into the bill, not unlike Northern Shoveler. Blue-winged Teal shows a slight rising forehead so the head appears squarer than the head of Cinnamon Teal. Bill shape can be a subtle but important difference. Cinnamon Teal has a longer, wider bill that has a broader spoon-like appearance. The bill of Blue-winged Teal, though close to the bills of most other dabblers, has a hint of spatulate tip, but not as wide as the spatulate look of Cinnamon Teal.

When dealing with a difficult teal, it is also important to evaluate the overall color of the bird. Blue-winged Teal tend to be brown-gray overall and give a cold impression. Cinnamon Teal are slightly darker brown with a strong rusty wash which gives them a much warmer look.

As for plumage details, Blue-winged Teal have a

sharply defined face pattern, with a pair of large white eye-arcs, a strong brown eyeline and a clear pale loral patch at the base of the bill. The loral patch is usually connected to the pale throat, and is reminiscent of the male's white crescent. In contrast, Cinnamon Teal have a diffuse face pattern, usually lacking noticeable eye-arcs. The eyeline looks washed out and the loral patch is buffy. Sometimes, Cinnamon Teal completely lack the loral patch, but when present, they do not have the definition shown by Blue-winged Teal. Overall, dark facial markings are more distinct in Blue-winged than the browner, blended face of Cinnamon.

By using a combination of these characteristics, most difficult teal shouldn't be too challenging. Birds with mixed features are better left unidentified. Male hybrids between these two species occur somewhat regularly, so there are certainly some female hybrids as well, although they may be impossible to distinguish without a genetic test.

There is also the remote problem of female Garganey, usually differentiated by that species' two dark lines on the face, loral spot (as opposed to patch), and hint of white throat patch.

Sex ratio: Male-dominated (56-60%).

YEAR IN THE LIFE

Blue-winged Teal are common and widespread in North America part of the year, but retreat to warmer climates mostly south of the U.S. for the winter. They are among our longest-distance waterfowl migrants, reaching south to the northern half of South America for the winter. Several bands have even been recovered south of the equator in Brazil and Peru.

Because they travel a long way on their migrations, they are one of the last species to return to the breeding grounds in the spring, and one of the earliest to leave in the fall. They are most abundant passing through the Central and Mississippi Flyways on the way to and from northern South America, where the majority of the population winters in coastal areas, often in rice fields, freshwater and brackish marshes. Blue-winged Teal forages on plant matter, consuming an array of seeds, aquatic plants, duckweeds, algae, and occasionally agricultural grains.

Pair bonds form later than other dabblers, often in January-March. Like other dabblers, groups of males often court one female; they swim after her as they perform an array of displays. These courting displays include ritualized dabbling, a swimming-shake, head-dipping, and the common turning-the-back-of-the-head. Males often take to the air after the female in short jump flights, with hopeful males leap-frogging rivals to get a better chance for female consideration. Spring migration kicks off in January and February, vacating Panama in by April and Mexico by early May. Once pairs arrive at the shallow ponds and seasonal wetlands where they breed, the female selects a territory. Curiously, Blue-winged Teal exhibit very little fidelity to breeding areas; instead, they will venture into new areas when habitat conditions permit.

The hen will pick a wetland with an abundance of invertebrates for her and the brood to eat. Her mate actively defends the territory, while she eats aquatic invertebrates to meet the protein requirements for egg production. She may spend several days flying over prospective nest sites. Once she chooses a spot, she'll line a scrape with nearby grasses, add some down and start laying the clutch shortly after. The hen lays one egg a day, in the morning, until the clutch is complete. In many areas, more than 90% of the nests fail because mammalian predators. If the clutch is lost, Blue-winged Teal are not likely to renest, unlike other prairie nesting ducks.

For successful clutches, the male stays with the female, defending the territory, until late in the incubation period, when the male takes off for a molting site. By mid-summer, molting birds concentrate in large marshes, including the Pel-Kutawagan marshes in Saskatchewan, Freezout Lake in Montana, and Delta Marsh in Manitoba.

Females with broods hatching early in the season tend to young until they are capable of flight, while late-hatching broods are abandoned earlier at 3-4 weeks after hatch. In late July or early August, most broods are ready to fly at 36-40 days old. Unlike males, females take off to molt at a nearby wetland, typically not traveling as far as the males. Here, they are flightless for about 3 weeks.

After the wing molt, Blue-winged Teal are one of the first ducks to head south in the fall with adult males showing up at staging grounds in Gulf Coast marshes in early August. Numbers peak in coastal areas of Louisiana and Texas in the first two weeks of October, but numbers decline drastically by the end of the month. The adult males head south first, allowing them to get to the wintering grounds and stake out their winter territory before the females and juveniles arrive. By mid-August, they may all be abundant in the Gulf Coast marshes. There are several major migration routes are established, one from Manitoba/Minnesota through Florida, another from Saskatchewan south-southeast to eastern Texas/Louisiana, and from western prairies south to southwest coast of Guerro, Mexico.

GEOGRAPHIC VARIATION

No subspecies are recognized.

SOUNDS

Blue-winged Teal is a quiet duck. Males: Listen for the high-pitched *kip*. The males give a long series of these peeping, clear whistles that are frequently heard during courtship. Early in the fall and winter, prior to pair formation, males give a series of evenly spaced, descending quacks. Females: Give a variety of *quack* calls, similar to other dabblers. Their decrescendo call is a descending series of *quacks* speeding up at the end. They give a persistent *quack*, which is a long series of monotone, evenly spaced notes given just before laying. Low quacks are also given when leading a brood or when disturbed.

HUNTING

Bluewings are such early fall migrants that they rank as the dabblers least exposed to hunting, even with special teal seasons that last a week or two. Most of the population also winters south of the U.S. Historically, harvests account for about only 11% of all annual mortality, very low among game ducks. Annually, the harvest numbers may fluctuate, at about 1 million birds.

These teal tend to jet into the decoys close and fast like a swarm of bees! They decoy well to Mallard decoys, or, better yet, smaller-bodied decoys, without calling. Hunting methods are not much different than for most of the dabblers, but a majority of successful hunters use nasally teal quacks and whistle calls. The immatures do not learn the ropes of survival fast enough; they are twice as vulnerable to hunting as adults. Favored hunting locations include the coastal marshes of Louisiana and Texas.

DIET AND FEEDING BEHAVIOR

Blue-winged Teal feeding behavior includes dabbling with the bill or the head submersed, gleaning invertebrates from submerged or floating vegetation, up-ending, and, very rarely, diving. Primarily these teal dabble in shallow water (about a foot deep) and will also forage on mudflats. Blue-winged Teal limit foraging to aquatic areas where their diet would be dominated by plant matter, particularly seeds. But they will consume a wide array of aquatic invertebrates, vegetative parts of aquatic plants, duckweeds, algae, and, on occasion, grains from agricultural crops. Animal matter, mainly insect larva and snails, will dominate the diet of breeding females.

NESTING

Site: Breeds by small waters – potholes, ponds, sloughs, and marshes – in grassy areas. Nest on the ground, usually near water and well-concealed rarely using brushy nesting cover. (Nest sites have shorter and less dense nesting cover than those of Mallard and Gadwall.)

Nest description: A hollow lined with dry grasses and nearby vegetation, with an inner lining of down. Nearby cover often arched over nest, concealing it from the top and multiple sides. (Down tufts are drab brown, similar to those of Cinnamon Teal, but lighter and larger than those of Green-winged Teal, with large whitish centers.) Nest size averages, 5 inches in inside diameter, 8 inches in outside diameter, and 2 inches in depth.

Clutch size: Usually 8-12, sometimes 6-14.

Egg description: Elliptical to subelliptical. Smooth and slightly glossy. Dull white, creamy white, or with pale olive tint. 47 X 33 mm.

Incubation duration: 23-24 days, but may be 19-29 days.

Brood parasitism: Rare host, because nests are dispersed and well-concealed, occasionally parasitized by Ring-necked Pheasant.

POPULATION AND CONSERVATION

Blue-winged Teal numbers fluctuate from 2.8 to 8.9 million in response to conditions on the prairie nesting grounds. Population over the past decade averaged at about 7 million. In 2016, the population estimate was almost 6.7 million, which was 34% above the long-term average and over the NAWMP target population of 4.7 million breeding ducks. This was good news after 1990 when the population hit a 40-year low of 2.8 million after several dry years. These ducks were major beneficiaries of CRP because they readily nest in restored grasslands, however, loss of habitat is still a major threat to Blue-winged Teal.

Local populations are affected by nest success and brood survival as well. They have the highest mortality rate (65%) of all dabblers, which is probably because of habitat loss and their long-range migration route. Like other prairie nesting ducks Blue-wings are affected by the unnaturally high numbers of predators on the prairies. In many areas, more than 90% of the nests fail because of mammalian predators. Each year, many nests and incubating females are taken by predators, therefore they benefit from predator removal programs that restore the predator population to a more natural level. Blue-winged Teal is also at risk of encountering powerful pesticides (that have been banned in the US), while on their wintering grounds in Central and South America. They also encounter unregulated hunting in South America, where techniques used in the market hunting days are still in practice.

Cinnamon Teal
CITE *Spatula cyanoptera*

Plates Page 144

OTHER COMMON OR REGIONAL NAMES
Red teal, red-breasted teal, teal
(Mexico: cerceta canela, zarceta, coyota, chichito)

MEASUREMENTS
Length: Male – 15.3-17.0 in, av 16.0 in (40.6 cm); Female – 14.5-16.3 in, av 15.5 in (39.4 cm)
Wing: Male – av 7.6 in (19.2 cm); Female – av 7.2 in (18.3 cm)
Weight: Male – av 0.75 lbs (340 g); Female – av 0.78 lbs (354 g)
Bill: Male – av 44.2mm; Female – av 42.9 mm

FIRST IMPRESSIONS
This highly sought-after dabbler is stately and handsome. Deep-chestnut-colored males are often not far from warm-brown females on small lakes and alkaline ponds with lots of vegetation. Males are dark overall, a deep rusty-brown that appears a rich cinnamon color in good light. Females are a fairly warm brown with a plain face and patterned body. Size and shape: Very similar to the slightly smaller Blue-winged Teal. Oval-shaped head is large and rounded, with almost no forehead, grading into a long bill reminiscent of Northern Shoveler. That bill is more spatulate than that of a Blue-winged Teal, but far less spatulate than that of a Northern Shoveler. This teal has a thinish neck and relatively long body. Flight: Shape is almost like a small-billed shoveler. Head projects in front of its rounded body and wings are thin. Males have chalky blue upperwing coverts, which contrast sharply with the cinnamon body. Notice the broad white border to blue wing coverts. Females are light brown with a duller blue wing patch. Bill is tilted slightly downward. Cinnamon Teal are often in small, tight flocks consisting of several pairs. Wingbeats are quick and fluid, but strong. They often twist and dip like other teal, but not to the extent of Green-wings.

ID: IN DEPTH AND SIMILAR SPECIES
Most breed in their first-year, so they become difficult to age after they complete their molt in the fall because they all look like adults in the field. Ducklings are similar to Mallard and Blue-winged Teal, with longer bills and many are lighter yellow overall. They are lighter gray with more pink on the bill than Blue-winged Teal. Juvenile plumage is fully grown by about 7 weeks. And the irises become deep reddish-orange when males are about two months old.

Initially, juvenile plumage is crisp with even patterns. Once they begin to replace juvenile plumage in July, juveniles appear motley as their juvenile plumage wears out and fades, contrasting with newer feathers. First-years molt out of juvenile plumage starting in June. They often replace their head feathers first and continue with body feathers, sometimes replacing the last of the juvenile plumage in February. Look for finely-speckled underparts.

First-year females are separated from adult females by the presence of worn juvenile plumage. Greater covert pattern can also be useful. Females undergo a body molt from January-March, becoming even more camouflaged before incubation. After raising a brood, females undergo a wing molt, and replace some body and tail feathers.

First-year males sometimes retain a few juvenile feathers into the winter; however, most males look like adults with a mostly chestnut plumage and red eyes by October or November. Reduced white (a few dark tips) in the greater coverts and narrower tertials can be an indication of a young bird. Adult males are distinct with their stunning chestnut body and red eyes. Their greater coverts are pure white. After the breeding season, males replace their body plumage into eclipse plumage from May-August. Eclipse males become entirely mottled brown, but are noticeably darker overall than females. Their head, sides, back, and undertail all have dark centers to the feathers. Look for their bright red eyes. During the molt, in and out of eclipse, rusty or chestnut-colored feathers are mixed in. Males undergo a wing molt and are flightless for about 3 weeks in July or August as they replace their primaries and secondaries. Males molt into their bright chestnut plumage starting as early as July. Many males obtain a bright plumage by October, while others continue to molt until January. Males that obtain breeding plumage earlier in season may be more successful finding a mate for the season and are presumably older males.

Similar species: Separating female and young Cinnamon and Blue-winged Teal can be difficult and will require paying attention to details. Juvenile Cinnamons are paler in overall color than Blue-winged Teal; this is distinguishable even if they aren't very close to each other. Blue-winged Teal may look "cold," while Cinnamon Teal appear "warmer." Blue-winged Teal have a sharply defined face pattern, while the face pattern in Cinnamon Teal is diffuse. In Cinnamon Teal, the face is "blander"; any eyeline is indistinct and the pale patch at the base of the bill is less pronounced. Remember to look for the degree of spoon-shape to the bill. Cinnamons are also thicker-necked.

Beware, in the early fall (through October) some individual Blue-winged Teal can be exceptionally bright and a small number have rusty staining on their body plumage. In the East, these are often mistaken for Cinnamon Teal.

There are also Blue-wing x Cinnamon hybrids to watch out for. Adult males can either look more like Bluewings or more like Cinnamons. They have rusty bodies with dark spots, a buffy patch on the rear; head is rusty with slaty-blue above the eye or entirely bluish, red eye, and part or all of a white crescent behind the bill. In recent years, there have been more hybrids than pure birds turning up in the East.

Sex ratios: Male-dominated (54-56%).

YEAR IN THE LIFE

Cinnamon Teal are widespread across western North American and South America. They are most common in the Pacific and Central Flyways, but a not nearly as common as most other ducks. Cinnamon Teal is the least abundant of all our native puddle ducks. The origin of birds found outside their normal range — e.g., in the East — is often questioned because they may be escapees from captivity. Cinnamon Teal range south all the way the tip of South America. Large concentrations are typically found at Bear River NWR and Fish Springs NWR in Utah from late June through early October.

The North American population winters primarily in Mexico and southwestern U.S. They forage where there is plenty of submerged vegetation from flooded fields, to tidal estuaries, freshwater and saltwater marshes, agricultural fields and mangroves.

Most courting activity picks up in the mid-winter and new pair bonds begin forming in late February and most pairs are established by May. Male courtship displays include ritual preening, lateral dabbling (a mock feeding), repeated calls, turning-the-back-of-the head, head dipping, and up-ending. The female will often respond with a typical incite movement.

Cinnamons are an early spring migrant, heading towards their breeding grounds as early as February. They move into California in numbers in late February and early March. The majority arrive in Utah by late April and reach the northern edge of their range in Alberta in early May.

Cinnamons breed in marshes, ponds and shallow lakes of the Great Basin and mountainous regions in the west. Unlike other dabblers, they often use highly alkaline water. Incubating females are typically abandoned by their mates by the third week of incubation. There is no pronounced molt migration. Many males head to off to molt relatively short distances away, while others will molt in the vicinity of the breeding grounds. Females stay with and defend their young until they fledge at seven weeks old.

In the fall, they depart earlier than other dabblers, with numbers dropping sharply after early September. Males and unsuccessful females depart first, followed by first-years and brood-rearing females. Some individuals move from Utah head to California's Central Valley to stage, and then head to Mexico. Cinnamons begin arriving on their wintering grounds in Mexico in numbers by mid-September; almost all are in western Mexico by November.

GEOGRAPHIC VARIATION

Cinnamon Teal has one subspecies in North America and four in South America. In general, South American subspecies tend to have more black spots on the breast and sides and a darker belly than the North American subspecies.

S. c. septentrionalium occurs in North America and ranges south to Mexico. In South America, four subspecies have been described: *S. c. tropicus* inhabits Colombian lowlands and is the smallest subspecies, *S. c. borreroi* is known from east slope of the Colombian Andes, *A. c. orinomus* inhabits the high Andes from Peru to northern Chile and is largest subspecies, *S. c. cyanoptera* is found in from southern Peru and southern Brazil to Tierra del Fuego and the Falkland Islands.

SOUNDS

Cinnamon Teal is a quiet dabbler. Males: Give a dry series of clicks and rattles during courtship and while head-pumping. This is similar to the call given by Northern Shoveler during courtship. Males also utter a low, whistled *peep*. Females: Give a shrill *quack*, mainly during courtship and with brood. They also give a low *quack* much like Blue-winged Teal. Females give a quiet, rattling *rrrr* while flicking their bill up during the inciting display. They infrequently deliver a decrescendo call *gack-gack-ga-ga*, much like Northern Shoveler.

DIET AND FEEDING BEHAVIOR

Cinnamon Teal feed by dabbling in shallow water (about a foot deep in freshwater, brackish, and highly alkaline waters of the Great Basin), pecking at the surface, and ducking their heads under water to reach submerged vegetation. Omnivorous feeders, they will eat seeds and aquatic vegetation, insects, snails, and zooplankton. Shoveler-like social feeding, in which groups of teal follow each other while surface dabbling in water stirred up by the bird in front, can occur at any time of year.

NESTING

Site: Breeds near shallow water, freshwater, and highly alkaline seasonal and semipermanent wetlands – often lake edges, pools, and areas where tule is present. The nest, in dense vegetation, may be covered by the water's edge, or at some distance. Usually very well concealed, deep in growing herbage, or in marsh or waterside plants on the ground.

Nest description: A hollow, usually with a lining of plant material – often dry, residual stems of rushes, saltgrass, bulrushes, or grasses. Nest in marsh vegetation may also be built up above water level. The nest lined with down, drab or dark brown with light centers. (The down tufts are similar to those of Blue-winged Teal.) Nest size averages, 5 inches in inside diameter, 7 inches in outside diameter, and 2 inches in depth.

Clutch size: 8-12 eggs, sometimes 4-16.

Egg description: Elliptical to subelliptical or oval. Smooth and slightly glossy. White, creamy-white, creamy-buff, or warm buff. 47 X 34 mm.

Incubation duration: 21-25 days.

Brood parasitism: Fairly commonly parasitized by Redhead.

HUNTING

This is a prized species by hunters in North and South America. However, relatively few are harvested each year in the U.S. and Canada because many depart the region before the hunting season opens. In Utah, females and immatures comprise the bulk of the harvest because adult males have already left the region. Hunting does not appear to have as great of an impact on their population, but their populations are not well monitored, so the effect of hunting is unclear. Moreover, harvest figures for Cinnamon Teal in the U.S. are combined with those of Blue-winged Teal, complicating matters. Still, many Cinnamons are harvested incidentally, while hunters are in pursuit of other species.

Favored hunting locations include: The western highlands of Jalisco (particularly Lake Chapala) and Michoacán, Baja California and lagoons of coastal Sinaloa, Mexico. In the U.S., Utah's Great Salt Lake and California's San Joaquin and Sacramento Valley are among the favorites.

POPULATION AND CONSERVATION

Cinnamon Teal is one of the least abundant dabbling ducks in North America. There is surprisingly little known about the population of this western species because most individuals inhabit areas that are not covered during breeding and wintering surveys. Their population is limited in part by the availability and quality of wetlands and nearby uplands for breeding. Issues connected with water scarcity and competition – e.g., municipalities, agriculture, and industry – complicate matters. The population of Cinnamon Teal in North America appears to be stable, but long-term datasets that closely monitoring their population are not available. Estimates suggest there are somewhere between 260,000 and 300,000 individuals breeding in western North America.

Past numbers from Mexico suggest a serious decline, at least between 1991 and 2000.

Green-winged Teal
GWTE *Anas crecca*

Plates Page 148

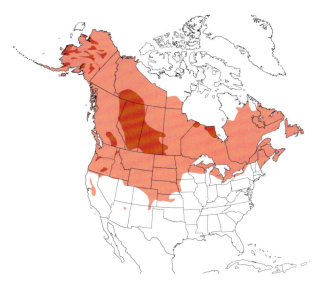
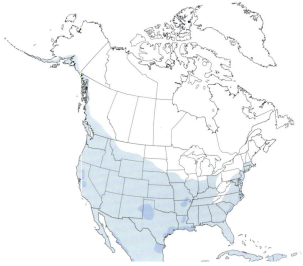

OTHER COMMON OR REGIONAL NAMES
Green-wing, American green-winged teal, greeny, common teal, teal
(Arctic: tengesqaarag [YK], tengesqaar [NS], qaiffiq [NWS], sarpak [N])
(Québec: sarcelle d'hiver)
(Mexico: cerceta de alas verdes)

MEASUREMENTS
Length: Male – 13.7-15.5 in, av 14.7 in (37.3 cm); Female – 13.0-14.5 in, av 13.9 in (35.3 cm)
Wing: Male – av 7.3 in (18.5 cm); Female – av 7.0 in (17.8 cm)
Weight: Male – av 0.71 lbs (322 g); Female – av 0.68 lbs (308 g)
Bill: Male – av 38.2 mm; Female – av 36.5 mm

FIRST IMPRESSIONS
This tiny dabbler, our smallest dabbler, often acts more like a shorebird than a duck as it walks along mudflats. Often in small flocks, Green-wings look dark overall, at any distance, the males green swash behind the eye and rusty head, just blend together. Green-wings often appear dark with little contrast in their coloration, unless they are close and in bright light. Males have rusty heads with a broad green swash through the eye, brown breast, gray body with a black-bordered and obvious creamy-colored butt. Females are an even colored, cold brown. Size and shape: A tiny, round-bodied duck with a short and thin neck and squarish head. (Other teal look flatter-headed.) It has a distinctive shape and sits high in the water. Flight: Small-bodied, compact dabbler with thinish neck and bigger head. It bursts up in a vertical takeoff. It appears dark overall and plain-winged, lacking the pale blue forewings of Blue-winged and Cinnamon Teal, but with a green-and-black speculum bordered with white and rufous. At any distance, notice the small size and sweptback wings. The erratic behavior of the tight flock is also an excellent clue. They will come in for a quick landing, crashing in at high speeds apparently out of control. Tight flocks are constantly changing position within the flock as individuals twist and turn, causing the shape of the flock to change quickly. During migration, flock size varies, often from a handful to roughly 30-60. Green-winged Teal are so small that they have very quick wingbeats and are quite the little speedsters!

ID: IN DEPTH AND SIMILAR SPECIES
Most of these teal attempt to breed in their first year and attain adult-like plumage their first fall, which makes them generally difficult to age. Ducklings have a color pattern similar to Mallard, but are significantly paler, very light yellow on the face and a bolder cheek stripe. Juvenile plumage begins to appear presumably at 3 weeks and is fully grown at 6-7 weeks. It looks much like adult female, but look for finely patterned underparts. First-years begin a molt out of juvenile plumage in August, body molt continues into September and October, sometimes lasting until December. They can always be separated from adults by any remaining juvenile plumage. However, they are difficult to age after October if juvenile plumage is not apparent.

Adult females are difficult to separate from first-year females if there are not any traces of juvenile plumage. A female will have a distinct dark eyeline often with a cheek stripe on a uniform brown speckled face. She will also have a pale buff wedge by the undertail coverts in contrast with the speckled rear flanks.

Females undergo a partial body molt February-April

to become more camouflaged on the nest. After their broods fledge in mid-to late summer, females initiate a wing molt, typically on the breeding grounds, and are flightless for three weeks. This is followed by a complete body molt which can span until October.

First-year males begin to become identifiable in September. Those appearing with a row or two of brown feathers with buffy internal markings along the top of the flanks after mid-November or December are likely first-year males.

Adult males have green wash behind the eye, rusty head, spotted breast, gray sides with a creamy patch at the butt. Look for the distinctive vertical white line down the side of the breast. They undergo partial molt (<50% of body feathers) into eclipse plumage from mid May-June-July; initiated after leaving incubating female. After molt-migration, undergoes a simultaneous flight feather molt, with a 21-day flightless period in the summer. Eclipse males look a lot like females, but have a coarser gray pattern on the face, with a dark area around the eye. Also, look for the buffy stripe under the tail.

They will undergo a complete body molt into bright plumage acquired in the fall, which is mostly complete by late October, and worn throughout the winter until after the breeding season.

Similar species: Females could be confused with other female teal and small female dabblers, but the Green-winged Teals' angular head shape and darker brown coloration will distinguish them. Blue-winged Teal have a more rounded head shape and a plainer face. If their wing is spread look for the chalky blue upperwing coverts, lacking in Green-winged Teal. Female Garganey is extremely rare in North America, but has a longer bill and dark stripe through the cheek. For more on Green-wing vs. the rare Garganey check out p. 411 or in comparison with the even rarer Baikal Teal, see p. 412.

Sex ratio: Males dominate at 52-55%.

YEAR IN THE LIFE

Green-winged Teal span the Northern Hemisphere, where they are abundant through their range, breeding across northern Europe, Iceland, Greenland, northern Russia, and Japan. In North America, they migrate south in large numbers to central Mexico, and others will trickle down all they way to Costa Rica and sporadically south to Colombia. They also winter in the Caribbean. Green-wings are most abundant in the Mississippi Flyway, where large numbers winter in coastal marshes and rice fields of Louisiana and Texas. They are common in each flyway in the spring, but in the fall Pacific Flyway birds tend to use the Central and Mississippi flyways when they head north in the spring. Large wintering concentrations of over 10,000 birds are found, for example, at E. B. Forsythe NWR in New Jersey, Bear River Refuge in Utah, William L. Finley NWR in Oregon, bays in northern Puget Sound of Washington. Cap Tourmente in Quebec also has high counts of High counts in migration mid-to-late September.

Green-wings in their winter range prefer to forage in shallow wetlands, freshwater marshes and tidal creeks associated with estuaries. Courtship begins early in the year, in the fall from late September-November. Most pair bonds form pair bonds on wintering grounds. But courtship may initially involve two dozen males attempting to attract the attention of one female or several females. Males use a remarkable variety of movements, many of which are also used by other dabblers. Some of the frequently observed male displays include burping, grunt-whistle, head-up-tail-up, bill-down, turning-the-back-of-the-head, bridling (with the head moved slowly backward and the chest stuck out), and head shake. Jump-flight movements, where one male leaps over his rivals to get a better chance at getting the female's attention is also frequently observed.

Spring migration starts up in February through April, with some lingering in the southern part of the wintering range into late April. The majority have left from the northern part of the wintering range by early May.

Their breeding grounds are pretty far north in wooded ponds, potholes and tundra pools. The first pairs arrive on the southern part of their breeding range from early March to early April. They reach the Northwest Territories and Yukon Delta from late April to mid-May. Females are very attentive at their nests during incubation and are very reluctant to leave the nests. Molt-migration starts off with males of early-nesters, followed by the males of late-nesters and unsuccessful females. Even females with broods may occasionally delay wing molt until after a short migration.

Fall migration timing varies greatly, from early birds heading south in late August and other leaving in mid-October, with some lingering until freeze-up. Peak migration days on Lake Ontario are one day after cold front passes. Green-wings arrive on in the southern portion of their wintering grounds from late September through late November, even into December. Alaskan breeders typically winter in British Columbia and in coastal regions of North America, following and inland and coastal migration corridor.

GEOGRAPHIC VARIATION

Three subspecies are recognized, *A. c. carolinensis* spans across North America, *A. c. nimia* is on the Aleutians and *A. c. crecca* in Eurasia. Nominate *A. c. crecca* is regular to western Alaska, uncommon to fairly common on Aleutians and Pribilofs, rare to St. Lawrence Island and mainland western Alaska, very rare on West Coast, regular to Newfoundland in winter; casual elsewhere. *A. c. nimia*, year-round residents of the Aleutian Islands of Alaska teeters between subspecific status and clinal variation; they average slightly larger than *A. c. crecca*, lacking a vertical white stripe on the breast of *carolinensis*.

Male Common Teal, *A. c. crecca* are distinguished by a broad white horizontal stripe along the bottom edge of the scapulars and bolder white face lines on the head pattern. They lack a vertical white stripe between the breast and sides. The vermiculation on the sides is also courser. Females are difficult to identify with certainty. *Crecca* typically lacks the darker horizontal cheek stripe that is usually shown by *carolinensis*. This is not diagnostic, but it is suggestive, particularly if the female is accompanied by a male or if narrower white tips on the secondaries on *crecca* can be seen. Females with less than 3mm of white on the tip of their secondaries are very likely to be *crecca*. This may best be determined in the hand or with good photos. Reportedly, there is a clinal size difference within *A. c. crecca*, with birds in the eastern Palearctic the largest.

SOUNDS

Green-winged Teal is a fairly vocal species. Male whistles are frequently heard rising above a mixed flock of waterfowl. Males: Give a sharp, rolling whistle *preep, preep, preep, preep*, similar to Northern Pintail, but thinner. The whistle is not unlike the sound of a spring peeper. Also, they utter low grunting calls during grunt-whistle display. Rapid 'chittering' given with bill-up display. Females: Utter a raspy, thin *quack* often given in a descending series of 4-7 notes, *kre-KEE-ka-gaga*. Call like that of female Mallard and other puddle ducks, but not as loud or forceful. Quacking series given in many contexts from courtship, to distractions displays and on wintering grounds. Harsh, rattling call given while inciting.

DIET AND FEEDING BEHAVIOR

Green-winged Teal feed by walking on mudflats or by dabbling in shallow water. They prefer to feed on exposed wet mud and usually feed in waters under a foot deep, but they will also show greater flexibility in depth of feeding than many other species of dabbling ducks (e.g., Mallard and Northern Pintail), responding to food availability. Their small bill, with dense lamellae, allows them to select small invertebrates and seeds that are available in shallow water or mudflats. They typically feed on a heavy diet of seeds – smartweeds, sedges, pondweeds, and grasses – and also on aquatic insects, mollusks, crustaceans, and tadpoles. While being major seed-eaters, animal matter may still range between about 10% and 35% of their diet, depending upon season and availability. Green-winged teal are also known to forage in agricultural areas (e.g., corn or rice) in winter.

NESTING

Site: Breeds on islands in lakes, the edges of lakes, lagoons, and sloughs. Also on higher ground, a little distance from water – sedge meadows, grasslands, brush thickets, or even woods. Nest usually found within 220 yard of water. The nest is on the ground, well concealed in long grass or under bushes or low trees. The female continues building the nest throughout the egg-laying process.

Nest description: A hollow, lined with dry grasses, sedges, or leaves, depending on surrounding material, with a lining of small feathers and down. The down is small and very dark with white centers. Nest size of about 6-7 inches in inside diameter, 9-10 inches in outside diameter, and 3-6 inches in depth.

Clutch size: Average 8 eggs, sometimes 6-9.

Egg description: Elliptical to short subelliptical. Smooth. Dull white, cream-colored, creamy-buff, or very pale olive-buff. 46 X 33 mm.

Incubation duration: 20-24 days.

Brood parasitism: Extremely rare to have another duck lay in their well-concealed nest.

HUNTING

Green-wings are a real challenge to hunt due to their fast, erratic flight and small size. They create more laughs in the blind and stories than most other ducks. Hunters may fail to get off a single shot, or they may miss completely as a flock of Green-wings buzzes the blind. All experienced hunters have similar stories. Tight flocks often come in close to decoys, buzzing by, right in front of the blind or coming from behind. When using a call for these teal, four to seven short and quick peeps in staccato may do the job. These ducks seem to come from nowhere and make a fast pass by the decoys, but tend not to lock in and land. They are fairly wary and sometimes responsive to whistle calls.

Regardless of the difficulty of the hunt, these charming teal are still one of the most-harvested waterfowl in North America, behind Mallard and ahead of Gadwall. The harvest of Green-winged Teal in the U.S. over two years (2013 and 2014) averaged at about 1,731,500 birds; and for Canada the corresponding number was 69,600.

POPULATION AND CONSERVATION

The population is increasing in North America, though little is known about what effects the population size. Positive trends may be due to the fact that they breed farther north than major agricultural areas. The population estimate was almost 4.3 million in 2015, 107% above the long-term average. (Beyond North America, the population estimate for Eurasian Green-winged Teal is 2.25 – 3.27 million, with the Aleutian Green-winged Teal estimated at 10,000.)

Green-winged Teal are frequently missed during the aerial surveys because these small ducks forage in thick vegetation and are often under cover. More Green-wings end up in hunters bags than are counted on these surveys. In part, this is because so many nest in habitats that are not covered in aerial surveys. Regardless of the estimates, their population is seemingly doing well and has received little management effort.

Garganey
GARG *Spatula querquedula*

Plates Page 152

OTHER COMMON OR REGIONAL NAMES
None used in North America

MEASUREMENTS
Length: Male – c. 15.6 in (39.6 cm); Female – c. 15.0 in (38.1 cm)
Wing: Male – av 7.9 in (20.1 cm); Female – av 7.5 in (19.0 cm)
Weight: Male – av 0.88 lbs (400 g); Female – av 0.77 lbs (350 g)
Bill: Male – av 37.5 mm; Female – av 36.5 mm

FIRST IMPRESSIONS AND SIMILAR SPECIES
This snazzy Eurasian teal occasionally makes its way to North America, although its occurrence in the New World has been distinctly declining. A Garganey can be discovered in areas where there are lots of dabblers, particularly flocks of Blue-winged Teal.

Males are dark brown-breasted and purple-brown-headed with a prominent and wide white eyebrow. Sides are gray. Females are dark brown with solid brown upperparts having well-defined pale fringes. They have a bolder face pattern than any other teal. The hen has a dark crown, long and broad supercilium, pale spot below the eye (at the base of the bill), and pale chin exaggerated by a strong cheek stripe extending to the base of the bill: a striking face pattern. Eclipse males look almost like females but with pale gray upperwing coverts and green speculum of adult males. Size and shape: Similar to Blue-winged Teal, with a blockier head shape, slightly heavier bill, not unlike Cinnamon Teal, and a slightly longer tail. Flight: They are similar to other teal with fast and often indirect, twisting flight. Males can be picked out by the contrast between the dark breast and white belly, chalky blue upperwing, and broad white borders to the speculum, especially the white trailing edge to the secondaries. Females have paler gray coloration on the outer half of their wing, unlike the darker "hand" of Blue-winged and Green-winged Teal.

Similar species: Female and eclipse male Garganey can be confused with other teal. Even a quick look at the wing will settle any confusion, with a pale blue forewing in the Garganey. Also note the green speculum bordered by broad white borders on both sides in the male Garganey, and the pale "hand" – inner webs of primaries – on a female Garganey.

Wing patterns aside, Green-winged Teal, particularly Green-wings with bold facial patterns can be tricky. Garganey has a bolder facial pattern with darker eyeline and stripe across the cheek and heavier bill. Garganey is also noticeably larger and longer-bodied than Green-wing. A Garganey will also have white tertial edges, visible in a swimming bird, a feature not present on any other North American teal.

Sex ratio: Unknown.

BACKGROUND AND TIPS
Garganey is a common species in Eurasia, wintering in large flocks in West, Central, and eastern Africa, and in Asia from Pakistan east to southern China, south to the Philippines. A large portion of population winters in western Africa and in Australia. There, Garganey is a highly migratory species, much like our Blue-winged Teal, spanning two continents in a year.

It is a regular migrant to the western Aleutians, very rare on the Pribilofs and along the West Coast. It is a widespread vagrant elsewhere, having appeared in most states and provinces.

Garganey populations overall are apparently decreasing. The world population was estimated at 2,600,000-2,800,000 in 2006. In east Asia, counts have dropped from 90,000 birds during the 1970s to 22,000 birds by 2003. Garganey populations are threatened by habitat degradation and loss and by human disturbance (e.g., wetland drainage, early mowing of meadows, lead poisoning and hunting in Africa, dam construction, and large-scale river diversion).

Garganey could turn up almost anywhere there are concentrations of Blue-winged Teal and other puddle ducks, arriving in North America from both east and west. They are most often found in April and May, when males are most easily recognizable. South of Alaska (where they are discovered in spring and, less likely, in fall), there are good chances of encountering the bird on the Pacific coast (e.g., there are about two dozen records for California, mostly between 1975 and 2000 and mostly in fall and winter). But there are many other records scattered throughout North America (mostly in spring). Possibly correlated with their declining population, there have been significantly fewer records in North America since the turn of the century than the twenty years prior.

SOUNDS
Often rather quiet. Male gives a unique mechanical wooden rattle, not unlike running a finger across a comb or shaking a box of matches. No whistle-sounds are produced by the male. The female utters a harsh *quack*, resembling Green-winged Teal.

DIET AND FEEDING BEHAVIOR
This species feeds in shallow waters by swimming with head underwater, uncommonly by up-ending, and from the surface. In breeding season, the Garganey is omnivorous. During the rest of the year, times during which this species may appear in North America, these ducks are mainly vegetarian, with a diet dominated by seeds and other materials from pondweeds, smartweeds, wild rice, and grasses.

Baikal Teal

BATE *Sibirionetta formosa*

Plates Page 153

OTHER COMMON OR REGIONAL NAMES
Formosa teal, clucking teal, spectacled teal

MEASUREMENTS
Length: Male – c. 16.6 in (42.2 cm); Female – c. 15.9 in (40.3 cm)
Wing: Male – av 8.3 in (21.0 cm); Female – av 7.7 in (19.5 cm)
Weight: Male – av 0.96 lbs (437 g); Female – av 0.95 lbs (431 g)
Bill: Male – av 36.5 mm; Female – av 34.5 mm

FIRST IMPRESSIONS AND SIMILAR SPECIES-
Look for this Asian visitor's intricate face pattern and ornate scapulars in large flocks of Green-winged Teal or wigeon.

The male is a real stunner, and the specific name, "formosa," does not stand for the island, but actually means "beautifully formed." Males rival Harlequin Ducks with their unique head pattern; however, Baikal Teal can blend into a flock of Green-winged Teal surprisingly well. Males have a spotted rusty breast, gray sides, draped with long cinnamon scapulars, and a black butt. They can be picked out among Green-winged Teal by a glimpse of the elongated scapulars or yellowish cheek patch. Females are very much like female Green-winged Teal, but with warm brown fringing on many of the body feathers and head, with two short stripes on the face, and a conspicuous white loral spot – almost appearing dime-like – behind the bill. Also look for an extensive pale throat that extends up onto the face and pale sides to the undertail coverts. Size and shape: Larger than a Green-winged Teal, similar shape as Green-wing, even longer to the rear. Extremely long scapulars sometimes reach the water on a swimming bird. Flight: These are fast-flying little ducks. Males are most similar to Green-winged Teal, with an intricate head pattern that appears pale-faced at a distance. Upperwing pattern is relatively plain and dark, much like Green-winged Teal. Unique and bold underwing pattern has a dark leading edge, white stripe in the middle, and gray trailing edge. White belly is apparent in flight.

Similar Species: Females present the only real ID problem. Baikal Teal are only slightly larger, broader billed, and longer-tailed than Green–winged Teal. Look for Baikal's paler throat, bolder face pattern, darker crown, and stronger loral spot (encircled with darker border). Some female Green-winged Teal may have strongly patterned faces, which appear very similar to Baikal Teal, so it pays to be cautious and look at the size and shape as well. Even the most strongly patterned Green-wings generally do not show the sharply delineated pale loral spot of Baikal. Baikal is richer brown overall – especially about the breast – and has a whiter belly.

The upperwing pattern is much like Green-winged, but the narrow cinnamon-buff line (formed by the tips of the greater coverts) bordering the green secondaries is straight, not wedge shaped, and the white trailing edge of the secondaries is broader than Green-winged. The underwing is more extensively gray.

Sex ratio: Males dominate in Korea at 62%.

BACKGROUND AND TIPS
Baikal Teal are locally abundant in East Asia. They are very rare visitors to Alaska's outer Aleutians during migration and farther south along the West Coast in winter. (The majority of the population winters in eastern China and South Korea, some range north through Japan.) Most records for Alaska are between late August through December, although there are spring records. There are about a dozen records from British Columbia, Washington, Oregon, and California in the winter (mainly December-January). Curiously, Baikal Teal have been noted associating with wigeon, rather than with other teal. Baikal Teal are uncommon in captivity, but most individuals away from the West Coast might be escapes from collections.

The Baikal Teal population was formerly declining sharply, perhaps as low as 20,000 to 40,000 birds in the 1980s. Drops in numbers were ascribed to increased pesticides in staging area and especially massive over-hunting in parts of northeast Asia. But this duck appears to have rebounded dramatically in recent years and may have already become the commonest duck in South Korea. The recent discovery of enormous flocks in South Korea, for example, may help account for a bump in Alaska records. The worldwide population estimate is 500,000-700,000 (BirdLife).

SOUNDS
Males give a deep, repeated *wot-wot-wot*. Females give soft *quack*.

DIET AND FEEDING BEHAVIOR
Like other dabblers, Baikal Teal will forage by picking off the surface and tipping up to reach submerged vegetation. They also feed on the ground, taking seeds in the fields during winter. This teal will feed on seeds, leaves, and grass weeds, sedges, and aquatic vegetation, with small aquatic invertebrates, snails, and insects also consumed. In its native range in Asia, it dabbles by day and feeds in fields by night.

Canvasback
CANV *Aythya valisineria*

Plates Page 160

OTHER COMMON OR REGIONAL NAMES
Can, bull can (drake), canvas-backed duck, wedge-head (Québec: fuligule à dos blanc)
(Mexico: pato coacoxtle)

MEASUREMENTS
Length: Male – 20.0-21.9 in, av 20.7 in (52.7 cm); Female – 18.8-20.4 in, av 19.8 in (50.3 cm)
Wing: Male – av 10.4 in (26.4 cm); Female – av 9.0 in (22.9 cm)
Weight: Male – av 2.76 lbs (1252 g); Female – av 2.55 lbs (1157 g)

FIRST IMPRESSIONS
Widely considered the King of Ducks, Canvasbacks have a commanding presence and distinctive appearance. And what a fine name! In one word, it describes the immediate impression and captures a vision of the past: a waterfowl with a back that resembles traditional canvas, perhaps canvas used on a sailing vessel. The bright white backs and rusty heads of the male Canvasbacks bring ease to their identification from great distances. Their sloping foreheads produce a regal appearance. They tend to flock in rafts of hundreds, often mixed with scaup and Redheads. Males are white-backed with black breasts and butts. Their black and white bodies contrast greatly, whereas male Redheads have dark gray and black body and scaup have a gray back with white sides. Canvasbacks' deep chestnut angular heads appear dark in low-light or at a distance. And close up, their striking red eyes are a wonder. Females are warm brown overall, pallid and two-toned: gray body and brown head and neck. They are vaguely similar to female Redheads in coloration, but much paler and two-toned than Redheads. Size and shape: Canvasbacks, the largest of our bay ducks, have sloping foreheads, giving them wedge-shaped heads unlike other ducks. Their bills are also wedge-shaped, tapering toward the tip. In the water, these ducks appear large yet sleek. Flight: Canvasbacks' triangular head, long straight neck, broad pointed wings (held straight out, not angled back), and round body produce a distinctive shape, which in combination with the males' bright white color make them readily recognizable. That is true even from great distances. The long straight neck is sometimes held at a slight downward angle. The large wing bar is often not obvious because of overall paleness. In winter, females have a sharp delineation between the dark brown breasts and light gray bellies. Watch for huge feet splaying out to the side when they come into land, wings cupped, committed to drop onto the water. For takeoff, they run over the water to get some speed. Flocks tend to be fairly organized, either in a line or in a V. Canvasbacks are power-cruisers! They are fast flyers, with strong wingbeats, having a ground-speed estimated at 60-70 mph.

ID: IN DEPTH AND SIMILAR SPECIES
Canvasbacks have a very distinctive angular head shape, which usually leads to a quick ID to the species level. Even as downy young, they can be identified by their sloped forehead. Ducklings are straw yellow from their cheeks to their belly, and olive-brown from their crown to their tail, with a couple small yellow patches on their side/back. Even as ducklings a few weeks old, they will have the distinctive Canvasback head-profile. Juvenile plumage begins to grow two weeks after hatching and may be fully grown by four weeks. It's mainly brown and wears out quickly. Like the adult female plumage in summer, juveniles lack a clear demarcation between the dark brown breast and grayer sides. First-years replace most of their juvenile body feathers in the fall and winter, from September to March. They also replace some tertials and wing coverts and occasionally from 2-14 (all) tail feathers.

First-year females look like adult females starting in late winter, except for the presence of any juvenile body feathers and by examination of their upperwing coverts in-hand. Their plain, gray-to-brownish median and lesser coverts lack the fine flecking of adult females. Adult females undergo body molt during spring migration, when they obtain mottled brown and gray sides. By early in the breeding season, they are browner overall without the clean gray back and dark brown breast that they have in winter. They are mildly pale-throated, but the pale and smudgy teardrop behind the eye is distinctive. After breeding, they undergo a molt of all their wing and body feathers, from July to November. They are flightless for 3-4 weeks in the late summer during wing molt.

First-year males look like females when they are in juvenile plumage, until mid-October when they begin molting into a white and black adult-like plumage. By late December, they look like adults, but can be distinguished in-hand and careful field examination by their medium-gray upperwing coverts. Look for contrast between light gray/white tertials and darker gray greater coverts with less white vermiculation. They can also be aged by retained brown juvenile tails. Adult males have white to very pale gray upperwing coverts with fine vermiculation. From the late fall to early summer, males are striking with white and black bodies and rusty heads. After breeding, they undergo a molt-migration, generally starting at the end of June. Then they replace their body feathers, molting into an eclipse plumage. Eclipse males have dusky gray backs and sides, dark brown breast, and a reddish-brown head. While they are in eclipse plumage, they replace their wing feathers and are flightless for about 4 weeks. By late July or early August, they are able to fly again and are molting their body feathers with patches of white and black feathers coming in the body. During fall migration, their molt is more intense than any other time of the year. By late October or early November, they usually are in a perfect breeding plumage.

Typically, molt does not overlap with other energy-demanding events, such as migration and breeding. Studies of Canvasback molt challenge this concept. During the courting season, which is primarily during spring migration, Canvasbacks of all ages and sexes actually increase the number of feathers they are growing. In many ducks, it is only the females that are known to molt in the spring. It is likely that males of other species also have a fairly extensive spring body molt that has been overlooked or underappreciated.

Similar species: Given their distinctive triangular head shape, Canvasbacks are generally not confused with other species. In coloration, they are closest to Redhead, but males are significantly lighter-backed and females can be readily separated by head shape. The long sloping forehead of any Canvasback is a dead giveaway, as is the long black bill (vs. the shorter tricolored, mostly pale blue [male] or slate [female] bill in the Redhead). Basically, if they are not pale, and they are not sleek, they are not Canvasback.

Common Pochard, a Eurasian species rare in Alaska and even rarer elsewhere, is another possibility, with the head shape and general coloration approaching that of Canvasback. For more on Common Pochard, see p. 168.

Sex ratio: These are male-biased (c.53-85%), but they vary with location and season. Along with the highly rare Common Pochard, these ducks probably show the greatest disparity.

GEOGRAPHIC VARIATION
No subspecies recognized.

SOUNDS
Canvasbacks are usually silent, except during some of their displays. In winter, both sexes give a wheezing *rrrr-rrrr-rrrrr* when other Canvasbacks approach their feeding area. Males: Give a soft cooing, *go-grWHO-oooo*, first two syllables in rapid succession, the third syllable is soft and descending. Females: Their inciting display includes a guttural *krrr-krrr* and raspy rattlings *hrrrr*. To collect her brood, gives soft, *low kuk-kuk-kuk-kuk* and alarm call, a harsh *kurr*. Also, utters loud quack during takeoff and long, whine *whaa-aaa-aaa* or *graack-graack-graack-graack* in flight when a male is pursing her.

YEAR IN THE LIFE
Canvasbacks are found in large concentrations in some areas, but they are an uncommon duck throughout North America, ranging south to central Mexico. Wherever they are seen they are admired. They are held in high regard by hunters and birders alike.

A gregarious species during the winter, Canvasback are often seen in large flocks with other Aythya in habitats ranging from brackish bays and estuaries, freshwater lakes, and marshes. They often dive to snatch submerged vegetation, but their diet shifts seasonally.

They concentrate in large flocks in winter. Main wintering areas include the mid-Atlantic states, particularly the Chesapeake Bay, Pamlico Sound in North Carolina, and Mississippi River Delta in southern Louisiana. In the Pacific Flyway, they winter along the coast of California: San Francisco and San Pablo Bays host particularly large numbers. Historically the majority of the population wintered in Chesapeake Bay, but after loss of submergent vegetation in the bay, their range shifted south to the Lower Mississippi Alluvial Valley. They occasionally wander as far as Japan, Hawaii, Europe and are very rare winter visitors in the Caribbean.

Spring is the peak season for courting and mate selection for Canvasbacks. Many Canvasbacks display at stopover sites during spring migration from March to mid-April. Courtship display frequently performed during migration, include a fairly subtle neck-stretch, a sneak posture (with the male's head lowered and extended forward), a kinked-neck posture (and accompanying call), a head-throw with the head tossed backward, and a common turning-the-back of-the-head used by other species of waterfowl. These displays are very similar to those of Redhead.

Canvasbacks are early-nesting ducks. Pairs typically arrive on the breeding grounds by mid-to late May. They prefer the stable wetlands in the parklands, the transition zone in the northern part of the prairies where there is a mix of grass and trees. Upon arrival, to the deep-water mashes, small lakes, and bays of freshwater and alkali lakes where they breed, the female searches for a nest site.

They have incredible philopatry – females almost always return to where they hatched or where they nested in previous years. Canvasbacks choose deeper wetlands than many other ducks, where they are bound to have enough water and food resources to make it through the season. Males keep a watchful eye on their females through their first week of incubation, but they abandon them shortly thereafter. Occasionally the males will breed with a second female, and then depart on a molt-migration. Males undergo their molt-migration mostly traveling northward to concentrate in large, freshwater wetlands of aspen parklands and southern boreal forests region shortly after leaving their mate.

The females tend to their broods for varying lengths of time, depending how late it is in the season. Females with early-hatching broods may remain with the young until they are able to fly at 8-10 weeks old, while late-hatching broods may be abandoned at 2-3 weeks old. First-years and females usually head south in the fall before the adult males. Therefore, a skewed sex ratio is noticeable at stopover sites. Adult male Canvasbacks are among the last of the divers to head south, with the majority leaving northern staging areas in the Canadian prairies and parkland by mid-October.

DIET AND FEEDING BEHAVIOR

Canvasbacks generally dive for food at shallow depths from about 2 feet to 6 feet, but they will sometimes dive to depths of over 15 feet. In shallower water – under one foot – Canvasbacks will tip up or submerge their heads and necks. Canvasbacks are omnivorous, but they prefer plants yet depend on what is seasonally available. During winter and migration, they will eat mainly plants (e.g., wild celery, wigeon grass, eelgrass, varied rhizomes, and tubers of aquatic plants); when plant foods are limited, they will eat small clams and snails. In winter, some populations eat primarily fingernail clams, but during migration they feed on winter buds and rhizomes of wild celery (*Vallisneria americana*) for which their scientific name, *Aythya valisineria*, originates.

Degradation of the SAV (e.g., wild celery and sago pondweed) in the Chesapeake Bay had a huge impact the Canvasbacks wintering there, numbers which declined significantly when the habitat could not sustain the birds.

Throughout the breeding season, they will consume both plant and animal material (e.g., seeds, rhizomes, tubers, buds, leaves, and root stalks of aquatic plants, and snails, varied larvae, and damselfly and dragonfly nymphs). They will glean insects from the water surface, especially when insects are hatching, and will even snatch flying insects from the air.

NESTING

Site: In small lakes, deep-water marshes, sheltered bays of large lakes, varied ponds, sloughs, potholes, and other fresh waters with growing vegetation. Often concealed in vegetation growing in the water, but sometimes in more open sites in sedges or hidden in tall waterside plants.

Nest description: A large and bulky structure of stems and plant material (e.g., tule bulrush, cattail, reed grass, and whitetop grass). It may be topped with an overhanging canopy of vegetation. The cup is well-lined with down. (The down is light grayish-brown with indistinct centers, darker than that of Redhead.) In wet springs, if the water level crises, female Canvasbacks will continue to build the nest by folding over more cattails and other nearby vegetation. The resulting height or thickness of the nest base can be very large, even approaching 27 inches. Other dimensions are also correspondingly variable, including 5-10 inches in inside diameter, 12-35 inches in outside diameter, and 2-6.5 inches in depth.

Clutch size: Normally range 7-10, average 8.

Egg description: Elliptical to subelliptical or oval. Smooth. Dull green, bluish-green, olive-green, or grayish-olive. 63 X 45mm.

Incubation duration: 24-29 days.

Brood parasitism: Frequently dump in nests of other Canvasbacks, with some studies showing a third of the nests conspecifically parasitized. Often Redheads and less frequently Ruddy Ducks will lay in their nest.

HUNTING

Cans reign as the King of Ducks. It's the bird most waterfowl hunters dream about. They are the bird that keeps hunters in the blind waiting for hours on days when toes feel like they are about to freeze off. It's the bird that hunters remember the first one shot, and possibly every one after. It's not just the beauty of a bull Can, the female's graceful lines, or the incredible speed of a flock passing over the decoys; their taste is delectable. Market gunners knew.

Canvasbacks are excellent table fare, which made them the most prized duck in the market gunning days. In the late 1800s their meat would sell for $5-7 per pair. That was an era when that amount was about half to two-thirds the median wage of an industrial blue-collar worker for a week.

Their historic population in the Chesapeake Bay region was devastated, but they managed to rebound after market hunting and move into other areas after habitat degradation in the region. In general, their population is closely monitored and changes are quickly reflected in bag limits and harvest numbers. For example, the season on Canvasbacks was closed in 1936-36, 1960-63, 1972, and 1988. In addition, Cans seriously declined after a prairie drought in the spring of 2002, and it was not legal to shoot a Can in the 2002-2003 hunting season in the U.S. After low counts in the spring of 2008 they were again off limits in the 2008-2009 season.

The harvest of Canvasbacks in the U.S. over two years (2013 and 2014) averaged at about 134,000 birds; and for Canada the corresponding number was 16,700.

Cans are fast fliers, so it can be hard to keep up with them, but they are good decoying ducks. They generally lock onto large diver decoys from a great distance and readily drop into the decoys if you give them a pocket to land. Calling in Cans may not be the best strategy for the most part, but some guides claim a Mallard highball attracts Canvasbacks and scaup into the decoys. Mallard calls can also be used to mimic a diver call with a three-note prrrt-prrrt-prrrt.

Favorite hunting locations include Chesapeake Bay, Upper Mississippi River in Wisconsin and Iowa, and Catahoula Lake in Louisiana, Lake St. Claire, Ontario/Michigan.

POPULATION AND CONSERVATION

The population is rebounding after low numbers in late 1980s and early 1990s, due to a loss of habitat (breeding and wintering) and lead poisoning from ingesting spent shot. (Canvasbacks, bottom-feeding species, had some of the highest rates of lead shot ingestion.) The lead poisoning threat eventually will become negligible because the use of lead shot in waterfowl hunting was banned across the U.S. in 1991 and in Canada in 1997 (over water) and in 1999 (over farmfields).

Canvasbacks are susceptible to the accumulation of other contaminants, but so far not at levels to cause impairment, let alone affecting Canvasbacks at the population level. Still, Canvasbacks are our least abundant of the widely distributed hunted ducks in North America.

And, as indicated previously, Canvasbacks are highly sensitive to drought years (e.g., 1959-63, 1971-72, 1978, 1985-94, and 2002).

In 2007, the population estimate was 865,000, the highest recorded to date. Yet, in response to low counts during the 2008 spring surveys when 489,000 where tallied, the harvest was halted with a zero Canvasback limit in the 2008-2009 season. In 2016, the estimate was 736,000, 26% above the long-term average (1955-2015).

Due to their strong tendency to return to the same area they hatched or nested in previous years, hunting a breeding population can lead to local extinctions. This has happened in some areas. Biologists are able to reestablish them in some places by transferring young into the area.

In Canada, the species has been on the Blue List (for species that may be of concern) from 1975 to 1981. And Canvasback was on the list of Species of Concern in 1982 and 1986.

Redhead

REDH *Aythya americana*

Plates Page 164

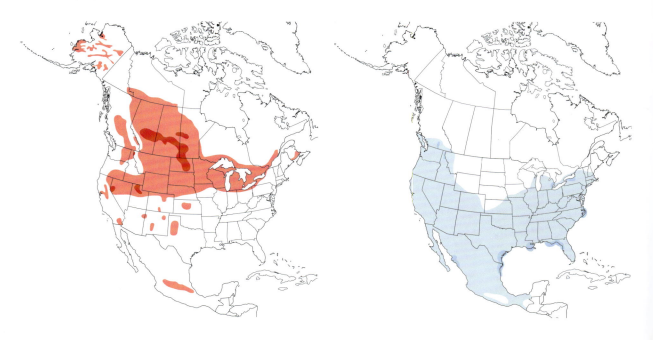

OTHER COMMON OR REGIONAL NAMES

Red-headed duck, red, red-headed-pochard, pochard, raft duck
(Québec: fuligule à tête rouge)
(Mexico: pato de cabeza roja)

MEASUREMENTS

Length: Male – 18.1-21.7 in, av 20.0 in (50.8 cm);

Female – 18.0-20.5 in, av 19.0 in (48.3 cm)
Wing: Male – av 9.2 in (23.4 cm); Female – av 8.8 in (22.4 cm)
Weight: Male – av 2.44 lbs (1107g); Female – av 2.14 lbs (971 g)
Bill: Male – av 47.7 mm; Female – av 46.1 mm

FIRST IMPRESSIONS

Huge flocks of these rufous-headed, gray-bodied drakes, sprinkled with dull-tawny-brown females, will raft together in the Laguna Madre of Texas and Mexico in the winter. Outside the core of their wintering range, Redheads are often in large rafts of divers, mixed with scaup and/or Canvasbacks. Males have rusty-red heads with dark gray on the back and sides, bracketed by black breast and butt. Females are a warm brown, paler on the head, especially behind the bill. Both sexes have tricolored bills: extensive gray-based, white-ringed, and black-tipped. Size and shape: A big-headed and large-bodied duck a little smaller than a Mallard. Redheads have puffy heads that are smoothly rounded, with steep forehead, flattish crown and thick neck. The body rides high on the water. Generally, the shape is similar to that of other *Aythya* ducks, but strikingly different from Canvasback. Flight: Notice their large-rounded head, thick neck, round body, and broad wings, creating Redhead's stocky appearance. Flocks move quickly, often fairly low over the water. Flocks traveling high that commit to landing will plunge to the surface, falling like heavy leaves, then put on the breaks, stick out their feet to ease the landing. Listen for the incredible ripping sound like jets passing over as the air escapes their wings during this maneuver. Redhead run over the water to get airborne, and they have a direct flight with rapid wingbeats, but not as fast as scaup or Canvasback.

ID: IN DEPTH AND SIMILAR SPECIES

Both sexes typically breed in their first-year, so they reach adult-like plumage quickly.

Ducklings are yellow overall, with a plain yellow face. They are the yellowest and plainest of all our wild ducklings. Juvenile plumage begins to appear at about two weeks old and is fully-grown by eight weeks. Most birds attain first flight between 55 and 70 days of age. Juveniles are pale brown overall with a buffy face like females. First-years replace juvenile plumage from September to March, with males changing greatly in appearance in October and November.

First-year females for the most part, can not be readily picked out in the field. They are slightly paler than adult females as their feathers wear. Adult females are brown-bodied with a dark brown breast in winter. In April-May, they molt some head, body, and inner wing coverts. This has the overall effect of becoming browner with less contrast between the breast and sides. Sometime between July-November, they will replace their wing, body, and tail feathers. The timing of this molt depends on their nesting success. Nonbreeding or unsuccessful breeders may undergo wing molt in Aug-late September, while females who raised a brood molt primarily late September-October. Some females will initiate wing molt while tending to their broods. As wing molt is finishing, they undergo body molt to attain a crisp winter plumage. Their face is paler than the crown, and they will often have a hint of a buffy eyering. Their bill is mainly light blue with a thin white band and dark tip. If you look carefully at large flocks, you may notice flecks of white feathers on the nape. This is rarely even more extensive, with white flecks also on the face.

First-year males have molted into a bright plumage by early December. Males attain an adult-like head first, followed by the back and sides, the incoming dark breast seems to be one of the last parts to molt. While most appear adult-like by December, some will retain a trace of juvenile plumage in the tail, belly, or elsewhere going into the year. After breeding, most adult males undergo a partial body molt into eclipse plumage in June and July. Their heads and necks becomes browner, with brown feathers mottling their breast and back. Later in the summer, they molt their wing feathers and are flightless for about 3 weeks. They replace all of their body feathers from July-November and attain their bright red, gray, and black plumage once again.

Similar species: Canvasback is the most similar species to Redhead in many ways; however, the two have very different head shapes. Redhead also has a more rounded head, opposed to Canvasback's sloped forehead and triangular head. The bill ridge and forehead in Redhead combine to create a concave shape from the bill tip up to the crown; this is essentially straight in a Canvasback. Males of both species have a rusty-red head, but Redhead has a bright, evenly reddish head, while Canvasback has a darker rusty-colored head with a dark crown. Male Redheads are darker gray on the back than Canvasback. Male Redheads have yellow eyes; male Canvasbacks have striking red eyes.

Female Redheads can be confused with scaup or Ring-necked Duck. Female Redheads can be tricky, in part, because their overall head and face pattern is very plain and changes throughout the year with molt and wear. People often key into females of Greater and Lesser Scaup, with their clearly defined white patches at the base of the bill. Redhead, however, is palest at the base of the bill the whitish patch is usually more washed out and sometimes whitish on the throat. Scaup also lack the pale line behind the eye in Redheads, and they are darker overall. Female Ring-necked Duck can be separated by their peaked head (opposed to Redhead's rounded forehead with a hint of a flat crown), paler sides, and darker back. Overall, female Ring-necked Duck has more contrast, whereas Redhead's body is more uniform in coloration.

Common Pochard, a Eurasian species extremely rare anywhere outside of Alaska, is another possibility to consider. A few are kept in captivity. That species' sloping head shape and general coloration is closer to that of Canvasback. In addition, the pale gray center of the bill, in both male and female Common Pochard, as opposed to the narrow pale ring bordering the black tip in Redhead, is important to consider.

Sex ratio: Males dominate at 51-59%, but may be much higher (e.g., 69%) at some seasons.

GEOGRAPHIC VARIATION
No subspecies are recognized.

SOUNDS
Redhead is generally silent, except during courtship displays. The call of the male Redhead is readily picked out in a cacophony of courting ducks in wetlands in the spring. Males: Give wheezy *whee-ough* or catlike *meow*, often given with head-throw displays during spring migration and upon arrival to the breeding grounds. *Meows* are emitted during courtship, pair greetings, after disturbance, or post copulation. When threatened by an intruding Redhead, males sometimes give quiet *err* call. On the wintering grounds, males give a soft *zoom-zoom* call at night. Females: Give soft, repeated *err* sounds when inciting a male. Also, utters deep, guttural *kurr-kurr-kurr* usually during breeding season. Sometimes females emit a loud *squak* when taking off. They also give a low *kuk-kuk-kuk* during hatching and when leading their brood.

YEAR IN THE LIFE
Redheads are common and widespread in North America, ranging south to central Mexico where there is an isolated, non-migratory breeding population. They rarely stray to Bermuda, Hawaii, or the United Kingdom. Redheads are primarily a duck of the Central and Mississippi flyways. An estimated 90% of the population winters along the Gulf of Mexico particularly in the Laguna Madres of Texas and Tamaulipas, Mexico. Next highest wintering counts (10,000+) are from Cayuga Lake in New York. Highest counts on migration are from Wolfe Island and Long Point in Ontario.

Each winter, Redheads return to the same site where they dive to feed on seagrasses.

In the spring, they begin leaving the wintering grounds in late January. Migration peaks on the southern prairies in mid-March. Each year the adults and first-years form new pair bonds while on the wintering grounds or during the northward spring migration. At this time, male displays activities include those shared with other *Aythya* divers. These displays are accompanied by vocalizations and include kinked-neck and turning-the-back-of-the-head. The head-throw of Redhead is more exaggerated than that of any other *Aythya*. Females often respond in an inciting display. Both birds will also engage in mutual neck-stretching, often while facing each other and in physical contact.

When choosing a breeding location, they respond to water conditions each year, so they often do not breed in the same location like other ducks.

Redheads have a different breeding strategy than most other ducks; they don't put all their eggs in one nest. In fact, up to 75% of all Redhead eggs are not laid in their own nest, but laid parasitically to benefit from another female's investment in building a nest and incubating a clutch. There are actually three strategies for female Redheads, which they choose based on how favorable conditions are for a given breeding season. They can have a "typical nest" where they can build their own nest, lay and incubate their clutch. They can lay in other female's nest, before building a nest and incubating their own clutch. They tend to pick this strategy when breeding conditions are good (wet years on the prairies) and are able to produce more ducklings than a normal clutch size would allow. Or they can lay in the nest of others, which tends to be the strategy in years when nesting conditions are poor.

Female Redheads don't stay with their broods as long as many other ducks. They are often with their brood for 6-8 weeks, although some are abandoned at three weeks. The broods, however, tend to stick together until they can fly at 8-10 weeks old.

Males and unsuccessful females undergo a molt-migration north to where they concentrate at traditional molting lakes in Canada such as Lake Winnipegosis, Manitoba, where up to 80,000 gather. They first arrive at these lakes in June or early July. Peak numbers are in October after the flightless period, just before the onset of fall migration.

Fall migration peaks in the southern prairies in mid-to-late October. They arrive in numbers on the Gulf Coast in early November.

DIET AND FEEDING BEHAVIOR
Redheads will generally dive for food at shallow depths, at or below 3 feet, infrequently up to 10 feet. This is a shallower preference than that of all other *Aythya*, perhaps with the exception of Ring-necked Duck. They will also engage in dabbler-like tipping or immersing their heads, or simply gleaning foods from water surface. They are the vegetarians of the diving ducks with fairly specific habitat needs. Redheads are also active feeders at night. Once they reach the breeding grounds, they depend primarily on pond weed and musk grass, although in breeding season they will also feed on animal matter, from larvae to snails. In migration they are also rely mainly on vegetable matter. And they are dependent in winter on several key coastal areas with abundant seagrasses (especially shoalgrass, but also manateegrass, turtlegrass, and other grasses) as well as various tubers and seeds.

NESTING

Site: In fresh water, usually in emergent taller vegetation bordering lakes or sloughs, occasionally in more open sites in similar areas, on land, or even on a muskrat lodge. Cattails and hard-stem bulrush are nesting covers chosen most often. (*Aythya* ducks will usually nest over water in emergent vegetation, but Redheads and Lesser Scaup may choose dry-land sites.)

Nest description: A solidly woven nest – the most solid of our diving ducks – with a substantial cup in wet sites, but a hollow sparsely lined with plant material in drier sites. Nest may be topped with an arched cover of bending vegetation. The cup is also lined with down. (The down tufts are very pale, grayish-white and paler than that of Canvasback.) The height is usually about 7-10 inches, but it can be variable, depending on water depth changes during incubation. Other variable dimensions are about 5-10 inches in inside diameter, 10-28 inches in outside diameter, and 3 inches in depth.

Clutch size: Average 10-11 eggs, range 7-14, difficult to determine due to parasitism, average for unparasitized nest 7-8.

Egg description: Elliptical to subelliptical. Smooth. Greenish to pale olive or olive gray, sometimes a buffy brown. (See Mallard egg description.) 61 X 43mm.

Incubation duration: 24-25 days

Brood parasitism: Frequently lay eggs in nests of Canvasbacks and other Redheads. Occasionally lay eggs in nests of puddle ducks (Mallard, Northern Pintail, Gadwall, American Wigeon, Northern Shoveler, Blue-winged and Cinnamon Teal) and other *Aythya* (e.g., Lesser Scaup and Ring-necked Duck), and Ruddy Duck. This apparent parasitism strategy is more common in Redhead than in any other North American duck.

HUNTING

Redheads are big water ducks in fall migration and winter. They are often in hunted in mixed flocks with scaup. They are drawn to large numbers of diver decoys. In particular, long, J-shaped arrangements that give the Redheads a pocket to land in is often a good strategy. Redheads respond readily to particular weather conditions, which will make or break a Redhead hunt. On "good" weather days when winds are whipping and a front is moving through, they will drop from high in the sky and at high speed, roaring into the decoys. Successful hunts often happen when there is this sort of weather or when hunters find a freshwater source that the Redhead need when they are rafting on saltwater.

Bag limits shift regularly in response to population estimates. Bag limits were highly restrictive in the 1960s and 1970s, even with a complete ban from 1960 to 1963. Into the early 1990s, there were several years of closure on multiple flyways.

As with other ducks nesting in the potholes, their breeding success fluctuates greatly in response to water conditions on the prairies. Relative to other divers, Redhead is one of the more well-understood and more easily monitored species. However, compared to many dabblers they still have a relatively small population, so wildlife managers keep a close watch on breeding success and corresponding bag limits.

The harvest of Redheads in the U.S. over two years (2013 and 2014) averaged at about 321,000 birds; and for Canada the corresponding number was 26,300.

Favored hunting locations include the Laguna Madre in Gulf Coast of Texas and Mexico, Long Point Ontario, Lake St. Claire, Ontario/Michigan, and other sites in the Great Lakes region.

POPULATION AND CONSERVATION

The species had experienced a dramatic decline in the early part of the 20th century, with competent observers, by the late 1930s, believing that extinction was a real possibility. As late as 1961, official breeding population estimates were only 323,000. Redheads, bottom-feeding species, had also exhibited some of the highest rates of lead shot ingestion.

Fortunately, the Redhead population has been increasing since the early 1990s, although annual counts fluctuate in response to conditions on the breeding grounds. Redheads rely on prairie wetlands for successful breeding and ample food resources on the wintering grounds, particularly shoalgrass beds. Any declines in seagrass beds can be especially damaging to Redheads, since they have not shown the ability to switch to alternate foods.

Hunting regulations are closely correlated to survey results and breeding success the previous year, in effort to protect this species with a relatively small population compared to other waterfowl.

While the increase in Redhead numbers can still be regarded as a success, remaining dangers – such as botulism, avian cholera, and other diseases – have significantly affected Redhead numbers in the recent past.

In 2015, the population estimate was an encouraging 1.2 million, 71% above the long-term average (1955-2015).

Common Pochard
COMP *Aythya ferina*

Plates Page 168

OTHER COMMON OR REGIONAL NAMES
Pochard, Eurasian pochard

MEASUREMENTS
    Length: Male – c. 18.8 in (47.2 cm); Female – c. 17.2 in (43.7cm)
    Wing: Male – av 8.6 in (21.75 cm); Female – av 8.2 in (20.8 cm)
    Weight: Male – av 2.15 lbs (975 g); Female – av 1.93 lbs (875 g)
    Bill: Male – av 47.0 mm; Female – av 45.0 mm

FIRST IMPRESSIONS AND SIMILAR SPECIES
Common Pochard is a very rare visitor from Eurasia that looks like almost the perfect cross between Canvasback and Redhead, with a robust rusty head of a Redhead and pale back color of Canvasback.

    Males have a chestnut head, black breast, and light gray body, similar to Canvasback. Pay attention to the bill on the male. It has a dark base and black tip separated by thick whitish-blue band in the center. Females have a mottled gray and brown body and a brown breast. The head is light brown with a pale throat and lores that are paler than the face. The bill has a pale band in the center. Size and shape: Heavily built *Aythya* with a short, thick neck, high crown and sloping forehead grading smoothly into a long broad bill. It's a ski-jump slope from the forehead down to concave culmen. Flight: Appears chunkier than Canvasback with short, rounded wings and a heavy body. Common Pochard has a clumsy appearance in flight; a word no one would ever use to describe a Canvasback in flight. Wings are uniform gray with no wing stripe. They run over water to get airborne, and their wingbeats are strong and quick, producing a whistling sound.

    Similar species: A Common Pochard can be easily overlooked in a group of Canvasbacks or Redheads. In comparison, male Canvasback has a less concave head profile, lighter gray back and has a blackish crown. Female Canvasback has a lighter gray back as well. Female Canvasback lacks the different-toned bill sections, especially the noticeable pale gray bill-center, seen in Common Pochard. In addition, the pale gray bill-center, in both male and female Common Pochard, is very different from the narrow and almost indistinct ring bordering the black tip in Redhead. Also, female Redheads do not have gray on the sides and back like Common Pochard. Canvasback X Redhead hybrids are very rare. They can, however, appear very similar to Common Pochard, but they lack Common Pochard's unique bill pattern.

    Sex ratio: Males dominate in Europe at 59-73%, in Japan at c. 65%. Along with Canvasback, these ducks probably show the greatest disparity.

SOUNDS
Generally silent, except during courtship rituals, when males give weak calls, whispered, nasal *wiwieer* and louder, descending *kil-kil-ki*l. Females give a variety of one-syllable raspy calls.

BACKGROUND AND TIPS
Common Pochards are widespread breeders in western Europe and range broadly eastward to Lake Baikal in Siberia and northeastern China. Northern populations are highly migratory; southern populations, including those in parts of western or southern Europe, are largely sedentary.

    Although the species breeds occasionally in Iceland, the lion's share of North American records are from the other end of this bird's range, from North American areas closer to Asia.

    The western and central Aleutian Islands of Alaska or areas around the Bering Sea have produced this species in the spring, but even during other seasons. They are very rare in coastal southern Alaska and extremely rare in southern California. Still, previous records suggest that it is possible that one could turn up anywhere along the West Coast. There is also a chance of finding one on the eastern seaboard, with only one record thusfar in Quebec.

    Counts of breeding population in Europe are generally increasing, but wintering counts are decreasing. Worldwide, the population trend appears to be decreasing, but the population is large enough not to be alarming. The world's population estimate is 2,200,000-2,500,00 (BirdLife). Current threats, depending on locale, appear to be overhunting, water-based recreation, coastal development, predation (e.g., mink in Europe), ingesting lead shot (e.g., Spain) and drowning in fishing nets (e.g., China).

DIET AND FEEDING BEHAVIOR
The Common Pochard is an omnivorous diver, usually foraging at depths of 3 to 10 feet. It may sometimes up-end in shallower water. It will feed with head and neck immersed or will even dabble on the surface. The duck prefers diving in extensive areas of open water under 18 feet deep, lacking floating vegetation. A Common Pochard diet consists of seeds, roots, rhizomes, and parts of grasses, sedges, and other aquatic plants. This duck also consumes aquatic insects and larvae, worms, mollusks, crustaceans, amphibians, and small fish. The Common Pochard can be crepuscular in the winter, and it often feeds at night.

Tufted Duck
TUDU *Aythya fuligula*

Plates Page 169

OTHER COMMON OR REGIONAL NAMES
Tuftie
(Québec: fuligule morillon)

MEASUREMENTS
 Length: Male – c. 17.1 in (43.5 cm); Female – 15.5 in (39.3 cm)
 Wing: Male – av 8.1 in (20.7 cm); Female – av 7.9 in (20.0 cm)
 Weight: Male – av 1.76 lbs (800 g); Female – av 1.60 lbs (725 g)
 Bill: Male – av 39.9 mm; Female – av 38.6 mm

FIRST IMPRESSIONS AND SIMILAR SPECIES
Tufted Ducks from Europe and Asia turn up in flocks of scaup and Ring-necked Ducks, where handsome males stand out with their black backs and white sides, and females appear dark brown overall.

 Males have black heads, backs, and breasts, with accompanying clean white sides. They have distinct tufts, extending down the back of their heads. Females are dark brown overall: heads, breasts, and backs, with slightly lighter brown sides. Adult females will have smaller tufts on the back of their heads. First-winter males typically have a short tuft (can be absent) and a brownish tinge to their sides, not perfect white. Size and shape: Very similar to scaup with a big, rounded head, somewhat exaggerated by the long drooping tuft. Males have long tufts, and females have short, shaggy tufts. With their short tufts, females can appear somewhat flat-headed. Flight: Males have a dark head and upperparts, along with a bold white stripe down the wings—a wing pattern that is similar to that of Greater Scaup (but note the back differences). Females appear dark overall with a striking white stripe on their dark wings. They run over the water to get airborne.

 Similar species: Tufted Duck shares many characteristics with scaup and Ring-necked Duck which can cause ID challenges. Adult male Ring-necked Ducks share a jet black back, like Tufted Duck. However, Ring-necked Ducks have light grayish sides and lack that droopy tuft on the back of the head. Females Tufted Ducks have more rounded heads with short tufts, unlike Ring-necked Duck, with their peaked hind-crowns. Tufted's head is darker and even throughout, whereas Ring-necked Duck has a dark crown, contrasting with a paler (often grayish cheek). Female Ring-necked Duck has a pronounced white ring on top of her bill; female Tufted will only have a subdued ring. Beware: female Tufted Ducks will occasionally have a scaup-like whitish patch or even extensive white at the base of the bill (although not as much as Greater Scaup).

 Tufted Duck occasionally hybridizes with scaup or Ring-necked Ducks. Male Ring-necked × Tufted hybrids will have an accentuated crest. Their forehead slopes up to a peak like Ring-necked, but the peak is almost a cardinal-like crest – its pretty striking on a duck! The white ring on top of the bill is extensive. Look for sides that are paler and a more even gray than in Ring-necked Duck. Male Tufted × Greater Scaup look superficially like scaup with broad white sides, gray back and glossy greenish head, however, the back is darker gray than on scaup and the head usually has a pointy crest. The vermiculation on the back is finer and diffuse on hybrids. Watch out for female Tufted × scaup hybrids showing intermediate structural characteristics and darker backs (lacking lots of gray vermiculation and contrasting with the flanks) than scaup and more extensive black tip on the bill than you would normally see on scaup (which is limited to the nail).

 Sex ratio: Males dominate in Europe at 54-59%, in Japan as high as 70%.

BACKGROUND AND TIPS
Tufted Ducks are widespread across Eurasia and regularly wander to coastal states and provinces and elsewhere in North America each winter. The odds of discovering one are best in Alaska, the Pacific Northwest, and California. They are also encountered on the East Coast as well, with Atlantic Canada, New England, and Lake Ontario being particularly good places. They are prone to join in with large flocks of *Aythya* when they wander to North America.

 Tufted Ducks expanded their range westward in Europe in the 19th century. They are doing well in part because they have adapted to using man-made habitats, yet they still face a series a series of threats (e.g., habitat degradation and excessive hunting). There is little definitive information on the status of their populations, with their Eurasian population estimated at 2.6-2.9 million.

SOUNDS
Generally quiet. Males: During courtship utter drawn-out, musical whistle WHEE oo Females: Call is softer than other *Aythya*. Give a croaking distress call.

DIET AND FEEDING BEHAVIOR
Like other *Aythya*, the Tufted Duck feeds by diving, and it will accompany scaup and Ring-necked Ducks in feeding. It dives in a forward leap where the water depth is usually 2 to 6 feet deep. But it will also dive to depths of 10-45 feet to feed from the bottom. It will also up-end and dabble. While the species is omnivorous, the major part of its diet consists of mollusks, gastropods, crustaceans, and aquatic insects. It will also eat vegetable matter, occasionally wading in shallow water and walking on shore to feed. Sometimes, it will feed at night.

Ring-necked Duck
RNDU *Aythya collaris*

Plates Page 170

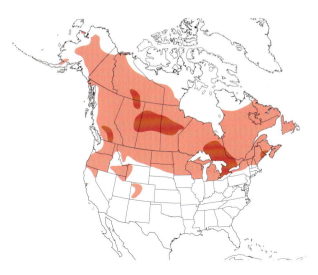

OTHER COMMON OR REGIONAL NAMES
Ringer, ringbill, ring-billed duck, jack, blackjack
(Québec: fuligule à collier)
(Mexico: pato anillado, pato boludo, pato prieto, pato de pico anillado)

MEASUREMENTS
Length: Male – 16.1-18.3 in, av 17.2 in (43.7 cm); Female – 15.6-17.5 in, av 16.6 in (42.2 cm)
Wing: Male – av 8.0 in (20.3 cm); Female – av 7.6 in (19.3 cm)
Weight: Male – av 1.64 lbs (744 g); Female – av 1.48 lbs (671 g)
Bill: Male – av 47.5 mm; Female – av 44.5 mm

FIRST IMPRESSIONS
This is a dapper diver, a duck of small lakes, beaver ponds, and bays. Ring-necked Ducks will often share habitats with puddle ducks, rather than divers. They can maneuver in tight spaces with many surrounding trees with apparent ease, unlike many other divers. Males have dark heads, black backs, and gray sides with a white vertical wedge, or "spur," behind the dark breast. Females are cold gray-and-brown, with paler sides and a pale patch at the base of the bill. The species might have been more appropriately named the "Ring-billed Duck," since the ring on the male's neck is an inconspicuous maroon or chestnut-brown. The white ring on the bill, however, is prominent. Size and Shape: This is a compact diver with a proportionately large head. Look for the distinctive sloping forehead with a peaked rear crown. They flatten their crown, however, when diving. Flight: Ring-necked Duck has rounded body and compact shape of a small diver. They have big heads and thinish necks. Look for the uniform gray wing bar, distinguishing the Ring-necked Duck from either scaup, but not unlike Redhead. Ring-necked Duck tends to travel in small flocks (smaller groups than scaup) of 15-20 birds, often fewer. They are quick and agile, seemingly designed to maneuver around small bodies of water and dropping steeply into confined spaces. They run along the water to get airborne, and their wingbeats are deep but rapid.

ID: IN DEPTH AND SIMILAR SPECIES
Ring-necked Ducks breed in their first-year. They acquire an adult-like plumage quickly, so it becomes very difficult to age them after November. There are subtle differences in the wing coverts if they are in-hand. In the field, look for a worn brownish tail, which is often the most visible marker for a first-year bird.

Ducklings have a bright yellow face with a brown crown extending down the nape. They have the most extensive dorsal spots of any North American duck (note, especially shoulders and rump spots). The crown is darker brown than that of a Redhead. While their color pattern is similar to that of a Canvasback, which has a line of brown running from the crown to the top of the bill, Canvasbacks have a distinctive triangular head shape even at a very young age. Juvenile plumage begins to appear at about two weeks old. It is fully-grown at 7-8 weeks when they are able to fly. Juvenile plumage is plain brown overall, darker on the back. Males eye color begins to change from dark brown to yellow at 5 weeks. First-years replace juvenile plumage from September to March, including head, neck and most of the body, and some to all of the tail. First-years retaining juvenile plumage can be picked out by paler brown plumage than adults and they are browner-faced. First-year females are difficult to separate from adult females once most juvenile plumage has been replaced.

Adult females are dark brown above, paler brown

sides and breast. They have a dark cap and paler cheek, which is a cold-toned gray. Look for a white smudge at the base of the bill and a distinctive soft white eyering, usually visible with an accompanying pale line extending back from the eye. Note the prominent white ring near the end of the bill. Adult females molt some head, body, and inner wing coverts in April-May. Their body becomes darker brown, even brown from the breast along the sides. After breeding, from July-November they replace their wing, body, and tail feathers. The timing of this molt depends on nesting success. Non-breeding or unsuccessful breeders may undergo wing molt in August-late September, while females who raised a brood may molt primarily late September-October.

First-year males transition from a plain brown juvenile plumage to an adult-like plumage between September and November. First, they get a dark head and a yellow eye. Next, they molt in a black breast and gray sides, at which point (often by November) first-years look like adult males. Any retained juvenile tail feathers or wing coverts will give away their age. Generally, the bird looks like a "grungy" or "dirty" adult male with darkish flanks and a bill that lacks white tracing at the base. Adult males are clean cut with solid black backs, gray sides, and small white wedges right behind their black breasts. Look for the fine white tracing lines at the base of the bill. The ring on the neck is merely where the navy blue head blends into a maroon collar. While this can be seen in good light on a close bird, it is best viewed in-hand. After breeding, males undergo a partial molt of body feathers into eclipse plumage in June and July. Eclipse males have brown heads, very dark backs, and brownish sides. They have yellow eyes. They undergo wing molt in the July and August and are flightless presumably for about 3 weeks. They replace all of their body feathers from July-November into their striking breeding plumage.

Similar species: Ring-necked Duck is most similar to Tufted Duck, which is rare in North America. Separating female Ring-necked from scaup, particularly female Lesser Scaup, is a more frequently encountered challenge. Lesser Scaup and Greater Scaup are roughly similar in shape and color pattern to Ring-necked Duck. Ring-necked Duck is noticeably smaller than Greater Scaup and slightly smaller than Lesser Scaup. Always look for differences in head shape—Ring-necked Duck has a flatter crown, peaking in the rear, giving it a pointy-headed look. Lesser Scaup has a steeper forehead and flat-topped head. Head shape changes when the birds are diving, however. With practice, this feature is particularly useful when separating immature birds that have more muted face patterns and dull-colored bills. Male Lesser Scaup are grayish on the back, whereas Ring-necked Ducks are jet black on the back. In general, female Lesser Scaup have even-colored brown heads, lacking contrast between a dark crown and paler (grayish) cheek. Female Redheads are paler, warm brown overall and often have a paler, buffy cheek. They are larger in size and have a smoothly rounded head. A female Redhead can have a pale area at the base of the bill and faint eyering, but it's not as bold or clearly defined as the female Ring-necked Duck's white patch and bolder eyering. Very rarely male Ring-necked × scaup hybrids are encountered, which are scaup-like with an oddly peaked head, brighter ring on the bill and darker gray back than a pure scaup.

Tufted Duck is an exciting find in North America. Male Tufted Duck and Ring-necked Duck both have entirely black backs and dark heads. Adult male Tufted Ducks have stark white sides, much brighter than the gray sides of Ring-necked Duck. First-year male Tufted Ducks lack a long tuft and can have more brown on the sides. They are most likely to be confused with Ring-necked Ducks. Even at this age, Tufted Duck has a fuller, more rounded head, not peaked at the rear like Ring-necked Duck. Separating females can be difficult, and watch out for hybrids. These challenges are addressed in the Tufted Duck account.

Sex ratio: Males dominate at c. 61%, but may occasionally occur as high as 86%.

GEOGRAPHIC VARIATION
No subspecies are recognized.

SOUNDS
Relatively quiet ducks, these birds are generally silent except during the courting season when small groups of males gather around a female to display. Males: During courtship displays, they give a mellow *woow woow* that is similar to Redhead, but weaker. It is given in combination with a neck stretch or head throw. Females: Give a series of short, pig-like grunts when being pursed by displaying males. An alarm call given to the brood is a short, quiet *cut-cut-cut*.

YEAR IN THE LIFE
Ring-necked Ducks are widespread in freshwater marshes and shallow ponds and lakes across all the flyways spanning to southern Mexico. The largest concentration may be near Rice Lake in Minnesota where hundreds of thousands stage for fall migration. They also concentrate in flocks of over 1,000 in during migration at Montezuma NWR in New York and Missiquoi NWR in Vermont, and Long Point in Ontario. Comparably-sized large wintering groups are found in locations as southwest Louisiana, coastal South Carolina, and central Florida.

In winter, Ring-necked Ducks use a variety of wetlands from marshes and shallow lakes to estuaries and water treatment facilities or even flooded fields.

Most pair bonds form in the late winter and during spring migration in March and April. Courting behaviors observed at this time are similar to those of other *Aythya* ducks, including neck-stretching, bill-dipping, and head-throwing. Female inciting is also common, with head raised and lowered, oriented in direction of the male intruder.

The majority of Ring-necks are in place on their breeding grounds by late April or early May. The greatest breeding numbers are in Canadian boreal forests, with some spreading into subarctic and prairie regions.

Males leave their incubating mates later than most ducks to head to poorly known locations where they can molt their wing feathers. Males often gather in groups to molt, but not in huge numbers. Typically, fewer than 300 males will head to a favored wetland. The female remains with the brood until the young are capable of flight, at about 8 weeks. In some areas, females molt near where they raised their brood. Otherwise, they headed to remote northern lakes and marshes to replace their wing feathers.

Ring-necked Ducks head south in the fall at a fairly normal time, relative to other species. Large numbers are seen in the wild-rice lakes of Minnesota and Wisconsin in October where they stage before continuing south.

DIET AND FEEDING BEHAVIOR

Ring-necked Ducks feed at shallower depths than almost all other divers, close to the behavior of Redheads. Ring-necks forage by diving in shallow water (usually under 5 feet) to snatch seeds of aquatic plants, tubers and invertebrates. They will also feed sometimes by tipping up, dabbling at and below the water surface, and snapping at items on the surface. They eat a wider-variety of plant parts than other species of *Aythya* which likely explains why they have taken to bogs, sewage lagoons, and other habitats that appear not as productive as classic wetlands inhabited by their close relatives. Besides their preference for parts of many submerged, floating, and emergent aquatic plants (e.g., rice, water bulrush, bur reeds, and pondweed), they will also eat animal food (e.g., worms, leeches, midges, snails, clams, larvae, and flies).

NESTING

Site: Ring-necked Ducks will construct nests in northern bogs and sedge meadows over fresh water – often on islets of floating marsh plants – in dense emergent vegetation, especially sedges, but mixed with other leafy plants. Most locations are within a few feet of openings in sedge marshes.

Nest description: A hollow lined with grasses and plant material. In wet places in particular, the nest material will be built up. The nest is lined with down. (The down tufts are warm medium brown with whitish centers.) The height is usually about 4-8 inches, but it can be much higher, depending on rising water. A ramp is constructed to facilitate climbing into the nest. Other variable dimensions are about 5-7 inches in inside diameter, 6.5-11 inches in outside diameter, and 2-4 inches in depth.

Clutch size: Average 8-9 eggs, range 6-14.

Egg description: Elliptical to subelliptical. Smooth. Very pale olive, grayish-olive, or greenish. 57 X 40 mm.

Incubation duration: Average 26 days, range 25-29 days.

Brood parasitism: Occasionally parasitized by Redhead, Canvasbacks, and probably other Ring-necked Ducks. Parasitism is less common in Ring-neck than other *Aythya*.

HUNTING

Blackjacks behave more like Hooded Mergansers in their preference for smaller waters than they do their closer relatives, including scaup and Canvasbacks. Ring-necked Ducks are often active early in the morning, flying fast in tight flocks, low over the reeds. Ringbills don't decoy in the classic diver fashion of scaup or Canvasbacks, but they are definitely attracted to decoys. Ring-necks typically decoy easily to any type of decoy. They don't have the status in the hunting community of a Northern Pintail or Canvasback, but they can still be a fine duck to hunt.

The harvest of Ring-necked Ducks in the U.S. over two years (2013 and 2014) averaged at about 498,000 birds; and for Canada the corresponding number was 29,400.

POPULATION AND CONSERVATION

The breeding range of Ring-necked Duck has expanded east of the Great Lakes since the 1930s. During the 1980s, they spread northwest into Alaska and the Yukon Territory. (There has also been a notable increase in records in the United Kingdom and throughout Europe since the mid-1970s.) Much of their breeding range is not included in the traditional survey areas, so there are gaps in information about any population trend. However, their population seems to have increased in the 1980s and early 1990s when most other North American ducks, especially prairie-nesters, were declining. Since they can breed in poor-quality habitats outside the Prairie Pothole Region, they have not experienced the stresses of other waterfowl breeding on the prairies. Contaminants are not a real problem when it comes to breeding Ring-necked Ducks, since their primary breeding range is away from major agricultural and urban areas. Still, Ring-necked Ducks are vulnerable to overharvest and, even today, ingesting spent lead shot. In 2007, an estimated 600,000 Ring-necks were present in the eastern wintering survey areas, and the continental population was averaging (2002-2011) at just under 2.1 million.

Lesser Scaup
LESC *Aythya affinis*

Plates Page 174

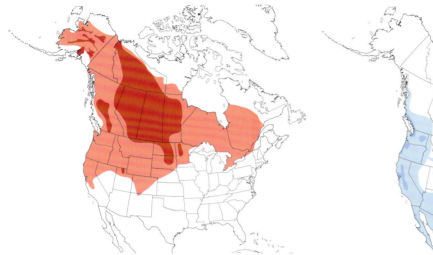

OTHER COMMON OR REGIONAL NAMES
Bluebill, little bluebill, broadbill, scaup, jack, blackhead, dos gris (Louisiana)
(Arctic: qaqjuktuuq [NWS])
(Québec: petit fuligule)
(Mexico: pato boludo menor, pato boludo chico, boox-pool)

MEASUREMENTS
Length: Male – 15.8-17.9 in, av 17.0 in (43.2 cm); Female – 15.2-17.5 in, av 16.5 in (41.9 cm)
Wing: Male – av 8.2 in (20.8 cm); Female – av 8.0 in (20.3 cm)
Weight: Male – av 1.82 lbs (826 g); Female – av 1.65 lbs (748 g)
Bill: Male – av 40.0 mm; Female – av 38.0 mm

FIRST IMPRESSIONS
Hundreds of these "little bluebills" often gather in tight flocks to feed and rest in large ponds, lakes, reservoirs, and rivers. The male's white sides, gray back, and dark head stand out from great distances. Looking closer, the brown females are peppered throughout the flock and sometimes Greater Scaup, Redhead, and Ring-necked Ducks are mixed in as well. Males have pale blue bills, dark heads, black breast, gray back, and often whitish sides with a black butt. Females are brown overall, with a darker brown head and white patch behind the bill. Size and shape: Medium-sized duck, noticeably smaller-bodies (perhaps 10%) than Greater Scaup, with a narrow head, angular crown with a peak in the front, giving the bird a balanced square-headed feel. Also looks straighter-bodied and thin neck. ed Flight: Well-proportioned duck with a round body, thin neck, and thinish wings. Males are dark-headed with paler backs, white bellies, and grayish wings with a pale stripe. Females are dark brown overall. White on forehead may or may not be apparent, depending on distance. Like other divers, scaup need a considerable runway to take off; they do not lift into the air without several seconds of running and flapping on the surface of the water. The white stripe is bold on the secondaries and only faint on the primaries. Flocks of scaup ball up at the front of the flock, with a tail lagging behind. They shift positions frequently and move as swiftly as a unit. Flock sizes vary, often from 5-75. They usually aren't too high off the surface of the water, but often not right on the deck either. Once aloft, they look like they are moving fast, and they are!

ID: IN DEPTH AND SIMILAR SPECIES
Both males and females can breed at one year-old and obtain an adult-like plumage by the spring courting season. Ducklings are dusky gray-bodied with a pale yellow face and breast; some have a dusky wash on their faces. Their eyes are olive-gray, paler than other species of ducks, except Greater Scaup. Juvenile plumage is fully grown at 7-8 weeks; it is a plain even brown. Juveniles have olive to grayish-brown eyes, which become yellower in the fall. Juveniles are flying at 6.5-8.5 weeks. First-years replace their brown juvenile plumage (including head, neck and body feathers) primarily in October and November. They often retain tail feathers, which become faded brown by the winter with notches at the tip.

First-year females can be separated from adult females by the presence of any retained juvenile plumage, which by the late fall starts to look worn and faded. Any remaining feathering in the winter or spring contrasts sharply with newer feathers. First-year females tend to have lighter brown heads, olive-brown eyes, worn juvenile tail feathers, and faded juvenile feathers on their sides. Adult females have darker brown heads than most first-years, at least while they are on the wintering grounds. They have yellowish eyes. They molt some head, body, and inner wing coverts in early March-April, giving them browner, less contrasting plumage for the breeding season. By the summer, adult females also look worn and their head color fades. After the breeding season, in the late summer-early fall they replaces their wing and tail feathers. Timing of this molt depends on nesting success and ranges from late August-September in nonbreeding or unsuccessful breeders, to late September-October for successful females raising a brood. Females will initiate wing molt while tending to brood. Lessers complete their molt earlier than Greater Scaup.

First-year males transition from looking like females in the early fall to near adult males by the spring. In September they are primarily in brown juvenile plumage. By late October, they have significant amount of black feathers on the breast, a dark head (it usually appears green rather than purple) and vermiculated whitish feathers on the back and sides. They often retain at least a few dusky-brown juvenile feathers on the sides until March, and in general do not look as sharp as quickly in the fall as adult males. Adult males go through some interesting plumage shifts throughout the year. In the fall, they molt into a crisp plumage with a black breast, dark purplish or green gloss to the head, vermiculated whitish back and sides. However, even apparent adult males will often have some dusky smudging on the side. In the early spring, around March, they apparently have a partial molt of the head and body and obtain a purplish sheen to the head, loose any dusky smudging on the sides and their back and sides are whiter with finer light gray vermiculation. After breeding, adults and first-years, depart in June-July to molt in boreal lakes. They molt some body feathers to become more camouflaged. Eclipse males have dusky heads, sometimes with white at the base of the bill (like females) with a brownish breast. Molt is heaviest in July and August as they undergo wing molt and are flightless for 2.5-3 weeks. Then they molt their body feathers, so that by October they are in their bright plumage once again.

Similar species: Separating Greater and Lesser Scaup is a classic identification conundrum. Like anything difficult, it takes practice and time to unravel, watching these species to learn them well through the year. Scaup are most difficult to separate in the summer when they are frequently misidentified. Summer is when their head feathers are worn, changing the entire look of the head. In general, head shape and size is a key feature to study, a feature sometimes noticeable even in flight. Lesser Scaup has a more angular head. It has a steep rise to the forehead, flat-top, little tuft on the back of the head. Greater has a more rounded head with a smooth peak in the front. As for head color, Lesser has a dark purplish (often mixed with green) gloss to the head; Greater has a green head – often appearing black – but never purple. Be careful: shape and color may not be easily discernable on slick and wet divers.

In time, you should notice a number of other helpful characteristics. For example, looking head-on, Greater also has jowls. It has a much heftier head and broader bill. The bill on Greater flares out at then end, but Lesser is much less dramatic. The black on the bill is usually confined to the nail on a Lesser; it extends off the nail to the leading edge of the bill in a Greater.

The best way to practice scaup ID, is when both species are in a flock together, allowing for direct comparison. Greaters are much bigger, with slightly brighter flanks. When you see a Greater, you know it. Its large bill and big, rounded head gives it away. This means, Lesser Scaup are far more likely to be misidentified as a Greater than vice versa.

Size is also useful if other *Aythya* are nearby. For example, if the mystery scaup is the same size as nearby Redheads, its Greater, because Lessers are smaller than Redheads. If it's close in size to the nearby Ring-necked, it's Lesser; Greater is significantly larger than Ring-necked.

Wing pattern is also useful, but takes practice in the field. It's important to note, that the boldness of the white stripe varies with age and sex, as well as, by species. Many observers don't take into account that an adult male Lesser will have a very similar wing pattern to a first-year female Greater. Lesser Scaup show contrast between the intensity of the white stripe between the primaries and secondaries. The primaries are much grayer, with less white, than the bolder secondaries. On Greater, however, the white strip is bold from the secondaries all the way out to the outer primaries.

Sex ratio: Males dominate, usually between 57-68%, but sometimes as high as 70-87%.

GEOGRAPHIC VARIATION
No subspecies are recognized.

SOUNDS
Lesser Scaup are generally silent. Males: Give soft sounds including whistled *whew* and faint *whee-ooo* during courtship displays. Females: Females are more vocal than the males. They give a repeating *grrr- grrr- grrr* or *purr-purr-purrr* primarily on the breeding grounds or late during spring migration. The call is nasal, grating and typically given in a long series. It is often given during courtship rituals, pre-laying or if disturbed.

YEAR IN THE LIFE
Lesser Scaup are common and widespread breeders in North America, wintering south to northern Colombia. They are rare wanderers elsewhere in South America and Europe. A large portion of the population migrates via the Central and Mississippi Flyway to winter near the Gulf of Mexico. Others head east to the Great Lakes and Atlantic coast via the Atlantic Flyway. A few end up in Hawaii, and even fewer turn up in Greenland, Britain, and the Netherlands.

In the winter, large flocks form on lakes, reservoirs

and coastal lagoons. They prefer wetlands with lots of emergent vegetation.

Spring movement is one of the most drawn out migrations among North American ducks in spring. Some begin to leave their winter range in early February as ice thaws, while other are still en route in May. Peak movements through upper Midwest and West in April. Most of the courting activity also takes place during migration, later than most ducks with pair bonds forming in April or early May. Courting behaviors are similar to those of other *Aythya*, particularly, Greater Scaup, with kinked-neck, head-throw, and turning-the-back-of-the-head among them. Also the female's inciting display shows preference for a particular male and rejection of others rivals. She stretches her neck, lifts her chin, and makes movements of her bill while giving a low call.

Spring staging on the prairies is a critical time for females to build enough fat reserves to migrate and then lay their eggs.

Most arrive on their breeding grounds in the boreal forest from mid-April to mid-May. They prefer lakes, pools, sedge meadows, and large permanent potholes in the western prairies. Scaup are late nesters, and males abandon females midway through the incubation. Female tends to the brood until the young are capable of flight, when they are 7-9 weeks old. Creching occurs in successful areas, and typically consists of 15-40 ducklings with 2-3 females. Molt-migration males and nonbreeding females depart breeding grounds in June-July to molt in boreal lakes. Successful females typically remain to molt near brood-rearing areas. Large molting flocks, with up to 300,000 individuals, gather in late summer in north-central Saskatchewan Plain, on Lake McCallum; also many (10,000-15,000) have been recorded on Great Slave Lake in Northwest Territories.

In the fall, Lessers are the last *Aythya* to move south as weather permits. They remain on the breeding and molting grounds until mid to late September. Migration peaks through Canada mid-October to mid-November, and through south-central U.S. in late November. Peak migration days on Lake Ontario are usually two days after a cold front passes.

DIET AND FEEDING BEHAVIOR

Lesser Scaup will forage by diving, sometimes in depths of only a few feet, in ponds and flooded fields, to 15-40 feet in offshore saltwater. Mostly, they will feed in water from 10 to 25 feet deep. Except for sea ducks, they feed in deeper waters than do other diving species. They will feed mainly on aquatic invertebrates (e.g., insects, crustaceans, and mollusks), usually consuming their prey underwater. The availability of zebra mussels in the Great Lakes has become a diet mainstay of Lesser Scaup. Seeds — of pondweed, wigeon grass, wild rice, sedges, and bulrushes — and leafy structures of aquatic plants can be important in certain areas.

NESTING

Site: Lesser Scaup nest in wetland areas, but, like Redhead, are more likely than most other *Aythya* ducks to nest in upland areas adjacent to these freshwater ponds, sloughs, and creeks, or lake islands. Nest on the ground under cover, usually near water in tall and new grasses, sedges, or waterside plants (e.g., bulrushes), exceptionally in some vegetation growing in water.

Nest description: A hollow, usually lined with plant material, and with an inner lining of sparse down (less than most ducks) and some feathers. (The down tufts are dark brown with indistinct pale centers.)

Clutch size: Average 8-10 eggs. Usually 8-12, sometimes 6-15.

Egg description: Elliptical to subelliptical. Smooth and slightly glossy. Pale olive or greenish, to olive buff. 58 X 40 mm.

Incubation duration: 21-27 days.

Brood parasitism: Parasitized by Redheads, Gadwall, White-winged Scoter, Ruddy Ducks, Red-breasted Mergansers and Canvasback, lays in nests of other Lesser Scaup.

HUNTING

Little bluebills have been favored by hunters for generations due to their attraction to decoys. These scaup are one of the easiest species to decoy, and they prefer more decoys than puddle ducks. Setting up the decoys in a J-hook with a long tail can lead them into the center of the spread with a pocket for them to land at the bottom of the J. They often make multiple passes (three passes is not unusual) before coming in to land. Calling is generally not particularly effective.

Bag limits for both scaup species have been continually reduced since the mid-1980s when, unlike other species, their numbers did not rebound after severe prairie droughts. The causes of the decline or the reasons why the population is not rebounding are uncertain, and the decline has not been strongly tied to hunter harvests.

The harvest of Lesser Scaup in the U.S. over two years (2013 and 2014) averaged at about 284,000 birds; and for Canada the corresponding number was 29,100.

They tend to come into decoys spread out and bunch up into a ball as they leave. Known for being excellent decoyers, cupped wings, feet out, ready to land. The *SssswoooooshH* sound of a flock buzzing through the decoys, which makes any hunter's day.

POPULATION AND CONSERVATION

Populations have been in general decline since 1980, falling from about 6.3 million in 1970s to 4.4 million in 2015. Despite considerable research efforts, biologists are unsure of the cause or a solution. Some biologists think it is due to poor wintering habitat, while others argue its suboptimal staging and breeding habitat. If staging areas on the prairies also have a depleted food resource, the ducks will not be in good condition for the breeding season. If ponds on the breeding grounds in the boreal forest are warming up earlier, it may mean the food situation is not appropriately timed for the breeders or the brood. Lower hen survival and nest success may point to predators. Contaminants and parasites may also be factors. Increases in selenium levels among Lesser Scaup have been attributed to the increased zebra mussels available in the Great Lakes, since the mussels are efficient filter feeders, and they naturally bio-accumulate contaminants.

The population in western Canadian boreal forest in the region experiencing the most dramatic decline.

Other areas seem to be in better shape, with high breeding densities, such as sites in North Dakota.

Complicating the situation, surveys often do not distinguish between Greater and Lesser Scaup, so estimates are often combined totals. The combined scaup population estimate in 2016, was just under 5 million, 13% below the long-term average (1955-2016). (Lesser Scaup are estimated to constitute about 89% of the continental scaup population, or just over 4.4 million.) More attention has been directed toward Lesser Scaup over the years.

Greater Scaup

GRSC *Aythya marila*

Plates Page 178

OTHER COMMON OR REGIONAL NAMES
Bluebill, big bluebill, broadbill, scaup, jack, blackhead
(Arctic: kep'alek [YK, NS], qaqtuqpalik [NS], qaqjukpalik NWS])
(Québec: fuligule milouinan)
(Mexico: pato boludo mayor)

MEASUREMENTS
Length: Male – 16.5-20.2 in, av 18.6 in (47.2 cm); Female – 15.5-18.7 in, av 17.0 in (43.2 cm)
Wing: Male – av 8.8 in (22.3 centimeters); Female – av 8.5 in (21.5 cm)
Weight: Male – av 2.32 lbs (1052 g); Female – av 2.15 lbs (975 g)
Bill: Male – av 26.7 mm; Female – av 25.6 mm

FIRST IMPRESSIONS
Massive wintering flocks of these waterfowl cluster together to form thick rafts of scaup with bold white sides and dark heads that blanket the water. (The dark-and-white mixture is captured in the specific name: *marila*, from the Greek, marile, for charcoal embers or coal dust.) Dark brown females and the occasional Redhead blend in surprisingly well. Stark white sides and dark heads of adult males stand out. Dark chocolate-colored females with white patches behind the bill, blend in to the water remarkably well from a distance. First-years have a motley appearance; males have some dusky wash on the sides and females are lighter brown. Size and shape: Big rounded head is proportionality large on a noticeably thick neck and robust body. When the head is viewed squared-on, the bird's cheeks puff out with hefty, pit-bull-like jowls. At such an angle, the bill also looks wide and the edges flare out Daffy-Duck style. Flight: Large rounded head, thick neck and extensive white in the wings characterize Greaters. The white stripe in the wing extends from the secondaries well into the primaries. It can be hard to judge the amount of white in the wings on these fast fliers, however, look for how bold the white is toward the tip. Greaters have less contrast between the amount of white in secondaries and primaries than do Lessers. Flocks are always shifting clusters, often a tight ball at the front of the flock with some individuals strung out in the tail. Often travel with 25-300 or more. Frequently mix with Redhead that tend to bring up the rear of the flock. Occasionally flock with Canvasbacks and Lesser Scaup. They run over the water to get airborne, and often fly not too far off the water's surface. Wingbeats are fast and steady. Flocks move at a quick pace.

ID: IN DEPTH AND SIMILAR SPECIES
Some individuals are capable of breeding in their first-year, although the majority breed in their second-year. Ducklings are dusky gray-bodied with paler dusky-yellow face and breast. Eyes are very pale, even yellowish in males, which is a unique trait of Greater Scaup. Juvenile plumage is very plain and uniform in coloration from head

to tail. First-years replace juvenile plumage from September through March, including most head and body feathers, sometimes a few tertials and some or all of the tail feathers. Many first-years do not acquire a crisp breeding plumage in their first winter, so with practice and a good look at the feathers, most first-years can be separated from adults in the winter by the presence of worn juvenile feathers.

First-year females are generally paler brown and more mottled than adult females and can be separated by the presence of worn juvenile plumage. First-year females become worn with a lighter brown head and often mostly brown body. Adult females from roughly September-March have a dark brown breast, contrasting with grayer sides with gray flecking on the sides and back. Adults also have a more extensive white cheek patch behind the bill. Adult females molt some body feathers in April-May, at which point their breasts become richer brown and blend into browner sides. In this plumage they are more uniform in coloration and are more camouflaged for nesting. After breeding, females replace their wing feathers; this is often in early August, later than males going through wing molt. They continue body molt through November, acquiring grayer sides and back once again.

First-year males start off in the early fall with a mostly brown juvenile plumage. They molt many body feathers from September-November and acquire an adult-looking plumage with white feathers on the sides, a dark head and gray back feathers. Their eyes are also yellower by the late fall. They often retain some dusky feathers on the sides or other juvenile feathers into the late winter or spring. Adult males are boldly marked with dark green heads, white sides, white back with coarse black vermiculation that gives them a gray-backed appearance. After breeding, they molt body feathers in June and July into an eclipse plumage. Eclipse males are washed out with brown and gray on the sides and back. Their breast and head are dull brown-to-black. During wing molt, they are flightless. The majority is flightless from the last week of July through early August. Males are flying again by the third week of August and continue body molt until November.

Similar species: Greaters can be very difficult to separate from Lesser Scaup. The main thing is that Greaters are a bigger duck, with a more robust head and bill with a blacker nail. Males appear whiter overall, with cleaner white flanks, and less fine black barring on the back. In flight, primaries and secondaries are extensively white in Greater, but white only in secondaries in Lesser. See Lesser Scaup for a more thorough comparison of these two species.

Sex ratio: Males dominate at 58%.

GEOGRAPHIC VARIATION
Two subspecies are recognized, although they are not very different in appearance. *A. m. nearctica* (or *A. m. mariloides*) breeds and winters in North America and eastern Asia. The Eurasian subspecies, *A. m. marila* breeds across northern Eurasia, wintering south to the Mediterranean region and India.

There are only specimen records of *A. m. marila* in North America, from Alaskan outposts. Males from the Eurasian subspecies have been described as being less coarsely barred on the back than our subspecies. These subspecies are weakly differentiated at best and may be better described simply as geographic variations rather than distinct subspecies.

SOUNDS
Greaters are generally silent unless they are on the breeding grounds or courting during spring migration. Males: Give a raspy, low *kurr-kurr-kur-kur-kurr* that is repeated sometimes for minutes while pursuing a female. Also utters a soft, quick whistle *week-week-whew* or *wah'hoooo* while courting and after copulation. Female: Gives a low *arrr* while inciting and a *tuc-tuc-turra-tuc*, in response to male's neck-stretching display. When alarmed or showing aggression, females gives a *kaup kaup kaup* or *scaup scaup scaup* call for which the species was named.

YEAR IN THE LIFE
Greater Scaup is the only circumpolar *Aythya*, occupying the cooler regions of the Northern Hemisphere. In the Americas, they winter primarily in large bodies of salt water and the Great Lakes, spanning south just into northern Mexico. They often appear in large rafts, mixed with other *Aythya* in each flyway. Some of the highest wintering counts are from Dead Horse Bay in Kings County, New York, where even in recent years there have regularly been over 35,000. The northern Chesapeake Bay, also holds some of the highest concentrations, but they are also prominent at a number of sites around Lake Ontario, Sandy Hook in New Jersey, near Milwaukee in Wisconsin, the shore of Connecticut, and the San Francisco Bay area, California.

Greaters winter in bays, estuaries, and deep inland lakes and rivers where they dive to reach a combination of plant and animal matter. Their diet shifts depending on what is available.

Spring migration begins is full swing by mid-March continuing through mid-April in the mid-Atlantic region. In the west, most Greaters have left their wintering range by late March. Most pair bonds form in February and March, before spring migration is under way. Some pairs form later in April en route north. Courtship usually involves multiple drakes gathering around one hen. Calls are frequent, and displays include head-throws and turning-the-back-of-the-head, activities also commonly observed in other *Aythya* ducks.

Pairs reach the tundra pools and lakes on their Alaskan breeding grounds in mid-May. The male stays with the female until or midway through the incubation, before they take off to molt. Flocks of males start to form by late June on freshwater ponds and lakes. Females stay with their brood until they are about three-quarters grown, before they can fly.

After breeding, males gear up to replace their wing feathers by gathering on nearby lakes in June. By mid- to-late July hundreds of males head in molt-migration to larger, isolated lakes, often far away from their breeding marshes. At some locations, including large tundra lakes on the Yukon-Kuskokwim Delta and the Old Crow Flats upwards of 1,000 males gather.

Fall migration begins with a departure from the breeding grounds from mid-September to late October. The bulk of the population migrates to the Atlantic coast, via the Great Lakes where numbers peak in the second week of October, usually highest following cold fronts. High counts occur from late October to early November in the mid-Atlantic region. On the West Coast, peak concentrations pass through southern British Columbia mid- to late October.

DIET AND FEEDING BEHAVIOR

Greater Scaup are serious divers whose diet consists of both plant animal matter, which could include bivalves, snails, crustaceans, aquatic insects, seeds, aquatic plant parts, depending on the season and what is available. In winter, clams may constitute the principal items consumed. Zebra mussels in the Great Lakes have also provided a new food source for migrant waterfowl, increasingly including wintering Greater Scaup. Mostly a diurnal feeder, Greater Scaup will shift to nocturnal feeding in fall and winter if their daytime activity is disturbed. They will usually feed in less than 6 feet of depth, although often on or near the surface in breeding season. They will also dive for food to a depth of about 24 feet.

NESTING

Site: Greater Scaup breed by fresh water on open ridges and tundra, often using lake islands. In their most important Arctic breeding areas, they favor marshy, lowland tundra. They nest on the ground, and the presence of the previous year's growth of grass or sedge is important. They usually nest near water in fairly open sites, with little or no cover. They may nest sociably, with many pairs together.

Nest description: A simple hollow lined with nearby grasses, down, and feathers. (The down tufts are sooty-brown with indistinct pale centers.) The height of the nest may be up to 7 inches, but it can be variable. Other variable dimensions are about 7-8 inches in inside diameter, 9-12 inches in outside diameter, and 3-5 inches in depth.

Clutch size: Typically 8-9 eggs 6-15.

Egg description: Elliptical to subelliptical. Smooth but not glossy. Pale-greenish to olive-gray. 63 X 43 mm.

Incubation duration: 24-28 days.

Brood parasitism: Regularly parasitized by other species of ducks (e.g., Lesser Scaup, Long-tailed Duck, Gadwall, Mallard, Northern Pintail, and Northern Shoveler) and other Greater Scaup.

HUNTING

For many hunters, there may be nothing that excites them more than watching a flock of big bluebills come roaring into their decoys, wings cupped and feet dangling. Flocks commit to the decoys from a long way out and approach at great speeds, bringing a flurry of excitement and the sound of fighter jets to the blind. Greaters tend to be wary, but they do come into decoys. Like Lessers, they favor diving-duck decoys and prefer more decoys than puddle ducks do. Compared to Lesser decoys, lighter flanks on these decoys may be a smart modification.

Bag limits for both scaup have been reduced since the mid-1980s when unlike other species, they did not rebound. The cause of the decline, or the reason why the population is not rebounding, is uncertain. However, this is a species in which adult mortality due to hunting may impact their breeding population.

The harvest of Greater Scaup in the U.S. over two years (2013 and 2014) averaged at about 72,200 birds; and for Canada the corresponding number was 9,200.

POPULATION AND CONSERVATION

Greater and Lesser Scaup populations are in a long-term decline, which is noticeable on their wintering grounds. Biologists are struggling to pin down exactly what is causing the decline. An estimated 80% of the Greater Scaup population in winter is concentrated in the urbanized northern portion of the Atlantic Flyway, a location where the species may be exposed to physical disturbances, habitat degradation, and various contaminants. Greater Scaup are also sensitive to disturbance on their breeding grounds, although much of their breeding range is largely inaccessible to humans.

Increased zebra mussel diets in the Great Lakes may contribute contaminant exposure through mussel bioaccumulation.

Surveys often do not distinguish between Greater and Lesser, so estimates are often combined totals. The combined scaup population estimate in 2015, was 4.4 million, 13% below the long term average (1955-2015). (Greater Scaup are estimated to constitute about 11% of the continental scaup population, or about 484,000.)

Steller's Eider
STEI *Polysticta stelleri*

Plates Page 188

OTHER COMMON OR REGIONAL NAMES
Steller's
(Arctic: caqiaraq [YK], igfiqauqtuq [NS],ifnigqauqtuq, igniqauqtuq [NWS])

MEASUREMENTS
Length: Male – 17.5-18.5 in, av 18.1 in (46.0 cm); Female – 17.1-18.1 in, av 17.5 in (44.5 cm)
Wing: Male – av 8.4 in (21.3 cm); Female – av 8.3 in (21.1 cm)
Weight: Male – av 1.92 lbs (871 g); Female – av 1.89 lbs (857 g)
Bill: Male – av 26.4 mm; Female – av 27.5 mm

FIRST IMPRESSIONS
One of the most distinctive and bizarre species of ducks in North America, Steller's Eider is not only the smallest of our four eider species, but it is one that does not fit the commonly held profile of an eider. (Its distinct genus, *Polysticta*, comes from a pair of Greek words meaning "many spotted.") Looking at its bill shape, one would not be surprised that the species was originally described as a dabbling duck, *Anas stelleri* (by Pallas in 1769.) The male's white head is marked by black eye-patch, collar, and chin. The striking black-and-white males with buff-breasts and dark brown females will huddle in tight groups where they feed and rest in lagoons, tundra pools, and sheltered bays of Alaska. Winter flocks on the water stay closer together than any other diver. They also dive synchronously- with an entire group diving under or resurfacing in a span of seconds. They dive with their wings out (like Harlequin Ducks) and kick up a splash as they go. These behaviors allow them to be identified at great distances. Males have large white patches on the forewing. Females are an even dark brown. On the water, they often show white borders to the dark blue speculum, because they don't always tuck their wings back under their side feather after diving. Size and shape: Shaped much like a dabbler, they have stocky round bodies with a bit longer tail than most dabblers. Head is relatively large and rectangular, with an odd bump on the rear of the crown. Bill is thick and more like a dabbling duck bill – nothing like other eider species' bills. Flight: Stocky with a thick neck and potbelly. Wings are relatively long. Males are largely white above (lots of white on the forewing) with chestnut bellies you may not see unless the birds are in flight, banking. Females look really dark with the exception of the bold white borders on the speculum. At a distance, the male's white forewing stands out, and the female looks very dark. Steller's Eiders often travels in small, tight groups of fewer than 20, flying low over the water. They have quick wingbeats; unlike slower, belabored wingbeats of other eiders. They are the fastest-flying eiders, and they can twist and turn deftly, much like other smaller divers.

ID: IN DEPTH AND SIMILAR SPECIES
Steller's are slow to mature and do not breed until they are at least two years old, possibly three.

Ducklings are darker overall than most species. They are dark gray on the body and head, with a paler eyebrow (with some brown tones) and a whitish throat. Juvenile plumage is entirely dark brown like females with short, plain tertials, presumably fully grown at 6 weeks. First-years replace juvenile plumage during the winter from October-March. Second-years (two year olds) undergo some body molt in May-June, followed by wing molt in August and body molt extends into the fall.

First-year females are separated from adults by less extensive white borders to the speculum. They have narrow white tips on the greater coverts and secondaries. Their tertials are plain and not curved. Adult females are dark brown, much darker than a female Mallard, with bold white tips on the greater coverts and tips of the secondaries. They molt some body feathers prior to breeding, May-June. Breeding females are the last to arrive on the molting grounds, where they replace their wing feathers and are flightless for about 4 weeks; body molt continues from September to December. Nonbreeding females start body molt in mid-summer when they are still on the tundra, then migrate to the molting grounds for wing molt.

First-year males are generally female-like, showing some signs of male characteristics in winter with a paler head and breast. Adult males are almost clown-like with their odd spots, around the eye, back of the head and on the breast. They have a soft buffy wash on the breast and sides, darkening to a spectacular chestnut on the belly. Adult males start body molt in mid-summer when they are still on the tundra. Males molt body feathers into eclipse plumage from May-July. Eclipse males loose their white body plumage almost entirely, retaining white wing coverts. After their molt-migration they are flightless for about 4 weeks while they replace wing feathers. Body molt into a bright plumage takes place from September-December.

Similar species: The male may appear unique, but the female, out of context or out of her normal range can certainly be a head-scratcher. Look for the female Steller's pale, and almost blurred, eyering. Still, females can look like a number of other species, especially if you aren't ready for a female Steller's Eider to appear. Those immediate impressions might include scaup, Harlequin Duck, and scoters. Among scoters, the dark coloration and shape could resemble that of a Black Scoter, but Steller's lacks the pale cheek. They share the white borders to the blue speculum with female Mallard, however Steller's shape and behaviors bear little resemblance to Mallard. Steller's thick, blue-gray bill, cool curved tertials and relatively little patterning on the body are also features unlike Mallard or other female dabblers.

Sex ratio: This is highly variable and with limited information. In large numbers of banded Alaskan birds in the 1960s the males were 54%. In Finland, spring migrants were 39% males, and 61% brown-colored females or juveniles. In wintering flocks in Norway, the proportion was almost 50-50%.

YEAR IN THE LIFE

Steller's Eider is an uncommon and declining species that breeds along the Arctic Coastal Plain of Russia and Alaska. During the winter, birds from Alaska and Russia congregate in the southern Bering Sea. In Alaska, large wintering concentrations are on the peninsula, Kodiak Island, the eastern Aleutians and lower Cook Inlet (particularly near Homer Spit). They are very rare outside Alaskan waters, where they have turned up in British Columbia and in the Pacific states. There are a handful of eastern records, including from Quebec, Maine, Massachusetts, and Baffin Island.

Steller's Eiders have a strong tendency to return the same wintering, staging, and molting sites year after year as described here.

In winter, they prefer protected lagoons with tidal flats, with some eiders remaining in molting areas and others wintering in the Aleutian Islands, the southern coast of the Alaska Peninsula, the Kodiak Archipelago, and southern Cook Inlet.

By spring, courtship activities have kicked into gear. They will concentrate in the Kuskokwim Bay and Bristol Bay areas and Izembek Lagoon, for example. They form courting groups of one female and 3-7 males where the males display. Their display is fairly low-key with subtle movements and soft vocalizations. Males frequently rise up in the water, showing their chestnut belly. They also move their head back, but not particularly quickly, it's a slower motion than, say, Common Goldeneye's head-toss. Most pair bonds form before they head to the breeding grounds. Courting displays can be dramatic and are different from those of other eiders. Males will sequentially engage in an alert posture with neck stretched and tail cocked, the begin shaking and rushing rapidly toward the female while engaging in head-turning. The male then halts and steams rapidly away from the female while again performing lateral head-turning.

Migration is in full swing by early April. Most pairs arrive on their Alaskan breeding grounds in early June. They nest on tundra and areas with numerous connected ponds. When females start incubating, males gather on nearby feeding areas. When breeding conditions are good, they may stay there for a month until mid-July before leaving, along with failed females and subadults, for the molting grounds. Curiously, nonbreeding and failed-breeding females will linger in small flocks near incubating females, which is actually a useful indication there is an active nest nearby. Molt-migration to northern Kuskokwim Bay near Cape Avinof, along coastal Nunivak Island, and at the north side of the Alaska Peninsula (e.g., Nelson and Izembek Lagoons) starts off with subadults in July and peaks in early August. Successful females are the last to show up there in mid-September. (Steller's Eiders that nested in Alaska are accompanied in these locations by far more numerous Steller's Eiders from the Russian Pacific population. See Population and Conservation.)

Steller's will stage at many of the molting sites into the fall, through late September and October. Highest counts are in mid-September. On 10 September 1980, over 79,300 Steller's were counted at Alaska Peninsula sites. In October, 57,000 were present. After the wing molt, they begin to disperse and arrive on wintering grounds from late October-November. By February, there were only 5,900 at Nelson and Izembek Lagoons. Numbers are on the rise again in March, with 27,100 in 1980. It is unlikely that these counts would top these numbers in the near future, however, it's a good indication of when the birds utilize these traditional sites, which is clearly an extremely important habitat for Steller's Eiders.

GEOGRAPHIC VARIATION

No subspecies are recognized. There are two distinct populations. One nests on the North Slope of Alaska and eastern Siberia that winters in Pacific waters. There is one small Atlantic population that breeds in western Russia and winters in northern Europe from Finnmark and Norway to the eastern Taymyr Peninsula of Russia.

SOUNDS

Not particularly vocal. Steller's give mostly quiet calls during the courting season. Both sexes resemble a barking or growling small dog. Males: Do not give a cooing call like other eiders. Females: Vocalize in winter flocks, giving a rapid guttural call. Inciting call, loud *qua-haa* or *cooay*. Utters growling noise, similar to female wigeon. In flight, their wings produce a loud whistling sound, actually louder than that of Common Goldeneye.

DIET AND FEEDING BEHAVIOR

In winter, Steller's Eiders will feed in protected lagoons with relatively shallow areas, often less than 30 feet deep where they dive and dabble to forage on crustaceans, worms, gastropods, and mollusks when in marine waters. On the tundra breeding grounds, they will feed almost 90% on animal matter (e.g., on macroinvertebrate larvae, water beetles, water boatmen, fairy shrimp, and tadpole shrimp) and the remainder on vegetation (e.g., seeds, pondweed, and crowberry). At molting sites, mussels will dominate the diet when the birds are flightless. Except in breeding season, their diet is very limited; they are essentially specialists with a limited ability to pursue a variety of food resources. They forage more often by dabbling and up-ending than do other sea ducks. But when feeding in a flock, they are especially noted for their diving synchrony, a simultaneous activity.

NESTING

Site: On the ground in tundra by pools, lagoons, or higher edges of pond margins. The nests will often be on polygonal tundra and areas where there are shallow ponds that are connected. These pond areas are dominated by pendant grass and sedges. Steller's typically nest within about 15 miles of the coast, but occasionally 15-60 miles inland.

Nest description: A hollow lined with nearby materials (e.g., grass, moss, weeds, and lichen), down, and some feathers. Dimensions are highly variable, such as the height: 5-10 inches. Other dimensions can be 5-6 inches in inside diameter, 9-20 inches in outside diameter, and 2-4 inches in depth.

Clutch size: 6-8 eggs normally, occasionally ranges to 10.

Egg description: Short subelliptical. Pale yellowish-olive, greenish, or olive-buff and smooth. 61 x 42mm.

Incubation duration: 26-27 days.

Brood parasitism: Very little known, but conspecific brood parasitism has been observed.

HUNTING

Federally listed as a Threatened, this species is closed to hunting and subsistence harvest. Even when legal, their hunting was uncommon, given the eider's somewhat unpleasant taste. A few are still taken illegally as part of subsistence hunting in Alaska, perhaps a few dozen per year. But the harvest in Russia can be substantial, perhaps several thousand per year.

POPULATION AND CONSERVATION

Steller's populations are declining quickly and leaving few clues to explain their disappearance worldwide. In 1997, they were listed as a Threatened Species in the United States. Their 2010 IUCN Red List status is considered Vulnerable. The world population estimate is 110,000-125,000 individuals.

There has been a marked decline in Alaskan breeding population since the 1960s from an estimated 400,000-500,000 to 220,000 in the late 1990s. In 2009, a global population estimate by Birdlife International was only 110,000-125,000. They formerly bred in the Yukon-Kuskokwim River Delta, with an estimated 3,500 pairs in the 1950s and 1960s, but only 5 nests could be found in an intensive study in the 1990s. Population estimates of wintering concentrations along Alaskan Peninsula (including the much more numerous birds that are Russian breeders) and springtime surveys reveal seriously dropping numbers. Still, more Steller's Eiders are located near Barrow, Alaska, than any other single Alaska location.

Spring migration surveys at staging areas from 1992 to 2003 showed declines of 6% annually, from 137,904 to 77,369. The Alaska breeding population may now be as low as the hundreds on the Arctic Coastal Plain (between Wainwright and Prudhoe Bay) and possibly dozens in the Yukon Kuskokwim Delta. The NAWMP average estimate (2002-2011) of 500 breeding pairs may actually be optimistic.

Molt-migration sites, especially along the Alaska Peninsula and in southwest Alaska, include mostly birds from Russia. Total survey numbers average about 82,000 birds, with some stable numbers from 2003 to 2011.

Reasons for the decline of Steller's Eiders remain a mystery, but these may include subsistence harvesting, illegal hunting in Russia, lead poisoning (from shot remaining in wetland sediment), incidental take from gillnet fisheries, predation (e.g. arctic foxes), oil-development interference, and sea level rise. Finally, the consequences of climate change for this and other Arctic-favoring species are not fully understood.

The Steller's Eider Recovery Team (SERT) is developing a reintroduction program for the Y-K Delta. Because the Y-K Delta sub-population is virtually extirpated, it is unlikely to meet conservation recovery goals without re-establishing a breeding population. Re-establishing a viable sub-population of Steller's Eiders on the Y-K Delta could take decades to accomplish.

Spectacled Eider
SPEI *Somateria fischeri*

Plates Page 192

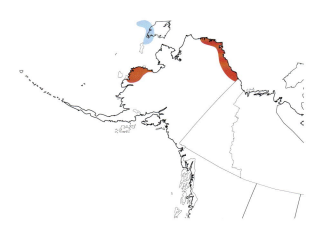

OTHER COMMON OR REGIONAL NAMES
Spec, spectacled, sea duck, eider
(Arctic: qaugeq [YK, NS], qavaasuk [NWS])

MEASUREMENTS
Length: Male – c. 20.7 in (52.7 cm); Female – 19.6 in (49.9 cm)
Wing: Male – av 9.8 in (24.9 cm); Female – av 9.6 in (24.4 cm)
Weight: Male – av 3.29 lbs (1492 g); Female – av 3.21 lbs (1456 g)
Bill: Male – av 23.5 mm; Female – av 22.5 mm

FIRST IMPRESSIONS
All the male eiders are substantial black-and-white sea ducks. And the male Spectacled Eider only emphasizes that first impression. The males have striking white patches around their eyes, hence the "spectacles," surrounded by almost lime-green hoods and accentuated by bright orange bills. These males are black from the breast all the way to the undertail, and their back is white, with broad white tertials that curl over the sides. Females are brown with dark barring, palest around the eye where they have subdued but discernible ghost-patterns of "spectacles." Pairs and small flocks are scarcely sprinkled over Alaska's tundra on the North Slope and on the Yukon-Kuskokwim Delta. In the summer, they can be found up-ending and dipping their heads underwater to feed in shallow tundra pools—a stark contrast to their feeding on wintering grounds! There they gather by the thousands to feed in holes in the Bering Sea ice by taking deep dives to feed on clams. Size and shape: Smaller than Common and King Eiders, with a trapezoidal head, long sloped forehead ending in a small bill mostly covered with feathers. Flight: They are reminiscent of Common Eider, but significantly smaller. Wings are set back on the body. The males' black belly and breast, with black extending up to the neck, gives the birds a distinctly different look than King and Common Eider, particularly when they are too far away to discern their head pattern. They also lack the dark capped look of Common Eider. On males, upperwing coverts are white and primaries and secondaries are dark, so the wing is distinctly two-toned. Females are even brown with pale spectacles that are noticeable at fairly close range. Spectacled Eiders are usually seen in pairs or flocks of fewer than 10 birds.

ID: IN DEPTH AND SIMILAR SPECIES
Spectacled Eiders breed in their second-year or older; about half the females breed in their second-year. In general, their molt has not been well-studied. Where and when they travel for their molt-migration was discovered in the 1990s from satellite telemetry work. Presumably their molt follows a pattern similar to other *Somateria*.

Ducklings even have the distinct shadow of the pale spectacles around their eye and a pale throat, along with a triangular head and feathering that extends down the bill.

Juvenile plumage starts appearing on the back after two weeks. Juveniles are warm brown on the body with even dark markings on the sides and back, and pale spectacles of course. The dark marks give more of a blotchy or scalloped appearance than even, crisp barring on adult females. In late summer (July-September), when juveniles are present, adult female look very work with pale patches on their breast, sides and back and worn tertials; quite different than even brown juveniles. First-years replace some juvenile plumage from October through March. Some body feathers are retained until following spring for females, summer for males. Primaries and secondaries are molted for the first time at sea in the summer when the birds are a year old. Second-years (two year olds) undergo a limited body molt from May-July. From late July to October they have a complete replacement of wing and body feathers. By early fall, they have acquired their first adult plumage.

First-year females are readily separated from adult females by their tertials, which are more tapered and pointed than adults. Adult females have even dark barring on their breast, back and sides, particularly as they are arriving on their breeding grounds. Their tertials are broader with a white tip and have a bit of a curve. Adult females undergo body molt from April-June. By late summer, they have less of a distinction between the pale spectacle and the nape and their face is contrastingly darker brown in front of the spectacle. After breeding, they head out to sea and replace their wing feathers. Their body molt can span September to December.

First-year males are almost entirely dark brown with some white feathers coming in by mid-winter. Their bill changes from slaty gray to acquiring dull pink or pale orange tones over the course of the winter. Second-year males are primarily white and black on the body, looking generally like adult males, but with dusky gray tertials. Adult males are stunning with extensive green on the head and orange bill. Later in the summer, the green above the bill in particular wears to brown. With an exceptionally close view, you can appreciate their bright blue irises. Their tertials are white, attenuated and curved. Adult males undergo a limited body molt from June-August into eclipse plumage, which is followed by a complete body and wing molt from September-December. Eclipse males have heavy brown mottling in their black and white plumage. Their neck is becomes washed with gray, the green above their bill turns brownish, they grow slaty gray feathers on the back. They retain white upperwing coverts and the bill becomes dull orange.

Similar species: Spectacled Eiders in North America are fundamentally Alaskan birds. In regions of Alaska where King and Common Eiders also occur, look for Spectacled Eider's smaller size, distinctive bill shape and signature pale spectacles. Female King Eider does not have the trapezoidal head of Spectacled with feathers covering much of the bill. Even as females become worn in the summer, Spectacled Eider will have contrast between darker brown feathers above the bill and paler feathers around the eye, whereas King Eider is a more even brown head.

In flight, male Spectacled Eiders have a similar predominately white upperwing pattern as Common Eiders. However, the black on their belly comes right up to the base of the throat, while on Common Eider it comes up no further than the base of the breast. King Eider has a pale breast and less white on the upperparts.

Sex ratio: There is very little information, but birds were equal on the Yukon Kuskokwim Delta during spring arrival in the late 1970s

YEAR IN THE LIFE

Spectacled Eiders are uncommon and declining in their small Arctic breeding range.

There are three breeding populations: western Alaska, northern Alaska, and Sakha Republic, within the Russian Federation, in coastal areas from Kolyma Delta to Yana Delta. The entire population winters primarily in the Bering Sea, south of St. Lawrence Island. They have not been recorded in the U.S. or Canada outside of Alaska. A few vagrants outside Pacific Rim have been recorded many years ago in Norway in December of 1933, and flock of four in Finland in March of 1938 (present day Russia).

Winter areas were only found in 1995, in open leads and holes in Bering Sea pack ice (polynyas) or open water. These locations were between St. Lawrence and St. Mathew Islands at locations where depths were up to 230 feet. They forage by diving to reach benthic invertebrates, primarily clams. Males spend about 11 months of the year at sea, females spend 8-9 months there. Most nonbreeding subadults probably remain at sea when one year old, and they first arrive at breeding areas as 2- or 3-year-olds. Pairs form prior to arrival on the breeding grounds and may reunite in subsequent years. Their courtship displays have been observed but not thoroughly studied. Recorded male displays include neck-stretching, head-forward rearing, bill-toss, and neck-jerk activities.

Spectacled Eiders do not migrate very far to reach their breeding grounds; therefore, the onset of spring migration and their arrival near their nest site is a narrow window of time. As soon as water opens up in the Bering and Chuckchi Seas, they are on the move. They arrive in western Alaska in early-to-mid May. Others head to eastern Siberia in early-to-mid June and arrive in northern Alaska, via Beaufort Sea from late May-early June. Females are highly philopatric to their breeding areas, often reusing previous nest-bowls.

Breed in coastal wetlands and tundra. Males depart for sea shortly after the clutch is complete. The brood fledges at 50-52 days. Females and young stay on breeding grounds until ponds begin to freeze, usually departing from late August to early September. Then they head out for a molt-migration, arriving on the molting grounds about ten days later.

Males in June and females in August take off on a molt-migration from their breeding areas to bays and other coastal habitats in the Chukchi and Bering Sea (north of St. Lawrence Island). There they molt, anywhere from a half-mile to thirty miles from shore. They are generally at four main sites from July-October: Ledyard Bay (northwest Alaska), Norton Sound (south of Seward Peninsula), and two in Russia (north of St. Lawrence Island at Mechingmenskiy Bay and further east of the Indigirka and Kolyma River Deltas).

Fall migration lasts only 1-2 weeks. It begins with departure of males and unsuccessful females in late September or early October. An exceptional count of 4,375 from Gambell, Alaska on 28 September 2010 was virtually all adult males. Unsuccessful females arrive on wintering grounds south of St. Lawrence Island around October 10, males around October 23, successful breeding females around November 7.

GEOGRAPHIC VARIATION

No subspecies are recognized.

SOUNDS

Spectacled Eider is a very quiet species. Even when males are displaying, they give only a very soft vocalization, so quiet many researchers studying them didn't even hear any vocalization. Males give a faint *hoo-hoo* when they display by moving their head forward. Females: Give a guttural croak as an alarm call when attending a nest or brood to distract predators. This causes the ducklings to flee and hide. When females greet a mate, other females, or to summon a brood, they give a rapid two-syllable clucking, emphasizing the second syllable, *buckBUCK buckBUCK buckBUCK*. Ducklings: Give rapid, slurred two-syllable whistle.

DIET AND FEEDING BEHAVIOR

During nesting season, Spectacled Eiders will up-end and dip their heads underwater to reach insects, small mollusks, and vegetation (e.g., seeds, mosses, sedges, and crowberries) in shallow tundra pools. In winter, their feeding is remarkably different: they will gather by the thousands to feed in large openings – or polynya – in the Bering Sea ice by taking deep dives (up to 230 feet deep, but usually 80-190 feet deep) to feed mostly (87-99%) on clams, but also crustaceans and snails. (Along with King Eiders, White-winged Scoters, and Long-tailed Ducks, Spectacled Eiders are among our deepest-diving ducks.) This remote wintering area – and corresponding diet – was discovered in 1995. It is assumed that Spectacled Eiders consume these clams under the water.

NESTING

Site: On the ground on coastal marshes or tundra: pond shorelines, small islands, peninsulas, and drier areas in wet meadows. Set on a drier site or tussock near water, but often concealed by vegetation.

Nest description: A hollow lined with grasses, plant debris, and moss. The inner lining is made with down and small feathers. Average size is 5.5 inches in inside diameter, 9.5 inches in outside diameter, and 2 inches in depth.

Clutch size: Usually 5-7, sometimes 3-9.

Egg description: Elliptical to subelliptical. Smooth and green, light olive-green, or olive-buff. 67 x 45mm.

Incubation duration: 23-24 days.

Brood parasitism: Small percentage parasitized by Cackling Geese, Black Brant, Common Eider and Greater Scaup. Occasionally lay in nests of other species resulting in eider ducklings in broods of Cackling Geese and Arctic Loon. Very rarely known to lay eggs in nest of conspecifics.

HUNTING

Specs are listed as a federally Threatened species in the United States, therefore, they are off-limits to sport and subsistence hunting. Despite strict regulations, some are poached (tens to hundreds) at breeding sites and during migration in western Alaska at St. Lawrence Island and northern Alaska. There is also an unspecified number (roughly estimated at 10,000-14,000) taken each year in Arctic Russia.

POPULATION AND CONSERVATION

Spectacled Eider is a species of great concern because their populations have been seriously declining. Unfortunately, there is little long-term data available for this Threatened species. The western Alaska population declined 96% from 1953-1993. In the 1970s alone, nesting females dropped from 50,000 to <4,000. These figures resulted in listing them as Threatened under the U.S. Endangered Species Act in 1993. By the mid-1990s, both Alaska populations were estimated at <4,000 breeding pairs. Today, they are higher, perhaps as high as 9,200 breeding pairs. The Russian population is the stronghold with >140,000 individuals. The global population may only be slightly over 300,000 birds.

Hunting, lead poisoning, habitat loss, increased predation, disease, and complex change in invertebrate populations in the Bering Sea are all threats to the Spectacled Eider. Hunting in this case means the take in Russia and the poaching in the U.S. Lead poisoning is caused by the consumption of spent lead shot – remaining in wetland sediments over many years. Such lead exposure was evident, widespread in the 1990s (estimated at 25-37% of the population) and persistent. Low survival of adult females during brood rearing and the lead exposure to juveniles may yet impede recovery of local Spectacled Eider populations. Habitat loss includes the construction of on-land and off-shore structures, towers, and power-lines that create collision risks. It also includes coastal erosion, salinization from storm surges, and thawing permafrost, all potentially altering the value of current nesting areas in particular. Diseases, such as infectious bursal disease virus (IBDV) may be a serious threat as it attacks the developing lymphoid tissue of young Spectacled Eiders, compromising their immune system.

The long-term impact – on breeding habitat and winter feeding – of climate change for this and other Arctic-favoring species deserves further inquiry. Clearly, the changing climate has led to a decrease in the amount of Bering Sea ice and reduced the amount of prey available for wintering eiders. It also opens up their habitat for bottom trawling, which could also affect the prey available. At night, the eiders save energy by resting on the sea ice; however, the future loss of sea ice available for resting could cause them to expend more energy than in the past, a situation exacerbated by the potential loss of prey.

The total continental population according to the NAWMP was 17,000 (a 2002-2011 average), a figure that may be optimistic today. Still, after years of decline, Spectacled Eider populations in North America are experiencing some steady but slow recovery, especially at the main breeding ares on the Yukon-Kuskokwim (Y-K) Delta.

King Eider
KIEI *Somateria spectabilis*

Plates Page 196

OTHER COMMON OR REGIONAL NAMES
King, sea duck, eider
(Arctic: qengallek [YK,NS], qifalik [NWS, N], kingalik, kchingalik, quingalaaq [N])
(Québec: eider à tête grise)

MEASUREMENTS
Length: Male – 21.7-25.0 in, av 22.7 in (57.7 cm); Female – 18.5-22.5 in, av 21.1 in (53.6 cm)

Wing: Male – av 10.7 in (27.3 cm); Female – av 10.4 in (26.3 cm)

Weight: Male – av 3.68 lbs (1669 g); Female – av 3.45 lbs (1565 g)

Bill: Male – av 32.0 mm; Female – average 33.5 mm

FIRST IMPRESSIONS
A rapidly declining Arctic sea duck that is often found in small groups or pairs on picturesque tundra pools or migrating past St. Lawrence Island or Point Barrow in Alaska. Away from the heart of their arctic range, singles or small groups mix with flocks of Common Eiders and scoters. Adult males have dark backs and bellies, creamy breast and colorful head with pale blue crown and nape, orange knob, red bill, and green wash under the eye. This wonderful combination is captured in the scientific name, since *spectabilis* comes from the Latin, meaning conspicuous or spectacular. Females and immature males are brown overall with some black mottling. Size and shape: A large sea duck, slightly smaller and more compact than Common Eider. King Eiders have big rectangular heads, short thick necks and robust bodies. Adult males have a bulbous knob on top of their bill. Flight: Heavy in the belly and rear, with almost a pear-shaped body. They appear to be dragging their butts and hold their heads higher. Males look pale-headed, buff-breasted with a dark belly and undertail. Wings are dark with a white oval patch. Females are an even dark brown overall. At key migration sites, groups of thousands can be seen to migrate together, clustered in the front and trailing at the end. Flocks usually travel at a reasonable distance above the water, abreast in long lines, instead of flying one behind the other. Their wingbeats are powerful, like other large sea ducks, but a bit snappier than Common Eider with a slightly thinner-winged look.

ID: IN DEPTH AND SIMILAR SPECIES
King Eiders typically breed in their third-year, although some may breed in their second-year. Once first-year males acquire some black or white feathers it is easy to determine the sex.

Ducklings are gray overall, whitish on the breast with a distinctive light and broad strip above the eye and whitish throat and cheek. Juvenile plumage begins to grow at two weeks; it is paler brown than adult females and wears out quickly. First-years replace some juvenile plumage over the course of the winter from October to March. They have a limited body molt from May-July before undergoing their first wing molt.

First-year females are paler and more washed out overall than adult females. By late fall, they their retained juvenile plumage is worn and their belly has faded to pale brown. The combination of the worn juvenile feathers and new adult-like feathers gives first-year females a scruffier, mottled appearance. Adult females are richer, warmer brown overall with crisp patterns on their body feathers. They molt head and neck feathers in April and May. Nonbreeding and unsuccessful females may join males for a molt-migration; they undergo a complete molt of wing and body feathers earlier than successful breeding females. Females undergo wing molt from late August to October in western Greenland. Wing molt is followed by body molt from September to December.

First-year males are dark brown overall in the fall, palest on the breast with a pale bill. They undergo body molt from October to March. By fall, many first-year males have whitish feathers on the breast, which readily separates them from females. By the late winter, they have a nearly black head, and some individuals have a mostly off-white breast, black body, and small white patch behind their leg. In their first summer, their head and body is plain dark brown to black with white speckling on breast (which can be extensive), and their bill is dull pink with a small orange frontal lobe. Second-year males have all the same main colors as adult males, but they have a duller head and smaller frontal lobe. Early in their second-winter some have brown smudging on the head (particularly on the face), nape and breast. Their body is black with "fins" on the back and white patch near their legs. Second-years have a complete molt of wing and body feathers in July-

October at which point they are adults. Adult males are stunning in the winter and spring when they have bulbous orange bills and blue heads. In June and July, they molt some body feathers to obtain an eclipse plumage. Eclipse males are mostly chocolate brown. White feathers grow in throughout the fall. The bill remains pale but the bulge on their bill shrinks and becomes duller. They retain white upperwing coverts. Bill color and lobe size separates them from first-years. They retain white upperwing coverts. Adult males undergo a molt-migration out to sea in July and August, where they replace their wing feathers and are flightless. They molt body feathers from September to December to attain a stunning blue, white, and black plumage once again.

Similar species: Distinguishing female King from Common Eider is often tricky and requires careful consideration of a few features. Common Eider has a long sloping forehead, lending to a triangular-shaped profile. Looking more closely, the shape of the bill and frontal lobes is helpful – King Eider has a black bill with short pointed frontal lobes, Common has a gray bill with pale tip. If you need to get into some plumage details, the internal markings on the side feathers are dark chevrons in King; Common has dark barring on the sides. This gives Common a neatly arranged look to the barring on the sides, while King's pattern has a disheveled look.

In flight, King Eiders drag their butts; their heads are held higher than their rears. Common Eiders are on an even keel, horizontal head to rear. If you are lucky enough to be in a place where Spectacled Eiders occur, look for head pattern differences. King Eider also has more white on the breast and more black in the upperwing coverts, so it's just a white oval on King, not the entirely white upperwing coverts of Spectacled.

Sex ratio: Proportions are largely equal during migration and arriving at breeding areas, but at some spring migration passage sites, males may dominate at 52-57%.

YEAR IN THE LIFE

King Eider is a circumpolar Arctic breeder, nesting in northern Alaska, the east and west coasts of northern Greenland across Russia and in lower density in northern Finland, Sweden and Norway. The largest wintering concentrations are along the southern edge of the sea ice in the Bering Sea. Smaller numbers trickle down to the eastern Great Lakes and Atlantic Coast south to Maryland almost every year. There are a few more extraordinary records from Texas, Louisiana, and British Columbia, Washington, Oregon, and California.

In winter, King Eiders forage on the edge of sea ice or in coastal areas where water is shallow enough to dive for their food.

Courting rituals are in full swing in the late winter and during spring migration, which begins in April. Male displays commonly include a "pushing" action, with head angled downward, chin close to the breast, and back arched. There is also upward stretching, wing-flapping, and head-turning involved. The female will often respond by preening, bill-dipping, and dramatic wing-flapping.

In early spring, the western North American population heads north, leaving wintering areas in the north Pacific and Bering Sea. When the birds reach the Bering Strait, the route divides and some head west toward Russia, while others go east to Alaska and northwestern Canada. They follow leads and polynyas in the sea ice from April to June, moving through the Chuckchi Sea to the west coast of Alaska.

King Eiders migrate in spectacularly large flocks, which makes their migrations an extraordinary scene. The enormous flocks, sometimes exceeding 10,000 ducks in a group, will pass by Point Barrow, Alaska. A record count occurred May 26, 1976 when 360,000 passed in a 10-hour period with 113,000 in 30 minutes! Given King Eider's significant population decline, it's an event that may not be repeatable ever, or at least for many years if they do begin to rebound.

Pairs arrive on breeding grounds in mid-June. Females return to the same area each year, often choosing a site within 9 miles of where they nested the previous year. Males, however, move to a different location each year, sometimes moving over 620 miles from where they bred the previous year. Interestingly, they will return to the same molting site for multiple years.

Females choose nest sites on the tundra A male will leave his mate after she is about a week into the incubation, and he will head northward on a molt-migration. Once the brood is out of the nest, the hen and young are on the move traveling overland with to reach shallow ponds with sedges or deep ponds with pendant grass. These areas can be fresh or salt water. By the time the young fledge they are using saltwater habitats. Females often undergo a molt-migration and join the males, but occasionally they will molt near the nesting area.

Molt-migration of males and nonbreeding or unsuccessful females starts 3-4 weeks after end of spring migration. Among breeders, it begins in early July, with adult males heading out first, followed by adult females and young birds in August and September. For example, as the eiders leave the Beaufort Sea thousands pass Point Barrow, heading southwest across the Chukchi Sea. By late August the males have passed and are staging in the eastern Chuckchi Sea.

Over a third of the King Eiders in the Bering Sea do not migrate after completing their wing molt and winter in the same spot or nearby where they molted. Those that do undergo a fall migration may take anywhere from a week to several months to reach their wintering grounds. The eiders shift as sea ice forms from October through December. Many move considerable distances throughout the winter, somewhat responding to shifts in weather and food availability, but not necessarily. They seem to be checking out other location in case conditions at their main location become unfavorable.

GEOGRAPHIC VARIATION

No subspecies are recognized, however, there are two North American populations in the eastern and western Arctic that look the same. These two widely separated populations show no genetic differences, although banding data suggests they do not mix.

Western North American breeders winter in Russia from Kamchatka to the Kuril Islands, as well as, the Aleutians in Alaska. Eastern Siberian breeders winter in the Bering Sea. Breeders from western Siberia, Scandinavia, and Spitsbergen winter from White Sea to western Norway and eastern Iceland, with small numbers in Great Britain and Ireland. The majority of eastern North American breeders winter at sea from Labrador to Newfoundland.

SOUNDS

This is a relatively quiet species, although commonly heard during courtship. Males: During courtship display, give a soft, dove-like, rolling, and two-part *coo-ooo* while tucking their chins and pushing their heads forward. They also give a threat call when with mate, *kwack*. Females: Give murmuring growls in flight in migration. Occasionally respond to displaying males with low chattering *kuck* given in series. Call is reminiscent of Least Bittern's chuckle call, but is given more forcefully and in longer series. When they feel threatened with brood, females utter an angry growl. Their wings whistle during flight.

DIET AND FEEDING BEHAVIOR

During the breeding season, a King Eider diet will consist primarily of vegetable matter. Females and young, in particular, will eat midge larvae, fresh willow parts, seeds, sedges, and moss, all in fresh water areas. Among our deepest divers, King Eiders are known for their diving ability at sea. In winter, King Eiders will dive anywhere from a several feet to 40 feet or even 150 feet to reach mollusks, crustaceans, echinoderms, and some vegetable matter (e.g., eelgrass, widgeon grass, and algae). They regularly dive deeper than Common Eiders. At molting sites, they prefer feeding on mollusks.

NESTING

Site: On the ground in tundra, often in marshy areas, polygonal wetland, in grass meadows, near lakes or ponds, and near the sea. At times they will nest on barren tundra or at a considerable distance inland from the coast.

Nest Description: A hollow lined with nearby plants. Inner lining of substantial dull-gray down and some feathers. Average outside diameter is 10 inches.

Clutch size: 4-7 eggs, clutches of more than 7 eggs assumed to be from more than one female.

Egg description: Subelliptical. Pale olive and glossy. 66 × 44mm.

Incubation duration: 22-24 days.

Brood parasitism: Uncommon within species (see clutch size above), rarely parasitized by another species.

HUNTING

A small number of these birds are taken by sport hunters, perhaps 400-500 per year combined for the U.S. and Canada. These ducks are highly prized. Although official sport-hunting bag limits are kept to a minimum, the impact on local populations is unknown.

The subsistence harvests in Alaska and Canada are substantial and important for those communities involved. Many are poorly monitored, however, and there is unregulated harvesting of thousands of birds (including during their molt-migration) by native communities in Alaska and Canada (e.g., western Victoria Island). An estimated 25,000 King Eiders are harvested annually in Alaska and in northwestern Canada by subsistence hunters. In eastern Canada, the annual harvest is closer to 19,400.

POPULATION AND CONSERVATION

King Eider populations have declined both in eastern and western North America in recent decades. The total continental population, according to the NAWMP, is roughly averaged (2002-2011) at 600,000 birds, with 200,000 in the East and 400,000 in the West.

Unfortunately, their populations have not been closely monitored, so the magnitude of the decline isn't fully understood. Results from studies in the mid-1990s were quite alarming, showing counts of migrants at Point Barrow declined 55% from 1976 to 1996. Counts in 2002-2003 were similar to the mid-1990s tallies, suggesting a stabilized, but not increasing, population.

The reasons for their decline are not well-understood, but these may include habitat changes, lead poisoning, hunting pressure, and increased predation while nesting. Periods of food deprivation during spring migration may cause some of the population to die (e.g., 10%) of starvation or be in poor body condition that negatively affects reproductive success, which varies greatly from year to year. King Eiders face many threats, including chronic oil pollution, and they are at high risk for a catastrophic oil spill in the Bering Sea. Oil exploration degrades their food resources. They are also subject to high rates of human disturbance from unregulated shipping (mainly of oil transfer) through their molting and wintering grounds.

Previously mentioned overexploitation takes a huge toll on their populations. In the case of the southwest Greenland population, 10-20% of these birds are killed each winter in commercial harvest. This is a situation that is not sustainable. Others die from drowning in gill nets each spring. The Alaska birds are shot 24/7, under the midnight sun, during spring migration, molt-migration, and fall migration when they pass Point Barrow and some other native communities.

A significant portion of the handful of King Eiders that reaches the eastern U.S. is probably taken by hunters. They are truly rare birds in the East, yet they have somehow eluded more serious protection by falling under the "eider" umbrella.

Further monitoring and studies are very much needed in order to sort out what is causing these population declines. In this specie's case, increased protection from hunting pressures and the subsistence harvest could be a good place to start.

Common Eider
COEI *Somateria mollissima*

Plates Page 202

OTHER COMMON OR REGIONAL NAMES
American eider, northern eider, Pacific eider (Arctic: metraq [YK], amaullik [NS], amauligaaluk [NWS], mitiq [NS,NWS, N], mitivik, mitshek [N])
(Québec: eider à duvet)

MEASUREMENTS
Length: Male – 21.7-26.8 in, av 23.78 in (60.4 cm); Female – 21.0-24.7 in, av 23.2 in (58.9 cm)
Wing: Male – av 11.2 in (28.6 cm); Female – av 10.8 in (27.3 cm)
Weight: Male – av 4.95 lbs (2245 g); Female – av 4.40 lbs (1995 g)
Bill: Male – av 55.0 mm; Female – av 50.5 mm

FIRST IMPRESSIONS
Common Eiders are in their element weaving around rocky coastlines in small flocks, low to the water. The sturdy and dapper black-and-white males intermix with rich brown females pumping with slow wingbeats and achieving great speeds. On the water or loafing on sandbars or jetties, eider flocks are distinguished by the males' stunning black sides and white backs mixed with warm-brown females. Adult males have black sides and white backs, a broad black swath through the eye and light green wash on the cheek and nape. Females are generally an evenly mottled, rich brown. The overall brown body coloration varies between subspecies. Size and Shape: As the largest duck in the Northern Hemisphere, Common Eider is robust – almost the size as a Brant, larger than a scoter or a Common Merganser. It has a unique profile, with a long and sloping bill and peaked forehead, above and in front of the eye. Its wedge-shaped head is reminiscent of Canvasback. It has a thick neck and a long and wide body. Flight: Once they take to the air, their large size is readily apparent in their laborious wingbeats. But, they are moving faster than they look! The white back and wing coverts and half-black wings are also prominent. The head and neck are held straight out, and the wedge-shaped head helps separate female Common from King Eider. Also, notice the body is held horizontal, whereas a King appears to be dragging its butt. Small flocks are often strung out in a waving line cruising low over the water. Wingbeats are deliberate and powerful.

ID: IN DEPTH AND SIMILAR SPECIES
These long-lived sea ducks take three years to mature. Common Eiders follow a similar molt pattern as other sea ducks. This a great species to learn sea duck molt patterns because you can often study the male's plumage progression from brown juveniles to black-and-white adults.

Ducklings are various shades of gray with a whitish stripe above the eye and a lighter belly. Juvenile plumage is fully-grown at 7-8 weeks. It is brownish overall with a paler crescent above the eye; the overall color and patterns are duller and more muted than adult females. First-years often replace a large portion juvenile body plumage from October to March. They retain their wing coverts until they are about a year old.

First-year females can be picked out from adult females by retained juvenile plumage, which gives them a mottled look as they begin to replace feathers in October and continue during their first-winter. First-years have very limited white tips of the greater coverts, whereas adult females have broad white tips on the greater coverts. Adult females are warm brown with even and intricate dark barring on their sides. They have a crisp, uniform look to their sides and back in the fall and winter, a pattern which you do not see on first-year females. In flight, you may notice two narrow wing bars. Adult females replace some body feathers in April and May, before they initiate nesting.

After breeding, females replace their wing feathers and are flightless for several weeks. Once they regain flight, they continue molting body feathers until about October.

First-year males start off with a dark brown juvenile plumage. They molt throughout the fall and winter and attain black sides and a partially white breast. By late winter, some individuals have an entirely white breast, black sides and white mottling on the back, contrasting with their brown head. Some individuals, however, do not attain any black or white feathers until March-April. Their bills are pale, dull green with thinner bill extensions or lobes than adults. Second-year males can vary in appearance from a full adult-like plumage to extensive brown mottling on the breast, belly, and sides. They are most easily aged by brown tertials. (They are white in adults.) Second-years typically have well-developed lobes though slightly narrower and paler than older birds. Look for a dusky wash on the face and nape. Second-years and non-breeders undergo wing molt and body molt from July to October. Adult males have a clean white breast and back, contrasting with black sides. They molt into a partial eclipse plumage in June-July after leaving the incubating hen. Eclipse males from July to October will be blackish-brown with white flecking on the breast, white upperwing and underwing coverts, and olive-to-orangish bills. They are flightless during wing molt; then they replace their body feathers, by which time they are in a perfect, bright plumage once again.

Similar species: Separating female eiders can be a real problem, but with a close look at a few structural and plumage details, ID problems can be overcome. When it comes to female eiders, study the head shapes. King has a short bill, with a steep rising forehead, whereas Common has an even sloping forehead. If you look closely at the pattern of the feathers, Common has barring on the sides and King has chevron-shaped markings. See the King Eider account for more on separating these species.

Sex ratio: Close to even.

GEOGRAPHIC VARIATION

Common Eider has extensive geographic variation, with six subspecies recognized, four of which occur in North America: *S. m. dresseri* (Atlantic or American), *borealis* (Northern), *v-nigrum* (Pacific), and *sedentaria* (Hudson Bay). Nominate *mollissima* (European or Eurasian Eider) and *S. m. faeroeensis* (found only on the Faeroe Islands) have not been recorded in North America.

For the most part, *sedentaria* – given its appropriate subspecies name – doesn't leave the Hudson Bay, *v-nigrum* (Pacific Eider) stays in Alaska, and *dresseri* is by far the most common eider seen on the East Coast. This leaves us with *borealis*, whose broad distribution is not as easily defined in northeastern North America. Read on for more specifics on their distribution and plumage details to help you separate them, if for some reason you can't figure it out based on the accompanying range map.

S. m. dresseri, Dresser's, Atlantic, or American Eider, is widespread in the eastern US and Canada, breeding from Labrador to Maine and wintering south to the mid-Atlantic states with stragglers all the way to Florida. They are medium-sized, with an olive-green to greenish-yellow bill with broad bill projections – frontal lobes extending toward the eyes – that are rounded at the top. Males have fairly extensive green on the nape and rear cheek. Females are a warm, or almost reddish, brown.

S. m. borealis, Northern or Boreal Eider, is the smallest of the four North American subspecies. Males have a bright, banana yellow to yellow-orange bill with bill lobes that are rather pointed and tapered at the tips (unlike the broadly rounded lobes of Dresser's). The head has a flat-crowned appearance and bumped forehead (unlike the even crown of Dresser's). Northern Eider has limited green on the head, concentrated on the nape, giving it a white-cheeked appearance. It has paler pink blush on the breast, so the breast appears whiter than Dresser's. The white feathering below the lobes comes to a blunt point, unlike the rounded circular area that is shown in Hudson Bay Eider. Females are a medium brown, averaging buffier in general plumage tone than Dresser's. Several specimen records from Maine and Massachusetts and recent observations suggest it may occur south to New England with regularity. It has recently been discovered almost annually in Maine and Massachusetts among winter flocks of Dresser's, so despite relatively few documented records it is probably rare but regular in winter as far south as Cape Cod.

S. m. v-nigrum, Pacific Eider, is found primarily in Alaska and is the largest subspecies. The bill is bright orange or yellow-orange, with short lobes extending upward that are narrow and pointed. Pacific Eider has a heavy green wash extending from under eye to the nape. Most males have fine black V under their chin. The black V, often hard to see, is not entirely unique to v-nigrum; it is occasionally seen on Dresser's, Northern, European Eider, and King Eider.

S. m. sedentaria, Hudson Bay Eider, is a resident of Hudson and James Bays. They are very similar to Dresser's and some have considered them the same subspecies. Males have ochre yellow bills with wide lobes, very similar to those of dresseri. Most Hudson Bay females are distinctly pale, frosted gray. However, there is variation, and a few are browner. They winter primarily in any remaining open water west of the Belcher Islands. There are two exceptional specimen records, one from Lincoln County, Nebraska and one from Niagara Falls, Ontario. Large die-offs occur in severe winters.

SOUNDS

Flocks of courting males can be heard from great distances. If alarmed, both sexes give a series of hoarse, grating, kor-korr-korr notes. Males: Give a ghostly low, *ahOOOOoo* during courtship displays and an *A-coo* or *Woo-hoo* call is also given. Females: Give a quiet *Roo* and grating *krrrr* of varying length and tempo during feeding and courtship. When in search of nest sites, they give a mixture of croaking and groaning noises.

YEAR IN THE LIFE

Common Eiders are at home within the intertidal and subtidal zones of the Northeast and far north. There they forage by diving and plucking mollusks and crustaceans from the bottom of shallow waters near ledges, shallow reefs, and jetties of rocky coastlines. Look for the largest wintering concentrations near Nantucket and Monomoy NWR in Massachusetts and Montauk Point in New York. They are very rare on the Great Lakes, and rare in winter on the Atlantic coast from North Carolina to Florida. On the Pacific coast, *S. m. v-nigrum* is common in southern Alaska, rare in British Columbia, and extremely rare in the Pacific states, and is known to wander east to Greenland and Newfoundland. *S. m. sedentaria* is extremely rare outside Hudson and James Bay.

The majority of the courtship displays are performed from the fall to early spring. Females can breed at age two. Males are out of the breeding pool until they are at least three years old. Males congregate and display with elaborate head throws and their head held high, neck outstretched, accompanying their soft chorus of cooing and vigorous ritualized wing-flapping. Pair bonds will have formed prior to arrival on the breeding grounds. Unlike most other ducks, it is likely that some pairs reunite for multiple breeding seasons.

Pairs reach the coastal breeding colonies anywhere from early April for early nesters to mid-June for Arctic breeders. Females are highly faithful to breeding areas, often returning to the very same nest site year after year. They typically initiate nesting at about the same time as other females nearby. Once the brood hatches, females look after the ducklings, often joined by nonbreeding females, called "aunts." Broods frequently come together to form crèches averaging 20-30 ducklings. Record large crèches can reach 150 young! Females remain with the crèche for variable periods of time; some will stay with the brood until they fledge, others are with them for a very short time. After breeding, females take off to molting sites in late August-September.

The molt-migration of adult males, immature birds, and non-breeders occurs in June-July; breeding females do not follow until August or September. The journey is a considerable migration for some subspecies, both in terms of distance traveled and the number of individuals that molt in one area. It is well-described for some subspecies, but less so for others. Northern Eider that breed along north coast of Ungava and northern Labrador move to areas in Ungava Bay, while those from the High Arctic likely travel to Greenland. In Alaska, thousands of Paciic Eider travel east pass Point Barrow in July and gather in large flocks on the coast of the Beaufort Sea. In September and October, they head west past Barrow after completing their flight feather molt. Dresser's Eider is believed to molt in general vicinity of nesting colonies, although farther offshore. Some Dresser's molt along north shore of St. Lawrence estuary and gulf, but the origin of this group is unknown. The Hudson Bay Eider in Hudson Bay do not undertake a real molt migration, but simply move offshore to remote islands, including near King George Island.

By October, fall migration has largely wrapped up, and most Common Eiders are settled on their wintering grounds.

DIET AND FEEDING BEHAVIOR

The winter diet of Common Eider consists mostly of mollusks, especially larger blue mussels which maximizes the eider's short-term energy intake. Some researchers claim that no other duck species depends so heavily on a single food source. Very little plant food is consumed by Common Eider. This eider feeds by diving and selecting food from bottom (c. 30 feet deep, not as deep as King Eiders). They may forage at any time of day and usually dive deeper in winter than in summer. Most prey items are brought to the surface for handling and swallowing. On nests, females will feed very little and may actually become emaciated. Once the females are attending ducklings they will all feed extensively on periwinkles. When they molt, they will feed in shallow waters close to shore.

NESTING

Site: On the ground often close to the coast, otherwise on an island (often a rocky island or barrier island), by a lake or river farther from the coast. The nests are often exposed and in dense colonies. Colonies range in size, but can be as large as 10,000 to 15,000 birds.

Nest description: A hollow lined with plant material or seaweed. Inner lining contains much down and feathers. The sizes are variable, but may be about 8 inches in inside diameter, 10 inches in outside diameter, and 3 inches in depth.

Clutch size: 4-6 eggs, sometimes 3-10.

Egg description: Variable shape, from elliptical, to subelliptical, to oval. Smooth and slightly glossy. Variable in color, from pale green or olive, to bluish or grayish. 77 x 52 mm.

Incubation duration: 24-27 days.

Brood parasitism: Frequent, especially in denser colonies, often 1-3 parasitic eggs per nest. Occasionally parasitized by other species (e.g., Brant, Canada Goose, Snow Goose).

HUNTING

The Migratory Bird Treaty placed a moratorium on hunting common eiders, one which lasted a decade. Maine, where hunting eiders had been popular, extended the closed season on eiders through 1932. The recovery was slow. In the 1940s, the Maine nesting population had built to 2,100 pairs. Certainly by the 1970s, aided by improved coastal island protection, about 20,000 pairs were nesting.

Adults and eggs are commonly taken under substance harvests in the Alaska and Canada, but these harvests have been difficult to quantify. High harvests in west Greenland, where 90% Northern Eider can occur, may not be sustainable, despite recent regulation, international cooperation, and some local population increases. (And for other related Canadian harvest issues and the status of down harvest, see Population and Conservation.)

The classic eider hunt either takes place on picturesque rocky coastlines on days with biting winds and salt spray filling the sky, or they occur several miles from shore with converted lobster boats setting up smaller hunting vessles and a large decoy spreads. Eiders are most frequently hunted in Nova Scotia and Maine from half-tide ledges. Knowing the daily feeding habits of the local flocks in relation to the ever-shifting tides is key to a successful eider hunt. Lumbering flocks readily change coarse in response to a string of sea-duck decoys.

Just like other sea ducks, they are susceptible to being over-hunted in a region, and their populations are in long-term decline. With the popularity of sea duck hunting on the rise, harvest numbers may no longer be at a sustainable level. Bag limits are dropping in some states, a trend that will likely continue.

POPULATION AND CONSERVATION

Common Eider has been exploited throughout its range. The population on the Atlantic coast was nearly extirpated after excessive commercial hunting for valuable eider down in the nineteenth century. (Curiously, the specific name, *mollissima*, derives from the superlative of Latin, mollis, very soft.) The Migratory Bird Treaty in 1916 offered a blanket of safeguards, with special protection for eiders. While the Atlantic population has made an incredible recovery, it still faces hunting pressure and habitat threats. At some Canadian locations (e.g., places in Newfoundland and Labrador), there are excessive and illegal hunts and even selling of harvested Common Eiders, despite efforts to curtail these activities.

Local threats include those to ducklings and smaller eiders, especially by gulls and Bald Eagles.

They are threatened by chronic oil contamination near international shipping lanes, unknown affects of bio-accumulation of toxins (including heavy metals), habitat degradation (caused in part by the increase in recreational use of islands and inshore waters), commercial fishing (the large-scale harvest of blue mussels and sea urchins in Maine and being drowned in gill nets) and the subsistence harvest (including eggs) in parts of Canada and Alaska. They also have remarkably high rates of lead shot embedded in their bodies. About 50% of nesting females in southern Labrador had pellets in their body, indicating they were surviving cripples.

The commercial harvest of eiderdown has a rich history and has been conducted in parts of eastern Canada for about six decades. It is not detrimentally impacting the populations there. (The harvest must take place during the nesting season, while the female is incubating.) This takes place on the Lower North Shore in Quebec (in the St. Lawrence Estuary) and less-so in northern Quebec (at islands dotting the Nunavik coast) and occasionally in Nunavut (e.g., Belcher Islands).

Outbreaks of avian cholera have hit nesting colonies of Common Eider in eastern Canada and Maine. These have been attributed to high nesting densities.

Common Eider joins the other sea ducks on the list of species in long-term decline. The Sea Duck Joint Venture regards the Dresser's Eider among its highest-priority sea ducks, right after the scoters and Long-tailed Duck. The remaining populations are declining. The total continental population, according to the NAWMP, averaged (2002-2011) at over 1.2 million: 300,000 Dresser's, 550,000 Northern, 150,000 Pacific, and 260,000 Hudson Bay.

Finally, the consequences of climate change for this and other Arctic-favoring species need to be pursued. For Common Eider, this includes a potential shift in shellfish distribution, since this duck is tightly associated with mussel distribution, adapted as it is to cold waters.

Harlequin Duck

HADU *Histrionicus histrionicus*

Plates Page 214

OTHER COMMON OR REGIONAL NAMES
Harley, sea mouse, squeeker
(Arctic: cetuskaraq [YK], sagvaq'tifmiaq, [NS, NWS], sabvaq'siuyuk [NWS], tulajun [N])
(Québec: arlequin plongeur)

MEASUREMENTS
Length: Male – 16.2-21.2 in, av 18.7 in (47.5 cm); Female – 14.6-17.2 in, av 15.9 in (40.4 cm)

Wing: Male – av 7.7 in (19.6 cm); Female – av 7.4 in (18.9 cm)

Weight: Male – av 1.44 lbs (653 g); Female – av 1.22 lbs (553 g)

Bill: Male – av 27.5 mm; Female – av 25.6 mm

FIRST IMPRESSIONS
Harlequin Ducks are boldly patterned little ducks that thrive in turbulent water. They are often found in small groups in near-shore coastal waters and in mountain streams where they breed. On coasts, these compact ducks may frequent breakwaters and jetties, rocky areas, and even sunken shipwrecks. They dive with their wings out and buoyantly pop to the surface like corks. Both sexes have stubby bills, oval-shaped heads with steep foreheads, thick muscular-looking necks, and long tails.

This sea duck is structurally unique with its steep, rounded forehead, stubby bill, and chunky body. The male has an obvious clown-like appearance for which the species is named (*histrionicus* comes from Latin and histrionic, related to histrio, a stage-player).

Male Harlequin Ducks appear dark overall with strikingly bold white markings, particularly about the head. In good light, the male's blue-gray tones above and chestnut sides are obvious, but at a distance or in poor light these patterns become diffuse and appear dark overall. Females appear dark brown, but with a couple of bold spots or pale areas about the face. First-year males appear more subdued than adult males, particularly about the head, and they have brownish wings. Size and shape: These small Harlequin Ducks have a unique structure with a compact body and long tail. They have an oval-shaped head with a steep forehead and bulging mane. Flight: Females can resemble female Buffleheads given their small body and short wings, but Harlequin Ducks have darker wings. Harlequins have stubby wings, rounded bodies, and long tails. Their wings are entirely dark, except adult males, which have small white spots on a few coverts. Females often appear dark overall; their whitish belly and white facial patterns are often not noticeable in flight. They tend to fly in small flocks, often tightly packed, low over the water, and are generally seen moving short distances between feeding areas. They have wickedly fast, stiff wingbeats.

ID: IN DEPTH AND SIMILAR SPECIES
Harlequin Ducks do not breed until they are two years old or older; first-year birds, particularly males, can be readily picked out in the field.

Ducklings are dark gray above and white below with a big white cheek patch and a few white spots on back and sides. The tail is relatively long or tapered. The legs are dark gray; the dark gray bill has a brownish-pink nail. Juvenile plumage starts to grow at 2-3 weeks old and is fully grown by 6 weeks. It is lighter brown than adult females, with poorly defined pale spots on the head. First-years replace variable amounts of juvenile plumage starting in late fall, or as early as late September, continuing through March. This molt includes only body feathers (no replacement of wing or tail). The timing and extent of this molt is highly variable.

First-year females are often difficult to separate from adult females, but if they are hauled out on sea-rocks, look for patches of juvenile plumage on the belly of first-years. They replace a portion of their juvenile body plumage from September-March. They also molt body feathers from June-August before undergoing wing molt. This is followed by a body molt into adult plumage. On average, the head pattern may be more pronounced on adult females and they are a shade darker brown overall. Adult females molt some body feathers from May-July when they reach the breeding grounds. After breeding, they molt their wing feathers and are flightless for about 4.5 weeks, followed by a body molt. These molts span from August-October. Non-breeding females molt primarily in August, whereas breeding females molt in September. They retain that plumage until they reach the breeding grounds the following the spring.

First-year males start off the fall in a dark brown juvenile plumage and molt into a duller version of an adult-like plumage from September to March. By mid-December, they typically are readily recognizable males. To separate them from adult males, look for retained juvenile feathers on the breast and belly. Their color patterns are not as crisp and bright as adult males. Some second-year males (two year olds) do not obtain a perfect adult plumage; they still have some brown feathers mixed into their otherwise chestnut sides. Adult males are colorful with their distinctive bold patterns that lead to their name "Harlequin," coming from the comedic and nimble characters of traditional French comedy and pantomime. After breeding, adult males begin molt of body feathers into eclipse plumage upon arrival to the molting grounds from mid-June to July. Eclipse males are very dark overall with small white patches on the face similar to females. Look for remnants of the breeding plumage, such as white on the scapulars or a white line on the breast. They molt their wing feathers simultaneously and, like adult females, are flightless for about 4.5 weeks, followed by a body molt, a process that cumulatively spans August-October.

Similar species: The bold head pattern of Harlequin Ducks is unique for males and females. But at a distance in flight, female-plumaged birds may resemble Bufflehead in size and shape, particularly when they are too far away to see any head pattern. A Harlequin Duck is thicker-necked than Bufflehead with a darker body, and longer, pointed tail. Also, the Harlequin Duck is smaller in overall size, with a smaller bill and steeper forehead than any female scoters. A chunky body, proportionally tiny bill, spots on the face, and proportionally longer tail will quickly separate a female Harlequin Duck from a female Black Scoter.

Sex ratio: The Eastern population is, essentially even. In the West, the males are dominant at about 60%.

YEAR IN THE LIFE

Harlequin Ducks can be fairly common in certain parts of North America, Iceland, and Eastern Asia. There are significantly more Harlequin Ducks on the West Coast than on the East Coast. In winter, they are rare on the Great Lakes and extremely rare south to Florida and on the Gulf Coast of Texas. One of the largest concentrations is 12,000-15,000 individuals. They gather in the Strait of Georgia between Vancouver Island and mainland British Columbia. Smaller numbers winter farther south to northern California, and very few individuals have wandered south to southern California and Baja California.

Harlequin Ducks winter in near-shore, shallow intertidal zones of rocky coastlines where they can often be seen hauled out on the rocks, resting.

Both males and females are highly faithful to wintering sites, and, unlike most other ducks, Harleys are known to reunite with their mate year after year each fall or winter. Courtship activities begin in October, but well established pairs often do not partake in the rituals. The most common display is head-nodding; the male flips his bill upward with his neck outstretched. Bachelor males will test established pairs, rushing the female and perform head-nodding. Studies have shown that males that complete their molt earliest are most likely to attract a female. Males guard their mates very closely on the wintering and breeding grounds. Watch for them scurrying across the surface of the water chasing rival males away during aggressive encounters. Even some paired females will guard their mates vigorously.

In spring, Harlequin Ducks move inland —and/or northward — from the coasts, departing April to mid-May (East) and late march for mid-May (West). But nonbreeders will often remain along the coast throughout the year.

Harlequin Ducks breed in areas where there are clear, fast-flowing mountain streams and rivers. Some females breed in their second-year, although nest success is low until their fifth-year. For younger males, finding a mate may take considerable time; some acquire mates in their second year, although most form their first pair bonds in their third year or older. Both males and females show strong fidelity to their breeding sites. Females tend to brood for at least a couple weeks, but the point at which she abandons the young is variable; some females leave brood before fledging, but others lead them to wintering grounds.

Molt-migration of males starts in late June. Harlequin Ducks return to same sites to molt each year. In the East, males and immature females molt in several specific locations, including parts of Labrador, eastern Quebec, and even Greenland. Molting sites of females are uncertain, though some molt on the wintering grounds in Maine. In the West, molt sites are more widespread than in the East. Breeding females molt at same locations as males and immature females, but typically 4-8 weeks later.

In fall, males gather before departing for the coast. The first males arrive in southwest British Columbia and south-central Alaska in late May through July. Females appear in July-September, and young show up in late July-August, reaching southwest British Columbia coast in August, late July in south-central Alaska. In the East, the schedule occurs about a month later.

GEOGRAPHIC VARIATION

No subspecies are recognized, but there are two distinct populations: one in eastern and one in western North America. While these populations are genetically isolated, there is little genetic difference between them, and they are morphologically the same.

SOUNDS

Harlequin Ducks are vocal for sea ducks. Listen for their high-pitched nasal squeak, a mouse-like *gia*, which is commonly given by both sexes. The pitch and intensity vary depending on the social context. Females: Give harsh *ek-ek-ek* when looking for a brood or mate. Also, utters lower, softer squeak during aggressive interactions and with her brood.

DIET AND FEEDING BEHAVIOR

The Harlequin Duck diet consists almost entirely of animal matter. During the breeding season, the young and adults eat aquatic insects and also insect larva from rocky bottoms. (Some studies have shown that where there are fish in streams and rivers where these ducks breed, the competition for food impacts the Harlequin Ducks negatively.) In the winter, they dramatically shift, eating a variety of animals, including amphipods, snails, small crabs, barnacles, and, occasionally, fish. This diet is more varied than that of other sea ducks. Some mollusks preferred by this species are rarely consumed by other sea ducks, since the mollusks are attached so firmly to rocks as to make them difficult to loosen. Harlequin Ducks dive into the water with their wings open and are able to maneuver with great agility in turbulent water. The depth of their dives is usually under 15 feet. Occasionally, Harlequin Ducks will also dabble.

NESTING

Site: By swift-flowing streams and rivers, in forested, alpine, arctic and subarctic habitats, on the ground on rocky islands, banks, cliff ledges, tree cavities, or on stumps, usually less than 16 feet from water and concealed in thick shrub cover.

Nest description: A hollow, lined with little plant material (grass and dry leaves) and with down and feathers. Down tufts are light brown with pale centers. Size of nest is variable, with an outside diameter of 8-11 inches, and an inside diameter of c. 5 inches, usually depending on the cavity or opening dimensions.

Clutch size: Average 5-6, occasionally 3-9.

Egg description: Subelliptical to elliptical. Pale creamy to pale buff. 58 X 43 mm.

Incubation duration: 27-29 days.

Brood parasitism: Not reported in North America, but occurs where nesting is denser, such as in Iceland.

HUNTING

Harleys are trophy ducks; they are tightly regulated, given that hunting may significantly impact the population. In eastern Canada, the hunting season began closing in 1987 in some provinces, and was completely shut by 1990. This is when the entire eastern population was estimated near 1,000. In the eastern U.S., the season was shut by 1990. It remains shut for the Atlantic Flyway.

Small numbers are hunted annually in the West primarily in Alaska (c. 1,200 birds) and western Washington (c. 100 birds). The subsistence harvest in Alaska is not large (c. 2,200 birds). In response to concerns about low abundance, both Washington and British Columbia established a series of sequential limitations on bag limits, starting in the late 1990s.

Harlequin Ducks are easily attracted to decoys mimicking their own kind, which is not too surprising given that they are a relatively tame species and social by nature. Decoys are usually placed over areas where these wild birds feed, exceptionally close to shore. The ducks move from feeding site to feeding site, so being near their food source, such as a bed of mussels, is key. Favored hunting locations include Kodiak Island, Alaska, and the Puget Sound region of Washington.

POPULATION AND CONSERVATION

Harlequin Duck populations are relatively small and probably declining, but there aren't any comprehensive population surveys. Harlequin Ducks also have a very specific habitat needs and are not readily adapting to changes in the environment. Overall, their range is shrinking because of local extirpations on the breeding grounds. The eastern population is listed under SARA in Canada as a Species of Special Concern. Many studies are underway to better understand and conserve this imperiled species.

Historical information indicates that the eastern population may have peaked at about 5,000-10,000 before it began to decline due to hunting and other pressures. The population estimate was under 1,000 by 1989, at which point hunting in the East was banned. The eastern population is slowly recovering. Winter estimates were just under 1,800 in 2007, but total breeding population may be closer to 4,000 birds. More optimistic numbers suggest 5,000-10,000 birds wintering in Greenland, many of which originate from breeding areas in eastern Canada, and up to 3,500 birds wintering in North America.

The West Coast population hosts the majority of the continent's Harlequin Ducks, with an estimated population of 200,000-300,000.

Harlequin Ducks are threatened by human disturbance and habitat loss on their breeding, molting, and wintering habitats, which is taking its toll. The West Coast population is particularly threatened by development pressure in the Strait of Georgia (near Vancouver) and disturbance from recreational activities.

Harlequin Ducks are slow to mature, have low reproductive capabilities and a very low rate of dispersal, which are limiting factors to population growth or recovery after high mortality in an area, such overharvest or a disaster like an oil spill. While all sea ducks are susceptible to harm from oil spills, Harleys can be especially vulnerable; their nearshore foraging behavior can expose them to oil residue long after the initial spill.

Thousands were lost from Alaska's Prince William Sound population in 1989 after the Exxon-Valdez oil spill. The death toll was not only from the initial mortality, but as benthic feeders, the birds continued to be exposed to oil residing on the bottom. A quarter of a century after the disaster, the population had yet to rebound to pre-spill numbers.

Black Scoter

BLSC *Melanitta americana*

Plates Page 218

OTHER COMMON OR REGIONAL NAMES
American scoter, common scoter, singing scoter, black coot, sea coot, black duck, yellow nose, scoter
(Arctic: kukumyaraq [YK], kukumyeq [NS], tuunbaabrupiaq [NWS])
(Québec: macreuse noire)
(Mexico: negreta negra)

MEASUREMENTS
Length: Male – 18.0-20.9 in, av 19.7 in (50.0 cm); Female – 17.0-19.0 in, av 18.5 in (47.0 cm)
Wing: Male – av 9.0 in (22.9 cm); Female – av 8.7 in (22.1 cm)
Weight: Male – av 2.50 lbs (1134 g); Female – av 2.20 lbs (998 g)
Bill: Male –av 43.7 mm; Female – av 40.9 mm

FIRST IMPRESSIONS
In the early spring, Black Scoters are the sirens of coastal bays, as several males cluster around a female serenading her with their whistles. It is no accident that they have a common name, or nickname, of "singing scoter." Their particularly vocal courtship ritual and propensity to travel in masses during migration are two impressive Black Scoter behaviors. Adult males are all black with an orange knob on their bill. Females and first-year males are dark-bodied with a paler gray cheek and dark cap. Size and shape: Black Scoters are a medium-sized duck, the smallest and chunkiest of the three North American scoters. They have round heads, blunt faces, and round bodies. Their tails are sometimes cocked up, like a stiff-tailed duck, or lying flat on the water. Flight: Black Scoter is a dark compact duck with a potbelly. The orange knob on the male's bill is visible at close range, but disappears quickly with distance, leaving a blunt-headed look. The female's pale cheek can be visible at great distances and is a useful mark in flight. In spring, the primaries wear to brown and become translucent. In flight, the blackish wing-linings contrast with the paler primaries. Black Scoters often travel in large flocks of hundreds or thousands, particularly during fall migration in the mid-Atlantic coast. Flocks form a ball in the front and taper out into a long, trailing line. This distinctive formation is a classic behavior of Black and Surf Scoter flocks. They tend to fly low over the water's surface. They have even wingbeats, steady on the wing.

ID: IN DEPTH AND SIMILAR SPECIES
Black Scoters are slow to mature, presumably not breeding until 2 or 3 years of age.

Ducklings are dark gray overall. They are light gray below with very dark caps and have light gray cheeks and rounded heads. Juvenile plumage is fully grown by the time they are about 8.5 weeks old and is sooty brown overall, darker on the cap. First-years replace juvenile plumage in a protracted molt from October-May. They start off replacing the head and breast, proceeding to sides and back feathers. This is variable in timing and extent and can be suspended from December-February.

First-year females are like adult females but duller with a pale belly, often becoming white by the summer. Look for light brown, retained juvenile belly feathers, which can be spotted on first-year birds even into the spring. First-year birds typically have all-dark, but not black, bills.

Adult females have dark brown bodies with a dark cap and paler gray cheeks. They have a hint of yellow-to-orange on the bill; sometimes this looks like just a line of color near the nostrils. Between April and June, they molt some head feathers and loose the strong contrast between the crown and the cheeks and the bill becomes duller to a limited amount of yellow. After breeding, adult females are flightless for 3-4 weeks during their simultaneous wing molt. Their wing molt usually begins later than males in August-September. Body molt continues from October through December.

First-year males start off the fall very brown and female-like, but by spring there is extensive black on their bodies and some yellow or orange on the top of their bills. Look for light brown, retained juvenile belly feathers, which can be spotted on first-year birds even into the spring. This pale belly can be easy to see in flight. Adult males are black with bulbous orange to yellowish knobs on the top of their bill. They sometimes have a limited body molt in the spring from late March to early May. After breeding, they undergo a molt-migration and being a complete body and wing molt. They are flightless for 3-4 weeks during their wing molt, which falls sometime between mid-July and mid-September. Body molt continues in the fall from September-December.

Similar species: Black Scoter can be difficult to separate from Surf Scoter in flight during migration when both species frequently travel together in flocks. Compared to Surf Scoter, Black has a pot-bellied appearance, shorter and more rounded wingtips, and usually shows a stronger silver flash on the underside of the primaries. One of the best ways to pick out flying Black Scoter is head shape, even when the birds are too far to see the head color pattern. The rounded head of Black Scoter that ends abruptly at a flat forehead. This is quite different from the long, sloping foreheads accentuated by the longer necks of the other two scoters. As Black Scoter primaries wear they become significantly paler a feature that is most useful in the spring (especially for adult males), and this also separates Black from the two other scoters.

Watch for their distinctive diving behavior; Black Scoters do a small leap up, wings held closed unlike other scoters, then go under. While swimming, they often rear out of the water, dip their head down, and perform a rapid series of wingbeats. Other species of scoters hold their head up when they stretch their wings.

The different landing styles of scoters are distinctive, even at distances. Black Scoters do a crash landing. They hit the water with a belly-flop, head arched back and wings staying tucked in, spraying water everywhere. Surf Scoters, on the other hand, will land more serenely with feet first and wings held pointed skyward as if waiting for applause. White-wings are intermediate.

Finally, the closely-related Common Scoter has to be considered. Refer to that species' treatment to unravel the similarities and differences.

Sex ratio: Males dominate, at an estimated 63%.

YEAR IN THE LIFE

Black Scoter is one of the most neglected North American ducks when it comes to attracting the attention of researchers. Relatively few studies have been conducted in North American. Their fall migration, however, is a spectacle that has attracted the attention of admirers and is among the most impressive and predictable bird migrations you can witness. Flocks of thousands, one right after another, for example, pass Long Island and New Jersey, heading toward their wintering grounds in a couple days in late October.

In the winter, large concentrations (over 10,000 individuals) in the East are often around Montauk Point in New York and offshore in Pamlico Sound in North Carolina. In the West, high counts are usually more in hundreds, concentrating around Homer and Kodiak Island, Alaska, and Queen Charlotte Islands in British Columbia. Black Scoters are rare in the interior and along the Gulf Coast. They are rare in southern California and Baja. During migration and wintering, Black Scoters primarily use inshore bays and inlets along the coasts. During migration, occasionally small flocks or individuals turn up on interior lakes and reservoirs.

Black Scoters have exciting courtship rituals that are most intense during spring migration but go on for much of the winter. Several males gather around a female, serenading her with whistles and propelling themselves across the surface with a series of awkward flaps, a behavior called "steaming" or "rushing," resulting in a water-spray. Other actions include an upward stretch, a tail-snap (with the tail quickly raised, neck upright, and bill horizontal), a water-flicking (using the bill to flick water), and a breast-preen. Males that win approval are chosen before they reach the breeding grounds. She will indicate her preference by a head-stretch posture, by following her mate, and by aggressive rejection toward other males. Their spring migration takes place mostly at night. Numbers peak in mid-Atlantic region in early April and in Canadian Maritime Provinces in early May. Migration begins in earlier in the west, with the onset in early March in California.

Pairs arrive on the tundra where they breed as the ice thaws. This is around the third-week of May in northern Quebec. Shortly after arrival, the female sets out to find a nest site. Females tend to their brood for several weeks, then leave them to molt before they fledge at 45-50 days old.

A molt-migration of males and some females occurs in late June. Known sites include: James and Hudson Bays for the eastern population, and bays of the Alaska Peninsula and coastal locations in western Canadian Arctic for the western population. One count on the west coast of the James and Hudson Bays was 88,700 males, July 23-24, 1977.

Fall migration begins in September, peaking in the mid-Atlantic in a short time frame from late October to early November. It peaks in British Columbia in early November. Observations suggest that males arrive on the wintering grounds before females and immatures. They tend to move in a span of several days past Avalon, New Jersey. The most-impressive days usually fall in the last week of October, regardless of weather conditions. The record single day count is 156,000 scoters (at least 48% Black) passing Avalon, New Jersey, October 26, 2007.

GEOGRAPHIC VARIATION

Black Scoter and Common Scoter of Eurasia were split as distinct species by the AOU (now AOS) in 2010.

Today, there are no subspecies of Black Scoter recognized. There are, nonetheless, two independent populations recognized and studied in North America: an eastern and western population.

SOUNDS

The constant mellow, plaintive whistling sound of the males can be heard for miles. Black Scoter is the only scoter species you are likely to hear away from the breeding grounds. Males: In late winter groups of 5-30 males follow females almost continuously giving a long, mournful whistle; a musical *cour-cour-cour-loo-cour-lour* or drawn-out *whuuuuuw*. Generally, they sound like children just learning to whistle. A less frequently given call is a rattling *tuka-tuka-tuka-tuk*. Females: Utter a *pe-e-e-e-e-e-ut* when flushed from nest, and reedy *tooooo-it-tooooo* in flight or as low growl-like call.

As with other scoters, the wings produce a strong whistling noise.

DIET AND FEEDING BEHAVIOR

When Black Scoters arrive on the breeding area, their diet will include eelgrass, muskgrass, widgeon grass, pondweeds, and algae. During migration and in winter, small flocks of Black Scoters will form around jetties and rocky points to feed mainly on animal life, including mollusks, crustaceans, and small fish. Generalists, they will feed on both bottom-surface or burrowing creatures, depending on the habitat. Blue mussel is often heavily favored. Birds feed by diving underwater, usually swallowing prey underwater, unless the food is bulky (e.g., large mollusks). The depth of the dive is usually under 20 feet, but can be as deep as 33-40 feet. Major molting sites are also characterized by an abundance of shellfish resources, especially clams and mussels.

NESTING

Site: On ground in large clumps of tundra grass, in the boreal forest/tundra zone, usually close to freshwater site by tundra pools, lakes and rivers, or coastal marsh.

Nest description: A mound with a hollow containing plant material, variable amount of down, and feathers. Approximately, 4-6 inches in height, 6-8 inches in inside diameter, 9-11 inches in outside diameter, and 4-5 inches in depth.

Clutch size: Usually 6-9, occasionally 5-10.

Egg description: Subelliptical. Smooth. Pale creamy to creamy-buff. 65 X 45mm.

Incubation duration: 27-31 days

Brood parasitism: Not documented in North America.

HUNTING

'Sea coots' are perceived to be of little interest to hunters, which possibly explains why they have been poorly studied. Even if they don't rank highly on many hunters' favorites lists, hunting is still the main source of mortality for the Atlantic Flyway population. As a result of apparent population declines, hunting is restricted in the flyway. Bag limits have been reduced by a third. Their reproductive success is variable each year and they take several years to mature, therefore, adult survival is crucial to maintaining a stable population. This means Black Scoter is exceptionally sensitive to hunting mortality because their population cannot recover quickly from overharvest in a region.

They decoy well in response to sea duck decoys and small dark flags being held up. Scoters are not particularly wary. They always come in low over the water. Winter concentrations include Pamlico Sound, North Carolina, where there is prime hunting after mid-November.

POPULATION AND CONSERVATION

Black Scoter it is both the least common of the three scoter species and the species least studied. Concern for the North American population is rising due to contaminants in the food chain, both subsistence and sport hunting pressures along the Atlantic Flyway, slow reproductive potential (as with other sea ducks), susceptibility to oil spills (particularly around large molting and wintering concentrations), chronic oil pollution, human disturbance, and the degradation of food recourses from oil exploration. Also, increased mussel harvests lead to a diminishing food supply.

In the Atlantic Flyway, juvenile-to-adult harvest ratios raise some concern, with 0.3 juveniles shot for every adult in 2014, suggesting declining breeding success or an increase in adult female mortality.

The Sea Duck Joint Venture regards Black Scoter as one of its four highest-priority species (the scoters and Long-tailed Duck).

It is very difficult to survey scoters on the breeding grounds and most winter surveys lump all three species of scoter together. Therefore, there are insufficient population estimates to determine the species status, but it is believed to be gradually declining. The total continental population for Black Scoter, according to the NAWMP (2012), was averaged (2002-2011) at half a million birds, with 200,00 in the western population and 300,000 in the eastern population. Still, these numbers are rough, but the estimates do indicate declines in both populations.

Common Scoter

COSC *Melanitta nigra*

Plates Page 231

OTHER COMMON OR REGIONAL NAMES
(Québec: macreuse noire)

MEASUREMENTS
Length: Male – c. 22.5 in (57.2 cm); Female – 20.4 in (51.9 cm)

Wing: Male – av 9.3 in (23.6 cm); Female – av 9.0 in (22.8 cm)

Weight: Male – av 2.42 lbs (1100 g); Female – av 2.09 lbs (950 g)

Bill: Male –av 47.5 mm; Female – av 43.4 mm

FIRST IMPRESSIONS AND SIMILAR SPECIES
This mega-rarity most closely resembles Black Scoter. The Common Scoter male has a larger knob at the base of its bill, which is black, and the bill itself has a broad central yellow patch, opposed to the orange-yellow knob present on the Black Scoter. Females and first-year males are dark-bodied with a paler gray cheek and dark cap and are very difficult to separate from female and first-year Black Scoter.

Observers should also look for finer bill details, orbital-ring color, and the impression of comparative bulk in the water.

The nail at the end of the bill in Common Scoter is thinner and, on average, less decurved than that of Black Scoter. This subtle difference is true of many females as well as males. (It is also good to know that female Common Scoters rarely show the yellow in the bill that all adult female Black Scoters show.) The orbital ring in Common Scoter regularly shows a yellowish or orange-yellow color, and is slightly thicker. First-year male Common Scoter lacks the orange bill protrusion of Black Scoter. But they, like females, are very difficult to distinguish from Black Scoters. Darker feathers surround the base of the bill on both sexes.

Size and shape: Common Scoters are similarly-sized to Black Scoters, but structurally there are several subtle differences. Common Scoter tails are more pointed and longer; they are sometimes held cocked up. Common Scoters also appear sleeker on the water among Black Scoters. Part of that perceived difference is attributed to Black's tendency to "ride higher" in the water. Commons have noticeably longer necks, and their heads appear smaller, also adding to a sleeker appearance. Commons, particularly female-types, have a steeper forehead emphasized by a narrower-based bill (with a straight culmen). This creates a very different look, even at a distance.

Flight: Like Black Scoter, Common Scoter is a dark compact duck with a potbelly. In close comparison, the head and neck shape in flight can be very helpful for all sexes. Common has a slimmer or thinner head and neck; Black appeared larger-headed and thicker-necked. Under ideal circumstances the wingtips of Common appear more pointed than those of Black Scoter.

Similar Species: See additional comments about other scoters under Black Scoter.

Sex ratio: Males dominate.

BACKGROUND AND TIPS
Confusion in identifying Common Scoter and Black Scoter is understandable. They were alternately considered separate species, then, in the early 20th century, considered conspecific, only to be split again in 2010.

Common Scoter, is found across the Palearctic. It winters in northwestern Europe – including Baltic Sea, North Sea, and some around Iceland (where some also breed). Our own Black Scoter is now recorded annually from northwest Europe, always with flocks of Common Scoter. But the opposite is not true! Common Scoter has thus far only been recorded twice in North America, curiously in Northern California (2015) and Oregon (2016). But it is likely that careful inspection along the East Coast in winter will turn up more.

The northwest European population is estimated at 1,600,000 birds, a majority of which winters in the Baltic. Populations in some areas are in serious decline.

SOUNDS
The main vocalization of Common Scoter is a series of short single repeated notes, *pju* or *pjut*, also described as *pee-peeu*. This is quite different from the drawn-out mellow or plaintive whistles of Black Scoter: higher in pitch and four to seven times shorter. Their wings also whistle.

DIET AND FEEDING BEHAVIOR
In winter, when we might be lucky enough to find one, Common Scoters feed principally on animal life, mainly marine mollusks, in locations where animal food is abundantly available. They feed by diving; the depth of the dive can be as deep as 33-44 feet, but usually shallower.

Surf Scoter
SUSC *Melanitta perspicillata*

Plates Page 222

OTHER COMMON OR REGIONAL NAMES
Skunkhead, skunk-head coot, sea coot, horsehead, horsehead coot, candy-bill, scoter
(Arctic: tuungaagruk [NS], tuunbaabruk [NWS])
(Québec: macreuse à front blanc)
(Mexico: negreta de nuca blanca, negreta de marejada)

MEASUREMENTS
Length: Male – 18.0-20.9 in, av 19.7 in (50.0 cm); Female – 17.0-19.0 in, av 18.5 in (47.0 cm)
Wing: Male – av 9.5 in (24.1 cm); Female – av 8.9 in (22.6 cm)
Weight: Male – av 2.20 lbs (998 g); Female – av 2.00 lbs (907 g)
Bill: Male – av 35.8 mm; Female – av 38.8 mm

FIRST IMPRESSIONS
These dark ducks can have an almost sinister look with their pale eyes and strange bills as they patrol harbors and bays. Another very different impression can suggest a clown-like look for the male of this fascinating species. In any case, males can be obvious (*perspicillata* comes from the Latin, meaning conspicuous or spectacular). First-years and females have a motley appearance, but males are quite striking with their colorful bills. As a gregarious species, Surf Scoters are often in large flocks mixed with other scoters during migration and winter. Adult males are black with a white patch on the nape and a very colorful bill. Females are dark brown with a capped appearance and a couple of pale patches about the face. Size and shape: Surf Scoter has a large, pointed head. Their bill is thick at the base and where it protrudes from the head, then it tapers to a tip. The general shape is long-bodied and long necked. The size is larger than Black Scoter but smaller than White-winged Scoter. Flight: The body is plump and rounded in the undercarriage, with the weight toward the rear, and with a short tail. With a long and slim neck, pointed head, and slim wings angled back and pointed, the Surf Scoter has a sleek look. At close distances, the white on the males' head is visible, but it can be surprisingly hard to see. Their wings and body appear dark overall, although first-years have paler bellies. Surf Scoter migrates along the East Coast in large flocks often with hundreds or thousands of Black Scoter and fewer White-wingeds. Flock formations are distinctive and irregular with a mass of birds at the front with a long tail of trailing lines, sort of tadpole-shaped. Flocks and trailing lines are usually not high off the water's surface. Wingbeats are strong and steady.

ID: IN DEPTH AND SIMILAR SPECIES
Surf Scoters take a couple years to mature. They often breed in their second or third year. With a good view, most Surf Scoters can be readily aged and sexed.

Ducklings have dark gray overall on the upperparts and whitish below. They have dark faces, small light gray cheek patch and angular-shaped heads. Juvenile plumage is fully-grown at about 55 days. Juvenile plumage is dark brown, darkest on the cap with two smudgy white patches on the face and no hint of whitish nape patch. First-years replace juvenile body plumage from October to May. They often retain their juvenile belly feathers, which contrast with darker side and back feathers. From July-October, first-years molt all their body and wing feathers, attaining their first adult plumage.

First-year females are separated from adult females by their contrastingly pale juvenile belly feathers and the presence of any other faded juvenile feathers. Adult females begin body molt in spring, continuing through summer. They are flightless during their wing molt for 4-5 weeks, which usually begins in August and finishes up in late summer or fall. The body is a dark brown with a pronounced darker cap. The bill is blackish-gray. The forward of the two white patches on the face is larger, vertically-shaped, and close to the bill; the second is smaller and on the auricular. She will often have a whitish patch on the nape. She has a squared-off feathered edge at the base of the bill, subtly different from the more extensive feathered area between the bill and the eye in White-winged Scoter.

First-year males are readily picked out in the winter and spring by their mottled appearance as they transition from brown to mostly black with some white on the nape. Their bill becomes brighter throughout the winter, but is always duller than the adult male's bill. Look for paler plumage on the belly. Adult males are black with a white patch on the forehead and nape. Their bill is stunning with deep red, orange and white tones. Their eyes are white. Adult males have a very limited (if at all) molt in the spring from March-May. After breeding, they undergo a limited molt into eclipse plumage. Eclipse males have duller soft part colors, sooty feathers on the forehead and white patch on the back of the head only. Once they arrive on the molting grounds, they undergo a simultaneous wing molt and are flightless for 4-5 weeks. After wing molt, they replace their body feathers from September-November and attain their bright plumage once again.

Similar species: Surf Scoters are most likely to be confused with Black or White-winged Scoter. Shape (especially head shape) and the color pattern of the face are a great way to separate confusing females and immature males. White-winged Scoters have a more evenly tapered, triangular head that slopes into the bill. Black Scoters have a more rounded head and bill that looks like a separate unit. Surf Scoter has a thick bill at the base that awkwardly protrudes from the head. Beware of some first-winter females that can have pale cheeks like Black Scoter; head shape is a great way to separate these birds.

In flight, Surf Scoters are noticeably smaller than White-winged Scoter, which is reflected in faster wingbeats. They also lack the white wing patches on the wing. Separating Surf and Black Scoter in flight can be more difficult. At closer ranges, you can see color patterns, for example the pale cheek of a female Black Scoter or the white nape of a male Surf Scoter, which is helpful. At a distance or in poor light, Black Scoter has a much more centered, pot-bellied look than Surf Scoter, with the Surf Scoter's weight farther back in the undercarriage. Surf also has more pointed wings; the wings look sweptback and come to a point, unlike a broader, more rounded look of Black Scoter wing shape. Surf Scoter may appear lankier than Black Scoter. Also, by spring, the primaries on male Black Scoters have worn to brown and the brown primaries contrast with blacker body feathers. If you can see the legs and feet of Surf Scoter, they will be orangish, not dark, like in Black Scoter. Finally, when landing on the water, Surf Scoter will tend to have its wings held pointing skyward, not at a 45-degree angle like a White-winged Scoter.

Sex ratio: Strong male-dominance, at about 66%.

YEAR IN THE LIFE

Surf Scoters are an exclusively North American duck. Their breeding and wintering range is entirely within the U.S., Canada, and northwestern Mexico. Surf Scoters didn't capture the attention of waterfowl biologists until the mid-1980s when many aspects of their natural history were described for the first time. They are common on the coasts in winter, most numerous on the West Coast, rare in the Gulf Coast and interior U.S. They are extremely rare in the United Kingdom and Greenland.

Some of the largest wintering concentrations are along the Pacific Coast, including Alexander Archipelago in southeast Alaska, Vancouver Island in British Columbia, and San Diego in California. On the East Coast they congregate in the Chesapeake Bay and Pamlico Sound and to a lesser extent the Delaware Bay.

Winters in bays, estuaries and saltwater habitats less than 35 feet deep, often with pebble or sandy bottom. Pair bonds form on the wintering grounds and staging areas. Courtship rituals can be intricate. The male may adopt a sentinel posture (swimming back and forth and dipping his bill in the water occasionally), breast-scooping (lateral head-shaking and breast-preening), tail-lifting, and a unique chest-lifting (with head thrown back and chest out of the water). There is also a fly-away display, which involved stretching the neck and raising the wings upon landing. Females will respond in mutual chin-lifting. These pair bonds may last for more than one season.

In spring, Surf Scoter migration takes place mostly overland at night. It kicks off in March and peaks in April. A large portion of the eastern population stages in the St. Lawrence gulf from late April to mid-May as they head toward the breeding grounds.

Surf Scoters reach their breeding grounds in May. They nest on shallow lakes, often with rocky shores. Females usually leave their brood before they are able to fly, which is when they are about 55 days old. Broods often join together, forming crèches.

Males abandon their incubating mates and undergo a molt-migration to coastal salt-water habitats. Those heading to the East Coast congregate along Labrador coast and St. Lawrence estuary and gulf. The majority of West Coast scoters molt in coastal British Columbia and Alaska, some go to the Bering and Beaufort Seas. Others molt in the Hudson Bay. Padilla Bay, Washington and the Fraser River Delta to south to Boundary Bay, British Columbia hosts 10,000 molting scoters each year. Later in the fall, females and immatures join the males. Females end up molting their wings on average three-four weeks later.

Fall movements on Atlantic coast can be incredible because they travel in large flocks with Black Scoter and in a narrow window of time. A cold front bringing northwest winds can push the majority of the eastern population to their wintering grounds. Migration begins in late August, peaking in early November in California and late October in the mid-Atlantic. Record single day count 156,000 scoter (at least 43% Surf) passed Avalon, New Jersey, on October 25, 2007. Numbers build on the wintering grounds build in from late October through November as migrants arrive.

GEOGRAPHIC VARIATION

No subspecies are recognized.

SOUNDS

Surf Scoters are a quiet species that usually only vocalize during courtship and when females are defending their broods. Males: Give a liquid, gurgling call, explosive *puk-puk* during breast-scooping display. A guttural croaking, *krrraak krrraak* is given during the chin-lifting display as a threat. Females: Utter a harsh, crow-like *crahh* when defending their broods.

DIET AND FEEDING BEHAVIOR

Surf Scoters dive to feed on mollusks, especially younger and smaller blue mussels, on the wintering, molting, and staging grounds. (Adults on the Great Lakes are known to eat the invasive zebra mussels.) Like Black Scoters, and unlike White-winged Scoters, they are generalists; they feed on both bottom-surface or burrowing creatures, depending on the habitat. They will feed in flocks in bays, estuaries, and saltwater habitats up to about 33 feet deep, but usually under 16 feet and usually over pebble or sand substrate. When feeding, most flocks will dive synchronously and surface simultaneously. They eat herring eggs if available during spring migration, particularly on the West Coast. On the breeding grounds, they switch and feed on freshwater invertebrates. At molting sites, they prefer shellfish, especially clams and mussels.

NESTING

Site: On the ground by ponds, lakes (often with rocky shores), and rivers, mostly in wooded and open boreal forests, but also in boggy and tundra areas. The nest site will usually be sheltered by surrounding vegetation.

Nest description: A hollow lined with a little plant material, down, and some feathers.

Clutch size: 6-8 eggs, occasionally 5-10. The nest size averages 7 inches in inside diameter, 12 inches in outside diameter, and 2 inches in depth.

Egg description: Subelliptical to oval. Pale creamy to creamy-buff. Smooth and slightly glossy. 66 x 46 mm.

Incubation duration: Estimated at 27-31, has not been thoroughly studied.

Brood parasitism: Very rare, if it occurs at all.

HUNTING

Skunkheads are primarily hunted as a trophy duck on their wintering grounds these days. Historically, scoter hunting was a big business on the Atlantic coast.

The number taken each year has been dropping, which may actually be key to sustaining their populations. Surf Scoter is exceptionally sensitive to adult mortality from overhunting, and they recover very slowly under those circumstances. The annual take averages 25,000-30,000, with 80-90% of it occurring on the Atlantic Flyway.

Surfs decoy well in response to sea duck decoys and dark flags held up. They are not particularly wary. Winter concentrations include Pamlico Sound, North Carolina, where there is prime hunting after mid-November. Also, around commercial mussel beds in Washington State in the Puget Sound.

POPULATION AND CONSERVATION

Traditional survey techniques are not well-suited for monitoring scoters, so there is not precise long-term set of population estimates. In western North America, all three scoter species have declined 50% since the 1950s, but for reasons that are poorly understood. Changes in wintering areas including developments for energy, shellfish aquaculture, heavy metal contamination from industry and oil spills could be playing a role. The condition and affects of global warming of the boreal forest where they breed could be attributed to their decline. Scoters molting in southern British Columbia and Washington are also subject to great human disturbance during their wing molt.

The Sea Duck Joint Venture regards Surf Scoter as one of its four highest-priority species (the three scoters and Long-tailed Duck).

There have been fewer immatures harvested each year since the 1960s, which is indicative of decreasing breeding success or an increase in adult female mortality. Efforts are underway to better understand and monitor sea duck populations, which will hopefully lead to effective management strategies in the future.

The rough North American population estimate is 600,000 to 1.0 million birds, with a 2012 NAWMP figure averaging at 700,000. These estimates are admittedly poor, especially since this species' breeding range is incompletely surveyed.

White-winged Scoter
WWSC *Melanitta fusca*

Plates Page 226

OTHER COMMON OR REGIONAL NAMES
White-wing, white-winged coot, sea coot scoter
(Arctic: uyufiaqtuyuut [NS], killalik [NWS])
(Québec: macreuse à ailes blanches, macreuse brune)
(Mexico: negreta de ala blanca)

MEASUREMENTS
Length: Male – 20.7-23.0 in, av 21.6 in (54.9 cm); Female – 19.0-23.6 in, av 20.6 in (52.3 cm)

Wing: Male – av 11.1 in (28.2 cm); Female – av 10.5 in (26.7 cm)

Weight: Male – av 3.50 lbs (1288 g); Female – av 2.60 lbs (1179 g)

Bill: Male – av 43.5 mm; Female – av 40.5 mm

FIRST IMPRESSIONS
White-winged Scoter is a huge black sea duck with a large patch of white in the wing, which can often be seen while on the water. The birds tend to be seen in small groups flying low over oceans, the Great Lakes, or large coastal bays. They have a distinctive dive, flicking their wings open as they go underwater. Males are black with an inverted white comma under their eyes and pink-tipped bills. The eye-patch, head shape, and thick neck can give this scoter a particularly "mean" look. They have a white patch of secondaries in all plumages and ages. Females are a dark brown with pale patches on the face. They lack the dark contrasting caps and paler faces of the two other female scoters. Size and shape: Note the big head, bulbous bill, thick neck, and chunky body. This scoter's head is long and pointed, concave from the forehead to the bill. Flight: Robust – a big-bodied, thick-necked and broad-winged duck. Their body is entirely dark and the white wing patch is prominent in flight and hard to miss. First-years have paler bellies from the worn juvenile plumage. At a distance, the white secondaries begin to disappear, so their wings look very narrow. White-winged Scoters need a longer water-runway than most ducks to take off. Flocks are often strung out in irregular wavering lines, low over water, and with fewer than 20 individuals. Wingbeats are strong and steady.

ID: IN DEPTH AND SIMILAR SPECIES
White-winged Scoters take several years to mature. First-years can be readily separated from adults. They typically breed for the first time in their second or third year.

Ducklings have a white cheek with dark gray breast band and upperparts. Their underparts are white. White-wingeds are the most strongly marked of the scoter ducklings, resembling goldeneye, but separated by the shape the white patch on cheek that curves up around the ear on White-wings. Juvenile plumage is fully-grown when the young fledge at about 10 weeks old. Juveniles are browner than adults with a white patch behind the eye and a buffy-white patch in front of the eye. The brightness and shape of these patches changes as their feathers wear. First-years replace juvenile body and tail feathers throughout the fall, winter, and into spring. During the winter, the birds become increasingly mottled as new darker feathers replace the worn juvenile plumage. First-years also have contrastingly pale bellies that are worn, retained juvenile feathers that become almost whitish by the spring.

First-year females can be separated from adult females by the presence of any worn juvenile plumage, which is particularly noticeable on the belly. The head also continues to wear to lighter brown with less well-defined whitish patches during the winter and will be paler than adult female head color. Adult females are uniform dark brown in the fall and winter, at a time when many first-years have a mottled appearance and are paler on average. They have two fairly well-defined white patches on the head. Adult females have a blackish bill, sometimes with pinkish tones on the sides. They sometimes show a small bulge at the base of the bill. They have an extensive feathered area between the bill and the eye, different from the squared-off feathered edge at the base of the bill in Surf Scoter. In spring, the females begin body molt continuing through summer. Females are flightless during wing molt, which usually begins in August and finishes up 4-5 weeks later.

First-year males are brown in the fall until they replace juvenile plumage with blackish feathers. First-year males are particularly noticeable when they are acquiring blacker head feathers, and the head looks mottled with brown and black. They will often loose most of the white patch behind the eye and still have some white in front of the bill. Their body is typically still mottled with black and brown throughout the winter. They often retain brown juvenile belly feathers into the spring, feathers that get lighter as they fade throughout the year. Their pale bellies can be easy to pick out in flight. Some first-years have a small white dash around the eyes, and most acquire some pinkish color on the bills. Their eyes are often smoky gray-brown through their first winter. Adult males are velvety black with glaring white eyes with a dash of white feathers through the eye. Look carefully to notice that their sides are actually dark brown, not quite black (a feature that distinguishes the North American from Eurasian subspecies). Adult males begin body molt in spring, followed by wing molt in the summer. They are flightless for 4-5 weeks, during wing molt. Eclipse males appear similar to their plumage the rest of the year, but with duller-colored bills. They often have very worn, brown tertials or other feathers in the summer. After wing molt, they replace their body feathers in the fall, attaining a crisp black plumage once again.

Similar species: Separating a sitting scoter can be surprisingly tricky, because Surf and White-winged share pale patches on the face. These vary greatly based on time of year and with different ages and sexes. Their head shapes can appear remarkably similar. Notice that White-winged has feathers right down to the nostril, while Surf has a straight vertical line diving the bill and nearby feathers. Black Scoter has a more rounded head shape and single pale cheek patch. And White-winged has a distinctive landing with wings held at 45-degrees, as opposed to Surf Scoter which will land with wings pointed skyward.

In fight, look for white secondaries on White-winged Scoter. In some lighting conditions, the white in the wing disappears into the background and they appear extremely narrow-winged, much narrower winged than other species of scoters.

Sex ratio: Males dominate at 60-72%.

YEAR IN THE LIFE

White-winged Scoters have a nearly circumpolar breeding range with populations breeding in northern Europe and northern Asia. These sea ducks are most common in the winter in coastal regions of Atlantic and Pacific Flyways and Great Lakes region. Large wintering concentrations are found in Massachusetts, Chesapeake Bay, Puget Sound of Washington, and British Columbia. White-winged is the most abundant scoter wintering on the Great Lakes and other inland locations. They are very rare in the interior U.S. and Gulf Coast.

In the winter, White-wings dive to favoring coastal estuaries, bays, and areas with sand or gravel bottoms where there are shellfish beds. On the Great Lakes, they have increased in winter since the spread of zebra mussels, an introduced invasive species.

Pair bonds are likely to form during spring migration and pairs may reunite for multiple years, but their courtship rituals have not been well-studied. Apparently, the displays are also the most reserved of the scoters. Activities include a neck-stretching with the head and about a 65-degree angle, wing-flapping (by both sexes, perhaps to display the white secondaries), an upward stretch with bill held high, and a "false drinking," where the bill is dipped in the water and then suddenly jerked up. Females also respond with this false drinking and with chin-lifting. White-wings breed in their second or third year; a number of first-years remain near coastal areas and molt after the adults head inland.

White-winged Scoters are slow to progress through the breeding season. They are among the latest of waterfowl to migrate and initiate nesting. In late April or May, pairs reach their breeding grounds, which are typically not far from where the females were born or raised young in previous year. Nesting may even begin in mid-June. The female selects a nest site which may be identical to previous years.

After hatching, the brood has a long development period relative to other ducks. The young are finally able to fly after 63-67 days. Females normally leave their brood after one to three weeks, but the brood often remains together for another one to three weeks more and frequently join with other broods. Successful females molt while attending their brood, but females that are unsuccessful depart breeding sites early and molt. Molt-migration males would have left the incubating females during her early incubation to molt at undetermined saltwater locations.

Fall migration is underway by September, peaking in November in coastal regions, and with numbers building on wintering grounds through December.

GEOGRAPHIC VARIATION

There are three subspecies that are likely to be elevated to species status at some point and have been treated as separate subspecies in the past. *M. f. deglandi* is widespread in North America. *M. f. stejnergeri* is found in Siberia and eastern Asia and is very rare in western Alaska. *M. f. fusca* is found in Europe and western Russia. It has not been recorded in North America yet. All three subspecies are readily identifiable with distinct ranges, and there is no evidence of interbreeding.

M. f. deglandi, White-winged Scoter, differs from other subspecies by its brownish sides, primarily pinkish-red bills, and a larger white comma below eye than other subspecies. Outside of North America, *deglandi* has been recorded in Iceland and northeast Asia.

M. f. stejnegeri, Siberian or Stejneger's Scoter, is now-recorded annually in small numbers from St. Lawrence Island and less regularly from Nome, Alaska. Broader coverage in western Alaska will presumably show it to be annual in small numbers. Males have a protruding dark hump or knob on their bills, which is more prominent than White-winged Scoter. Their bill shape is so strange and large that 'Hump-nosed Scoter' is the closest English translation of their Russian name. They are also distinguished by a thin yellow line on edge of the bill, in addition to some pink and red tones like White-winged. Their sides are jet black, unlike brownish-black sides on *deglandi*. The comma under their eye is long and thin. Siberian Scoter breeds from River Yenisey east to Pacific coast of Asia. It winters in Bering Sea and northern Pacific Ocean. There are a handful of recent records from Europe.

M. f. fusca, Velvet Scoter, breeds in Europe and western Asia, east to River Yenisey. It winters off coast of Iceland and Scandinavia and is very rare in Greenland. Be alert. There is a good chance it will be found in North America someday. Male Velvet Scoter has orange-yellow along the sides of the otherwise black. Its body feathers are all black. The white dash under they eye is smaller than White-winged Scoter, more like a hyphen rather than an inverted comma. It has only a slight bump at the base of the bill. The head shape is concave from the forehead to the bill tip (think Canvasback, but not that elegant).

SOUNDS

White-winged Scoter is a very quiet species that rarely vocalizes; perhaps it is not surprising that their vocalizations are not well known. Males: May give a whistling note during their display. Females: Give a low, repeated *guck, guck, guck*. They may give a whistled note with their chin-lifting display. White-winged vocalizations are typically heard when paired females incite mates or when females alert their broods to danger, including attacking gulls and other predators. Their wings make a whistling sound which, especially when considering flocks, can be heard far away.

DIET AND FEEDING BEHAVIOR

White-winged Scoters dive up to about 40 feet in depth, but usually dive under 16 feet to feed off the bottom primarily by snatching mollusks (about 75% of all foods) and crustaceans. White-winged Scoters usually use deeper water sites farther from shore than those of Surf and Black Scoters. (In winter, White-winged Scoters usually feed at depths between 16 feet and 65 feet, but have been reported at diving depths as far as 100 feet.) White-winged Scoters have a more specialized diet — emphasizing mollusks and larger prey — than Surf and Black Scoters, both generalist foragers. Animal matter, dominated by mollusks, may take up about 95% of the White-winged Scoter diet, with plants the remaining 5%. On the Great Lakes, these scoters may congregate in areas where zebra mussels are abundant. There in winter, they have increased since the spread of zebra mussels. In breeding areas, White-winged Scoters may rely heavily on small freshwater or brackish amphipod crustaceans for their diet. They prefer shellfish resources at molting sites, but avoid mussels preferred by the other two scoter species.

NESTING

Site: On the ground in a variety of locations, from islands on freshwater lakes, in open boreal forest, brushy areas, or, more rarely, on open coastal plain, sometimes far from the water's edge. The nest is usually located under dense cover. These scoters will reuse bowls over multiple years and take over nest sites from other waterfowl.

Nest description: A hollow lined with nearby plant material, including leaves or twigs, with an inner lining of down and some feathers. Dimensions are poorly known, with few measurements: a few nest bowls have averaged 8 inches in inside diameter and about 3-4 inches deep.

Clutch size: Usually 7-9, occasionally up to 11.

Egg description: Nearly elliptical. Pale creamy to buff. Smooth and nonglossy. 67 × 46 mm. (After Common Eider, White-winged Scoter eggs are the second-largest duck eggs in North America.)

Incubation duration: 27-30 days.

Brood parasitism: Laying in "dump nest" of White-wings is common in areas with high nesting density. Interspecific parasitism has been recorded (e.g., Gadwall, Lesser Scaup, Blue-winged Teal, and Mallard).

HUNTING

Sea coots, meaning scoters in general, are not at the top of the hunters' list of prized ducks, but hunting pressure still has a significant impact on their population.

White-wings are good decoyers when the decoys are strung out. For this generation of hunters, they are hunted over decoys. Back in the "gold old days" White-wings were hunted by placing boats every 60-100 yards and pass-shooting on the "coot line." The birds are not particularly wary, but generally an inaccessible duck for most hunters these days. Traditionally White-wings are hunted primarily on the Atlantic Coast, particularly the Pamlico Sound of North Carolina, which is prime hunting after mid-November.

Annual harvest for the U.S. is about 8,500 birds; for Canada it is about 2,200 birds.

Subsistence harvest is not strongly followed, but the numbers for the mid-2000s was about 5,000 scoters in Alaska, and 3,000 in Canada. These are particularly important birds for the First Nations of Canada's western boreal forest.

POPULATION AND CONSERVATION

The population dynamics of White-winged Scoter in North America are poorly understood, partly because surveys do not differentiate between the three species of scoter. There has been a recent population decline in scoters overall, but relatively little attention has been directed toward understanding this species in particular. White-wings were formerly much more abundant and had a larger breeding range, even extending into North Dakota and southern Manitoba. (Decreases in the Canadian prairies since the 1950s may be as much as 75%.) Changes are likely due to shifting land-use and habitat loss. Climate change cannot be dismissed in this case.

Several other factors certainly affect their populations. White-winged Scoters are susceptible to some hunting pressure, mainly along the Atlantic Coast. Their population has a low recruitment rates because of low annual productivity and late maturation of young. In addition, they return to the same nesting areas each year, so disturbance in their breeding area — e.g., petrochemical development or logging — can extirpate local populations.

Generally, there is little good data to generate population estimates. Concern is widespread, and the Sea Duck Joint Venture regards White-winged Scoter among its four highest-priority species (the scoters and Long-tailed Duck). The total continental population, according to the NAWMP, is averaged (2002-2011) at 400,000.

Long-tailed Duck
LTDU *Clangula hyemalis*

Plates Page 236

OTHER COMMON OR REGIONAL NAMES
Oldsquaw, long-tail, sea pintail, cockertail, sea duck, coween, cockawee, quandy
(Arctic: aarraangiiq [YK], aahaaliq [NS, NWS], aaqhaailq [NWS], aahanngiq, ahaanliq [N])
(Québec: harelde kakawi)
(Mexico: pato colilargo)

MEASUREMENTS
Length: Male – 19.0-22.6 in, av 20.8 in (52.8 cm)*; Female – 14.8-17.2 in, average 15.6 in (39.6 cm)
Wing: Male – av 8.7 in (22.1 cm); Female – av 8.3 in (21.1 cm)
Weight: Male – av 2.11 lbs (957 g); Female – av 1.74 lbs (787 g)
Bill: Male – av 28.9 mm; Female – av 27.3 mm
*Includes up to 5 in (13 cm) of tail extension in males.

FIRST IMPRESSIONS
The clamor of wintering flocks carries for miles over open water as male Long-tailed Ducks call while holding their white heads high. Males dart after other males that are getting too close to their preferred female. These males change their plumage considerably throughout the year, but they are either very white-headed (in winter) or exceptionally dark on the front half of their body (spring and summer). Females have a white face with a dark patch behind and below the eye. Females have bluish bills. In winter, their breasts are plain light brown, back dark brown, and sides white. Size and shape: A compact sea duck with a rounded body, giving a generally dainty and elegant impression. The head is rounded, peaked in the front with a long neck and exceptionally long tail on the adult male. Females and young males are short-tailed. Flight: Long-tailed Ducks have a distinctive appearance — their black triangular wings are sweptback, and they have a long graceful trailing tail. In the winter, males are white-headed with pointy, black wings. At great distances, the males are still distinct with white heads and breasts and dark elsewhere. Long-tails land with a distinct splash, bouncing off the surface after almost hovering for a second before dropping a couple of feet into the water. For takeoff, they will run along the water. Small clusters fly low over the water in a careening flight style, rocking from side to side with quick wing beats. They look like they are moving really fast.

ID: IN DEPTH AND SIMILAR SPECIES
Long-tailed Duck breeds at two-years old, attaining their adult plumage when they are about a year old. Long-tailed Duck has a unique and complex molt strategy and their appearance changes more throughout the year than most other ducks. Another unique feature is that the number of tail feathers varies from 12-16; 90% will have 14.

Ducklings are dark gray overall with a big white cheek patch and several small white dots around the eye. This is the only North American duckling with white underparts and dark unpatterned upperparts. Juvenile plumage begins to appear 11 days after hatching and is fully grown by 5-6 weeks. Juveniles are light brown on the breast and back with gray sides. The face lacks white and has a dusky gray wash overall and a dark cap. First-years replace some juvenile plumage starting in the fall, continuing into December and obtain a largely white head. They retain their wing feathers until the following summer when they undergo their first complete wing and body molt.

Aging and sexing Long-tailed Ducks has often caused confusion, and there is still much to learn. Much of the confusion is because of the large variation in color. This is most notable on the upperparts, with some being very rufous, others being a cold brown. The scapulars are usually white or pale gray, but can be rufous or dull brown. This range of colors – some might even call morphs – is similar to other cryptic, tundra breeders such as Sanderling and Red Knot.

Females have a thin dusky crown, dark patch at the back of the white face, whitish flanks, and a brown back; but are highly variable. Between February and May, they change from their winter plumage with a mostly white face to a mostly dusky face, appearing better camouflaged for nesting. The spring molt also includes some breast, body, and back feathers.

After breeding, they molt their wing, tail, and some body feathers in late summer and fall. Adult females are flightless for about 4 weeks during wing molt in mid-August. They begin a gradual body molt in September–October, continuing into November or December; this plumage is retained until April.

First-year males in winter look much like females, but males sometimes have a whiter breast, and females always have a dark crown. Only male Long-tails attain pink in the bill; first-years typically get some pink by the middle of winter. This is the safest and easiest way to sex Long-tails. First-year males also show longer and narrower scapulars than females; adult males should be obvious.

Adult males change their plumage considerably throughout the year. There are several features present year-round: a pale gray-brown patch on the back of the face, black breast, light gray sides, fading to white undertail. In winter, they have white crowns, napes, and necks, which make their heads seems very white, even at a great distance. They have light gray backs and scapulars in winter plumage. For the breeding season, they molt into a darker plumage, obtaining a black crown, nape and neck. Their scapulars are dark-centered with broad rusty edges.

Adult males molt their scapulars a remarkable three times a year; in spring, prior to wing molt, and after wing molt. They undergo a partial body molt of their head, neck, breast and back in spring. After breeding, they head to the molting grounds for a wing molt. Adult males are flightless late July-early August for about 4 weeks. They gradual body molt begins September–October, continuing into November or December. At this time, they get their white-headed winter plumage, which they retain until March-April.

Similar species: Female is somewhat similar to female Harlequin, but look for the Harlequin's dark, sides, steep forehead, rounded head, and spotted face pattern. Female Steller's Eider is darker overall with a plain face, white-edged speculum, and curved tertials. In flight, guillemots, can actually cause confusion in the winter, as they are quick erratic fliers, and appear predominately white-headed and bodied. Look for the guillemots' bold white wing patches, unlike black wings of Long-tailed Duck.

Sex ratio: Usually male-biased, but counting is made difficult when differentiating first-year males and females. The number of males may be 51-60%.

YEAR IN THE LIFE

Long-tailed Ducks are circumpolar breeders spanning the Arctic tundra from coastal Greenland to Svalbard and the north coast of arctic Russia, U.S., and Canada. In Eurasia, they winter primarily in the Baltic Sea and Kamchatka Peninsula, Bering Strait, Japan, and northeast Korea. In North America, they are primarily in coastal areas and the Great Lakes, stretching south to Washington and Virginia. There are exceptional wintering counts on Nantucket Island in Massachusetts, upwards of 350,000. They also congregate in masses on the eastern shore of Lake Michigan and the western end of Lake Ontario.

In winter, Long-tailed Ducks occupy marine waters and large freshwater lakes, where they dive for food off or near the bottom.

Pair bonds form on the wintering grounds. Courtship displays can be very impressive, with lateral head-shaking and bill tossing (both accompanied by vocalizations), a kind of porpoising (with dips of the head and neck under the surface followed by rearing up), and rear-end display (with hindquarters raised above the water and the long tail and white rump revealed). Short flights, and heavy splashing falls, are also used and are directed toward the female, with black breast most visible. At least some pairs reunite on the wintering grounds. They breed when they are two-years old, but often unsuccessfully in the first couple of years.

During spring migration, pairs migrate north together. Thousands congregate at coastal sites in southwest Alaska during spring migration, heading inland to nest from Lancaster Sound and Baffin Bay in mid-to late June. Migration on the East Coast starts between late March and early April. Long-tailed Ducks on the West Coast begin to head north in late February. Most have departed by May in west and Great Lakes. Numbers of Long-taileds flying east observed at Point Barrow peak in early June. Peak numbers are observed on the northwest coast of the Northwest Territories and Yukon in late May. Exceptional single day counts are from the Great Lakes.

The timing of arrival on the breeding grounds depends on the availability of open water and the distance from the coast. It ranges from mid-May in southerly breeding areas to mid- to late June in northern regions. They nest on Subarctic and Arctic freshwater wetlands. The male follows the female as she picks a nest site, scrapes away any debris and lays the first egg within about an hour. The males abandon the female partway through incubation. After the young hatch, the female tends to the brood. Large crèches are common. One hen was recorded with 32 ducklings accompanying her.

Molt-migration begins in late June with a westward

movement of males along the northern Alaska coast, peaking in early July. Females move to molting grounds several weeks later. The locations of molting grounds are not well known, but concentrations have been noted around St. Lawrence Island and in coastal lagoons on west and north coast of Alaska. Many Alaskan and western Canadian breeders probably also travel to the coast of Siberia to undergo the molt; eastern birds have used the coasts north-central Nunavut and probably head off to the northwestern coast of Greenland.

Fall migration is relatively late, peaking on the U.S. Coasts and the Great Lakes in late November and December. Exceptional migration days on Lake Ontario occur two days after cold front passes. Adult males typically arrive on the wintering grounds first, starting in mid-October on Great Lakes and in British Columbia.

GEOGRAPHIC VARIATION
No subspecies are recognized.

SOUNDS
Long-tailed Ducks are among the most vocal of ducks. Heard frequently and at a distance, especially in noisy winter flocks. Males: Utter nasal, loud, yodeling, three part, *ahr-ahr-ahroulit* given mostly during courtship displays (bill-tossing and head-shaking), pair bond, and mate defense, *ahr-ahr-ahroulit*, *ahang-ahóo*, *ow owooolee*, *ow ow owoolik*, or *unk-on-alik*. Females: give *gut-gut-goo'ah-goo'ah*, when interacting with mates during bill-tossing display. Also, barking *urk* or *uk* given when potential predator is present. Both sexes: give soft *gut* or *gut-gut* when feeding, which may be a contact call.

DIET AND FEEDING BEHAVIOR
Long-tailed Ducks, with their deep-diving reputation, feed primarily on animals, and their generalist preferences will vary with local abundance. While they may usually dive to depths of 15 to 50 feet and almost regularly to 75 feet, they are among our deepest divers, having been recorded at phenomenal depths of 195-215 feet. They forage with wings partly open, but propel themselves mainly by wing propulsion. Long-tailed Ducks eat mostly crustaceans (amphipods, mysids, and isopods) when in saltwater, and, when in freshwater, they will feast on amphipods, fish, mollusks or oligochaeta worms. Since most prey items are small, they are likely consumed underwater; the larger items are brought to surface. Their diet shifts in the summer to aquatic insects, crustaceans, fish roe, and vegetable matter. At molt-sites, the birds will feed heavily on tidal crustaceans in lagoon systems. The invasion of nonnative zebra and quagga mussels into the Great Lakes has provided Long-tailed Ducks with food, but apparently not at particularly high levels.

NESTING
Site: On the ground, near freshwater, on forest edge and arctic and subarctic tundra, often concealed by vegetation or rocks. They may nest solitarily or in colonies.

Nest Description: A hollow lined with some nearby plant material (e.g., dried dwarf birch and dwarf willow leaves), down, and feathers. About 5 inches in inside diameter, 7 inches in outside diameter, and 3 inches in depth.

Clutch size: usually 5-9, occasionally up to 11.

Egg description: Subelliptical to elliptical, sometimes oval. Yellowish with a slight olive tint or greenish. 53 × 38mm.

Incubation duration: 23-25 days.

Brood parasitism: Very rare, but reported by Greater Scaup and Red-breasted Merganser.

HUNTING
Long-tailed Ducks are attracted to decoys of their own species and other sea ducks. Strings of decoys are usually floated behind boat or anchored to shore. The bird often make a single pass by decoys moving slightly off course, broadly circle or completely ignore decoys. They make a pass to investigate, but generally do not commit to the decoys. Not particularly wary of people and boats. Calling typically not practiced. Due to fishy diet in the winter, the flavor of meat ranks low among ducks, with a tough texture and excessive fishy-tasting fat. The East Coast from the Chesapeake Bay to Maine is the prime hunting zone for Long-tailed Ducks. As the challenge of sea-duck hunting grows in popularity, some New England states have established more restrictive bag limits than federal frameworks actually require.

This species is not heavily hunted by sportsmen. The harvest of Long-tailed Ducks in the U.S. over two years (2013 and 2014) averaged 21,200 birds; and for Canada the corresponding number averaged under 2,000 birds. Recent subsistence estimates are about 11,000 ducks in Alaska, and 6,000 birds in Canada (mostly in the east).

While recent harvest regulations for Long-tailed Ducks have become more restrictive, it is probably time to take an even closer examination of the issue. Long-tails and other sea ducks are not able to compensate easily from the impact of hunting mortality. Dabbling ducks and prairie pothole breeders have large clutches, breed in their first-year, often move into new breeding areas in different years, renest frequently, so they have multiple ways to recover from years of drought or harsh weather; this also allows them to recover from a substantial annual harvest. On the other hand, Long-tailed Ducks and other sea ducks don't have adaptions to recover from a heavy harvest or oil spill in a specific region or across their population, even long after stricter regulations are in place. One complicating factor in setting bag limits and management strategies is the opposition of some groups to hunting species for which crippling losses are thought to be high, and it is uncertain how many of these birds are not recovered.

POPULATION AND CONSERVATION
Little long-term monitoring has been done for sea ducks

in the Americas, partly because it is so difficult to survey their breeding and wintering grounds. Long-tailed Duck is no exception; their population trends are not well-understood and better population estimates are needed. They are not included in the traditional duck surveys conducted across the continent each year.

The Sea Duck Joint Venture regards Long-tailed Duck as one of its four highest-priority species, along with the three scoters.

Anecdotal observations and stories from the mid-twentieth century certainly indicate there has been a staggering decline in their North American population. Counts from the West Coast suggest a drastic decline; figures from the East Coast show a slight decline. The breeding population in Alaska has declined 75% since 1977. The 1999, estimate was 72,100 individuals breeding in Alaska. Midwinter inventories on Atlantic coast of U.S. also indicate serious declines. In the Atlantic Flyway, juvenile-to-adult harvest ratios raise some concern, with 0.4 juveniles shot for every adult in 2014, suggesting declining breeding success or an increase in adult female mortality.

The total continental population, according to the NAWMP, is averaging (2002-2011) at 1.0 million. Even though Long-tailed Ducks are considered to be the most abundant Arctic sea duck, this population estimate is considered to be rough.

Long-tailed Ducks are vulnerable to overhunting (heavy subsistence harvest devastating local populations), disease, oil spills, habitat loss and degradation and, histori-cally, fishing nets. Contaminants (e.g., lead, mercury, cadmium, and organochlorines) have also turned up at high levels among these ducks in eastern Canada and Alaska. One Canadian study indicated that after mergansers, Long-tailed Ducks had the highest levels of organochlorines among sea ducks.

Overhunting is a potential problem, depending on the region and local population. Dramatic over-harvesting events have certainly dropped, but, over time, so has the population of Long-tailed Ducks. A closer examination and reconsideration of bag limits may be in order, since Long-tailed Ducks – and other sea duck populations – do not seem to rebound easily from hunting pressures. Even if this is only one problem impacting Long-tailed Ducks, the harvest is still one thing that can be controlled.

Avian cholera has caused substantial mortality in wintering Long-tailed Ducks, particularly from the 1970s to the 1990s (e.g., in the Chesapeake Bay).

One recent concern involves ocean acidification, a result of the uptake of human-caused carbon dioxide into the oceans, with the upshot being the increase of the oceans' acidity. A recent study on Long-tailed Ducks in the Baltic Sea revealed a population decline from 4 to 1.5 million over 15 years. Acidification is thought to be the culprit, a factor that is seen to accelerate thiamine deficiency in the birds. This certainly deserves further study.

Another area deserving study, of course, is the impact of climate change on Long-tailed Duck and other Arctic-favoring waterfowl.

Bufflehead
BUFF *Bucephala albeola*

Plates Page 240

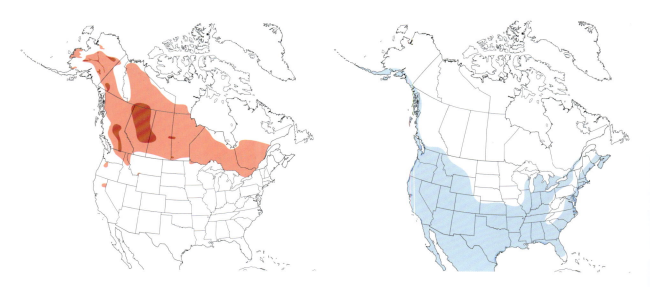

OTHER COMMON OR REGIONAL NAMES

Butterball, dipper, buffy, buffalo-head, helldiver
(Arctic: pugtaqutayagaq [YK], nunuqsigiilaq [NS], nunuqsibi-ixaq [NWS])
(Québec: petit garrot)
(Mexico: pato monjita, pato monja, pato chillón)

MEASUREMENTS

Length: Male — 14.0-15.6 in, av 14.8 in (37.5 cm); Female — 12.7-13.7 in, av 13.1 in (33.3 cm)
Wing: Male — av 6.7 in (17.0 cm); Female — av 6.1 in (15.5 cm)
Weight: Male — av 1.14 lbs (517 g); Female — av 0.68 lbs (308 g)
Bill: Male — av 28.7 mm; Female — av 26.0 mm

FIRST IMPRESSIONS

Little flocks or pairs of feisty, active, and squat Buffleheads, with their oversized-looking heads, can be found in almost any habitat with open water, anywhere from the ocean to a flooded field. Groups of 5-20 of these energetic, chunky ducks are often dominated by dull gray female-plumaged birds and accompanied by several stunning black-and-white drakes. The male has a big white patch on his otherwise black head. This stands out from great distances, along with his bright white sides, and black back. The female and first-year male will be dark gray-brown with a dark head that has a small whitish patch behind and below the eye. Size and shape: This tiny duck is very compact with a large, almost oversized, head, small bill, and short body. They ride low in the water, often with their tails awash. Flight: Buffleheads rock! Not just because they are cool little ducks, but also because they tip from one side to another in flight. They have the most rapid wingbeats of all waterfowl. They look heavy in the rear. Males appear very white in flight, given that about a third of their wing is white. Females and first-year males appear dark gray with minimal white in the wing. Buffleheads land gracefully with an upright posture, sticking their feet out to put on the breaks as their upright body crash-lands into the water. For takeoff, they need a short runway. Clusters or lines of just a handful of birds fly low over the water. At a distance, the blur of their wingbeats — in addition to their color pattern — helps give away their identity.

ID: IN DEPTH AND SIMILAR SPECIES

Buffleheads breed in their second-year, so males do not attain an adult plumage until they are over a year old. With the exception of adult males, aging and sexing Bufflehead is typically difficult, though not impossible, in the field.

Ducklings are very similar to downy goldeneyes with their dark caps and white cheeks, but the smaller Bufflehead ducklings have all-black wings and backs. The tapered bill is smaller than that of Common Goldeneye with a smaller reddish-gray nail. Juvenile plumage grows in about 50-55 days and looks like that of an adult female, but it is even more diffuse and wears out quickly. First years begin replacing juvenile plumage shortly after fledging in August, continuing through March. They molt a variable amounts of body feathers and all their tail feathers. Their appearance typically does not change appreciably.

First-year females are not readily distinguished in the field from adult females.

Looking very closely at a wing in the hand, narrow and more worn greater coverts can separate a first-year bird from adult females. Adults undergo a complete molt from August-October on molting grounds.

First-year males look generally like females. They typically have slightly larger white cheek patches that almost touche the eye. First-year males are slightly larger than first-year females, which is discernable in-hand by measuring the wing chord and is also sometimes noticeable in the field. The head can often look significantly larger than females. By March or April, males average whiter on the breast and some get a larger white cheek patch.

Adult males are sharply colored black-and-white. Although the heads appear black, they are actually an iridescent green-and-purple. Their bills are bluish-gray. After breeding, some males molt body feathers in June-July into an eclipse plumage. Eclipse males have a dark brownish head with a smudgy white patch behind the eye. Their breast and sides are pale brown to dusky gray. The back is dark brownish-gray, and the bill fades to dark gray. They retain the gleaming white upperwing coverts.

Similar species: In flight, female-plumaged Bufflehead can be easy to confuse with other small dark ducks. With all dark wings and a mostly dark head they have similar color pattern to Hooded Merganser, Ruddy Duck, and Harlequin Duck. Therefore, size and shape are the best features to separate these species, in addition to the probability of these other species occurring in the same area and/or season.

Sex ratio: It clearly favors males, but since young males resemble females, the exact ratio is difficult to determine. It is probably 60% male.

YEAR IN THE LIFE

Buffleheads are a common and widespread North American breeder, that can be found in nearly any habitat with water deep enough to dive for inviting food. They are most abundant in the Pacific and Atlantic Flyways. Large wintering concentrations form along the Pacific coast in southern British Columbia, Washington, and California. Along the Atlantic, they congregate from New Jersey to North Carolina. Inland concentrations can be found in the Klamath Basin (northern California), Yazoo NWR (Mississippi) and the Pecos River (New Mexico). They are accidental wanders to Japan, Greenland, the British Isles, and other European countries and Hawaii, Cuba, and other parts of the Caribbean.

Bufflehead winter in wide range of open water habitats, including sheltered bays, estuary systems, rivers, and lakes. Pair bonds usually form in March-April, prior to arrival on the breeding grounds. (Some pairs will reunite consecutive years.) Courtship activity peaks during spring migration. Several males often congregate around a female or two. Their display is more subtle than their close relatives. Rapid head bobbing and quick chases on the water and in the air are often observed. Fly-over-and-landing displays can still be impressive, where the male landing on the water, crest erect, "skis" with his feet pointing ahead and displays his obvious black-and-white upper plumage and even his bright pink feet.

Both sexes breed in their second-year, although first-year females will travel to the breeding grounds in search of prospective nest cavities near the area where they were born.

During spring migration, they travel at night and begin to head north in February. Most arrive in the boreal forest and aspen parklands between early April and early May. Pairs settle near small lakes and ponds as the female seeks a good cavity.

Females exhibit strong fidelity to their breeding areas, often returning year after year. They normally lay one egg every 1.5 days, although this ranges from one egg every 1-3 days. After the ducklings hatch, females lead them to an area to feed. She'll defend a territory for them to feed from other Bufflehead and goldeneyes. Broods often merge or mix when females are fighting territorial disputes. After the fight, the winning female will often end up with more ducklings or the entire brood. When the young are 5-6 weeks old the female abandons them and takes off to molt. Broods often congregate after they are abandoned in June-July until they can fly at 50-55 days old. Males undergo a molt-migration to a suitable lake to molt their wing feathers. However, the distance they travel or where they go is not well studied.

With the onset of cool fall temperatures, migration will often begin in late October. Numbers on the wintering grounds increase until early December. Peak migration days on the Great Lakes are often two days after a cold front passes.

GEOGRAPHIC VARIATION
No subspecies are recognized.

SOUNDS
Buffleheads are quiet ducks; only when they are courting are you likely to hear one if you listen closely. Males: During head-bobbing display, males give a loud chattering. Also, gives low squealing or growling in late winter or spring. Females: Follow males during the leading display and give loud, guttural call, *ec-ec-ec-ec*. Give low, buzzy note to call ducklings, *cuc-cuc-cuc*. Also a similar call is given as alarm call if separated from brood or disturbance at the nest. When prospecting for nest sites, give guttural, loud, quick *cuk-cuk-cuk* while circling around potential sites. Unlike their cogeners, the goldeneyes, Buffleheads do not make a whistling sound from their wings when in flight.

DIET AND FEEDING BEHAVIOR
Buffleheads feed mostly on animal matter (c. 80%) on freshwater lakes, rivers, estuaries, and inshore coastal waters. In breeding season, they dive for insect larvae and amphipods. In winter, when the birds are primarily coastal, they will feed on crustaceans and mollusks in shallow-water bays and inlets. Zebra mussels are consumed, but at modest amounts (in contrast to both scaup). Buffleheads favor waters that are no more than 10 feet deep, but sometimes to 15 feet. As divers, they are underwater feeders, and they avoid emergent or dense submerged vegetation. Buffleheads swim low in the water when feeding. Competition for breeding-area food regularly promotes territorial aggression between Barrow's Goldeneye and Buffleheads, with the smaller Buffleheads the losers.

NESTING
Site: Buffleheads nest by ponds,lakes, and slow rivers in boreal forest, sometimes in open muskeg with a few trees. Bufflehead will nest in a cavity or broken snag, woodpecker hole (often a Northern Flicker hole, with an entrance 2.75-3.5 inches in diameter), or nestbox, 2-11 feet up (but sometimes much higher). See the appendix at the end of this book for Bufflehead nest-box details and dimensions.

Nest description: No material added to the cavity nests, but down and sometimes feathers are added. (Down tufts are pale gray, tinted purplish or brownish and with indistinct pale centers.)

Clutch size: Average 9 eggs, normal range 6-12.

Egg description: Elliptical to oval. Smooth and slightly glossy. Creamy-white, yellowish-cream, or pale olive-buff. 51 × 36 mm.

Incubation duration: 28-33 days.

Brood parasitism: Other Bufflehead eggs are dumped in 5-8% of nests, much less frequently than among goldeneyes. But Bufflehead eggs occasionally laid and hatch in goldeneye nests. Interspecific brood parasitism by both goldeneyes.

HUNTING
Hunting Butterballs was actually prohibited in the U.S. from 1932 through 1937, in response to presumed population decline. The next year, hunting was reestablished, but serious restrictions were imposed. These were overwhelmingly lifted in 1944. By the next decade, Buffleheads had clearly recovered.

Today, they are not a particularly sought-after-species by hunters. The meat has a fishy flavor. The harvest of Buffleheads in the U.S. over two years (2013 and 2014) averaged at about 215,000 birds; and for Canada the corresponding number was 15,800.

They swing into decoys of their own kind or other diving ducks in small groups, but they are often just out of range in big water. They fly fairly low over the water.

POPULATION AND CONSERVATION

Bufflehead is one a few species of ducks to increase in numbers greatly since the mid-1950s, continent-wide. Buffleheads are still vulnerable to overhunting, in part because they frequent areas close to shore in the fall and winter. They are susceptible to local extirpation because the females strongly favor breeding in their natal areas, and both sexes return to same wintering areas each year. If a population is overharvested or becomes locally extirpated, it takes years to re-colonize and recover. Also, replacement may lag because the birds do not renest if a clutch is lost.

Contaminants (e.g., PCBs and mercury) have been found in Buffleheads, but at relatively low levels.

Loss of habitat in the boreal forest is a significant threat to their population. Buffleheads need large, mature trees with cavities. These areas are threatened by increased industrial activity, including agriculture, logging, and gas development.

Buffleheads readily use nestboxes, which could be a successful management practice in areas where their habitat has been destroyed by logging. Boxes have the best success in areas thick with conifers.

It is difficult to estimate the population size, as it is with other species that breed in the boreal forest due to limited access and difficulty of conducting surveys using traditional methods. Available numbers still suggest successfully stable or increasing populations. In 2004, the population was estimated at 1.4 million, and today is estimated at almost 1.7 million.

Common Goldeneye
COGO *Bucephala clangula*

Plates Page 244

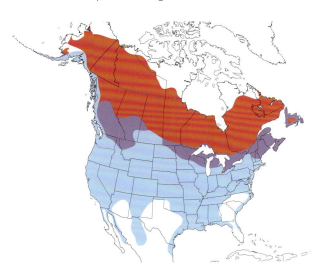

OTHER COMMON OR REGIONAL NAMES
Goldeneye, whistler, golden-eye duck, sizzle-britches (Arctic: qamiqurpak [YK], anarniilnguq [NWS], kabvirtok [N])
(Québec: Garrot à oeil d'or)
(Mexico: pato ojos dorados común, ojodorado común, pato chillón de ojos dorados)

MEASUREMENTS
Length: Male – 17.9-20.2 in, av 19.2 in (48.8 cm); Female – 15.7-19.7 in, av 17.0 in (43.2 cm)

Wing: Male – av 9.0 in (22.8 cm); Female – av 8.3 in (12.0 cm)

Weight: Male – av 2.37 lbs (1075 g); Female – av 1.74 lbs (789 g)

Bill: Male – av 34.3 mm; Female – average 33.6 mm

FIRST IMPRESSIONS
Common Goldeneyes are often found in small flocks or pairs where the striking black-and-white males stand out compared to the gray-bodied and brown-headed females. Males are black above and white below with dark green heads and a white oval cheek patch behind the bill. Females have gray bodies and brown heads, with a touch of light pink at the bill tip. Adults have bright yellow eyes that can be seen at close distances. Size and shape: A medium-to-large-sized diver with a triangular-shaped head. Flight: Common Goldeneye has a fairly distinctive shape with an oversized triangular head, long thin neck, wings in the center of the body, and a fairly long tapered tail. They only need a short runway for takeoff, with just a few strides. Their wings whistle as they beat, louder than any other duck. Flocks are loosely assembled, also typically small and scattered in migration. They sometimes form larger congregations on the wintering grounds. Wingbeats are tight and quick.

ID: IN DEPTH AND SIMILAR SPECIES
Common Goldeneyes typically do not breed until their second-year. They can often be aged and sexed in the field.

Ducklings have black caps that extend below the eye, white cheek, gray breast and dark gray body with several white patches. These look like Barrow's Goldeneye downy young, but the bill is longer and squarer. Unlike Bufflehead, they have white spots on the body. Juvenile plumage begins to appear on the sides and back at about

3 weeks. By 7-8 weeks the young are fully grown. Their heads are brownish with grayish-brown necks and grayish bodies. Their eyes are dark brown and their bills are dark. First-years replace some to most of their juvenile body plumage from August to March and often many of their tail feathers. In first-year males, this replacement is readily apparent, whereas in females it is more difficult to discern.

First-year females have the same overall color pattern as adult females, but their heads are slightly lighter brown and their bodies are a bit duskier gray, often with a mottled appearance. Their eyes are darker, starting brown as juveniles, changing to a dull yellow-green for the fall and most of the winter, and eventually turning bright yellow.

Adult females have rich brown heads, clean white necks, and even gray bodies. Their bills are dark with a pink band across the tip. Rarely, females have all orangey bills. After breeding, females molt their wing feathers and are flightless for 3-4 weeks. Wing molt is followed by a body molt that wraps up by November.

First-year males acquire their adult-like plumage throughout their first winter. They undergo a noticeable transition from a female-like juvenile plumage with brown eyes to an adult male-like plumage with yellow eyes. In the late fall and early winter, they acquire their first black and white feathers, starting with a white flecking on the cheek in the fall, followed by some white scapulars and breast feathers. By late winter or early spring, they often are mostly black and white, but typically still have some mottling in their plumage. Adult males have a crisp, bold black-and-white color pattern almost year-round. After breeding, some males replace some head and back feathers in June-July, attaining a partial eclipse plumage. In the late summer, around July, they undergo wing molt, followed by a complete body molt into their white and black plumage, which finishes up in November.

Similar species: Common Goldeneye is most likely to be confused with Barrow's Goldeneye. More often than not, Commons are misidentified as Barrow's than vice versa. This stems in part from Barrow's being the scarcer and more sought-after of the pair. However, when you see a Barrow's, it usually jumps out at you. This species pair is treated in the Similar Species section of the Barrow's Goldeneye account.

Sex ratio: Data is sparse, probably because of difficulty differentiating first-year immature males from females. Ultimately, males may dominate at almost 60%.

GEOGRAPHIC VARIATION

Two subspecies are recognized *B. c. americana* of North America is slightly larger and thicker-billed than nominate *B. c. clangula* of Eurasia. Identification in the field is probably not possible. Some authors do not believe there are sufficient grounds for subspecific status.

YEAR IN THE LIFE

Common Goldeneyes span the Northern Hemisphere. They are fairly common across North America, reaching south to northern Mexico in small numbers during the winter. Beyond North America, they breed mainly in a coniferous forest zone from Scandinavia to Kamchatka, also in wooded tundra and arctic-alpine zones south to wooded steppe.

Their wintering habitats range from large freshwater lakes to estuaries and coastal bays. They have a particular affinity for tidal zones and river mouths.

Courtship rituals begin in December and continue through April. It is possible that pairs reunite for more than one year, just like five other species of sea ducks, but this has not been confirmed. Males gather to display in small groups, often with four males for each female. Over a dozen dramatic displays have been described, but the most common display is a "head-throw" or "head-throw-kicks" display when the male flings his head forward, then throws it over his back pointing his bill skyward, calls, and thrusts his head forward while kicking the water. There are also displays of nodding, head-flicks, head-up pumping, and "masthead," a jerky movement with the lowering and stretching of the male's head parallel to the water surface and then withdrawing it, making a circular path with his bill.

Pairs migrate in the spring to the open lakes with nearby woodlands. It can be tough competition to find a good nesting cavity, and females often return to the same cavity each year. Females do not breed until their second-year, but they are known to search for cavities the summer before they breed. Breeding females have a slower rate of egg laying than most ducks, laying one egg every other day or even one every three days! Once the clutch is complete and females are incubating, males will abandon the female to take off on a short molt migration to molting grounds. These are usually larger lakes, bays, and rivers not far from the nesting area.

Females tend to the brood for their first 5-6 weeks. Broods often merge, forming crèches when a brood is abandoned or when ducklings get mixed up as females fight over feeding territories. After dispute, some or all of the brood joins the female holding the territory. Females often abandon their broods before they are able to fly. Adult females are the last to undergo a molt-migration after the breeding season.

In the fall, these birds are often the last waterfowl to begin moving south. Western-breeding birds (Saskatchewan and west) move toward Pacific coast, whereas eastern-breeding birds move to Atlantic coast. Juveniles may arrive on wintering grounds in October, but adults follow the first freeze. Fall migration in New England and Atlantic coast peaks early December. Pacific coast movements span from late October- early December, peaking in California in the third week of November.

SOUNDS

A quiet duck, except when males are displaying. Males: Give soft, short, and buzzy two-part *pre-preent* during courtship displays that can carry surprising distances. A grunt is given post copulation. Females: Gives harsh croak, *gack*, when disturbed. May utter a series of short *cuk* calls when searching for prospective nests.

The sounds produced by flying Common Goldeneyes are not vocalizations at all, but the whirring whistle noise of their wings.

DIET AND FEEDING BEHAVIOR

Common Goldeneyes will feed on a variety of waters, from large freshwater lakes to estuaries and sheltered coastal bays, usually less than 14 feet deep, sometimes up to 24 feet deep. Common Goldeneyes feed by diving, with parts of swimming flocks often diving underwater in unison. They often put their heads downward before jumping up to dive, and they will resurface in a sitting posture, not necessarily head-first. In winter, they dive in both fresh and marine waters to feed on mollusks, crustaceans, insects, and, occasionally, small fish. Zebra mussels in the Great Lakes have become a serious part of the species' diet when Common Goldeneye are passing through. Their primary diet shifts during the breeding season when they eat mostly aquatic insects, crustaceans, and aquatic plants. It is no accident that breeding-area lakes and ponds are most often without potentially competing fish. At the same time, vegetable matter (seeds, tubers) comprises less than a quarter of the diet.

NESTING

Site: Common Goldeneye will breed in boreal forested country, preferring areas close to fishless lakes, with aquatic invertebrates, and slow rivers. They will use tree cavities, abandoned woodpecker holes, tree stumps (often top snags), or nestboxes. The site is usually 6-45 feet up. See the appendix at the end of this book for Common Goldeneye nest-box details and dimensions.

Nest description: No material added, but grayish-white down and some feathers may be present. Size of interior nest is variable, depending on the available space, with an inside average diameter of 8 inches.

Clutch size: Average 7-10 eggs.

Egg description: Elliptical to oval. Smooth and slightly glossy. Bluish-green. (See Barrow's Goldeneye.) 60 × 43 mm.

Incubation duration: 27-32 days.

Brood parasitism: Frequent, more common earlier in the season, and in areas where cavities are in greater demand.

HUNTING

Whistlers, as Common Goldeneyes are sometimes called, often come into decoys of their own kind, if they react to decoys at all. Decoy placement usually requires more decoys per spread, usually in a fishhook pattern. They typically stay just out of range over big water. Females and immatures more likely to shift their flight path in response to decoys, but they generally stay high and keep their distance.

The harvest of Common Goldeneyes is hard to determine, since numbers are blended with Barrow's Goldeneye. In the U.S. over two years (2013 and 2014) harvest averaged about 79,000 birds; and for Canada the corresponding number may be close to 15,000.

An annual subsistence harvest for Canada is estimated at about 11,000, but under 1,500 for Alaska.

POPULATION AND CONSERVATION

Goldeneye populations are believed to be stable, however, precise population estimates are not available, in part due to the difficulty of surveying forested areas. If a local population is overhunted, or if its local breeding habitat is destroyed, a very slow recovery process follows. This is because female goldeneyes are highly philopatric, returning to the area where they were born to nest each year, and they will not renest. There is also the risk of exposure to pollutants, particularly from oil spills. Elevated levels of PCBs and selenium in Common Goldeneyes in the Great Lakes have been associated with zebra mussel diets.

Loss of breeding habitat – due to logging, agriculture, and urban expansion – is an ongoing threat. At the same time, Common Goldeneye readily use nestboxes, which might be a good strategy for increasing local breeding populations, particularly in areas where there are wetlands but few suitable large trees with natural cavities.

Population estimates are rough, and range from 500,000 to almost 1.4 million. The combined goldeneye (Barrow's and Common) population is probably closer to the top number, with the Common Goldeneye continental population, according to the NAWMP, averaging (2002-2011) at 1.2 milliion.

Barrow's Goldeneye
BAGO *Bucephala islandica*

Plates Page 250

OTHER COMMON OR REGIONAL NAMES
Whistler, Rocky Mountain whistler
(Arctic: anarnissakaq [YK])
(Québec: garrot d'islande)

MEASUREMENTS
Length: Male – 18.6-19.9 in, av 19.2 in (48.8 cm); Female – 16.2-17.7 in, av 17.0 in (43.2 cm)
Wing: Male – av 9.2 in (23.4 cm); Female – av 8.3 in (21.2 cm)
Weight: Male – av 2.13 lbs (966 g); Female – av 1.31 lbs (595 g)
Bill: Male – av 34.3 mm; Female – av 31.7 mm

FIRST IMPRESSIONS
These handsome ducks are found breeding on freshwater lakes and ponds, often at high elevations, and wintering in small groups of individuals in salt or fresh water. They often frequent ferry docks or harbors in winter, moving with the tide to feed at optimal sites. The male is a striking black-and-white medium-to-large-sized duck, having a large-looking head, dark purplish (not green), with a white crescent behind the short bill. He has a clean white flank interrupted by a black 'spur' that extends down into the breast and a black back with white patches on the scapulars. Females are brown-and-gray birds, with brown heads and gray bodies, most easily identified by their oval-shaped heads with steep foreheads. Adult females have bright orange bills in winter. Size and shape: The head is striking, with and oval-shaped and swollen mane. Large head, short neck, and long body sloping downward into the water. Look for the steep forehead and puffed-out nape area. Subtly more compact than Common Goldeneye. Flight: A large head and long thick neck stick out in front of wings. Oval-shaped body tapers to a long tail. Body angles up slightly. A male Barrow's will appear darker in flight than a Common Goldeneye, because it has a darker back and less white on the upper wing coverts. Specific covert patterns are hard to judge on moving birds, so look for a general impression of how much white and black is present. Females are even more difficult to separate, but they also have less white in wings than Common Goldeneyes, but the prominent orange bill is the best clue during winter months. Wings make a distinctive, loud whistle in flight. Small flocks (usually fewer than 20) are often seen moving short distances from one feeding area to another. They need a short runway to take off, but once in the air, their wingbeats are quick and stiff.

ID: IN DEPTH AND SIMILAR SPECIES
Barrow's Goldeneyes take at least two years to mature, sometimes not breeding until their third year. Therefore, first-year males can be picked out through much of the winter, and some young females can be distinguished as well.

Ducklings have black caps that extends below their eyes, white cheeks, gray breasts, and dark gray bodies with several white patches. Very similar to Common Goldeneye, but the bill is shorter, more tapering, with a wider nail. Juveniles plumage begins to appear at about 3 weeks old and is fully grown by 8 weeks. Juveniles have a brown heads, dusky breasts, and dusky gray bodies. Their bills are black and eyes are dark brown. They have an overall duller and muted appearance than the adult females. First-years replace juvenile plumage gradually from late fall to early spring. They undergo a complete body and wing molt in the summer at about a year old, attaining their first full adult plumage by the late fall.

First-year females are replacing body feathers, which gives them a mottled appearance on their body. Adult females have even, clean gray bodies in winter, brighter yellow eyes than first-years, entirely orange bills, and darker brown heads. Their bill color begins to fade in March and by the time they are incubating their bills are very dark. After raising a brood, adult females undergo a complete molt of body and wing feathers in early July through late September.

First-year males transition from brown-headed, gray-bodied juveniles to having extensive patches of white and black on their body by the spring. Their eyes also change from brown in the fall to yellow or dull yellow by the winter. Black-and-white scapulars are some of the first adult-like feathers to appear, along with white on the breast and an incomplete white – or shaded – crescent behind the bill. Males have black bills year-round. Adult males are black-and-white overall. After breeding and a molt-migration, they molt body feathers into eclipse plumage. Eclipse males are dusky overall with a dark brown head and neck, with only some have white feathers on the head in the former crescent. They have a simultaneous wing molt and are flightless for 3-4 weeks around mid-July to late August. Body molt continues through late September as they attain a black-and-white plumage.

Similar species: Separating female Barrow's and Common Goldeneye is a classic ID challenge. Head shape is a consistent way to differentiate the species in all age and sex classes (with the exception of juveniles whose head shape may not be fully developed in the early fall). Common has a triangular to trapezoidal-shaped head, while Barrow's is reminiscent of an oval with a trailing mane. Barrow's will have a steeper forehead and much more puffed-out nape area when the neck is held erect. Bill size and shape – often appearing shorter and stubbier in Barrow's Goldeneye – has often been noted as a separating feature, but their measurements are very similar and some overlap.

Juveniles that are fully grown and still largely in juvenile plumage and unaccompanied by an adult female are by far the most difficult to identify. In this time frame, late July-September, juveniles of both species and sexes have dark eyes and dark bills. Because they are in juvenile plumage, they do not have a well-defined border between their brown head and white neck, so that field mark is not helpful. Juveniles do not have fully developed skulls, making head shape an unreliable field mark in their first summer and early fall. They also have fewer, shorter feathers on their head than adults, which also makes head shape harder to judge.

Females from October-April have bill color that matches what you might expect. While Commons will have a dull pink band across the tip of the bill, adult female Barrow's will have a bright orange bill. First-year female Barrow's Goldeneyes have duller orange bills, but the bill is still primarily orangey. Pitfall for the unwary: First, note that a very small percentage (less than 1%) of adult female Common Goldeneyes have orange bills! This has led astray many observers in the East astray, trying to find a rarer Barrow's. Also, by March, adult female Barrow's start to loose the bright orange bill color so they will be more camouflaged on the nest. By mid-summer their bills can be all black. At this point, go for head shape. Another very useful mark is how far down the brown goes on the throat. Posture also needs to be taken into account. Barrow's will often have a short-necked look, because their brown head color extends down the font of the neck. The point where the head become the neck is brown on Barrow's, cutting straight across, whereas on Common, the front of the neck is white.

Males typically present clear-cut identification. First-year males can still be separated by the shape of the incoming white patch at the base of the bill and the pattern of the scaupulars. There is a brief time when first-year male Commons have an incomplete patch that can look like a crescent. A Barrow's crescent, however, should extend above the top of the bill and eye. Adult male Barrow's also will have a black 'spur' or 'thumb' that sticks down between their breast and flanks, which, in combination with a darker back overall, will help to pick them out in flocks of Commons.

Hybrids are rare, but there are a number of records. A female hybrid would be impossible to identify in the field with certainty without knowing the parents. However, male hybrids can often quite easily be identified with certainty. Hybrid males usually have intermediate characteristics of both species. The white patch on the face is an oblong oval, not a pointed crescent. Their black "spur" is shorter than in Barrow's, and their scapular pattern is intermediate (see mystery photos).

Sex ratio: Data limited, but may be 55% male. In the East the number may be 58-68% male, in the West 55-58% male.

YEAR IN THE LIFE

Barrow's Goldeneyes are uncommon throughout their range in North America and Iceland. There are two populations in North America; one that breeds in the mountains of the West and winters along the West Coast, another significantly smaller population that breeds in Québec and winters in New England and the Maritime Providences. The main wintering area in the East is along the northern coast of the St. Lawrence estuary. The bulk of the western population winters from Kodiak Island, Alaska to the Puget Sound of Washington. In the East, their wintering sites are very local, in flocks of varying size (typically 4-40) or in pairs, but rarely are the birds found in groups of more than 100 individuals. Barrow's is very rare in the Great Lakes region in winter and in the central plains. There are significantly fewer records in the East from south of Long Island to Virginia. Since the mid-1970s they have wintered regularly on lower Colorado River in Arizona.

Barrow's winter primarily in sheltered coastal waters primarily; a few will winter at inland sites in lakes and rivers. Male Barrow's are the only waterfowl known to defend a winter territory. Within its range, Barrow's typically will not associate closely with other waterfowl. Vagrants are found in flocks of Common Goldeneyes.

New pair bonds are formed in the winter. Males display in small groups from November-February to earn the approval of a female. "Rotary-pumping" is a common courtship display, with the male's head lifted back, the neck straightened and then moved forward and downward to make a pear-shaped or oval figure. Existing pairs often re-established their bond in fall, despite long periods of separation. Most pairs are formed before spring migration in late March.

Pairs often depart for spring migration early in the season, starting in late February on the Pacific coast, with the majority passing in late March-early April. Barrow's depart Maine and Massachusetts from mid-March through the first week of April. They leave Québec from the last week of April through the second week of May.

Females lead their mates to the open lakes and small

ponds where nesting cavities are present. Barrow's are likely to breed in second or third year. Hens have high fidelity to previous nest sites, especially those where they were successful in prior years. Competition for sites can be intense. Females without breeding experience prospect for potential nest cavities in the summer prior to their first nesting attempt. Older females regularly return to established breeding sites earlier than younger females.

The female typically lays an egg every other day. That's a very slow rate, similar to that of other *Bucephala*.

The male remains on territory with his mate for the first 7-10 days of incubation. She joins him to feed and preen during incubation breaks. Once the eggs hatch, the female leads the brood to a feeding territory, which she will adamantly defend tirelessly for her brood. During fights between females, ducklings sometimes get scrambled or lost to the other female. This is one scenario that results in the merging of multiple broods, known as créching. The female typically abandons her brood when the young are 5-6 weeks old, before they are capable of flight, and she will take off to molt with others on larger lakes nearby. Some females molt with their brood.

Males undergo a molt-migration in mid-June. Molting areas can be located many hundreds of miles from breeding areas. Known molting sites for the western population include the Old Crow Flats in the Yukon, several lakes in Alaska, some lakes in central Alberta, and Stum Lake and Charlie Lake in central British Columbia. Molting sites for males from the eastern population include Nain Bay on the coast of Labrador, Ungava Bay, and the Hudson Bay east of Belcher Islands.

In the fall, Barrow's return in numbers on Pacific coast from late October-early November. They arrive on East Coast in Massachusetts and Maine in late November-early December.

GEOGRAPHIC VARIATION
No subspecies are recognized.

SOUNDS
Generally silent, even their courtship calls are relatively quiet and unremarkable. Males: During courtship, may give soft, grunt *ka-KAA*. Females: Give a harsh *gack*, not unlike Common Goldeneye, when disturbed. They also give a soft *cuc-cuc-cuc* when communicating with the brood. Groups of females in search of a nest sites utter one-syllable calls, similar to the *cuc* call.

Although not vocalization, their wings make a discernible whistling sound in flight.

DIET AND FEEDING BEHAVIOR
Barrow's Goldeneye feed by diving, primarily during daylight but also on moonlit nights. Their diet is similar to that of Common Goldeneye, except that the Barrow's will rely more on insects (breeding season) and mollusks while consuming fewer crustraceans. Outside the breeding season, Barrow's Goldeneye will disperse to ice-free rivers and lakes and along inshore coastal waters, where they will usually feed in waters under 14 feet in depth. In winter they forage in saltwater where they dive to pluck prey from bottom and pry mollusks from rocks and pilings while floating on the surface. Vegetable matter is less than 20% of their diet. In breeding season, however, insects will form over three-quarters of the adult diet. These breeding-area ponds are most often without fish, and may be more saline than those used by Common Goldeneye. At the same time, competition for food during the breeding season probably promotes territorial aggression between Barrow's Goldeneye and Buffleheads.

NESTING
Site: Barrow's Goldeneye breed by lakes, pools, and rivers, often in forested or montane country (in the Rocky Mountains, sometimes up to 9,800 feet). Pond areas preferred are usually more saline than those preferred by Common Goldeneye. Surrounding waters must be at least 3 feet deep. Barrow's Goldeneye will nest in tree cavities, nestboxes, old woodpecker holes (often made by Pileated Woodpecker), occasionally rock crevice, or cliff ledge. The cavity may be as high as 65 feet up. See the appendix at the end of this book for Barrow's Goldeneye nest-box details and dimensions.

Nest description: No material is added, but nest lined with significant white down and some feathers.

Clutch size: 6-12 eggs, sometimes to 14 (perhaps the result of two females).

Egg description: Elliptical to oval. Smooth. Green or bluish-green. 62 × 44 mm.

Incubation duration: Averages 30 days.

Brood parasitism: Eggs are frequently dumped in the nests of other females (30-64% of the time), therefore, clutches with more than 13 eggs indicate another female has laid in the cavity. Eggs of other cavity nesting species (e.g. Common Goldeneye, Hooded Merganser, and Bufflehead) are also frequently laid in their nest.

HUNTING
There are limited opportunities to harvest Barrow's Goldeneye partly because they have a fairly small winter range, but also because they are protected from over-hunting on the much of the eastern seaboard. While U.S. federal frameworks for the Atlantic Flyway have no specific restrictions on this species, the season has been closed in Maine. In Atlantic Canada, very restrictive limits have been established, and a complete ban has been considered.

On the West Coast, with some concerns over the western population, restrictive daily bag limits were established in British Columbia in 1990 and western Washington in 2010.

The overall harvest of Barrow's Goldeneyes is hard to determine, since numbers are blended with Common Goldeneye. In the U.S. over two years (2013 and 2014) harvest average may have been close to 5,000 birds; and for Canada the corresponding number could be about

1,000. This does not include estimated subsistence harvest of 2,000 for Alaska and 950 for Canada, numbers from the recent past.

There are some premier hunting opportunities on West Coast, particularly in Alaska. Popular hunting localities include: Kodiak Island, Alaska, and the Puget Sound in Washington.

They are hunted in much the same manner as Common Goldeneyes. Individuals readily come into decoys of their own species, decoying more easily than Common Goldeneye. Females and first-year males are more susceptible to hunting mortality than adult males. Local wintering populations are susceptible to over-hunting and even local extinctions because they return to the same wintering areas each year and reproduce slowly.

POPULATION AND CONSERVATION

Barrow's Goldeneye has a relatively small population, compared to most other North American ducks. The total continental population, according to the Sea Duck Joint Venture, was estimated at 204,000, although NAWMP put it at an average of 258,000 (2002-2011). The western population (at about a quarter of a million) is apparently stable, although data suggests that the eastern population (at 4,000-8,000) is declining. The eastern population was listed under SARA in Canada as a Species of Special Concern in 2001.

In general, these birds are not closely monitored, because they are difficult to count on the breeding grounds, and they are lumped with Common Goldeneye in some instances. Lack of information is one of the greatest concerns for this species.

Given their small population, they should be watched more carefully. They are at risk of oil spills when they are congregated on their wintering grounds, accumulation of heavy metals in their prey, loss of habitat from logging (particularly large trees with suitable nesting cavities). The logging problem may be particularly troublesome in western Canada. They are also in danger of being over-harvested in areas (e.g., Northeast). Given that they do not breed until they are two years old, females do not disperse widely from their natal area, and they typically will not renest, local populations are very slow to recover from a significant loss of adults. Barrow's Goldeneyes readily take to nestboxes, which could assist local populations and represent significant local conservation efforts addressing a number of these problems.

Smew

Plates Page 272

SMEW *Mergellus albellus*

OTHER COMMON OR REGIONAL NAMES
None used in North America

MEASUREMENTS
     Length: Male – c. 17.3 in (44.0 cm); Female – c. 15.2 in (39 cm)
     Wing: Male – av 8.0 in (20.3 cm); Female – av 7.3 in (18.5 cm)
     Weight: Male – av 1.49 lbs (676 g); Female – av 1.29 lbs (585 g)
     Bill: Male – av 29.0 mm; Female – av 26.5 mm

FIRST IMPRESSIONS AND SIMILAR SPECIES

This is one sleek little merganser! Smew is a small and peculiar Eurasian merganser that is very rare in North America.

Adult males are a bold white with a black mask and dark patch behind the eye, also with several black lines on the body. Females have a gray body, brown head, darker around the eye and white cheek. First-year males are gray with white cheeks and fairly obvious rusty-brown caps and a black patch between the bill and eye. Size and shape: Small, compact duck with a thinish neck and slightly crested head. These birds are shorter and thicker-billed than other mergansers. Flight: Males have bold white and black pattern, like Bufflehead but with a whiter head. Females show the dark cap, white cheek, gray breast band, white body and white oval (like wigeon's patch) on a dark gray wing. After a short – or no – running takeoff, these small size will produce some very fast wingbeats. Also note the extended straight neck in flight.

Similar species: Under most circumstances, Smew are hard to misidentify. Adult male Smew have more white on them then any other duck. The almost entirely white head in particular, separates them from Bufflehead and goldeneye, which share striking black-and-white body coloration. Females may give the impression of a miniature Common Merganser. And females and first-year males with their white cheek patches might suggest Ruddy Duck. Occasionally Smew hybridizes with Common Goldeneye, presenting confusing, yet remote, possibilities.

Sex ratio: Unknown

BACKGROUND AND TIPS

This rare visitor seldom strays far from its usual haunts in Europe and Asia. (Smew winters in western Europe, Middle East, China, and Japan, feeding in sheltered coasts and inland lakes.)

In North America, they may be discovered in the west and central Aleutians from mid-March-May and October through early winter. Smew has also showed up elsewhere in Alaska, and some have reached the Lower-48 (mostly between November and March).

This lovely species is sometimes kept in captivity; therefore, the origin of individuals is often questioned for sightings away from the Alaska or away from the coast. There are several records from south of Alaska, including California, Missouri, Washington, British Columbia, Wisconsin, New York, Rhode Island, Ontario, and Québec.

Smew populations went through a long-term decline in Eurasia, but are apparently stable these days. The global population, estimated at 130,000 individuals, is relatively small compared to most ducks. These birds are vulnerable to oil pollution, habitat loss and degradation from logging and agriculture, and excessive hunting pressure.

SOUNDS
Generally silent and infrequently heard, except during courtship displays. Males: Give a prolonged deep, frog-like grunting that accelerates to end with a hiccup. Females: Give a shorter hoarse grating or rattling.

DIET AND FEEDING BEHAVIOR
Smew feed by diving, usually with a forward jump and with frequency. Outside the breeding season, Smew use freshwater lakes, estuaries, and sheltered coastal bays to feed. During the winter and in early spring, seasons when we may find the species in North America, Smew mainly feed on fish. Smew will usually dive less than 13 feet below the surface to reach food.

Hooded Merganser
HOME *Lophodytes cucullatus*

Plates Page 256

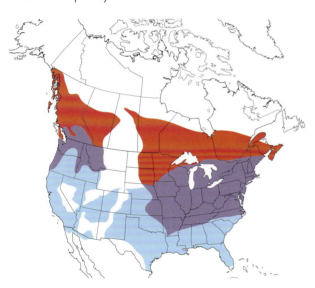

OTHER COMMON OR REGIONAL NAMES
Hoody, sawbill, fish duck, fanhead, hair-head, hairyhead, hoary-crested, frog-duck
(Québec: harle couronné)
(Mexico: mergo de caperuza, mergo cresta blanca)

MEASUREMENTS
Length: Male – 17.0-19.2 in, av 18.1 in (46.0 cm); Female – 16.0-18.0 in, av 17.1 in (43.4 cm)
Wing: Male – av 7.7 in (19.6 cm); Female – av 7.4 in (18.8 cm)
Weight: Male – av 1.60 lbs (726 g); Female – av 1.50 lbs (680 g)
Bill: Male – av 39.6 mm; Female – av 38.3 mm

FIRST IMPRESSIONS
When male Hooded Mergansers fan their crests, it's hard not to be stopped in your tracks. The huge whiteand-black crest is impressive, and not only to the female Hoodeds. Pairs and small flocks huddle in tranquil ponds and lakes. At a distance, males appear dark overall until they fan their white crests. Their chestnut sides fade away. Females are dark-brown overall with pale bellies and usually obvious, brown, bushy crests. Size and shape: A small and slim duck, with a big crested-head, and long, broad tail that usually slopes into the water. Flight: Hunch-backed and head down, they plow ahead. Wings are short, but moving so fast in shallow wingbeats, that they are a blur. They fly with their fan compressed, but they still have a large-headed and thin-billed appearance. Their body is slender; tail is long and broad. They are dark above with white bellies. Males have some white on the secondaries, but it is limited and indistinct in flight. At a distance, their wings look like they are moving a million miles and hour and body is dark. Little groups fly on the same horizontal plane, often a good distance above the water.

ID: IN DEPTH AND SIMILAR SPECIES
Hoodies do not breed until they are at least two years old. First-year year males are slow to mature but can be separated from females with a close look. In general, more

study is needed to gain a clearer understanding of the timing and extent of molts in Hooded Merganser. Ducklings are dusky-brown overall with a dark brown crown, buffy cheek and breast. They are more darkly colored than our other mergansers. Their bills are orangey along the lower edge. Juvenile plumage is entirely brown. They replace some juvenile plumage from August-March. First-years are difficult to separate from adult females. They appear warm on the crest and darkest around the eye. First-years also have duller tertials and wing coverts, which is helpful mainly in-hand.

First-year females are extremely difficult to separate from adult females in the field. Their tertials are plainer with a white stripe running down the center. Adult females have crisper white stripes with blacker borders. Adult females do not look appreciably different over the course of a year, which is one reason their molts are not well-understood. They have a partial body molt from May to July; little is known about the extent and timing of this molt. Breeders undergo complete body and wing molt from August to October.

First-year males are much like females, but with some white in the center of the crest, a yellow eye, and sometimes dark flecking on the head. Their bills blacken throughout the fall and winter as their eye become brighter yellow. Adult males are stunning with their unique white fan, bold black-and-white stripes across the breast and on their tertials. After breeding, they molt body feathers into an eclipse plumage. Eclipse males have a dusky-brown crest, often still showing some white in their fan. They are very dark brown on the back. They loose the white breast, but they still have bright yellow eyes, dark bills, and the same upperwing pattern as the rest of the year. Adults have a partial body molt from May to July; not much is known about the extent and timing of this molt. Breeders undergo complete body and wing molt from August to October.

Similar species: Females and first-year males could be mistaken for other mergansers with their thin bills. Distant birds in flight can be confused with Wood Duck, in part because they share the same wooded habitats and both have long tails. Wood Ducks, however, have much slower wingbeats than Hooded Merganser, and they tend to hold their head high, avoided the hunch-backed look of Hooded. Female Bufflehead are also small, dark ducks with quick wingbeats, but look for the white cheek patch on a Bufflehead, in addition to their more compact look overall.

Sex ratio: Not well studied, but thought to be even.

GEOGRAPHIC VARIATION
No subspecies are recognized.

SOUNDS
Hooded Merganser is a quiet species, most often heard when courting and around the nest site. Males: Utter a rolling croaking *braaaa-brrrraaaooo* given with a fanned crest and head toss. It's a very low, drawn out call that bears no resemblance to other duck calls and sounds. It's more like a frog. The rolling croak is often preceded or followed by a loud pop. Females: Give a hoarse *croo-croo-crook*, sometimes given in rapid succession while flying around nest site or calling to ducklings. They also give a harsh *gack* during courtship.

YEAR IN THE LIFE
Hooded Mergansers are fairly common in a broad band through the middle of North America. The majority of the population winters in the Mississippi Flyway, especially in Mississippi Alluvial Valley. There are some concentrations in the Atlantic Flyway in coastal waters south of Maryland. The highest counts reaching a thousand or more are from Wheeler NWR in Alabama, Falls Lake in North Carolina, Thomas Hill Reservoir in Missouri, and Big Lake WMA in Arkansas.

Hoodeds are rare south of their range in Baja California, Veracruz, Distrito Federal, Coahuila, and throughout Caribbean, even rarer in Hawaii and the Yucatan Peninsula. They are uncommon, north of the core of their breeding range in southeast Alaska and rare elsewhere in Alaska and Newfoundland. They are also a very rare visitor to the British Isles, West Germany, Scandinavia, and Iceland.

During the winter, they prefer forested freshwater wetlands, brackish estuaries, and tidal creeks. They forage by diving to capture prey, including small fish, aquatic insects, and crustaceans (particularly crayfish). Pair bonds form primarily in winter when stunning males fan their crest and call to entice a mate. Males in small groups will display to attract the attention of one or a few females. The elaborate behavior involves crest-raising (with males bringing their heads backward to touch their backs), wing flaps, ritualized drinking, head shakes, and a rotary pumping with the bill tracing circles in space.

Hoodeds are early migrants the spring, pushing north as ice thaws. In the southeast they start heading north in early February. In the Pacific Northwest, they remain in coastal areas until mid-April.

They arrive on the breeding grounds just days after the ice breaks up. They prefer forested areas where nest cavities are available. The females exhibit strong site-fidelity, usually returning to previous nesting areas. Breeding kicks off in early February in southeast Missouri to late March in the Great Lakes, mid-April in British Columbia and Quebec. The female picks out a suitable cavity, which she may even scout out the summer before. Males abandon females shortly after they begin incubating, and they take off to find a place to molt their wing feathers. Females take more incubation breaks than other diving ducks. They to the brood until they are ready to take off and undergo wing molt. The youngsters begin to fly at 10 weeks old. Some juveniles hatching early in the season disperse north (up to 435 miles, based on band recoveries), before moving south again for the winter. Little is known about adult molt migration, although it is probably of short distance.

Fall migration typically gets off to a late start. In Minnesota, the peak is from the last week of October through the first week of November. The peak is in mid-November in New England. Numbers on the wintering grounds in Florida, peak in late December. Hoodeds depart British Columbia in the third week of October. They begin arriving on wintering areas in California and Pacific Northwest in mid-November.

DIET AND FEEDING BEHAVIOR

Hooded Mergansers feed by diving in relatively shallow waters, usually estimated at under 5 feet but perhaps deeper. They will feed on rivers and small lakes, estuaries, coastal lagoons, and sometimes on coastal waters. Unlike other mergansers which feed almost entirely on fish, these mergansers have a more diverse diet, where fish comprise about half their food. Diving and seizing small fish is important, but the birds also eat aquatic insects, mollusks, and crustaceans, especially crayfish, grasping them with their thin, serrated bills.

NESTING

Site: Hooded Mergansers will breed by slow rivers, ponds, and small lakes in forested regions with both live and dead trees (e.g., beaver ponds). Hooded Merganser nests are found in natural cavities in trees, stumps, and in nestboxes. Usually 15-20 feet up, but sometimes as high as 80 feet. The preferred entrance hole is about 3 x 4 inches in diameter. See the appendix at the end of this book for Hooded Merganser nest-box details and dimensions.

Nest description: No material is added to the cavity nests, but they will be lined with down and some feathers. (Down tufts very pale gray, with centers a little lighter.)

Clutch size: average 9-13 eggs, sometimes as few as 5.

Egg description: Short elliptical to short subelliptical. Smooth and glossy. White. 54 x 44 mm.

Incubation duration: Often 31-33 days, ranges widely from 26-41 days.

Brood parasitism: common, with over a third of nests parasitized by other Hoodeds. They parasitize and are parasitized by Common Goldeneye, Common Mergansers, Wood Ducks.

HUNTING

Hoodies are usually considered trophy ducks that are hunted opportunistically. It's usually not a target duck and is a bonus if the hunter is able to add a drake to the bag. Fanheads are consistent with the merganser practice of not being particularly attracted to decoys. A single hen might decoy readily, but flocks often flight right over. Most shots tend to be pass shooting for trophy drakes as they buzz by. These are generally not wary ducks.

Compared to other mergansers, bag limits for Hooded Mergansers have remained conservative. Recently, the harvest of Hooded Mergansers in the U.S. over two years (2013 and 2014) averaged at about 98,200 birds; for Canada the corresponding number was 9,500.

POPULATION AND CONSERVATION

Hooded Merganser populations are apparently stable, possibly increasing in some areas. Population estimates vary for the continent. According to the NAWMP, averaged (2002-2011) at over 1.1 million but other estimates have been as low as 485,000. This is an byproduct of the difficulty of getting reliable count-numbers. Still, the population is thought to be stable, if not increasing.

The earliest ornithological records indicate that Hoodeds likely bred throughout eastern U.S. and mountainous western states. They occupy most of their ancestral range today, although in lower densities and more localized areas. An inferred population crash started in the 1880s due to logging of old forests, which reduced the number of cavities available. At the time, unregulated hunting, over many years, was a real problem. Even today, deforestation remains a main threat to this merganser's population, with hunting not a real concern.

Nestbox efforts and the appropriate management of beavers (which help creative attractive wetlands) are two local management tools.

Red-breasted Merganser
RBME *Mergus serrator*

Plates Page 260

OTHER COMMON OR REGIONAL NAMES
Sawbill, fish duck, merganser, merg
(Arctic: payirpak [YK], paisugruk [NS, NWS], nujaralik, pitiulayurak [N])
(Québec: harle huppé)
(Mexico: mergo pecho rojo, mergo copetón)

MEASUREMENTS
Length: Male — 22.8-25.2 in, av 24.0 in (60.9 cm); Female — 20.1-22.1 in, av 21.1 in (57.3 cm)
Wing: Male — av 9.8 in (24.8 cm); Female — av 9.4 in (22.4 cm)
Weight: Male — av 2.55 lbs (1157 g); Female — av 2.03 lbs (925 g)
Bill: Male — av 58.8 mm; Female — av 53.7 mm

FIRST IMPRESSIONS
Red-breasted Mergansers are the wolves of the water. They cruise large lakes, estuaries, and oceans in packs, diving synchronously in a coordinated effort to snatch fish. In between dives, they are peering under water, head down, crest sticking straight up, as they plan their next attack. Other times, they are on solo missions as they work harbors and bays. Males are dark-headed with a broad white collar, thick speckled brown breast-band, and gray sides. Females have warm brown heads and gray bodies; their whole appearance is rough around the edges, with a washed-out plumage and scruffy crest. Size and Shape: These are long and lanky mergansers with thin necks, shaggy crests, and skinny bills. Flight: They look like a shooting arrow through the sky, with a long body and neck outstretched. The male is dark-headed with a thick white collar, a dark breast, white belly, and with big white patches in the wing seen even at a distance. The female looks pale brown-headed and largely white-breasted and white-bellied, with large white patches in the wing. When they turn to land, the feet flare out to the sides, and wings look long, thin, and tapered at the tips. Red-breasted Mergansers are often in groups of fewer than 30, except on big migration days. They run along the water for takeoff and move stealthily, low over the water, with wingbeats snappy, shallow, and stiff.

ID: IN DEPTH AND SIMILAR SPECIES
Red-breasted Mergansers usually breed in their second-year. In general, with the exception of adult males, they are difficult to age and sex.

Ducklings are dark brown with a reddish head, white cheek and two dark stripes on the face. They are extremely similar to downy Common Mergansers, but Red-breasted tend to have more reddish heads that are more peaked or triangular.

Juvenile plumage is gray on the body with a brown head. First-years replace juvenile plumage slowly from August through March. Both sexes look alike, initially showing no black around the eye. Later in winter, first-year males molt in dark feathers around the eye and are very difficult to age from adult females. Literature states that birds with black around the eye are first-year males. However, most adult female Red-breasted Merganser also show some black around the eye. This increases with age. Whether this is linked to estrogen senescence remains to be determined. Spring, when pairs form, is a great time for you to test the variability of this face pattern. (Female European Red-breasts may not show black in the face.)

Red-breasted Mergs can also be aged by tapered, gray tertials coverts on first-years versus the shiny black, rounded tertials of the adults. Adult females have pale forenecks and chins, more extensive and less well-defined than that on female Common Merganser. Their plumage does not change appreciably throughout the year. They are more worn in the summer while they are tending to their brood. Females molt some body feathers from May-July. In July and August, they undergo a complete wing molt and are flightless for 30-33 days.

First-year males look like females. They molt in darker feathers around the eye later in winter and spring and look almost identical to adult females. In spring, a few young males molt in adult-type bright feathers, such as on the flanks and breast. Beware: eclipse adults look very similar!

Adults males are in their bright plumage from late-fall to summer. They will molt body feathers into eclipse plumage from May-July, with males looking almost identical to females in this plumage. By July and August, they undergo a complete wing molt and are flightless for 30-33 days. (Note that one-year-old males initiate their wing molt earlier than the breeding males and females.) We rarely see Red-breasted Mergansers in eclipse. They are very secretive in breeding season, and their breeding distribution is poorly known. Additionally, many nest in remote areas in the north. Moreover, Adult males are slower to come out of eclipse plumage than most other waterfowl. Some will still look mottled into December. This is very late!

Similar species: The female Red-breasted Merganser is most similar to Common Merganser; they share a rusty-brown head, gray body and thin reddish bill. Common Merganser, however, has a thicker bill, bigger head, and larger body than Red-breasted. Red-breasted is a sleek and slender bird overall. Female Common has a crisper plumage and a clean-cut appearance overall with a shorter crest and a clearly delineated whitish throat. Red-breasted is rough around the edges, with duskier and more diffuse plumage, almost appearing "blurred," and a shaggy crest. Female Hooded Merganser is entirely brown, smaller in size with a fluffier, fuller crest.

Sex ratio: Difficult to determine, due to identification of subadults. Males may perhaps account for 60-63%.

YEAR IN THE LIFE

Red-breasted Mergansers are widespread in North America and northern parts of Europe and Asia, however, they are really a bird of the coasts and big lakes in winter. They winter from Alaska to Baja California and from Nova Scotia to Florida and south Texas. They are rare in winter in the Caribbean and in Nayarit, Veracruz, and northern Yucatán. High counts on fall migration on the south shore of Lake Erie, west of Cleveland, Ohio, as well as, the southern end of Lake Michigan and south shore of Lake Ontario.

In winter, they prefer sheltered bays, estuaries, harbors and other marine habitats. Flocks often move through areas, diving to catch their prey.

Red-breasted Mergansers are on a later schedule than most ducks. They take two years to reach an adult plumage and breed. Once they are finally ready to breed, they acquire their snazzy breeding plumage late in the fall (or early winter), they pick a mate later in the spring, then linger during spring migration, and initiate nesting after all the other ducks.

Red-breasted Mergansers have very elaborate courtship rituals that are readily observed during spring migration. Groups of males gather around females as they perform the salute-curtsy and head-shake over and over inter-mixed with dashing across the surface in short spurts creating a splash. The salute-curtsy involves a raised crest that is suddenly depressed, the head dropped to the water's surface and then raised in a "salute," and then the chest and neck are submerged into the water and the tail is bent under to touch the surface.

As a late breeder, Red-breasted Mergansers arrive on the breeding grounds from mid-to late May. Females tend to return to the same nesting area yearly. Females leave their broods relatively early in their development, some are abandoned within a week of hatching, so many broods join together and form large crèches. The theory explaining this behavior is that the females are in poor condition after a long incubation period with only short periods off the nest, so they need to spend time feeding. Given their late nesting schedule, they are also running out of time to head to a suitable place to go through their wing molt.

Males take off on a relatively short molt-migration and join the second-year birds on at key molting sites, particularly the St. Lawrence River mouth in the East.

In the fall, they pass through the Great Lakes in the first two weeks of November, with numbers increasing in mid-Atlantic in early November. Large numbers remain on the Great Lakes well into the winter in some years.

GEOGRAPHIC VARIATION

No subspecies are recognized.

SOUNDS

Red-breasted Mergansers are not considered to be accomplished vocalists at all and are generally quiet, except during courtship and giving alarms around the nest or brood. Males: During display, give a catlike *yeow-yeow* or single *yeow* or loud, rough purring. Females: During displays give raspy croaking *krrrr-krrr* call. Occasionally females will croak flying to and from nest. Alarm call is low *garr*. They will call to their young with a low, husky, distinctive *kha-kha-kha*.

DIET AND FEEDING BEHAVIOR

Red-breasted Mergansers will feed almost entirely on inshore tidal waters, chiefly estuary mouths and shallow coastal bays, but also on freshwater lakes in migration.

They are similar in ecology to the Common Merganser but, in contrast, they feed more commonly in winter in salt water and estuaries, and they will dive more frequently. With bills having lamellae modified to grasp their prey, these mergansers will eat mainly small fish (4-6 inches in length) but also crustaceans (e.g., shrimp and crayfish), worms, insects, and amphibians. Red-breasted Mergansers will feed by diving (sometimes as deep as 30 feet), and when feeding will swim low in the water. They will often engage in cooperative herding, where a line of the mergansers will push and feed upon schools of small fish.

NESTING

Site: Red-breasted Mergansers will nest in woodlands near fresh water or in sheltered coastal areas. These mergansers will breed by estuaries, rivers and lakes in wooded country north to the edges of tundra. They nest exclusively on the on ground, sometimes in shallow cavities or under cover including under low branches, driftwood, drooping conifers, near water (usually within 75 feet).

Nest description: A hollow lined with nearby plant material, down, and some feathers. Down tufts darker gray than Common Merganser's, brown-tinged with pale centers and pale tips. Inside diameter 7-8 inches, outside diameter 12-14 inches, depth of 3 inches.

Clutch size: Average 9-10 eggs, sometimes 7-12.

Egg description: Elliptical to subelliptical. Smooth and non-glossy or slightly glossy. Smoke-gray to greenish-buff. 63 × 45 mm.

Incubation duration: 30-31 days, ranges from 28-35 days.

Brood parasitism: Frequently parasitizes other Red-breasted Mergansers, especially (64%) where nest-densities are high. Will parasitize others (e.g., Barrow's Goldeneye, Harlequin Duck, Mallard, Gadwall, Lesser Scaup).

HUNTING

Hunters were previously allowed very generous bag limits when it came to Red-breasted Mergansers. The birds were considered to be excessive fish predators, although not as egregious as Common Mergansers. These bag limits have now been curtailed.

Sawbills today are not considered prized ducks by most hunters and are typically not the main focus of a hunt. Mergansers don't exhibit the classic decoying tendencies of many other species. Despite their low ranking with hunters and a low total sport and subsistence harvest, hunting is still an important source of mortality.

POPULATION AND CONSERVATION

A precise population estimate is not available for Red-breasted Merganser since waterfowl surveys do not differentiate between merganser species. Available data suggest at least stable populations since the 1970s. The average total continental population (2002-2011), according to the NAWMP, was estimated at 400,000. Global population estimate is roughly 510,000- 610,000. Trend studies including all three merganser species (Common, Red-breasted, and Hooded) indicate that merganser populations are stable or increasing. In some areas (e.g., in the southern portion of their breeding range), Red-breasted Mergansers may be experiencing a decline. Red-breasted Merganser is threatened by degradation and loss of habitat, particularly water pollution, dam construction, and logging. They are also sometimes shot illegally due to the belief that mergansers negatively impact fish stocks.

Common Merganser
COME *Mergus merganser*

Plates Page 264

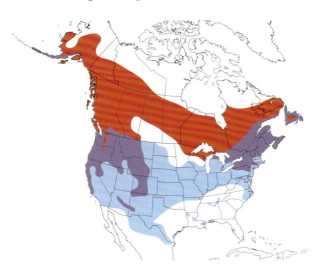

OTHER COMMON OR REGIONAL NAMES
 merganser, common merg, merg, sawbill, fish duck, American goosander, hell diver, sheldrake
(Arctic: payiq [YK], payit [NS], aqpaqsruyuuq [NWS])
(Québec: grand harle)
(Mexico: mergo común, mergo mayor)

MEASUREMENTS
Length: Male – 23.5-27.1 in, av 25.5 in (64.8 cm); Female – 21.3-26.6 in, av 22.9 in (58.2 cm)

Wing: Male – av 10.5 in (26.7 cm); Female – av 9.8 in (24.9 cm)

Weight: Male – av 3.64 lbs (1651 g); Female – av 2.73 lbs (1238 g)

Bill: Male – av 55.8 mm; Female – av 49.2 mm

FIRST IMPRESSIONS

Pairs and small flocks of this hardy merganser are regularly seen along raging streams or loafing on chunks of ice in winter lakes. Common Mergansers are usually found only on freshwater. In winter, they form large single-species flocks that are often tightly packed, facing the same direction. The bright white body and dark head of the male is striking even at great distances. That dark head is actually green, but can look black. The female has a gray body and rufous head. Her neck-line is defined by a sharp border, and she has a well-defined white chin. Size and Shape: This is a big duck! Common Merganser has a long, sleek body. Its head is oddly-shaped, almost trapezoidal with a thin bill. Its long, flat body rides low in the water. When swimming, the head is held low, so it looks like it doesn't have a neck. Clearly, this merganser looks front-heavy. Flight: As very large duck, the body appears to have some heft to it, rounding out the undercarriage. The neck is out-stretched. Males appear very white on the body with the clean-cut dark head. Females have a prominent brown head, and the white belly is apparent. Both sexes have large white patches in the wing that are prominent in flight. They tend to fly in steady single-file lines with individuals evenly spaced. Generally, these mergansers travel in relatively small flocks, often fewer than 30 individuals, and rarely joining mixed species flocks. They usually run along the water for takeoff and have stiff shallow wingbeats, holding their wings rather flat, not moving much above or below the horizontal.

ID: IN DEPTH AND SIMILAR SPECIES

Common Mergansers are slow to mature; they breed in their second-year (or later), and it is difficult or impossible to separate first-year birds from adult females in the field. First-year males often do not attain more than a few flecks of dark feathers on the head or white body feathers until they are nearly a year old. Old females can also have dark flecking on the throat, which makes confidently aging and sexing Common Mergansers very difficult in fall and winter.

Ducklings are dark brown, with a reddish head, white cheek, two dark stripes on the face, and short dark bill. Juvenile plumage begins to grow at 3-4 weeks and the young are fully feathered at about 5.5 weeks when they resemble adult females, but they have a lighter brown head with pale lores and lack a clearly defined white throat. They molt partly out of juvenile plumage from September-November, replacing head, body, and tail feathers (retaining wing feathers). Their overall appearance changes very little, except loosing the pale stripe on the lores. It seems as though they do not molt much during the winter (December-March), but they molt additional body feathers in the spring. At about one year-old, they molt wing feathers, followed by their first complete body molt.

First-year females and adult females are very similar, with rusty brown heads, white throats and gray bodies. In-hand, look for adult females shiny black tertial coverts versus first-years gray-black and worn tertial coverts. After breeding, adult females shed their wing feathers and are flightless for about one month, around August. They continue to grow tail and body feathers into October.

First-year males are virtually indistinguishable from females until sometime between February and May (or even later) when they will get their first white feathers in the body and darker head feathers. They molt a new set of wing and body feathers in the summer and fall, attaining their first mature adult plumage at the end of their second fall. Adult males are distinctive with bright red bills, dark green head, salmon-colored wash on the breast, white sides, and a dark gray back. After breeding, they molt their head and body feathers from mid-June to early August into eclipse plumage. Eclipse males have a dark brown head, white throat, gray breast, and gray and black on the back. In comparison to females, they have a thicker, brighter red bill and redder legs. In July or early August, they shed their wing and tail feathers and are flightless for about a month, until sometime between August and mid-September. At this time, they are molting in white body and dark green head feathers. By December, they are in stunning breeding plumage once again.

Similar species: Female Red-breasted Mergansers are most likely to be confused with female or first-year male Common Mergansers. Size and shape is an excellent place to start. Common is a heftier bird with a larger head and thicker bill. The crest on Red-breasted is also longer and spikier, while the Common Merganser is usually "flattened down." Look at the overall color pattern; the white throat patch is clearly defined on Common Merganser.

Sex ratio: Not well known, especially given the difficulty of sexing subadults. Males still seem to dominate at 65-67%.

GEOGRAPHIC VARIATION

Three subspecies are recognized.

M. m. americanus, is found across North America and exhibits no geographic variation.

M. m. merganser, the widespread subspecies of Eurasia, commonly referred to as Goosander is a migrant to the western Aleutian Islands. It is most readily separated by a thinner bill, most noticeably at the base, with a hooked tip. The nail is a different shape. The head shape appears more irregular, with a small flat crown, indentation toward the back of the head.. Our North American appears more sleek-headed.

M. m. orientalis, (also known as *M. m. comatus*) breeds south of *M. m. merganser* from northeast Afghanistan to western China, and is the largest subspecies distinguished by a shorter, narrower bill, longer wings, paler rump, and more black on the tertials and humerals.

SOUNDS

This species is generally quiet, but low grunts uttered by alarmed birds are regularly heard. Males: Call when alarmed and during courtship. Give a weak, high-pitched, bell-like note during salute display, a twanging *uig-a* during neck stretch, and a *kragagagagagaa* during courtship flight. Alarm call is a hoarse *grrr* or *wak*, sometimes given as a low chuckle, *guk-gu-ga-guck-guck-guck*. Females: Alarm call is a harsh *krr* or *gruk*, or *gruk gruk gruk* given in rapid succession. With brood, females utter higher pitched, rapid *cro cro cro* to call the young from the nest. She often hisses when with brood or in the nest when concerned.

YEAR IN THE LIFE

Common Mergansers span the Holarctic; breeding across the forested boreal parts of North American and in widespread areas across northern Eurasia. Common Merganser is fairly common and widespread in winter, remaining farther north than most species of waterfowl. High counts are from Shiawassee NWR in Michigan, Salt Plains

NWR in Oklahoma, Caballo Lake SP in New Mexico, and Lovewell Reservoir SP in Kansas.

On the southern Great Plains in winter, they'll flock by the thousands on reservoirs as far north as they can find open water. They are often seen snorkeling as they cruise shorelines of large lakes, rivers, and reservoirs. In contrast to Red-breasted Merganser, Common Mergansers are found primarily on freshwater, though they will use coastal bays, estuaries, and harbors.

Courtship rituals begin in late winter, and soon mates are selected for the breeding season. Their displays are not as elaborate as other mergansers; often several males and a female or more gather to court. The displays involve an intent-posture with the male extending his neck forward, head feathers erect, while circling the female. There are also wing-flaps and upward shakes involved. Even if a pair bond has already formed they will engage in these displays. Pairs in the southernmost part of the wintering range begin heading north in mid-February.

In the spring, they undergo a relatively short migration, heading overland at night and along seacoasts or river systems by day. Males often get a head start on migration, either by wintering farther north or heading north a few weeks before the females.

Once pairs reach the clear rivers and woodland lakes where they breed, the female seeks a tree cavity, box, cliff crevice, or site on the ground to nest. The female generally breeds for the first time in her second year. She is accompanied by her mate until partway through incubation, at which point the male takes off for a larger body of water to molt. The female tends to the brood ,often for 30-50 days after they hatch, before they are able to fly. It is common to see broods merge together to form large crèches. Females go through wing molt with or near the broods. Molt-migration of males is generally local movements, opposed to a long distance trek. Males breeding in Britain are a known exception, as they undergo a 1,250-mile molt-migration to northern Norway.

Fall migration is not a dramatic event, numbers just begin to build on the wintering grounds as water bodies to the north freeze over. Birds arrive on wintering grounds in the southeast in mid-Nov and build through December.

DIET AND FEEDING BEHAVIOR

Common Merganser, whose bills have lamellae modified to grasp fish, will feed mostly in freshwater habitats, including large lakes, and locally on estuaries and brackish waters, basically avoiding coastal waters of high salinity. They will even gather to feed at power stations. They are fairly deep divers, but will also forage in shallow water by swimming with their faces submerged looking for prey, not unlike a snorkeler. Their diet varies with season and location. As adept divers, they are able to capture fish, amphibians, crustaceans, mollusks, and other invertebrates. They are top predators in the aquatic food chain, feeding mostly on small to medium-sized slim fish (usually 4-12 inches long) of various species. (Their fish prey is usually larger than that of Red-breasted Mergansers.) Common Mergansers can forage cooperatively, drifting fish ahead of them. Their skill in catching fish has put them in the spotlight for studies of their impact on salmonid populations. Common Merganser will feed in waters up to 14 feet deep.

NESTING

Site: Common Merganser will nest near large lakes and rivers in northern forested freshwater rivers and lakes, sometimes over a quarter of a mile away from water. Common Merganser nests are found in a tree cavity, either live or dead (including holes created by Pileated Woodpeckers), by broken tree limbs or hollow tops of standing trees, cliff, or on the ground (under some cover). The nests in trees are usually 15-50 feet up. Common Merganser will take to man-made nestboxes. See the appendix at the end of this book for Common Merganser nest-box details and dimensions.

Nest description: The outside nests are hollows lined with nearby plants. Cavity nests have no added material. The nests are lined with pale gray down, paler than that of Red-breasted Merganser. Inside diameter c. 7.5 inches, outside diameter c. 12 inches, depth 4 inches. Entrance holes are about 5 inches in diameter.

Clutch size: Usually 9-12, sometimes 7-14.

Egg description: Elliptical to subelliptical. Smooth and slightly glossy. Creamy-white to yellowish. 66 × 46 mm.

Incubation duration: Average 32 days, ranging from 28-35 days.

Brood parasitism: Very frequently dumps in nest of conspecifics (sometime 20%), and occasionally in nests of Common Goldeneye and Hooded Merganser. In turn, regularly parasitized by those same two species.

HUNTING

Using the rationale of protecting economic fisheries, hunters were previously granted very generous bag limits when it came to Common Mergansers. (Common Mergansers were considered even more damaging as fish predators than were Red-breasted Mergansers.) This erroneous and excessive practice has been curtailed.

Sawbills today are certainly not a prized game species. Most are taken incidentally. Sport and subsistence harvest is low; there were, perhaps, 11,000 harvested in the United States in 2013 and in 2014.

Mergs often do not head directly into decoys, but will "take a look" and circle high over the decoys. They may respond to Mallard calls probably because the calling adds life to the decoys. They are fast fliers and known as a pass-shooting duck.

POPULATION AND CONSERVATION

Waterfowl surveys do not differentiate between merganser species, so estimates include all three: Common, Red-breasted, and Hooded Mergansers. Therefore, precise population estimates are not available. However, trend studies indicate that merganser populations appear to be stable or increasing. The total continental population, according to the NAWMP averaged (2002-2011) at over 1.2 million, while the global population estimate is 1.7–2.4 million.

The availability of nest cavities has a major impact on merganser populations, and widespread logging can have a negative effect on the birds by removing larger trees for nesting.

Because of this bird's fish diet, it is a significant indicator of contamination pathways and also the health of aquatic habitat. Elevated levels of contaminants (e.g., PCBs, dioxins, and mercury) have been found in mergansers in the Great Lakes and other sites. While troublesome, the levels have not yet had substantial adverse impact on Common Mergansers. Continued monitoring is justified.

Common Mergansers have been a focus of small-scale management efforts in the past when programs were instated to eradicate local populations, ostensibly to protect local salmonids fisheries or hatcheries. Local populations took years to recover, and there was minimal benefit to young salmonid populations.

Masked Duck

MADU *Nomonyx dominica*

Plates Page 273

OTHER COMMON OR REGIONAL NAMES
None used in North America
(Mexico: pato enmascarado)

MEASUREMENTS
Length: Male – 13.6-13.8 in, av 13.7 in (34.8 cm); Female – 13.2-13.9 in, av 13.6 in (34.4 cm)
Wing: Male – av 5.6 in (14.1 cm); Female – av 5.5 in (13.9 cm)
Weight: Male – av 0.80 lbs (365 g); Female – av 0.78 lbs (352 g)
Bill: Male – av 33.3 mm; Female – av 32.8 mm

FIRST IMPRESSIONS
Look carefully to find one or two shy Masked Ducks lurking quietly in dense vegetation at small, secret ponds in Texas and, perhaps Louisiana and Florida. Breeding males are a rich brown with a black face and baby-blue bill. Females and first-year males are barred brown with bold lines across the face, one through the eye and one across the middle of a creamy, pale cheek and dark bill. Size and Shape: Similar to their close relative Ruddy Duck, with a long stiff tail and big head with a fat bill. Bill proportions are slightly smaller and stubbier than those of Ruddy Duck. The sloping forehead leads to a fairly flattened crown. The head appears quite large, the body almost neckless. Flight: They are not seen flying often, but males and females have a white patch in the secondaries that sets them apart from Ruddy Duck. When observed, they fly low, often dropping into heavy vegetation. Relatively light birds, with a low wing load, they lift off the water almost vertically, without a running start. (They may actually get a boost in lift-off with a pre-flight shallow dive, using the forward propulsion of their feet and gaining momentum to leave the water sharply.)

ID: IN DEPTH AND SIMILAR SPECIES
Masked Ducks breed in their second-year, and males do not acquire their stunning adult plumage until they are two years old. Non-breeding males closely resemble females. Therefore, there are far more brown, female-looking, Masked Ducks found. Aging and sexing these brown ducks with striped faces is very difficult given what is currently known about their molt cycles. And little is known about the timing and locations of Masked Duck molt.

Ducklings are like miniature females, with dark brown bodies, yellow faces with two dark stripes, one through the eye and one across the cheek.

Juvenile plumage is replaced, starting with back and scapulars, then sides of breast and uppertail coverts. The birds undergo a wing molt later in the year.

First-year females are, apparently, much like the Adult females, with two dark stripes across the face, darkish brown crown, body mottled dark brown and tawny brown, also giving the back a finely-barred look. First-year males can be picked out from other female-types by looking for upperparts that are rufous-edged from the back to the uppertail coverts, or rufous feathers on the sides of breast, rufous-edged tertials and scapulars. Also, these birds may have black mottling on face. Adult males in breeding plumage are distinguished by their black faces and reddish-brown heads. Their bodies are generally reddish-brown and blackish. Their hefty blue-gray bills are black-tipped. Breeding males will have a pale blue orbital ring.

As an essentially tropical species, much of this duck's breeding, feeding, and molt timing are reliant on seasonal patterns, especially water levels. As a result, breeding and molt is not restricted. This is typical of southern hemisphere waterfowl. Normally, the Masked Ducks undergo simultaneous wing molt and will molt into an eclipse plumage before their wing molt. In eclipse plumage (usually November-April), males will appear much like females but with a bolder face pattern and stronger contrasting colors, especially with paler eyebrow..

Similar species: Males in their bold black and rufous-brown breeding colors should present no problems. Difficulties occur when considering males in other plumages or females, at which point Ruddy Duck should be considered. For those birds, always look for the two dark stripes across the face and the brown cap (not a solid dark crown to include the eye) in the Masked Duck. Masked Duck also tends to swim with its tail submerged, while Ruddy Duck is more likely to hold the tail raised. Habitat is a good clue: Masked Duck in southern wetlands with dense vegetation, Ruddy Duck in more open waters. Also, be aware that Black-bellied Whistling-Duck ducklings can look remarkably like female and first-year Masked Ducks!

Sex ratio: Unknown, but probably favors males.

YEAR IN THE LIFE

Masked Duck is a tropical species, found sporadically in the United States in southern and southeast Texas, casual in Louisiana and Florida. (There are a few exceptional records from elsewhere in the Eastern U.S.) It normally ranges from southernmost Texas south to central Argentina. They forage primarily in thickly-vegetated ponds and small lakes, sometimes in rice.

Even though Masked Ducks are not truly migratory, they do disperse, which contributes to their tendency to show up north of their normal range. They are also considered nomadic, partly due to water-level fluctuations.

The courting display is not well-studied, but may involve the male approaching the females with neck held low and neck engorged.

Nest timing varies throughout this species' range, but generally is during the wet seasons. In Texas, young have been observed from February to mid-November. The male remains with female until partway through incubation, leaving the female to tend to the brood.

GEOGRAPHIC VARIATION

No subspecies are recognized.

SOUNDS

Masked Ducks are quiet – so quiet that very little is known about their vocalizations. Male: Several courtship calls described as *coo-coo-coo*, *ooo-ooo-ooo*, *du-du-du*, *kirroo-kirroo*. Also, utters very low, soft *oo-oo-oo*. When alarmed, male gives loud *kuri-kuroo*, often repeated. Female: Reported to hiss.

DIET AND FEEDING BEHAVIOR

Masked Duck feed mostly along edges of floating mats of vegetation and in shallow water in overgrown ponds and densely vegetated lakes. Their near-vertical take-off allows them to feed in small ponds and wetlands. They feed by tipping-up and slipping below the surface. Unlike Ruddy Duck, foraging dives are not preceded by any forward leaps. Depth of dives are shallow, but these have also been estimated at about 6 feet. While feeding, only the tip of the Masked Duck's tail and head may be visible. The diet is presumed to be vegetable matter – seeds, stems, leaves, and roots of aquatic plants – with little or no animal matter.

NESTING

Site: Masked Duck will breed in ponds, usually small and always thickly vegetated. In dense beds of reeds, close to the water.

Nest description: An elaborately built flat platform of green reeds, roofed-over, with little or no down lining. Clutch size: 3-4. Sometimes 2-6.

Egg description: Oval to subelliptical. Lightly granular (smoother than those of Ruddy Duck). Cream-colored, buffy white, or even pale bluish-white. 54 X 41 mm.

Incubation duration: Uncertain, likely 23-24 days.

Brood parasitism: Dumping by conspecifics is likely.

HUNTING

There are very few hunting opportunities in the United States, although the species is legal to harvest in Texas. With so few in the U.S., extra protection for their limited population might be valuable to manage – and increase – this little-known species.

POPULATION AND CONSERVATION

The population across their wide range is estimated at 25,000 – 100,000 birds. This stiff-tailed duck is thought to be declining, but the rate is not known. Most Texas records (from November through April) appear to be cyclic, with 4 major invasions: late 1880s and early 1890s, 1930s, late 1960s and early 1970s, and 1990s. Peaks of such invasions often corresponded to sightings in Florida and Louisiana. Florida birds are assumed to be visitors from the West Indies (mostly from from November to February). In coastal Texas in a year considered one of Masked Duck invasion, 1992-1993, 47 individuals were counted, and when that was extrapolated to other blocks of suitable habitat in the region, it was estimated that there could have been over 3,800 Masked Ducks in the U.S. in that period.

Ruddy Duck
RUDU *Oxyura jamaicensis*

Plates Page 274

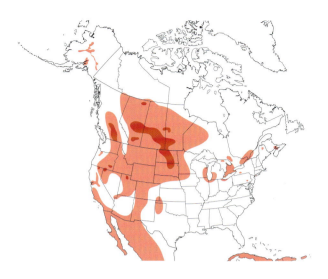
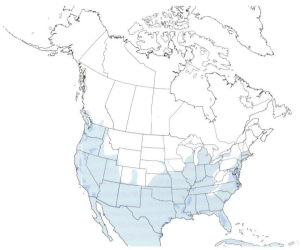

OTHER COMMON OR REGIONAL NAMES
Ruddy, stiff-tail, bull-necked teal, butterball, shot-pouch, wire-tail, dollar duck
(Québec: érismature rousse)
(Mexico: pato tepalcate)

MEASUREMENTS
    Length: Male — 14.7-16.0 in, av 15.4 in (39.1 cm); Female — 14.5-16.2 in, av 15.1 in (38.1 cm)
    Wing: Male — av 5.8 in (14.7 cm); Female — av 5.5 in (14.0 cm)
    Weight: Male — av 1.38 lbs (629 g); Female — av 1.17 lbs (532 g)
    Bill: Male — av 41.5 mm; Female — av 41.5 mm

FIRST IMPRESSIONS
The male's white cheek patch is a dead giveaway to ID wherever these stocky, compact, and distinctive ducks cluster in tight groups. Males have white cheek patches, blackish crowns, and gray-brown flanks in winter. In the summer months, males have bright chestnut-colored bodies and baby blue bills. Females and first-year males are brown overall, with darker caps and lines below the eye and across the cheek. Size and shape: Look for a small, round body, big head, broad bill, thick neck, and a long, fan-shaped or cocked tail. The concave bill is relatively large for the size of the body. Flight: Ruddy Ducks are not often seen in flight for a few good reasons. When they are disturbed they tend to dive instead of fly away. They migrate in small flocks at night. When they do take off to dart across a small body of water, they require a long runway with feet draggin behind. The long runway is required due to their high wing load (ratio of body weight to wing area), the highest among our waterfowl.

Their unique shape is especially apparent in flight, with head held high, thick neck, potbelly, long tail, and short broad wings. Flocks moving short distances string out low over the water to move between feeding areas. Wingbeats are swift and direct.

ID: IN DEPTH AND SIMILAR SPECIES
Both sexes are presumed to breed in their first-year. Aging and sexing female-plumaged birds is very difficult, if not impossible in many cases.

    Ducklings are dark gray overall. They have whitish cheeks with gray lines across them, blackish crown and large broad bill. They have heavy, round bodies, long stiff tails, and dark, coarse down. The nail on the bill is hooked sharply downward and angled backward. Juvenile plumage begins to appear at about 2.5 weeks and is fully grown at 8-9 weeks. Unlike most ducks, Ruddy Ducks lack an extensive molt out of juvenile plumage in late fall and winter (late Oct-late Feb). In most individuals, juvenile plumage is retained through the winter and early spring. Ruddy Ducks have more durable feathers that do not wear out as quickly.

    First-year females are most easily separated from adult females by retained juvenile tail feathers. Adult females are brown — with some chestnut tones in breeding. The brown is two-toned, especially in non-breeding, with darker brown above, paler below. The cheek stripe is always obvious; the bill is usually black, sometimes paler in breeding.

    First-year males are really hard (if not impossible) to separate from females, because they do not acquire a white cheek patch until December or later.

    Adult males are gray-brown bodied in the winter and chestnut-bodied in the summer. Look for a blackish cap and white cheek patch. Extremely rarely they will have patches of black in the white cheek patch or an all-dark cheek. The term "eclipse" doesn't really apply to Ruddy Duck, because their plumages follow more a traditional winter/summer pattern, similar to when a loon or grebe switches from breeding to non-breeding plumages. In northern California, adult males arrive on breeding grounds in late March, and undergo a body molt to attain a chestnut-colored plumage before pairing. In Manitoba, males arrive in mid- to late April, already in their bright rufous plumage. After breeding, males undergo a molt-migration, and they will replace their wing feathers simultaneously, followed by a body molt into their gray-brown winter plumage.

There are some unique features associated with molt in Ruddy Ducks: 1) males acquire a breeding plumage during the late winter and early spring, 2) the wing feathers are molted twice annually in some birds, and 3) the tail feathers are molted asynchronously.

Similar species: The distinctive shape with a stocky body and long tail, often held cocked up is often a dead give-away for Ruddy Duck. Their closest North American relative is the very rare Masked Duck, found primarily in South Texas. Masked Duck shares the shape and some stripes on the face, but is warmer brown overall than a female-plumaged Ruddy Duck. There is also limited white in the secondaries of a Masked Duck. See the Masked Duck account on p. 478 for a full treatment of this species pair.

Sex ratio: One of the highest male-biased ratios among waterfowl with 62-67%, but as high as 75%.

YEAR IN THE LIFE

Ruddy Duck is North America's misfit duck in many ways, with bizarre life-history traits. They are widespread, spanning the Americas south to the tip of South America. They can reach north occasionally to the interior lakes of eastern Alaska and rarely to Newfoundland.

Ruddies winter on lakes, bays, and salt marshes. When it comes to breeding, their pair bonds are not formed until their arrival on their breeding areas. These bonds are of short duration, and some do not form pair bonds at all. Males will display on the breeding grounds and mate with more than one female in a breeding season. Some males are truly polygynous and tend to multiple females at the same time.

In spring, migration begins in early February. Males arrive about a week earlier than females on the breeding grounds. After arriving, sometime from late March to May, males will begin to display. Ruddy Ducks have one of the craziest displays, the distinctive bubbling display. This is most the common courtship display in which a male raises crests (horns), inflates neck, and beats his bill slowly against his chest, pushing air out of its feathers, forming bubbles in the water, and at end, flicks his tail over back and emits a belching sound. The display is also used in aggressive interactions. A courtship display flight is also used and directed at females. In this display, the male holds his head and tail erect, quickly lowers his tail into the water, and runs across water's surface for a few yards with his back hunched, head and neck held forward and slightly downward, and beating his wings as if to take flight. His feet can actually make a popping noise slapping the water.

Ruddy Ducks take a liking to breeding on freshwater wetlands with dense emergent vegetation. About 3-5 weeks after the females arrive, they build a nest and lay a clutch of eggs. Their eggs are proportionally very large compared to their small body size, the largest eggs in proportion to their body size of all waterfowl. Males usually abandon females early on in incubation, but, unlike most other ducks, female Ruddy Ducks with broods are sometimes accompanied by males. (This is probably and extension of a pair bond and does not reflect any form of brood care.) Females typically leave broods well before they are capable of flight They fledge at 6-7 weeks. Some females will stay and molt with their brood. Molt-migration of males starts as early as August, when they travel (usually a short distance) to molt their flight feathers. Females follow several weeks later. There are several major molting sites that have been discovered, including Lake Winnipegosis in north-central Manitoba.

Fall migration kicks in earlier than other divers, beginning in late August, peaking from mid-September to late October. Many Ruddy Ducks arrive on wintering grounds in December.

GEOGRAPHIC VARIATION

Some authors have described two weakly differentiated subspecies; the mainland North American birds *Oxyura jamaicensis rubida* and a resident West Indies birds *O. j. jamaicensis*. However, the only morphological difference measured on a small sample of museum specimens is shorter wings in the West Indies specimens.

SOUNDS

Generally silent, except during courtship. Males: During their main courtship display, males give belching, *raa-anh* sound as part of the unique bubbling display. Produced when the male slaps his bill on an inflated throat and upper breast, the sound has also been described as a muffled ticking or popping-like *jif jif jif jif jijjijji werrrr* sound. The sound made during this display seems very unducklike. Females: Gives nasal raanh to call brood or in threat, and high-pitched *E* given when chased by males attempting force-copulations.

DIET AND FEEDING BEHAVIOR

Ruddy Ducks are skilled divers and omnivorous feeders. They forage by diving and occasionally dabble. Their diving is usually no deeper than 3 feet, sometimes to 10 feet, very shallow water for a diving duck. They will occasionally feed by skimming the water surface or immersing their heads, straining food from water. They feed close to emergent vegetation during breeding season, but during migration and winter, they feed mainly in open waters, near submerged vegetation. They will dive obliquely, in a leap-dive, and their diet consists mainly of aquatic insects, crustaceans, zooplankton, and other invertebrates. Their invertebrate diet predominates in the breeding season, but Ruddy Ducks also typically consume a variety of aquatic vegetation and seeds, especially at other times of the year.

NESTING

Site: Ruddy Ducks breed on freshwater lakes, ponds, stock ponds, sloughs, and marshes of varied sizes, where open water is bordered by tall plants growing in water.

Nest description: A partly floating and elaborate structure attached to growing plants, well woven, well concealed, and built up above the water level (10-12 inches deep), with plants pulled together over it. Rarely built on dry land. Built of reed stems, weeds, or other nearby plants. Usually without down. Nest size variable, but may be 4-12 inches in inside diameter, 8-13 inches in outside diameter, and 1-5 inches in depth.

Clutch size: Normally 6-10. Rarely to 18.

Egg description: Elliptical or subelliptical. Rough and granular. Dull white. 64 X 42 mm.

Incubation duration: Average 23-24 days.

Brood parasitism: Uncommon, but known to lay in Canvasback, Mallard, Northern Pintail, Cinnamon Teal, and Redhead nests. And, occasionally parasitized by Cinnamon Teal and Redhead, as well as other Ruddy Ducks. (Higher clutch sizes may actually indicate this parasitism.).

HUNTING

Stiff-tails were not particularly desirable game birds, known as "trash ducks" in the market-hunting era. Even today, they are not particularly prized by hunters. The harvest of Ruddy Ducks in the U.S. over two years (2013 and 2014) averaged about 53,700 birds; and for Canada the corresponding number was 2,500.

They decoy well in some circumstances, such as when they are first arriving in an area. They may be attracted over shallower and protected waters, using puddler methods. Generally, they don't fly much once they are settled into an area, and they are unlikely to pick up and make a pass at the decoys. Migrating birds in large bodies of water are typically found in the middle of open water, not near a shoreline blind and often will not fly in closer.

POPULATION AND CONSERVATION

Historically, Ruddy Duck was much more abundant. Their population took a significant toll during the market-hunting days. But Ruddy Ducks only became popular in the later stages of the market-hunting days, when populations of the other species had seriously declined. By then, there were still lots of Ruddy Ducks to harvest. They also became primary targets in part because they were relatively easy to harvest; they would dive to escape predators as opposed to flying. Although their numbers have seemed to have fluctuated since the mid-1950s, they have generally rebounded, and their population has been increasing slightly since the 1970s in North America. (Numbers may be slightly slipping in Canada.)

As diving ducks, these birds are prone to accumulate contaminants.

The average total continental population (2002-2011), according to the NAWMP, was estimated at 1.2 million.

MYSTERY PHOTO ANSWERS

With mystery photos, generally our first impulse is to look at an image, slap an answer on it, and then look to see if we are correct. Learning in this way may be quick, but it will not help you become a better naturalist and observer. The purpose of the waterfowl plates in this book is to help you practice identifying these birds in a way that can help you increase your skills in the field. This way, you can really go through this book, cover to cover, as a workbook.

As previously mentioned, nothing beats the real thing. Practicing with these images, however, is the next-best thing. To maximize this opportunity, consider the following:

1) Take your time! The best are the best because they put the time into the process. The challenge is to work out each bird's age, sex, and identity – if possible. These mystery photos are fun. It is important to recognize that we learn more when we don't know all the answers.

2) Study each bird very carefully. Learn the bird – its size, shape, and variations in plumage. A fun thing to try is to look away and draw or write a detailed description of the bird. Doing this well is much harder than it sounds, but it will improve your understanding of a bird's appearance and ultimately its identity.

3) Read the text and compare each waterfowl with other images in the book. This book offers many tools to help you work out the answers. Even after you feel that you know the waterfowl in question, compare it with others of the same species. You probably notice that no two will be the same. It is important to note that field guides give only a representative image. Here, you are able to see a wide range of variation shown by most species.

Watching and knowing waterfowl is a voyage of discovery. It is not about being right or wrong. Try to learn something from each image. And when it really comes down to it, try to appreciate not just the waterfowl, but everything else: the habitat, the other birds and animals, and how we interact with them. In the process, we should be able to appreciate, understand, and conserve these wonderful creatures around us. It's all great – you just have to see it!

Aging and sexing, p. 28
Bottom left: Surf Scoter. 1st-yr male. It is sexed by bill pattern, iris color, and newly-molted black adult feathers; aged by old pale-tipped and narrow juvenile feathers. The narrow, pointed, and pale-tipped tail feathers are typical of juvenile.
Bottom center: Redhead. 1st-yr male. It is superficially adult-like but with a few retained brown juv feathers, scattered throughout the body.
Bottom right: Ring-necked Duck. Adult female. The broad and blunt-tipped feathers are all adult. The gray face is also typical of adult females.

Mystery Swans, Seattle, pp. 42-43.
1) Adult Trumpeter Swan. Long neck, kinked backwards, V-shaped forehead, long triangular bill.
2) Juv Trumpeter, aged by small dusky feathers. Same size and shape as 1.
3) Adult Tundra Swan. Smaller size/bill with yellow spot.
4) Juv Trumpeter. Tricky one! Still in juv plumage, though faded. Large bill, straight culmen.
5) Adult Trumpeter. Large size with rounded back. Extensive black around eye, straight line to bill.
6) Three adult Tundras. Smaller size and different shape, compared to sitting Trumpeter (5). All three have yellow eye-spot and isolated eye.
7) Adult Trumpeter. Large bill. No yellow on large bill. Black on bill "absorbs" the eye. Extensive white on forehead. Note rust-staining.
8) Adult Tundra. Yellow on bill. Confirmed by size, shape, including arched-forward neck.
9) Adult Tundra. U-shaped forehead and yellow eye-spot (barely visible).
10) Juv Trumpeter (presumed). In full juv plumage; Tundras usually molted by Feb. Back also look like Trump-esque.
11) Adult. Shows mixed features. Hard to judge size and shape. Curved neck and curved culmen suggest Tundra. Lack of yellow spot suggests Trumpeter. Don't be afraid to say, "I'm not sure."
12) Juv Trumpeter. Juv plumage, extra-long neck, large wedge-shaped head.
13) Adult Tundras, four. Tough one! Shorter necks, bill more squared-off with isolated eye.

Mystery Swans, Great Lakes, pp. 44-45.
1) Adult male Mute Swan. ID by orange bill, extra-large know sexes it. Long tail.
2) Adult Trumpeter Swan. Size, shape, all-black bill.
3) Trumpeter Swan. Long neck. Shape of black around eye and bill. Bill looks big with broad base.
4) Tundra Swan. Shortish tail, eliminates Mute. Size and shape strongly suggests Tundra. Sleeping swan to the right looks noticeably larger and is presumably a Trumpeter.
5) Trumpeter Swan: juv left, adult right. Size, shape (including bill), and lack of yellow spot indicate Trumpeter. Left bird still in mostly juv plumage.
6) Tundra Swans, three. All 1st-yr, with mostly adult-type body feathers and contrasting gray neck. Note the still-juv bills.
7) Adult Tundra. Size, shape, and obvious yellow bill-spot give it away.
8) Tundra Swans, ten. Although distant, size and shape point to Tundra. Squared-off bill and isolated eye. (See birds 5 and 7.)

Looking for Rarities, p. 50-51.
Two Ross's, closest lower left birds. Canada Goose behind right. Ross's directly behind the Canada's back. One Ross's closest lower right bird, with another behind feeding with dark-morph Ross's x Snow Goose hybrid. Notice the

larger size of the hybrid and the intermediate bill shape; the wart on the bill is an obvious Ross's feature. Row of six birds behind – left-most bird is a Ross's. Directly behind, is a White-front, with another, peeking out, five birds to the right. And a Cackling Goose nine bird to the right of this. Look up, close Ross's flying over, top right (p. 68).

Mystery White-fronts, pp. 56-57.

1 and 3) These are pale with little contrast in neck and head makes them 'Pacific' White-fronts. Pale bellies – lacking speckles – and retained juv coverts makes them 1st-winters.

2, 4, and 5) Really dark head and neck, contrasting strongly with underparts makes these three birds Tules. Note how 4 stands 'tall.' All adults, with large squared-ended upperpart feathers.

6. Adult Pacific. Pale head and neck identifies to subspecies. Uniform adult-type wing feathers and barred belly ages bird to adult.

7. Pacific White-front. ID by pale head and neck.

8. Adult Pacific. Structure alone identifies this. Also, solid black belly is probably never seen in Tule. Pale head and neck.

9. All flying White-fronts are Pacifics, most showing low contrast between belly and the head and neck. Extensive dark bellies on two individuals is also strongly suggestive of Pacific. Did you see the Northern Harrier flying right?

Mystery Brant, pp. 66-67.

1) Adult 'Black' Brant. Very bold complete necklace. Extensive and dark underparts.

2) Adult 'Gray-bellied' Brant. Extensive and fairly darkish belly, but only a partial necklace.

3 and 5) Adult 'Pale-bellied' Brant. Very pale underparts, partial necklace.

4) 1st-yr Pale-bellied Brant. ID by pale belly. Aged by white-tipped wing coverts.

6) One Black with seven Pale-bellies. Darker upperparts and underparts accentuate white flanks on Black. Even the necklace is visible at this distance.

7) Four Pale-bellied Brant. ID by pale bellies. Two right bird are juvs, aged by slightly darker underparts pale-tipped coverts.

8) All Pale-bellies.

9) Top-middle Brant is a Black. Obviously darker with strong contrast with the vent. Beware: shadows can create the illusion of dark.

10) One Black Brant underneath the red ship on the right.

The Anchorage Conundrum, pp. 76-77.

Front left: the same color or slightly darker than most of the geese. But it's larger! It's a 'Dusky' Canada. Front left, center: Smaller and paler-breasted with a small bill. This is a 'Taverner's' Cackling Goose. Front right, center: This bird, and the one behind it and slightly left, noticeably smaller than the accompanying 'Lesser' Canadas. In fact, it's tiny, with a stubby little bill. The two are also one year old with retained, faded, juv belly feathers. The two lack neck collars. Everything points to 'Cacklers' (*B.h. minima*).

Mystery Geese in Flight, pp. 80-81.

1) Two adult Snows. Large bill with obvious grinning patch.

2) Four Snows and two Ross's in the flying birds. The Ross's is in the middle, upper left. Smaller, shorter-necked, stubby little bill.

3) The smallest looking bird, third from the right, has a dark trailing edge to the wing. This means it's a juv Snow. The rest are all Snows, based on size. Ross's would be smaller and shorter-necked.

4) Large, slim, long-necked, with long bills. These white-cheeked geese are Canadas.

5) Smaller than 4, with short fat necks and a stubby bill. The upper parts look frostier. These are Cackling Geese, appearing to be 'Richardson's.'

6) These are Canadas, rangy and long-necked.

7) It's a Canada, big and long-billed.

North Slope with Goslings, p. 82-83.

The four species are Greater White-fronted Goose, Brant, Snow, and 'Taverner's' Cackling Goose. Parasitic Jaeger are always bombing around.

Mystery Wigon, p. 129.

1) Adult drake Eurasian. The green behind the eye is common in this species.

2) Adult drake Eurasian. Orange head, pink breast, gray-and-white flanks. Again, no sign of hybridization.

3) Adult male American. Adult male head. Lacking juv feathers anywhere.

4) Adult hen American. Grayish head, lacking orange-brown tones. Black around base of bill. No juv feathers.

5 and 6) Adult male American. Bold color patterns.

7) Hen American with gray head.

8) Hen Eurasian, with unicolored reddish-brown head and chest.

9) 1st-year female American. Female wigeon with gray head. The tail and other feathers are worn and old. These are juv.

10) Hen Eurasian. Again, notice how uniform the head and body are.

11) Same as 2.

12) One adult drake Eurasian with Americans.

13) Same as 12.

14) Upper right bird has dark auxiliaries and dark head. It's a male Eurasian.

15) Adult male American x Eurasian hybrid. Reddish head with extensive green. Flanks with extensive pink, mixed with gray and white. All intermediate characters.

Northern Pintail, pp. 132-133.

Green-winged Teal, American Wigeon, and Northern Shoveler are the three other species.

Northern Shoveler, pp. 138-139.
No Blue-winged Teal.

Cinnamon Teal, pp. 146-147.
No Blue-winged Teal.

Mystery Teal, p. 154.
Lower left six birds in water: Front - Green-wing, two Blue-wing, and one Cinnamon. The Green-wing is the smallest, with square head, stong face pattern, and, importantly, a white horizontal stripe at the base of the tail. Look closely, and you will note all the birds behind the Mallard have these same characteristics.

Two are boldly-patterned drakes. The birds in flight also are Green-wings. The of the two swimming Blue-wings has a vague crescent moon on face, a male. The tail and other flank feathers are juv, indicating a 1st-yr bird. The second Blue-wing appears to be a female, although some of the colors suggest Cinnamon. The accompanying drake Cinnamon has a nice long bill, flat-headed look, red iris, and some russet on the flanks.

p. 155.
Bottom: the boldly patterned drake Blue-wings have the same breast pattern as the two sleeping Blue-wings. The two other standing teal appear to be the same size; their boldly patterned underparts are indicative of adult females. The pale loral area, prominent eyelid on an otherwise bland face indicate Blue-winged Teal. The flapping bird has a Green-winged wing pattern. The Square head, small bill with pale sides, and different face pattern confirm the ID. Mid-group of swimming birds: a nice boldly patterned drake Cinnamon, accompanying four similar-looking female teal. Their bill shape, bland face, warm tones, and size/shape are all a perfect complement the male. Hiding behind and to the right is a similar-sized and cold-toned teal. It has a bold face pattern with strong eyeline and a cheekstripe. It's a Garganey!

Next row of swimmers: the two front birds have pale lines in front of the tail. All the other characters are also good for Green-wing. The three birds in line behind are slightly larger and longer. They lack the pale line, and have pale loral spots, pale eyelids, and are Blue-wings. The other teal behind, one male in the water and three flying, are all Blue-wings.

Hybrid Dabblers, pp. 156-157.
The place is Oak Hammock Marsh; the building is the Duck Unlimited, Canada, HQ. D.U. are in this book out of recognition for the great job they do for conservation.

Greater Scaup, p. 180.
The other species are Long-tailed Duck, Bufflehead, Red-breasted Merganser, Canvasback, Mallard, and Mute Swan. A couple of female scaup in the background suggest Lesser, but are best left unidentified… until we get a better look! Never feel compelled to put a name to birds you are not sure of - however much pressure you feel you are under.

Mystery Aythya, pp. 182-183.
1) From l to r: Gadwall, Redhead, Ring-necked Duck, American Wigeon, Ring-necked Duck
2) There are one Gadwall, five Common Goldeneye, four Greater Scaup, one Lesser Scaup (next to Gadwall), and three Redheads. Note the smaller size, different head shape, and black restricted to the nail on the Lesser Scaup.
3) These are six Canvasbacks, all in the same pose but at different angles. Hint, hint… These are all decoys! If you got this, great job!
4) Mixed group of Redheads, Canvasbacks, and both scaup.
5) The three front scaup are noticeably smaller than the four scaup behind them. They have peaked crowns; they are Lessers. The four are Greaters. There is also a Canvasback (l) and Redhead (r).
6) There are seven Greater Scaup and four Redheads.
7) All Bufflehead, except for three Lesser Scaup and a Redhead.
8.) All Buffleheads.

Mystery Aythya Flight, pp. 184-185.
1) All Redheads.
2) Left, 1st-yr male Greater Scaup. Right two birds, Lesser Scaup; both smaller with two-toned wingbars.
3) Seven Greater Scaup, white clearly extended onto primaries on all.
4) Fifteen Canvasbacks.
5) All Redheads, except two male Canvasbacks. One close landing bird and a drake swimming in center.
6) Five Ring-necked Ducks.
7) Six more Ring-necks. Almost impossible to separate from Redhead from this view.
8) Five Canvasbacks and two Redheads (upper and lower center).

Mystery Scoter, pp. 232-233.
There are six White-winged Scoters on the plate: front right, adult female; four birds behind, adult male; right back, rear, adult female; left page, center, swimming right, adult female; center, swiming left, 1st-yr female (white cheek-patches and pale juv flank feathers). Sixth bird flying, top right.

Mystery Goldeneye, pp. 254-255.
1) Female Common, large all-dark bill.
2) Female Barrow's, stubby bill and head shape.
3) Adult drake Barrow's.
4) Female Barrow's, small yellow bill and head shape.
5) Female Common, long-looking mostly black bill and head shape.
6) Same as 5, but two Common.
7) Hybrid adult male. Face patch and scapular spots intermediate.
8) All Commons, except one male Barrow's on left.
9, 10, 11, and 12) All Common.
13) Common or Hybrid? Broad-based bill with extensive

yellow suggests Barrow's. But the bill is large! The wing covert pattern is Common Goldeneye. Bird was photographed where Barrow's is very rare.

Mystery Mergansers, pp. 268-269.
p. 268 - Lower left: Common, 1st-yr. Note serrated bill, designed to hold fish. Three swimming Red-breasted. On the ice, four Common Mergs, one Hoodie.
p. 269 - Three Commons and one Red-breast in the water. Three Commons on the ice.

Mergansers in the Bay, pp. 268-269.
Hooded: seven; Red-breasted: eleven; Common: fourteen.

Distant Ducks on a Mountain Pond, pp. 278-279.
1) Ring-necked Duck.
2) Common Merganser.
3 and 4) Common Goldeneye.
5) Common Merganser.
6) Wood Duck.
7) Ring-necked Duck.
8 and 9) Barrow's Goldeneye.
10 and 11) Common Merganser.

Prairie Potholes, pp. 280-281.
1) Ring-necked Duck.
2) Canvasback with Osprey..
3) Canvasback.
4) Gadwall.
5 and 6) Bufflehead.
7) Ruddy Duck.
8) Lesser Scaup.
9) Canvasback.
10) Redhead.
Also: five Bank Swallows, five Barn Swallows, two Great Blue Herons, two Black Terns.

Rust-stained Birds, pp. 284-285.
1) Pintail.
2) Green-winged Teal.
3, 4, 5, and 6) Blue-winged Teal.
7) Green-winged Teal.
8) Adult Tundra Swan.
9) Adult Northern Pintail.
10) Green-winged Teal.
11) Mallard.
12) Northern Pintail.

Mystery Freshwater Bellies, pp. 286-287.
1, 2, and 3) Gadwall.
4, 5, and 6) Mostly Gadwall, with two Mallards, and one American Wigeon.
7 and 8) All American Wigeon.
9) Four Northern Shovelers.
10) Four Hooded Mergansers.
11 and 12) All Wood Ducks.
13 and 14) Northern Pintail.
15) Green-winged Teal.
16) Northern Shoveler.

Overhead Bellies, pp. 288-289.
1) Six Green-winged Teal and two Blue-winged Teal (on top).
2.) Cinnamon Teal.
3 and 5) Northern Shoveler.
4) Hooded Merganser.
6) Wood Ducks.
7, 8, and 11) American Wigeon.
9) Gadwall.
10) Eurasian Wigeon.

Mystery Teal in Flight, pp. 290-291.
p. 290 - These are mostly Green-winged Teal, eleven in fact. There are three Blue-wings; only the Blue-wing at the bottom of the page doesn't show its blue wing coverts. One Cinnamon. One non-teal, an American Wigeon.
p. 291 - The three lower birds are Blue-winged Teal. The middle bird is female by wing-covert pattern; the other two, males. Adult male Blue-wing in the center of the page. Left and right are two more Blue-wings with leading edge to underwing solidly dark. The rest of the teal are Green-wings. There is a Gadwall and a Northern Shoveler (center-right). The distant birds in the flock are Mallards with four American Black Ducks (or hybrids).

Mystery Freshwater Marsh, pp. 292-293.
P. 292 - Mostly Northern Pintail. Bottom bird is a Greater White-fronted Goose. Mixed in are Canada Goose (1), American Wigeon (2), Northern Shoveler (3), Hooded Merganser (2), Bufflehead (1), Lesser Scaup (4).
P. 293 - More Pintail and even more birds mixed in! Ring-necked Duck (27), Blue-winged Teal (3), Cinnamon Teal (2), Green-winged Teal (1), American Wigeon (2), Black Duck (2), and Bufflehead (2).

Flying away in Buffalo, pp. 294-295.
1 and 2) Green-winged Teal.
3) Mallard (moribund – very dead).
4) Gadwall.
5) Mallard.
6) Lesser Scaup.
7) Ring-necked Duck.
8) Gadwall.
9) Mallard.
10) Mallard x Black Duck hybrid.
11) Black Duck.
12) Common Meransers.
13 and 15) American Wigeon.
14) Gadwall.
16) Hooded Mergansers.
17) American Wigeon.
18) Shoveler.
19) Pintail.
20) American Wigeon.

21) Ring-necked Ducks.
22) American Wigeon.
23) Shoveler.
24 and 25) Pintail.

Flying Away Bay Ducks, pp. 296-297
1) Unidentified scaup.
2) Long-tailed Duck.
3 and 5) Greater Scaup.
4) Redhead.
6) Long-tailed Ducks.
7) All Greater Scaup.
8) Common Goldeneye.
9) Red-breasted Mergansers.
10) Canvasback.
11) Redhead.
12) Red-breasted Merganser.
11) Common Goldeneye.

Squadrons, pp. 298-299
P. 298
Close Common Goldeneye with five mergansers behind: 4 Common, 1 Red-breasted. The Common Goldeneye flock above includes two hens that appear to be Barrow's at the bottom. Four Hoodies.

p. 299
Two close Bufflehead. The two lower mergansers are Red-breasted. With a distant flock of Common Goldeneye. Above the two Redhead are a Red-breasted Merg and Common Merg. The tight flight of mergansers are all Commons.

Landing, pp. 300-301.
p. 300
All the close lower birds are Northern Shovelers, except for the two Gadwall on the right. There are three descending American Wigeon, close together. The three landing, with feet dangling are tricky. The lower left is a Redhead. The other two are Gadwall. There are two more distant Gadwall, landing behind and a Mallard in the upper left.

p. 301
Lots of Green-wings up close landing, with a bright-plumaged Blue-wing. Four Common Mergs and a Bufflehead landing behind the teal. The distant birds are all Green-winged Teal. The two birds dropping down from high are Shoveler and Red-breasted Merg. It's always great to see Peregrines; this one is a young bird.

Dabblers taking off, pp. 302-303.
p. 302
The three Northern Shovelers are the last to take off, except for the still stilling Hooded Merganser, with its head sticking up. All the rest are Gadwall, except for the close male Mallard.

p. 303
The close bird flying to the right is a Pintail. There are lots more Gadwall taking off. The top two birds are a hen Mallard and a male Hoodie.

SAVING WATERFOWL AND WETLANDS

Being able to fully enjoy North America's waterfowl is certainly enhanced by being able to appreciate the amazing story of North American waterfowl conservation, a story that has had, decade by decade, its ups and downs, its zig-zags and detours, its dead ends and reversals. The lessons involved are not only important for waterfowl; they have implications for other birds, too.

You could skip this section of our book and still do very well identifying our waterfowl. But you would miss understanding and appreciating the many decades of hard work it took to save these birds, and you would miss why this experience should be built upon for the future of waterfowl and their habitats.

The waterfowl story that cuts across the last century and a quarter - at least back to the late 1880s - is a one that can certainly be appreciated by birders, hunters, policy makers, wetland conservationists, educators, and environmentalists of all stripes. The story involves three long-term trends or crises:

1) the efforts to stop the reckless, commercial slaughter of birds for the feather trade and table,

2) the reaction to a wholesale habitat crisis which devastated wetland, riparian, and bottomland habitats, and

3) the response to excess pesticide and chemical externalities on those habitats.

The lessons that are involved in North America's long waterfowl experience and the responses to these three crises actually touch on seven trends: exploitation, devastation, confusion, depression, reconstruction, recovery, and smart management. And we can examine each of those power-packed trends sequentially:

Exploitation: The "common wisdom" of the latter half of the 19th century assumed the existence of near-endless resources in a new continent, bounty available for the picking from coast to coast, from sea to shining sea. This feeling, however, began to be questioned as the 19th century was approaching an end. As part of the evidence of the problem, certainly by the close of the 19th century, waterfowl number began to drop perceptively. There were multiple causes, of course, including the feather trade, unrestricted market hunting, spring shooting, grain-baiting, the advent of repeating shotguns, and habitat loss. While the first of these, the feather trade, was one of these factors influencing waterfowl declines, that business was also devastating other waterbirds like egrets, herons, Brown Pelicans, Roseate Spoonbills, gulls, and terns which were impacted more than waterfowl. Still the effort for bird protection, stopping the feather-trade, the roots of the first long-term crisis in American bird conservation, impacted beleaguered waterfowl, as well. And, if observers at the time were neglecting the loss of valuable habitat during this part of our history, that's probably because the excesses in the uncontrolled harvest of our birdlife was so much more obvious.

The Labrador Duck, endemic to the northeastern coast of North America, had already slipped away. It disappeared by 1875, known to science for only about 100 years. No certain causes can be cited to explain its extinction. A specialized diet, exposure to introduced mammalian predators at nesting sites, and market hunting may all have been contributing factors, and the mystery persists.

By the late 1800s, sportsmen went to great lengths to distinguish themselves from the market hunters and the feather-harvesters. Those people killed without restraint and for purely financial gain.

Dr. George Bird Grinnell, the original inspirational godfather of the early Audubon movement, wrote in the pages of his own *Forest and Stream* in early 1894:

The game supply which makes possible the general indulgence in field sports is of incalculable advantage to individuals and the nation; but a game supply which makes possible the traffic in game as a luxury has no such importance. If this is granted, public policy demands that the traffic in game be abolished… We suggest this declaration, the sale of game should be forbidden at all seasons, as a plank in the platform of that vast body of men scattered in hosts over the country… interested in preserving the game of the continent.

Soon, the burgeoning Audubon societies, the American Ornithologists' Union (especially through their Model Law), and concerned hunters (e.g., the Boone and Crockett Club) were pressuring for state and federal game laws, seasonal restraint on hunting, and other moves to curtail an unrestricted harvest of waterfowl. Most often, however, when regulations were present, they would follow, rather than anticipate, problems in the field.

The passage of the Lacey Act (1900) and the creation of the first Wildlife Refuges (starting with Pelican Island, in 1903, created by President Theodore Roosevelt) helped to resolve this first crisis in bird conservation in North America, the struggle over the feather trade and market hunting.

Still, the demise of these twin threats to birds, including waterfowl, was not secure until about 100 years ago, with the signing of the Migratory Bird Treaty in 1916, its adoption by Canada in 1917 (the Migratory Birds Convention Act), its U.S. congressional passage in 1918 (the Migratory Bird Treaty Act), and its legitimacy confirmed by the U.S. Supreme Court in 1920. These actions made both U.S. and Canadian federal governments legally responsible for migratory birds.

Before the Treaty, there were few restrictions on bag limits, hunting hours, gun size, or the number of shells each gun could hold. Spring hunting was common; live ducks were used as decoys, and the sale of harvested waterfowl was fully legal. For example, and to confirm that market hunting was not simply an eastern phenomenon, waterfowl sold in markets in San Francisco and Los Angeles during the 1910-11 season numbered over 185,000 birds. Although the Migratory Bird Treaty was under fire between its signing in 1916 and the Supreme Court decision of 1920 - mainly from states' rights advocates and market hunters clinging to the past - a basic issue was being resolved with the treaty, and a fundamental shift had occurred in bird conservation.

This major achievement promised a brighter future, but many observers were still deeply troubled. Unless the circumstances on the ground improved quickly, they argued, waterfowl would still be seriously threatened.

Devastation: As the first crisis in North American birdlife (feather trade and market hunting) was coming to resolution with the successes of the early bird-protection movement, the second long-term crisis in birdlife, came to the fore. This was the waterfowl-and-wetland crisis. If it was late in getting attention, that's because any serious focus on saving habitat had taken a back seat in the first crisis. That oversight was no longer possible. This second crisis would be persistent, from at least the 'teens into at least the early 1940s. The encouragement to "farm to the fencelines" had spread quickly with the start of the 20th century.

The Great Plains and prairies were open to settlement as long as homesteaders were willing to break the land for agriculture. That expectation went beyond the norm, and became a veritable compulsion, with U.S. entry into WWI, there was the imperative to supply the troops and American allies with food (especially staple grains) during the Great War. Land here was being exhausted; waterfowl was being evicted. Wetlands continued to be drained for agricultural use. Soon, waterfowl became trapped between thoroughly drained habitat and eager hunters, still insufficiently restrained.

Confusion: The 1920s saw a lengthy - and ultimately non-productive — series of debates among bird conservationists of all stripes. The core question actually revolved around whether to save habitat or restrict hunting. The debate was embittered, and, mostly because "wildlife management" itself was not yet a recognized profession, emotions and confusion often ruled.

One debate concerned the relative merits of replicating the European model of raising waterfowl for release - stocking — in the wild.

A second lively debate was over charging waterfowlers a fee at the federal level to reinvest in waterfowl habitat and management. Furthermore, if waterfowl hunters were to be charged, it could be a possible fee of a dollar-a-year or a penny-a-shell. There were multiple options.

Another controversy swirled around expanding the Refuge System and whether such locations would embrace "public shooting grounds."

Men and women of good will were on all sides of these issues, and sometimes leading proponents would switch sides. All the while, habitat devastation — centered around draining for agriculture — continued apace. Some species, especially some of our dabbling or puddle-ducks, had experienced precipitous decline, with the devastation of native prairie and potholes. And the draining of bottomland hardwood habitat had its impact on many resident and wintering waterfowl species. The problem was ubiquitous. For example, along the Atlantic Coast, Canvasbacks were often the favorite targets through the end of the market-hunting period, if only because their meat was considered particularly tasty. It was called "king of the ducks" for that reason. And Wood Ducks were particularly hard hit across their range, with rumors of near-extinction by the turn of the last century. It was no accident then that Wood Duck was the only duck species singled out for total protection at the start of the Migratory Bird Treaty Act (total protection that lasted until the early 1940s). Curiously, and without much supportive science, there were few accurate population numbers to point to and no overall management recommendations to embrace.

At the same time, hunting expanded: in 1911, there were 1.5 million state hunting licenses issued; in 1922 it was 4.5 million; in 1928 it was 6.5 million.

Depression: The Crash of 1929 not only marked an economic collapse, it virtually marked a reality-check over the previous decade's obvious failures to make advances for waterfowl and wetland conservation. What started as over-farming and wetland draining to supply the troops with food (especially staple grains) during World War I peaked in a frenzy of draining the 1920s only to crash dramatically in the dirty 30s and The Dust Bowl. In the far West this also was also evident with the channeling of waterways to tame the land, but with dire bird-and-wildlife consequences. Waterfowl habitats in Canada were not immune from the trend. In one estimate, cultivated land — with the loss of waterfowl habitat — in the prairie regions of Canada had expanded from 1.5 million hectares in 1901 to 16.4 million hectares by 1931. The pressure was unrelenting.

Here was the core of our second crisis in bird conservation in modern times, that waterfowl-and-wetland crisis. The second crisis revealed that laws alone, or an international treaty, or even the most stringent regulations, however well-intentioned and strongly applied in the aftermath of the first crisis, could not save waterfowl without additional actions.

The U.S. and Canada were confronting a multi-faceted economic Depression, and it was emotionally dispiriting and depressing for conservationists, too. Hunter-conservationists had already acknowledged that our waterfowl was not everlasting, and, indeed, was under major duress. By one respected estimate, 1934 marked an all-time low for migratory waterfowl numbers, a mere 27 million birds. There was an aura of despair among conservationists of all stripes. In fact, there was even a serious discussion of instituting a hunting ban for a year.

In January 1935, the American Game Conference held its 21st annual meeting, organized through the American Game Association (forerunner of the Wildlife Management Institute). More than 800 delegates debated for four hours the issue of whether or not to completely close the next waterfowl hunting season. Although the resolution to close the season was defeated, the debate actually illustrated how dire the situation had become. More than a third of the committee members voted to close the hunting season.

By 1936, duck seasons were reduced to 30 days, and several species – including Canvasback, Redhead, and "Atlantic" Brant – were added to the list of birds protected from shooting.

Reconstruction: Clearly, the conflicting arguments of the 1920s and the early 1930s had to be resolved, before the waterfowl consequences became even more horrific. Many of the different stances of the past decade were actually combined, finances and manpower marshaled.

The issue of raising waterfowl for release was mainly set aside, with a few exceptions. There was the example of "recovering" Canada Geese, from which we now have the ongoing problem of "resident" Canada Geese across many areas of North America. For Trumpeter Swans there was a combination of captive breeding, translocation, and reintroduction in the 1930s and 1940s, redoubled since the 1980s.

Concerning the debate over what to charge hunters on the federal level to reinvest in habitat and management, ultimately, both proposed solutions were applied.

The dollar-a-year argument found a home with the pursuit of a federal license – or stamp – paid for by waterfowl hunters. Bills for a federal license had been defeated in 1921 and 1924, and side-tracked in 1929 (the applicable portion having been removed from the Migratory Bird Conservation Act of 1929). Only with the passage of the Migratory Bird Hunting Stamp Act of 1934 was there a federal fee imposed and a funding vehicle created. The 1934 law, commonly referred to as the duck stamp act, required any persons 16 years of age or older hunting ducks, geese, or swans, to have a $1 federal stamp and valid state hunting license. Jay Norwood "Ding" Darling, cartoonist, conservationist, and newly appointed head of the U.S. Biological Survey, drew the artwork for the first stamp. Over the decades, the stamp (since 1977, renamed the Migratory Bird Hunting and Conservation Stamp) would bring in over $980 million, and this funding mechanism would secure over 6.0 million acres of valuable wetland and grassland habitat for the National Wildlife Refuge System.

A version of the penny-a-shell argument was also adopted. With the passage of the Pittman-Robertson Act of 1937 (official name, Federal Aid in Wildlife Restoration Act), wildlife funds were collected on the federal level

The 1934-35 Migratory Bird Hunting Stamp.

and distributed to the states. Pittman-Robertson took over a pre-existing 11 percent excise tax on firearms and ammunition. But instead of having those funds disappear into the U.S. Treasury, as had been done in the past, the funds would be kept separate so that the Secretary of the Interior could distribute them to the states for wildlife conservation. Over the decades, the state wildlife agencies have used much of these funds for waterfowl and wetland support.

The debate over expanding the Refuge System and whether refuges would include "public shooting grounds" was resolved. The "inviolate sanctuary" approach of the 1929 Migratory Bird Conservation Act was the original guide. (Later, the permissible hunting bumped up on refuge refuges lands - first to 25% in the late 1940s and then 40% in the mid-1960s.) Clearly, refuges were the main beneficiary of the reconstruction that emerged toward the end of the 1930s.

There finally was a funding mechanism for growing a refuge "system," vital for waterfowl. The stamp starting bringing in dollars, and Darling was able to cajole significant starter funds from the Franklin Delano Roosevelt administration. The priorities for habitat acquisition were based on the vision of Frederick C. Lincoln's "flyways" (articulated by 1935), the growth of wildlife management as a science, and the persistence of Darling's first lieutenants, Ira N. Gabrielson and J. Clark Salyer.

The existence of the Civilian Conservation Corps (CCC) which mobilized the manpower of as many as three million young men (between 1933 to 1942) certainly didn't hurt, either. Not only did this army of eager and semi-skilled manual labor contribute to the conservation and development of natural resources in mostly rural lands owned by federal, state, and local governments, but waterfowl especially benefitted. Many parks, forests, and refuges were "built" through the CCC. And the dikes, impoundments, and other projects constructed or restored waterfowl habitats from coast to coast.

Before the big drought of the 1930s, before the stamp, the U.S. federal government managed about 744,000 acres for the conservation of all kinds of wildlife.

By 1942, nearly 3,000,000 acres had been accumulated for waterfowl alone.

This period of "reconstruction" also marked a flurry of citizen action in favor of waterfowl and wetlands. By the mid-1930s, an organization called More Game Birds in America Foundation transformed itself into Ducks Unlimited, Inc., and a parallel organization, Ducks Unlimited Canada was founded in 1938. The initial drive was to conserve waterfowl habitats in Canada, but by 1984 DU Inc. initiated highly successful conservation projects in the U.S. as well. Also in the late 1930s in Manitoba, the Delta Duck Station was established, later to evolve into the Delta Waterfowl Foundation.

Species started to respond, numbers picking up in nesting, stopover, and wintering areas.

Recovery: The first tentative waterfowl census was not published until 1930. Only with reliable numbers could the growing cadre of waterfowl-and-wetland managers make informed decisions concerning habitat acquisition, hunting regulations, and future expectations. The parallel growth of wildlife management as a science and a profession was essential. Inspired by Aldo Leopold and his colleagues, the goal was to restore and improve habitat and to educate the professional biologists and the land managers about the clear limits of the resources which informed their interests.

Even aircraft was used as a way to count waterfowl numbers. Experimentation began in 1931 with Frederick Lincoln, and the procedure was tried for the next 20 years. But it was the end of WWII, with the availability of military-trained pilots and surplus military aircraft, along with the accumulated experience of aerial reconnaissance, which made aerial surveys readily achievable. Every spring and summer, since 1955, cooperators in the U.S. Fish and Wildlife Service, the Canadian Wildlife Service, state and provincial biologists, and non-governmental partners engage in the Waterfowl Breeding Population and Habitat Survey (WBPHS). Beginning in 1948, flyways – Atlantic, Mississippi, Central, and Pacific - began to be codified as convenient administrative units to assist in waterfowl management, serving as the basis for managing harvest and other regulation and decision-making processes. By 1952, all four Flyway Councils were in place. These flyway efforts grew to cover both the U.S. and Canada.

If anything, the 1940s and 1950s represented a period of vital information-gathering, consolidation, professionalization, and experience in the waterfowl-and-wetland world.

When the protection of the Wood Duck was lifted in 1941, Frank Bellrose, waterfowl chronicler extraordinaire, regarded its recovery as nothing short of miraculous. Following World War II, nest boxes began to play a significant role in the continued recovery of this species. If Wood Duck could recover, then other waterfowl species could, too.

Smart management: Just because there was a postwar growth in professionalism and experience, just because wetlands were being secured across North America, doesn't mean that there were not serious problems and downturns in waterfowl populations.

In fact, there were troublesome cycles of downturn, particularly in the late 1950s, the early 1960s, the late 1970s, and the mid-1980s. By 1985, many waterfowl populations had dropped again to disturbingly low numbers, impacting Mallard, Northern Pintail, American Black Duck, American Wigeon, and Blue-winged Teal. At the same time, sea ducks, more difficult to watch and to count, were clearly in some trouble.

A smart-management response emerged. There were, in fact, four significant innovations in the 1980s and the start of the 1990s which would help secure a better future for waterfowl.

The first was the introduction of conservation innovations in the 1985 Farm Bill, elements which became very important for grassland and wetland conservation and for waterfowl. The bill was officially called the Food Security Act of 1985, and much of the content reflected the agricultural-support of the past. For far too long, the U.S. Department of Agriculture had been providing assistance – monetary and technical – for drainage of properties that were actually important waterfowl habitat. At the same time, moderate – but clearly insufficient - efforts, such as the Soil Bank Program going back to the mid-1950s, were focused on lands that were at high risk of erosion. These cross-purposes began to be resolved with the Farm Bill of 1985, which contained provisions for significant landscape conservation in the Conservation Reserve Program (CRP). CRP would subsidize new planted grassland cover on agricultural lands, effectively removing the land from agricultural production and protecting highly erodible land while producing soil-enriching growth and wildlife cover. "Swampbuster" in the 1985 bill also discouraged the conversion of wetlands to cropland use, with producers losing eligibility for several federal farm program benefits if they engaged in such conversions. This was extremely important for waterfowl, as was the similar and parallel Wetlands Reserve Program (WRP) established in the next Farm Bill (1990). WRP became another voluntary program for landowners, providing them the opportunity to protect and restore wetlands on their property. Both CRP and WRP have been boons for waterfowl (as well as an entire suite of wetland and grassland species – from shorebirds to long-legged waders, to grassland songbirds). With the 2014 version of the Farm Bill, the WRP was combined with other protection programs into a new Agricultural Conservation Easement Program, but it functions with similar results.

The second was the North American Waterfowl Management Plan (NAWMP) in 1986. This plan set out a blueprint for waterfowl conservation and restoration across the continent (first between the U.S. and Canada, and in 1994, to include Mexico). The ambitious original plan sought to focus and coordinate existing conservation programs, approach waterfowl conservation on a landscape level, set population goals for waterfowl, and launch a new partnership institution. This key waterfowl plan has since served as a model for other plans for other suites of species, including shorebirds, non-waterfowl waterbirds, and Neotropical migrant landbirds.

The third innovation was the establishment of those recommended partnership institutions, the Migratory Bird Joint Ventures. A Migratory Bird Joint Venture (JV) is a collaborative, regional partnership of government agencies, non-profit organizations, corporations, tribes, and individuals to conserve habitat for priority bird species. Six JVs were created in 1987, located in portions of North America - the Prairie Pothole Region of the U.S. and Canada, the Central Valley of California, the Lower Mississippi Valley, Gulf Coast, Atlantic Coast, and Great Lakes/St. Lawrence Basin — deemed the highest priority habitats of concern for waterfowl.

Since then, and especially with the next innovation, NAWCA (North American Wetlands Conservation Act) the primary funding mechanism for NAWMP activities, JV partnerships have invested $8.5 billion to conserve 26.5 million acres of critical habitat. The two dozen Joint Ventures existing today cover virtually all of the continental U.S., the lion's share of Canada, and large parts of northern Mexico.

The fourth innovation was the passage and funding of the North American Wetlands Conservation Act of 1989. NAWCA provides matching grants for partnerships that have developed to carry out wetlands conservation projects in the United States, Canada, and Mexico for the benefit of wetlands-associated migratory birds and other wildlife. The Act was passed, in large part, to sustain activities under the North American Waterfowl Management Plan, for the long-term protection of wetlands and associated habitats needed by our waterfowl and other migratory birds. From September 1990 through September 2015, 5,467 partners in 2,553 projects have received more than $1.4 billion in NAWCA grants. In addition, these have leveraged nearly another $3 billion in matching funds to impact almost 30.8 million acres of habitat. Canadian projects alone have accounted for nearly $2 billion in initial funds and partner contributions. Funding from this act is split 50% to The U.S., 45% to Canada and 5% to Mexico, in recognition of the continental habitat needs of these migratory species.

These four innovations initiated in the 1980s and early 1990s have made for real advances in saving waterfowl and saving wetlands since then. But problems persist. Notable waterfowl species that have experienced long-term declines or remain well below NAWMP population objectives include American Black Duck, Northern Pintail, and Lesser Scaup. Recently, Greater Scaup and American Wigeon have exhibited some declines, raising concerns. Spectacled and Steller's Eider (both classified as Threatened species under the Endangered Species Act in the 1990s) continue in deep trouble. Other species, such as Emperor Goose in the West and Harlequin Duck in the East deserve special attention. Brant on both coasts may be stabilized after dips in the 1970s and 1980s, but may be is too soon to say if they are truly out of trouble.

At the same time, there are some major success stories among waterfowl in the past few decades. Some of them include the following: the population and range expansion of Black-bellied Whistling Duck, the growth of Cackling Goose (especially the recovery of the Aleutian subspecies), the expansion in the east of Gadwall and Northern Shoveler, and the considerable increases in Bufflehead.

It is important to realize that a third long-term crisis in American bird conservation, focusing on a sensitivity to pesticides and chemicals, an awareness following Rachel Carson's *Silent Spring*, had impacted waterfowl and their habitat, too. Indeed, the rise of environmentalism, and the extent to which all things in the natural world are interconnected, did not bypass the waterfowl community. Whether it has been measuring levels of contaminant exposure, the pursuit of clean water — indeed, much of the "habitat" which surrounds a duck's life! — or the banning of lead in the environment (with lead shot banned in waterfowl hunting in 1991), the connections have been important and ongoing.

In short, however, the story of waterfowl conservation is the story that runs from shocking abuse to TLC, tender loving care. At times, this entire experience seems under-appreciated outside of waterfowl circles. It shouldn't be.

What's more, there are some important areas of intersection between waterfowlers and non-waterfowlers that merit consideration. The North American Waterfowl Management Plan (NAWMP), a leading model for international bird conservation plans, was revised and officially signed in late May 2012.

The ambitious 2012 Revision of NAWMP sets forth three overarching goals for waterfowl conservation:

1) maintain abundant and resilient waterfowl populations to support hunting and other uses without imperiling habitat;

2) support wetlands and related habitats sufficient to sustain waterfowl populations at desired levels, while providing places to recreate and ecological services that benefit society; and

3) increase the number of North American citizens who enjoy and actively support waterfowl and wetlands conservation.

The first two goals had always been part of the NAWMP. They are often addressed when considering the areas of greatest significance for waterfowl (see coverage starting on p. 500). The third goal is new and very exciting, and it underscores the importance of people to the success of waterfowl and wetlands conservation. In fact, the NAWMP revision went on to elaborate on the issue (p. 9):

The number of people who make a dedicated effort to view waterfowl is now ten times the number of waterfowl hunters, and their numbers continue to grow. This phenomenon creates an opportunity to increase support for conservation as well as a responsibility to ensure the needs of this growing clientele are being addressed.

Clearly, waterfowl-watchers and waterfowl avitourists are becoming increasingly important for thoughtful waterfowl conservationists. The conclusion is obvious, insofar as the 2011 report of the U.S. Fish and Wildlife Service, *Birding in the United States: A Demographic and Economic Analysis*, indicated that the most popular group of watched birds in the U.S. was waterfowl.

If there are swans, geese, and ducks tomorrow, it will be because of the responses to the major bird crises over the past century and a quarter – bird protection and the attempt to stop the slaughter, the long-term mid-century wetland emergency, and the rise of environmental concern. The whole ethic of stewardship - from waterfowl hunters, to professional wildlife managers, to concerned birders, to all sorts of other conservationists and environmentalists – has become an integral part of how waterfowl and wetlands are approached today. Waterfowl has benefitted, and so have we.

What You Can Do

It is essential that we continue to protect waterfowl populations in the 21st century. We all can help preserve ducks and waterfowl by taking even small steps. Below are some of the possibilities to consider:

1) Purchase a Duck Stamp. If you could only do one thing - buy this book or get a duck stamp, we'd prefer you try the latter. It's officially called the Migratory Bird Hunting and Conservation Stamp, but often just called the duck stamp. That said, we also hope you are far enough along in this book to already have purchased it! Please don't return it. Get a duck stamp, too! Yes, federal duck stamps function as a national license in the U.S. to hunt waterfowl, but they are much more. Stamps will also cover your entry fee into any National Wildlife Refuge. Since 1934 duck stamps sales have raised more than $980 million that has been used to secure over 6.0 million acres of habitat for the National Wildlife Refuge System. Purchasing a duck stamp is also easy. They now cost $25 each and are available at U.S. Post Offices, most sporting goods stores that sell hunting and fishing licenses, and online at: http://duckstamp.com/. It has been estimated that 25% of all duck stamps sold are purchased by someone who did not hunt waterfowl that year.

There are also state duck stamps in the U.S. dedicated to different conservation efforts, depending on the state.

In Canada, the equivalent is the Canadian Wildlife Habitat Conservation Stamp. This effort started in 1984, 50 years after the U.S. Duck Stamp. The revenue from this Canadian stamp funds the conservation and grant programs of Wildlife Habitat Canada, a national charitable non-profit conservation organization. The stamp, costing $8.50, is purchased primarily by waterfowl hunters to validate their Migratory Game Bird Hunting Permits. You can secure your own Canadian Wildlife Habitat Conservation Stamp at Canadian Post Offices, at Rousseau Collections Stamps and Coins at Hudson's Bay in Montreal, and also online, with details here: http://whc.org/online-store/

2) Support the Jr. Duck Stamp effort. The Jr. Duck Stamp program began in 1989 as a companion to the Duck Stamp. The program is an art- and science-based curriculum that teaches wetland and waterfowl conservation to students in kindergarten through high school. It is linked to many state and a national student art contest. The program encourages students to explore their nature, investigate biology and wildlife management, and encourages them to express and share what they have learned with others.

3) Join organizations dedicated to preserving waterfowl and their habitats. These organizations and others pool the efforts of tens of thousands of people, making large-scale land management and acquisitions possible. Some of our favorite organizations include Ducks Unlimited Inc, Ducks Unlimited Canada, Delta Waterfowl, and The Nature Conservancy.

4) Make your property wildlife-friendly. If you have some large property or property adjoining waterfowl habitat, you can play a significant role. There are many opportunities for private land owners to manage in favor of waterfowl. Conservation easements are one major vehicle as are elements of the Farm Bill. Don't forget local land trusts. And even with small properties, it is always good to remember that when it comes to water quality, ducks and other water-loving birds live downstream from you!

5) Cooperate in a nest-box project for waterfowl. Many organizations participated in nest-box projects, providing nesting sites for Wood Ducks, mergansers, goldeneye, and other ducks. These projects are often run by refuge or park Friends Groups, duck clubs, scout groups, and others. It's a wonderful way to get your hands and feet dirty, and to make a difference near where you live. See the nest-box section which follows for ideas.

6) Be a responsible hunter. Follow the rules; you should know what they are. Most importantly, learn waterfowl identification. Now hunters will do what their mentors teach them. The regulations are there to protect ducks and ensure they'll be flying by your blind next year and for years to come. And remember that honest reporting of harvest numbers – through the Harvest Information Program (HIP) – allows biologists to better monitor duck populations, allowing for appropriate bag limits and healthy, sustainable waterfowl populations.

7) Be a responsible birder and wildlife photographer. Viewing and photographing waterfowl – and other wildlife – is wonderful, but behaving responsibly in the field is a must. Viewers and photographers have an obligation at all times to think of acting in ways that benefit the birds, the natural environment, and the rights of others. For decades, the American Birding Association has promoted its fine "code of ethics." Details include four general areas of concern:

1. Promoting the welfare of birds and their environment.
2. Respecting the law, and the rights of others.
3. Ensuring that feeders, nest structures, and other artificial bird environments are safe.
4. Awareness that group birding, whether organized or impromptu, requires special care.

They are explained in detail, with examples here: *http://www.aba.org/about/ethics.html*

The North American Nature Photography Association also has a useful code of ethical field practices, particular to issues confronting nature photographers. These involve the knowledge of subject and place, knowledge of rules and laws, and the development of individual expertise and related responsibilities: *http://www.nanpa.org/wp-content/uploads/NANPA-Ethical-Practices.pdf*

8) Participate in waterfowl banding and neck-collar recovery. Each waterfowl that is banded receives a piece of "jewelry" or "bling," a uniquely numbered aluminum ring clamped onto its leg, so individuals can be recognized in the future. Each time a banded bird is recaptured or the band is reported by a hunter, it provides biologists with valuable information. Banding data has been essential in working out migration routes, how productive the breeding season was, how long birds are surviving, and establishing harvest information for the future. Reporting is simple. In a matter of minutes, you can report a band, in one of three ways:

Online: *www.reportband.gov*
Call Toll-Free: 1-800-327-BAND
Write: Bird Banding Laboratory, 12100 Beech Forest Road, Laurel, MD 20708

Much like bands, plastic neck collars are used to track individual geese and swans. They come in various colors with large-print numbers and letters that can be read from a long way away. Sightings of birds with neck collars can be reported like bird bands on the Bird Banding Lab's website.

9) Submit your notes: Taking field notes is important. If you want to become better at identifying birds, the fastest way to improve is by taking notes while watching birds in the field. If you sketch or describe a bird at the moment you are watching it, you'll notice things you've never seen before. You will build knowledge of what birds look like and how they behave. These notes, including numbers and locations become particularly valuable when you enter you field checklists into eBird: *www.ebird.org*

Using eBird is simple, and it's a free online checklist program where your observations contribute to a worldwide database of bird sightings, used by scientists, conservationists, and anyone who wants to explore the information.

If your observations are significant enough – covering rarities, observed seasonal trends, or significant movements of waterfowl, you can also submit the detailed information to the regional editor for North American Birds. You can find particulars here: *http://publications.aba.org/north-american-birds/*

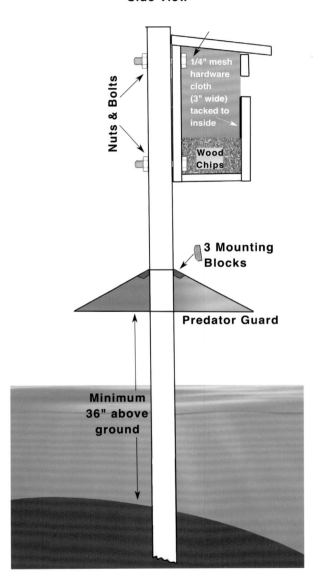

Nestboxes

Nestboxes for cavity-nesting ducks can be extremely beneficial for local waterfowl populations. In fact, starting in the late 1930s, nest-boxes became essential in recovering Wood Ducks across North America. Today, some cavity-nesting species (e.g., Common Goldeneye, Barrow's Goldeneye, Bufflehead, and even wild Muscovy Duck) are limited by the availability of natural nesting cavities.

HINGE FOR CLEANING

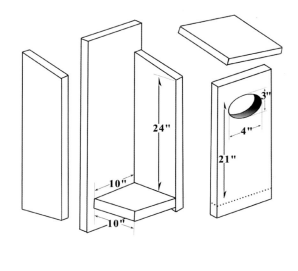

Hooded Merganser Nestbox

These species could benefit substantially from organized regional nest-box efforts, an important management practice where habitat has been destroyed by logging or other human pressures. Of course, local-scale changes in waterfowl populations may actually reflect larger scale, regional or continental, shifts in population size.

While most suitable cavities occur in living trees (60% or more originate from broken branches or heart rot), completely dead trees rarely remain standing long enough to provide regular nesting sites year after year.

The placement and monitoring of the boxes are not only helpful, but they can also be simple fun! Nestbox projects can be wonderful experience for families, bird clubs, duck clubs, scout troops, refuge/park friends groups, and others. The projects have something for everything: building, placement, cleaning, repair, monitoring, and, especially, witnessing the results. Being able to point to the outcome of such work — producing more ducks — can be incredibly gratifying.

Once nestboxes are claimed they may be used by the same female in subsequent years. Young may also return to the same area to seek out available cavities, so the success of a nest-box program often depends on a good start!

Our cavity-nesting waterfowl also have stronger-shelled eggs than other waterfowl, presumably for durability. And while these birds are resilient, they need safe and secure nest sites. This is where nestboxes come into play for eight species of our cavity-nesting ducks.

The chart below shows essential interior dimensions for the boxes. The exterior requirements – i.e., larger back to assist in fastening, overhanging roof (at 2-4 inches), and access door for cleaning and monitoring – are not on the chart. These features are variable and often stylistic; work them into your assembly plans. Also, not on the chart is placement height, a subject covered under each of the eight species descriptions that follow. The height, whether down to the ground or to the water surface, is measured from the center of the box's entry hole. Finally, almost all of the entry holes are elliptical.

As for the egg descriptions, clutch size, incubation duration, brood parasitism, and other nesting details, see the book's individual species accounts, all cross-referenced in the pages that follow.

Species	Floor	Front/Back	Height to Entrance Top	Entrance (height x length)
Black-bellied Whistling-Duck	12" x 12"	22" / 20"	19"	4" x 5"
Muscovy Duck	16" x 16"	24" / 22"	21"	7 3/4" x 7 3/4"
Wood Duck	10" x 10"	24" / 26"	21"	3 1/2" x 4"
Bufflehead	7" x 7"	15" / 17"	12"	2 3/4" x 3"
Common Goldeneye	10" x 10"	28" / 30"	21"	3 3/4" x 4 3/4"
Barrow's Goldeneye	11" x 11"	17" / 19"	12"	4 1/2" x 5"
Hooded Merganser	10" x 10"	24" / 26"	21"	3" x 4"
Common Merganser	10" x 10"	32" / 34"	129"	5" x 5"

The model shown on the left - which just happens to be for Hooded Merganser - is a standard example of what almost all nestboxes should look like. Its dimensions correspond with those outlined for the Hoodie the chart on the bottom of the previous page.

Black-bellied Whistling-Duck – p. 362 - This species regularly nests 8-30 feet up among live oak, ebony, and willow. Nestboxes can help in securing a stable population for this spreading species. Both male and female will search for a cavity. South Texas researchers found that predator-proof boxes were 77% successful for Black-bellied Whistling-Ducks; unprotected boxes and natural cavities were 46% and 44% successful, respectively. Also, predator-proof nestboxes resulted in a 19% renesting success – a second clutch - for this species. As indicated in the dimensions chart, the front of the nestbox is actually higher than the back! Odd as it may seem, this is a proven design for this species. Placement may be best at wooded pond or wetland area edges, on land or over water. Natural tree-perches near the box entrance can increase box use. It should be at least 6 feet above water. Boxes in open areas and in close proximity invite unwanted brood parasitism. Isolated placement is essential. Post: Often a 2-inch-diameter well-pipe, best with a conical sheetmetal predator guard.

Muscovy Duck – p. 367 - Cavities used by Muscovy Ducks can be found 9 to 65 feet up, at or near water in the Neotropics. Similar to the nest-boxes for the Black-bellied Whistling-Duck, with the front of the box higher than the back! Ducks Unlimited Mexico has pioneered this design with great success in Mexico. In the very limited range for Muscovy Duck along the Rio Grande in South Texas, the standard, but smaller, whistling-duck box has attracted the attention of Muscovies. A specific Muscovy Duck box, with more exacting requirements, should do even better. Placement in riparian areas, along narrow river side channels, by resacas (oxbows), and at ponds may be ideal. The box entrance should be 6-7 feet from the ground or the water. Muscovies can use a small bit of hardware cloth on the lip of the entrance hole as well as down the inside, providing a gripping entrance on the edge for adults as well as a functional ladder on the inside for young. More boxes along the Rio Grande may help this local and rare species hold on to – or increase – a very limited range in Texas. Post: Posts are either of 2-inch pipe or four-by-four-inch wood, always set with cone predator-guards.

Wood Duck – p. 369 - The variety of model boxes for Wood Ducks is astounding, including standard wooden boxes (which we favor), vertical metal cylinders, horizontal metal cylinders, and plastic containers of various sizes. That variety is an outgrowth of the 20th-century Wood Duck nest-box effort, starting in the 1930s. Nest success in nestboxes is considerably higher than in natural cavities. Hooded Mergansers and both goldeneyes have used boxes designed for Wood Ducks. Wood Ducks prefer natural nesting sites that average 24 feet up. The male accompanies the female in search of nest cavities, but plays no role in selection. Searching may take several days, but normally done in early mornings. Nestboxes should be placed close to or over the water, by ponds, lakes, marshes, or rivers. Boxes should face the water and be at least 6 feet up. We recommend boxes that are 11-inches square at the base, slightly larger than most. These slightly larger models have produce more ducklings. Ideally, boxes should be placed at least 200 yards from each other, or where when one stands at any given box, other boxes cannot be seen. This reduces nest-dumping and brood parasitism. Post: If placed on posts, they should be at least 3 feet over the high-water mark, always with predator-guards.

Bufflehead – p. 460 - These small ducks use small boxes! In areas of mixed coniferous and deciduous woodlands, Bufflehead will typically use old Northern Flicker holes, occasionally old Pileated Woodpecker holes. Holes are usually 2-11 feet up in natural settings, uncommonly up to 45 feet, often in poplars, aspens, and sometimes pines. Bufflehead numbers are limited by the availability of natural cavities. Nestboxes placement can address this situation and contribute to population gains. Once a female chooses on a box, she will usually return the next year. (Return rates are between 57% and 83%.) Buffleheads will use larger boxes for other species, but boxes specifically built for Buffleheads, with exact entrances, will more likely benefit Buffleheads and thwart competing Wood Ducks and Hooded Mergansers. Buffleheads have also been known to avoid larger cavities or with larger entrance-holes to avoid local competition from goldeneyes. Female Buffleheads in larger cavities have been displaced or even killed by goldeneyes! Successful boxes have been placed in trees whose trunks are at least 8 inches in diameter (at breast height), often about 10 feet up, within riparian zones. Such boxes should be placed at least 80 yards from each other. Success rates are best in areas thick with trees, less so at edges of beaver ponds, lakes, and waterfowl impoundments. Like goldeneyes, young female Buffleheads, usually in a group, will scout out potential nesting cavities for use next year. This probably developed to deal with the scarcity of quality cavities. Posts: Boxes often attached to trees. Successful boxes have been on posts in areas with fewer trees.

Common Goldeneye – p. 463 - Common Goldeneyes will use boxes with Wood Duck dimensions, but prefer boxes that are longer and with slightly larger openings. Usually, they are found nesting 6-45 feet up, traditionally in maples or elms. Original cavities are often made by Pileated Woodpeckers. Natural cavities nest-trees in maritime Canada have been large, averaging 23 inches in diameter (at breast height). Common Goldeneyes are limited by the availability of natural nesting cavities.

Experienced females are faithful to previous nest sites, including old nestboxes. Younger and inexperienced females may often group together to seek out potential nest cavities the summer before a nesting attempt. Therefore, using nestboxes in the right habitat may contribute to population gains. Shoreline boxes seem to be preferred, as well as placement above 18 feet in trees. When multiple boxes are available, females prefer located on wetlands with many aquatic invertebrates (commonly fishless) and on isolated wetlands. Boxes should be placed at least 80 yards from each other in trees adjacent to large wetlands. The box should face open water for easy access. Posts: On trees trunks more than 8 inches in diameter (at breast height) within riparian zones. Also use boxes on posts, usually 8 feet up or higher (uncommonly as low as 6 feet up), and protected by predator guards

Barrow's Goldeneye – p. 466 - Cavities are found from 6 to 50 feet up, rarely to 65 feet, often in aspen, cottonwood, birch, Douglas fir, or ponderosa pine. Sites are normally near shallow lakes or ponds with submerged aquatic and marsh vegetation, within 100 feet of water. Pileated Woodpecker cavities are often used, as are Northern Flicker cavities enlarged by natural decay. Experienced females will return to previous successful nest sites. Inexperienced Females are suspected to prospect for nest cavities in the summer before their actual use. Both returning and new females favor boxes occupied the previous year. Rivalry can be lessened by providing alternate choices in the area. Boxes should be placed no closer than 80 yards from each other. Especially in the East where they are declining, and in western Canada where clear-cutting is practiced, Barrow's populations could be assisted with nestbox programs. Posts: Most boxes have been placed on trees in fairly remote areas, 12 to 16 feet up, but usually on the lower end of this range.

Hooded Merganser – p. 470 - Hooded Mergansers will use the same box type as Wood Ducks, although recommendation here for a Hoodie opening is more exact with a base is slightly smaller. Use this size specifically to attract Hooded Mergansers. While Hooded Mergansers are comfortable using the same style boxes as Wood Ducks, they are more easily disturbed by human impact and more sensitive to water quality decline than Wood Ducks. At the same time, Hooded Mergansers are not demanding over cavity height or tree species; they will use cavities between 15-20 feet up, sometimes as high as 80 feet. Beaver pond sites can be particularly attractive. Female cavity selection may start the summer before a breeding attempt. Nestboxes should be placed 6 feet above the ground or at least 3 feet above the high-water level. Nestboxes containing wood shavings (always recommended) and boxes used the previous year are preferred. Hooded Mergansers select nestboxes that are nearest to water and may prefer west-facing entrances. Post: Always use a predator-guard.

Common Merganser – p. 475 - Cavities used by Common Mergansers are often 15-50 feet up, often made by Pileated Woodpeckers. Sites are often close to water, but sometimes as far as 200 yards from shore. Common Mergansers prefer nesting near large water bodies surrounded by conifers or mixed forests. Some of the best results are 12-17 feet high in trees, on the water's edge, or 8 feet above the waterline on dead trees. Experienced females will return to same nest sites, but they will also prospect for new sites while rearing a brood or once the brood has fledged. Inexperienced females may group together to prospect for future nest sites the summer before a nesting attempt is made. While entry-perches are never recommended for any nestbox, a small slab of wood with the bark attached and placed directly under the entrance hole has helped Common Mergansers gain easy access. Common Mergansers have been known to use smaller boxes intended for Common Goldeneyes. Post: If raccoons or other predators are a problem, a post that is 10 or 12 feet high may work, as long as it has a predator-guard.

Mallard – p. 372 - Finally, we have Mallards, waterfowl that do not qualify as traditional cavity-nesters at all. And they aren't! But they have been known to use "hen houses" quite successfully, especially in the Prairie Pothole Region. Mallards will readily nest in locations well over water, more so than any other species of dabbler. These sites may include fallen logs, stumps, snags, and dead tree tops. The modern hen house is a take-off of historic nest baskets used for Mallards in Great Britain and the Netherlands, probably for over 300 years. These nest baskets were large pitcher-shaped objects woven of willow shoots. Baskets mounted 6 feet or higher above the ground were well used. Cone-shaped baskets have been used successfully in many states and provinces. In North America, the highly effective hen house variation has been promoted by Delta Waterfowl, and other conservation groups have taken up the cause. The modern unit is, in practical terms, a 3-foot-long wire-mesh cylinder that is a foot in diameter. Lined with flax straw (or equivalent). Placement about 3 feet over water deters most mammalian predators. A hen house looks like a straw barrel, open at both ends, resting on a post! They are relatively inexpensive and low-maintenance. Most significantly, in some regions, the rate of occupancy and the rate of nest success is greater than 70%. Successes in some areas (e.g., farmed areas in western Manitoba) can be impressive. Occupancy rates tend to be low during the first years after placement, but rates increase thereafter once females that have successfully nested. Offspring return to nest in the same or nearby hen houses. In 2013, Delta Waterfowl estimated a tally of 6,900 hen houses that they placed in 12 states and five Canadian provinces. That number does not include nearly 3,000 more that Delta has merely assisted with, nor does it include any privately or independently constructed units. While the vast majority of occupants of these houses (~95%) are Mallards, other waterfowl have used them. They include Lesser Scaup, Canvasback, and Redheads (Manitoba), Wood Ducks (Minnesota, Pennsylvania, Ontario), Gadwall and Blue-winged Teal (Utah), and, rarely, Common Goldeneye (Manitoba). Be warned that if the inside diameter of the roll is larger than 12 inches, your hen house could attract Canada Geese. Post: The baskets were placed on small islands, tree crotches, and on posts. The unit is usually supported by a metal T-post. You can find building instructions here, from Delta Waterfowl: www.deltawaterfowl.org/henhouses/build.php

BUILDING, PLACEMENT, AND ESSENTIALS:

Door, lid, or side-opening - Your box must include a door or lid to allow you to clean the box and add nesting material, such as wood chips. A side door (as shown in the illustration on p. 496) is preferred. Top openings are adequate, but require an awkward topside approach when monitoring or cleaning. Avoid a hook-and-eye to keep the door closed. Raccoons are clever, and they can open boxes so secured!

Drain Holes - Four 3/8 inch diameter holes should be drilled in the bottom of each box for drainage.

Duckling Ladder – Always apply a 4-inch-wide strip of ¼-inch hardware cloth long enough to reach from the interior wood-chip bedding to the entrance hole. The hardware cloth should be cut out with the cut edges folded back. Attach this strip to the inside to serve as a ladder for newly hatched ducklings. Alternately, you can add kerf cuts to the wood up to the entrance. These grooves, cut into the wood, can act as steps to assist exiting ducklings. In either case, some sort of rough "ladder" is required to allow the ducklings to exit the box successfully. (If rough-cut unfinished limber is used in construction, you may skip the ladder; ducklings will have little trouble climbing out under those circumstances.)

Fasteners - Deck screws or concrete coated nails are recommended for construction. Avoid galvanized nails; they have a tendency to loosen with wood expansion. (See Mounting.)

Maintenance - Nestboxes should be cleaned out in the fall or early winter, with the previous season's nest material, egg shells, and any unhatched eggs removed, and the box refreshed with new wood chips. (In one recent Wood Ducks study, maintenance increased duckling production by 30%.) This is also ideal for simultaneous repairs. When female ducks find a good place to nest, they will often return the following year. Regular maintenance is a must!

Monitoring - Long-term data concerning nestboxes is invaluable, simply crucial for researchers in helping understand habitat, productivity, and population changes. Although hundreds of thousands of nestboxes have been provided to help waterfowl, many are infrequently monitored. Gathering basic data on cavity-nesting waterfowl is fundamental citizen science. Only if data is collected can it be subject to scientific scrutiny. Ask about state, provincial, or regional data collection or birding or hunt club collection on waterfowl nesting. Or simply connect with the Cornell Lab or Ornithology and their excellent Nestwatch Resource Center: www.birds.cornell.edu/nestinginfo

Mounting - U-bolts should be used for mounting a nestbox on a pipe post. Bolts can be used on pre-drilled 8-foot metal signposts. And 3 ½-inch lag bolts can be used for mounting on wooden posts. If you must attach the nestbox to a tree, use four 3 ½-inch lag bolts. (See Posts and Predator-guard.)

Other Species - Depending on geography, location, placement, and the size of the unit, your boxes may host other occupants. Some are desirable; many are not. Your boxes may host screech-owls, Saw-whet Owls, American Kestrel, squirrels, raccoons, mice, wasps, and bees. European Starlings may try to make your nestbox a home. Remove their nests and eggs whenever these undesirable birds try to move in!

Perches - It's simple: don't install perches on nestboxes. Perches allow access by predators. (See Muscovy Duck and Common Merganser for minor exceptions.)

Posts - Attaching nestboxes to posts is recommended; trees are too predator-accessible. Posts are regularly used for at least for half the species here: Black-bellied Whistling-Duck, Muscovy Duck, Wood Duck, and Hooded Merganser. Posts have been shown to work for the other four species, but tree-placement for those species has been more customary. For nest-box placement on posts, 2-inch pipes are often used, especially in water. Also, 4"x4" cedar posts can be used or standard 8-foot treated landscaping timbers. One easily acquired post is a used 8-foot metal highway signpost. These sometimes can be obtained free from local or district highway maintenance offices. Like the 2-inch pipes, they can be pounded into the ground (about 2 feet) using a post-pounder. When considering any posts, predator-guards always included in plans. (See Mounting, Predators, and Predator-guard.)

Predators - Predators on cavity-nesting ducks, are mostly tree-climbers. Precise entrance-hole dimensions can discourage access by some predators. Mammals that can enter or break into boxes are a continual problem. In such cases, the duck's eggs are in jeopardy. Predatory mammals can be raccoons, opossums, bobcats, fishers, pine martens, mink, or squirrels. Black bears can even be a threat to cavity-nesting ducks in nestboxes! As for non-mammals, snakes can also get into boxes and will feast on eggs. These all can be deterred – perhaps with the exception of the bears – when predator-guards are used with the nestboxes. (See Mounting, Posts, and Predator-guard.)

Predator-guard - Many nest-box stewards use 3-inch-diameter or 4-inch-diameter PVC pipe at least 4 feet long as functional shields around metal or wooden posts. Such predator-guards (with makeshift closures on the top ends, up against the pipe/wood) work fairly well, but never as well as sheetmetal conical baffles. Likewise, a sheetmetal wrap around a tree, or a stovepipe around a post, is a minor deterrent, but not as effective as a sheetmetal conical baffle. Another wrap-guard used recently is a very flexible and inexpensive children's plastic "crazy carpet" snow-rider, found in most toy stores. Wrap it around the tree and nail it in place! If beavers are in the habitat, you might avoid placing your tree-mounted box on birch, aspen, cottonwood, willow, maple, beech, poplar, or alder trees. That doesn't leave much, but be aware that beavers find them yummy! The best metal conical baffles can be easy to make, and they are good for nestboxes mounted on either pipes or wooden posts. These predator-guards should be placed 6-12 inches below the nestbox. If the cone is large enough (recommended at 36 inches in diameter), it can deter most predators. Find plans here: *www.birds.cornell.edu/nestinginfo/downloads/guardcon.pdf*

To deter egg-loving snakes, make sure that the conical predator-guard is sealed tightly against the pole (A square piece of 1/4-inch hardware cloth as a screen next to the pole and beneath the cone will fill any gap.) (See Mounting, Posts, and Predator-guard.)

Ventilation - Ventilation is not required for these nestboxes, but you can incorporate some openings in the process of construction. For example, at the top of the side door, keep it dropped down a 1/4" to avoid binding on the door. This gap will also provide a little ventilation in hot weather. (See Drain holes.)

Wood - Nestboxes should be made from rough-cut cypress, cedar, redwood, or other rot-resistant wood. Cedar is best and will last a decade. One-inch white pine is fine, but avoid plywood. Do not paint, stain, or treat a box with creosote. Shun wood for your boxes that has been treated with preservative.

Wood chips - Use wood chips at the bottom of all these nest-boxes. The chips should be at least 3 inches deep. Chips can be obtained from a woodworking shop or bought from pet stores as pet bedding (e.g., for hamsters, rabbits, or guinea pigs). Use chips or shavings, not sawdust! (Fine sawdust can suffocate ducklings.)

Areas of Greatest Significance

The availability of safe, plentiful, and food-rich habitat is the greatest limiting factor facing waterfowl in North America. This map on p. 500 and quick review of corresponding 43 areas of most significance to North American waterfowl is a byproduct of the 2012 North American Waterfowl Management Plan (NAWMP) revision. The map was prepared by the NAWMP Science Support Team (NSST) based on information provided by Migratory Bird Joint Venture Coordinators, Joint Venture Science Coordinators, and NSST members.

Identifying significant areas to continental waterfowl populations was not easy for the NSST. For example, comparing the relative importance of smaller areas with high waterfowl densities to larger areas with abundant waterfowl at low densities was not simple. Comparisons were difficult when different needs for different species were evaluated across the annual cycle. Clearly, the protection of breeding and wintering habitats is insufficient without also securing migratory stopover points.

In addition, some areas were identified as critical to a single species of high concern, while others were considered important because they were used by many species. Other considerations arose; for example, certain arid locations provide high value to waterfowl, but these are inconsistent over the years (e.g., playa wetlands).

Finally, the NSST recognized that many other areas of North America certainly attract large numbers of waterfowl. Although they are significant at smaller scales, they are not considered of "great significance" at a continental scale.

Almost all of these 43 Areas of Greatest Continental Significance correspond or overlap with Important Bird Areas (IBAs) as defined by BirdLife International standards. As IBAs, moreover, they are often vital for species other than waterfowl. These species are often shorebirds, long-legged waders, rails, gulls and terns, raptors, and/or songbirds.

Not unlike IBA standards, these Areas of Greatest Continental Significance meet certain measurement requirements. In this case it's usually 25% of a species population in spring or winter or 5% of a total waterfowl population.

The 43 areas of greatest continental significance to our waterfowl and their outstanding characteristics (concerning species or habitat) indicated on map – with some brief justifications - are as follows:

1. Prairie Pothole Region – Covering a large portion of the U.S. northern Great Plains and the Prairie Provinces of Canada, this is the most important breeding area for ducks on the continent. Among dabblers, it is crucial for Mallard, Northern Pintail, Blue-winged Teal, Northern Shoveler, and Gadwall. Among the pochards, the PPR is vital for Canvasbacks and Redheads while increasing numbers of Ring-necked Ducks and smaller numbers of Lesser Scaup breed there too. The vast majority of North American Ruddy Ducks nest in this region as well. It is a major stopover region in spring and fall.

2. Boreal Plain and Shield – Heavily forested and non-forested lakes are critical. Particularly important for breeding Common Goldeneye, American Wigeon, Green-winged Teal, Ring-necked Duck, and Bufflehead. Large segments, such as the Peace-Athabasca Delta, are extremely significant waterfowl staging areas. When drought strikes the Prairie Pothole Region, waterfowl may shift northward to this region to nest.

3. Taiga Plain and Shield - More thinly treed areas with wetland habitats. Important breeding areas for several duck species, including sea ducks, such as Black and White-winged Scoters.

4. Northern Great Plains – Especially important for

breeding when drought conditions impact the PPR. Several hundred thousand shallow stock ponds and large expanses of relatively contiguous grassland result in excellent nest success. Breeding population estimates from 1986-2005 averaged 1.3 million breeding ducks, with a composition similar to that of the PPR. Species have been Blue-winged Teal (28%), followed by Mallards (22%), Gadwall (19%), Northern Pintail (8%), American Wigeon (7%), Northern Shoveler (6%), and other species (10%). The area is also important as a migratory stopover for many waterfowl species.

5. Sandhills – Nebraska's Sandhills have been considered as the most important area for breeding ducks south of the PPR, particularly for Mallard, Blue-winged Teal, Gadwall, Northern Shoveler, and Northern Pintail.

6. Platte River and Rainwater Basin – Key migration (spring staging) area for geese and ducks in the Central Flyway (almost 9 million), including 90% of the mid-continent Greater White-fronted Geese, 50% of the Mallards, and almost a third of the continent's Northern Pintails. Half a million Canada Geese also pass through here.

7. Central Kansas Marshes – At least 500,000 waterfowl pass through this area, particularly in spring.

8. Playa Wetlands Region – High wetland density and importance to nonbreeding ducks and geese. These include over 2 million wintering dabblers, migrating Aythya (i.e., Redhead, Lesser Scaup, and Canvasback, and breeding teal (Blue-winged and Cinnamon).

9. Central Rivers – Key migration areas for geese and ducks in the Mississippi Flyway, with a total of about 4 million. This includes 30-70% of the eastern prairie population of Canada Geese.

10. Mississippi Alluvial Valley – The crucial MAV, a rich alluvial floodplain and agricultural landscape, can support as many as 8 million migrating and wintering ducks and geese. It is the most important wintering area for Mallards (2-4 million, or 20-40% of the continental population). In winter, the MAV also can sustain large concentrations of Northern Pintails, Wood Ducks, Green-winged Teals, Northern Shovelers, White-fronted Geese, "Lesser" Snow Geese, and 10-20% of the continent's Canvasback population. The MAV is also a key breeding area for Wood Ducks. Invertebrate and general foraging conditions in the MAV are also ideal for pre-migratory spring staging.

11. Gulf Coast Region – Over 14 million ducks and 2 million geese can winter along the Gulf Coast, probably the most important waterfowl wintering area in North America. An estimated 80% of the continent's Gadwalls, Green-winged Teals, and Redheads winter here. More than 90% of the Mottled Ducks of North America are year-round residents here. Three species of increasing concern – Northern Pintails, Greater Scaup, and Lesser Scaup – also winter in this region in large numbers. The Mexican portion of this region supports a third of the country's waterfowl and is particularly significant for wintering Redhead and Ruddy Duck. Also, this part of the region hosts meaningful numbers of resident Muscovy Duck and Masked Duck.

12. Lagos y Lagunas Centro/Humedales del Valle de Mexico – Important for Green-winged Teal, Northern Shoveler, and Northern Pintail. It's a priority site for permanent-resident Mexican Duck, and important for wintering Canvasback.

13. Tierras Altas Norte – Supports about 11% of Mexico's wintering waterfowl. Important for "Lesser" Snow Goose and smaller numbers of Greater White-fronted Goose. Dabblers, such as Green-winged Teal and Northern Pintail, are present in significant numbers. The region is also very important for permanent-resident Mexican Duck and for breeding Cinnamon Teal.

14. Costa del Pacifico – Large numbers of western "Lesser" Snow Geese and about 20 % the "Black" Brant population winter here, as do a substantial number of dabblers, especially Northern Pintail, but also Northern Shoveler and Green-winged Teal.

15. Baja California – About 60-80% of the "Black" Brant population can winter along the west coast of Baja California, especially at 3 Lagoons: San Quintin, San Ignacio, and Ojo de Liebre (aka Scammon´s Lagoon). Smaller but significant numbers of divers (Redhead, scaup and Bufflehead) and scoters also occur in this region.

16. Central Valley - Made up of the Sacramento Valley and the San Joaquin Valley, this area has huge numbers of wintering geese and ducks (estimated at 10-12 million), including more than half the Tundra Swans and Northern Pintails in the West and, among geese, most of the "Aleutian" Cackling Geese and all the "Tule" Greater White-fronted Geese. Very large numbers of American Wigeon, Mallards, Green-winged Teal, and Northern Shovelers winter here. Breeders include Mallard, Cinnamon Teal, Gadwall, and Redhead.

17. San Francisco Bay – This is probably the most biologically significant estuary on the Pacific Coast, between Mexico and Canada. Close to half (46%) the populations of migrating West Coast divers may stop by or winter in the Bay Estuary. These include Canvasback but also Redheads, Ruddy Ducks, both scaup, and some sea ducks (e.g. scoters).

18. Pacific Coast – Tidal wetlands, adjacent agricultural fields, river estuaries, and immediate offshore area all provide important wintering habitat for Trumpeter Swans, wintering and migrating "Black" Brant and "Lesser" Snow Geese. Here are found high densities of wintering Barrow's Goldeneye, Harlequin Duck, scoters (all 3), Long-tailed Duck, and dabblers (e.g., Mallard, Northern Pintail, and American Wigeon).

19. Southern Oregon Northeast California Wetlands Basin and Carson Sink – Up to 80% of western Tundra Swans may migrate through here. Also, large numbers of Snow and Cackling Geese and half the Greater White-fronted Goose population of the Pacific Flyway migrate through here. Also half the Canvasbacks of the Pacific Flyway also come through here. It is a regionally important area for breeding Cinnamon Teal, Redhead, and Gadwall.

Waterfowl areas of Greatest Continental Significance - These are the 43 areas designated by the North American Waterfowl Management Plan (NAWMP) in 2012.

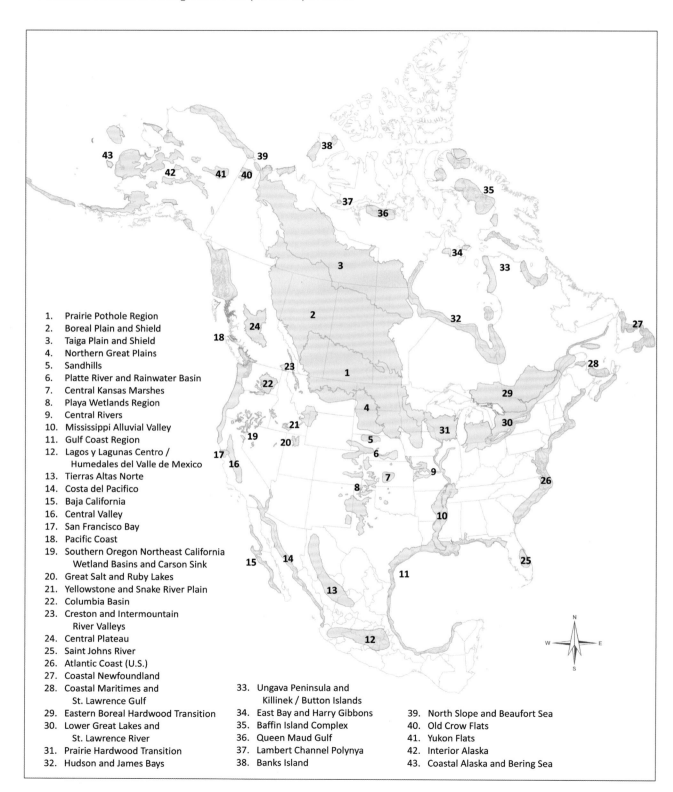

1. Prairie Pothole Region
2. Boreal Plain and Shield
3. Taiga Plain and Shield
4. Northern Great Plains
5. Sandhills
6. Platte River and Rainwater Basin
7. Central Kansas Marshes
8. Playa Wetlands Region
9. Central Rivers
10. Mississippi Alluvial Valley
11. Gulf Coast Region
12. Lagos y Lagunas Centro / Humedales del Valle de Mexico
13. Tierras Altas Norte
14. Costa del Pacifico
15. Baja California
16. Central Valley
17. San Francisco Bay
18. Pacific Coast
19. Southern Oregon Northeast California Wetland Basins and Carson Sink
20. Great Salt and Ruby Lakes
21. Yellowstone and Snake River Plain
22. Columbia Basin
23. Creston and Intermountain River Valleys
24. Central Plateau
25. Saint Johns River
26. Atlantic Coast (U.S.)
27. Coastal Newfoundland
28. Coastal Maritimes and St. Lawrence Gulf
29. Eastern Boreal Hardwood Transition
30. Lower Great Lakes and St. Lawrence River
31. Prairie Hardwood Transition
32. Hudson and James Bays
33. Ungava Peninsula and Killinek / Button Islands
34. East Bay and Harry Gibbons
35. Baffin Island Complex
36. Queen Maud Gulf
37. Lambert Channel Polynya
38. Banks Island
39. North Slope and Beaufort Sea
40. Old Crow Flats
41. Yukon Flats
42. Interior Alaska
43. Coastal Alaska and Bering Sea

20. Great Salt and Ruby Lakes – This area is particularly important for migrating Tundra Swans (for perhaps 30% of the population) and for Northern Pintails. A significant number of Cinnamon Teals breed here.

21. Yellowstone and Snake River Plain – Crucial for swans – migrating Tundra and Trumpeter and about 80% of the breeding Trumpeters of the Rocky Mountain population.

22. Columbia Basin – About 8% of the continental population of Mallards migrate through here. It is also particularly important for Tundra Swans and Northern Pintails.

23. Creston and Intermountain River Valleys – Floodplain wetlands provide stopovers for migrating Trumpeter and Tundra Swans, Canada Geese, and dabblers as well as Redhead and Ring-necked Duck.

24. Central Plateau – There are migrating waterfowl in the fall in numbers, especially Mallard and American Wigeon. It is also an important for wintering Trumpeter Swans and breeding Barrow's Goldeneye.

25. Saint Johns River – This river floodplain and adjacent coastal area provides wintering habitat for about 400,000 ducks. About 75% are Lesser Scaup using open water habitats associated with seagrass beds. Other wintering species include Ring-necked Duck, Northern Pintail, Blue-winged Teal, American Wigeon, and Mottled Duck. Breeding populations supported include Black-bellied Whistling-Duck and Mottled Duck.

26. Atlantic Coast (U.S.) – This area covers crucial coastal marshlands, important for migrant ducks and geese, and for breeding and wintering American Black Ducks. The Chesapeake Bay alone can account for more than a million ducks and geese – about 35% of the Atlantic Flyway population – in winter. Bays and estuaries along the entire coast provide stopover and wintering areas for huge numbers of waterfowl. The area from the Chesapeake through the North Carolina Outer Banks can be crucial for wintering Tundra Swans. In the 1970s, it was maintained that the most abundant waterfowl species as migrants along the coastal waters were White-winged, Surf, and Black Scoters, Brant, Common Eider, and Black Duck. All these species today are either in trouble or barely recovering from past population drops. This area is also vital for eastern population of Harlequin Duck.

27. Coastal Newfoundland – Among other species, large numbers of Common Eiders nest and winter here.

28. Coastal Maritimes and St. Lawrence Gulf – This area is important breeding are for the American Common Eider (S. m. dresseri). It is also important for Common Eider (S. m. borealis) wintering along the North Shore of the Gulf and Anticosti Island. This area also winters large concentrations of Long-tailed Ducks, Red-breasted Mergansers, Common Goldeneyes, and most of the eastern population of Barrow's Goldeneyes. The Bay of Chaleur is an important spring staging sites for the 3 scoter species. The St. Lawrence Estuary is an important molting and fall staging area for Surf and White-wing Scoters.

29. Eastern Boreal Hardwood Transition – High densities of breeding American Black Duck, Ring-necked Ducks, Hooded Mergansers, and other waterfowl benefitting from abundant beaver ponds. The eastern portion of this area also hosts most of the wintering Barrow's Goldeneyes in eastern North America.

30. Lower Great Lakes and St. Lawrence River – A major staging area with nearly 10 million waterfowl in the fall flight, of which the Greater Snow Goose, Canada Goose, and several dabblers, plus some sea ducks (e.g. White-winged Scoters) concentrate in the Great Lakes. American Black Ducks and other dabblers nest at high densities in the St. Lawrence lowlands. The north shore of the St. Lawrence is an important spring staging area for all 3 scoter species.

31. Prairie Hardwood Transition – Over 2 million ducks and geese use this area for nesting, including primarily Mallards, Wood Ducks, and over 30% of Mississippi Flyway Giant Canada Geese. Significant portions of the continental population of Ring-necked Ducks (30%), Common Goldeneye (30%), Tundra Swan (>30%), Southern James Bay Population and Mississippi Valley Population Canada Geese (>50%), and Canvasback (>50%) pass through this region.

32. Hudson and James Bays – All 3 scoters, but especially Black Scoters, stage in this area during spring and fall migration, and males from the eastern population of Black Scoters molt here. The Hudson Bay Common Eiders (S. m. sedentaria) spend their entire life-cycle within this area, and significant colonies of Lesser Snow Geese breed here. The area is also very important for migrating Brant and an important staging area for Long-tailed Ducks and Greater Scaup.

33. Ungava Peninsula and Killinek/Button Islands – A large portion of the northern sub-species of Common Eider (S. m. borealis) stage and breeding along the Baffin and Ungava coasts of Hudson Straight. The largest concentration of wintering King Eiders in eastern North America may occur in the area around the Killinek/Button Islands. This is also an important area for a number of molting sea ducks, such as scoters and goldeneyes.

34. East Bay and Harry Gibbons – Significant for breeding "Lesser" Snow Geese. Also important for breeding Common Eider and "Atlantic" Brant breeding here. Cackling Geese concentrations are important and increasing here. Lesser numbers of other waterfowl, such as Ross's Geese, King Eiders, and Long-tailed Ducks.

35. Baffin Island Complex – Key nesting, molting, and wintering area for sea ducks, including breeding and molting Common Eiders. "Greater" Snow Geese also nest and molt here in very large numbers. At least 160,000 Cackling Geese nest here, and large number of "Lesser" Snow Geese nest here.

36. Queen Maud Gulf – Large Numbers of the Ross's Goose population (>80%) and about 15% of the "Lesser" Snow Goose population of Canada nest here. Also, about 6% of the west/central North American King Eider population may nest here.

37. Lambert Channel Polynya – This is an important feeding area prior to nesting for "Pacific" Eider (perhaps for 60-70% of the Canadian population). Large numbers of Long-tailed Ducks also use this area.

38. Banks Island — This is important for multiple geese (Ross's, "Lesser" Snow, Goose, "Richardson's" Cackling, and "Black" Brant). Long-tailed Duck and King Eider nest, and both King and Common Eider use it as a staging area.

39. North Slope and Beaufort Sea — Coastal lagoon systems and coastal plain are particularly important for migrating and molting Long-tailed Ducks, Common Eiders, and Surf and White-winged Scoters. Polynya and other ice-free areas are important during spring migration. Onshore nesting habitats support multiple geese (Snow, Greater White-fronted, and "Black" Brant). Wetlands from Cape Simpson to Cape Halkett are especially important for breeding Spectacled Eiders, and wetlands near Barrow are important for Steller's Eiders. The Teshekpuk Lake area is one of the most important molting habitats in the entire circumpolar Arctic for geese (e.g., Greater White-fronted Geese and Brant.)

40. Old Crow Flats — Over 2,000 lakes and ponds, surrounded by sedge marshes and shrub thicket habitat. Significant numbers breeding duck species (in order of abundance) are scoters (mostly White-winged and Surf), both scaup, American Wigeon, Northern Pintail, Green-winged teal, Northern Shoveler, Long-tailed Duck, Mallard, and Canvasback. Primary molt migrants are goldeneyes and Canvasback.

41. Yukon Flats — Open spruce forests, shrubs, lakes, bogs, and streams host the largest combined population of breeding ducks in Alaska. The primary breeding duck species (in order of abundance) are Lesser Scaup, Northern Pintail, American Wigeon, Green-winged Teal, Mallard, scoters (White-winged and Surf), Northern Shoveler, Canvasback, Long-tailed Duck , Bufflehead, and both goldeneyes. Increasing numbers of Trumpeter Swans also breed here.

42. Interior Alaska — This area includes lake, stream, river, mixed forest, and shrub habitats, with an estimate of 2.5 million ducks and over 100,000 geese found in the fall flight. The primary breeding duck species (in order of abundance) are Lesser Scaup, Northern Pintail, scoters (White-winged and Surf), American Wigeon, Green-winged Teal, Mallard, Canvasback, Northern Shoveler, Bufflehead, Goldeneyes (Common and Barrow's), and Long-tailed Duck. A large proportion of the increasing Alaska breeding Trumpeter Swan population occurs here.

43. Coastal Alaska and Bering Sea — This huge area of about 50,000 square miles covers such crucial sites as the Yukon-Kuskokwim Delta, Bristol Bay-Kvichak Bay, Alaska Peninsula (including Izembek Lagoon), the Aleutian Islands, and the Bering Sea Ice Leads. Fall flights are about 4 million ducks, 600,000 geese, and 70,000 tundra swans. Primary breeding duck species are Northern Pintail, Long-tailed Duck, Greater Scaup, Green-winged Teal, American Wigeon, Mallard, Black Scoter, and eiders (Spectacled and Common). All Pacific Flyway Cackling Geese and Greater White-fronted Geese and up to 80% of "Black" Brant and over 90% of Emperor Geese breed here. Marine estuaries and shoreline habitats, especially along the Alaska Peninsula, are essential for migrating, molting, and wintering waterfowl (notably "Black" Brant, Emperor Geese, and Steller's Eiders). Bering Sea islands (Pribilof, Nunivak, St. Matthew and St Lawrence islands) include an estimated 4,000 square miles of important waterfowl habitats.

Each of these 43 areas of greatest continental significance requires special care and protection. Virtually all of them are included inside the areas of responsibility for the Migratory Bird Joint Ventures and correspond with Important Bird Areas (IBAs) for waterfowl as well as other bird species. Each of the 43 would benefit from increased monitoring and wetland habitat management. Not surprisingly, they are connected in a web of mutual dependence: a bird that may nest or molt in a northern area of concern will use areas in the middle areas for migratory stopover, and may end up in the southern areas of significance for wintering. Indeed, they do!

ACKNOWLEDGMENTS

It is impossible to name all the people who have helped with this project—on so many levels. Indeed, the information gathered between this book's two covers must rely on the collective and individual contributions of myriad of observers, writers, computer whizzes, and researchers. These have been acquired over a lifetime from so many people. A lot of these are close friends, others with a big influence were just people we met in passing who were generous enough to help with advice or information.

Some are mentioned in passing in the Introduction, especially since understanding waterfowl has been so collaborative over the decades. In fact, one cannot attempt to approach this subject without a serious nod to the incredible works of Samuel M. Carney, Paul A. Johnsgard, Sebastien Reeber, and, especially, the late Guy Baldassarre and Frank C. Bellrose.

Since this Crossley ID Guide is so ambitious, we are indebted to a particularly large group of colleagues who provided advice, review, and assistance.

A number of waterfowl experts have shared decades of work. Some of these went to extra lengths to help. These include Craig Ely, Pat Kehoe, Jim Leafloor, Bruce MacTavish, and John Pierce. Steve Mlodinow helped with his many hybrid photos and discussions of tricky ID problems. Tony Leukering provided excellent editing skills.

Our partners, spouses, and daughters have to put up with us on a daily basis: Debra, Sophie and Samantha Crossley, Yvonne, Judith, and Sara Baicich (who also provided artwork on pp. 495-6), and Chris Wood. Sophie Crossley helped with all aspects of the book, from it's initial layout, to packaging it for the printers, and was the go-to person whenever stuck! My parents Brian and Margaret Crossley, as always supported and encouraged me. My father's artistic influence has been the cornerstone of my appreciation for color and patterns.

The following people took time out of their very busy, and influential, lives to review this book and provide quotes: John Devney, Bob Ford, John Fitzpatrick, Karla Guyn, Dale Hall, Mike Parr and Wayne Peterson.

It is impossible to acknowledge all the people who have helped with this project– at so many levels. A book like this involves so many different skills, These have been acquired over a lifetime from so many people. Many are close friends, other were those whom we met in passing, helpful in graciously giving advice and information. We thank them all and apologize to anyone unintentionally omitted from the list which follows. Most of our helpers and reviewers include the following: Ray Alskauskas, George Armistead, Michael Anderson, Brad Arner, Peter Barthel, Adrian Binns, Karen Bollinger, Jeff Bouton, Tim Bowman, David Brakhage, Michael Brasher, Gwen Brewer, Joseph Brin, Steven Brock, Tink and Corey Bryan, Dan Buffett, Steve Cardiff, Vinnie Carrissimi, Mike Carter, Gordon Court, Cameron Cox, Mike Crewe, James Currie, Marcel Darveau, John Devney, Jon Dunn, Megan Edwards, Michael Eichholz, Vincent Elia, Rob Faucett, Shawneen Finnegan, Bob Fogg, Don Frieday, Christian Friis, Hugh Gallagher, Mark Garland, Grant Gilchrist, Scott Gililand, David Govatski, Mary Gustafson, Carol Henderson, Paul Holt, Ryuhei Honma, Steve Howell, Julian Hough, Samuel Iverson, Tom Johnson, Kevin Karlson, Satoe Kasahara, Ken Kriese, Kazuo Koyama, Mike Lanzone, Josee Lefebvre, Joe Liebezeit, David La Puma, Michael Lanzone, Paul Lehman, Jerry Liguori, Derrek and Jeannette Lovitch, Tim Lucas, Keith McKnight, Anne Mini, Clive Minton, Molly Monroe, Artie Morris, Ted Nichols, Michael O'Brien, Leigh Patterson, Wayne Petersen, David Povey, Bill Pranty, James and Debbie Provenzano, Peter Pyle, Sebastion Reeber, Jim Ringelman, Sievert Rohwer, Will Russell, Ken Sambor, Jean-Pierre Savard, Stuart Slattery, Bill Schmoker, Arnold and Debbie Schouten, Keith Seager, Paul Schmidt, Cathy Sheeter, Gary Shugart, Octavia Sola, Greg Soulliere, Lloyd Spitalnik, Shawn Stephenson, Roger Strand, Brian Sullivan, Roy Sutton, J. F. Therrien, Dave and Kathy Tetlow, David Ward, Mary Whalen, Dave Wheeler, Scott Whittle, Jim Williams, Jeff Wells, Barry Wilson, Chris Wood (UWBM), Scott Yaich, Louise Zemaitis.

Also these institutions were also particularly helpful: The Slater Museum of Natural History (University of Puget Sound), University of Washington Burke Museum (UWBM), Patuxent Refuge Research Library (USGS), Ducks Unlimited, Delta Waterfowl, Cornell Lab of Ornithology, and Livingston Ripley Waterfowl Conservancy.

Virtually all the photos in this book were taken by RC. We are grateful to the following friends for completing the 'picture' in some of the plates for the following species.

Jessie Barry: many of the wing specimens
Johan Buckens: TABG
Jon Buxton: GARG
Raymond De Smet: SMEW
Doug Gochfeld: LTDU
Bruce Mactavish: MABO, ESBD, COEI, AMWIxMALL, RNDUxLESC, RNDUxLESC, GADWxNOPI
Steve Mlodinow: AMWIxGADW, AMWIxNOSH, CAGOxROGO, CAGOxSNGO, ROGOxCAGO, BRGOxCAGO, NOSHxGADW, BWTExCITE, MUDUxMALL, REDHxRNDU
Tom Johnson: BLGO, PFGO, ROPT, SNGOxROGO, COEI, SPEI, NOPIxMALL
Bill Schmoker: COGOXBAGO, COGOxHOME
Debbie Schouten: BAGO, BUFF, COGO, COME, COMExKIEI, HADU, RBME, SPEI, STEI, WWSC.
Lyn Topinka: WODU
Lloyd Spitalnik EUWIxAMWI

Index

Numbers in bold refer to color plates

Aix sponsa		**98**	*369*
Alopochen aegyptiacus		**86**	*361*
Anas			
	acuta	**130**	*392*
	bahamensis	**134**	*395*
	crecca	**148**	*408*
	diazi	**108**	*376*
	fulvigula	**114**	*381*
	platyrhynchos	**102**	*372*
	rubripes	**110**	*378*
	zonorhyncha	**135**	*396*
Anser			
	albifrons	**52**	*336*
	anser	**59**	*340*
	brachyrhynchus	**58**	*342*
	caerulescens	**46**	*330*
	canagica	**60**	*345*
	erythropus	**59**	*339*
	fabalis	**59**	*341*
	rossii	**48**	*333*
	serrirostris	**59**	*341*
Aythya			
	affinis	**174**	*425*
	americana	**164**	*416*
	collaris	**170**	*422*
	ferina	**168**	*420*
	fuligula	**169**	*421*
	marila	**178**	*428*
	valisineria	**160**	*413*
Brant (BRAN)		**62**	*347*
Branta			
	bernicla	**62**	*347*
	canadensis	**68**	*351*
	hutchinsii	**72**	*357*
	leucopsis	**65**	*350*
Bucephala			
	albeola	**240**	*460*
	clangula	**244**	*463*
	islandica	**250**	*466*
Bufflehead (BUFF)		**240**	*460*

Cairina moschata		**96**	*367*
Canvasback (CANV)		**160**	*413*
Clangula hyemalis		**236**	*457*
Cygnus			
	buccinator	**36**	*324*
	columbianus	**34**	*320*
	cygnus	**38**	*329*
	olor	**40**	*326*
Dendrocygna			
	autumnalis	**90**	*362*
	bicolor	**92**	*365*
Duck			
	American Black (ABDU)	**110**	*378*
	Eastern Spot-billed (ESBD)	**135**	*396*
	Falcated (FADU)	**135**	*397*
	Harlequin (HARD)	**214**	*444*
	Long-tailed (LTDU)	**236**	*457*
	Masked (MADU)	**273**	*478*
	Mexican (MEDU)	**108**	*376*
	Mottled (MODU)	**114**	*381*
	Muscovy (MUDU)	**96**	*367*
	Ring-necked (RNDU)	**170**	*422*
	Ruddy (RUDU)	**274**	*480*
	Tufted (TUDU)	**169**	*421*
	Wood (WODU)	**98**	*369*
Eider			
	Common (COEI)	**202**	*440*
	King (KIEI)	**196**	*437*
	Spectacled (SPEI)	**192**	*434*
	Steller's (STEI)	**188**	*431*
Gadwall (GADW)		**118**	*384*
Garganey (GARG)		**152**	*411*
Goldeneye			
	Barrow's (BAGO)	**250**	*466*
	Common (COGO)	**244**	*463*
Goose			
	Barnacle (BARG)	**65**	*350*
	Brant (BRAN)	**62**	*347*
	Cackling (CACG)	**72**	*357*
	Canada (CANG)	**68**	*351*
	Egyptian (EGGO)	**86**	*361*
	Emperor (EMGO)	**60**	*345*
	Graylag (GRGO)	**59**	*340*
	Greater White-fronted (GWFG)	**52**	*336*
	Lesser White-fronted (LWFG)	**59**	*339*
	Pink-footed (PFGO)	**58**	*342*
	Ross's (ROGO)	**48**	*333*

Snow (SNGO) **46** *330*
Taiga Bean (TABG) **59** *341*
Tundra Bean (TUBG) **59** *341*

Histrionicus histrionicus **214** *444*

Lophodytes cucullatus **256** *470*

Mallard (MALL) **102** *372*

Mareca
   americana **124** *387*
   falcata **135** *397*
   penelope **128** *390*
   strepera **118** *384*

Melanitta
   americana **218** *447*
   fusca **226** *454*
   nigra **231** *450*
   perspicillata **222** *451*

Merganser
   Common (COME) **264** *475*
   Hooded (HOME) **256** *470*
   Red-breasted (RBME) **260** *473*

Mergellus albellus **272** *469*

Mergus
   merganser **264** *475*
   serrator **260** *473*

Nomonyx dominicus **273** *478*

Oxyura jamaicensis **274** *480*

Pintail
   Northern (NOPI) **130** *392*
   White-cheeked (WCHP) **134** *395*

Polysticta stelleri **188** *431*

Pochard, Common (COMP) **168** *420*

Redhead (REDH) **164** *416*

Scaup
   Lesser (LESC) **174** *425*
   Greater (GRSC) **178** *428*

Scoter
   Black (BLSC) **218** *447*
   Common (COSC) **231** *450*
   Surf (SUSC) **222** *451*
   White-winged (WWSC) **226** *454*

Shelduck
   Common (COMS) **59** *343*
   Ruddy (RUSH) **59** *344*

Shoveler, Northern (NSHO) **136** *398*

Smew (SMEW) **272** *469*

Sibirionetta
   formosa **153** *412*

Somateria
   fischeri **192** *434*
   mollissima **202** *440*
   spectabilis **196** *437*

Spatuala
   clypeata **136** *398*
   cyanoptera **144** *405*
   discors **140** *401*
   querquedula **152** *411*

Swan
   Bewick's **38** *321n*
   Mute (MUSW) **40** *326*
   Trumpeter (TRUS) **36** *324*
   Tundra (TUSW) **34** *320*
   Whooper (WHOS) **38** *329*

Tadorna
   ferruginea **59** *344*
   tadorna **59** *343*

Teal
   Baikal (BATE) **153** *412*
   Blue-winged (BWTE) **140** *401*
   Cinnamon (CITE) **144** *405*
   Green-winged (GWTE) **148** *408*

Whistling-Duck
   Black-bellied (BBWD) **90** *362*
   Fulvous (FUWD) **92** *365*

Wigeon
   American (AMWI) **124** *387*
   Eurasian (EUWI) **128** *390*

Swan Heads	**39**
Mystery Swans in February, Seattle, WA	**42**
Mystery Swans in February, Great Lakes, NY	**44**
Looking for Rarities	**50**
Mystery White-fronts in the West	**56**
Rare Gray Geese and Shelducks	**59**
Mystery Brant	**66**
The Anchorage Conundrum	**76**
Growing Up and Oddballs	**78**
Mystery Geese in Flight	**80**
North Slope Goslings	**82**
Hybrid Geese	**84**
Attracting Mates	**104**
What Creates Color in Feathers?	**106**
Mallard x American Black Duck Hybrid	**112**
Mottled Duck x Mallard Hybrid	**116**
Mystery Wigeon	**129**
Mystery Teal	**154**
Hybrid Dabblers	**156**
Mystery Aythya Sitting	**182**
Myestery Aythya Flight	**184**
Hybrid Diving Ducks	**186**
What is He Doing?	**200**
Eider Beauty	**210**
Mystery Eider	**212**
Scoter Landing Styles	**230**
Mystery Scoter on the Coast or Great Lakes	**232**
Mystery Scoter	**234**
Displays	**246**
Mystery Goldeneye	**254**
Mystery Merganser	**268**
Mergansers in the Bay	**270**
Distant Ducks on a Mountain Pond	**278**
Prairie Potholes	**280**
Senescent Hen Waterfowl	**282**
Rust-stained Birds	**284**
Mystery Freshwater 'Bellies'	**286**
Overhead 'Bellies'	**288**
Mystery Teal in Flight	**290**
Mystery Flight in Fall	**292**
Flying Away in Buffalo, NY	**294**
Flying Away Bay Ducks	**296**
Squadrons	**298**
Landing	**230**
Dabblers Taking Off	**302**
Exotics	**304**
Duck Look-alikes	**306**
Widespread and Common	**308**
Wingspreads	**310**